China – Central and Eastern Europe Cross-Cultural Dialogue

Society, Business and Education in Transition

CHIŃSKIE DROGI

Series editor: Joanna Wardęga

China – Central and Eastern Europe Cross-Cultural Dialogue

Society, Business and Education in Transition

Edited by Joanna Wardęga

Jagiellonian University Press

Series: Chińskie Drogi

This publication was supported by the Jagiellonian University Centre for Chinese Language and Culture "Confucius Institute in Krakow"

REVIEWER
ks. prof. dr hab. Krzysztof Kościelniak
prof. Zhao Gang

COVER DESIGN
Ewa Skrzypiec

Photo on the cover: Robert Pipała

ISBN 978-83-233-4111-6
ISBN 978-83-233-9450-1 (e-book)

www.wuj.pl

Jagiellonian University Press
Editorial Offices: ul. Michałowskiego 9/2, 31-126 Kraków
Phone: +48 12 663 23 80, +48 12 663 23 82, Fax: +48 12 663 23 83
Distribution: Phone: +48 12 631 01 97, Fax: +48 12 631 01 98
Cell Phone: + 48 506 006 674, e-mail: sprzedaz@wuj.pl
Bank: PEKAO SA, IBAN PL 80 1240 4722 1111 0000 4856 3325

Contents

PART TWO. Economy and Markets in Transition

PART THREE. Education in Transition

Foreword

Socio-cultural, economic and political transformations have altered both the Chinese and Eastern European societies over the last few decades, creating a new context in which both these regions continue to undergo important changes and meet future challenges, such as economic reforms, social inequality, aging population, sustainable development, environmental problems, legal issues, educational challenges, and others. In the fields of economics, culture, and education, many possibilities to meet partners from geographically distant areas have recently appeared. These encounters between different cultures entail various challenges. What are the effects of contacts between representatives of different countries of Eastern and Central Europe and China? A comprehensive analysis of these spheres could offer great opportunities for interdisciplinary comparative research. This text explores the dynamics of dialogue between China and CEE in a number of areas.

The study of the Chinese presence in Central and Eastern Europe and the relations between these two regions was initiated as a result of intensifying exchange between academics both from China and many countries of the region. The second stage was the intellectually stimulating Conference on China-Central and Eastern Europe (CEE) Cross-Cultural Dialogue, Education and Business organized by the Confucius Institute in Krakow and the Institute of Middle and Far Eastern Studies at the Jagiellonian University on September 22–24, 2015. The conference was supported by the Beijing Foreign Studies University, Confucius Institutes in Budapest, Bucharest, Lancaster, Ljubljana, Olomouc, Skopje, and Sofia, the Faculty of Economics at the University of Ljubljana, the Institute of European Studies at the Chinese Academy of Social Sciences, the Shanghai University of International Business & Economics, and the Alliance of Chinese and European Business Schools.

This book, as well as the conference, aimed to promote cross-disciplinary, academic, educational, and professional dialogue concerning all kinds of China-CEE subject areas. The main idea was to use a comparative approach and combine diverse experiences and different research approaches and perspectives across various disciplines in order to analyze similarities between the two regions, as well as to address future challenges related to socio-economic and institutional transformations. Despite the great distance that separates them, as well as obvious cultural differences, these two regions also have important common traits and can learn from each other.

This book is divided into three sections. Part One, "Society and Cultures in Transition", contains nine articles. Its contributors present a wide range of topics, including the differences and similarities in the field of ethics, law and government systems, a comparative analysis of solutions to environmental and population problems, the development of Chinese presence in some of the countries of the region, as well as the perception of China in media and among students.

Part Two, "Economy and Markets in Transition", focuses on economics. Its nine contributors of different backgrounds cover the issues of the Chinese economic influence on Central and Eastern Europe, including foreign direct investments, potential development of markets, and the expected impact of the New Silk Road and the Asian Infrastructure Investment Bank on CEE economies. Their interests also include the comparison between China and CEE in the field of innovation and development patterns.

Part Three, "Education in Transition", contains eight articles, written by authors who combine practical experience with an analysis of education issues. Their research presents a picture of Chinese teaching, including issues pertaining to the Chinese language and culture classes provided by Confucius Institutes, and a comparative analysis of teaching styles. The two final articles are links to history, showing the historical perspective of Eastern European Jesuits working in China.

I would like to extend special thanks and appreciation not only to the contributors, but also to Ms. Danijela Voljč and Dr. Matevž Rašković, University of Ljubljana, for their original idea of networking. I would also like to express my gratitude to Prof. Krzysztof Kościelniak, Prof. Adam W. Jelonek, Prof. Zhao Gang, and Prof. Bogdan Góralczyk for their support and guidance. Finally, I would like to thank Ms. Katarzyna Liwosz, Assistant Conference Coordinator, for her great commitment to the organization of the conference.

Joanna Wardęga

PART ONE

SOCIETY AND CULTURE IN TRANSITION

József Poór, Péter Fodor, Péter Kollár, Attila Farkas, János Fehér,
Patrick Woock

Idealism and Relativism in Ethics: Comparing China and Central Eastern Europe (CEE)

Introduction
The CEE region

Central and Eastern Europe (CEE) or Eastern and Central Europe are terms frequently used in science, politics, and daily life alike. They are customarily used in connection with the part of Europe which differs in more significant respects – social, economic, cultural, and political – from both Western and Eastern Europe. According to Halecki (1980), Europe is divided into four parts for historical reasons: Western Europe, West Central Europe, East Central Europe, and Eastern Europe. CEE countries are situated geographically in the centre, one part lying within a bloc comprising Sweden, Germany and Italy, and the other between Russia and Turkey. Over the centuries, peoples of very diverse backgrounds have established their own independent states or even empires. In their relationships with Western and Eastern Europe they developed distinctive national cultures, and these have contributed greatly to the development of European civilization. The use of the term CEE as a definition in the political structure of the region strongly emphasizes that these states represent cultures different from those of Eastern Europe – more specifically, Russia (and, later, the Soviet Union) which ruled the whole territory after the Second World War. The anti-Soviet, anti-bolshevist argument can claim many serious protagonists, such as Bibó (1946) or Kundera (1984).

A single European culture is an abstract ideal, but this does not mean that it has no influence on the mentality of people. The sources of European culture are Greek philosophy, Roman law and monotheistic religions – in particular, Christianity – which are integrated into the traditional culture of various peoples. Progress and modernization took root and flourished in these. The most significant steps on the long journey towards modernization were the Renaissance, Humanism, the Reformation, and the Enlightenment. According to various authors, the Enlightenment in particular can be considered as the great intellectual movement and historical era that helped establish modernity (Himmelfarb, 2005; Israel, 2002). The impact of the (ongoing) debate on the nature of science, world-view and the characteristics and consequences of individualistic secular morality is more profound. The basic difference between the CEE region and Eastern Europe is that such movements have more influence in CEE then in the East. The roots of this difference go back to the period when CEE lay clearly in the orbit of Western Christianity, whilst Eastern Europe was a solid part of Eastern Orthodoxy. According to Huntington (2007), not only did the consequences of this difference in the history of religion determine past events, but they also have an impact on the future. From the perspective of economic development, the CEE region differs significantly from Western Europe. Although the Industrial Revolution reached CEE, the huge distance from the Atlantic Ocean prevented the region from trading with the New World as openly as in the case of Western Europe. Capitalism appeared in the region later and in a somewhat modified form – affecting political changes as well.

During their history, the peoples of CEE were ruined by different empires (German, Austrian, Russian, Ottoman), or, at least, they had relations which endangered their sovereignty. This delayed their development as nation-states, in some cases postponing their foundation to the 1990s. The peace treaty that ended First World War had a significant effect on the position of the region: empires were dismantled, new states were established, although some were not nation-states and experienced serious ethnic problems. Some became stronger, whilst others, especially Hungary, lost. The mutual distrust among states made it impossible to harmonize interests (Friedmann, 2015). After First World War, democracy was in crisis. Western Europe came out of the crisis after Second World War and achieved gigantic economic success within a relatively stable democratic political framework. This was associated with the fact that distribution conditions were agreed on by the majority as reasonably fair. Due to its dependency on the Soviet Union, the CEE area embarked on a politico-economic path whose economic, political, and moral damage is still felt today. The end of the Cold War and the triumph of the West were experienced in CEE states as their own, but these were generated illusions of which only democracy was realised, whilst economic 'catch-up', western prosperity levels and a more equitable society were not. To several people the slow and difficult process of joining the European Union was also disappointing. The situation has been aggravated by the economic crisis, which arose in 2008 – the worst since 1929. Today it is clear that this crisis, just like the one in 1929–33, was not only economic, but also social and moral. Albeit to different extents, all countries of the region were affected deeply by the crisis. The handling and reconstruction of the effects is a huge burden for individual states and also for the EU. There are two economic-philosophies: neo-liberalism and Keynesianism, plus a third practical possibility: a mixture of the two. At the end of the 20th century, it seemed that Keynesianism had disappeared from European economic policy (Parsons, 2005), but, according to many, there is a need for its revival (Krugman, 2014; Skidelsky, 2010).

In the CEE region, the failure of communism and the development of the capitalist economy resulted in a transition crisis, which also had its moral effects. The communist system was not supported by the majority of people, who simply tolerated it, as there was no better option. They were, in reality, waiting for a free market economy to emerge, but they soon felt the related injustice, the growth of social differences (which were spectacular but difficult to justify), and the spread of poverty, the exclusion of middle classes, the increasing level of corruption and the criminalization of the economy. Communism was essentially strange to the people of the region. One of its disruptive effects was that it restricted the survival of tradition. During the transition, societies were compelled to re-discover and revive traditions and to apply them in the new situation. All of this has led to a situation where there is a worldwide feeling that morality and economy, morality and business, and morality and welfare are conflicting, incompatible concepts – a feeling which has recently intensified.

Chinese culture and history

The Qin's wars of unification were a series of military campaigns launched in the late 3rd century BC by the Qin state against other six major provinces – Han, Zhao, Yan, Wei, Chu, and Qi – within the territories which form modern China (Kiser & Cai, 2003). The Qin dynasty was the first imperial dynasty of China, lasting from 221 to 206 BC and was formed after the conquest of the six other states. The name was derived from its heartland of Qin, in modern-day Gansu and Shaanxi (Huang, 2015).

During its reign in China, the Qin sought to create an imperial state unified by a highly structured political apparatus. The Qin central government sought to minimize the role of local warlords and have direct administrative control over peasantry, who constituted the majority of the population (Tanner, 2010). This control enabled ambitious construction projects, such as the Great Wall of China.

Qin set the stage for how future dynasties would rule, via centralized government, while allowing considerable regional autonomy (Edmonds, 1985). Historically speaking, the control of the Chinese Central Government over its populace has been weak, with regional autonomy and little loyalty. Additionally, China's topography isolated it for much of its history, and because of this isolation, it was not until the late 11th century that China started to experience Western influence via the Silk Road (Ma, 1998). This early influence was most notably attributed to Marco Polo and Matteo Ricci.

Marco Polo (September 15, 1254 – January 8–9, 1324) was an Italian merchant traveller whose travels are recorded in *Livres des merveilles du monde* (*Book of the Marvels of the World*, also known as *The Travels of Marco Polo*, c. 1300), a book that introduced Europeans to Central Asia and China. Polo's influence during the Yuan dynasty opened the door to future foreign emissaries from Italy – most notably, Matteo Ricci (Burgan, 2002).

Matteo Ricci (October 6, 1552 – May 11, 1610), was an Italian Jesuit priest and one of the founding figures of the Jesuit China missions. In 1601 Ricci was invited to become an adviser to the imperial court of the Wanli Emperor; the first Westerner to be invited into the Forbidden City. This honour was in cognition of Ricci's scientific abilities, chiefly his predictions of solar eclipses, which were significant events in the Chinese world (Hsia, 2010). He established the Cathedral of the Immaculate Conception in Beijing, the oldest Catholic Church in the city (Lu, 2011).

By the 1940s, China's imperial government power had begun to wane, and it was at this time that Communist revolutionaries under Mao Zedong began to wage war on the KMT – the Chinese Nationalist Party and the titular government of China – although the two entities had been allies against the invading Japanese. On October 1, 1949, with the retreat of the KMT to Taiwan, Mao Zedong established the Peoples' Republic of China (PRC). The PRC completely changed the culture and social geography of the Chinese people. It implemented five-year plans, which consisted of land reform, social and cultural reform and economic planning. One of Mao's early policies was to encourage the Chinese to have large families. In 1949 he proclaimed: "Of all things in the world, people are the most precious." The communist government condemned birth control and banned imports of contraceptives. At the beginning of Mao's policy, China's population was 541 million (1949), but thirty years later it stood at 969 million (1979).

By the late 1970s, the founders of the PRC were slowly dying out, including Mao Zedong himself. Deng Xiaoping took the opportunity and seized power. He was eventually nominated Chairman on March 8, 1978. Deng brought a new philosophy and policies. One important policy was the 'One-child policy', which was implemented on September 18, 1980, thus reversing Mao's policy (Greenhalgh, 2008).

Modern Day China (similarities and differences between CEE and China)

Similarities

Individualism (Little Emperors): Repercussions of the 'One-child' policy. The Little Emperor Syndrome is one aspect of the 'One-child policy', where only children gain seemingly excessive amounts of attention from their parents and grandparents. One factor frequently associated with the Little Emperor effect is the "four-two-one" family structure, which refers to the collapse of the traditionally expanded Chinese family into four grandparents and two parents doting on one child (Feng, Cai & Gu, 2013). It is believed to be one of the side effects of the 'One-child' rule. There is a different behavioural attitude among the only-child population compared with the previous generation: "If you've lived in the Chinese society for a long time, you can sense the difference as people become more individualistic" (Meng, 2013). The 'One-child policy' has led to a more individual way of thinking among the Chinese youth, similar to that of CEE youth.

Christianity: Another modern issue with its roots in China's past is Christianity. The introduction of Christianity goes back to Marco Polo and Matteo Ricci, but, with the assent of the Communist Party in 1949, Chairman Mao was determined to stamp out any kind of religion. He stated: "Religion is poison." During the Cultural Revolution of 1967–1976, many religious leaders were imprisoned or sent to labour camps, while places of worship were routinely destroyed. However, in the years following Mao's death, greater tolerance was offered. Today, the communist nation is often cited as having the fastest growing Christian populace. Estimates vary, but there are thought to be between 50 and 100 million Chinese believers, with up to 10,000 people converting to faith across the country every single day (Yang, 2005).

Differences

Human rights: Human Rights in China have taken a back seat in the government's policy. Typically, the implementation of policies is left to local administrators. This allows for greater interpretation and flexibility therein, although, when society comes into direct conflict with government policy, the government will use all resources at its disposal, including military, to ensure that its policy is implemented – without regard for human rights. One example is the Bobai crackdown: in 2007, riots broke out in Bobai County in China's southwestern Guangxi province. Under pressure from higher authorities to meet birth targets (established by the 'One-child policy'), local officials had launched a vicious crackdown on family-planning violators. Squads rounded up 17,000 women and subjected them to sterilizations (Feng, Cai & Gu, 2013).

Democracy: Chinese Central government has always kept a firm hand on individuals' rights. The most significant example is the Tiananmen Square protests of 1989 (Ruan & Xu, 1989), which were student-led popular demonstrations in Beijing that took place in the spring of 1989 and received broad support from city residents. Hardline leaders ordered the military to enforce martial law in the country's capital and forcibly suppressed the protests. The crackdown was initiated on June 3–4 and brought troops with assault rifles and tanks who inflicted casualties on civilians trying to block the military's advance towards Tiananmen Square in the heart of Beijing, which students and other demonstrators had been occupying for seven weeks (Cunningham & Wasserstrom, 2011).

Ethical positions in the light of cultural dimensions

In one of the first cross-cultural explorations of the ethical ideology among physicians, authors from six countries conducted a study which involved the total of 1,109 physicians from Canada, China, India, Ireland, Japan, and Thailand. The Ethics Position Questionnaire was used for this exercise. The authors undertook a comprehensive Bayesian Confirmatory Factor Analysis and demonstrated the robust nature of the ethical dimensions of idealism and relativism as fundamental across cultures, with noteworthy cross-cultural variations (MacNab et al., 2011).

Hofstede (1980) developed a universal framework for understanding cultural differences based on a worldwide survey. He originally identified four dimensions: *power distance (PDI)* shows the extent to which inequalities among people are seen as normal; *uncertainty avoidance*

(*UAI*) refers to a preference for structured versus unstructured situations; *individualism-collectivism* (*IND*) considers whether individuals are used to acting as individuals or as a part of cohesive groups; the *masculinity-femininity* (*MAS*) dimension distinguishes between hard values, such as assertiveness and competition and soft or feminine values of personal relations, quality of life and caring about others (Jackson, 2011). These elements of national culture in the countries studied according to Hofstede's theory appear in Figure 1.

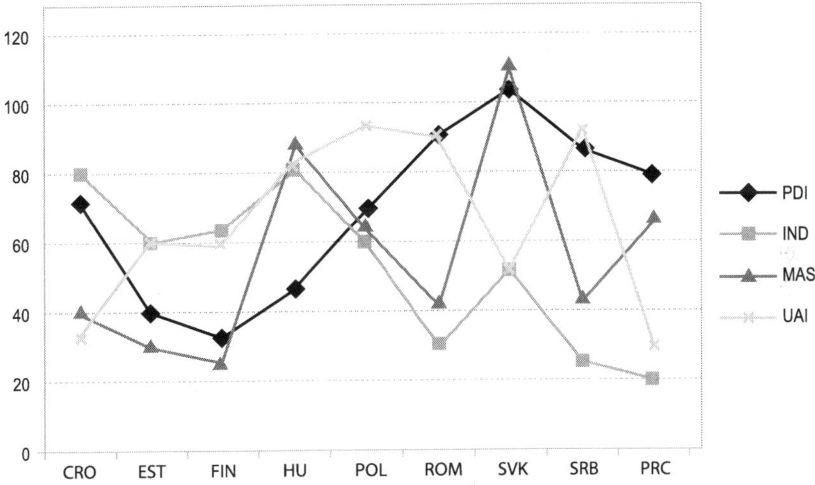

Figure 1: Elements of national culture of the countries examined according to Hofstede

Source: http://geert-hofstede.com (accessed 15/10/2-15)
Comments: CRO: Croatia; EST: Estonia; FIN: Finland; HU: Hungary; POL: Poland; ROM: Romania; SVK: Slovakia; SRB: Serbia; PRC: China.
PDI: Power Distance; IND: Individualism-Collectivism; MAS: Masculinity-Femininity, and UAI: Uncertainty Avoidance.

The data show that, among the nine countries studied, there are very significant differences in terms of all four of Hofstede's dimensions. Slovakia and Romania show a high Power Distance Index, whilst in Finland and Estonia people do not accept social inequalities. Serbs and Romanians are collectivistic nations, whilst in Hungary and Croatia individual interests come before the collective. In Estonia and Finland feminine values dominate, whilst in Slovakia and Hungary hard masculine values are more important. People in Slovakia, Croatia, Finland, and Estonia accept uncertainty, whilst in Poland, Serbia, and Hungary they prefer structured situations.

We can compare China to the CEE region due to China's physical size, topographical location (isolated) and population. There are not many "true" Chinese values reflecting these factors. However, in general, the Chinese tend to be more risk-adverse (avoiding uncertainty), a reflection of which can be seen in the Chinese proverb "the tallest tree gets cut first" – meaning that those who stand out will be first to be removed. Moreover, China's culture, which is deeply intertwined with its historical feudal system (high power-distance), has not been affected by recent experiments in communism. In fact, Deng's adaptation of the 'one country, two systems' policy – relating to Hong Kong – has increased the Power Distance between China's elite and the working class.

Rawwas, Arjoon, and Sidani (2013) asserted that, according to Hofstede, on the one hand, relativists are focused on risk-taking, earnings, competition, advancement, challenge, and individual decision-making, and are more likely to violate societal norms for personal gain and to excuse self-benefiting unethical practice than idealistic individuals (Barnett et al., 1996). Cultural relativists state that "there are no ultimate universal ethical principles and that all value judgments are relative to particular cultural contexts. Cultural relativists refer not only to cultural differences in moral standards, but also to the way in which people reason about morality" (McDonald, 2010, p. 453). On the other hand, according to idealists, especially ethical absolutists, despite differences in socio-cultural and political factors, ethical beliefs based on moral standards vary little from culture to culture. The commonality of ethical beliefs hints at the possibility of common moral standards and supports the notion of absolutism (McDonald, 2010).

Idealism and relativism in ethics

CEE countries have more common features at a certain abstract level, but these countries are quite different with regard to their ethical values. The derogations come from the differences in national cultures, and these differences are expressed also in the judgment of ethical idealism and ethical relativism. This subject is presented in a comparatively detailed way in research reported by Poór et al. (2015). The research applied the method developed by Forsyth (1980) in conjunction with Hofstede's (1980) method regarding cultural dimensions. The EPQ contains 20 statements, and if the person who answers agrees on the first 10 (at least in part), then it refers to ethical idealism; if they do not agree, then it shows relativism. In the second 10 statements this is reversed, as agreement to some degree shows relativism, and non-agreement shows idealism. Forsyth (1980) recommends a four-fold classification based on both these dimensions. Individuals who are highly relativist and highly idealistic are called *situationists*; they feel that people should strive to produce the best consequences possible, but that moral rules cannot be applied to all situations. *Absolutists,* same as situationists, are also idealistic; they approve of actions which yield many positive, desirable results. However, unlike situationists, absolutists are not relativist. They feel that some ethical absolutes are so important that they must be included in all codes of ethics. *Subjectivists* reject moral rules (high relativism) and are also less idealistic about the possibility of achieving humanitarian goals. *Exceptionists* are low in both relativism and idealism; they believe that moral rules should guide our behaviour, but that actions which yield some negative results should not necessarily be condemned. Hence, they are willing to make exceptions to their moral principles. Hofstede (1980) suggests a four dimensions-examination to understand cultural differences. Power distance (PDI) shows the extent of the social differences which can be accepted; uncertainty-avoidance (UIA) refers to the preference for structured or un-structured situations. Individualism-collectivism (IND) considers whether individuals are used to acting as individuals or as a part of cohesive groups; masculinity-femininity (MAS) distinguishes between hard values, such as assertiveness and competition, and soft values of personal relations, quality of life and caring about others.

According to the research, nations in CEE countries have rather idealistic values (3.96) as opposed to relativism (3.74). However, there are significant differences among countries consequent on the different national culture, even if they border geographically – e.g. Hungary, Serbia, Romania, and Slovakia – but there is a considerable similarity in the case of Estonia and Finland. There is a significant difference between the ethical position of ethnic Hungarians living in Hungary, Slovakia, Serbia, and Romania. Hungarian citizens, as such, show higher idealism and lower relativism values than people of, simply, Hungarian ethnicity. It seems that the ethical position of ethnic Hungarians living in the neighbouring countries (Slovakia, Serbia or Romania) has been significantly influenced by the more relativist environment of these countries. Considering Hofstede's cultural dimensions, the data analysis produced some interesting results, although it should be emphasized that we found a significant correlation only in the UA cultural dimension. We assumed that the nations with high UA values would be the most idealistic, as they prefer structured situations and, therefore, avoid engaging in activities which conflict with their beliefs, thus indicating signs of high idealism. This assumption proved to be true for Poles and Serbs. At the same time, the value of relativism was the lowest for Serbs, whereas Poland ranks high when it comes to relativist values. Hence, the presumption concerning the UAI and idealistic dimensions is at least partly true. However, it is hard to find a relationship between the cultural dimensions and ethical positions of other nations. A large number of Hungarian citizens belong to the absolutist (high idealism and low relativism) sector. A significant number of Slovakian citizens are subjectivists and situationists (medium idealism and relativism and high idealism and medium relativism respectively). A significant number of Serbian respondents are situationists (high idealism and medium relativism). Most Romanians are subjectivists (medium idealism and relativism). Finnish and Estonian respondents tend to be subjectivists (medium idealism and relativism), while a significant number of Polish respondents are situationists (high idealism and medium relativism). Croatians are prevailingly absolutists (high idealism and low relativism).

Our methodology

To investigate the respondents' moral philosophy, we used the Ethical Position Questionnaire (EPQ), developed by D.R. Forsyth. It contains 20 statements and requires individuals to indicate their acceptance of these statements, which vary in terms of relativism and idealism. The relativism scale, on the one hand, includes assertions such as "Different types of morality cannot be compared in terms of 'rightness'" and "What is ethical varies according to the situation." On the other hand, it measures an individual's perspective on positive and negative consequences with such assertions as "Individuals should ensure that their actions are free of any intent to harm others – even to the slightest degree" and "If an action could harm an innocent third party, it should not be taken" (Forsyth, 1980).

In the current questionnaire each statement was rated on a 5-point Likert scale from 1 (strongly disagree) to 5 (strongly agree). To show the idealism and relativism scales, we counted the arithmetic means of items 1–10 (idealism) and items 11–20 (relativism). Higher scores represent higher levels of idealism or relativism.

Empirical research results

To test the reliability of the idealism and relativism scales, Cronbach's alpha was used. According to Table 1, we can accept the alpha measure of the reliability of the idealism and relativism scales.

Table 1: Reliability Statistics of the relativism scales

Scales	Cronbach's Alpha	N of Items
Idealism	0.821	10
Relativism	0.770	10

Source: Authors' own research.

The research was conducted in eight European countries (Hungary, Slovakia, Romania, Serbia, Croatia, Poland, Estonia, Finland) and in China. Our sample comprises the total of 2,735 respondents from these countries, recruited among financial circles and groups of business students, as well as the general public. The structure of our sample in terms of nationality and citizenship is shown in Table 2.

Table 2: Sample

		Country									Total
		HUN	SVK	SRB	RO	FIN	EST	PRC	POL	CRO	
NAT	HUN	268	221	66	96	0	0	0	0	0	651
	SVK	0	296	0	0	0	0	0	0	0	296
	SRB	0	0	119	0	0	0	0	0	0	119
	RO	0	0	0	25	0	0	0	0	0	25
	FIN	0	0	0	0	200	0	0	0	0	200
	EST	0	0	0	0	0	326	0	0	0	326
	PRC	0	4	0	0	0	0	183	0	0	187
	POL	0	0	0	0	0	0	0	819	0	819
	CRO	0	0	0	0	0	0	0	0	112	112
Total		268	521	185	121	200	326	183	819	112	2735

Source: Authors' own research.

To investigate the difference between male and female respondents' idealism and relativism values, the Independent Samples T-Test was used. The requirements of this test are normality and equal variances. According to the Kolmogorov-Smirnov test, the variable does not meet the requirement of normality, and so we had to transform and standardize the dataset. According to Levene's test, the requirement of equal variances is met only in the case of the relativism scale.

Table 3 shows the means for male and female groups. According to the Table, we can see that women are more idealistic than men, but the difference is only 0.2. In terms of relativism, this gap is not significant.

Table 3: Descriptive statistics of Independent Samples T-Test

	GENDER	N	Mean	Std. Deviation	Std. Error Mean
IDEAL	MALE	1015	3.860	0.6836	0.0215
	FEMALE	1719	4.024	0.5778	0.0139
RELAT	MALE	1015	3.480	0.6195	0.0194
	FEMALE	1719	3.489	0.6159	0.0149

Source: Authors' own research.

Table 4 shows the results of the Independent Samples T-Test and Welch's d-test. According to Levene's test, equal variances do not meet the requirements in the case of the idealism scale. Sig. value is 0,000. It means that equal variances are not assumed. So we can use Welch's d-test in the second row. According to the result, we can determine that the means of the categories are not significantly different in the relativism scale. Equal variances are assumed. The result shows that there is no significant difference between men's and women's relativism values.

To investigate relationships between age and idealism as well as relativism, Pearson's correlation was used. Table 5 shows that there is a positive relationship between age and idealism, but the correlations are very weak at 1% significant level. We can say that younger respondents are less idealistic than older respondents. We must note, however, that this statement should be accepted with some reservations.

Table 4: Independent Samples T-Test and Welch's d-test

		Levene's Test for Equality of Variances		T-Test for Equality of Means						
		F	Sig.	T	df	Sig. (2-tailed)	Mean Difference	Std. Error Difference	95% Confidence Interval of the Difference Lower	Upper
IDEAL	Equal variances assumed	41.027	.000	−6.693	2732	0000	−.1641	.0245	−.2121	−.1160
	Equal variances not assumed			−6.412	1855.007	.000	−.1641	.0256	−.2142	−.1139
RELAT	Equal variances assumed	.087	.768	−.337	2732	.736	−.0082	.0244	−.0561	.0397
	Equal variances not assumed			−.337	2117.401	.736	−.0082	.0245	−.0562	.0398

Source: Authors' own research.

Table 5: Results of Pearson Correlation

		AGE	IDEAL	RELAT
AGE	Pearson Correlation		.217[**]	−.052[**]
	Sig. (2-tailed)		.000	.009
	N		2468	2468
IDEAL	Pearson Correlation	.217[**]		
	Sig. (2-tailed)	.000		
	N	2468		
RELAT	Pearson Correlation	−.052[**]		
	Sig. (2-tailed)	.009		
	N	2468		

** Correlation is significant at the 0.01 level (2-tailed).

Source: Authors' own research.

This research also includes work experience. We tried to answer the question: what kind of relationship is there between idealism, relativism variables, and work experience?

To explore the effect of this experience on idealism and relativism scales, ANOVA was used. According to the homogeneity of the variance test, the requirement is met in respect of the idealism scale.

Table 6: Effect of work experience on idealism and relativism scales

	POWE	IDEAL	RELAT
PUB	Mean	4.109	3.497
	N	426	426
	Std. Deviation	.6560	.6739
PRI	Mean	3.987	3.458
	N	1040	1040
	Std. Deviation	.6489	.6272
BOTH	Mean	4.064	3.476
	N	541	541
	Std. Deviation	.5814	.6328
NONE	Mean	3.756	3.572
	N	461	461
	Std. Deviation	.5819	.5639
Total	Mean	3.982	3.490
	N	2468	2468
	Std. Deviation	.6343	.6266

Source: Authors' own research.

If we look at Table 6, we can see that the most idealistic respondents are those who have work experience in the public sector. In the case of the idealism scale, an analysis of variance resulted in significant differences between the means of this category. According to Table 7, the effect of work experience on the idealism scale is also significant (F=3.647; df=3; sig.: 0.01) but the relationship is very weak. (Table 8: Eta 0.066).

We assume this correspondence can be explained rather by the effect of age on idealism and relativism. If we aggregate private, public and both categories, we can see that all those who have some work experience are more idealistic than who have none.

Table 7: Effect of work experience on idealism

		Sum of Squares	Df	Mean Square	F	Sig.
IDEAL * POWE	Between Groups (Combined)	34.053	3	11.351	29.175	.000
	Within Groups	958.647	2464	.389		
	Total	992.700	2467			
RELAT * POWE	Between Groups (Combined)	4.281	3	1.427	3.647	.012
	Within Groups	964.234	2464	.391		
	Total	968.516	2467			

Source: Authors' own research.

Table 8: Effect of work experience on idealism and relativism

	Eta	Eta Squared
IDEAL * POWE	.185	.034
RELAT * POWE	.066	.004

Source: Authors' own research.

We have tried to explore the differences between the nationalities of the respondents on the idealism and relativism scales. According to the results of our variance analysis (Table 9), the effect of nationality on both scales is significant.

According to Figure 2, Croatian and Polish respondents are the most idealistic (blue line). Slovakian, Serbian and Chinese respondents are less idealistic, but their idealism scores are 4. The least idealistic are the Hungarian, Romanian, Finnish, and Estonian respondents with 3.7–3.8 idealism scores. If we look at the red line and the average scores, we can see that the most relativist respondents are the Romanian, Polish, and Chinese. The Hungarian, Slovakian, Finnish and Estonian respondents are less relativist. Their relativism scores range from 3.4 to 3.5. The least relativist respondents are Serbians and Croatians with 33 and 3.2 respectively.

Table 9: Results of the variance analysis

		Sum of Squares	df	Mean Square	F	Sig.
IDEAL	Between Groups	61.282	8	7.660	20.789	.000
	Within Groups	1004.460	2726	.368		
	Total	1065.742	2734			
RELAT	Between Groups	32.657	8	4.082	11.012	.000
	Within Groups	1010.510	2726	.371		
	Total	1043.166	2734			

Source: Authors' own research.

Due to the high number of respondents, we used the K-mean cluster method to classify the respondents in terms of clusters, and, in accordance with the established practice, we determined 4 hypothetical clusters among Forsyth's theory of ethical position.

We then attempted to interpret the emerging clusters. In the first one, the respondents scored low in both idealism and relativism (Exceptionists), whilst in the second one, the level of relativism was higher than that of idealism (Subjectivists). In the third cluster, the respondents displayed a high level of idealism and a high level of relativism (Situationist), whereas in the fourth cluster, the levels of idealism were high and those of relativism were low (Absolutists). Table 10 shows the final cluster centres.

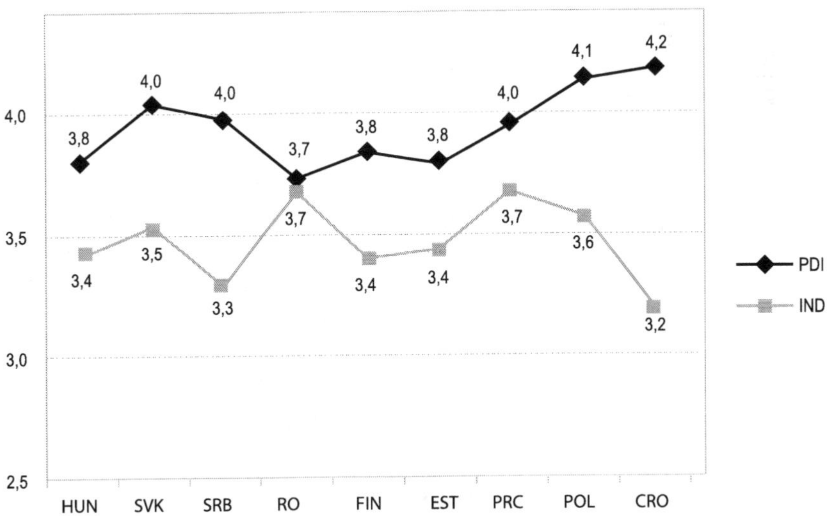

Figure 2: Means of idealism and relativism scales, according to nationality

Source: Authors' own research.

Table 10: Final cluster centres

	Cluster			
	Exceptionists	**Subjectivists**	**Situationists**	**Absolutists**
IDEAL	2,6	3,5	4,4	4,2
RELAT	2,7	3,6	4,0	2,9

Source: Authors' own research.

This research also includes the relationships between cluster membership and nationality. We have used crosstab analysis and Pearson's chi-square test to explore the association between the category of cluster and nationality. According to the results, Pearson's chi-square test eventuated in significant relationship (sig.: 0.000) between these variables. The Contingency Coefficient for measuring the association is 0.3 at sig.: 0.000 level.

According to Table 11, large numbers of the Hungarian, Romanian, Finnish, and Estonian belong to the subjectivist cluster (lower level of idealism and high relativism). A significant number of Serbian and Croatian respondents are absolutists (high idealism and low relativism). Chinese, Slovakian, and Polish respondents tend to be situationists (high idealism and high relativism).

Conclusion

By way of a summary of our intercultural research into the ethical positions of businessmen and business students in our target countries, we can conclude that idealistic values, attitudes and behaviours are more characteristic than their relativist counterparts.

Our investigation of ethical positions in these countries and nations has led us to the conclusion that cultural and historical backgrounds influence the ethical position, just as the ethical views of the dominant nations influence minorities' attitudes to universal rules and standards. The data obtained partly confirms our initial hypothesis: differences in national cultures and history inevitably mean that ethical positions also differ...

Our intercultural research into the ethical views of businessmen and business students in the Baltic-Nordic countries and PRC shows that idealistic values, attitudes and behaviours are more characteristic than their relativist counterparts.

As regards a comparison between male and female groups, the differences found do not meet the requirements in respect of idealism. At the same time, we have not found any significant differences between men and women in terms of relativism values.

According to the results of our analysis, the variance effect of nationality on both individualism and relativism is significant.

The research found a significant relationship between the membership of clusters alongside Forsyth's theory of ethical position and nationality.

The data obtained partly confirms our initial hypothesis: idealism and scale values and cluster membership vary across countries with different national cultures and history.

Over the last 40 years, China has shifted away from being an isolated country to being a country well connected to the world around it. Chinese traditional isolationist values have shifted, in many cases reflecting similarities to CEE countries. The earlier exposure to Christianity is now taking root, and will have a long-term impact on how the Chinese see issues on morality. Additionally, the 'One-child policy' has created a substantial sub-group of the Chinese who are more individually-minded, and see themselves as important, breaking away from more traditional fatal thinking.

Certain differences remain between China and the CEE region. For instance, China's position on human rights, implementing such western systems as "free and independent" courts with the size of China's population, could end up in a disaster. Also, allowing a population of 1.3 billion to expand unchecked could potentially outstrip China's (Potts, 2006) and even world's resources. Nevertheless, over the last 40 years, CEE and China's values have become more aligned then in any previous period in history.

Table 11: Cross-table of cluster membership and nationality

			ClusterN				Total
			Exceptionists	Subjectivits	Situationists	Absolutists	
NAT	HUN	Count	39	296	142	174	651
		% within NAT	6.0%	45.5%	21.8%	26.7%	100.0%
		% within ClusterN	26.4%	32.9%	14.8%	23.9%	23.8%
		Adjusted Residual	.7	7.8	−8.1	.1	
	SVK	Count	8	87	127	74	296
		% within NAT	2.7%	29.4%	42.9%	25.0%	100.0%
		% within ClusterN	5.4%	9.7%	13.2%	10.2%	10.8%
		Adjusted Residual	−2.2	−1.4	3.0	−.7	
	SRB	Count	3	37	31	48	119
		% within NAT	2.5%	31.1%	26.1%	40.3%	100.0%
		% within ClusterN	2.0%	4.1%	3.2%	6.6%	4.4%
		Adjusted Residual	−1.4	−.4	−2.1	3.5	
	RO	Count	1	15	5	4	25
		% within NAT	4.0%	60.0%	20.0%	16.0%	100.0%
		% within ClusterN	0.7%	1.7%	0.5%	0.6%	0.9%
		Adjusted Residual	−.3	2.9	−1.6	−1.2	
	FIN	Count	12	80	53	55	200
		% within NAT	6.0%	40.0%	26.5%	27.5%	100.0%
		% within ClusterN	8.1%	8.9%	5.5%	7.6%	7.3%
		Adjusted Residual	.4	2.2	−2.6	.3	

NAT			ClusterN				Total
			Exceptionists	Subjectivits	Situationists	Absolutists	
EST	Count		17	135	76	98	326
	% within NAT		5.2%	41.4%	23.3%	30.1%	100.0%
	% within ClusterN		11.5%	15.0%	7.9%	13.5%	11.9%
	Adjusted Residual		-.2	3.5	-4.8	1.5	
PRC	Count		13	69	82	23	187
	% within NAT		7.0%	36.9%	43.9%	12.3%	100.0%
	% within ClusterN		8.8%	7.7%	8.5%	3.2%	6.8%
	Adjusted Residual		1.0	1.2	2.6	-4.6	
POL	Count		52	158	410	199	819
	% within NAT		6.3%	19.3%	50.1%	24.3%	100.0%
	% within ClusterN		35.1%	17.6%	42.7%	27.4%	29.9%
	Adjusted Residual		1.4	-9.9	10.7	-1.8	
CRO	Count		3	23	34	52	112
	% within NAT		2.7%	20.5%	30.4%	46.4%	100.0%
	% within ClusterN		2.0%	2.6%	3.5%	7.2%	4.1%
	Adjusted Residual		-1.3	-2.8	-1.1	4.9	
Total	Count		148	900	960	727	2735
	% within NAT		5.4%	32.9%	35.1%	26.6%	100.0%
	% within ClusterN		100.0%	100.0%	100.0%	100.0%	100.0%

Source: Authors' own research.

References

Barnett, T., Bass, K., & Brown, G. (1996). Religiosity, ethical ideology, and intentions to report a peer's wrongdoing. *Journal of Business Ethics, 15*(11), 1161–1174.

Bergreen, L. (2007). *Marco Polo: From Venice to Xanadu.* London: Quercus.

Bibó, I. (1946). *Poverty in Small East European States* (In Hungarian). Retrieved from http://mek.oszk.hu/02000/02043/html/194.html (accessed 15/10/2015).

Burgan, M. (2002). *Marco Polo: Marco Polo and the Silk Road to China.* Mankato: Compass Point Books.

Cunningham, M.E. & Wasserstrom, J.N. (2011). Interpreting protest in modern China. *Dissent, 58*(1), 13–18.

Edmonds, R.L. (1985). *Northern frontiers of Qing China and Tokugawa Japan: a comparative study of frontier policy.* Committee on Geographical Studies.

Feng, W., Cai, Y. & Gu, B. (2013). Population, policy, and politics: How will history judge China's one-child policy? *Population and Development Review, 38*(1), 115–129.

Fong, V.L. (2002). China's one child policy and the empowerment of urban daughters. *American Anthropologist, 104*(4), 1098–1109.

Forsyth, D. (1980). A taxonomy of ethical ideologies. *Journal of Personality and Social Psychology, 39*(1), 175–184.

Friedman, G. (2015). *Flashpoints – The Emerging Crisis in Europe.* Melbourne: Penguin Random House.

Fukuyama, F. (2006). *The End of History and the Last Man* (2nd edition). New York: Free Press.

Greenhalgh, S. (2008). *Just One Child: Science and Policy in Deng's China.* Berkeley: University of California Press.

Halecki, O. (1980). *Borderlands of Western Civilization: A History of East Central Europe.* Safety Harbour, FL: Simon Publications.

Harris, G.L. (1966). The Mission of Matteo Ricci, SJ: A Case Study of an Effort at Guided Culture Change in China in the Sixteenth Century. *Monumenta Serica*, 1–168.

Himmelfarb, G. (2005). *The Roads to Modernity: The British, French, and American Enlightenment.* New York: Alfred A. Knopf.

Hofstede, G. (1980). *Culture's Consequences: International Differences in Work-related Values.* Newbury Park, CA: Sage.

Hsia Po-Chia, R. (2010). *A Jesuit in the Forbidden City.* Nova Iorque: Oxford University Press.

Huang, R. (2015). *China: A Macro History.* London: Routledge.

Hucker, C.O. (1975). *China's Imperial Past: An Introduction to Chinese History and Culture.* Stanford, CA: Stanford University Press.

Huntington, S.P. (2007). *The Clash of Civilizations and the Remaking of World Order* (2nd edition). New York: Simon and Schuster.

Israel, J. (2002). *Radical Enlightenment: Philosophy and the Making of Modernity (1650–1750)*. Oxford: Oxford University Press.

Jackson, T. (2011). *International Management Ethics – A Critical, Cross-Cultural Perspectives*. Cambridge: Cambridge University Press.

Kiser, E. & Cai Yong (2003). War and bureaucratization in Qin China: Exploring an anomalous case. *American Sociological Review*, 511–539.

Krugman, P. (2014). Keynes is slowly winning. *The New York Times*, 26 November.

Kundera, M. (1984). The tragedy of Central Europe. *New York Review of Books*, 26 April, 33–38.

Lu Caitlin (2011). Matteo Ricci and the Jesuit Mission in China 1583–1610. *Concord Review*, 1.

Ma Debin (1998). *The Great Silk Exchange: How the World Was Connected and Developed*. London: Routledge.

MacNab, Y.C., Malloy, D.C., Hadjistavropoulos, T., Sevigny, P.R., McCarthy, E.F., Murakami, M., Paholpak, S., Natarajan, S., & Liu, P.L. (2011). Idealism and relativism across cultures. A cross-cultural examination of physicians' responses on the ethics position questionnaire (EPQ). *Journal of Cross-Cultural Psychology*, 42(7), 1272–1278.

McDonald, G. (2010). Ethical relativism *vs* absolutism: research implications. *European Business Review*, 22(4), 446–464.

Parsons, W. (2005). Politics and markets: Keynes and his Critics. In: Ball, T. & Bellamy, R. (eds). *The Cambridge History of Twentieth Century Political Thought* (pp. 45–69). Cambridge: Cambridge University Press.

Poór, J., Ruth, A., Vanhala, S., Kollár, P., Slavic, A., Berber, N., Slocinska, A., Kerekes, K., Zaharie, M., Ferencikova, S. & Barasic, A. (2015). Idealism and relativism in ethics: the results of empirical research in seven CEE countries and one North European country. *Journal of East European Management Studies* (under publication in November 2015).

Qian Yingyi (2000). The process of China's market transition (1978–1998): The evolutionary, historical, and comparative perspectives. *Journal of Institutional and Theoretical Economics (JITE) / Zeitschrift für die gesamte Staatswissenschaft*, 151–171.

Rawwas, M.Y.A., Arjoon, S. & Sidani, Y. (2013). An introduction of epistemology to business ethics: A study of marketing middle-managers. *Journal of Business Ethics*, 117(3), 525–539.

Ruan, M. & Xu, G. (1989). *Tell the World: What Happened in China and Why*. New York: Pantheon.

Skidelsky, R. (2010). *Keynes: The Return of the Master*. London: Penguin.

Spence, J.D. (1985). *The Memory Palace of Matteo Ricci*. Harmondsworth: Penguin Books.

Tanner, H.M. (2010). *China: From the Great Qing Empire through the People's Republic of China 1644–2009* (Vol. 2). Cambridge: Hackett Publishing.

Yang, F. (2005). Lost in the market, saved at McDonald's: Conversion to Christianity in urban China. *Journal for the Scientific Study of Religion*, 44(4), 423–441.

József Poór, Péter Fodor, Péter Kollár, Attila Farkas, János Fehér, Patrick Woock

Web-source:

http://www.hungarianhistory.com/lib/halecki/halecki.pdf (accessed 15/10/2015).
http://krugman.blogs.nytimes.com/2014/11/26/keynes-is-slowly-winning/?_r=0
    (accessed 15/10/2015).
http://geert-hofstede.com (accessed 15/10/2015).

Balázs Sárvári

China's Role in the New World Order

Introduction

Chinese cultural heritage may provide missing messages for global institutions: how to reach long-term sustainability and efficiency, and how to accommodate to Eastern cultures. These are the two basic pillars of global peace, or otherwise of enhancing the normative convergence all around the world. We would not like to suggest that western religious tradition needs the East to solve the problems of the world (as Voltaire suggested), but we state that both sides have to have the ability to understand and co-operate with each other. Basically, this means global harmony of all high cultures in the world, which may be the foundation of global institutions in the current wave of globalisation; as Buzan says:

> "Peaceful rise involves a two-way process in which the rising power accommodates itself to rules and structures of international society, while at the same time other powers accommodate some changes in those rules and structures by way of adjusting to the new disposition of power and status." (Buzan, 2010, p. 5)

"Peaceful rise" itself is not a historical fact, it's an idealistic goal that is based on all levels of international cooperation – this is the meaning of the term "two-way process". Since this goal is impossible to be achieved by China alone, it requires continuous harmony among the actors of the international arena to create the necessary conditions. This proves that the common global interests are the sources of competitiveness.

Confucian and Taoist values, China's history and its solutions for creating a unity within the Great Wall serves as an example for global powers in the 21st century in forming a sustainable method of solving global and regional issues. This is the most important source of China's own developing model that differentiates it from:

1. Western countries;
2. those emerging countries that adapted the Western suggestions and best practices without any reservations;
3. leading global powers that are historically more integrated into global issues (e.g. Russia).

Although China is increasingly included in globalization, the concrete process is a matter of how China joins globalization rather than how China modifies the current workflow. In other words, "China is seeking to 'supplement' the existing international order rather than to revise it" (Godement, 2015, p. 2) – this restructuring does not mean the weakening of the USA, but a turn to global partnership, which empowers developing countries. The aim of this paper is to highlight the possibilities for global partnership in the Chinese tradition and policymaking.

By means of a political economic approach (that focuses on how to achieve political goals with economic tools – where *political* refers to high culture and philosophical aspects rather than party politics), we will describe the Chinese case with its external and internal challenges. Then we will continue with China's global aspirations and its relation to the EU, which is an essential milestone on the road China accepts to pursue within the global framework. In relation to the latter as a study case, we will highlight the most important conclusions of our research on the Political Economics of the Modern Silk Road project.[1]

1. The Chinese case

China is the world's oldest civilization that has continuously preserved its characteristics. This unique path of development motivated Fukuyama to start his new bestseller, *The Origins of Political Order*, with analysis of Chinese tradition. It may seem revolutionary to those who derive state or even the prototype of global governance from such examples as the Ancient Greece or Vatican City.

With this notion Fukuyama is arguing against the narrative: "the competitiveness of China comes from the efficiency of the operation of capitalism". However, the import of capitalism is a term based on cultural hierarchy. The 21st century shows that:

---

[1] The core of the paper is a summary of the presentation held at the 2nd Conference on China-Central and Eastern Europe (Krakow, Poland, 2015).

1. there is no hierarchy among high cultures since each of them may establish sustainable political and economic institutions in the long run in any technological environment
2. the Western institutions in the 90s failed to establish a globally acceptable model of development that would neglect the exclusion of regions and nations from the highest level of welfare.

Modern argumentations seem to assume that Confucian values are basically in harmony with the global market. This combination of "Confucian Capitalism" refers not only to an economic system, but to the whole view of the Chinese economic and political role in the world. It provides the whole concept for international issues and a competitor for the classic Western practices.

As a matter of fact, not only the West cannot rely simply on its own previous practices, but China also needs foreign experiences in establishing its national, regional and global policies.

As Fukuyama assumes, "neither the Chinese economic nor political models are sustainable in the long run" (Fukuyama, 2014). On the one hand, China's slowing growth rate narrows the opportunities for the middle class, which can easily lead to political instability; but on the other hand, there is no leading Chinese supporter to form a Western welfare state as Alan Greenspan envisioned: "The current Chinese middle class is not motivated in any fundamental political change toward democracy" (Greenspan, 2007). All these factors add up to a development in which China will not choose between the two obvious options, namely the Western democracy and authoritarianism, but it will form its own model – this is the so called *China's Political Trilemma*. The basic requirement of this third option is to befit the Chinese tradition as well as the needs of the modern era.

"China should take its own path in enhancing democracy. We never view socialism and democracy as something that is mutually exclusive". As this quote from Wen Jiabao (Premier of the People's Republic of China) demonstrates, China is looking for a politically sustainable transition process that (1) maintains the central power; (2) controls the pressure from the opposition that aims to achieve more power even by risking the stability of the state; (3) enhances economic growth. From this point of view the experience related to the transition of the Post-Soviet countries, like Slovakia or Hungary, is highly relevant to China right now.

Without strict regulations, it is impossible to achieve the needed growth, but those may lead to turmoil. Meanwhile, liberalization may prevent political turnover, but pose a threat to cooperation within the country. Since the population has no experience with freedom to speak, it could possibly lead to wide societal conflicts and dramatic decline.

1.1. External challenges

China is currently a combination of authoritarian government and a partially market-driven economy. The upcoming development of this system will not only affect the Chinese and the international political and economic arena, but the term *good governance* as well.

China suffers from a long list of unstable or potentially unstable factors. As a definitive regional power, China induces India, Japan and South-Korea to be sensitive against any initiatives broadening its sphere of influence. The prevention of the official formation of an *opposition triangle* in the region by these countries is a priority.

An export driven economy provides an opportunity for development but weakens its foreign assertions. To convert this external challenge to an internal one by inspiring consumption will free up its manoeuvres against USA, EU, and will clear its position towards Russia. Last but not least, we have to note that China is the largest and fastest-growing export market and investor in sub-Saharan Africa and Latin America, which is related to the global responsibility plan.

1.2. Internal challenges

The level of poverty is extreme in China, bringing it to the top of international comparisons – even with the decreasing Gini-coefficient. The middle-class suffers from even more serious unemployment than low-skilled workers do, which is accompanied by significant worries as to the quality of Chinese higher education outside of the elite universities like Tsinghua. The one-child policy destroyed the classic forms of Chinese family, which can lead to the reduction of the standards of living.

Nevertheless, the demographic problem is also a race against time: the biggest challenge is that the country is likely *to grow old before it grows rich* causing the unsustainability of its current progress and an unavoidable collapse.

On the one hand, social injustice may easily provoke unrest, but we must not "underestimate how much legitimacy the government gets as a result of rising Chinese nationalism" (Fukuyama, 2014). At this stage, Beijing steps between the Chinese population and the oligarchs, since the latter has two basic tools to oppress the population: *corruption* and *pollution*. China's environmental responsibility is highly above the usual level of any developing country – a pronounced motif of this role was the US-China Climate Change Agreement announced on November 12, 2014.

The significance of this agreement for this paper is to show how the central power positions itself and gradually cuts the oppressing power of the elites and rearranges political power toward the population. This process emphasises the fact that the Communist Party of China is resolutely moving forward the economic reforms even if doing so may provoke fundamental changes in the political sphere as well. Although Singapore is the only example of how to maintain economic growth with centralised power without oil resources, Japan and Sweden also show historical political stability – also in party politics. That recognition motivates China to investigate these systems substantially.

On the basis of the above, we conclude that the historical and cultural heritage as well as the economic reality inspires Chinese policymakers to lead rather than to fight political changes within the country as well as at regional and global levels – basically all economic moves are potential tools for that purpose.

2. Global aspirations

"The five years between 2005 and 2010, for example, have marked the appearance of three distinctive sets of literature whose academic and policy influence is likely to grow: neo-Tianxiaism[2] (tianxia is a Chinese term usually translated as 'all under heaven') symbolized by the philosopher Zhao Tingyang, the project on China's pre-Qin thoughts of international relations led by Yan Xuetong at Tsinghua University, and the 'China model' literature with inputs from Pan Wei at Peking University and various other scholars." (Zhang, 2013, p. 2)

On a global level, China's political economic strategy is built upon its concept of world order. By the second half of the 1970s, the deterioration of the Marxist theories and the political opening of China led to an ideological vacuum that was filled by the teachings of Confucius on all levels of society. The Chinese refer to the whole world as Tianxia ("all-under-heaven"). As Yanli Gao notes, "the term of 'all-under-heaven' is the ideal and aspiration inherent in it for a certain 'world institution' or 'world government' based on this ideal" (Gao, 2008, p. 256).

China's unique history that has preserved its civilization for thousands of years may be a supplement to the Western concepts of how to rule the world in the 21st century. China is relevant not only because of its massive population and territory, but also because of its exemplary traditions, which could be used as a model for stability in the world.

---

[2] In this paper we investigate only the term *neo-Tianxiaism*.

"Although since the mid- to late 1990s Chinese analysts have characterized the world power configuration as 'one superpower (the United States), many great powers (Europe, Japan, China, and Russia)', they expect the rise of China and other countries to transform US unipolarity into some sort of multipolarity in which China would play a greater role." (Zhang, 2013, p. 12)

China and its relations with Russia are among the characteristics that shape the 21st century and the restructuring of the global political and economic power. In that way China's rise does not only depend on its massive population and territory but also on its unique construction; hence, it *represents a potentially antagonistic balance against American dominance.*

In accordance with Putin's speech at Sochi (*Valdai*) in 2014, the new global order is real – only the transition may be a topic to investigate. On that field, China's approach, tools and global concept are highly relevant, focusing light on the traditional sources and modern forms of Chinese leadership. Chinese development does not necessary fall into war conflicts. Thus we may argue against the "Chinese track" ideology, as Fukuyama does:

"I believe that the analogies between China and pre-WWI Wilhelmine Germany, while obviously oversimplified, are correct in one essential sense. Like Germany after 1871 but unlike either Nazi Germany or the former Soviet Union, present-day China is not an imperialist power with unlimited global ambitions, nor is it driven by a millenarian, universalistic ideology." (Fukuyama, 2014, p. 1)

3. Chinese-European relations

The Sino-European partnership has a vast strategic potential. China currently has interests in a multipolar world instead of an America-dominated unipolar one that highlights the role of a prosperous and strong EU since "it is the most likely candidate to become another pole" (Turcsányi, 2014). As Geeraerts expresses: "The unipolar moment is definitely fading and slowly giving way to an international system characterized by multi-layered and culturally diversified polarity" (Geeraerts, 2011, p. 57).

China is increasingly suspected to be the Trojan horse in the European Union since its growing activity may weaken the continent's political economic power. However, this is far from Chinese interests. China has mainly bilateral relations with Western EU members and negotiates with the smaller and less influential CEE (Central & Eastern Europe) countries on a multilateral platform called 16+1. From one point of view, this process seems to form a new Berlin wall; therefore, this logic suggests that China's strategic goal is to undermine EU's power to rule it through dividing its unity.

China's growing presence certainly reshapes not only Europe, but the world as well. It became the biggest economy in the world, with low consumption rate, which means that China depends on external markets to maintain its growth. Necessarily, this transition induces conflicts – as it used to be said: what is common in Chinese businesses over CEE is that they are not German. Nevertheless, literature shows that this competition means cooperation instead of scramble.

In the European countries there was a big lack of investments and a need to alter their relations after the economic downturn of 2007. These intensions motivate them to intensify relations with China. Nowadays, China's economic presence in the region is highly connected to the modern Silk Road concept. The vision of Xi Jinping provokes dynamic competition in the CEE region, since all countries are intent on becoming the bridge between China and EU through this commercial project. Nonetheless, the main fact is that China's regional presence is dominated by contracts with multinational firms rather than national companies or states.

The complexity of the phenomenon is the following: (1) China is not a leading power in Europe; (2) it does not have the capacity to serve as a dividing force. Essentially the suspicious rhetoric does not harmonize with the Chinese foreign policy guidelines that provoke strong and united Europe, since only this can maintain the international environment for sustainable development of the Chinese economy and society.

Ultimately, China's European strategy is built upon its concept of world order. The meaning of *Tianxia*, or the Confucian harmony, is built upon the world-as-one and fits the Western traditions. This was also proved to be true for Christian missionaries who "encountered many similarities between the teachings of Jesus and Confucius" (Gao, 2008), opening the possibility for intercultural understanding.

Even if these concepts seemed to be well founded, we should admit both sides of the Chinese benefits due to its presence in the region: a short-term goal of economic self-enrichment and long term (geo)political goals. "China wants to secure the critical geopolitical space between Germany and Russia" (Turcsányi, 2014, p. 3).[3] Only time will tell how China will use its influence to push its interests.

---

[3] Based on an interview with MEP Adrian Severin, 27 November 2013, European Parliament, Brussels.

3.1. The global relevance of the Silk Road Project

The main similarity between the Ancient and Modern Silk Road initiative is that they both overshadow the pure trade route concept.[4] The historical one served as a corridor through which influential Western thoughts and at least seven religions arrived to China (Juhász, 2015). However, the differences between them are the attributes that show the real geopolitical targets of the "One Belt, One Road" (*yidai yilu*, hereafter OBOR) concept. Compared to the ancient trade route, which was demand-led, the current project is a supply-driven concept that targets:

1. development of its poor Western regions by introducing them into the world economy,
2. diversity of China's overdependence on sea transportation in foreign trade,
3. development of strong partnership with the EU that fits the new global order,
4. pacification of (potential) conflict zones where routes will cross with market rules.

The concept had evolved from a speech given by the Chinese Premier Xi Jinping in Kazakhstan in 2013. Originally, it targeted the development of China's bilateral relations with its neighbours; however, the initiative has since then traversed the region's borders and become a global project. Thus, the Silk Road became a key element of Xi Jinping's global vision. Nevertheless, it is essential to differentiate the OBOR from any alliances, since there are no direct political strings attached.

The proposal is not solely economic and trade-related. China has numerous interests in promoting the Silk Road Economic Belt. In essence, this initiative will enclose social, cultural, and security areas as well, contributing to the normative convergence of the partner countries. Most importantly, it serves as development of the Western regions; China sees the Silk Road and the establishment of transportation infrastructure as the answer to the development of its western region and the neighboring Central Asian nations. This is the primary goal and in itself – the political side of the OBOR.

The Belt and the Road together would "create an economic cooperation area that stretches from the Western Pacific to the Baltic Sea" (Fung Business Intelligence Centre, 2015, p. 3). The Belt railroad has various proposed routes (outlined in the following section) but in general it is directed from the Chinese coast towards the West, through China's Xinjiang province, through the Central Asian countries into Eastern Europe;

---

[4] Further details of our related research may be found in: Sárvári & Szeidovitz, 2016.

destination: the Baltic Sea. The Maritime Silk Road is a sea-trade route to Europe, which complements the Belt, but incorporates China's Southeast Asian neighbors and the Indian Ocean's coastal states. The two together would not only tie China unconditionally into the trade circuit of Europe and Asia, but also promote it as a country that acts unambiguously upon its global responsibility.

Another reason as to why this initiative is important to China is the questionable future of the Chinese economy. The main concerns are about economic growth. However, it is quite popular to state that China is giving up its export-oriented model – this is far from reality. The current trend in the Chinese economy is that as a result of the global economic crises and the emergence of its middle class, the government urged a shift to a consumption-led economy; this does not mean, however, that China gives up on its targets in export. As Inotai argues, China will shift its economic policy from a simply export-driven one (that China had chosen as a single country among the big developing states) to a more balanced structure (Inotai, 2011). The Chinese export will not decrease while the government motivates consumption to gradually increase it hand in hand with import.

The Chinese OBOR program in essence provides a structure for Chinese diplomatic, commercial, and foreign infrastructure policies around the world to expand Chinese exports and access to raw materials, and obtain new markets for Chinese trade and investment.[5] China can, in effect, concurrently contribute to Eastern Europe's rise and in that way to a new, more balanced Europe.

Between East Asia and Europe 95–96% of the trade is conducted through sea and only 3–3.5% through railroads. This is mainly because transport by land is significantly more expensive than transportation by sea. This is primarily due to the long delays at the borders caused by bureaucracy, tariffs and logistical ineptitude. While maritime transportation takes roughly 2.5–3 weeks, it only takes 13–15 days by land.

When analyzing the pros and cons of various forms of transport, in the end, transportation by land is more expensive; thus, currently this route is reserved for more expensive and valuable commodities, which are immune to colder weather, but are sensitive to sea-travel. What spikes up the cost of transportation by railway is the lack of goods on the return journeys from Europe and the inefficient modes of transport of various goods. Furthermore, government subsidies of various Chinese provinces' hubs have led to distorted prices and unbalanced competition on the market (Liu, 2014, p. 8).

---

[5] van der Putten & Meijnders, 2015, p. 29.

Many scholars (e.g. Anbound, Xu Gao) state that the new concept of three commercial directions (east, west, and south) is beyond the Chinese capacity. This micro- and macroeconomic approach leads to significant criticism of Chinese plans. It is pointed out that although the western route is logical, further diversification will disperse Chinese resources; meanwhile, China does not have an advantage in competitiveness compared to ASEAN countries. Xu Gao (2014) calls this project a "micro-hazard" since investments in infrastructure already represent a quarter of China's total investments and especially because such projects offer low direct returns and thus increase the threat of a potential debt-crisis.

Regardless of the expenses, in terms of Chinese goals, the primary purpose of rejuvenating the Silk Road through the OBOR is not to be cost-efficient but to contribute to the establishment of a new, multipolar world order. Based on all these factors, the New Silk Road proves that China is already a globally responsible power rather than a developing country that only extracts the possibilities of the America-financed global infrastructure. All this is underlined by the timing of the OBOR. It may be completed in about 35 years, which will fall on the centenary of the foundation of the People's Republic of China (2049).

Conclusion

The source of China's current economic policy is rooted in its understanding of the distribution of global power in the 21st century. China decided to accept the law of globalization and fill the given void. China in that way adapts to the change in global governance. This is an element that turns the OBOR concept into contribution to the stability of the new world order.

The main goal of the presentation and this paper was to contribute to the discussion on the possibility of the harmonisation of different high cultures in order to create a basis for global cooperation and sustainable development, or, in other words, to find a common "language" for the political debates of 21st century and the Confucian tradition. It is expressed in the Chinese meaning of harmony, which refers to "the message that China is increasingly and deliberately attempting to convey about itself to the world at large" (Brzeziński, 2012).

As Sino-expert Gyula Jordán concludes:

> "However there are unique experiences of the Chinese development, but these do not imply a complete model and may not be transferred to other countries easily. China is rather forming a model in the elastic adaptation of foreign practices by shaping a hybrid outcome as they accommodate these with the given environment." (Jordán, 2010, p. 80)

References

Brzeziński, Z.K. (2012). *Strategic Vision: America and the Crisis of Global Power*. New York: Basic Books.

Buzan, B. (2010). China in international society: Is 'peaceful rise' possible? *The Chinese Journal of International Politics, 3*, 5–36.

Chen Jie, Lu Chunlong (2001). Democratization and the middle class in China: The middle class's Attitudes toward democracy. *Political Research Quarterly, 64*(3), 705–719.

Fukuyama, F. (2014). Dealing with China. *Hoover Institution Press*. Available: http://www.hoover.org/sites/default/files/fukuyama_dealingwithchina.pdf (accessed: 04/06/2015).

Fung Business Intelligence Centre (2015). The Silk Road Economic Belt and the 21st Century Maritime Silk Road. Available: https://www.fbicgroup.com/?q=publication/silk-road-economic-belt-and-21st-century-maritime-silk-road (accessed: 20/01/2016).

Gao Yanli (2008). China's world view and world historical studies. *Dimensioni e problemi della ricerca storica*, 255–268.

Geeraerts, G. (2011). China, the EU, and the new multipolarity. *European Review, 19*(1), 57–67.

Godement, F. (2015). "One belt, one road": China's great leap outward. *European Council on Foreign Relations. China Analysis*, June, 18.

Greenspan, A. (2007). *The Age of Turbulence: Adventures in a New World*. New York: The Penguin Press.

Inotai, A. (2011). The strengthening of China's role in world economy and the future of the export-oriented "model". *Köz-gazdaság, 6*(1), 215–218.

Jordán, G. (2010). Washington Consensus vs Beijing Consensus. *Kül-Világ 2–3*, 60–80.

Juhász, O. (2015). A Selyemúton oda-vissza. *Remény*, 2. Retrieved from: http://www.remeny.org/remeny/2015–2-szam/juhasz-otto-a-selyemuton-oda-vissza/ (accessed: 20/01/2016).

van der Putten, F.P., Meijnders, M. (2015). China, Europe and the Maritime Silk Road. Clingendael report March 2015. *Netherlands Institute of International Relations Clingendael*. Retrieved from http://www.clingendael.nl/sites/default/files/China%20Europe%20and%20the%20Maritime%20Silk%20Road.pdf (accessed: 20/01/2016).

Sárvári, B., Szeidovitz, A. (2016). The political economics of the New Silk Road. *Baltic Journal of European Studies, 6.1*(20), 3–27.

Turcsányi, R. (2014). Central and Eastern Europe's courtship with China: Trojan horse within the EU? Retrieved from: http://www.eias.org/sites/default/files/EU-Asia-at-a-glance-Richard-Turcsanyi-China-CEE.pdf (accessed: 20/01/2016).

Zhang Feng (2013). The rise of Chinese exceptionalism in international relations. *European Journal of International Relations, 19*.

Xinhua News Agency (2007). *"Wen Jiabao: Guanyu shehuizhuyi chuji jieduan de lishi renwu he wo guo dui wai zhengce de ji ge wenti"* ("Wen Jiabao: Several Questions Concerning the Historical Duty of the Primary Stages of Socialism and Our Nation's Foreign Policy"), February 26. Retrieved from http://news.xinhuanet.com (accessed: 20/01/2016).

Xu Gao (2014). Looking at the 'One Belt, One Road' strategy from a return on investment point of view. *Financial Times* (Chinese version), 20.11.2014.

Natalia Ożegalska-Łukasik

Redefining and Elderly Caregiving in the 21st Century China and Poland

The family has been the central unit of the Chinese social organization for thousands of years. Traditionally, elders were looked after by the young with minimal state interventions. The Confucian filial piety that bound children to obey and serve their parents was treated as the highest of all virtues (Cheng & Chan, 2006, p. 262). However, it is a fact that recently the Confucian idea of filial piety has received lots of criticism, particularly from anthropologists and sociologists, who focus on the area of "family studies" (Slote & de Vos, 1998). Apart from a few exceptions, commentators have been critical of the idea to such an extent that one might wonder if it still has any relevance for the twenty-first century Chinese society. Nevertheless, as in the case of most concepts and ideas in ancient Chinese philosophy, this is all a matter of interpretation.

Polish families used to be traditionally large, with elders representing an important link with the past. The practice of respecting elders has its roots in the Christian culture. As observed by Robert Bellah (1970), "it is on the basis of authority derived from God that parents and rulers should be reverenced". It is not due to religious observance, however, that the value of deference to elders is significant to the majority of Poles. Older people are perceived in the Polish culture as the embodiment of wisdom and virtues, and as such, they are to be followed (Kukołowicz, 2002).

Nowadays, in the face of significant changes both of the mentioned countries have been undergoing since the 80s of 20th century – through reforms, marketization, and social phenomena like migration, and the ageing processes – a question arises about the impact of these changes on the pattern and structure of social relationships. A relevant indicator of social change in the Chinese society is located between the sense and content of the obligation that individuals feel to others, especially in the context of the relationship with parents. As noted by Mao and Chi (2011), there is a plethora of studies on filial piety which focuses on its factorial constituents (e.g. Sung, 1998), its role in intergenerational bonds and support exchange (e.g. Chow, 2001; Miller, 2004; Zhan, 2004), and its influence on parental caregiving (e.g. Chappel & Kusch, 2007; Hseuh, 2001; Lai, 2010) as well as presumptions of filial piety cultivated by parents and the implementation of this piety by their grownup children (Cheng & Chan, 2006; Philips et al., 2008). While the problem of ageing is frequently studied in the context of the Polish society, the issue of filial piety is occasionally mentioned in primary sources. It is dominated by studies of caregiving strategies (Bień & Wojszel, 2007), the position of elderly within the family and society (Czekanowski, 2011) and the determinants of life satisfaction among the elderly (Angelini et al., 2012).

The present paper discusses the way in which the concept of filial piety, which is deeply rooted in the Chinese and Polish cultures, is adapted to the ever-changing contemporary reality. Apart from analyzing the role of elders and elderly care, it principally covers the actions of the Communist Party of China (CPC) promoting its persistence. As a case study, the paper also examines the content of selected social campaigns created to promote and reshape the idea of filial piety.

Elders and the concept of filial piety in China

At the moment, China is still a relatively young country, with the average age of around 30; however, it is aging at an unprecedented rate and on an extraordinary scale due to the one-child policy (implemented between 1979 and 2015), the improvement of life expectancy and the large base population. In 2013, the average life expectancy at birth for the Chinese reached 75 years and the total fertility rate dropped to 1.5, well below the replacement level (United Nations Population Division, 2013). While in 1990 China had 67 million people aged 65 and older, this number climbed to 88 million in 2000, and then to 114 million in 2010. It is projected to reach 235 million (about 16.2% of the entire population) by 2030 (ibid.). At this rate in 2030 the country will have more elderly dependents than children, whereas in most of the other developing countries this relation will be opposite. In the early 1980s Wu Cangping, an academic at the Population and Development Resarch Centre at the Renmin University in Beijing, predicted a problem of "getting old before getting rich" in People's Republic of China (*The Economist*, 2009). Since then, however,

China has become a lot richer (with an income per person of about $7500 at ppp) and Chinese demographers might now argue that the phrase should be changed to "getting old while getting rich" (ibid.).

The socioeconomic changes in the country are shifting the condition and nature of familial and individual values. For centuries, family has played a central role in the elderly care in China. In addition, the Chinese Constitution and a series of laws were passed in the late 1990s that stipulate that family members have the primary responsibility to take care of their elderly parents, including arranging suitable housing (Zhang et al., 2004). These traditions are also reflected in many language idioms, for example: *happiness for the elderly comes from their children, who please them by living with them* (Chin. *cheng huan xi xia*), *having three generations living together under one roof* (Chin. *san dai tong tang*), and *insisting that harmony in the family is the basis for success in any undertaking* (Chin. *jia he wan shi xing*) (Chyi & Mao, 2012). Furthermore, care for the elder within a family also constitutes a cultural expectation based on the Confucian tradition of respect for age and experience.

Traditional cultural patterns in terms of norms, roles, and relationships have been deeply embedded in the Chinese society for millennia. With respect to family relations, sentiments and practices where associated in particular with *xiao* (filial piety), which included respect, obedience, and the obligation to care for elderly parents and respond to their needs (Deutsch, 2006). Attitudes and behaviors towards parents to ensure their well-being have contributed to keeping different generations connected and have led to an inherent sense of a child's obligation to support their parents in the ever-changing Chinese context (Mao & Chi, 2011). The classic of filial piety, Confucius (551–447 B.C.) said: "In serving his parents, a filial son revers them in daily life, he makes them happy while he nourishes them; he takes anxious care of them in sickness, he shows great sorrow over their death; and he sacrifices himself to them with solemnity" (Chai & Chai, 1965, p. 331). Adult children are also encouraged to avoid travelling far away from their parents (ibid.). Family obligation as filial piety was institutionalized in imperial China in a moral culture based on the Confucian philosophy and sustained by laws which preferred seniors (Xu, 2001).

During the Mao era and specifically throughout the Cultural Revolution, a lot of efforts were made to uproot these traditional cultural values. Extensive and deliberate campaigns were launched to transpose loyalty from traditional kinship to the Communist Party and its apparatus. Confucian ideology was heavily criticized and the Maoist thought relating to class struggle, revolution and self-sacrifice to build a perfect collectivist society was strongly supported. The rectifications campaigns of 1950s that were continued until 1970s resulted in the loss of the traditional notion of filial piety on both the ideological and institutional ground (Yan, 2009, p. 172). Still, despite the fact that the customary legitimation of this virtue was unsettled, family obligation itself was left unharmed. Even though clashes between the family and the Party resulted in favoring the Party, the Party still emphasized the enduring significance of family associations for individual welfare in the newly-reformed China (Qi, 2014, p. 146).

In spite of the enormous changes that have taken place in China since the beginning of the 1980s, it is remarkable that the importance of the Confucian notion of *xiao* ersists to this day. Even though the ethos and practice of familial obligations play a major role in determining the behavior of both parents and children, the meaning of *xiao* has been re-interpreted in various ways. What is more, the institutional basis of the familial obligation in present-day China represents the interest of the party-state and the context-based motives for self-preservation of its citizens (Qi, 2015). The familial obligation and filial piety were weakened during the reform period. Those who support the individualization factor point to the cultural acceptance of an ideological shift from self-sacrifice in the name of kinship or collective needs to self-realization and self-interest (Yan, 2009). The psychological mechanism hidden behind filial piety may be understood in different terms. Ho (1994) regards the character of filial piety as authoritarian and believes it has influence on the absolute parental authority over children. Contrary to this, Yang (1996) views filial piety through a society-oriented lens which has the reciprocity function of the reification of the concept of filial piety and which treats the relationship to which this term refers as grounded in politico-legal, social and normative frameworks in which an individual creates innovative strategies (Qi, 2014, p. 145).

Elders and the concept of filial piety in Poland

The demographic situation in Poland has recently caused a lot of concerns, which were not only expressed by researchers working in social sciences but also politicians. This is due to the fact that Poland is ageing very fast. According to the World Bank statistics, the average age in Poland in 2012 was 38 years, and this number will grow to 51 in 2050 (Devictor, 2012). Low birth rates and emigration are the two main factors which lead to Poland's population decline. In 2013, the average life expectancy of Poles reached 76 years – which is a similar figure than the one for China. At the same time, the total fertility rate dropped dramatically to 1.3 (United Nations Population Division, 2013). At the same time, the Polish Central Statistical Office estimates that the number of long-term Polish emigrants has risen from 0.7 million in 2002 to the peak number of almost 2.3 million in 2007, and currently oscillates around 2 million (Central Statistical Office, 2013). The facts mentioned above are important not only when it comes to the quantitative population analysis, but also when examining the strains within Polish family structure as well as the position of the elderly and the state of elderly care.

Traditionally, Polish families consisted of three generations: children, parents, and grandparents living under one roof – which was similar to a Chinese family. The customary respect for the elderly, as is still seen today, takes the most varied forms – from the esteem-ridden nickname "Grandpa" (Dziadek) has (it appears next to the names of prominent persons, such as Kazimierz Lisiecki, a teacher, creator of educational centers, and marshal Józef Piłsudski) (Kukołowicz, 2002), to the special position of the eldest in the given chamber in the Parliament.

However, the attitude towards the elderly is also changing. First of all, they are frequently no longer the residents of the same household as their grown-up children. Still, if both of the parents work, grandparents are the ones who take care of their grandchildren. The life expectancy is increasing, although this also means that other household members have to provide long-term assistance for increasingly disabled and dependent elders. This leads to the feeling of solitude and often discrimination among the elder.

The issue of the perception of old age, ageing and discrimination in Poland was evaluated in a public survey conducted by the Public Opinion Research Center (Pol. Centrum Badania Opinii Społecznej) in 1998, 2000, 2007, 2009, and 2010. It was also studied in various scientific contributions (Szukalski, 2004; Szatur-Jaworska, 2000). However, it was noted by Piotr Szukalski (2008), that those studies lacked a wider perspective. The results of the surveys mentioned above point to the fact that respectful attitude towards elders prevails in family (79%) and neighborhood (79%). The lowest level of respect was towards elders in medical (39%) and governmental institutions (32%) or on the street (25%). One per four respondents reported a feeling of indifference and lack of preoccupation in their living environment (Prokop & Ożegalska-Łukasik, 2014). Still, 87% of the Poles who were questioned believed that elders were indispensable to the society; conversely, only 9% treated them as a burden to others (Public Opinion Research Center, 2009). It is worth mentioning that the majority of elders lean toward the second opinion. It is also a widely held judgment among old-aged respondents that they experience discrimination in the work place and face serious difficulties in finding a job due to old age (The Academy for the Development of Philanthropy, 2007).

The role of the CPC in the redefinition of filial piety

Within its contemporary meaning, filial piety refers to unconditional, material and emotional support for parents. It is expressed by caring for parents and showing respect, obedience, providing them with financial support, greeting and pleasing them (Ng, 2002). It provides, therefore, not only financial support and instrumental care, two widely recognized forms of filial obligation and responsibility, but also the filial virtues specified by Confucianism: 1) taking care of parents, 2) being obedient, 3) showing love and respect, 4) being courteous, 5) concealing or ignoring parents' faults, 6) mourning parents' death in persistent, spontaneous, cohesive, and mutually consented ways (Lin, 1992). The latter components, once associated with the practice of rituals and submission to parental authority, are no longer elements of the contemporary conception of filial piety (Cheng & Chan, 2006; Cheung, Lee, & Chan, 1994; Ho, 1996).

As it has already been indicated, China has a long standing tradition of caring for the elderly; this care should be the sole responsibility of family members – never that of the government or society in general. Furthermore, China has never had a wide-ranging welfare infrastructure, and there is practically no comprehensive system that would provide care for the elderly in today's mainland China. It is relevant to note that neither the Communist Revolution nor the post-1978 reforms resulted in any significant breakaway from this tradition (Ikels, 1993, p. 307). At the beginning of the new millennium, care homes managed by the state and collective units provided beds for only 0.8% of the target population (Wong, 2008, p. 90). The number of beds per 1 000 senior citizens was growing steadily (as shown in Figure 1) and reached over 21 beds in 2012 (National Bureau of Statistics, 2013). This level of enrollment is still much lower than the 50–70 score observed in the developing countries. It should be noted, however that, as demonstrated in Figure 1, in 2010 China surpassed Poland in the number of beds in elderly care institutions for the first time (since 2005, Poland has maintained a steady figure of 17 beds per 1000 elders).

At the same time, only the childless Chinese elderly are allowed to benefit from the state-provided system of "five guarantees", which include: food, housing, clothing and health care as well as burial costs. All of those are provided at the lowest possible subsistence level (Thogarsen

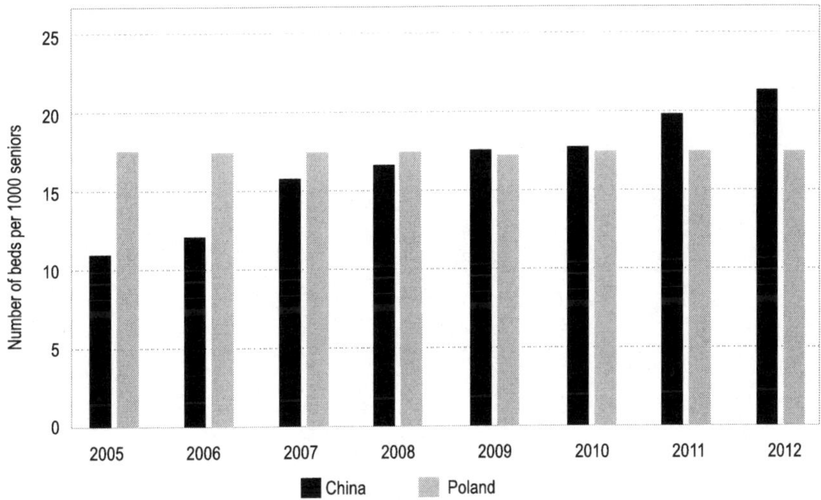

Figure 1. Number of beds in Chinese and Polish elderly care institutions per 1,000 senior/over 65 years old/citizens

Source: Author's own work based on National Bureau of Statistics, 2013, and OECD, 2016.

& Ni, 2008, p. 13). The Chinese government has persistently strengthened the emphasis on the responsibility of family members for the care for the elderly through media campaigns and legal means as a substitute for accepting the responsibility of the welfare program.

The Communist Party of China (CPC) has recently been promoting filial piety with a vast range of actions. Some of them will be listed and covered below:

I.   TV programs (e.g. Filial Piety Awards)
II. Modern Filial Piety Culture Museum
III. Education through documents (e.g. "Standard for Being a Good Pupil and Child")
IV. Creating a legal obligation of filial piety:
     a) "Protection of the Rights and Interests of Elderly People" includes a chapter entitled "Maintenance and Support by Families" with specific instructions
     b) "Family Support Agreement"
V.   Creating business opportunities for entrepreneurs to invest in elderly-related endeavors
VI. Ordering social campaigns aired on TV and distributed through the Internet (Youku, Weibo).

TV programs and award ceremonies such as the Chinese Filial Piety Awards Ceremony or the annual Chinese Filial Piety Writing Contest, attempt to emphasize the importance of filial devotion and celebrate its outstanding forms of expression. The Filial Piety Awards, just like other competitions, was set up to promote the virtue of filial piety through examples from real life.

Another initiative – Modern Filial Piety Culture Museum – was established in 2014 for more than one million US dollars and it constitutes part of government-backed efforts to "pass on the value" – as the banner over the entrance exhorts. It uses traditional Chinese architecture as a backdrop and showcases stories of filial piety by detailing narratives in which children sacrificed the most important things in life to honor and respect their parents.

Another important component of the governmental promotion of filial piety is through education and fostering of a collection of Confucian sayings which emphasize filial piety. President Xi Jinping is urging officials to read *Standards for being a Good Pupil and Child (Di Zi Gui)* written in Qing Dynasty by Li Yuxiu. Filial piety is also taught at school at different levels of education.

Special consideration should be also given to the legal aspects of filial piety in contemporary China. By mid-1980s, in order to ensure parental support, the Family Support Agreement (*jiating shanyang xieyi*) was introduced. Until the end of 2005, FSA has been signed by more than 13 million rural families across China and is now working its way into cities. FSA is a voluntary contract between parents and adult children giving formal grounds to parental care (Chou, 2010). Although the FSA is a voluntary contract, supporting one's parents is also mandated by law. According to Article 49 of the Constitution, "Parents have the duty to rear and educate their children who are minors; and children who have come of age have the duty to support and assist parents" (National People's Congress of The People's Republic of China, 1982). Articles 20, 21, and 22 of the Marriage Law extend the duty of mutual support from parents and children through adoptive, foster or stepparents and children, all the way to grandparents and grandchildren (National People's Congress of the People's Republic of China, 2001).

The assertion of filiality in other forms at the level of government was also notable in 2012 and 2013, when China's National Bureau of Senior Affairs (*Quanguo Laoling Ban*) released the New 24 Filial Exemplars. Another legal document, entitled "Protection of the Rights and Interest of Elderly People", includes nine clauses that lay down the duties of children and their obligation to tend to the "spiritual needs of the elderly". In order to provide additional motivation, some regional representations of the CPC (e.g. in Hunan) also indicated that applicants who did not provide sufficient care for their parents would be ineligible for party membership (Zhuang, 2012).

As mentioned above, two major forms of old-age support exist in China today. The more significant informal support is mainly provided by adult children and their spouses. The formal support is offered by public social welfare programs and public or enterprise-based pension systems (Pei & Pillai, 1999). However, according to a document issued on November 24, 2014 by the Ministry of Commerce and the Ministry of Civil Affairs, foreign investors are also very strongly encouraged to run commercial elderly care facilities, including nursing homes and recreation centers.

The last of the discussed types of measures taken by the CPC are social campaigns. They will be covered more broadly, as they constitute some of the most effective tools of reshaping the concept of filial piety.

Case study: Social campaigns as a means of filial piety's reinforcement in China

This research has conceptualized the social campaign as a specific element of the public sphere in contemporary societies world-wide. For the purposes of the research, social campaigns were conceptualized as social acts aimed at introducing a social change to broad social groups. Since social campaigns exert influence mostly by visual means, visual materials used in filial piety campaigns were operationalized as communicative tools employed in the process of the social change. The aim of this part of the research was to examine the content of the campaigns promoting the idea of filial piety which were ordered by one of the main actors who shaped the actual definition of filial piety. We wanted to explore social measures in the area of changing the cognitive, emotional, and behavioral components of social attitudes towards elders.

In the study, the analysis of visual materials was concentrated on their content. The objective was to answer the main research questions: What kind of message do those campaigns try to deliver? What specific elements can be identified in Chinese campaigns? How do social campaigns try to shape the concept of filial piety?

Visual materials from 15 filial piety campaigns were examined within the study. The materials were collected from Internet resources, portals offering collections of international social campaigns and local Internet resources. The majority of the visual materials analyzed herein were obtained from Youku. The materials were transcribed, encoded and analyzed with a help of the qualitative analysis program MaxQda, according to the above-described schema.

Most of the analyzed visual materials gathered for this exploratory research were produced by renowned Western agencies, such as Saatchi & Saatchi, and were commissioned by public institutions. One of the most successful examples of social campaigns promoting filial piety was a triptych called "The Aged Care", produced by Saatchi & Saatchi. It consists of three separate social ads concentrated on different aspects of elderly care. The success of those campaigns, aired in CCTV, is indisputable. The campaigns were launched on January 19th 2013 and were very frequently broadcast during Chinese New Year and later on throughout the year on 20 CCTV channels at different times of the day. The campaigns generated 1 million views on the first day of airing and a set of social media were abuzz with comments on the social network exceeding 2 million in 2 weeks. The films reached more than 500 million views. The main message was to raise awareness of the importance of connecting with relatives and loved ones in these increasingly selfish times. Each campaign of this triptych touched upon a different problem potentially experienced by the elderly. "Father's Lie" tells a story of an old man lying to his daughter to conceal the real difficulties he is experiencing in his old age. The second one, entitled "Take away", shows the story of a father suffering from Alzheimer's who forgets basic everyday things, but remembers the eating habits of his son. The advertisement is concluded with a meaningful tagline: "He's forgotten a lot of things. But he'll never forget he loves you". The third one of this series, called "Mum's wait", draws the viewers' attention to the problem of leaving parents due to economic migration. It starts with a picture of a young mother and her son who are transforming through ages, with the continuous thread of eternal and unconditional love linking each other.

The Confucian responsibility for ill parents is stressed in the campaign "Let love go back home". A father who was always seen as a hero by his son is turned into a person detached from reality due to Alzheimer's disease. The adult son is trying to face the problem of losing contact with his father, shows his involvement by trying to find his father who lost his way back home. This social advertisement ends with the message: "Pay attention to patients with Alzheimer's. Take care of and love your parents. Let love go back home". Another ad bringing tears to the eyes of many and viewed millions of times presents an image of a dying mother. "Lunch" – as it is entitled – mostly revolves around cooking and eating food – the de facto shared language of most Chinese families.

Another campaign called "63 years after the Reunion" highlights generational connections as an elderly man pays his respects to his late mother. The old man living in Taiwan is coming to visit his brother and other family members who live in mainland China for Chinese New Year.

After finishing a meal together, he is having some personal moments with a photograph of his mother.

The distinctive feature of most Chinese campaigns analyzed within the framework of this paper revolve around the challenges of facing the suffering of elderly people, induced by loneliness, health problems or a difficult financial situation, and especially – around the way they cope with their old age. At the same time, it is interesting that those stories are mostly told from the perspective of the third person (however, we can get a feeling that a story is presented by someone who sees situation of the elderly person from a wider perspective and with greater objectivity). A person dealing with old age is usually shown in a context of his/her relations with others, as in campaigns concerning Alzheimer's disease ("Let love go back home" or "Take away").

Elderly life within the studied campaigns is usually presented in a descriptive way, sometimes with the use of metaphors. For instance, the campaign "Let love go back home" shows a bicycle as a symbol of an elderly father's lost abilities, and the campaign "Take away" *jiaozi* (Chinese dumpling) uses the symbol of a son's favorite food – the last thing his father clearly remembers. Another characteristic motif which appears in some campaigns is related to internal migration and its consequences – mainly leaving the family home and ageing parents. They emphasize the necessity of visiting parents at least during Chinese New Year.

In general, the described campaigns convey messages in an emotional way. It is not surprising that Chinese campaigns typically promote social support – especially from loved ones – and acceptance as the anticipated social norms. The main message we can identify in the analyzed visual materials was a call for emotional support for parents. Finally, it is also stressed that attachment to home and family constitutes a moral obligation. What should also be noted is that none of the analyzed campaigns expressed a direct suggestion for providing help in an economic sense. Another characteristic feature of the studied campaigns is the fact that all of them consist of long video sequences and in order to understand the final message one should watch them from the beginning. Finally, a very interesting reference which could be distinguished was the cultural practice of eating together, as in the campaigns "Lunch", "63 years after reunion", and "Take away".

Conclusion

Filial piety understood as a cultural value is strictly codified and supported by legal sanctions, which results in the creation of limitations to
actions available to people and in building a scheme for the interpretation of other people's actions (Abramson, 2012, p. 173). The structural
foundation of familial obligation in contemporary China and Poland is
a continued dependence on family members when caring for the elderly
due to the absence of adequate state-provided welfare. Nevertheless, the
emotional commitment of mature children today, especially those living
far away from their hometown, might be perceived more in the context of
their private relations than their relations with parents. The shift in the
primary emotional responsibility does not mean that mature children
feel that they have no obligation to care for their parents' well-being, be it
physical or emotional. Familial obligation, particularly in terms of material support, will continue to play an important role in the Chinese and
Polish societies in the future. But it does not mean that past structures
and patterns of familial obligation and filial piety will remain unchanged.
The question which should arise is not whether adult children would sac-
rifice themselves for their parents but rather what form of support adult
children would feel obliged to provide to their elderly parents and on what
basis. Familial obligation and filial piety remain the core elements of the
culture system, which interacts with the politico-legal and social context
in which it operates. In China, the CPC undoubtedly plays a major role in
creating a new image of filial piety conforming to the contemporary Chinese reality. It holds in its hands a range of tools, such as the legal system
and incentives both for caregivers and investors willing to contribute to
the elderly care system. Finally, measures taken by the media, including
social campaigns distributed on television and on the Internet, represent
an effective means of reshaping the concept of filial piety. As observed
herein, recent social campaigns in this area seem to be professionally prepared, with a significant involvement of renowned media agencies. Consequently, they attract a lot of attention and appear to fulfill their goals.
The content of the campaigns refers to culturally meaningful motifs like
family, food, Chinese New Year Eve, dedication of parents to children etc.
The key to their success is that they build up on emotions and refer to
daily life of a Chinese adult living in contemporary China.

References

Abramson, C. (2012). From "either-or" to "when and how": A context-dependent model of culture in action. *Journal for the Theory of Social Behaviour, 42,* 155–180.

The Academy for the Development of Philanthropy (2007). *Rynek pracy a osoby bezrobotne 50+. Bariery i szanse.* Available online: http://www.rynekpracy. pl/pliki/pdf/3.pdf (accessed: 01/02/2016).

Angelini, V., Cavapozzi, D., Corazzini, L., Paccagnella, O. (2012). Age, health and life satisfaction among older Europeans. *Social Indicators Research, 105,* 293–308.

Bellah, R. (1970). Father and son in Christianity and Confucianism. In: Bellah, R. *Beyond Belief* (pp. 76–99). New York: Harper and Row.

Bień, B., Wojszel, B. (2007). Rural and urban caregivers for older adults in Poland: Perceptions of positive and negative impact of caregiving. *International Journal of Aging & Human Development, 65*(3), 185–202.

Central Statistical Office (2013). *Informacja o rozmiarach i kierunkach emigracji z Polski w latach 2004–2012.* Warszawa: Główny Urząd Statystyczny.

Chai Ch'u, Chai, W. (1965). *The Sacred Books of Confucius, and other Confucian Classics.* New Hyde Park, NY: University Books.

Chappel, N.L., Kusch, K. (2007). The gendered nature of filial piety – A study among Chinese Canadians. *Journal of Cross-Cultural Gerontology, 22*(1), 29–45.

Cheng Sheung-Tak, Chan, A.C.M. (2006). Filial piety and psychological well-being in well order Chinese. *Journal of Gerontology, 61B*(5), 262–269.

Cheung Chau-kiu, Lee Jik-joen, Chan Cheung-ming (1994). Explicating filial piety in relation to family cohesion. *Journal of Social Behavior and Personality, 9,* 565–580.

Chou, R. (2010). Filial piety by contract? The emergence, implementation and implications of the "Family Support Agreement" in China. *The Gerontology, 51*(1), 3–16.

Chow, N.W.S. (2001). The practice of filial piety among the Chinese in Hong Kong. In: Chi, I., Chappel, N.L., Lubben, J. (eds). *Elderly Chinese in Pacific Rim Countries: Social Support and Integration.* Hong Kong: Hong Kong University Press.

Chyi Hau, Mao Shangyi (2012). The determinants of happiness of China's elderly population. *Journal of Happiness Studies, 13*(1), 167–185.

Czekanowski, P. (2011). Implications of population ageing for family relations. In: Hoff, A. (ed.). *Population Ageing in Central and Eastern Europe: Societal and Policy Implications* (pp. 209–226). Farnham: Ashgate Publishing.

Deutsch, F.M. (2006). Filial piety, patrineality, and China's one child policy. *Journal of Family Issues, 27*(3), 366–389.

Devictor, X. (2012). *Poland: Aging and the Economy.* World Bank report. Available online: http://www.worldbank.org/en/news/opinion/2012/06/14/poland-aging-and-the-economy (accessed: 30/01/2016).

The Economist (2009). *China's predicament*, issue: Jun 25, 2009.

Ho, David Yau-Fai (1994). *Filial piety, authoritarian moralism and cognitive conservatism in Chinese society*. Genetic, Social, and General Psychology Monographs, vol. 120, pp. 347–365.

Hseuh Kuei-Hsiang (2001). *Family caregiving experiences and health status among Chinese in the United States*. PhD dissertation, Ann Arbor, MI, UMI Dissertation Services, ProQuest Information and Learning.

Ikels, C. (1993). Settling accounts: The intergenerational contract in an age of reform. In: Davis, D., Harell, S. (eds). *Chinese Families in the Post-Mao Era*. Berkeley: University of California Press.

Kukołowicz, T. (2002). Respect for women and the elderly and love of children. In: Dyczewski, T. (ed.). *Values in the Polish Cultural Tradition* (pp. 241–252). Washington: Council for Research in Values and Philosophy.

Lai, D.W.L. (2010). Filial piety, caregiving appraisal and caregiving burden. *Research on Ageing*, 32(2), 200–223.

Li Hong, Tracy, M.B. (1999). Family support, financial needs and health care needs of rural elderly in China: a field study. *Journal of Cross-Cultural Gerontology*, 15(4), 357–371.

Mao Weiyu, Chi, I. (2011). Filial piety of children as perceived by ageing parents in China. *International Journal of Social Welfare*, 20, S99-S108.

Miller, E.T. (2004). Filial daughters, filial sons: Comparison from rural North China. In: Ikels, C. (ed.). *Filial Piety – Practice and Discourse in Contemporary East Asia* (pp. 34–52). Stanford, CA: Stanford University Press.

Ministry of Commerce and the Ministry of Civil Affairs (2014). *Announcement of the Ministry of Commerce and the Ministry of Civil Affairs on Matters Relating to Foreign Investors' Establishment of For-profit Elderly Care Institutions*, November 27, 2014.

National Bureau of Statistics (2013). *China Statistical Yearbook 2013*. Beijing: China Statistics Press.

Ng, Anita Ching Ying, Philips, D.R., Lee, William Keng Mun (2002). Persistence and challenges to filial piety and informal support of older persons in modern chinese society: A case study in Tuen mun, Hong Kong. *Journal of Ageing Studies*, 16(2), 135–153.

Organization for Economic Co-operation and Development (OECD). *OECD Health Statistics 2015*. Available online: http://stats.oecd.org (accessed: 30/01/2016).

Pei Xiaomei, Pillai, V.K. (1999). Old age support in China: the role of the state and the family. *International Journal of Aging and Human Development*, 49, 197–212.

Qi Xiaoying (2014). Filial obligation in contemporary China: Evolution of the culture-system. *Journal for the Theory of Social Behaviour*, 45(1), 141–161.

Prokop, A., Ożegalska-Łukasik, N. (2014). Marketing społeczny a stygmatyzacja osób starszych z demencją i depresją oraz ich rodzin w wybranych krajach Europy. *Studia Sociologica*, 2, 86–106.

Public Opinion Research Center – CBOS (2009). *Polacy wobec ludzi starszych i starości. Komunikat z badań (nr BS/157/2009)*. Warsaw: CBOS. Available online: http://www.cbos.pl/SPISKOM.POL/2009/K_157_09.PDF (accessed: 30/01/2016).

Slote, W.H., De Vos, G.A. (eds) (1998). *Confucianism and the Family*. Albany, NY: State University of New York Press.

Sung Kyu-Taik (1998). An exploration of actions of filial piety. *Journal of Ageing Studies*, 12(4), 369–386.

Szatur-Jaworska, B. (2000). *Ludzie starzy i starość w polityce społecznej*. Warszawa: ASPRA-JR.

Szukalski, P. (2004). Uprzedzenia i dyskryminacja ze względu na wiek (ageizm) – przyczyny, przejawy, konsekwencje. *Polityka Społeczna*, vol. 2, 11–15.

Szukalski, P. (2008). *Ageizm – dyskryminacja ze względu na wiek*. In: Kowaleski, J.T., Szukalski, P. (eds). *Starzenie się ludności Polski – między demografią a gerontologią społeczną* (pp. 153–184). Łódź: Wydawnictwo Uniwersytetu Łódzkiego.

Thogarsen, S., Ni, A. (2008). He is he, and I am I: Individual and collective among China's rural elderly. *European Journal of East Asian Studies*, 7, 11–37.

United Nations Population Division (2013). *The World Population Prospects: the 2012 revision*. New York: United Nations.

Wong, L. (2008). The third sector and residential care for the elderly in China's transitional welfare economy. *The Australian Journal of Public Administration*, 67, 89–96.

Xu Yuebin (2001). Family support for old people in rural China. *Social Policy & Administration*, 35, 307–320.

Yan Yunxiang (2009). *The Individualization of Chinese Society*. Oxford: Berg Publishers.

Zhan Heying, J. (2004). Willingness and expectations: Intergenerational differences in attitudes toward filial responsibility in China. *Marriage and Family Review*, 36(1–2), 175–200.

Zhang Zhenmei, Gu Danan, Luo Ye (2014). Coresidence with elderly parents in contemporary China: The role of filial piety, reciprocity, socioeconomic resources, and parental needs. *Cross Cultural Gerontology*, 29, 259–276.

Zhuang Pinghui (2012). Respecting elders to gain fresh meaning. *South China Morning Post*, August 20ᵗʰ. Available online: http://www.scmp.com/news/china/article/1018761/new-standards-filial-piety-cause-unhappiness (accessed: 01/11/2015).

Łukasz Gacek

Roadmap for Moving to a Low Carbon Economy in China and Poland. Comparative Analysis

China and Poland underline the principle of maintaining a balance between population, resources, and environment. Considering similar energy structure with the dominant role of coal and significant environmental problems, both countries should initiate a revolution in the areas related to the production and the use of energy by promoting energy-efficient, low carbon development of the industry, as well as new and renewable sources of energy in building the country's energy security. They also have to establish a system for protection of arable lands, water resources and environmental protection management systems.

The need for greater diversification within the existing energy structure is forcing both China and Poland to take the activities related primarily to: restructuring the coal sector, which should result in increased competitiveness, and the promotion of clean coal technologies; promotion of energy efficiency; development of renewable energy sources as well as lifting capacity in nuclear power plants and increasing the importance of natural gas in the energy mix.

Main research questions posed in this paper concern the perception of low carbon development, the overall energy mix in China and Poland and their intensity for carbon reduction targets. The major goal of this paper is to present, firstly, that the transition to a low carbon economy in both countries leads to improving the environment. Secondly, that the environmental protection is a rising policy priority, both in China and Poland, and thirdly, that the renewable energy market dynamics combined with the efficiency improvement should enhance their bargaining position in the global energy market.

1. Global transition to a Low Carbon Economy

Low Carbon Economy (LCE) means the economy primarly character-ized by the separation of greenhouse gas emissions from the economic and social growth, mainly by reducing the use of fossil fuels, including coal, oil, and natural gas, that are currently the world's primary energy source. It is based mainly on the energy efficiency, the use of renewables and technological innovation help to limit greenhouse gas emissions. It is also an aleternative system of production and consumption, allowing to conserve the energy and to reduce greenhouse gas emissions (GHG).

This concept has its roots in the international environmental treaty *The United Nations Framework Convention on Climate Change* adopted at the United Nations Conference on Environment and Development (UNFCCC) in Rio de Janeiro in June 1992 (The United Nations Frame-work Convention on Climate Change, 1992). The strategy of reducing carbon emissions to protect and improve the natural environment, com-bined with the development of low carbon economy is identified within the concept of low-emission development strategies (LEDS). It refers to the national economic development plans that underline low-emission and climate resilient economic growth. This concept used to describe the objectives for the reduction of CO_2 emissions and other greenhouse gases. The term "low-emission development strategies" first emerged under The *United Nations Framework Convention on Climate Change* (UNFCCC) in 2008.

The Kyoto Protocol has promoted a low carbon development through the clean development mechanism. The document adopted in Kyoto in Japan, on 11th December 1997, required developed countries to *re-duce* their *GHG* emissions. Developing countries, like China, were not required to commit to the reductions because their per-capita green-house gas emissions are lower than those of the developed nations. The main aim was to create a global market system, supporting the transfer of technology and building a low carbon economy in developing coun-tries (Kyoto Protocol to the United Nations Framework Convention on Climate Change, 1998).

The next step towards building a low carbon economy was the cli-mate deal agreed by 195 countries. The Paris Agreement was adopted at the Paris UN Climate Change Conference, COP21 in December 2015. It supports transition to a low carbon economy. It provides an opportunity to development of innovations in low carbon energy. An international accord commits all countries to reduce greenhouse gas emissions (Adop-tion of the Paris Agreement, 2015).

2. Laws and policies for Low Carbon and Green Growth

2.1. China

The Chinese government officially endorsed Low Carbon Economy (LCE) in 2007, when the Ministry of Science and Technology, the Chinese Meteorological Administration and the Chinese Academy of Sciences started publishing annual reports on climate change in China – *China's National Assessment Report on Climate Change* (《气候变化国家评估报告》解读). China underlined, that development of nations must reflect common, but differentiated responsibilities and the principle of fairness. In this sense, developed countries should continue to take the lead position in emissions reduction actions, while developing countries should provide financial and technical support to enhance the capacity of developing countries to address climate change. In the framework of sustainable development, developing countries should take efforts to transform the model of economic growth, to promote technological innovation, development of "low carbon economy" (低碳经济, *ditan jingji*), and reduction in greenhouse gas emissions (Qihou bianhua guojia pinggu baogao jiedu, 2007).

On December 26, 2009, China adopted an amendment to the "Renewable Energy Law", which was first passed on February 28, 2005. It introduces a law to boost development of alternative energy sources. *Renewable Energy Law of the People's Republic of China* (中华人民共和国可再生能源法) (Zhonghua Renmin Gongheguo ke zaisheng nengyuan fa, 2005, 2009) emphasized the development and utilization of renewable energy, increase in the supply of energy, improvement of the structure of energy, safeguarding the safety of energy, protection of the environment and realization of sustainable economic and social development. Priorities relate to the development and utilization of renewable energy in the energy development; the establishment and development of the renewable energy market; as well as the development and utilization of wind, solar, water, biomass, geothermal, and tidal wave energy as well as other renewable energy resources (Zhonghua Renmin Gongheguo ke zaisheng nengyuan fa, 2009).

The solutions adopted three years later were equally important. On October 24, 2012, China published a white paper on its energy policy, *China's Energy Policy 2012* (中国的能源政策（2012）白皮书). Most significant is its commitment to a strong *increase of renewable and low carbon energy, as well as to establishing a green, low carbon concept* (低碳发展理念, *ditan fazhan linian*) *to coordinate the development and utilization of energy resources and strengthen environmental protection. China set new targets of developing clean coal technologies and highly efficient power generation systems based on thermal power generation. It is worth to underline, that China declared to promote advanced supercritical and ultra-supercritical coal-fired power with higher steam parameters and increased efficiency* (Zhongguo de nengyuan zhengce (2012) Baipishu, 2012).

2.2. Poland

All issues related to the Poland's energy policy defines *The Act of April 10, 1997 – The Energy Law* (Ustawa z dnia 10 kwietnia 1997 r. Prawo energetyczne). It underlines the creation of fordable conditions for sustainable development of the country, ensuring energy security, rational use of energy, development of competition, counteracting the negative effects of natural monopolies, environmental protection, it also included the obligations under the international agreements and balancing the interests of energy companies and consumers (Ustawa z dnia 10 kwietnia 1997 r. Prawo energetyczne, 1997).

Plans for Low Carbon Economy to contribute to the achievement of the objectives set out in the EU's climate and energy package by 2020, relating to the reduction of greenhouse gas emissions, increasing the share of renewables in the energy mix and reducing final energy consumption by improving energy efficiency. The major aim included in *The Act of 15 April 2011 on energy efficiency* (Ustawa z dnia 15 kwietnia 2011 r. o efektywności energetycznej) has led to improvement in the energy efficiency and the rational use of existing energy resources in the perspective of increasing demand for energy. Poland sets its targets for energy savings, taking into account the role of the public sector, establishing mechanisms for supporting and monitoring system and collecting the necessary data (Ustawa z dnia 15 kwietnia 2011 r. o efektywności energetycznej, 2011).

The long-term energy sector development strategy was presented in *The Energy Policy of Poland until 2030* (Polityka energetyczna Polski do 2030 roku), adopted by the Ministry of Economy in November 2009. It set out the basic principles and directions for formulating energy policies by Poland. Particular emphasis was placed on improving the energy efficiency, increasing security of energy supplies, diversification of the electricity generation structure by introducing nuclear energy, development of renewable energy sources, including biofuels, development of competitive energy markets, as well as reducing energy sector's negative impact of on the environment. The document pointed out that the supply of renewable energy would allow to reduce Poland's dependency on energy imports and favour the diversification of energy supply. It also established conditions for the development of a distributed energy system (Polityka energetyczna Polski do 2030 roku, 2009). The sustainable scenario included in *Project of the Energy Policy till 2050* (Projekt Polityka energetyczna Polski do 2050 roku) has stated that coal and oil would remain a major source of energy. Despite this, the plan provides dynamic increase in the share of natural gas, nuclear power and renewables in the Polish energy mix (Projekt Polityka energetyczna Polski do 2050 roku, 2015).

On the 4th of July, 2015, Polish Ministry of Economy set up a project called *The National Programme for the Development of Low Carbon Economy* (Narodowy Programu Rozwoju Gospodarki Niskoemisyjnej, NPRGN). The major aim is to develop a low carbon economy and to ensure a sustainable development. The activities focus on low carbon energy generation, efficient resources and efficient waste management, sustainable production, low carbon transformation in the distribution and mobility, transition towards low carbon distribution and mobility as well as the promotion of sustainable consumption patterns (Narodowy Program Rozwoju Gospodarki Niskoemisyjnej, 2015).

In this comparison one should also refer to some interesting proposals included in a document prepared under the project called *Low-emission Poland 2050* (Niskoemisyjna Polska 2050). It presented possible paths for transformation of the Polish economy towards 2050, particularly in the context of estimating the potential costs and benefits of the implementation of climate policy in the perspective of the year 2050. The project carried out by the Warsaw Institute for Economic Studies and the Institute for Sustainable Development focused on the costs and benefits of conducting climate policy in Poland in the perspective of the year 2050. It is an important shift towards thinking in terms of modernization based on innovation, the efficiency and environmental friendliness. Authors of the report emphasized that climate policy should be a part of Poland's development policy. Everything depends on the scenario that Poland will choose. The ratio of coal in Poland's energy mix should gradually decrease. Poland will have to replace old and inefficient coal-fired plants with more efficient, modern power plants. Because Poland will have to close the old coal-fired power plants, there will be a problem concerning electricity supply. Therefore, the government should concentrate its activities on improvement of the efficiency and on the promotion of renewable energy. The implementation of low-emissions measures should have a positive impact on Polish economy, contributing to an increase in GDP of 0.5 percent by 2030 and more than 1 percent by 2050 (Bukowski, 2013).

3. China vs Poland Energy Consumption

The essence of low carbon economy is the efficient utilization of energy and development of clean energy. Modernization of the energy sector in Poland and China, where it now depends on fossil fuels to the extent of about 90 percent (Table 1), is needed. The current energy generation is a result of the national raw material base, which encompasses substantial hard coal and lignite resources. It also constitutes a legacy of the development paradigm that dominated in Poland and China, which saw economic prosperity in the development of the energy-intensive heavy industry and mining.

Table 1: Primary energy consumption in 2014

	China		Poland	
	2014 (percent)	2014 (Mtoe)	2014 (percent)	2014 (Mtoe)
Coal	66	1 656	53	49
Oil	22	549	28	26
Gas	7	169	16	15
Hydroelectricity	3	77	–	–
Nuclear	1	31	–	–
Biodiesel	–	–	1	1
Biomass and waste	–	–	1	1
Other Renewables	1	21	1	1
Total	100	2502,1	100	92,1

Source: The World Bank – World Development Indicators. Breakdown of Energy Consumption Statistics, Primary Energy Consumption in 2014 (China, Poland).

The electricity mix is heavily dependent on solid fuels. Coal is the most often used fuel to generate thermal electricity. The coal share of China's total electricity generation was at an estimated 72 percent, compared to Poland's 81 percent. As a result the diversification of the electricity mix in both countries is very low (Table 2).

Paradoxically, large coal reserves make both countries energy independent. China and Poland are characterized by a high energy independence, respectively at 84 percent and 72 percent. Poland's energy independence is among the highest in the EU (Energy Research Estore, 2014, China, Poland). According to the figures released by Eurostat (the statistical office of the European Union), the energy dependency rate of the EU rate was 53.2 percent in 2013. Poland was amongst the member states least dependent on energy imports. It's energy dependency in-

Table 2: Electricity production from all energy sources in 2014

	China		Poland	
	2014 (percent)	**2014 (TWh)**	**2014 (percent)**	**2014 (TWh)**
Coal	72	3 681	81	126
Hydroelectric	20	1 029	1	2
Gas	2	91	4	6
Nuclear	3	131	0	8
Wind	3	148	4	6
Biomass and waste	–	–	9	14
Others	1	65	1	2
Total	100	5145	100	155

Source: The World Bank – World Development Indicators. Breakdown of Electricity Generation by Energy Source, Electricity Production from All Energy Sources in 2014 (China, Poland).

dex was only 23.8 percent, compared to Estonia (11.9), Denmark (12.3), Romania (18.6) (Energy consumption in the EU down to its early 1990s level, 2015).

3.1. China

Coal amounts to nearly 70 percent of the domestic demand for energy in China. These reserves are one of the largest in the world. In terms of total coal reserves, China is second only to the United States and Russia. However, China controls almost a half of the world production. Despite this, production does not balance the domestic demand, which makes China a net coal importer.

In the future, coal mining will still remain the key sector of the economy, because the central authorities intend to implement a series of major projects, aimed at modernizing and introducing new technologies in the production of clean coal. The possibility of extracting energy from coal while reducing environmental pollution at the same time, is becoming an essential part of the ongoing restructuring of coal mining industry. In July 2012, China planned to construct 363 coal-fired power plants with a combined generating capacity of 557 gigawatts (Luo, Otto, & Maddocks, 2013). China focuses on the construction of large advanced units, more efficient and generating less pollution. China has just underlined a plan of building a super-critical and ultra-critical units operating at high pressures. In parallel with these activities, in December 2015 China has announced that it would reduce the emissions of major pollutants in the power sector by 60 percent by 2020 and annual carbon dioxide emissions from coal-fired power plants by 180 million tonnes per year by 2020 (Guojia li tui ran mei dianchang gaizao jiangdi wuran paifang, 2015). The problem is the inefficiency of the coal-power sector. While utilisation rates had fallen and reached a record low, surplus capacity is still very high. There is a discrepancy in implementation of the environmental policy at the central and local levels. Despite the fact that the central government intends to shut down the old, unsafe or energy inefficient plants, local governments continue to approve new capacity. For example, around 200 GW of capacity were approved for realization in the first half of 2015, only 5 GW of small and ageing plants were shut down in 2014 (Wong, Lewis, Stanway, & Chen, 2015).

Oil is the second source of energy used in China. It accounts for some 20 percent of the country energy mix. China is the second largest consumer of oil in the world, just after the United States. According to Wood Mackenzie, by the year 2020, 70 percent of China's oil demand will come from import. China will overtake the US as the world's biggest oil importer by 2017 (Heading in Opposite Directions: China and US Reliance on Oil Imports, 2013). Approximately two-thirds of the total oil supplies are imported, mainly form the Middle East and Africa.

The third source of energy in China is natural gas, which amounts to 6 percent of the energy mix. But China plans to increase the share of gas to 10 percent by 2020. Gas sector in China is rapidly growing, and its influence on the global markets will increase in the future. China has already become the world's third largest gas importer behind Japan and South Korea. In this case, China relied on imports to meet 25 percent of its needs. Central Asian countries are the major suppliers of gas to China, through the Central Asia-China pipeline system. Turkmenistan alone supplied nearly abovea half of China's gas imports (Mei, 2015). In 2006, China began importing liquefied natural gas. Now, China is the world's third-largest importer of LNG after Japan and South Korea. It has 13 LNG terminals in operation and three under construction. It is worth to remember, that China has the world's largest unconventional gas reserves, with especially significant shale gas potential.

Renewable energy is the fourth largest source of energy in China. This sector is growing faster than the fossil fuels sectors. According to *Renewables 2015 Global Status Report*, global investment in renewable energy reached more than 270 billion USD. China alone was responsible for 83.3 billion USD of investment, followed by the US and Europe. China is the fastest growing wind and solar PV market in the world. Only in 2014, China added 23 gigawatts of wind power (one third of the world's total) and 10 gigawatts of solar PV (one quarter of the world's total) (Renewables 2015 Global Status, 2015).

Because of the fast growth of oil and gas consumption in the industrialization and urbanization, China has to develop new energy sources and to promote the technology of new energy. In the long term, China's energy consumption will depend on coal, but later, it will be gradually replaced by clean and renewable energy like nuclear, solar, wind, ocean, geothermal and hydrogen (Zhou, 2011).

3.2. Poland

Poland's energy structure relies on domestic coal resources. Coal accounts for 54 percent of the country's energy mix. Poland is the largest producer of coal in the EU. Coal is a pillar of its energy security. Thanks to the huge coal reserves, Poland is the least dependent on external supplies of energy resources amongst all of the EU-28 countries. In the document *Energy Policy of Poland until 2030* coal was described as a stabilizer of the country's energy security in the face of economy dependency on gas and crude oil imports (respectively 70 and 95 percent) (Polityka energetyczna Polski do 2030 roku, 2009). Similar arguments, treating coal as a stabilizer of energy security were included in the *Project of the Energy Policy till 2050*. An important direction of the state energy policy will be related to increasing the competitiveness of this sector (Projekt Polityka energetyczna Polski do 2050 roku, 2015). During the parliamentary campaign in September 2015, the Prime Minister of Poland Beata Szydło said that "there is no future for the Polish economy without coal and there is also no future for coal without modern and clean technologies" (Wybory 2015: energia z węgla czy atomu? Spór między Kopacz a Szydło, z Piechocińskim w tle, 2015). In December 2015 Andrzej Duda, the President of the Republic of Poland, underlined that coal was a guarantee of Poland's energy sovereignty (Duda: Węgiel jest podstawą suwerenności energetycznej Polski, 2015).

These statements show, that Poland's energy policy is not fully compatible with the EU's climate and energy targets. Poland especially opposes the reforms of the EU emissions trading system (EU ETS), designed to boost the price of emissions permits. The structure of the energy consumption in the European Union relies heavily on hydrocarbon energy. The low share of coal at 18 percent arises from the EU's greenhouse gas emissions targets and promotion of the low carbon economic model. The EU aims to increase the energy efficiency, develop renewable energy sources, as well as to replace coal with natural gas and other renewables.

Oil is the second source of energy used in Poland. It constitutes 28 percent of the country's energy mix. The third energy source is natural gas, which accounts for 13 percent of the country's energy mix. Poland con-

Table 3: EU-28 primary energy consumption by fuel type (1990–2013)

	1990 (percent)	2013 (percent)
Coal and lignite	28.9	18.2
Natural gas	18.0	23.8
Oil (crude oil and petroleum products)	35.0	30.1
Nuclear energy	13.1	14.4
Renewable energy	4.5	12.6

Source: Primary energy consumption by fuel type (2015).

sumes almost 15 billion cubic meters of gas annually. Approximately two-thirds of total gas supply are imported, mainly from Russia. In October 2015 Poland opened its first LNG Terminal in Świnoujście. It allows to partially reduce the dependency on Russian gas supplies. This project is critical for Poland's energy security. The initial regasification capacity will be 5 billion cubic meters annually, what corresponds to approximately one third of Polish demand for natural gas. The terminal capacity would be expanded in the future to up to 7.5 billion cubic meters (Świnoujście: zgoda na przyjęcie pierwszej dostawy LNG, 2015). Poland also has potential and opportunities for exploitation of unconventional gas deposits. According to the study prepared by Poland's Geological Institute, shale gas resources in Poland could vary between 346 and 768 billion cubic meters (Ocena zasobów wydobywalnych gazu ziemnego i ropy naftowej w formacjach łupkowych dolnego paleozoiku w Polsce [basen bałtycko-podlasko-lubelski] – raport pierwszy, 2012), much less than the 5.3 trillion cubic meters estimated earlier by the U.S. Energy Information Administration.

Renewable energy is the fourth energy source in Poland. The share of renewable energy in gross final consumption of energy should reach 15 percent by 2020 (Polityka energetyczna Polski do 2030 roku, 2009; Krajowy Plan Działania w zakresie energii ze źródeł odnawialnych, 2010). Wind and biomass are the most important renewable energy source in Poland (Krajowy Plan Działania w zakresie energii ze źródeł odnawialnych, 2010). According to the *REmap 2030: Renewable Energy Prospects for Poland*, prepared by the International Renewable Energy Agency (IRENA) in association with the Polish Ministry of Economy, Poland can increase its share of renewable energy in power generation to nearly 38 percent and in total, the final energy consumption to nearly 25 percent by 2030 (compared to 7 percent in 2010). Cumulative wind capacities will reach 16GW, solar PV 5 GW, and bioenergy 5GW. Total renewable power generation should grow nearly eightfold between 2010 and 2030. Poland unveiled plans to cut carbon emissions by 8 percent by 2030 based on

2005 levels and by 22 percent compared to 1990 levels (REmap 2030: Renewable Energy Prospects for Poland, 2015).

4. Strategies to reduce greenhouse gas emissions

In the context of building a sustainable economy, issues relating to environmental protection are of a high importance. China and Poland have recognized the fact that development policy must also take into account its environmental costs. Implementation of the objectives requires the development of appropriate technology in a way that maintains the economic competitiveness of the state.

On the one hand, China is the largest carbon dioxide (CO_2) emitter in the world and it amounts to nearly 30 percent of the total. On the other hand, CO_2 emissions per capita in China are still much lower than that of the U.S. The major sectors contributing to China's carbon emissions like manufacturing and power generation, are responsible for 85 percent of country's total carbon emissions. Additionally, about 25 percent of carbon emissions in China are caused by manufacturing products that are consumed abroad (Zhu, 2015). Poland belongs to the largest carbon dioxide emitters in the EU-28, however, it reduced its greenhouse gas emissions by one third since 1988. Poland also significantly reduced its emissions per capita.

Table 4: CO_2 emissions from fossil fuel use and cement production 1970–2014 (ton (Mg) per capita and per year

	1980	1990	2000	2010	2014
China	27 648	2 411 402	3 746 109	9 009 136	10 540 750
Poland	430 972	357 727	309 303	322 664	298 131
EU-28	471 7045	4 345 210	4 066 865	3 865 298	3 415 235
World	19 847 474	22 515 632	25 610 746	33 607 885	35 669 108

Source: Global CO2 emissions from fossil fuel use and cement production 1970–2014 (2015).

Table 5: CO_2 per capita emissions from fossil fuel use and cement production 1970–2014 (ton (Mg) CO_2 per capita and per year)

	1980	1990	2000	2010	2014
China	1.6	2.1	2.9	6.6	7.6
Poland	12.1	9.4	8.1	8.4	7.8
World	–	4.2	4.2	4.9	4.9

Source: Global CO2 per capita emissions from fossil fuel use and cement production 1970–2014 (2015).

4.1. China

China intends to prepare a long-term strategy and a roadmap for low carbon development, that will be based mainly on improving Regional Strategies on climate change, building low carbon energy system, building energy efficient and low carbon industrial system, controlling emissions from building and transportation sectors, promoting the low carbon lifestyle, innovating low carbon development growth pattern, and promoting international cooperation on climate change.

The strategy for Building Low Carbon Energy System includes:
- controlling total coal consumption, enhancing the use of clean coal,
- increasing the share of natural gas consumption in the primary energy consumption to more than 10 percent by 2020,
- promoting the development of hydro power,
- developing nuclear power,
- developing wind power, solar power, geothermal energy, bio-energy, and tidal wave energy,
- scaling up distributed energy and strengthen the construction of smart grid (Qianghua yingdui qihou bianhua xingdong: Zhongguo guojia zizhu gongxian, 2015).

12th Five Year Plan (2011–2015) underlined the main objectives of improving the energy efficiency in the country. Key points related to the reduction of energy consumption per GDP unit by 16 percent within five years towards 2015, reduction of carbon dioxide emission by 17 percent in between 2010 and 2015, as well as reduction of carbon dioxide emission by 40–45 percent by 2020, compared to 2005 emission. China set a target to obtain 11.4 percent of its primary energy requirements from non-fossil fuels in overall primary energy use (China announces 16% cut in energy consumption per unit of GDP by 2015, 2011). In June 2015 the Premier of the State Council of the People's Republic of China Li Keqiang declared during his visit in Paris that China would aim to cut its GHG emissions per unit of gross domestic product by 60–65 percent of the 2005 level by 2030. China also would increase the share of non-fossil fuels in the primary energy consumption to around 20 percent by 2030, and peak CO_2 emissions around the same point (Zhongguo xuanbu hou 2020 qihou mubiao: tan paifang qiangdu xiajiang 60%-65%, 2015).

It confirms the assumptions contained in *China's Energy Policy 2012*, a first white paper on energy policy, which very clearly emphasized the importance of developing alternative energy sources. The document states that China's energy development should be based on the use of advanced technologies, low consumption of raw materials, smaller environmental pollution, economic efficiency, and energy security. The document mentioned a plan to reduce, by the end of 2015, the energy consumption per GDP unit by 16 percent in comparison to 2010 and a reduction of carbon dioxide emissions per GDP unit by 17 percent, in line with the Twelfth Five-Year Plan (2011–2015). China announced active promotion within the scope of the development of water, solar, wind, and nuclear power, as well as biomass and other renewable energy sources (Zhongguo de nengyuan zhengce [2012] Baipishu, 2012).

Considering the need for greater diversification within the existing energy structure, China's development strategy based on low carbon solutions, should focus on activities related primarily to: restructuring the coal sector, which should result in increased competitiveness, and the promotion of clean coal technologies; development of renewable energy sources; lifting capacity in nuclear power plants; as well as increasing the importance of natural gas in the energy mix (Gacek, 2015, p. 126). China also has to improve the monitoring system of greenhouse gas emissions and gradually create the basis for a national trading scheme for carbon dioxide emissions. It already launched seven local, pilot emissions trading schemes. These experiences will help a launch of a national carbon emissions trading market in 2017. It will cover sectors like power generation, steel industry, chemicals and cement production industries. The carbon market will help China to meet its goals of ensuring its emissions peak around 2030 (Volcovici, 2015). The system still has a number of weaknesses, like legal and administrative regulations, statistics, data collection, as well as monitoring and evaluation systems. Emission limits for different regions should be based on their economic development, industrial structure, and the citizens environmental issues awareness. Progress in this area will mainly depend on the determination of the authorities.

4.2. Poland

Poland strategy corresponds with that of the EU. The most important is the *EU 2020 Energy Strategy*, also known as 20/20/20 climate/energy targets by 2020 (3x20 policy). The plan assumes a reduction in the greenhouse gas emissions by 20 percent before 2020, compare to the 1990 emission level; increasing the energy efficiency by 20 percent to 2020; reaching 20 percent of energy from renewables in the total energy consumption in the EU by 2020; and reaching the 10 percent level of biofuels use in the total vehicle fuel consumption by 2020 (Communication from the Commission Europe 2020. A strategy for smart, sustainable and inclusive growth, 2010).

Considering the criterion of equal efforts of member states, Poland could increase its 14 percent emissions by 2020 compared to 2005 in sectors not included in the EU emissions trading system, because of the lower Gross Domestic Product (GDP) per capita comparatively to the EU average. Poland could also increase the share of the energy from renewable sources to 15 percent by 2020, instead of the EU's average of 20 percent, due to the limited resources and low efficiency of renewable energy sources used in Poland (Overview of Europe 2020 targets). The EU's energy policy is based on three pillars: competitiveness, sustainability and supply security (Communication from the Commission to the European Parliament, the Council, the European Economic and Social Committee and the Committee of the Regions, 2010). The priorities related to achieving an energy efficient Europe, building a truly pan-European, integrated energy market, empowering consumers and achieving the highest level of safety and security, extending Europe's leadership in energy technology and innovation, and strengthening the external dimension of the EU energy market (ibid.).

The second important strategy is the EU 2030 Energy Strategy, setting goals for the EU in 2030. It proposed a 40 percent cut in GHG emissions compared to 1990 levels; at least a 27 percent share of renewable energy consumption; as well as at least 27 percent improvement in the energy efficiency (Communication from the Commission to the European Parliament, the Council, the European Economic and Social Committee and the Committee of the Regions, 2014). In 2011, the European Commission underlined its ambitious climate targets in *A Roadmap for moving to a competitive low carbon economy in 2050*. The document set a long-term goal of reducing GHG emissions in the range of 80–95 percent below 1990 levels by the year 2050 (Communication from the Commission to the European Parliament, the Council, the European Economic and Social Committee, and the Committee of the Regions, 2011).

Generally, Poland supports the EU climate policy. However, measures to achieve these targets are contentious. Adjustment of the Polish economy to the requirements of environmental protection and climate, in the reduction of greenhouse gas emissions are associated with a need to invest in new and less emissive technology. Poland emphasizes that the EU solutions should take into account the specificity of all members of the EU and their different energy mixes (Wiceminister Pietrewicz o pakiecie klimatyczno-energetycznym, 2015).

The reform of the EU ETS is perceived as controversial by Poland. The economic slowdown and lower demand for electricity led to a large surplus of CO_2 permits, pushing their prices down. Poland strongly opposes the EU policy that lead to gaining a greater control of the market and permanent introduction of a back-loading mechanism of CO_2 allowances. In

2013, the EU decided to remove a total of 900 million allowances on auction from 2014 to 2016, before returning them to the market from 2019 to 2020 (Erbach, 2014). The aim is to increase the price of allowances. This solution is not beneficial for countries such as Poland, whose energy is based mainly on coal. The decision of the EU could cost the Polish budget as much as 1 billion EUR in lost revenues from 2013 to 2020 (Polska może stracić ok. 1 mld euro na zawieszeniu aukcji CO_2, 2012). According to the World Bank's report, the implementation of the European Union climate and energy package might reduce Polish GDP by 1.4 percent annually by 2020 (while the average for the EU-26 is 0.55 percent). It will also raise the unemployment rate in Poland by 0.57 percent, while in the EU-26 by 0.17 percent (Transition to a low-emissions economy in Poland).

The EU's climate and energy policy beyond the year 2020 could be a matter of intense debate in Poland. The result of the proposed new trading system for greenhouse gases may be a distortion of competition and finally, it could further increase the energy prices. The EU's policy leading to a growth in energy prices, has a double negative impact on the poorer European countries like Poland. In particular, the costs of the EU's climate policy impact mainly on the households. The share of the domestic energy costs in the total expenditure in Poland was 9.1 percent in 2012, second only to Slovakia (while the EU-27's average was only 4.5 percent). The energy prices for the industrial consumers are relatively higher in the poorest countries in EU (Koncepcja zmian w unijnej polityce energetyczno-klimatycznej oraz proponowane kierunki jej modyfikacji wraz z uzasadnieniem i oceną skutków, 2013).

References

Documents & Reports:
Adoption of the Paris Agreement (2015). United Nations Framework Convention on Climate Change. 12, 12.
Communication from the Commission Europe 2020. A strategy for smart, sustainable and inclusive growth (2010). European Commission. Brussels. 3, 3.
Communication from the Commission to the European Parliament, the Council, the European Economic and Social Committee and the Committee of the Regions (2010). Energy 2020 A strategy for competitive, sustainable and secure energy. European Commission. Brussels. 10, 11.
Communication from the Commission to the European Parliament, the Council, the European Economic and Social Committee and the Committee of the Regions (2011). A Roadmap for moving to a competitive low carbon economy in 2050. European Commission. Brussels. 8, 3.

Communication from the Commission to the European Parliament, the Council, the European Economic and Social Committee and the Committee of the Regions (2014). A policy framework for climate and energy in the period from 2020 to 2030. European Commission. Brussels. 22, 1.

Heading in Opposite Directions: China and US Reliance on Oil Imports (2013). Wood Mackenzie. 8. http://www.woodmac.com/content/portal/energy/highlights/wk3__13/Heading%20in%20Opposite%20Directions%20-%20China%20and%20US%20Reliance%20on%20Oil%20Imports.pdf (accessed: 30/01/2016).

Koncepcja zmian w unijnej polityce energetyczno-klimatycznej oraz proponowane kierunki jej modyfikacji wraz z uzasadnieniem i oceną skutków (The concept of change in the EU's energy and climate policy and proposed directions for its modification with justification and impact assessment). Załącznik 3 (Appendix 3): Porównanie krajów UE pod względem udziału przemysłu, kosztów energii w budżetach domowych i struktury cen energii elektrycznej (Comparison of EU countries in terms of share of industry, energy costs in household budgets and structure of electricity prices) (2013). Polish Chamber of Commerce. Warsaw. 10, 5.

Krajowy Plan Działania w zakresie energii ze źródeł odnawialnych (National Renewable Energy Action Plan) (2010). Ministry of Economy of the Republic of Poland. Warszawa. http://www.mg.gov.pl/files/upload/12326/KPD_RM.pdf (accessed: 30/01/2016).

Kyoto Protocol to the United Nations Framework Convention on Climate Change (1998). United Nations.

Narodowy Program Rozwoju Gospodarki Niskoemisyjnej (The National Programme for the Development of Low Carbon Economy) (2015). Ministry of Economy of the Republic of Poland. 4, 8.

Ocena zasobów wydobywalnych gazu ziemnego i ropy naftowej w formacjach łupkowych dolnego paleozoiku w Polsce (basen bałtycko-podlasko-lubelski) – raport pierwszy (Assessment of Recoverable Natural Gas and Crude Oil Resources in Lower Paleozoic Shale Formations of Poland [Baltic-Podlasie-Lublin Basin] – First Report) (2012). Polish Geological Institute – National Research Institute. Warsaw. 3, 5.

Polityka energetyczna Polski do 2030 roku (Energy Policy of Poland until 2030) (2009). Ministry of Economy of the Republic of Poland, Warsaw. 10, 11.

Projekt Polityka energetyczna Polski do 2050 roku (Project of the Energy Policy till 2050) (2015). Ministry of Economy of the Republic of Poland, Warsaw. 8.

Qianghua yingdui qihou bianhua xingdong: Zhongguo guojia zizhu gongxian (强化应对气候变化行动: 中国国家自主贡献, Enhanced Actions on Climate Change: China's Intended Nationally Determined Contributions) (2015). Xinhua. 30, 6.

Qihou bianhua guojia pinggu baogao jiedu (气候变化国家评估报告 解读, China's National Assessment Report on *Climate* Change) (2007). Ministry of Science and Technology of the People's Republic of China. 4, 9.

Overview of Europe 2020 targets. http://ec.europa.eu/europe2020/pdf/targets_en.pdf (accessed: 30/01/2016).

Renewables 2015 Global Status (2015). Renewable Energy Policy Network for the 21st Century (REN21).

REmap 2030: Renewable Energy Prospects for Poland (2015). IRENA. 10.

The United Nations Framework Convention on Climate Change (1992). United Nations.

Transition to a low-emissions economy in Poland (2011). The World Bank Poverty Reduction and Economic Management Unit, Europe and Central Asia Region, The World Bank. Washington. 2.

Zhongguo de nengyuan zhengce (2012) Baipishu (中国的能源政策（2012）白皮书, China's Energy Policy 2012) (2012). Central People's Government of the People's Republic of China. 24, 10.

Ustawa z dnia 10 kwietnia 1997 r. Prawo energetyczne (The Act of April 10, 1997 – the Energy Law) (1997). Dz.U. 1997, nr 54, poz. 348, The Office of Parliament.

Ustawa z dnia 15 kwietnia 2011 r. o efektywności energetycznej (The Act of 15 April 2011 on energy efficiency) (2011). Dz.U. 2011, nr 94, poz. 551, The Office of Parliament.

Zhongguo de nengyuan zhengce (2012) Baipishu (中国的能源政策 (2012) 白皮书, China's Energy Policy 2012) (2012).

Zhonghua Renmin Gongheguo ke zaisheng nengyuan fa (中华人民共和国可再生能源法, Renewable Energy Law of the People's Republic of China). Adopted at the 14th Meeting the Standing Committee of the Tenth National People's Congress on February 28, 2005; Amended according to the Decision of the 12th Meeting of the Standing Committee of the 11th National People's Congress of the People's Republic of China on December 26, 2009.

Zhonghua Renmin Gongheguo ke zaisheng nengyuan fa (中华人民共和国可再生能源法, Renewable Energy Law of the People's Republic of China) (2009). The National People's Congress of the People's Republic of China. 26, 12.

Zhu, Liu (2015). China's Carbon Emissions Report 2015, Belfer Center for Science and International Affairs, Harvard Kennedy School. 5. http://belfercenter.ksg.harvard.edu/files/carbon-emissions-report-2015-final.pdf (accessed: 30/01/2016).

Books:

Bukowski, M. (ed.) (2013). *2050.pl The Journey to the Low-emission Future*. Warsaw Institute for Economic Studies. Warsaw: Institute for Sustainable Development.

Gacek, Ł. (2015). *Zielona energia w Chinach. Zrównoważony rozwój – Ochrona środowiska – Gospodarka niskoemisyjna (Green Energy in China. Sustainable development – Environmental protection – Low-carbon economy)*. Kraków: Wydawnictwo Uniwersytetu Jagiellońskiego.

Zhou Tianyong (2011). *The China Dream and the China Path*. Singapore: World Scientific Publishing Co. Pte. Ltd.

Articles:

China announces 16% cut in energy consumption per unit of GDP by 2015 (2011). Xinhua. 5.03. http://news.xinhuanet.com/english2010/china/2011–03/05/c_13761876.htm (accessed: 30/01/2016).

Duda: Węgiel jest podstawą suwerenności energetycznej Polski (Coal is the Basis of Polish Energy Sovereignty) (2015). IAR. Forsal. 4.12. http://forsal.pl/artykuly/909360,duda-wegiel-jest-podstawa-suwerennosci-energetycznej-polski.html (accessed: 30/01/2016).

Erbach, G. (2014). Reform of the EU carbon market. From backloading to the market stability reserve. European Parlament. 10. http://www.europarl.europa.eu/RegData/etudes/BRIE/2014/538951/EPRS_BRI%282014%29538951_REV1_EN.pdf (accessed: 30/01/2016).

Guojia li tui ran mei dianchang gaizao jiangdi wuran paifang (国家力推燃煤电厂改造降低污染排放, Emissions Reduction through Upgrade of Coal Fired Power Plants) (2015). *Renmin Ribao* (人民日报). 3.12. http://energy.people.com.cn/n/2015/1203/c71661–27886647.html (accessed: 30/01/2016).

Luo Tianyi, Otto, B., Maddocks, A. (2013). *Majority of China's Proposed Coal-Fired Power Plants Located in Water-Stressed Regions*. World Resources Institute (WRI). 26.08. http://www.wri.org/blog/majority-china%E2%80%99s-proposed-coal-fired-power-plants-located-water-stressed-regions (accessed: 30/01/2016).

Mei Xinyu (2015). Gas trade for the better. *Beijing Review*, 23. 28.05.

Polska może stracić ok. 1 mld euro na zawieszeniu aukcji CO_2 (Poland may lose approx. 1 billion euros for suspending the auction of CO_2) (2012). PAP. *Rzeczpospolita*. 17.12. http://www.rp.pl/artykul/962331-Polska-moze-stracic-ok--1-mld-euro-na-zawieszeniu-aukcji-CO2.html (accessed: 30/01/2016).

Świnoujście: zgoda na przyjęcie pierwszej dostawy LNG (Świnoujście: Acceptance for the First Delivery of LNG) (2015). PAP. *Puls Biznesu*. 16.11. http://www.pb.pl/4357751,23857,swinoujscie-zgoda-na-przyjecie-pierwszej-dostawy-lng (accessed: 30/01/2016).

Volcovici, V. (2015). China to announce 2017 launch of carbon market, officials say. Reuters. 25.09.

Wong, Sue-Lin, Lewis, B., Stanway, D., Chen, K. (2015). China says to cut power sector emissions by 60 pct by 2020. Reuters. 3.12.

Wiceminister Pietrewicz o pakiecie klimatyczno-energetycznym (Deputy Minister Pietrewicz on Climate and Energy Package) (2015). Ministry of Economy of the Republic of Poland. 21, 10. http://www.mg.gov.pl/node/25278 (accessed: 30/01/2016).

Wybory 2015: energia z węgla czy atomu? Spór między Kopacz a Szydło, z Piechocińskim w tle (Election 2015: Energy from Coal or Atom? The Dispute between Kopacz and Szydło, with Piechociński in the background) (2015). Polskie Radio. PAP. 5.10. http://www.polskieradio.pl/42/3167/Artykul/1524977,Wybory-2015-energia-z-wegla-czy-atomu-Spor-miedzy-Kopacz-a-Szydlo-z--Piechocinskim-w-tle (accessed: 30/01/2016).

Zhongguo xuanbu hou 2020 qihou mubiao: tan paifang qiangdu xiajiang 60%-65% (中国宣布后2020气候目标：碳排放强度下降60%-65%, China has announced a target for 2020 to reduce the emissions intensity of its economy by 60–65 percent) (2015). Beijixing jieneng huanbao wang (北极星节能环保网). 1.07. http://huanbao.bjx.com.cn/news/20150701/636379.shtml (accessed: 30/01/2016).

Statistics:

Energy consumption in the EU down to its early 1990s level (2015). Eurostat. 9.02. http://ec.europa.eu/eurostat/documents/2995521/6614030/8-09022015-AP-EN.pdf/4f054a0a-7e59-439f-b184-1c1d05ea2f96 (accessed: 30/01/2016).

Energy Research Estore (2014). China Key Figures. https://estore.enerdata.net/china-energy.html, Energy Research Estore (2014). Poland Key Figures. https://estore.enerdata.net/poland-energy.html (accessed: 30/01/2016).

Global CO_2 emissions from fossil fuel use and cement production 1970–2014 (2015). EDGARv4.3, European Commission, Joint Research Centre (JRC)/PBL Netherlands Environmental Assessment Agency. Emission Database for Global Atmospheric Research (EDGAR). release version 4.3. http://edgar.jrc.ec.europe.eu, 2015 forthcoming. http://edgar.jrc.ec.europa.eu/overview.php?v=CO2ts1990–2014&sort=des9 (accessed: 30/01/2016).

Global per capita CO_2 emissions from fossil fuel use and cement production 1970–2014 (2015). EDGARv4.3, European Commission, Joint Research Centre (JRC)/PBL Netherlands Environmental Assessment Agency. Emission Database for Global Atmospheric. 25, 11. http://edgar.jrc.ec.europa.eu/overview.php?v=CO2ts_pc1990–2014 (accessed: 30/01/2016).

Primary energy consumption by fuel (2015). European Environment Agency. 21, 10. http://www.eea.europa.eu/data-and-maps/indicators/primary-energy-consumption-by-fuel-6/assessment (accessed: 30/01/2016).

The World Bank – World Development Indicators. Breakdown of Electricity Generation by Energy Source, Electricity Production from All Energy Sources in 2014 (China, Poland), The Shift Project Data Portal. http://tsp-data-portal.org/Breakdown-of-Electricity-Generation-by-Energy-Source#tspQvChart.

The World Bank – World Development Indicators. Breakdown of Energy Consumption Statistics, Primary Energy Consumption in 2014 (China, Poland). The Shift Project Data Portal. http://tsp-data-portal.org/Breakdown-of-Energy-Consumption-Statistics#tspQvChart (accessed: 30/01/2016).

Joanna Wardęga

Chinese Community in Poland – the Dynamics of its Development[1]

Poland is an ethnically homogeneous country, and traditional foreign national groups are those originating from the bordering countries, and in recent years also from the European Union. The immigrant population from Asia for many years has been dominated by the Vietnamese, quite well organized and integrated. Chinese immigration to Poland does not have a long history. Among all the groups of a foreign origin in Poland, the Chinese are of a relatively small number, around 2,5 percent. Despite that, a rapid development may be observed in last few decades. The presence of this national group is visible in clusters, mainly in Warsaw and some other cities, where the branches of Chinese enterprises are located. Only individuals have settled outside these centres. Due to the short history of migration and a relatively low level of integration with the host society, the Chinese have not created a stable organization nor active institutions that would support their functioning in the new country. The following text is an attempt to describe the size and the forms of immigration, settlement structure, and rare organizations in which they operate. It was also intended to outline the prospects for the future development of this national group in Poland on the basis of the existing forms of cohabitation.

Overview of the Chinese immigration to Poland

Historically, Central and Eastern Europe wasn't a traditional destination for the Chinese immigration. In the pre-war period, the number of the Chinese in Central Europe was negligible (Nyiri, 2007, p. 29). In the

---

[1] The article was a result of the research project "Socio-cultural identification of foreigners", led by prof. Jacek Schmidt (UAM).

first decades after Second World War, there was no growth either as only individuals were arriving there, such as for instance the exchange students. The Chinese arrived in this part of Europe in larger groups in 1989–1991, mainly due to the abolition of Hungarian visas. As a result, in a very short period of time in that country the number of the Chinese rose to 40,000 (Nyiri, 2007, p. 54). Later, many of them re-emigrated to Poland, the Czech Republic, Slovakia, and Romania. After the tightening of visa policy in Hungary, new destinations emerged: Romania and the Czech Republic (also as a trail of transfer to Western Europe), and subsequently Slovenia, Poland, Albania, Bulgaria, Ukraine, Lithuania. The number of the Chinese in Central and Eastern Europe can be estimated at around 50,000 (Nyiri, 2007, p. 137). They are mainly businesspersons, characterized by their high intensity of contacts with the country of origin and the relatively high mobility between countries of the region. This is one of the reasons, why it is difficult to assess the number of the Chinese population.

Until the beginning of the 21st century very few people of the Chinese nationality were arriving to Poland. According to Polish data, in 1999 there were only 617 Chinese living in Poland; 462 of them had temporary residence permits, and 155 had settlement permit/permanent residence permit (Grzymała-Kazłowska et al., 2002, p. 118). More dynamic development of Chinese immigration to Poland would start after the access to the European Union in 2004.

Data from the Central Statistical Office, the Border Guard and the Police present a rough idea of the size of the Chinese population in Poland. The Chinese population in the last few years may be estimated between 5 to 8 thousand people, who were staying in Poland on the basis of valid residence permits of different kinds. For instance, in January 2015, the number presented by The Office for Foreigners was 4782 Chinese (Urząd do spraw Cudzoziemców, 2015a). These data, however, are incomplete, because it is not determined how many foreigners remained in the country without permits or visas, and how many might have been smuggled across the borders. 2015 mid-year data shows that the Chinese population with valid documents confirming the right of residence on the territory of Poland is nearly 5,000 people, accounting for 2.5 percent of the foreigners. That makes them the eighth largest ethnic minority group in Poland, after the Ukrainians, Germans, Russians, Belarusians, Vietnamese, Italians, and the French (Urząd do spraw Cudzoziemców, 2015b). Although this number is much lower than other, far more numerous groups, last several years' growth rate was fast, and the population has doubled since 2009. In addition, a growing number of the Chinese people receive visas for Poland.

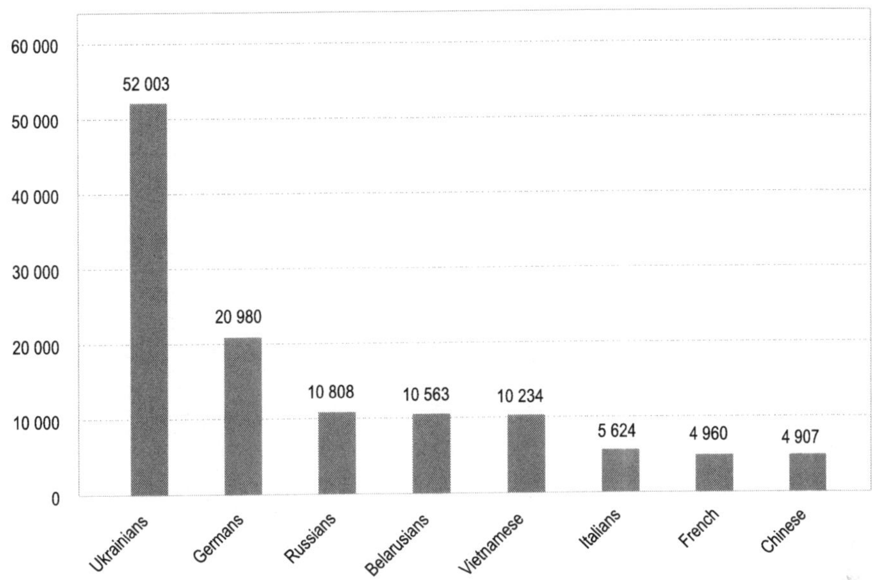

Graph 1: The size of the largest nationalities with valid permits in the Republic of Poland in mid-2015, as of 01/07/2015
Source: Urząd do spraw Cudzoziemców, 2015b.

Statistical data on the immigrants from China are often incomplete, as for many years they were not recognized by data collectors as a separate category distinctive from "the Asians". In some other data of the Central Statistical Office, Chinese from the Peoples Republic of China are counted together with the citizens of Hong Kong, Macau, and Taiwan. In 2009, the Chinese from the PRC were five times more numerous than the immigrants from Hong Kong, Macau, and Taiwan together: 2600 PRC citizens, 516 Taiwanese, and only 5 Hongkongers (Fundacja Rozwoju "Oprócz Granic", 2009, p. 41).

For comparison, preliminary data of the Office for Foreigners for mid-year 2015, shows that the number of the Chinese is growing, but number of the Taiwanese is much smaller. Therefore, the ratio of the Chinese to Taiwanese was 26: 1. In total, as of July 1, 2015:

- 4907 Chinese (494 permanent residence, 505 long-term EU residence, 3854 temporary residence, 35 residence for a family member of an EU citizen, 8 refugee status, 1 subsidiary protection, 4 humanitarian stay, and 4 tolerated stay;
- 186 Taiwanese (17 permanent residence, 15 long-term EU residence, 153 temporary residence, 1 residence for a family member of an EU citizen);
- 11 Hongkongers (1 permanent residence, 2 long-term EU residence, 8 temporary residence, 1 residence for a family member of an EU citizen) (Urząd do spraw Cudzoziemców, 2015b).

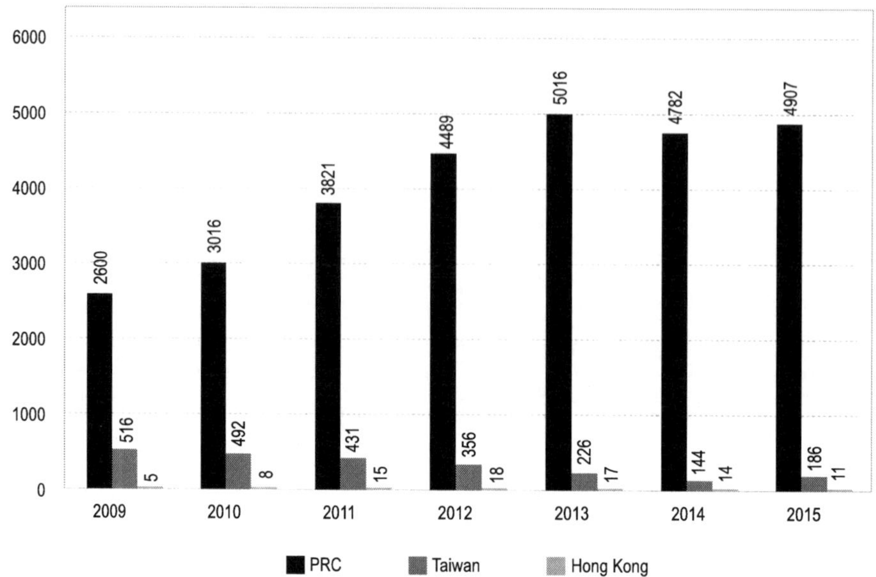

Graph 2: The number of citizens of the Peoples Republic of China, Taiwan and Hong Kong, holding valid residence cards from 2009 until 2015.

Source: Urząd do spraw Cudzoziemców, raports from 2009 to 2015.

The growth prospects of the Chinese arrivals to Poland is also shown by the number of invitations issued for the citizens of China: in the period of 2004–2006 total 318 invitations were issued (Departament Polityki Migracyjnej, 2008, p. 36), while a few years later, in 2013, the number increased to 1,010 per one year, and in 2014 to 1,104 invitations.

The number of the Chinese citizens who have received permission for a long-term residence has been significantly increased, as presented on the Graph 3. In 2014, it was 159 people, while a decade earlier only two (Główny Urząd Statystyczny, 2013, p. 484). The number of the Chinese, who received the other forms of permits is also increasing.

The Chinese seldom apply for Polish citizenship. For example, in 1992–2006 the President of the Republic of Poland has granted Polish citizenship to only 57 people of Chinese origin (Departament Polityki Migracyjnej, 2008, p. 39).

The total number of visas issued in the Polish consular offices in China is generally increasing. It is a result of a raise of interest in Poland amongst the Chinese entrepreneurs, investors, tourists, and students (Departament Konsularny, 2011, p. 20; Departament Konsularny, 2012, p. 21). A visible development in the number of travellers to Poland and to the other CCE countries as part of a group organized tourism (ADS), as well as within individual tourism is observed. Undoubtedly, Poland is better recognized among Chinese tourists than it was a few years ago (Departament

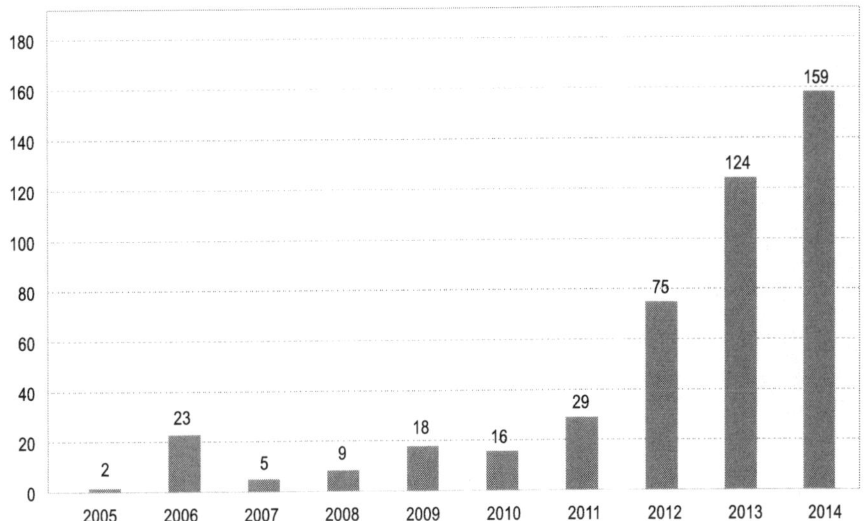

Graph 3: Number of permits for long-term resident granted to the Chinese people in Poland in the years 2005–2014.

Source: Urząd do spraw Cudzoziemców, raports from 2005 to 2015.

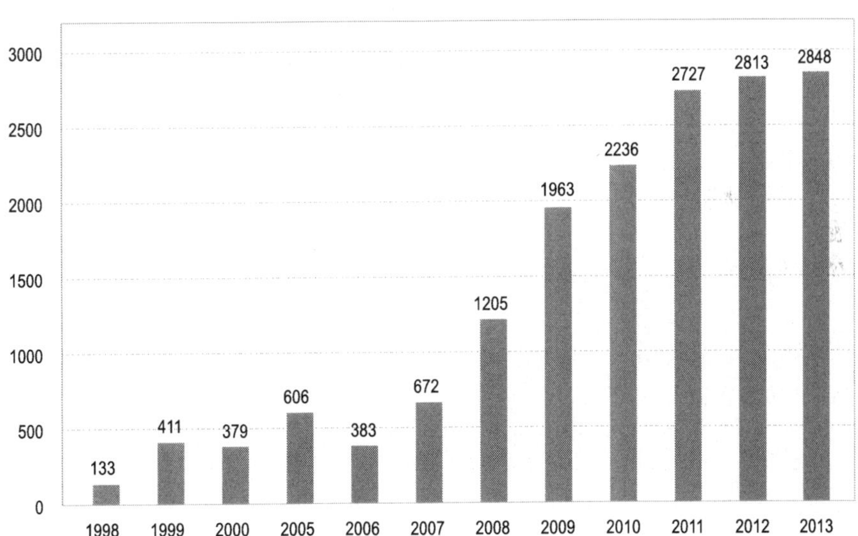

Graph 4: Number of residence permits for a fixed period of time granted to the Chinese people in Poland in the years 1998–2013

Source: Główny Urząd Statystyczny, 2013, p. 485; Główny Urząd Statystyczny, 2015, p. 503.

Konsularny, 2013, pp. 19–20). It is estimated, that a significant proportion (even about 50 percent) of all arrivals is on the visa-free basis. This may apply to approximately **8 million** holders of service passports, issued by a few dozens of government institutions in the PRC (Departament Polityki Konsularnej, 2008, p. 36). In 2014, the new Consulate General in Chengdu was added to the ones already existing in Beijing, Guangzhou, Shanghai, and Hong Kong (Departament Konsularny, 2014, p. 5).

It seems that the most Chinese living in Poland depend on the settlement of legal status, if only because of the physical stand out from the local environment, which results in controls of documents by the police. The Chinese, who are staying illegally in Poland, can legalize their status as part of the abolition: foreigners can apply to obtain a permit for temporary residence for 2 years and the possibility of legal employment. During the first abolition action in 2003, only 13 Chinese nationals applied for the permits (Departament Polityki Migracyjnej, 2008, p. 45), in 2007: 42 persons, while in 2012: 482 Chinese applied for the permits (Departament Polityki Migracyjnej, 2012, pp. 34–35). From the increasing number of applications we can come to the conclusion, that undetermined number of Chinese people of the status of illegal immigrants still remain on Polish territory. Nevertheless, relatively marginal number of the Chinese are expelled every year – only around 10 of them. The Chinese are the ninth national group in that category, counting less than 2 per cent of the foreigners obliged to leave Poland. In the last few years the number of Chinese citizens detained by the Border Guard for illegal crossing or attempting to cross the state border counts for around 20 per year. Interestingly, the majority has been stopped at the internal border of the European Union, mostly with Germany (Urząd do Spraw Cudzoziemców, 2015a).

Forms of migration and settlement structure

The oldest wave of Chinese immigration, associated with the enterprise of Chipolbrok, has focused on the coast (Gdańsk, Gdynia). Some of them were Chinese students, who studied in Poland in the sixties, and returned after the Cultural Revolution. At the turn of the eighties and nineties a relatively well-educated entrepreneurs from Eastern China arrived to Poland. Sometimes, they were founding the enterprises in two or three CEE countries, or were taking over the regional branches of the previously state-owned companies, using a network of contacts. Since the late nineties contract workers were employed on construction sites, and in restaurants, as well as centers of Chinese medicine (Wysieńska, 2012, pp. 88–89). Statistical data do not consist any information on the education level of 2/3 of the newly arrived Chinese. After the accession to the EU, Poland became more attractive for Chinese businesspersons, also those who arrived not directly from China, but from other countries in the region, such as Hungary, the Czech Republic, the countries of the former Yugoslavia (Wysieńska & Piłat, 2012, p. 105).

Similarly as in the case of Chinese immigrants, in other countries of Central and Eastern Europe, the Chinese have been concentrating in the capital city and surrounding areas of Mazowieckie voivodship. In 2013, the vast majority (3305 people, that is 66 percent) of Chinese people lived in Warsaw and the rest of the Mazowieckie voivodship. Rest of them lived in: Śląskie voivodship (340 Chinese), Pomorskie (199), Wielkopolskie (195), Dolnośląskie (175), Małopolskie (174), Łódzkie (165), Warmińsko-Mazurskie (105), Zachodniopomorskie (76), Kujawsko-Pomorskie (62), Lubuskie (59), Lubelskie (50), Świętokrzyskie (33), Opolskie and Podkarpackie (25 each), and Podlaskie (22 Chinese citizens) (Urząd do Spraw Cudzoziemców, 2014). Most of them live in the cities, although there are no districts inhabited mainly by the Chinese or having a form of Chinatowns.

Nevertheless, the concentrations of the Chinese population can be identified in several centers related to economic activity. This is primarily Lesznowola, a municipality with a large Chinese Trade Center located in Wólka Kosowska.[2] Other important clusters are Gdańsk and Gdynia, Jaworzno-Jeleń, Bydgoszcz, Stalowa Wola (Deloitte, 2012).

Migration networks play a very important role in supporting migrants informally. Many migrants aim to return to the country. Migration is rather individual, however, there are cases of inviting family members and employing them in small Chinese companies (Klaus, 2011, p. 42; Rossa, 2011, p. 182).

In the last few years, the number of the Chinese working in Poland is slightly decreasing, but it is still much higher than at the end of 20th century. In 2014, some 2133 PRC citizens received the work permits; 89 percent received A-type permit, which allows to work in the Polish territory on the basis of a contract with an employer, whose registered business is also located in Poland. Around 7 percent of the Chinese work on the basis of type C permit, which allows to work for a foreign employer and deployment in Polish territory for over 30 days in a the calendar year (Ministerstwo Pracy i Polityki Społecznej, 2015).

---

[2] Chinese Trade Center in Wólka Kosowska in Lesznowola municipality is located at the exit road from Warsaw to Kraków and Katowice. It was established in 1994, and has become the most important center of wholesale trade of goods imported from China, such as clothing, leather, footwear, toys, home furnishings, etc. Three largest halls (out of six) were financed by the Chinese, and the remaining ones by the Vietnamese, citizens of Turkey and India. About 1,000 tenants rent shops there. It is the largest shopping center of this type of in Central and Eastern Europe (Klorek & Szulecka, 2013; Piłat, 2013).

Table 1: Work permits received by the PRC citizens, divided by profession categories. Data of the Ministry of Labour and Social Policy

Year	Managers	Business owners	Specialist, experts	Teachers	Skilled workers	Unskilled workers	IT specialists	Medical workers	Artists	Lawyers	Others	TOTAL	Refusals	Permits repealed
1998	65	399	57	4	162	0	N/D	N/D	N/D	N/D	49	736	N/D	N/D
1999	80	334	57	5	151	24	N/D	N/D	N/D	N/D	34	685	N/D	N/D
2000	17	191	35	0	28	29	N/D	4	N/D	N/D	64	350	N/D	N/D
2008	771			3	823	111	99	1	3	0	N/D	2040	N/D	N/D
2009	1145			1	1558	570	125	1	1	0	N/D	4536	N/D	N/D
2010	1095			66	2072	241	117	12	7	2	N/D	6209	N/D	N/D
2011	1045			2	1154	931	108	21	2	0	N/D	5854	94	2824
2012	750			6	370	94	50	9	3	0	N/D	3247	27	705
2013	554			6	416	29	31	11	0	3	N/D	3089	7	650
2014	512			5	324	37	37	27	1	2	N/D	2133	8	464

Source: http://www.mpips.gov.pl/analizy-i-raporty/cudzoziemcy-pracujacy-w-polsce-statystyki/ (accessed: 21/01/2016).

The wholesale and retail trade dominate among the sectors of employment of the Chinese citizens (about 1/3 a few years ago, and over 2/3 in the last three years). Relatively many work in the construction sector, and in 2010–2011, every fifth citizen of China in Poland was employed there, which was connected with the activity of the Chinese companies, especially in the construction of highways (which, by the way, was unsuccessful, and reduced the level of confidence in Chinese companies). Hotels and restaurants have employed relatively few Chinese people – this number varies from 5 to 10 percent. The number of employees working in the manufacturing sector decreased from about 30 percent in 2008 to 2 percent in 2014. Approximately every fourth citizen of the PRC in Poland has been employed as a member of management, often in small Chinese companies.

The Chinese opt for self-employment and work in small businesses – for instance, according to data from the years 2008 and 2009, about 55 percent are employed in enterprises employing up to 9 people (Ministerstwo Pracy i Polityki Społecznej, 2010). These are usually the companies whose owners are also of Chinese nationality. A high level of intranational economic cooperation is observed, for example, the owners of

Table 2: Work permits received by the PRC citizens, divided by sectors of the economy. Data of the Ministry of Labour and Social Policy

Year	Agriculture, forestry, hunting and fishing	Manufacturing sector	Construction sector	Wholesale and retail trade	Transportation and storage	Hotels and restaurants	Information and communication	Finance and insurance	Professional, scientific and technical sector	Education	Healthcare	Workers employed in private households
2008	N/D	651	186	720	N/D	192	N/D	207*	N/D	5	13	N/D
2009	N/D	913	642	1766	N/D	405	N/D	653*	N/D	1	20	N/D
2010	49	649	1266	2084	17	347	41	78	513	6	17	19
2011	180	443	1260	2546	48	344	85	18	305	16	10	54
2012	36	141	128	2318	13	226	53	22	101	7	14	26
2013	4	77	179	2177	11	223	27	25	N/D	15	7	34
2014	0	43	110	1439	21	211	16	13	57	8	9	14

* and real estate services

Source: http://www.mpips.gov.pl/analizy-i-raporty/cudzoziemcy-pracujacy-w-polsce-statystyki/ (accessed: 21/01/2016).

Chinese travel agencies cooperate with the restaurants and hotels owned by other Chinese. The roots of this practice lie on the one hand, in the national solidarity, and on the other hand, in the attempt to avoid cultural barriers between the Chinese tourists and local companies.

Relatively few Chinese are interested in seasonal work in Poland, which is primarily due to the high cost of tickets between Poland and China, but also the communication problems, as lower-level staff cannot speak Polish, nor English. In 2009, only 41 visas for seasonal work were granted to the Chinese citizens (including 29 Schengen visas and 12 national), which can be compared to 4073 visas issued without work permission (including 2896 Schengen visas and 1177 Polish ones) (Krajowy Punkt Kontaktowy Europejskiej Sieci Migracyjnej, 2011, p. 43).

Chinese ethnic group is very flexible and prone to change their place of residence – both in China and abroad – if the situation requires that, or, if new business opportunities appear. Moreover, the low level of integration with the host society makes it even easier.

Special category: Chinese students in Poland

The number of Chinese studying in Poland is constantly growing. In the fifties, ten students from China came to Poland, later the number of Chinese students increased to about fifty. In the seventies, there were only a few people, because most of them were called back to China after the Cultural Revolution had begun. There is no institution that would assemble Chinese graduates of Polish universities – in 2013 Dom Polski (Polish House Club) proposed the creation of the Polish Universities Chinese Alumni Club and the Chinese Universities Polish Alumni Club, which would lobby for improvement of Polish-Chinese relations. The activities of these institutions are not yet visible. For a decade now, a promotional campaign "Study in Poland" addressed to young people in China has been run. At the same time, many Polish universities promoted their educational offer in English in China, in cooperation with the agencies recruiting Chinese students abroad or during educational fairs held in major Chinese cities. It should also be noted, that student visas are sometimes used as a path of illegal immigration not only to Poland, but also through Poland to other Schengen countries.

In the academic year 2013/2014, 670 students from the PRC and 413 from Taiwan studied in Poland (Główny Urząd Statystyczny, 2016, p. 505). As the Graph 5 shows, we can observe the growing tendency among Chinese candidates and decreasing among Taiwanese.[3]

In the academic year 2012/2013, students from the PRC and Taiwan together accounted for only 3.7 percent of foreign students in Poland, and in the year 2013/2014 even slightly less, 3 percent, due to the significant increase in the number of students from Ukraine. At the same time, they were the largest group amongst the students from Asia. If we count jointly students from China and Taiwan (total 1083), they would be the sixth national group – after the citizens of Ukraine, Belarus, Norway, Spain, and Sweden. If we consider Chinese students from the PRC alone, they would be less numerous not only than the above national groups, but also students from Lithuania, the United States, the Czech Republic, Russia, and Germany.

As non-European Union students, the Chinese pay the highest tuition fees, but, because of much higher costs of the higher education in West-

---

[3] After the accession to the European Union, the Taiwanese started to arrive at the medical schools in Poland. In 2011, about 300 Taiwanese studied medicine at the Medical University in Poznań, 30 percent of all foreign students of the university. They also studied in Katowice and Lodz. A significant reduction in the number of students from Taiwan was caused by factors unrelated to the Polish side, as the graduates of Taiwanese medical schools mobilized in defense of the labor market. After the change in legislation in 2012, nostrification of diplomas has been much more difficult, resulting in decline in the interest in medical studies in Poland.

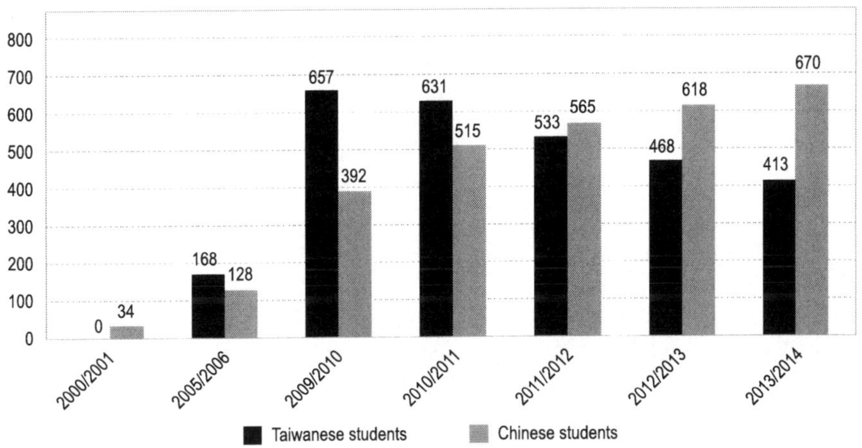

Graph 5: The number of Chinese and Taiwanese studying in Poland from the academic years 2000/2001 to 2013/2014

Source: Główny Urząd Statystyczny, 2016, p. 505.

ern Europe and America, the number of Chinese students in Poland is rising. This trend is expected to continue, especially if the Polish universities would be able to offer attractive curricula in English. Currently, the vast majority of young Chinese choose universities in English-speaking countries (the United States, the United Kingdom, Australia). In Poland, technical studies are the dominant fields of interest. With the popularity of Chopin's music in Asia, relatively many students choose Poland to study at the academies of music.

Educational cooperation between Poland and China is gradually being developed. During the official visit to China in December 2011, President Bronisław Komorowski and the Minister of Science and Higher Education, Barbara Kudrycka, signed an interdepartmental agreement on cooperation in the field of higher education. The agreement concerned the exchange of students (a slight increase in the scholarship exchange limit, to up to 40 per year) scientists networking, as well as joint research. Promotion of Polish language teaching in China and Chinese in Poland were also planned (Ministerstwo Nauki i Szkolnictwa Wyższego, 2011). Currently, Polish studies in China are conducted at the Beijing Foreign Studies University, Guangdong University of Foreign Studies, and Harbin Normal University. Chinese students of Polish philology are primarily the candidates for scholarships to Poland.

Most of the Chinese students come back to China after graduation. Some undertake higher education at other European universities, for instance in Germany. Global trends are evident: since the history of the Chinese studying abroad began (in early eighties), the proportion of the graduates returning to homeland is growing, as those who know foreign languages and have experience in an international environment, may find much more attractive professional opportunities in China than abroad (Sun & Liang, 2014).

Forms of organization

Within the Chinese community in Poland there are mainly informal groups, created on the basis of common interests (e.g. students, entrepreneurs). Some of these societies, especially of the older immigration, meet at the events organized by the Embassy of the PRC, for instance on the National Day or the Chinese New Year celebrations. The bonds are held primarily among the people from the similar waves of immigration or the same province of origin. Socializing is connected with meeting people's cultural needs (such as festivals), economic and professional (exchange of information, for example about employment opportunities, official procedures, assistance in translation), as well as cooking, or, generally speaking, supporting each other. These migration networks are not formalized. There are also Chinese (and often Vietnamese) entrepreneurs, providing goods and services for other Chinese and Vietnamese immigrants, for instance Asian food ingredients. Chinese students and teachers from Polish universities maintain intensive contacts with Chinese students in other European countries, contacting not only by internet social networks, but also visiting each other or traveling during the holidays.

Nevertheless, forms of social, political, economic, cultural organization, as well as any other institutions are rudimentary. In Poland, there are virtually no formal and actually active Chinese immigrant organizations focused on helping each other. The probable cause is that the history of immigration to Poland is too short.

The Chinese-Polish Joint Stock Shipping Company Chipolbrok, operating since 1951, played an important historical role in the development of Polish-Chinese relations. Chipolbrok has supported the Polish-Chinese cultural and educational projects, like the organization of the Polish school in Shanghai or publishing a magazine "Asia-Pacific" (in Polish).

In Poland, there are several institutions that promote cultural cooperation between Poland and China, but it's mostly the Poles working in them, and the activities are prepared rather for the local audience. The oldest organization of this type is Towarzystwo Przyjaźni Polsko-Chińskiej (TPPCh, the Association of Polish-Chinese Friendship, www.tppch.pl).

The Association was founded in the 50s of the 20th century (Góralczyk, 2008, pp. 232–237; Cyrzyk, 2008, pp. 238–245). It has been dealing mainly with cultural activities, organizing concerts, film screenings, exhibitions, lectures, Chinese lessons, publishing. Currently, it has formally nine regional offices: Warsaw, Kraków, Wielkopolska (Greater Poland), Bydgoszcz, Poznań, Śląsk (Silesia), Toruń, Zachodniopomorskie (West Pomeranian), and Pomorskie (Pomeranian), but they are not all active. The number of members can be estimated at several hundred people all together, the vast majority are Polish and the members of Polish-Chinese families. Occasionally, a number Chinese entrepreneurs or Oriental restaurant owners take part in the activities. In the times of its greatest development, branches of TPPCh existed in all voivodships, and had approximately 20 thousand members. Approximately one hundred organizations and companies were supporting its work, and it was financed from the state budget. The association had very prestigious headquarters in Blue Palace in Warsaw, hosting a club, library and a Chinese bar, organized lectures and Chinese lessons. TPPCh cooperated with a similar organization in China: the Association of Chinese-Polish Friendship. In the years 1964–1984, as a result of the relations between China and the Soviet Union cooling, the activity froze, but the organization has not been disbanded. In the mid-eighties the association was reactivated. In that time Klub Harbińczyków was also called into existence, gathering Poles repatriated from Harbin to Poland in the fifties and sixties. Again, in the second half of the nineties there was another collapse, caused by the interruption in funding from the budget and the loss of the Blue Palace location. Since that time, the Association focuses on low-profile cultural activities.

There are also some other cultural associations (for example Stowarzyszenie Polsko-Chińskie na Rzecz Kultury i Sztuki, Polish-Chinese Association for Culture and Arts), or business organizations, like Polsko-Chińskie Towarzystwo Gospodarczo-Kulturalne (Polish-Chinese Economic and Cultural Association), Polsko-Chińska Izba Gospodarcza (Polish-Chinese Chamber of Commerce), Polsko-Chińska Izba Przemysłowo-Handlowa (Polish-Chinese Chamber of Industry and Commerce), Stowarzyszenie Polsko-Chińskiej Promocji Ekonomicznej i Handlowej (Association of Polish-Chinese Economic and Trade Promotion). There are language schools in larger cities, employing native-speakers of the Chinese language, and occasionally engaging in the organization of cultural events.

Confucius Institutes, located in Kraków, Opole, Poznań, Wrocław, and Gdańsk, have been the most active cultural institutions promoting Chinese culture in the last decade. Although Confucius Institutes are not intended to support the Chinese community in Poland, they remain in touch with them, and the local Chinese communities participate in the cultural events (especially the Chinese New Year celebrations) as well as in the scientific events (conferences, open lectures), organized by these institutions. Sometimes, the local Chinese are employed as teachers or administrative staff. Institutes however; mostly employ teachers, who are being sent directly from China to Poland for 1–3-year contracts. In the academic year 2015/2016, the largest number of those native speakers (seven) are employed in the CI of the Jagiellonian University. There are, nevertheless, various experiences with the local Chinese communities within the network of 500 Confucius Institutes in the world: in the case of the institutes operating in countries with more numerous Chinese diaspora, institutes serve to the local Chinese as educational institutions, in which the second or the third generation of the Chinese learn Mandarin, or organize bilingual schools (in Italy, Hungary). Polish CIs do not fulfil this function yet, but perhaps in the future, along with the growth of the Chinese diaspora, these needs would arise.

When it comes to the institutions that would be established by the Chinese people for themselves, there are only few, and not really active. The first is Polskie Stowarzyszenie Chińczyków (the Polish Association of the Chinese), located in Wólka Kosowska, which was registered in 2006. The second, Stowarzyszenie Przedsiębiorców Chińskich w Polsce w Jaworznie (the Chinese Association of Entrepreneurs in Poland in Jaworzno), was also registered, but in reality it does not work.

There have been some attempts to involve Chinese community in religious activities, like the Chinese section of the Evangelical Reformed Ministry of Immigrants in Warsaw. In 2009, the section had about 30 members and 10 supporters. The activities focused on the Sunday services, religious meetings and social events. Representatives of the section were also in contact with Chinese Christians, staying in the Guarded Centre for Foreigners in Lesznowola near Grójec. Jehovah's Witnesses also propose the Chinese immigrants participation in the religious meetings in Wólka Kosowska and in Kraków.

It seems that the most active institution bringing the Chinese together is in the Internet: the portal www.plchinese.com. The website provides current news from Poland, tourists information, but mostly some practical information, instructing on visas, residence permits, work permits, diploma nostrification procedures. It also provides an information board to exchange the real estate announcements. A separate section of the Chinese cultural events in Poland is provided. This website serves also as a forum of exchange of experiences between the students, Polish-Chinese marriages, and opinions on the Polish people and realities. This website performs the functions of both formal and informal organizations.

Prospects for integration with Polish society – a preliminary analysis

The level of integration of the Chinese with the Polish society is quite low so far. Avoiding the efforts of learning Polish language seems to be a result of temporariness and transience of their status, and a rare intention of a permanent settlement in this country. Many of the Chinese manage to live in Poland without speaking Polish. Their school-age children often return to China for the primary and secondary education, and other attend school at the Embassy of the PRC in Warsaw. Even most of the Chinese students do not learn Polish language, because they find it too difficult and pointless, as the language of their curriculum is English, relations with their Polish peers are random, and they just have no plans to stay in Poland. Poland is not treated as a country of final destination of migration, and a further aim is to either migrate to the Western countries, or eventually – after graduation or collecting the expected capital – to return to China.

Little integration and a lack of knowledge of the Polish language makes the Chinese more willing to cooperate with the Vietnamese, who have a wider network of business contacts, thanks to a long tradition of living in Poland as well as their Polish language proficiency – mainly in second generation (Mroczek, Szulecka & Tulińska, 2008, pp. 190–191). Typically, the Chinese deal with the import of goods from China, because they have better *guanxi* there, while the Vietnamese dominate the retail trade (Klorek & Szulecka, 2013, pp. 54–56). Between these two communities conflicts sometimes break out, mainly on the economic basis, like disputes concerning rent increases in the Chinese Trade Center in Wólka Kosowska (Pytlakowski & Sowa, 2011).

There is no history of serious conflicts between the Chinese community and the local Polish inhabitants. The observed social isolation of immigrants is a kind of conflict-free strategy for their adaptation, especially in case of those, who do not plan to settle in Poland. The potential conflict area appears when the Chinese entrepreneurs employ the Poles – which concerns usually the positions where Polish proficiency, efficiency in the legal or bureaucratic realities are required – especially in direct contact with Polish customers, as salespeople or waiters. The offers in the Job Centers in some regions for people with proficiency in Chinese and English can give the impression that it is a way to obtain approval for the employment of a compatriot, rather than to find a local employee (Jóźwiak, 2012, p. 149). For example, in Piaseczno county in 2011 and 2012, 44 percent of the jobs contained a requirement of Chinese or Vietnamese language (Klorek & Szulecka, 2013, p. 38). The tension between the local population and Chinese entrepreneurs can occur where there is a business competition (Piłat, 2013, p. 5). Chinese entrepreneurs also report that the public institutions are inhospitable, that the procedures for obtaining permits are overly complicated and restrictive (Karpiński, 2012, p. 166). In addition, the Polish criminal groups may heighten unfavorable climate, impersonating representatives of the state institutions and extorting money.

Number of the Chinese among the foreigners suspected of committing crimes, and among the victims is limited. A small number of reports of crime victims may be a result of their reluctance to cooperate with the police, fear of complicated, time-consuming procedures and difficulties in communication. The number of people of the Chinese origin in police statistics has never exceeded 1 percent of all foreigners (Policja, 2013). It seems that in Poland, at least so far, the most widespread law abuses within this national category are fiscal: failing to register part of the business and illegal employment.

One of the evidences of effective integration would be Chinese-Polish marriages, as in the cases of such marriages, international social contacts are more complex than for the average Chinese living in Poland. Unfortunately, even in recent years the number of such marriages is negligible, a few per year. In addition, it is difficult to assess what part of them is only a result of a need to legalize the immigrant's status. Cultural differences may also be amongst the reasons for a small amount of Polish-Chinese marriages. In the discussion about the Polish men as potential husband candidates, on the plchinese.com forum, the opinions varied. Polish men were praised for courtesy, respect for women, caring for the house as well as for the accountability. But there were critical opinions on the culinary customs (too little fruits and vegetables), shorter life, addictions, infidelity and lack of stability in feelings, uncivilized behavior under the influence of alcohol, lack of habit of saving, and lack of tolerance for different cultures.[4]

Certainly, not only the Chinese side is responsible for the lack of deeper integration. Even in Lesznowola, which is inhabited by such a large Chinese minority, there were very little efforts to support the integration of foreigners. Municipal authorities organized Polish language classes and some intercultural events for them. In the years 2007 and 2008, the municipal schools conducted the "My neighbors come from Asia" project, during which a psychologist conducted intercultural workshops for pupils about the differences between Polish and Asian culture (Klorek

---

[4] Discussion (2012–2015) *Bolan nanren kaopu fou? [Are the Polish men reasonable?]*, plchinese.com, http://www.plchinese.com/thread-53746-1-1.html (accessed: 21/01/2016).

& Szulecka, 2013, p. 69). Not even once does the issue of multiculturalism or the presence of immigrants in the community appear in the 2011–2021 development strategy of the Lesznowola municipality (Górski, Barchański, Witosławski, Barchańska & Górska, 2011).

Conclusion

Poland, as a significant country in Central and Eastern Europe is becoming increasingly interesting for the Chinese. It is not only becoming more and more alluring tourist destination, but also a destination for those looking for a long-term settlement. Undoubtedly, Chinese entrepreneurs are attracted by an economic development, investment opportunities, relatively low labor costs and well-educated employees. The pragmatic Chinese appreciate the strategic geographic position of the country, and the privileges of membership in the European Union and the Schengen area. For Chinese students, the possibility to study in a European country, in English, with tuition and living expenses lower than the Western Europe, or even lower than in China, is a serious advantage. Those who came to know Poland better, generally appreciate the nature, culture and tradition, as well as the hospitality. Generally, however, little knowledge among the Chinese people about Poland, coexists with little knowledge of China among the Poles.

As a result of the previous analysis it can be expected that in the years to come, the number of the Chinese arriving to Poland will be increasing, and that at present, we are witnessing only an early stage of the development of Chinese immigration. Certainly in the future more study of this phenomenon would be needed.

References

Cyrzyk, L. (2008). U zarania Towarzystwa Przyjaźni Polsko-Chińskiej. *Azja-Pacyfik, 11.*

Deloitte (2012). Wejście smoka. Przypadki chińskich inwestycji w Polsce. Retrieved from http://www.deloittelegal.pl/sites/default/files/publications/chinapl_lekka_0.pdf (accessed: 21/01/2016).

Departament Konsularny (2011). *Raport Polskiej Służby Konsularnej za 2010 rok.* Warsaw: Ministerstwo Spraw Zagranicznych (Ministry of Foreign Affairs). Retrieved from: http://www.msz.gov.pl/resource/5ac6914e-f216–4ed2-a84b-53702a4067e7 (accessed: 21/01/2016).

Departament Konsularny (2012). *Raport Polskiej Służby Konsularnej za 2011 rok.* Warsaw: Ministerstwo Spraw Zagranicznych (Ministry of Foreign Affairs). Retrieved from: http://www.msz.gov.pl/resource/b6563c9e-f402-4cd8-b04b-17a7c44bae8f:JCR (accessed: 21/01/2016).

Departament Konsularny (2013). *Raport Polskiej Służby Konsularnej za 2012 rok.* Warsaw: Ministerstwo Spraw Zagranicznych (Ministry of Foreign Affairs). Retrieved from: http://www.msz.gov.pl/resource/dbfd4993-2a3b-4f0f-bb0c-f7c82a2ed9fc:JCR (accessed: 21/01/2016).

Departament Konsularny (2014). *Raport polskiej służby konsularnej za 2014 rok.* Warsaw: Ministerstwo Spraw Zagranicznych (Ministry of Foreign Affairs). Retrieved from: https://www.msz.gov.pl/pl/ministerstwo/publikacje/raport_ko nsularny_2014;jsessionid=278F41F545EDD46042C4D9671B9348DF.cmsap4p (accessed: 21/01/2016).

Departament Polityki Migracyjnej (Migration Police Department) (2008). *Migracje z Chin.* Warsaw: Ministerstwo Spraw Wewnętrznych i Administracji (The Ministry of Internal Affairs and Administration).

Departament Polityki Migracyjnej (Migration Police Department) (2012). *Polityka migracyjna Polski w odniesieniu do obywateli Republiki Białorusi, Ukrainy i Federacji Rosyjskiej.* Warsaw: Ministerstwo Spraw Wewnętrznych i Administracji (The Ministry of Internal Affairs and Administration). Retrieved from: https://emn.gov.pl/download/74/14029/Analizablokwschodniwersjaostateczna.pdf (accessed: 21/01/2016).

Fundacja Rozwoju "Oprócz Granic" (2009). *Nieuregulowane pobyty cudzoziemców w Polsce: próby rozwiązania problemu.*

Główny Urząd Statystyczny (Central Statistical Office) (2010). *Rocznik Demograficzny (Demographic Yearbook).*

Główny Urząd Statystyczny (Central Statistical Office) (2011). *Rocznik Demograficzny (Demographic Yearbook).*

Główny Urząd Statystyczny (Central Statistical Office) (2012). *Rocznik Demograficzny (Demographic Yearbook).*

Główny Urząd Statystyczny (Central Statistical Office) (2013). *Rocznik Demograficzny (Demographic Yearbook).*

Główny Urząd Statystyczny (Central Statistical Office) (2014). *Rocznik Demograficzny (Demographic Yearbook).*

Główny Urząd Statystyczny (Central Statistical Office) (2015). *Rocznik Demograficzny (Demographic Yearbook).*

Góralczyk, Z. (2008). Pięćdziesięciolecie Towarzystwa Przyjaźni Polsko-Chińskiej. *Azja-Pacyfik,* 11.

Grzymała-Kazłowska, A., Iglicka, K., Jaźwińska, E., Kaczmarczyk, P., Kępińska, E., Okólski, M., Weinar, A. (2002). Wpływ migracji zagranicznych w Warszawie na sytuację na społecznym rynku pracy. *Prace migracyjne,* 44. Warsaw: Instytut Studiów Społecznych, Uniwersytet Warszawski.

Jóźwiak, I. (2012). *„Nowa" imigracja z Chin i Wietnamu a społeczności lokalne – Jaworzno i Wólka Kosowska.* In: Wysieńska, K. (ed.). *Sprzedawać, gotować, budować? Plany i strategie Chińczyków i Wietnamczyków w Polsce* (pp. 139–162). Warsaw: Instytut Spraw Publicznych (Institute of Public Affairs).

Jóźwiak, J., Karpiński, Z., Piłat, A., Segeš Frelak J., Wysieńska, K. (2012). *Wnioski i rekomendacje*. In: Wysieńska, K. (ed.). *Sprzedawać, gotować, budować? Plany i strategie Chińczyków i Wietnamczyków w Polsce* (pp. 163–168). Warsaw: Instytut Spraw Publicznych (Institute of Public Affairs).

Klaus, W. (2011). *Przestrzeganie przez polskich pracodawców praw pracowników migrujących*. In: Klaus, W. (ed.). *Ziemia obiecana? Warunki pracy cudzoziemców w Polsce* (pp. 7–53). Warszawa: Stowarzyszenie Interwencji Prawnej. Retrieved from http://www.interwencjaprawna.pl/docs/ziemia-obiecana.pdf.

Klorek, N., Szulecka, M. (2013). *Migranckie instytucje ekonomiczne i ich wpływ na otoczenie. Przykład centrów handlowych w Wólce Kosowskiej. Raport z badań*. Warsaw: Stowarzyszenie Interwencji Prawnej, 2.

Krajowy Punkt Kontaktowy Europejskiej Sieci Migracyjnej (2011). *Migracja tymczasowa i cyrkulacyjna w Polsce: dotychczasowe doświadczenia, uregulowania prawne i opcje na przyszłość. Lata 2004–2009. Raport*. Retrieved from: http://ec.europa.eu/dgs/home-affairs/what-we-do/networks/european_migration_network/reports/docs/emn-studies/circular-migration/pl_study_on_temporary_and_circular_migration_pl_version_pl.pdf (accessed: 21/01/2016).

Mazuś, M. (2012). Źle się dzieje w Wólce Kosowskiej. Co iskrzy między boksami. *Polityka.pl*, 4.09.2012. Retrieved from: http://www.polityka.pl/tygodnikpolityka/kraj/1530081,1,zle-sie-dzieje-w-wolce-kosowskiej.read (accessed: 21/01/2016).

Ministerstwo Nauki i Szkolnictwa Wyższego (2011). *Minister Kudrycka w Pekinie: Zapraszamy do studiowania w Polsce*. Retrieved from: http://www.nauka.gov.pl/aktualnosci-ministerstwo/minister-kudrycka-w-pekinie-zapraszamy-do-studiowania-w-polsce,archiwum,1,akcja,pdf.html (accessed: 21/01/2016).

Ministerstwo Pracy i Polityki Społecznej (2010). *Cudzoziemcy pracujący w Polsce – statystyki, Dane zbiorcze 2009 r., Zezwolenia na pracę dla cudzoziemców według obywatelstwa, okresu ważności zezwolenia na pracę oraz wielkości przedsiębiorstwa*. Retrieved from: http://www.mpips.gov.pl/analizy-i-raporty/cudzoziemcy-pracujacy-w-polsce-statystyki/ (accessed: 21/01/2016).

Ministerstwo Pracy i Polityki Społecznej (2015). *Cudzoziemcy pracujący w Polsce – statystyki, Dane zbiorcze 2014 r., Zezwolenia na pracę dla cudzoziemców według obywatelstwa, okresu ważności zezwolenia na pracę oraz wielkości przedsiębiorstwa*. Retrieved from: http://www.mpips.gov.pl/analizy-i-raporty/cudzoziemcy-pracujacy-w-polsce-statystyki/ (accessed: 21/01/2016).

Nyiri, P. (2007). *Chinese in Eastern Europe and Russia. A Middleman Minority in a Transnational Era*. London and New York: Routledge.

Piłat, A. (2013). Między Warszawą a Wólką Kosowską. Cudzoziemscy mieszkańcy gminy Raszyn. *Biuletyn Migracyjny*, 44, listopad 2013, 4–6. Retrieved from: http://biuletynmigracyjny.uw.edu.pl/pliki/pdf/dodatek44.pdf (accessed: 21/01/2016).

Policja (2013). *Cudzoziemcy – przestępczość*. Retrieved from: http://statystyka.policja.pl/st/wybrane-statystyki/przestepczosc-cudzozie/50867,Cudzoziemcy-przestepczosc.html (accessed: 21/01/2016).

Polska – nowy kraj docelowy Chińczyków? *Biuletyn Migracyjny, 29* (May 2011). Retrieved from: http://biuletynmigracyjny.uw.edu.pl/29-maj-2011/polska-nowy-kraj-docelowy-chinczykow (accessed: 21/01/2016).

Pytlakowski, P., Sowa, A. (2011). Mała Azja. Duży problem z azjatycką mniejszością. *Polityka*, 24.05.2011. Retrieved from: http://www.polityka.pl/tygodnikpolityka/kraj/1515972,1,duzy-problem-z-azjatycka-mniejszoscia.read (accessed: 21/01/2016).

Rossa, M. (2011). Migranci w branży gastronomicznej w Polsce. In: Klaus, W. (ed.). *Ziemia obiecana? Warunki pracy cudzoziemców w Polsce*. Warszawa: Stowarzyszenie Interwencji Prawnej. Retrieved from: http://www.interwencjaprawna.pl/docs/ziemia-obiecana.pdf (accessed: 21/01/2016).

Sun Zhao, Liang Jun (2014). China sees overseas students returning at higher pace. *People's Daily Online*, 26.02.2014. Retrieved from: http://english.peopledaily.com.cn/98649/8546863.html (accessed: 21/01/2016).

Urząd do spraw Cudzoziemców (The Office for Foreigners) (2010). *Dane liczbowe dotyczące postępowań prowadzonych wobec cudzoziemców w 2009 r.* Retrieved from: http://udsc.gov.pl/statystyki/raporty-okresowe/zestawienia--roczne/ (accessed: 21/01/2016).

Urząd do spraw Cudzoziemców (The Office for Foreigners) (2014). *Dane liczbowe dotyczące postępowań prowadzonych wobec cudzoziemców w 2013 r.* Retrieved from: http://udsc.gov.pl/statystyki/raporty-okresowe/zestawienia-roczne/ (accessed: 21/01/2016).

Urząd do spraw Cudzoziemców (The Office for Foreigners) (2015a). *Zestawienie liczbowe dotyczące postępowań prowadzonych wobec cudzoziemców w 2014 roku.* Retrieved from: http://udsc.gov.pl/statystyki/raporty-okresowe/zestawienia-roczne/ (accessed: 21/01/2016).

Urząd do spraw Cudzoziemców (The Office for Foreigners) (2015b). *Dane liczbowe dotyczące postępowań prowadzonych wobec cudzoziemców w pierwszej połowie 2015 roku.* Retrieved from: http://udsc.gov.pl/statystyki/raporty-okresowe/zestawienia-roczne/ (accessed: 21/01/2016).

Wysieńska, K. (2012). Organizacje wietnamskie i chińskie w Polsce. Wstępna analiza instytucjonalnej kompletności społeczności wschodnioazjatyckich w Polsce. In: Wysieńska, K. (ed.). *Sprzedawać, gotować, budować? Plany i strategie Chińczyków i Wietnamczyków w Polsce* (pp. 77–96). Warsaw: Instytut Spraw Publicznych (Institute of Public Affairs). Retrieved from: http://www.isp.org.pl/uploads/filemanager/Rozne/Spoecznociwschodnioazjatyckiedruk.pdf (accessed: 21/01/2016).

Wysieńska, K., Piłat, A. (2012). Ekonomiczna adaptacja chińskich i wietnamskich migrantów zarobkowych. In: Wysieńska, K. (ed.). *Sprzedawać, gotować, budować? Plany i strategie Chińczyków i Wietnamczyków w Polsce* (p. 97–116). Warsaw: Instytut Spraw Publicznych (Institute of Public Affairs). Retrieved from: http://www.isp.org.pl/uploads/filemanager/Rozne/Spoecznociwschodnioazjatyckiedruk.pdf (accessed: 21/01/2016).

Tamás Matura, Ágnes Szunomár

Perceptions of China among Central and Eastern European University Students[1]

Even though the People's Republic of China (PRC) and most Central and Eastern European (CEE) countries established diplomatic relations as early as in the year 1949, the Cold War had caused them to driftaway from each other. Before the dawn of the 21st century, the nations of the CEE region and the PRC dealt with their own development and domestic problems. Only the last decade brought in a new momentum to the bilateral relations between the two sides, thanks to common political and economic interests. After the new millennium, as the world's economic centre of gravity shifts to the East, the relations between Central and Eastern Europe and China started to strengthen. This shift was followed by the economic crisis, which drew even more attention to the potential of Chinese economic relationship for the countries of the region, as they started to see a possibility for a recovery from a recession in the expansion and deepening of relations with the emerging China.

When China launched its new cooperation program with Central and Eastern European countries, it also invigorated the research on the relation of the PRC and the CEE region: economic and political aspects and potentials of the relation have been touched upon several times by academic scholars, PhD students and journalists. Now, it is time to assess the relations between the CEE region and the PRC with a special emphasis on public perceptions of China among the next generation of the CEE leaders. The research was motivated by our assumption, that high-level political relations have an impact on the perceptions of university students: better general political relations mean better understanding

---

[1] This paper was supported by the 2015 scholarship of the Sasakawa Young Leaders Fellowship Fund.

and acceptance among university students as well; furthermore, there is a positive correlation between the level and depth of economic cooperation between China and certain CEE countries and the attitude of university students toward China.

To thoroughly analyze the perceptions of China in the CEE countries, the paper presents the theory and literature on the topic, and provides an overview of the relations between China and the selected CEE countries, with a special emphasis on the general patterns. Following the description of the methodology, the paper's main section introduces the results of a public opinion survey conducted among Czech, Hungarian, Polish, and Slovak university students exclusively for this paper.[2] This quantitative research was taken on-line with a focus group of young university students to reveal public perceptions about the image of China, its international role and the 16+1 cooperation. Finally, the conclusion contains the authors' findings and recommendations on China-CEE relations.

1. Theory and literature review

The true meaning of the expression 'Central and Eastern Europe' is surprisingly blunt, yet still commonly used.[3] A huge variety of definitions and further names (Central Europe, East Central Europe, Middle Europe etc.) are well known in the academic circles, therefore it is hard to provide a single definition on what Central Europe really is. The definition varies according to the specific topic in question, thus, the CEE region is different from a cultural or from a geographic point of view, i.e. Central and Eastern Europe is a historically dynamic concept.[4] However, when it comes to modern politics the following definitions have to be considered.

Ronald Tiersky hailed the establishment of the Visegrad Cooperation (V4) by the Czech Republic, Hungary, Poland and Slovakia (still Czechoslovakia at that time) as a major achievement of Central European cooperation. The three presidents met in the former royal city of Visegrad in Hungary, to create a forum for cooperation of their respective states. After

---

[2] The authors would like to thank their colleagues in Visegrad countries, for their support and help in circulating the research questionnaire.

[3] This section is based on the paper of Tamas Matura: Central Europe and the Republic of Korea: Politics, Economy and Perceptions. *Journal of Contemporary Korean Studies*, 1(1), December 2014.

[4] International organizations usually embrace more pragmatic and less historic point of views. According to the OECD: Central and Eastern European Countries (CEECs) is an OECD term for the group of countries comprising Albania, Bulgaria, Croatia, the Czech Republic, Hungary, Poland, Romania, the Slovak Republic, Slovenia, and the three Baltic States: Estonia, Latvia, and Lithuania.

the peaceful split of the Czech Republic and Slovakia, the four countries became the engine of Central European EU accession aspirations. Even though the V4 failed to build a strong and sustainable common identity, these countries are still the main representatives of the CEE region, both in terms of the economic power and population number.

According to Peter Katzenstein, Central Europe is a way station in the Europeanization, represented by the transformation process of the Visegrad Group countries in different, though comparable ways. From a German point of view, 'Central European identity' means the divide between Roman Catholicism and Eastern Orthodoxy. Katzenstein also states that it is hard to decide whether the Baltic (Estonia, Latvia, and Lithuania) or the Balkan states (Bulgaria, Croatia Romania, Serbia, Slovenia, etc.) are parts of Central Europe or not.

And there are quite fresh assumptions about the meaning of the CEE region. The People's Republic of China (PRC) has implemented its 16+1 cooperation project, which aims at fostering better ties between China and sixteen Central and Eastern European countries. Beijing did not waste its time with academic definitions, rather pragmatically enlisted all countries recognized by the PRC, geographically stretching out between the members of the Commonwealth of Independent States and the "old EU member states" of Germany, Austria, and Italy. The cooperation embraces Albania, Bosnia-Hercegovina, Bulgaria, the Czech Republic, Croatia, Estonia, Hungary, Latvia, Lithuania, Macedonia, Montenegro, Poland, Romania, Serbia, Slovakia, and Slovenia. It is clear that the Chinese approach does not make historical, geographical, political or economic differentiation (11 of them are EU member states) between these countries. Beijing merely wanted to create a forum, where all the leaders of the 16+1 countries could negotiate with each other at the same time.

Regarding the literature on China-CEE relations, the number and depth of available international scientific publications and other resources is very limited. Majority of these publications (Jacoby, 2014; Woon, 2003; Song, 2014; Turcsányi, Matura & Fürst, 2014; Szunomár, Völgyi & Matura, 2014; Matura, 2012; Matura, 2013, etc.) deal with political and/or economic relations of China and Central and Eastern Europe, some of them try to estimate the future evolution of the relationship, but there has never been any attempt to gather primary data in the CEE region on the views and understanding of China's rise and its international role. Therefore, it was our priority to convey a public opinion survey among university students around the most relevant CEE countries in order to understand the present, and to predict the potential future of bilateral relations.

Our project is unique in terms of its geographical focus on the V4 countries, however, public opinion surveys about China have been conducted all around the World. The Pew Research Center publishes comprehensive survey results on a regular basis, and thus it is interesting to compare their results with our findings. One of their publications is especially interesting from our point of view, since it compares the attitude of the European youth and the 50+ generations' understanding of China. It is clear that young Europeans see China more favourably than elders do: 61 percent of youngsters have a positive view on China in France, while only 41 percent of elders do the same. In Poland, 37 percent of millennials and 29 percent of elders have a favourable view of China. At the same time, young Europeans are critical of Beijing's human rights record. A median of merely 17 percent in the countries surveyed believe, that China respects the personal freedoms of its people. Young Europeans are convinced that China has already replaced (or will replace one day) the United States as an economic and strategic super power; 79 percent of Spanish millennials and two-thirds of French and British young people see China as a global leader of the future. This perspective is much stronger among youngsters, than among elders in their respective countries (Pew, 2015).

2. Background of the relations

Exchanges between China and the CEE region date back to ancient times, as over 2,000 years ago, the Silk Road closely linked these regions together. Now, after a long break, the relationship is about to be revived. Of course, there were connections between China and the countries of the region during the Cold War and in the 90's as well. Some countries had better, some had less friendly ties, but generally, the region had no special role neither from Chinese or the CEE's point of view. Attitudes gradually began to change after the Millennium. On the one hand, the transformation of the global economy is responsible for growing Chinese interest in CEE, but on the other hand, CEE represents new challenges and new opportunities for China, too. The growth potential, institutional stability and the market size make the CEE region an attractive place for Chinese investments. As China became a major player in world economy and politics, CEE countries became more interested in developing relations with China. At the same time, China has also became increasingly interested towards the CEE region as the EU-accession process of the countries of the CEE region was launched.

The economic and financial crisis of 2008 was an additional impetus for both China and the CEE countries to strengthen their economic relations. CEE countries started to search for new opportunities in their recovery from the recession: we can observe increased interest of the CEEC's governments in boosting trade relations and attracting Chinese investors. For example, Hungary's "Opening to the East" policy was initiated after (and partly as a result of) the crisis, but the crisis also made Poland and – recently – the Czech Republic look eastward. In parallel, the crisis brought more overseas opportunities to Chinese companies to raise their share in the world economy, as the number of ailing or financially distressed firms has increased. China just took these opportunities, which can be the reason of the wider sectoral representation of Chinese firms in the CEECs in recent years.

Xi Jinping's tour as the Vice-President in 2009 to Europe signalled the real shift in the Chinese leadership's attitude toward the Central and Eastern European region, and marked the beginning of a new stage in their bilateral relations. Xi made an extended tour of Europe, visiting Belgium, Germany, Bulgaria, Romania, and Hungary, and he spent the most time in Budapest. This tour was framed as a visit to consolidate and develop cooperation in economic relations between China and the five countries, but Xi's visit to the Central and Eastern European countries told more about China's evolving "go-out" investment strategy, which indicated that the Chinese are eager to accelerate their diversification strategy through the emerging countries in the region.

In 2011, the Chinese Premier Wen Jiabao further appreciated the growing importance of Chinese-CEE relations in his speech at the initial 16+1 business forum, the "China-Central and Eastern European Countries Economic and Trade Forum" (Wen, 2011), held in Budapest. He said that China and the Central and Eastern European countries are not just good friends who stand by each other through thick and thin, but also good partners, that draw on each other's strengths and pursue win-win cooperation. Wen emphasized how cooperation areas have been expanding. And indeed, the CEE countries have more than doubled their exports to the PRC between 2009 and 2014, and have attracted more investments than ever before. Additionally, in recent years, China and the CEE countries have signed a series of bilateral agreements on a wide range of economic, industrial, scientific and technological cooperation, including agreements on investment protection and avoidance of double taxation.

Besides the traditional fields of trade and investment, the cooperation in finance, tourism, legal services, green economy and infrastructure has steadily increased. The two sides held various kinds of business forums, product exhibitions and trade fairs for entrepreneurs, providing important platforms for the business community to intensify exchange and cooperation. Besides, dozens of high or medium-level diplomatic delegations visited China and the CEE countries in recent years. Three years after Wen's visit in Budapest, Warsaw hosted the first summit of the heads of the CEE governments,[5] where the 12-measure initiative was presented. This step marked the official beginning of the 16+1 platform, which created a complex framework of contacts between the two sides (see Szczudlik-Tatar, 2013 and 2014).

In fact, Beijing perceives the Central and Eastern European region not only as one of its new frontiers for export expansion, but also as a strategic entry point for the wider European market. They chose this region because the CEE countries represent dynamic, largely developed, less saturated economies, which are directly connected to the EU common market. Chinese corporations can significantly cut their business costs in the CEE-countries, they get integrated into the industrial system within the EU, while there are less political expectations and fewer (or more silent) economic complaints compared to Western Europe. And, of course, Beijing's growing interest towards the Central and Eastern European markets could not be disconnected from some longstanding political and economic goals of China: to end the EU arms embargo on the PRC, and to grant it the market economy status. As a result, some may see China's engagement towards the CEE countries as an attempt to buy political support from Central European countries whose economies depend on increasingly scarce sources of FDI.

Before the global economic and financial crisis of 2008, many Central European countries had mixed feelings of closer economic ties with China. On the one hand, they actively wanted to attract Chinese FDI, and were anxious about losing out on trade and business opportunities with China. On the other hand, there were fears of the reliability of Chinese firms, for example as a result of the failure of Chinese company COVEC in Poland to complete a section of a highway project, or because of human rights issues such as the supposed exploitative labour conditions in Chinese-owned workplaces. Nowadays, more and more countries of the CEE region decide to put their doubts aside, and even the coldest relations (like the Czech-Chinese relations) start warming. However, it is true that despite the above-mentioned developments, most of the CEE governments lack a unified strategy towards China or Chinese companies. Hungary is one of the few exceptions, where in the spring of 2012 the government launched a new economic policy with special emphasis on the so-called "Eastern opening" (Éltető-Szunomár, 2014).[6]

---

[5] In 2013, the 16+1 summit took place in Bucharest, while in 2016 the summit was held in Beograd.

[6] This strategy puts emphasis on developing trade (and technology) relations with China and other emerging countries. Rapidly growing Asian countries are considered as ones able to provide several business opportunities and China is considered as an alternative source of external financing.

The question is, whether the growing Chinese interest towards the CEE region, as well as CEE governments' intention to be China's bridgehead in Europe will give sufficient impetus to intensify policy steps on the CEE's side too.

3. Methodology and limitations

As the concept of Central and Eastern Europe is rather broad, it would obviously be too complicated and too extensive to conduct a research on the relations of all countries of the region with the PRC. Therefore, we decided to concentrate our work on a fair selection of the CEE countries, considering their size, economy and political status. Members of the Visegrad Cooperation are the most developed and most important players of the region, all four of them are the EU and Schengen Area member states. These four countries are the home of 70 percent of the population and 70 percent of the economic output of the CEE region, and their trade equals to 80,3 percent of the region's total 64 billion USD trade with China (UNCTAD Stat). It is even more important that the Chinese side itself regards the V4 countries as their most important partners amongst all the CEE nations. According to the assessment of the Chinese Academy of Sciences, the most important adviser of the Ministry of Foreign Affairs on the CEE issues, Poland, Hungary, the Czech Republic and Slovakia are respectively the most important partners of China in the region (Liu, 2014).

The survey itself was circulated online among universities in several fields of sciences in the Czech Republic, Hungary, Poland, and Slovakia, where 80–90 percent of young people (age 16–29) use the internet on a daily basis (Eurostat, 2015). The language of the survey was English, since 81.8–98.8 percent of upper secondary school students learn the language in the V4 countries, and thus, almost all university students have to speak a certain level of English (Eurostat, 2013). Therefore we assume, that the survey has been filled by a fair sample of university students around the region. However, it has to be mentioned that students with an inherent interest in international relations or China might be overrepresented in the results.

The survey consisted of 29 questions, out of which six referred to the personal background of the respondents (sex, age, political attitude, etc.), while the remaining 23 questions covered the political and economic issues with regard to China.

While sending the survey to various universities in these countries we also launched a "control survey", using a control group of students from different parts of the world: the students of the Central European University (CEU). Since CEU students represent a heterogeneous group, coming from countries all around the World, their aggregate opinion serves as an important basis of comparison.

As always, the main question of our research was its reliability and representativeness. The results do not represent the opinion of the entirety of the V4 societies. Our aim was to conduct a research on the perception of young university students in the countries concerned. We received 257 responses from the four different countries in question altogether, out of the respondents, 248 were under the age of 35. The general composition of responses suggests a fair and comprehensive dissemination of the questionnaire, 52.5 percent of respondents were females, while 47.5 percent were males. Out of the total number of respondents, 89 percent were part of our target group with regard to age (yrs. 18–29) and 97.3 percent were either graduate or post-graduate students (those with a Ph.D. were excluded from the results). In order to check the reliability of answers, we had included a question about the political preferences of the respondents. Unfortunately, the overwhelming majority of responses arrived from leftist and liberal people, while the opinion of right winged, conservative people represents a minority (Graph 1). Even though the generally more liberal attitude of university students is common sense, the predominance of leftist/liberal responses had to be addressed.

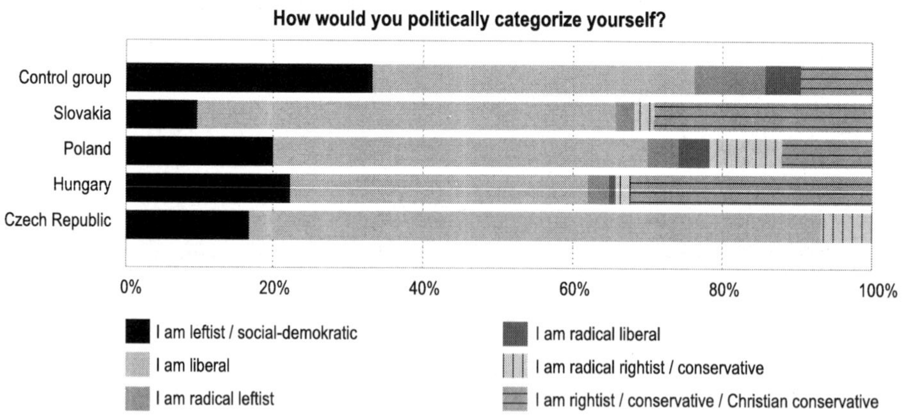

Graph 1: Political categorization of the respondents
Source: results of research.

Thus, to secure the reliability of the results and to mitigate imbalances we checked the correlation between the respondents' political preferences and their perceptions about China. Firstly, we separated responses coming from four different countries into three groups according to the political attitude of the respondents (i.e. groups of liberals, rightist-conservatives and leftist-socialists). Secondly, we calculated the average of responses for thirteen questions in all three groups. Thirdly, we calculated the difference between the highest average number and the lowest, to see whether political attitudes do have a considerable impact on responses or not. According to our calculations, political preferences have a surprisingly low impact on the perception of China in Hungary and in Poland (the averages of differences are 0.25 and 0.35 respectively on a 5 point scale), while in the Czech Republic and Slovakia political attitudes influence results to a higher extent (0.57 and 0.69 points respectively). Actually these partial results are in accordance with the general statement of the literature that there is a wide gap between the Czech left and right when it comes to China. Meanwhile, political sides all agree on the necessity of good relations with China in Hungary (Turcsányi-Matura-Fürst, 2014, pp. 129–130). To sum it up, we believe that the high share of liberal and leftist respondents does not influence final results to a considerable extent.

4. Analysis

The following chapter presents the final results and findings of our survey.

According to our results, 85.8 percent of the respondents have never been to mainland China, and 55 five percent of them does not have any friends or acquaintances of Chinese nationality. As a result of their international environment, 81 percent of the members of the control group (CEU students) do have a Chinese friend, which is in stark contrast with the V4 respondents. The overwhelming majority (66–90 percent) of students are aware of the form of government in China (people's republic), and literally everybody has heard about Confucius Institutes (CI) in their respective countries. However, 80–90 percent of them have never been to any events of a CI in the Czech Republic, Hungary and Poland. The figure is surprisingly different in the case of Slovakia, where 80 percent of the students have been to a CI event.

As for the political role of China and bilateral relations, most students seemingly embraced a rather pragmatic view. When it comes to the question of trust between China and the V4 countries, Polish students trust China the least (2.79 points out of 5), and the Hungarians the most (3.3 points). The difference is relatively low, and the control group produced a very similar level (3.28 points). China is considered as a partner by 77 percent of Hungarian and 50 percent of Czech students. It is remarkable that 7 percent of Czech university students think about China as an enemy. The results of the control group is again in line with the V4 countries (Graph 2).

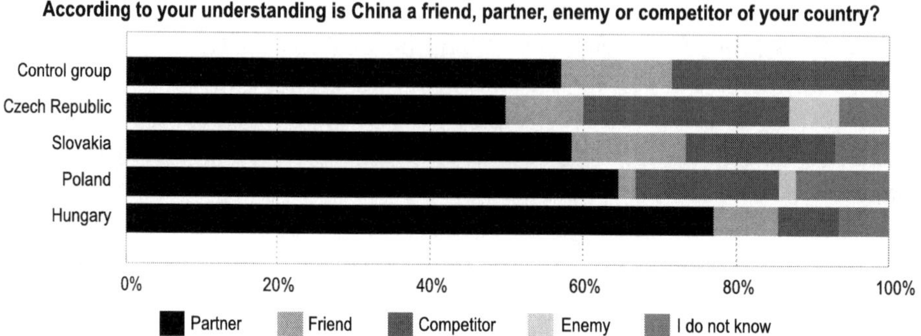

Graph 2: Opinions on bilateral relations
Source: results of research.

Respondents have a neutral opinion on the global role of Beijing (all countries between 3 and 3.5 points, including the control group), while the contribution of China to the World economy received better scores (3.5–4 points, Graph 3).

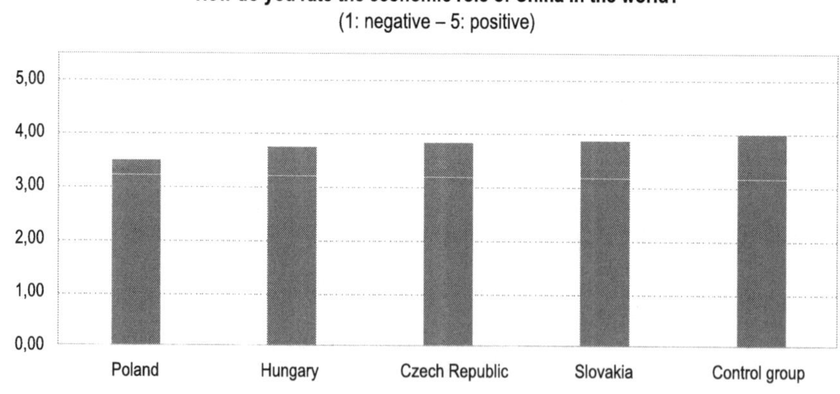

Graph 3: Opinions on economic role of China in the world
Source: results of research.

It seems that most students consider China as a promising economic partner, but as a less promising political actor at the same time. The importance of the economic relations received higher points in all of the V4 countries than the importance of bilateral political relations with China (Graph 4).

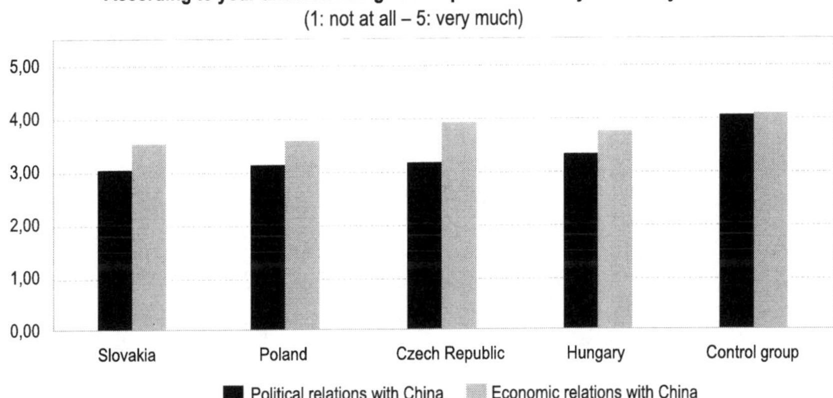

Graph 4: Opinions on political and economic relations with China

Source: results of research.

The less optimistic view about the political cooperation with Beijing is also reflected in Graph 5, where respondents from all the four countries believe that China does not really care about the interest of other nations (2.5–2.7 points), and it cares even less of the interest of the V4 countries (1.9–2.1 points).

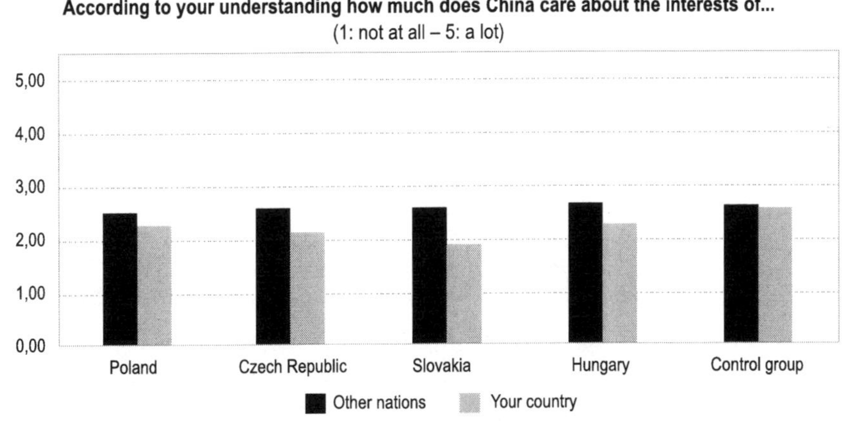

Graph 5: Opinions about political cooperation between China and CEE countries

Source: results of research.

Students in all of the V4 countries (and in the control group) have a rather negative opinion about the political system of China (2–2.5 points), but only a minority (19–24 percent) of them would promote political change there (Graph 6 and 7). International students of the control group are the most strong-minded, while there is a higher level of uncertain opinions in the V4 countries.

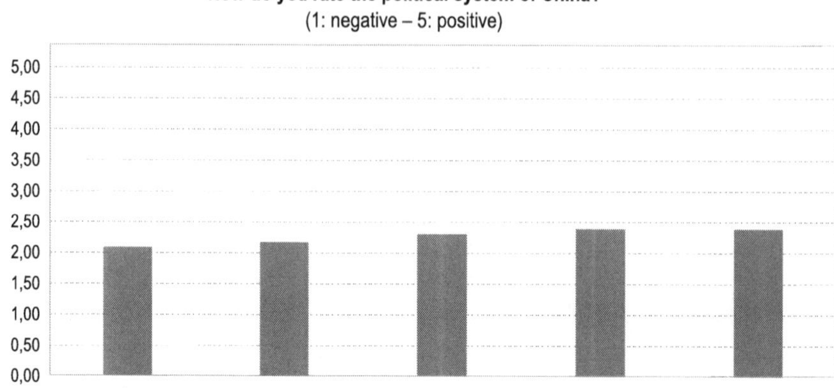

Graph 6: Opinions on the political system of China

Source: results of research.

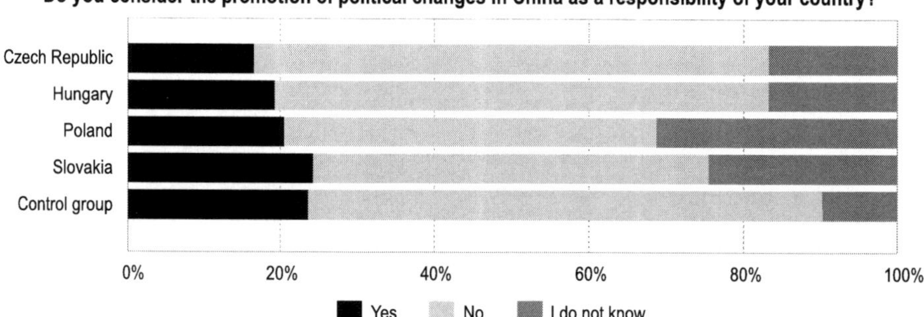

Graph 7: Opinions on promotion of political changes in China as a responsibility of the CEE countries

Source: results of research.

Similarly to the perceptions of the political system, the students have a rather negative opinion about the status of human rights in China, even compared to other developing countries (Graph 8). However, they clearly do understand the difference between human rights standards in developed and in developing countries.

Still, none of the V4 countries (or the control group) consider the support of human rights in China as their responsibility (Graph 9). Slovakia is somewhat different, as the supporters have a relative majority. At the same time, the international students of the control group very strongly reject the idea to take the support of human rights in China as their national responsibility.

When it comes to the question of Chinese investment in the V4 countries, the knowledge of respondents is rather limited, even though they consider economic relations with China to be important (Graph 10).

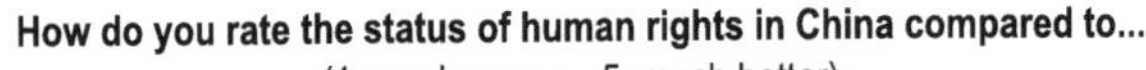

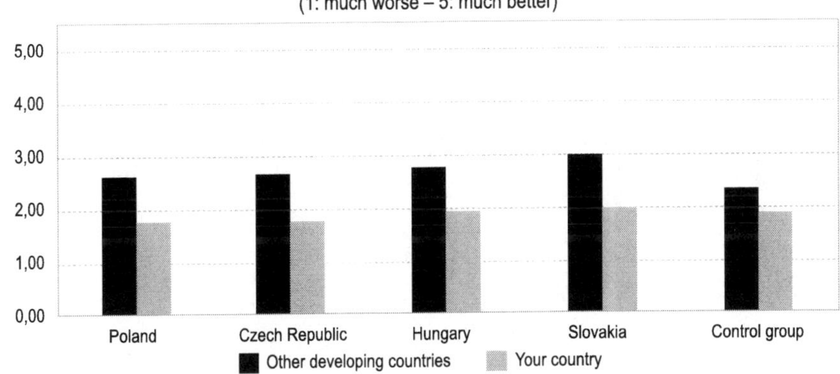

Graph 8: Opinions on human rights in China
Source: results of research.

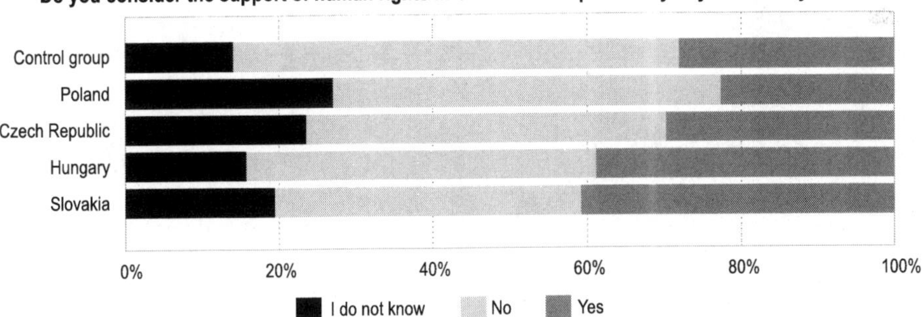

Graph 9: Opinions on supporting of human rights in China
Source: results of research.

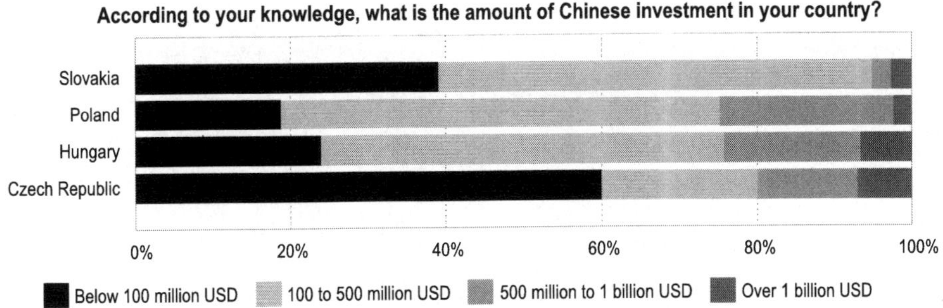

Graph 10: Opinions of the amount of Chinese investment in the CEE countries
Source: results of research.

The real amount of Chinese FDI stock in Slovakia is under 100 million USD, while the majority of students believe it is between 100 and 500 million USD. The stock is over 1 billion USD both in Poland and Hungary, still, only 2 and 6 percent of the respondents knew the correct answer. It seems that Czech students are more aware of reality, since 60 percent of them responded correctly that the amount is below 100 million USD (Heritage, 2015).

When it comes to stereotypes about the Chinese minorities living in the V4 countries, the picture is quite clear. Generally, the students have a relatively good opinion about them in all of the V4 countries (3.3–3.5 points), while the control group has a slightly lower esteem of the Chinese people (3.2 points) (Graph 11).

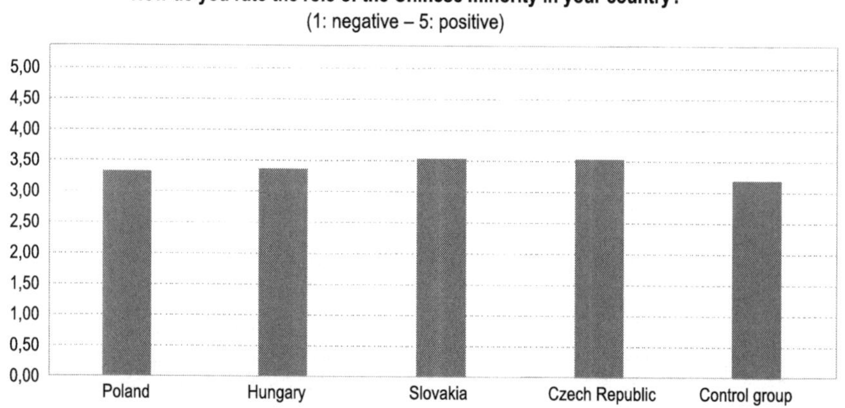

Graph 11: Opinions of the role of the Chinese minorities in the CEE countries
Source: results of research.

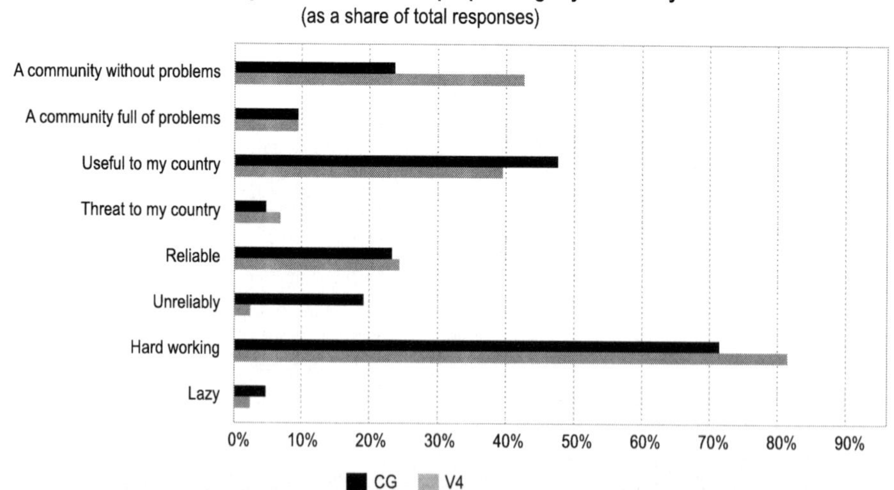

Graph 12: Opinions of the Chinese community in the CEE countries
Source: results of research.

Both the CEE and the control group respondents consider the Chinese people as hard working, useful for the host country, reliable and as a community without problems (Graph 12).

Last but not least, we were curious how Central and Eastern European students think about the future global power of China. Czechs are slightly pessimistic (2.9 points), Hungarians, Poles, and Slovakians and the students of the control group are neutral or slightly optimistic (3.0–3.37 points) regarding the impact of the rise of China (Graph 13).

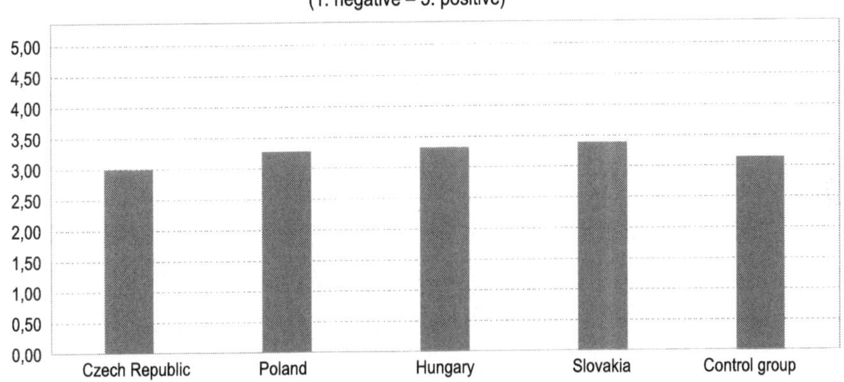

Graph 13: Opinions on the rise of China

Source: results of research.

Although all the countries (and the control group as well) still regard Washington as more powerful than Beijing (Graph 14), most respondents think that China will be the leader of the world in the 21st century. However, while the Czech, Slovakian and the control group students are certain about the shining future of China, the Hungarians, and the Poles give a similar probability to the continuing American leadership (Graph 15).

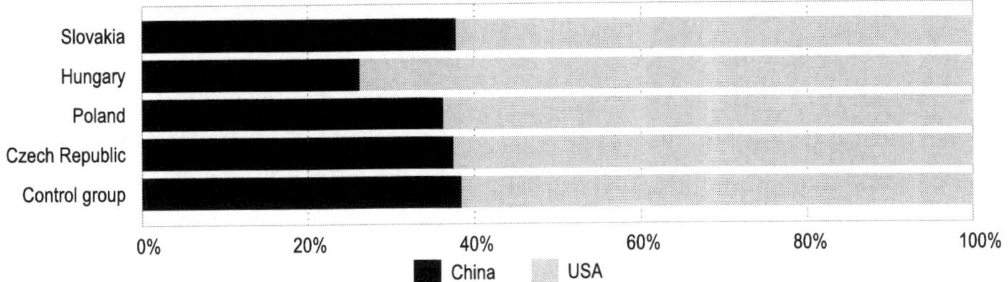

Graph 14: Comparison of China's and USA power

Source: results of research.

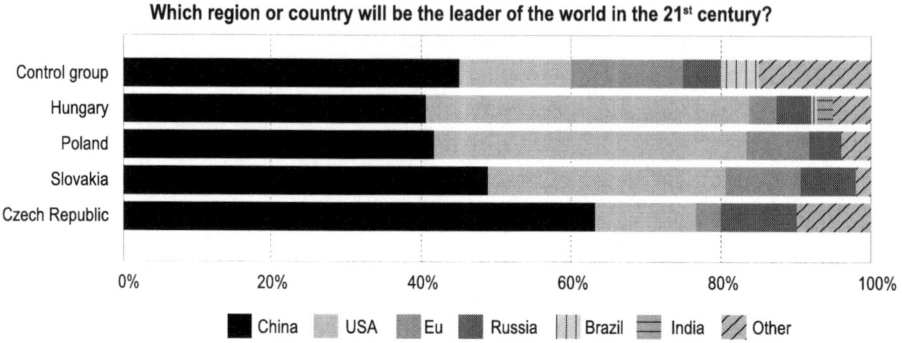

Graph 15: Predictions of future leader of the world
Source: results of research.

5. Conclusions

As mentioned above, there are more and more opportunities in the cooperation between the CEE region and China, but also, a lot of tasks to do in order to strengthen ties between them. Each of the CEE countries shows a great interest in developing relations with China, however, alone, they are not strong enough to do so. The countries of the CEE region – even if they are competitors of each other at the same time – must work together on deepening the relation between China and CEE, so that everyone could benefit from the successes of the cooperation.

According to our findings, Central and Eastern European university students have a rather neutral opinion vis-à-vis China when it comes to trust in and cooperation with China, and Beijing is mostly considered as a partner of their respective countries. The economic role of Beijing and bilateral economic relations between China and the Central European countries seems to be more important than politics to the university students. Even though they have an unfavourable view of the political system and human rights in China, only a small minority would support changes actively. They have a similarly neutral attitude towards the Chinese minority in their home countries, and about the potential effects of the rise of China as well. Even though most of them believe that the US is stronger than China for the time being, the majority thinks that China will eventually take over the US, which is in line with the mindset of other European countries (Pew, 2015).

To sum it up, there is a clear distinction between the perceived importance of political and economic relations with China, although the difference is small. Differences are also small when we compare the individual

Visegrad Four countries to each other, the Czech Republic and Slovakia are somewhat more critical, while Poland and Hungary are a bit more tolerant towards China. Surprisingly, the Czech and Slovak students are the most certain about the Chinese leadership in the 21st century, while the Hungarians and the Poles give an equal chance to the Chinese and the American supremacy. The relative neutrality of students might be the consequence of the huge geographic and cultural distance between Central Europe and China, and of the novelty of the 16+1 cooperation.

It is also important that Chinese soft power is weak in the region, Confucius Institutes barely reaches out to students. Confucius Institutes should consider this information as a constructive advice – rather than a critique – in order to focus and reschedule a bit more on this group of young people.

Of course, it would be desirable to conduct a nationwide, fully representative public opinion survey on China in all of the V4 or even all of the 16 CEE countries. It is an interesting and important question: how do the CEE societies think about China, since the cooperation between the region and Beijing will certainly grow even stronger in the coming years. Politicians should be aware of the mindset of their respective nations, while pursuing close relations with China. However, such an endeavor would need a strong financial and institutional background. In the upcoming years, it is our goal to find the necessary resources to conduct this regional survey about China.

References

Eurostat (2013). Pupils by education level and modern foreign language studied – absolute numbers and % of pupils by language studied. Dataset (accessed: 18/09/2015).

Eurostat (2015). Being young in Europe today. Statistical Books, p. 195.

Éltető, A., Szunomár, Á. (2015). Ties of Visegrád countries with East Asia – trade and investment. *Working Paper*, No. 215. Institute of World Economics – MTA KRTK.

Heritage (2015). China Global Investment Tracker. Heritage Foundation (accessed: 20/09/2015).

Jacoby, W. (2014). Different cases, different faces: Chinese investment in Central and Eastern Europe. *Asia Europe Journal*, 12, 199–214.

Liu Zuokui (2014). The analysis of China's investment in V4. In: *Current Trends and Perspectives in Development of China-V4 Trade and Investment*. University of Economics in Bratislava, Faculty of International Relations.

Matura, T. (2012). The Pattern of Chinese Investments in Central Europe. *International Journal of Business Insights and Transformation*, 5, Special Issue 3, July.

Matura, T. (2013). China's economic expansion into Central Europe. In: Matura, T. (ed.). *Asian Studies* (pp. 138–151). Budapest: Hungarian Institute of International Affairs.

Pew (2015). *European Millennials more likely than older generations to view China favourably*. Pew Research Center, February 18.

Song Lilei (2014). China's public diplomacy toward Visegrad countries: Beyond economic influence? In: Szunomár, Á. (ed.). *Chinese Investments and Financial Engagement in Visegrad Countries: Myth or Reality?* (pp. 108–126). Budapest: Institute of World Economics, Centre for Economic and Regional Studies, Hungarian Academy of Sciences.

Szunomár, Á., Völgyi, K., Matura, T. (2014). Chinese investments and financial engagement in Hungary. *Working Paper*, No. 208. Institute of World Economics – MTA KRTK.

Szczudlik-Tatar, J. (2013). China's Charm Offensive in Central and Eastern Europe: The implementation of its "12 Measures" strategy. *PISM Bulletin*, *106*(559), 4 October.

Szczudlik-Tatar, J. (2014). China and the CEE Look for New Development Opportunities. *PISM Bulletin*, *134*(729), 12 December.

Turcsányi, R.Q., Matura, T., Fürst, R. (2014). The Visegrad countries' political relations with China. In: Szunomár, Á. (ed.). *Chinese Investments and Financial Engagement in Visegrad Countries: Myth or Reality?* (pp. 127–141). Budapest: Institute of World Economics, Centre for Economic and Regional Studies, Hungarian Academy of Sciences.

Wen Jiabao (2011). Strengthen Traditional Friendship and Promote Common Development. Speech at the China-Central and Eastern European Countries Economic and Trade Forum, Budapest, June 25. Retrieved from: http://www.gov.cn/english/2011–06/26/content_1892994.htm (accessed: 21/09/2015).

Woon Lim Jia (2003). Asian FDI in Central and Eastern Europe and its impact on the host countries. *Asia Europe Journal*, *1*, 349–369.

Jarosław Jura, Kaja Kałużyńska

Transformation of the Dragon – China's Image in the Polish Media

This paper was written as a part of a wider research project, conducted in 2014[1] and aimed to establish the image of migrants and foreign ethnic groups in the Polish media. One of interesting findings of this research was a surprisingly positive image of China and the Chinese in the Polish media (at least during the period included in the research time frame – the second half of 2013). Such a relatively positive image was contradictory to the stereotypical belief that China is still being depicted in the Polish media mainly as a Communist and totalitarian, undeveloped country. Moreover, the problem of China and Chinese image in media content has not been popular among the scholars engaged in the Polish academic discourse. Actually, during our research we found only three articles referring to this issue: one referring strictly to image of China and the Chinese in the Polish media (Bukowski, 2014), and two of them focusing on the image of different ethnic groups in the Polish media (Mrozowski, 1997; Jóźwiak, Konieczna-Sałamatin & Tudorowski, 2010), where China was a minor point of interest.

Therefore, since our research interests include China's media image in the world, we decided to pay more attention to the outcome of the broader research and analyze the image of China in the Polish media in a more detailed way.

However, the very notion of a country image had been so widely discussed by numerous scholars from various fields, that we decided to provide a short overview of some of the definitions that had been worked out

---

[1] Moreover it is necessary to mention that the research was also a part of broader interdisciplinary project "High qualified migrants and the Polish labour market" financed by "European Fund for the Integration of third-country nationals".

by them. This notion is rooted, to some extent, in the Lippmann's stereotype, and had been used mostly in three contexts: tourism, marketing, and international relations. It is a bit ironic, though, since one of the first "imagologists", Kenneth Boulding, stated that "the national image is basically a lie, or at least a perspective distortion of the truth" (1959, p. 122). Quite frequently the term „national image" is substituted with „country image", but the latter should be applied in the tourism and marketing contexts. According to Jenes (2012), the proliferation of image-related academic project dates back to the early 2000's, but first such works were conducted in the USA as early as in 1930s (Katz & Braly, 1933). The national image itself has started to gain importance and popularity with the shortening distances between countries due to globalization, and countries' overall reputation has become a focal point in their domestic and international policies. In 1970, Nagashima defined the national image as "the picture, the reputation, the stereotype that businessmen and consumers attach to products of a specific country", such an image consisted of "representative products, national characteristics, economic and political background, history, and traditions" (quoted in Zhou, Chen & Wu, 2012, p. 767).

From the political and psychological perspective, Nimmo and Savage (1976) described the image as "a human construct imposed on array of perceived attributes projected by an object, event or a person", consisting of a subjective understanding of things (quoted in Newman, 1994, pp. 91–92). This definition emphasizes two aspects of an image – projection and perception and the fact, that these two do not necessarily have to be coherent or compatible. Such a cognitive perspective of an image is shared by many scholars (see for example Boulding, 1959; Wang, 2008). One of them is also Kunczik, who specifically defined a national image as a "cognitive representation that a person holds of a given country, what a person believes to be true about a nation and its people" (1997, p. 47). We believe, that the last definition suits our research attitude and, at least to some extent, is influenced by the image presented in the media.

Methodology of the research

The content of our database was a download from the on-line Polish media, both Internet news portals and on-line versions of popular journals and magazines. Table 1 presents the sources we used for gathering data for our research.

The initial database was created by downloading all the articles that contained chosen keywords related to particular countries, supplemented with more general words, such as "foreigner", "migrant", etc. and con-

Table 1: Data sources used in the analysis

Title	Media type	Average circulation	Characteristics[1]
Fakt	Daily newspaper	474 418	Tabloid
Super Express	Daily newspaper	260 743	Tabloid
Gazeta Wyborcza	Daily newspaper	278 300	Centrist-left, liberal
Gazeta Polska Codziennie	Daily newspaper	86 416	Rightist, conservative, with tabloid-like tendencies
Rzeczpospolita	Daily newspaper	69 256	Centrist, conservative
Nasz Dziennik	Daily newspaper	No data	Ultra-rightist, Roman-Catholic
Dziennik Gazeta Prawna	Daily newspaper	102 238	Centrist, conservative
Gość Niedzielny	Weekly magazine	200 113	Conservative, Roman-Catholic
Newsweek Polska	Weekly magazine	168 990	Centrist
Polityka	Weekly magazine	175 400	Centrist-leftist, liberal
Tygodnik Do Rzeczy	Weekly magazine	154 382	Rightist, conservative
Wprost	Weekly magazine	122 984	Centrist
Gazeta Polska	Weekly magazine	135 255	Rightist, conservative
Onet.pl	Internet news portal	5 205 141*	Centrist, various content
Gazeta.pl	Internet news portal	4 453 316*	Leftist tendencies, many articles from *Gazeta Wyborcza*
wp.pl	Internet news portal	5 994 541*	Centrist, mainly short news stories
Interia.pl	Internet news portal	2 239 893*	Rightist tendencies, short news, sparse longer editorials

[1] Due to the lack of professional, reliable sources concerning the ideological and/or political character of particular Polish newspapers, magazines and news portals, information about the character of these sources is based on Authors' own knowledge and statements published by some of these sources.

*Unique visitors in February 2013

Source: own elaboration, based on www.wirtualnemedia.pl, www.teleskop.org.pl (accessed: 20/11/2015).

sisted of 8096 articles. The scope of the initial research project was much broader and focused on different issues, therefore for the purpose of the present research we filtered this database on the basis of the presence of China-related codes, and analyzed only 220 cases in which China was mentioned in some way.

The whole coding and analysis process was performed by employing QDA Data Miner and QDA Wordstat software. In the first step, we created a concise dictionary, in which we included all the words that appeared in the initial database more than 50 times. All of them were either assigned as keywords to some category or categorized as irrelevant. Although this specific dictionary was created for the purpose of this particular research, most of the categories and subcategories to which the keywords were assigned, were been developed for other languages (namely English, Spanish, and Portuguese), during our earlier media-related research projects. Since our main research interest was focused on the issue of the emotional connotations, the first categories that were created consisted of keywords classified as either positive or negative. Apart from these "emotional" sets of keywords, many other categories, consisting of keywords related to various issues, like politics, economy, culture, conflicts, etc., were used as well.

Quantitative analysis

Data presented in Table 2 show that the focus of the Polish media is directed at Poland's neighbors: China, Russia, Ukraine, and at a country typically considered to be the world leading force – the USA. Despite the steady rise of the political and economic role of the People's Republic of China, this country does not draw too much attention of Polish news agencies; in the investigated period, the frequency of China-related references was lower than this of Hungary, Spain or Egypt.

There is one methodological remark that we need to make before proceeding to the next part of the analysis. On the one hand, while analyzing the content of China related articles in the database, we notice a prevalence of articles published by onet.pl (see Table 3), which might lead to the conclusion, that the overall image of China and the Chinese is strongly influenced by this information source. On the other hand, Onet is one of the biggest Polish Internet portals (with the number of unique visitors amounting to as many as 5 205 141 in February 2013). It might be assumed, that its place among Polish news sources would allow this the news portal to influence the Polish audience significantly, thus reducing the above-mentioned bias.

Table 2: Frequency of nations mentioned in the database

	Frequency	**Cases**	**% cases**
Russia	8755	1608	27,70
Germany	6677	1716	23,20
Ukraine	5067	775	10,50
USA	3367	1104	14,90
France	1806	708	9,60
Hungary	1389	412	5,60
Czech Republic	1114	439	5,90
UK	1058	503	6,80
Spain	972	412	5,60
Egypt	860	200	2,70
Syria	637	181	2,40
Italy	518	346	4,70
China	500	220	3,00
Bulgaria	494	233	3,10
Norway	486	234	3,20
Lithuania	483	230	3,10
Belarus	440	169	2,30

Source: results of research.

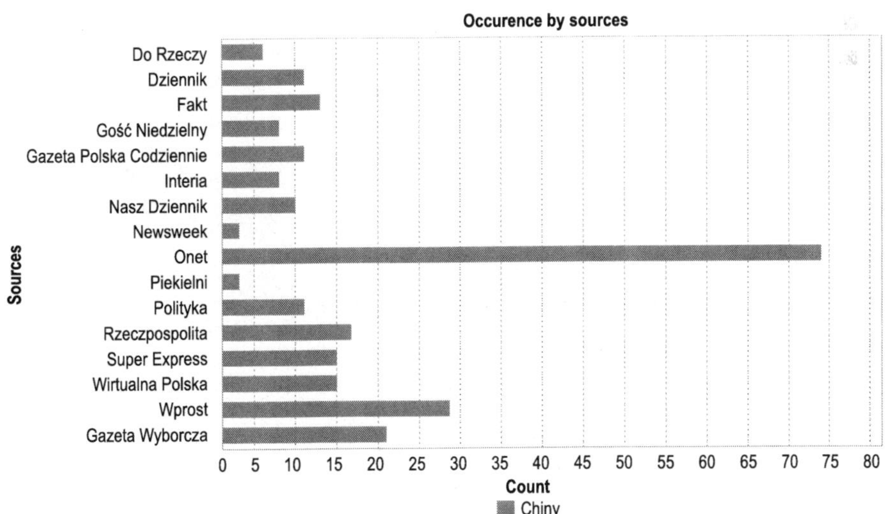

Graph 1: China-related articles by sources

Source: results of research.

Although China is far from being a point of focus of the Polish media, one of the most surprising findings of our study was the fact, that China actually was among the most positively depicted counties of the whole group which we took into account (see Table 3).

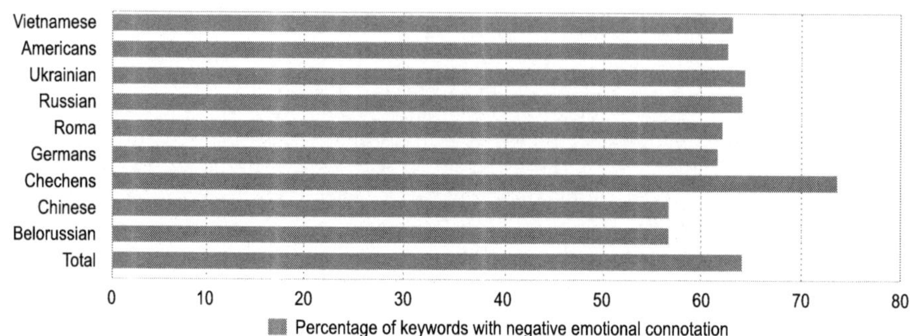

Graph 2: Ratio of keywords with negative connotation by nation
Source: results of research.

As we can see in Table 3, generally in the articles where preferences to particular countries have appeared, we are dealing with a slight prevalence of negatively associated keywords over the positive ones. It is probably related to the nature of contemporary media content, which is fo-

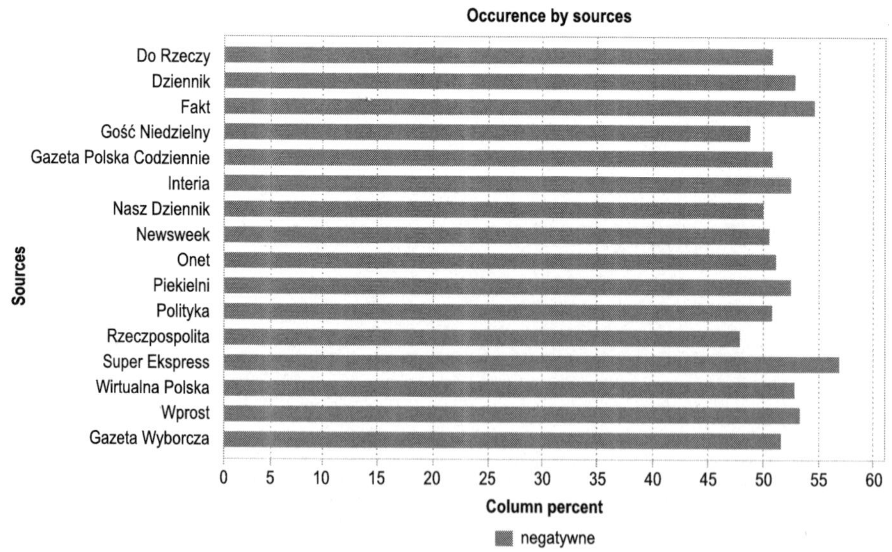

Graph 3: Ratio of keywords with negative connotation in China related articles by source
Source: results of research.

cused more on sensation, tragedy, or any other negative references over the positive ones. Nevertheless, the most positive reaction we can see in cases of Chinese and Belorussians, while the most negative was in the case of Chechens. It is worth to mention that it is probably related to the fact that China was presented mostly in a contemporary context, while the references to Ukraine, Russia and, to some extent Germany, were relatively often placed in some historical context, usually related to conflicts and their consequences. The Chechen image in the Polish media, on the other hand, was strongly influenced by terrorism-related issues.

There were no significant differences in the image of China and the Chinese between particular sources. However, it is worth to mention that in general, the most negative picture was presented by the tabloid press (which is generally related to sensational character of this media). At the other end of the continuum, there was the image created by "Rzeczpospolita", which is a newspaper with strong economical background (although recently of a rather conservative character).

Table 3: Most frequent categories in China-related articles

	Frequency	No cases	% cases
Law	179	73	30,50
Development	144	74	31,00
Lost/defficiency/lack/shortage	140	77	32,20
Success	124	65	27,20
Agreement	117	48	20,10
Cooperation	107	40	16,70
Attack	98	52	21,80
War	94	38	15,90
Problem	93	52	21,80
Help	85	42	17,60

Source: results of research.

The generally relatively positive image of China and the Chinese in the Polish media is supported by the above table, presenting the most frequent categories appearing in the articles where there were China- or the Chinese-related references. As it can be observed above, the dominant categories are those positively associated – mostly in the context of cooperation and development – which might suggest, that China is mostly perceived as a quickly developing country, and from the perspective of economic cooperation.

This reasoning is even clearer while analyzing the proximity plot above. The categories most frequently co-occurring with China category were

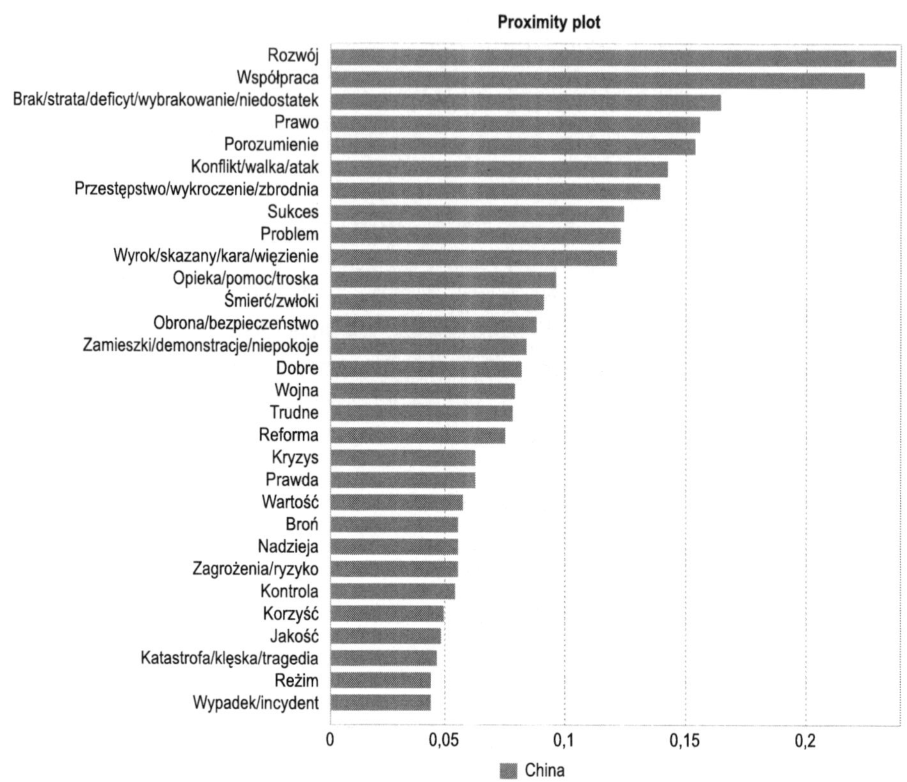

Graph 4: China and categories with positive and negative emotional connotation
Source: results of research.

related with cooperation and development. It seems to be a significantly strong argument supporting the hypotheses that nowadays in Poland, China is mainly presented from an economic and developmental perspective, which is in contradiction with the image of China widespread in the 1990s, namely the Communist regime, with violating the humans rights as one of its main features.

However, it is worth to mention that such a picture in some of the newspapers and magazines such as *Gazeta Wyborcza* (which is strongly associated with a pro-democratic approach), China is not presented from such a positive perspective, related to its economical position.

As it can be observed, the picture of China in *Gazeta Wyborcza* is much closer to the stereotypical one than the general image in the Polish media. China category most often co-occurs with negatively associated categories like prison, punishment, deficit, crime and conflict/attack. It seems that the image of China and the Chinese in *Gazeta*

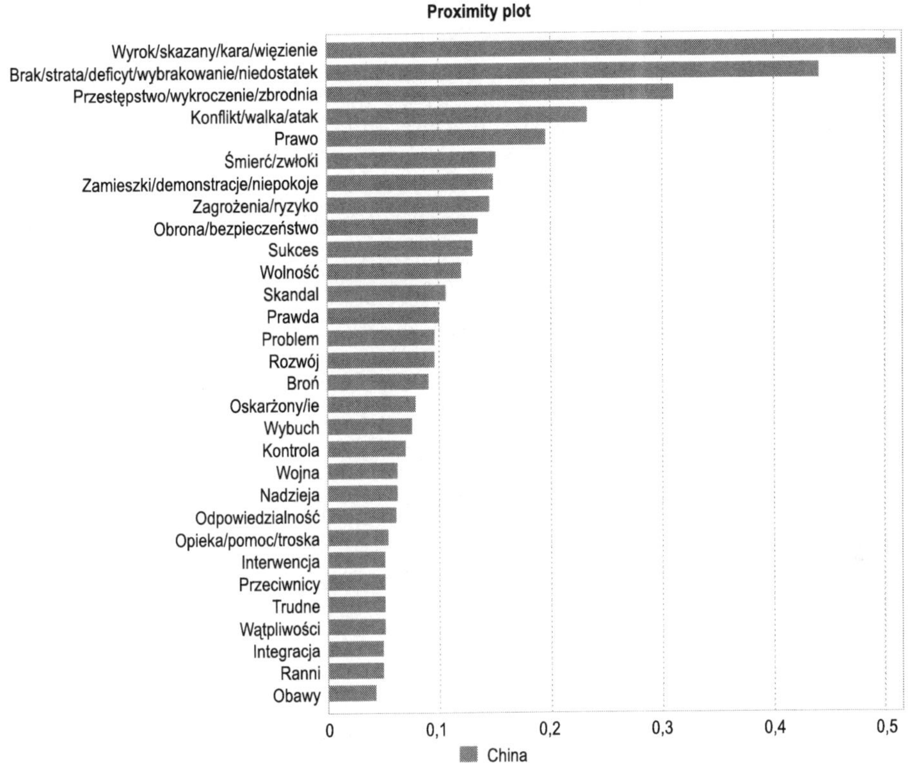

Graph 5: China and categories with positive and negative emotional connotation in *Gazeta Wyborcza*

Source: results of research.

Wyborcza has not changed significantly since 1990s. The overall image of China is much more positive and has changed its point of focus from political, human rights oriented discourse, to a much more pragmatic image, related to China's economic development and economic reforms success.

It is worth to mention that these remarks seem to correspond with the results of the authors' other research conducted in 2011, and related to the image of China and the Chinese in the Zambian and Angolan media (Jura & Kaluzyńska, 2013). In this particular article we provided arguments supporting the thesis that the source of the Chinese soft power in Africa does not consist (as it was argued by Nye [2004, location 299]) of issues related to politics (obviously, not the democracy either) nor culture, but with economy and investment in cooperation. The outputs of the quantitative analysis suggest that a similar situation exists also in Poland.

Qualitative analysis

After completing the quantitative part of the analysis, we decided to take a closer look at the details of the China-related articles from the Polish media. The whole database consisted of 220 articles. After reading all of them, we classified as many as 139 as either mentioning China in a most detailed way, or focusing on this country as the main subject.

This group was later on coded on the basis of the main context; some topics appeared more frequently, but there was also a group of codes that were assigned to only one article in the base. Each article was coded with only one code that best suited its general focus. Moreover, due to the different focus of the content, we decided to exclude the articles published by tabloids from the first part of the qualitative analysis, and analyze them separately.

During the analyzed period, China was most frequently mentioned (22 cases) as a country of an important position on the international scene, both in a regional context and also as a global country. Let us present and analyze some of the most interesting China-related remarks from this group.

"G20 is an informal club, founded in 2008, after the financial crisis. Among its members there are 19 biggest world economies and EU. Among them there are [...] China [...]." (Gość Niedzielny, 2013/09/05)

Numerous remarks about the place of the Chinese economy in the world and the fact that it belongs to the group of the biggest world economies appeared,; in some texts China was also mentioned as a member of other regional and international organizations of different character.

"Also the Chinese express their interest in Ukraine. [...] That's why president Wiktor Janukowycz has visited the Middle Kingdom, in spite of the political storm in Ukraine. [...] President Wiktor Janukowycz is lobbying in China to obtain loans and investments." (Polityka, 2013/12/05)

The above quotation appeared in a text that was not focused on China, but described "local", i.e. European issues. However, it could not be missed that China's economic position places this country on the top of the list of desired allies of any head of state that might get into troublesome situation, either due to the domestic or international issues. The importance of this information for an average Polish reader is rather high, since the situation of Ukraine had been widely present in all the media, therefore the fact that Janukowycz decided to leave the country in spite of the domestic unrest emphasizes the China's possible influence on the region's political situation.

> "The White House asked Beijing to put pressure on North Korea. [...] »It is obvious that China is able to influence North Korea«. We would like them to use that influence to change the Pyongyang's policy." (wp.pl, 2013/04/02)

As we can see, the importance of China is noticed not only by smaller countries. The word of the White House's representative prove that the Chinese are not only treated as equals by the Americans, but would also serve as the only mean to influence the biggest regional troublemaker, namely North Korea. Again, due to the Polish historical heritage, the issue of North Korea is rather well known to the Polish audience and the readers would be able to appreciate China's role in this type of international relations.

The next most numerous group of codes (16) was assigned to the texts that covered various topics, and their only common feature was the fact that China was mentioned there in some kind of culture-related context. Among them there were some topics related to history, more or less precisely described tourism etc. Again, we chose some of the most interesting quotations to include in this analysis.

> "From China to Tomaszów Mazowiecki. [...] Staff sergeant Karaszewski was born in 1915 in Harbin, China."

Above, we quoted only one sentence from the text about an important local hero. It could be assumed that most of the readers would not know about the Polish past of Harbin. However, after being exposed to the above information they might start to wonder, how is it possible that a person from Tomaszów Mazowiecki in central Poland, was born so far away; and possibly, eventually they might think about China as not such a distant country.

> "In the night the Taliban attacked the Nanga Parbat base. They shot nine climbers from Ukraine, China and Russia and a Nepali guide."

Although many Poles perceive China as a strange and exotic place (we will focus on that image in a while), the above sentence serves as an example of placing the Chinese among the "civilized" people, since they were mentioned as climbers, together with the Russians and Ukrainians, not with the local, Nepali guide.

> "Prices of Chinese art have been raising for the last 50 years. [...] During the Chinese wares auctions held by Desa, their public consists

mostly of the Chinese. [...] Art galleries of Warsaw are often visited by tourists from China. They do know what they are looking for, and they have knowledge about art."

Sometimes in Poland a phrase "the Ming dynasty china" is used as an idiom to describe something really valuable; this quotation presents the Chinese as not only the heirs of the long lasting tradition of producing art objects, but also as well-educated tourists, who not only could afford an inter-continental trip, but also buy rather pricey wares in Polish art galleries (and, therefore, they support the Polish economy).

Unfortunately, there are also some shades on the China's image we analyzed. So far the colors were maybe not bright, but at least not really dark. The next code, assigned to 11 cases, included articles in which China was presented as either a regime-supporting or an oppressive country.

"This cooperation broke down after the American invasion of Iraq, when Russia, together with Germany and France and such »advocates of human rights and international law« like communist China and Bashir Al-Asad's Syria, opposed this operation." (interia.pl, 2013/06/111)

This quotation not only places China in the same group as Russia, which could be harmful to this country's image in Poland anyway, but also mentions this country together with a well-known regime of Syria. Moreover, it employs irony, which is a rather infrequent phenomenon in the language used in short news published in the Internet news media. As we mentioned above, interia.pl is a right-oriented portal, negative opinions about China could be expected in the content published there, but this statement is surprisingly negative.

"Because of the deadlock within the Security Council, where all actions against the Syrian regime are being blocked by its supporters – Russia and China – the US president, Barack Obama requested the Congress to approve time- and scope limited military intervention in Syria." (onet.pl, 2013/09/04)

Again – China does support the Syrian regime and cooperates with Russia; such an information for the Polish audience usually would result in negative connotations.

"There is plenty of customers; new passports are being looked for by wealthy Russians, Chinese and Arabs. [...] Such an option is available to men of substance from China and other authoritarian countries." (wp.pl, 2013/09/26)

This quotation comes from a longer article describing the passport and citizenship trade. Wealthy residents of the authoritarian countries could get another citizenship, which would be useful in case of a domestic unrest. It is worth to emphasize the way that China was presented in this text. It's description as authoritarian is not really surprising, but the fact that the well-situated Chinese expect (or fear) problems which could make them flee from the country, might suggest that China's political system is weaker than it seems to be according the government's statements.

"The People's Republic of China, which is led by corrupted and criminal mafia, called the Communist Party of China, destroys dignity and tramples upon every human right at home, is also the source of evil in Asia. The Asian criminal, totalitarian regimes of North Korea, Vietnam and Laos could not exist without its support. China has also been fuelling civil wars all over the world, supporting the African regimes (for instance in Sudan and Zimbabwe)." (Gość Niedzielny, 2013/12/10)

The above fragment could not have been omitted in the present analysis. Negative remarks in *Gość Niedzielny*, a Roman-Catholic journal, could be expected, but not this type of language. In just a few sentences, the author managed to gather all the negative constituents of China's image in the world. Corrupted, communist, criminal, and the source of evil in Asia, and, as it could be understood, the root of evil in almost every third-world country.

But let's turn back for a while, to the positives. In spite of the rather outdated image of China as backward, held by the older generation of Poles, in 9 cases it was depicted as a modern country.

"A gene-repairing virus? [...] the European Commission approved a medicine by the name Glydera to be sold in Europe. [...] It is the first commercial medicine that employs gene therapy technology, produced in the West, and the second, after China, in the world. [...] Gene therapy, based on adding some genetic material into the system to prevent some disease or cure it, has brought high hopes in the world." (Nasz Dziennik, 2013/11/18)

Two facts in the above text are worth emphasizing. At first, China is mentioned as the first country in the world that employed a science-fiction like technology, gene therapy, for the production of commercial medicines. This suggests that it should no longer be treated only as the cradle of copycat products and might use new technologies on its own. The second important fact is the source of this news, *Nasz Dziennik*, could be expected to publish rather anti-China news, of the character such as the one from *Gość Niedzielny* quoted before. Therefore, an unnecessary positive remark about China is surprising, and might (but does not have to) indicate that the wind of changes would eventually influence the China's image in all the Polish media.

> "In the wine-producing countries of Europe, such as France, Italy or Spain, wine consumption decreases. However, the situation in the USA and China is quite the contrary. In these countries, wine is very fashionable and desired by the customers." (Wprost.pl, 2013/07/10)

This news is not of an extreme importance, but its communicate is clear: two totally different countries, that are sometimes depicted as less civilized than Europe (due to different reasons, of course), decided to follow the steps of the Western culture and introduce wine-drinking culture.

However, in an equally numerous group of remarks, China was presented as an opponent (or even a future enemy) of other global powers, namely Russia, the USA and NATO.

> "Turkish army will soon get 12 Chinese FD-2000 anti-aircraft rocket batteries as well as technology related to its production. Ankara published details of the 3.44 billion USD contract signed with China. This transaction was criticized by Washington, claiming that NATO countries should not buy military equipment from China." (Wprost. pl, 2013/10/04)

We decided to quote this article, since not only does it show tension between China and the USA/NATO, but also proves the already mentioned importance of China as a smaller countries' ally.

Traditionally, China being a distant country, has been perceived in Poland as exotic and strange. Such an image is still present in the media, and the strangeness-related code appeared 7 times in the database we analyzed. Let us quote two most significant texts.

> A huge house was built on the roof of a 26-floor building in Beijing. "A huge house, surrounded by rocks, gardens and waterfall occupies about 1000 square meters. [...] The police has not intervened because Zhang (the owner) has been a member of the Communist Party group in his district." (Wprost.pl, 2013/11/01)

The source of this quotation, a rather lengthy text, described an illegally built house, located on the roof of a tall apartment building. Even though in Poland illegal construction sites are not uncommon, the very idea of building a house on the top of such a building, creates the atmosphere of strangeness. Moreover, it mentions corruption related to the Communist Party, and such a picture would be met by the older part of the Polish audience with understanding.

"Social campaign against eating dog and cat meat raised a wave of protests among the people from Norther China. In Shenyang, the capital of Liaoning province, posters promoting the campaign were removed due to requests of the subway passengers. [...] One of the Chinese bloggers wrote »Do all these foundations think that while the Westerners do not eat dog and cat meat, they should be allowed to force the Chinese to do the same? Do they think they are gods? [...] In some regions of China, dog meat is believed to work as a cure or an anti-ghost remedy. [...] Dog meat is eaten mainly during winter, since the Chinese believe it to possess 'hot energy', needed during cold weather«." (Onet.pl, 2013/08/13)

One of the China-related stereotypes, present not only in the Western countries (see Jura & Kaluzyńska, 2015), presents the Chinese as dog-eaters. In Poland, even the horse meat is not popular due to the historically created bond with these animals; the fact that some people might not only consume dog and cat meat, but also do it openly and perceive it as perfectly normal, would be shocking for most of the Polish readers.

Two groups of codes were assigned to 7 cases each, namely: China's domestic problems and the Chinese expansion in the world. The first group of articles was focused on political issues, related mainly to Xinjiang, and social ones, such as the following:

"Chinese authorities introduced a law that obliges the youth to call and visit their parents frequently. [...] At present, China tries to solve the problem of providing medical care to numerous older citizens" (Wprost.pl, 2013/07/04)

"Many Uyghurs claim to be discriminated by the Chinese, as well as persecuted on the basis of their culture and religion. Beijing accuses Uyghur groups of terrorism and separatist tendencies." (Gazeta Wyborcza, 2013/08/13)

Articles of the second group are also interesting. They focus on the Chinese political and economic expansion, both in Asia and in the rest of the world, especially in Africa. These activities, however, were usually depicted as having negative consequences, either for local communities or for the international relations. The local issue is exceptionally visible in the content related to the Chinese presence in Africa.

"Economic expansion of China in Africa consists mainly of natural resources exploitation and infrastructure construction. [...] The Chinese are perceived as attractive partners by the African leaders because they do not mention the human rights, corruption nor democracy-related issues. [...] The main problem of the Sino-African cooperation is the fact that the Chinese ruthlessly take over local resources, using Chinese labour forces and equipment, but do not transfer technologies, therefore they do not support local development." (Gazeta Polska Codziennie, 2013/08/23)

As we can see, the Chinese do exploit Africa ruthlessly and do not care about the local people. Moreover, Chinese citizens migrate to African countries in large numbers:

"The African Union Seat in Addis Ababa – a Chinese 'gift'. »It took 3 years and 200 million USD to build a modern complex of conference halls for 2500 seats and 20-floor office building of a symbolic height of 99.9m (African Union got its present name on 1999/09/09). It was sponsored by the Chinese, who called it a 'gift'. This building will serve not only as a landmark of Addis Ababa, but also will become a symbol of Sino-African relationships. [...] At present, there are about 1 million Chinese workers in Africa. Chinese citizens visit Africa more and more often for tourism reasons – last year, 60 thousand of them spent their holidays in Kenya and 75 thousand in South Africa«." (Wp.pl, 2013/05/13)

However, the Chinese government does its best to sustain the Sino-African friendship and, by sponsoring large and noticeable buildings, marks its presence there.

The last three groups of codes refer to the issues that we expected to stumble upon more frequently, since they constitute the stereotypical image of China, namely: the problems related to the "made in China" fake wares, human rights, Tibet and the One-child Policy.

Manufacturing of fake ware in China results in consequences of not only economic character. Let us present a longer quotation concerning this problem.

"[...] famous Murano artists, Gianni Seguso, said: »We feel that our thousand year history has been trampled upon«. He and his fellow craftsmen say that it is often very difficult to say whether a specific product is original or fake, and the price might be the only indicator. [...] The case of Cremona luthiers is even more special, since the products of these craftsmen have been classified by UNESCO as a world heritage." (Onet.pl, 2013/07/14)

It touches upon two issues – a possible Chinese disrespect towards other cultures and their heritage, and surprisingly, the high quality of China-made fake wares. However, the next article we chose as worth quoting in length, is focused on the Chinese citizens' disrespect towards their own people and culture (namely, the food culture) as well.

"Local media informed that a criminal group, selling rats, foxes and martens as lamb was smashed by the police in China. 904 people were arrested. [...] Among the arrested, there are 63 people who occupied themselves with buying foxes, rats, martens and minks for meat. These types of meat, after being processed, with some addition of gelatin, were sold as lamb in Shanghai and at Jiangsu province markets. The police claims that more than 20 tonnes of this fake lamb meat was confiscated. [...] According to data provided by the Supreme Court of China, between 2010 and 2012 as many as 2088 people were sentenced in 1533 cases concerning crimes related to contaminated or possibly dangerous food." (Gazeta Wyborcza, 3/05/2013)

In the above text, China was depicted as a place in which more and more people try do make money without paying attention to the consequences of their actions for their co-citizens. A Polish reader might be convinced that the Chinese have nothing against consumption of exotic types of meat, however, the information about the increasing number of criminal cases related to food contamination would make them notice that such activities are not normal in China.

Another controversial issue that certainly influences China's image in the world (therefore in Poland as well) is the One-child policy. It was mentioned in a longer news story published at onet.pl describing problems rooted in this policy.

"[...] police rescued a group of more than 90 children, who were kidnapped by a human trafficking criminal group. About 300 suspects were arrested. In a result of this action, two kidnapped women were also freed. [...] Because of the restrictive one-child policy and parents' preferences, especially in the remote, countryside areas, where male children have been preferred, the number of children- and women-trafficking cases has been increasing in the last years. Women are being sold to male countryside residents, who, due to the gender imbalance, could not find a wife. The sociologists warn that the lack of gender balance creates a danger of increased number of sexual violence and human trafficking cases." (Onet.pl, 2013/09/06)

Apart from sustaining China's image as the place in which people are not allowed to have children, it presents social consequences of traditional Chinese preferences for male children and criminal face of this country.

The last code appearing more frequently in the database was related to the issue we expected to be much more frequent, namely – the human rights and Tibet. Only three articles of the whole database were focused mainly on this issue, and they were presented more as a report, rather than ethical statements. For instance:

"Diplomatic relationships between Oslo and Beijing have been frozen since 2010, when the Norway Nobel Prize Committee awarded the jailed Chinese dissident, Liu Xiaobo, its prize. [...] Norway tried to re-establish proper relationships, but Beijing's reaction was far from enthusiastic. The statement sent to media by the Chinese embassy in Oslo emphasized that the Nobel Committee decision „was a contempt for the independence of the Chinese juridical system as well as an involvement into domestic issues of China." (Gazeta Wyborcza, 2013/09/28)

The China-focused articles were published also by the tabloids – *Super Express* and *Fakt*, and they could be assigned to two main categories – general tabloid content, which might refer to any country of the world, and texts that presented some issues which are (or could be) perceived as specific for this country. The first group's catchphrases were as follows: "Male's suicide during shopping!", "Construction worker waiting 20 hrs. for being rescued from a concrete mixer!", "A plastic surgery clinic female customer sued by her husband for giving birth to ugly children!", "Stolen eyeballs!", etc. Although all these texts mentioned China, and had some influence on the reader's perception of this country, they might have substituted almost any other location. However, the other group carries a message "only in China!". An attentive reader of a Polish tabloid would think of China as a country in which, for instance, people visit hospitals to have huge worms removed from their brains, sell pills containing human ashes and tapeworm eggs (a specific version of the TCM), hang animals on trees for fun, have ridiculous laws, like regulations for an allowed number of flies per square meter in public toilets, and so forth.

Summary

China and the Chinese definitely still do not constitute the point of focus in the Polish media, which turn their attention more to the local European area and Poland's neighbours. Nevertheless, both quantitative and qualitative analysis of the content of our database showed that the media image of China in Poland is not negative. It consists mainly of the issues related to the economy and development, and is rather distant from the one held by the generations born in Poland before the 1970s. China is no longer a Communist country with human resources as its only wealth. It has been depicted as a global power, modernized and expanding its influence all over the world (perhaps not in the most ethical way). This picture is quite similar with Bukowski's (2014) findings. He emphasized the prevalence of the articles referring to the present economic and political situation and a slightly more negative picture (however, he was not presenting a comparison to other countries). On the other hand, in Mrozowski's article (1997), China was presented mostly from the perspective of illegal migration and fake goods, which could be treated as a kind of an indicator of significant changes in the image of China and the Chinese.

Of course, strictly negative issues like the human rights and supporting non-democratic regimes are parts of this image, but they are not prevalent. However, it is worth to stress that on the basis of the quantitative analysis result, it can be stated that such picture is still quite popular in some of the Polish media (for example *Gazeta Wyborcza*). The only rather predictable constituent of this image is the China's exoticism, its strangeness, which is based both on its cultural distance and the political system. As an Asian country, with "strange" customs, including the Chinese dietary habits, long-lasting tradition of corruption and so on, China could not get rid of the orientalist shades on its image (especially in tabloids and tabloid-like media).

References

Boulding, K.E. (1959). National images and international systems. *The Journal of Conflict Resolution*, 3(2), Junuary, 120–131.

Bukowski, M.M. (2014). The image of China in Polish media. In: Zemanek, A. (ed.). *Media in China. China in the Media* (p. 135–150). Krakow: Jagiellonian University Press.

Jenes, B. (2012). *Theoretical and Practical Issues in Measuring Country Image Dimensions and Measurement Model of Country Image and Country Brand,*

PhD thesis, Department of Marketing Research and Consumer Behaviour, Corvinus University of Budapest, Doctoral School of Business Administration.

Jóźwiak, I., Konieczna-Sałamatin, J., Tudorowski, M. (2010). *Bez cudzoziemców bylibyśmy ubożsi. Wizerunek obcokrajowców na łamach polskiej prasy (Without foreigners we would be impoverished. Image of foreigners in Polish Press)*. Warszawa: Instytut Spraw Publicznych.

Jura, J. & Kaluzynska, K. (2013). Not Confucius, nor Kung Fu: Economy and business as Chinese soft power in Africa. *African East-Asian Affairs. The China Monitor*, March, Issue 1, 42–69.

Katz, D. & Braly, K. (1933). Racial stereotypes of one hundred college students. *Journal of Abnormal and Social Psychology, 28*, 280–290.

Kunczik, M. (1997). *Images of Nations and International Public Relations*. Mahwah, NJ: Lawrence Erlbaum Associates.

Mrozowski, M. (1997). *Obraz imigranta na łamach prasy polskiej (The image of a Migrant in the Polish press)*. Prace migracyjne nr 1. Warszawa: ISS UW.

Newman, B. (1994). *The Marketing of the President: Political Marketing as Campaign Strategy*. Thousand Oaks, CA: Sage.

Nimmo, D. & Savage, R. (1976). *Candidates and Their Images*. Pacific Palisades: Goodyear.

Nye, J.S. (2004). *Soft Power: The Means to Success in World Politics* [Kindle DX Version]. New York: Public Affairs.

Wang Jian (2008). The power and limits of branding in national image communication in global society. *International Political Communication, 14*(2), 9–24.

Zhou He, Chen Xianhong & Wu Xing (2012). The image of the United States in the Chinese media: An examination of the evaluative component of framing. *Public Relations Review, 38*, 676–683.

Roxana Ribu

Bridges and Obstacles in "the Way of the Ideal Government":[1] the Transition from Mind Confucianism to Political Confucianism from Jiang Qing's Point of View

Ever since the dawn of the Chinese culture, great thinkers such as Mencius and Xun Zi expressed their concern for an ideal way of government. In this study we aim at pointing out why such ideas could not take the intended shape, whether they could have even been possible, and how these ideas were taken over and developed by our contemporary prominent promoter of "Political Confucianism" – Jiang Qing.

Jiang Qing, the centerpiece of our study, is the kind of thinker that went through different stages in his academic career as well as his intellectual pursuit. He puts forward a set of theories which promote a view on Chinese culture that looks upon its origins after hovering around for many decades, going as far as to demonstrate why Western liberal democracy could never work in China.

His critical approach to the "Mind Confucianism" that rose outside mainland China after 1949, obviously soaking in many Western ideas, underlines notions such as individuality, concern for the metaphysical and transcendent, undervalue of law and ritual, all of which mainly disconnected Confucianism from the real and historical China. That is why he leads the transition to a so called "Mainland China New Confucianism", which stresses the importance of the second half of the Confucian ideal, of the "outer king" (*wai wang* 外王) who should take precedence over "the inner sage" (*nei sheng* 内圣).

---

[1] The Romanian translation of Xun Zi's work, by Prof. Luminita Balan, bears the title: *Calea guvernarii ideale* ("the way of the ideal government").

Fundamental concepts like equality, human dignity, universal values or global ethics are critically discussed in many of Jiang Qing's works as well as in those of his critics. Thus, the many bridges between cultures sketched by thinkers on both sides of the Pacific (the Atlantic as well), along with the obstacles, are all just instances of vision and interpretation, and Jiang Qing spares no effort in stating his different views on these constructs. Nevertheless, there are many interesting connections to be analyzed between morality and governance, the transcendent and the immanent, the ideal and the real realm of society and culture.

Nowadays, liberal and democratic regimes face serious problems that can also point to the difference between the ideal kind of government and a pragmatic one, with roots in the history and tradition of the Chinese culture, on one side, and the European culture on the other, closely related to the changes that emerged within the last decades.

Jiang Qing's idealism offers a new view of the Chinese culture, which is in the process of recovering its strong foundation of the Confucian concepts, adapted to contemporary reality. Up until recently, a number of great thinkers dedicated their energy to reviving Chinese traditional thought, albeit in close contact with the core Western values. Jiang Qing stands firm ushering in a new era of thought, in the very soil of China's mainland, which is the reason why his ideas, as far from the possible world as they still are, must be discussed.

In our paper we aim at discussing the coordinates onto which the existence of the ideal city is projected, with emphasis on the individual versus the community, grounded on earth or in heaven, wrapped around needs and resources, ideals to be realized in the shining future as a mirror of the glorified past.

The story of Jiang Qing is generally known, which is why I am going to make only a very short account: after a period of Marxist frenzy, Jiang passes through stages of reading Confucian classics, Marxist reinterpretations and expressions of liberal democracy enthusiasm, which puts him in the position of being criticised in school. Afterwards, he takes refuge in Confucian humanism. Disappointed by the political manoeuvres at the immediate level, he then goes out in search of ultimate truths and meditates, in turns, about the Daoist, Buddhist and even Christian ideas.

Failing to find satisfying answers to his questions, or at least answers that are capable of resonating with what he calls "the spirit of Chinese culture", which he is deeply immersed in, Jiang becomes fascinated by the ideas of new Mind Confucianism, and this happens right after coming across Tang Junyi's work. The conclusions drawn make him assume the mission of reviving Confucianism on the mainland, in the form which was kept alive by the new Confucians outside of China. Liang Shuming is the very person who encourages him in this endeavour.

June 1989 however, becomes the sort of trigger that causes him to recalculate the relevance of Mind Confucian ideas such as self-cultivation, transcendence or metaphysics and, troubled by the lack of legitimacy of the political regime, he devotes himself to promoting Political Confucianism, deeply concerned with the betterment of social and political order, the very target of his criticism being those intellectuals who advocate the transplantation of Western liberal democracy on the Chinese ground, running the risk of seriously altering the spirit of the Chinese tradition.

Aware that the project he develops is on a very large scale, Jiang argues that such a political transition must draw its essence from the already existing cultural resources; only thus can an enduring constitutional order be legitimized.

What Jiang has to remonstrate about with Western democracy is a question of faulty premises. The total power belongs to democratically elected entities and is based on the separation of powers within the state, which poses serious problems in legitimization. This is because the sovereignty of the people, expressed by the electoral option, is amoral and centred upon the immediate interests, in the short term, thus representing a kind of secular absolutism where people replace God. The sacred values are not relevant any more, ideas like future or humanity as a whole wither in front of immediate needs.

In exchange, Jiang proposes a threefold legitimization, coming from three sources: heaven, earth and humanity. That is to say, this kind of legitimacy is grounded on the will of a transcendent authority, which functions in the sacred sense of natural morality, less on history and traditional culture, and the least on the will of the people. In a more concrete form, Jiang proposes a tricameral legislature formed from the House of the People, resembling a democratic parliament, the House of Ru (儒), bringing a sacred legitimacy as led by a renowned scholar and comprised of candidates nominated by a special scholar committee, having passed exams on classical scriptures and having been tested in the inferior forms of government; and the House of the Nation, lead by a direct descendant of Confucius.

This complex structure is based on a vision that goes to the deep structure of Chinese political tradition. According to Jiang, the Political Confucianism inspired by the Gongyang school starts with Xun Zi's ideas, then passes through Dong Zhongshu's redimensioning scheme in Han and Huang Zongxi's in late Ming and early Qing, to finally benefit from the contribution of Kang Youwei's argumentation. Jiang's concerns are thus directed towards sketching a Confucian constitutional order able to correspond thoroughly to the new dimensions of contemporary China.

Presently, we shall try to render some of the ideas that compose the political Confucianism orthodoxy in Jiang's view.

Xun Zi

Widely known for his seemingly pessimistic stance, but actually deeply pragmatic and concerned with the goodness of human innate nature, Xun Zi can, nevertheless, be labelled as an idealist. His teachings are imbued with exact data of the social and political circumstances of his own time, but what he advocates is a map of an ideal society, of a successful government, centred upon a figure of a ruler who acts through his virtues in a kingdom inhabited by superior men or ordinary people with idealized features. So, given the times he lives in, one may surely wonder about how Xun Zi was able to gather the necessary strength and energy to sketch such an Utopia and to draw the portrait of a ruler, but also of the ruled, who master the appropriate skill in order to function, according to the idealized model of the past.

As already stated, for Xun Zi, the ideal government pattern has as its main character the superior man, or the gentleman, who does not necessarily identify himself with a ruler who bears a special mandate from Heaven. The superior man is asked to make his contribution to the governing plan carried out by the ruler. His main instrument of action is the Rite, which has to be learned, understood and wisely applied. By means of Rites, he serves both Heaven and earth, he reveres his ancestors thus acknowledging his roots, and he venerates his king or his master.

Here is a small scale portrait of the gentleman in Xun Zi's view:

The gentleman is not necessary able to do a certain job but to behave and to listen, to speak and to work; he is honest, gentle, neat but also modest; although nobody asks him to become specialized in a certain domain, he is, nonetheless, a learned man, skilled in the art of learning and eager to learn more still.

> "A man who borrows a boat and paddles does not gain any new ability in water, but he can cut across rivers and seas." (Xun Zi 1:4)[2]

What he can do is use the vehicles at hand, that is, first and foremost, the superior cultural legacy.

---

[2] All English quotations from Xun Zi use the translation of John Knoblock, *Xunzi, a Translation and Study of the Complete Works* (Stanford: Stanford University Press, 1994).

Xun Zi's gentleman isn't what one would call a living collection of virtues; he can lack courage or even knowledge ("he realizes that the mind is small but the Way is great" 3:10), he can find himself in an inferior position, and sometimes be sad and poor. Nevertheless, in any situation he knows how to behave accordingly; by this he is a reference point in what concerns order and harmony, and that is so because he is attached to the moral and Ritual principles.

To be sure, the structure of the gentleman cannot be detached from virtues. And one of the most important of his virtues is sincerity, the one who allows him to nurture himself:

"For the gentleman, to nurture his mind, nothing is more excellent than truthfulness" (3:9a); this virtue ought to be achieved just like any other virtue and that, in its turn, nurtures the virtue of humaneness, thus giving it shape. Sincerity clarifies the sense of things, which leads to transformations but especially to the knowledge of order. It is considered the grounding virtue of governing exactly because of its transformational power. At the same time, it is the medium of communication beyond words.

The gentleman starts his programme by becoming devoted to wise men, admiring their superiority and yearning to follow in their footsteps.

> "Of the direct routes of learning, none is quicker than the devotion to a man of learning." (1.11) "When he has reached the limit of such perfection, he finds delight in it." (1:14)

Love thus described is rational and selective, by way of the heart-mind.

In developing his vision, we can see that Xun Zi does not dismantle hierarchy, nor does he seek to profess unfit equalitarianism.

The portrait of the petty man is as interesting as that of the gentleman, and can be seen as a very interesting counter-example. The petty man is not entirely dismissed, although he is asked to change his ways (and this is, probably, one of the strongest points in Xun Zi's account of the inborn nature – "The inborn nature of man is certainly that of the petty man" (4:10), he is, however, part of the world that the ruler has to govern. What differentiates the gentleman from the petty man is this yearning and choice to follow the right path, by learning, by observing the rites and persevering in sustaining his values.

> "Being a gentleman is properly called <good fortune>, and being a petty man is properly called »bad fortune«." (5:1)

Coming back to the wise ruler, he does not have to be original, but traditional, as he is not an innovator, an ingenious manager who is to come up with original policies, but one who continues the line of politics within the Confucian tradition, seasoned with a few influences from the Legalist school; he will only concentrate on learning and realizing the policies and the precedents which proved effective in the past, in the art of government practised by sage kings; at the core level, the emphasis is placed on assuming the correct posture and, especially, on concentrating on the virtue which makes people and things over which he rules place themselves in order. He is capable of inferring from what is near and recent that which is far, in space and time; by contemplating the Rites he can deduce the fundamental coordinates of the world and by help of the moral principles which he assumed, he manages to tell right from wrong, he can concentrate upon the essential, thus ensuring that the world is properly arranged.

Being capable of telling right from wrong and not mistaking good for evil is, nevertheless, proper for those simply called 'human beings'; it is the fundamental virtue which differentiates humans from other forms of existence.

> "What is it that makes a man human? I say that it lies in his ability to draw boundaries... to be fond of what is beneficial and to hate what is harmful – these characteristics man is born possessing and he does not have to wait to develop them." (5:4)

The process of governing can also be unsuccessful and unfortunate; the Heavenly mandate can dissolve at any time and these kinds of precedents are quoted in *Shijing*. In no case can the sovereign be seen as intangible and absolute:

> "A tradition says: the lord is the boat; his subjects the water. It is the water that sustains the boat, and it is the water that capsizes the boat." (9:4)

Yet Xun Zi finds reasonable solutions even for that which can be considered as faults of the ruler, as these wishes pertain to the restricted domain of "sufficiency":

> "If the lord of men desires to be secure no policy is as good as even-handed government and love of the people. If he desires glory, none is as good as the exalting of ritual principles and treating scholars with strict observance of forms of respect. If he desires to establish his fame and meritorious accomplishments, none is as good as advancing the worthy and bringing the capable into one's service." (9:4)

Among the virtues that the ruler has to cherish are "divine intelligence" (*shenming*), intuition and the capacity to ascertain the circumstances, together with purity or divine lucidity, pointing especially to understanding the Way.

As for the governed, Xun Zi says they are like fish and birds that leap and rejoice at hearing the zither playing, they gather around the ruler as if he were their father and they seek his protection.

On the one hand, ordinary men can live in society thanks to the principle of social position allocation, which is realized according to the moral sense and leads to harmony, unity and strength towards the exterior. Thus, everyone can leave peacefully, either in houses, or in palaces. On the other hand, lack of hierarchical order can lead to struggles and division and this induces vulnerability in front of foreign aggression.

The intrinsic principles which govern society, which is also made up of Rites and traditional moral values, are also of great use to the ruler, as the main scope is harmonization and synchronization. Actually, this idea of synchronization, of doing the right thing at the right time, is of great importance to Xun Zi's political teachings; he recommends that even the life of animals and plants be not interrupted but at the right time (9:16b), this being the key issue in the proper administration of the resources; even for correcting mistakes or trespasses there is a right time (9:16c).

Dong Zhongshu

Speaking of the context in which Dong Zhongshu's ideological intervention develops, one must remember the decrease in challenges and in the expansionist thrust, a context which left the necessary space for many rulers to search for guidance within the examples set by the sages of the past. On a larger scale, one can see that in Dong Zhongshu's times another model than the one represented by Qin comes to be cherished, and this is the Zhou model, which brings a series of changes in perspective, together with the religious practices of the king who shifts from venerating *wu di* 五帝 to worshipping Heaven – *Tian* 天.

Dong Zhongshu is the thinker who provides the new regime with the fundamental cosmological elements inspired by the times of the Warring States. Thus *Tian*, Heaven, the very ancestor of the ten thousand things, becomes the direct and natural source of authority and legitimacy of the ruling dynasty. The natural order, together with the moral and the political one, thus find their model in Heaven:

"The link between Heaven and Man is *Dao*, who also connects the past with the present." (Hanshu, apud Cheng, 2001, p. 236)

The ruler receives the symbolic and illustrative name in the character *"wang"* 王, which presents him as a central piece placed at the intersection of Heaven, Earth and Man. According to Dong Zhongshu's vision, the ruler must answer to Heaven and not to the people, as Mencius had once stated. Nevertheless, he has the duty of adjusting his governing system with Heavenly Dao. As Anne Cheng (2001) wrote:

"The genius of Dong Zhongshu and of all ideologists in Han times is that they referred the hierarchical socio-political order to the natural regularity of the Universe so that the political order stands on a cosmological, and not a formal or legal foundation". (Cheng, 2001, p. 237)

In Dong Zhongshu's political thought one can also observe the major importance of harmony and unity, resembling the cohesion within the members of one family, so that loyalty to the ruler is placed under the authority of the concept of filial piety (*xiao* 孝).

When governance goes astray, Heaven sends reprimands in the form of calamities and disasters, but ones that are controlled by the interpretations or forecasts, which remain under the scope of scholars. The age of Dong Zhongshu's systematizations, in search of a political and cultural unity, is centred upon the external dimension of rulership (*wai wang* 外王) and not so much on values like introspection and personal cultivation (*nei sheng* 内圣).

Kang Youwei

Considering that the reformist New Text school announced a certain need for renewal at the very beginning of the 18th century, in which Confucius was considered to be a great reformist who acknowledged the intention of the scholar to get involved in the political life, we can assume that Kang Youwei contributes first and foremost with his extraordinary enthusiasm, more often than not trapped into overreaction. But, without a doubt, he had the historic opportunity to come to the position of putting these reformist ideas – ideas that had been synthesised for over a century – into practice, even if for a short while.

As a supporter of the New Text School, Kang's conviction was that the Classical literature written in the ancient style was fake, and thus he started by taking apart the academic basis of the Qing scholars and forcing them to research the whole Confucian heritage in a new light. He adopted two of Wang Tao's ideas, namely the flexibility to change, displayed by the way of the ancient sages, affirming his confidence that

Confucius, if he were alive, would meet change with change; and the idea of progress, by which he understood not only a way of rearranging the classical precepts in order to adjust them to new situations but rather an ideal future-oriented order.

Kang Youwei's actions culminate in the short interval of three months, the summer of 1898, when he is summoned by the emperor Kangxi and entrusted with leadership over the government and with the launch of a reform campaign. In this period, he engages in drawing up laws that ultimately aim at modernizing China. Among these laws, the most important ones regard:

- the renewal of the bureaucratic system
- the inclusion of Western studies within educational standards for selecting state officials
- the reorganization of governmental positions so that they are compatible with the requirements of a modern state
- the establishment of a public educational system
- the organisation of public press
- the establishment, through popular vote, of local committees in order to create a parliamentary government.

Another move towards reform takes the shape of a strife for establishing a national religion for China, this being called "the Kong Jiao movement" (孔教运动).

In a memorial addressed to the Emperor in 1898, Kang warns that „the West relies on military power to conduct trade and missionary activities. Foreign churches can be found all over China, conflicts can be provoked. As one spark can set the whole plain on fire, one incident may lead to the end of the empire" (apud Gong, 2007, p. 301).

In this context, Kang proposes that Confucian churches should be built everywhere in China, from the prefecture level to small villages. These churches should be kept by Confucian clergy that would read to parishioners, on every Sunday, excerpts from the Classics. Confucius' day should become a national holiday and the calendar should not be centred upon emperors' periods of rule, but there should be a Confucian calendar drawn up instead. Thus Kang aimed at taking hold of the institutional power of Christianity replacing the theological content with Confucian ideas. Kang also suggested that the title of the Son of Heaven that the emperor holds should be replaced by Confucius as a symbol of the Chinese nation, as the spirit of the country, having the power to unite the Chinese and to inspire morality and national spirit, as was the case with European churches. In this way Kang wanted to create a national ideology and state that the Chinese nation was defined by its culture and its Confucian heritage. He aimed at creating a sense of religious-cultural community including the objective of propagating these ideas among the masses.

In 1901, Liang Qichao talks about his master as "an advocate of religiosity", who in his effort to recover the original state of Confucianism acts "like a Martin Luther of the Confucian religion" (Hsiao, 1975, p. 105).

As a student of Zhu Ciqi from Guangdong, and a supporter of the New Text School, Kang is keen on emphasizing the moral practice of Confucius' teachings. In fact, this school of thought believes in the prophetic character of Confucius' activity which reveals the true teachings of Heaven to humankind.

In Kang's work entitled "Thatched hall surrounded by ten thousand trees" (*Wan mu zaotang congshu*) he states that "The religious founders everywhere reformed institutions and established systems. All the moral institutions of China were founded by Confucius" (9:1a, apud de Bary, 1969, vol. 2, p. 68).

In his commentary to the Analects, an investigation on Confucius' constitutional reforms, Kang clearly sees Confucius as a religious founder, a sage king with spiritual intelligence, a partner of Heaven and Earth who nurtures all things. All human beings, events and moral principles are comprised in his great way. Thus he was the highest peak of perfection and the most supreme sage that humankind has ever had. And this is because of the six Classics, all the works of Confucius.

Jiang Qing

In Jiang Qing's view, a political transition must draw on already existing cultural resources in order to legitimize a long-lasting constitutional order. For more than a century, the Chinese people were placed in the very sensitive position of forsaking their traditional and cultural life in order to take up modern Marxism or Western liberalism. This is why Jiang draws a conclusion that the Chinese traditional culture cannot be maintained within a liberal democratic political framework.

The relationship between Mind Confucianism and Political Confucianism runs parallel to the relationship between the Greek rationalist tradition and the Judeo-Christian religious tradition. Political Confucianism was developed on the basis of rationalism just like the Greek rationalism that paved the way for the European enlightenment; whereas Mind Confucianism is founded on the kind of metaphysics similar to that of the Judeo-Christian one.

Nevertheless, in the line of thinking proper to Political Confucianism, the metaphysical aspect is not secondary, but the transcendent is affirmed through acts of filial piety and ancestral worship. A unit composed of ancestral deities and family bloodline realizes the connection between the transcendent and the immanent realm.

To put it otherwise, the fact that the emphasis is placed on the community rather than on the individual and holistic view changes the transcendent scheme, together with concepts about redemption or ultimate concern.

Just like Kang Youwei, Jiang strongly advocates Confucian religion.

According to the symmetry between the immanent and the transcendent, heavenly realm, an absolute God must be postulated as a peak of the heavenly hierarchy, same as the ancestral hierarchical order or any other kind of order that requires a "Premium" or the "highest" – an all encompassing superior authority the entire cosmic world of spirits.

Filial piety is the most important and concrete of the expressions of the Confucian faith, making people remember where they come from, and be thankful for the gift of life. To respect the father just like in Heaven and to respect ancestors actually means to respect their moral wishes, to avoid bringing humiliation and to glorify them by showing love and compassion, cultivate virtues and carry out social obligations.

The divine law refers to the moral obligations and the commandments which can no longer answer the question *why*, which comes contrary to the Rawlsian vision on equality and non-interference in the moral education of the simple person.

But most of all, keeping in line with both Dong Zhongshu and Kang Youwei, Jiang argues that a sacred authority is of Heaven as opposed to people, as people are "a secularized, limited and narrow collection of human desires" (Jiang, 2013, p. 30). Jiang feels the need to implement a transcendent, constitutionally established force that is powerful, not subject to the influence of either secular society or politics, and whose main target is to prevent corruption and ensure morality.

Jiang's ideas were met with a wide range of criticism, least of all sensing the degree of idealism which comes contrary to the real capabilities, be they political, moral or economical, of the world today.

The main point of discussing the opposition of idealism/realism in Jiang Qing's account may well be placed at the conjunction of the individual and the community.

As the saying goes: if one wants to order the state, they should first order the family, and within the family the individual must first be put in order. Yet this does not at all mean an emphasis on the individual. On the contrary, the scheme is perfectly understood if the individual is seen as a member of the community, expressed by family and the state. As a matter of fact, if one tries to answer the question "what went wrong with

these programmes of the ideal government, why could they not work?",
I believe that individualism would be the main reason. Just like a woman
has no meaning if estranged from her role of wife, mother or grandmoth-
er, the man is also seen as an impossible case should he choose the way of
solitude: an individual in a society cannot make sense unless he connects
to others, at a given time and along history. Any attempt to fulfil egotisti-
cal desires and wishes upsets the balance and ruins harmony. The individual is basically asked to get out of himself (or his self), to negate himself as a collection of needs and desires and to place himself at the service
of others, starting from the Universe itself, through the ruler and all the
way to his sons, nephews and neighbours, to fulfil his role in society.

This is also the reason why some see the Rite as overrated. It is not the
man that justifies the existence of Rite, as a means of communication and
harmonious communion, but it is the Rite that brings the individual into
existence from non-existence and selfishness, thus providing him with
the necessary means of communication.

In Jiang's view, the Western world offers exactly the reverse scenery
with liberalism and democracy emphasizing the importance of the individual and his inalienable rights, finding it very difficult to control the
ways of limiting these rights so that they do not infringe the rights of others. Concerned with the realization of the self in isolation from, and even
competition with, the others, the individual is more remote from reality
than from the idealistic community. The separation is pathological, just
like severing the channels to the source of existence. All that is left is the
relation of power by means of which the individual wins short-lived superiority while many detractors speed up his exit.

Thus, brutally and unnaturally turned over to the self and assimilated
into his basic needs which are impossible to satisfy and which rapidly
multiply just like cancer cells, he parts with any form of ritual and the historical past is a mere collection of errors that need to be reversed. Tradition is superstition, normal is overrated and any custom can be updated
by means of absurd combinations.

As Samuel Huntington (1997) reminds us, the real rulers of contemporary China use a new version of the substance/function scheme, with
capitalism and involvement in the global economy and political authoritarianism, doubled by the urge to get back to the values of traditional
culture.

Legitimacy comes from economic performance and the performance
of the nationalist tune emphasizing the distinct features of the Chinese
culture.

Then came Lee Kuan Yew, who remarked the progress of Asian societies versus the Western ones and who underscored the virtues of the East

Asian Confucian culture: order, discipline, family responsibilities, the ethics of hard work, the prevailing of the group and the nation versus the individual, as well as moderation; as for the faults of the Western style, he listed negligence in self-cultivation, carelessness, individualism, crime, inferior education, lack of respect for the authorities but most of all – mental stiffening. (These ideas can also be found within the "Manifesto for the appraisal of Confucianism..." issued in 1958 by the most prominent representatives of New Confucianism).

To the Chinese civilization, the individualism which, in my opinion, was invalidated many times in history by attempts such as those of Xun Zi, Kang Youwei and others to realize the ideal government, which are but a sum of accidents, does not at all represent "the pattern" and that is why it does not justify a more pessimistic approach of the thinkers. Such accidents are, basically, cases of estrangement from the Rites, examples of a lack of adjustment and of disobeying the commandment of Heaven on the way to self-satisfaction as well as the pursuit of happiness understood as the culmination of the self.

References

Cheng, A. (2001). *Istoria gândirii chineze* (*The History of Chinese Thought*; transl. F. Vișan & V. Vișan). Iași: Polirom.

de Bary, Wm. T., ed. (1964). *Sources of Chinese Tradition*, vol. II. New York: Columbia University Press.

Gong Guoqing (2007). *The Construction of Modern Political Civilisation: On Kang Youwei's thoughts of Political Reform in the 1898 Reform Movement.* Zhejiang: Shehui kexue wenxian chubanshe.

Hsiao Kong-ch'uan (1975). *A Modern China and a New World: K'ang Yu-wei, Reformer and Utopian.* Seattle: University of Washington Press.

Huntington, S.P. (1997). *The Clash of Civilizations and the Remaking of World Order.* New York: Touchstone.

Jiang Qing (2013). *A Confucian Constitutional Order*, ed. by D.A. Bell and R. Fan, transl. E. Ryden. Princeton: Princeton University Press.

Xun Zi (2004). *Calea guvernarii ideale* (*The Way of the Ideal Government*; transl. L. Balan). Iași: Polirom.

Xunzi (1994). *Xunzi. Translation and Study of the Complete Works.* Transl. J. Knoblock. Stanford: Stanford University Press.

Mateusz Stępień

Conceptualizations of Constitutionalism in Recent China's Debates: Preliminary Typologies

For many reasons, the lack of complete freedom of speech in China did not stop a wide range of schools of thought, ideologies and social and political doctrines from developing in China. According to He Li's position, some significant intellectual threads such as Liberalism, Neo-Authoritarianism, New Left, Democratic Socialism and New Confucianism have emerged (2015; see also e.g. Frenkiel, 2015). Each of them provides a different vision of a political system desirable for China. From the China's governing elite perspective, this relative pluralism of visions of political system is just as desirable as potentially destructive. That can be perfectly seen in the current mode of governance, where the need of experimenting and searching for new ideas on governance (including ideas regarding the form of official ideology) involves the risk that it may potentially lead to overthrowing of the ruling party. In fact, the role and significance of CCP's vision of political system and ideologies linked to them, does not exclude the possibility of searching for, and experimenting with unorthodox sources (due to the economic requirements, international commitments, situational necessities etc.). On the one hand, the eclectic and 'open' nature of the official political ideology which developed after 1978 provides relative flexibility, and on the other hand, it does not lead to the development of a coherent and stable ideological and axiological 'guidance' (Benedikter, 2014, p. 2). This is the perfect example of China's political practice known as 'guerrilla policy style' (Heilmann & Perry, 2011, pp. 12–13, 23).

With that in mind, let's focus on current debates among the Chinese intellectuals on constitutionalism, or the so called constitutional rule (*xianzheng* 宪政). For a long time, the role of the term *xianzheng* was rather marginal, though the term itself, along with the vision of political reforms related to it, was present in the debates on China's modernization since the late 19th century. Since 1978, other concepts, next to the official ones, dominated the narrative of the reforms (democracy, rule of law, human rights etc.). In the first and second decade of the 21st century, the idea of *xianzheng* became increasingly popular. A vibrant debate on that issue has developed, in which it is possible to distinguish three broad schools of thought: Liberal, Socialistic (or Sinized Marxist) and Confucian Constitutionalism (see e.g. Peng Chengyi, 2011b, 2011a, 2013).

This revival of interest in constitutionalism can be partly explained by the fact that in the 40s even Mao Zedong (albeit for a short period of time) was using the term (e.g. in the famous essay New Democratic Constitutionalism 新民主主义的宪政). This is a potential source of legitimacy for proponents of constitutionalism. Moreover, it is of great importance that in the PRC there is a rich constitutional tradition one might accommodate into the narrative of *xianzheng*. This conception never carried the negative connotations shaped in an earlier debate. Because the 'political' potential of *xianzheng* had not been definitively determined, it became easily adjustable to broader visions of the social and political system.

The aim of this paper is to make a contribution to the study on contemporary Chinese discourse on *xianzheng*. This time, I focus only on the ways in which the Chinese authors understood constitutionalism. A general hypothesis is that there are substantial differences between the proponents and the critics in the understanding of constitutionalism and the way it is framed. The subject of this pilot study are the selected articles of the Chinese authors about constitutionalism. This paper will focus on the articles, which had the biggest and the most meaningful impact on China's intellectual scene, published in 2013 during the intense debate on *xianzheng* that took place that year. I discuss three articles supporting constitutionalism (The Chinese Dream: A Dream of Constitutionalism and works of Wang Jianxun and Zhang Qianfan) and four critical works (by Yu Zhong, Yang Xiaoqing, Zhengzhi Xue, Wang Tingyou). However, reflections on a broader context and detailed description of the 2013' debate will be kept to a minimum, as it has already been discussed extensively by other authors (see Yuen, 2013; Creemers, 2015).

1. Understandings of Constitutionalism

The heated debate of 2013 resulted in a flood of works on *xianzheng*. In fact, a wide range of works represent competing approaches, contradictory viewpoints and fundamental differences in the understanding of the term 'constitutionalism'. Table 1 illustrates the definitions and main ele-

Table 1: Definitions of *xianzheng*

Author, title	Definitions/understandings of *xianzheng*
The Chinese Dream: A Dream of Constitutionalism (中国梦, 宪政梦) (2013)	The author treats constitutionalism as a broad social and political project, though he refrains from defining the term itself. He also highlights the direct link between *xianzheng* and freedom – 'Chinese people should be free, Chinese dream is the dream of *xianzheng*' (中国人本应就是自由人, 中国梦本应就是宪政梦).
Wang Jianxun (王建勋), *My view on Constitutionalism* (宪政之我见) (2013)	'*Xianzheng* is a kind of institutional and ideological concept of government limitations and protection of fundamental rights and freedoms of the individual' (宪政是一种限制政府权力, 保护个人基本权利和自由的制度安排和思想观念).
Zhang Qianfan (张千帆), Implementing the Constitution and Long Term Governance (宪法实施与长期执政) (2013)	'*Xianzheng* means implementing the Constitution and limiting the political power effectively' (宪政就是宪法获得实施并有效约束政治权力的一种状态).
Yu Zhong (喻中), *There is no one Path for Reform* (改革的路径不可能是单一的) (2013)	By asking 'what *xianzheng* really is' (那么,宪政又是什么呢?), the author describes its three elements: 'freedom, democracy and human rights' (自由, 民主, 人权).
Yang Xiaoqing (杨晓青), *Comparative Study on Constitutionalism and People's Democracy* (宪政与人民民主制度之比较研究) (2013)	Author believes that *xianzheng* comprises of: market economy, private property, multi-party parliamentary system, separation of powers (which serves to protect the people against the excesses of government), an independent judiciary and the army, which is politically neutral and controlled by the civilian sector.
Zhengzhi Xue (郑志学), *A Correct Understanding of "Constitutionalism"* (认清"宪政"的本质) (2013)	From the very beginning of his work, Zhengzhi Xue links *xianzheng* to 'the bourgeois constitution' (资产阶级宪法). The author believes that '«*xianzheng*» is a central concept that reflects the capitalist economy, political theory and practice' („宪政"就是反映资产阶级经济政治理论与实践的核心概念). It consists of: separation of powers, judicial independence, the existence of constitutional judiciary, a multi-party system, 'parliamentary budgeting', 'government with limited responsibilities', free market economy and universal values – freedom, democracy, rule of law, human rights, and finally, the nationalization of the army.
Wang Tingyou (汪亭友), *Views On Constitutionalism* (对宪政问题的一些看法) (2013)	The author uses the term 'Western capitalist *xianzheng*' (西方资本主义的宪政). Constitutionalism is associated with a particular social and economic order and culture circle. *Xianzheng* comprises of: 'separation of powers, democracy, rule of law, limitation of power through constitutional and legal system, protection of the fundamental civil rights' (分权、民主、法治，以宪法法律体系约束政府权力，保障公民的基本权利).

Source: Author's analysis.

ments of the presented approaches. Both the proponents (the first three papers in the table) as well as the critics (four other articles) conceptualized the idea of *xianzheng* differently. Both sides refer to the opposing meanings of the term 'constitutionalism.' As a result, the debate is asymmetrical and thus, it becomes inconclusive. Basing on the Chinese writings on *xianzheng*, three typologies might be proposed in order to identify the basic differences in the conceptualization of *xianzheng*. Remembering that these are only preliminary findings, let's take a look at each of the typologies.

1.1. Criterion of how the term *xianzheng* is specified

The main problem with all the works engaged in the debate on *xianzheng* are the significant differences in determining the necessary elements of constitutionalism. There is much controversy amongst the scholars over whether the distinctive features of *xianzheng* should be defined in a general or in a more detailed way. Therefore, we can distinguish a general and 'concrete' (identifying a number of more specific elements) understanding of this term.

The advocates of constitutionalism tend to define it in a general way, using a broad category of 'limiting the political power.' According to Wang Jianxun, constitutionalism is a concept relating primarily to limiting the government and promoting 'fundamental rights and freedoms of the individual.' Similarly, Zhang Qianfan believes that *xianzheng* functions when the Constitution is implemented and when it actually limits the political power.

Such a general understanding of *xianzheng* means that it cannot be reduced to a one catalogue of specific elements. Thus, *xianzheng* appears to be a general guideline for ruling, and only on such a general level it can be considered as universal. In this approach, constitutionalism is a very broad term and its empirical exemplifications may be very different. Moreover, it opens a door for adapting the idea of 'limiting the political power' to the existing local conditions. Also, a general understanding of *xianzheng* stimulates the discussion on specific alternatives to China's political system.

The critics of *xianzheng*, conversely, prefer a 'concrete' way of understanding *xianzheng*. They perceive constitutionalism as a peculiar model of society, which can be reduced to a set of various elements. Each of the cited authors propose a different catalogue of these elements (as shown in Table 1). Obviously, the main question is how were they selecting specific elements constituting *xianzheng*, but there is no reflection on this in their writings. It is worth noting that all the elements they mentioned, refer to the different levels of organization of social life. Some of them are not even commonly associated with constitutionalism ('nationalization of the army', 'government with limited responsibilities'). What is even more interesting, one of the two most common elements among all the definitions is democracy (multi-party system), which is not mentioned at all in any of the definitions presented by the advocates of *xianzheng*.

Treating constitutionalism as a very wide package of various elements has multiple consequences. This makes the copying of constitutionalism (or its comprehensive implementation) basically impossible to achieve. With so many complex and diverse elements present in the concept of *xianzheng*, it is not feasible to copy, nor to implement it in China anytime soon. Also, a consensus among scholars on all the necessary elements is difficult to reach. Increasing the number of elements constituting *xianzheng* leaves much less room for further debate on this topic.

1.2. Criterion of genus proximus

Next factor differentiating the understanding of *xianzheng* among the aforementioned authors, refers to the genus proximum used in its definitions. From this perspective, idea-centric and empirical approach can be distinguished. According to the first one, constitutionalism is a kind of a doctrine or ideology, concerning the standards of exercising the political power. However, according to the empirical approaches, *xianzheng* is a kind of a social praxis, a way of governing, a generalization of what really happens in the institutional realm.

Advocates of *xianzheng* employ the idea-centric understanding of this term. Constitutionalism is a general conception oriented towards the limitation of the political power. Hence, *xianzheng* is not linked to specific solutions and examples and, as a general concept, it may be implemented in many different ways. *Xianzheng* is a project that is universal only at the most general level. The Chinese Dream... argues that all the beautiful dreams require an institutional framework, which is to be provided by constitutionalism. According to that view, adapting common foundations to building a political system for all mankind, does not contradict the existence of 'particular' dreams. Thus, constitutionalism has been associated with a universal (but not necessarily Western) project, which can still keep its local shape and character.

Unlike the advocates of *xianzheng*, its critics focused on an understanding of constitutionalism closes to the empirical approaches. In contrast to their opponents, they see constitutionalism as a set of solutions already existing in the West. The authors (with the exception of Zhong Yu) clearly overlooked the fact that the solutions implemented in the West are not homogeneous, but quite the contrary – they have many different forms and features. Yet, the empirical approach has another important implication – constitutionalism becomes a rigid set of solutions applied in other countries. As it already identifies specific examples of states and institutions, it is clear that constitutionalism cannot be treated as a political model adaptable in many different forms. Moreover, from this empirical perspective, the reflections on *xianzheng* concern the general social systems, and for this reason, they may be easily contrasted. In consequence, it is possible to employ the concept as a tool involved in struggles between civilizations (see papers of Yang Xiaoqing i Zhengzhi Xue).

1.3. Criterion of genesis

The next criterion differentiating presented understandings of *xianzheng* refers to its genesis. On the one hand, some scholars consider ways of development of constitutionalism other than the Western ones, and accept the possibility of creating different political alternatives together with the presence of elements common to all forms of constitutionalism (the so called inclusive approach). On the other hand, the exclusive approach emphasizes the existence of a single form of constitutionalism, which is the one that was originally developed in the West (thesis of the genesis), and thus, constitutionalism is associated exclusively with the specific trajectory of the development of Western civilization (thesis of exclusivity).

The advocates of *xianzheng* refer to the inclusive approach. In Wang Jianxun's view, the Western achievements are only a source of inspiration rather than a model to copy. Similarly, Chinese Dream... mentions the Western ideas (including Anglo-Saxon constitutionalism) very broadly. The text does not encourage mindless imitation of the West, which has its own path of development. Instead, it focuses on building a 'new kind of civilization linking China and the West.' Zhang Qianfan develops a vision of 'socialist constitutionalism' based on implementing the constitution, which expresses the values promoted by the CCP. He states that *xianzheng* is not linked to capitalism, but is a kind of tool that can be used in various social and political systems, without undermining their distinctive features. Clearly, the increased emphasis on the existence of Chinese own resources related to constitutionalism is characteristic of Zhang Qianfan's vision. In this vision, nothing prevents constitutionalism from being developed in China on the basis of local resources (including Sino-Marxism). It also means that introducing *xianzheng* into China is not equal to implementing a Western model of constitutionalism.

In turn, a number of scholars criticizing *xianzheng* support the exclusive approach (in a form of the thesis of genesis and the thesis of exclusivity). The opponents of *xianzheng* adapted the idea that there is only one single western constitutionalism. Hence, *xianzheng* is being perceived as genetically linked to capitalism and the West, but not to socialism and China's 'people's democracy.' From this point, although openly criticized, it is possible to copy western constitutionalism, but it is far more difficult to create an indigenous Chinese version of *xianzheng*. This also applies to so called 'socialist constitutionalism' (社会主义宪政). Implementing constitutionalism symbolizes the rejection of China's own model, which is based on axiological foundations opposed to capitalism. Following its own path of development, China should not implement *xianzheng*. This view may be a side effect of a strategy, which favors maintaining the status quo, or an interesting and peculiar case of specific legal Auto-Orientalism (see Ruskola, 2002). Nevertheless, in the end the discussion on whether and in what form to adapt constitutionalism was reduced to the painful alternative – to implement western form of constitutionalism, or to follow China's own path?

Summary

The analysis of the selected texts documenting a fierce polemic against and for constitutionalism among the Chinese intellectuals in 2013 proved that there are significant differences in the understanding of *xianzheng* on both sides of the debate. Both advocates and critics of constitutionalism considered this concept differently. The differences were related mainly to: (1) how far the distinctive features of constitutionalism are being specified, (2) what is genus proximum of its definitions, and last, (3) where did constitutionalism originate (the genesis)? These major differences on how constitutionalism is conceptualized largely affect the direction and shape of Chinese intellectual discourse on *xianzheng*. In other words, each way of understanding and framing of *xianzheng* provides different starting point for further discussion. Its relevance for the process of forming a vision of reforms of the political system (with no freedom of speech) and developing social consciousness is undeniable (Jie Lu & Tianjian Shi, 2015).

To begin with, the advocates of constitutionalism express themselves strongly in favour of the general, idea-centric and inclusive approach.

This stimulates the discussion on different varieties of constitutionalism in China without the need for copying Western institutions. Furthermore, such understanding of *xianzheng* emphasizes its compatibility (or at least consistency) with the official political narrative, which greatly reduces the risk of discrediting it as a radical movement. To highlight non-confrontational side of *xianzheng*, authors made passing references to Xi Jinping's speech about the need of implementing the constitution, while emphasizing that referring to this concept does not challenge the power of the CCP, but quite the opposite.

But the critics chose the 'specific', empirical and exclusive understanding of *xianzheng*, which supported the thesis that capitalism and the West in general are inextricably linked to constitutionalism. As a result, they distinguished two conflicting paths of development – Western and Chinese, openly suggesting a rivalry between them. Hence numerous references to military metaphors (that we can find in all the critical papers with an exception of Yu Zhong's work), which are indeed a classic element of the CCP's narrative, are probably used to inspire respect and obedience among citizens, as well as to create an atmosphere of mobilization (Link, 2013, pp. 251–252). Using military metaphors in relation to *xianzheng* also emphasizes the confrontational nature of the discussion in which constitutionalism proves to be unequivocally negative. Moreover, according to the critics of *xianzheng*, with all its negative consequences, constitutionalism could be potentially implemented in China in its Western form, but it absolutely cannot be brought to life in its Chinese variation. Such an approach inevitably leads to the conclusion that *xianzheng* is radical and potentially destructive to the current political system.

It is to be hoped that the analysis carried out in this paper will contribute to our understanding of the Chinese political thought concerning *xianzheng* and will enable a more complete understanding of the contemporary intellectual discourse, as well as help to assess, what are the future prospects for constitutionalism in China's political reforms.

References

Benedikter, R. (2014). Xi Jinping's China. The motive behind China's current transition: Foreign success is changing domestic behavior. In: Benedikter, R. & Nowotny, V. (eds). *China's Road Ahead: Problems, Questions, Perspectives* (pp. 1–19). Dordrecht: Springer.

Creemers, R. (2015). China's constitutionalism debate: content, context and implications. *The China Journal, 74*, 91–109.

Frenkiel, E. (2015). *Conditional Democracy. The Contemporary Debate on Political Reform in Chinese Universities*. Colchester: ECPR Press.

Heilmann, S., Perry, E.J. (2011). Embracing uncertainty: guerrilla policy style and adaptive governance in China. In: Heilmann, S. & Perry, E.J. (eds). *Mao's Invisible Hand. The Political Foundations of Adaptive Governance in China* (pp. 1–29). Cambridge, MA and London: Harvard University Press.

He Li (2015). *Political Thought and China's Transformation*. Palgrave: New York.

Jie Lu, Tianjian Shi (2015). The battle of ideas and discourses before democratic transition: Different democratic conceptions in authoritarian China. *International Political Science Review, 36*(1), 20–41.

Link, P. (2013). *An Anatomy of Chinese. Rhythm, Metaphor, Politics*. Cambridge: Harvard University Press.

Peng Chengyi (2011a). Sinicized Marxist constitutionalism. *Global Discourse, 2*(1), 83–107.

Peng Chengyi (2011b). *Three Competing Constitutional Discourses for the 21st Century China*. Doctoral dissertation submitted to Department of Public and Social Administration, City University of Hong Kong.

Peng Chengyi (2013). Traditional Confucian constitutionalism: Current explorations and prospects. *Frontiers of Philosophy in China, 8*(1), 76–98.

Yuen, S. (2013). Debating constitutionalism in China: Dreaming of a liberal turn. *China Perspectives, 4*, 69–72.

Internet sources:

The Chinese Dream: A Dream of Constitutionalism (中国梦, 宪政梦). Retrieved from: http://www.inmediahk.net/2013-2 (accessed: 23/07/2015).

Wang Jianxun 王建勋 (2013). *My View on Constitutionalism* (宪政之我见). Retrieved from: http://www.yhcqw.com/html/wenzjc/2013/86/13861840455KFA092223F15K2I766IIAFJ.html (accessed: 23/07/2015).

Zhang Qianfan 张千帆 (2013). Implementing the Constitution and Long Term Governance (宪法实施与长期执政). Retrieved from: http://blog.sina.com.cn/s/blog_5fe6b5f90106ko8m.html (accessed: 23/07/2015).

Wang Tingyou 汪亭友 (2013). *Views On Constitutionalism* (对宪政问题的一些看法). Retrieved from: http://news.xinhuanet.com/politics/2013-06/09/c_124840106.htm (accessed: 23/07/2015).

Yang Xiaoqing 杨晓青 (2013). Comparative Study on Constitutionalism and People's Democracy (宪政与人民民主制度之比较研究). Retrieved from: http://www.qstheory.cn/hqwg/2013/201310/201305/t20130521_232618.htm (accessed: 23/07/2015).

Yu Zhong 喻中 (2013). There is no one Path for Reform (改革的路径不可能是单一的). Retrieved from: http://opinion.huanqiu.com/opinion_china/2013-01/3454136.html (accessed: 23/07/2015).

Zhengzhi Xue 郑志学 (2013). A Correct Understanding of "Constitutionalism" (认清"宪政"的本质). Retrieved from: http://bbs.tianya.cn/post-free-3351859-1.shtml (accessed: 23/07/2015).

PART TWO

ECONOMY AND MARKETS IN TRANSITION

Rafał Koszek

Chinese Economic Influence on the Central and Eastern Europe Countries

In recent years, China is becoming one of the most important players in the global economy. Its impressive growth, which is continuously realized for the last 35 years, has a great influence on the development of the modern world. This process accelerated significantly since 2001, when China acceded to the World Trade Organization. Two years earlier the PRC's government had announced the *go out* strategy. As a result, the Middle Kingdom developed international trade and began the process of transnational activity of Chinese companies. Although this led to an unprecedented economic growth of this country, the PRC is still in the period of transformation. It is seeking the best way to become a highly developed country.

As well as China, the Central and Eastern Europe countries[1] are in the process of transition. Obviously, their situation is relevantly different from the Middle Kingdom, because it was the political uprising that started the transformation course. The economic changes were possible due to the fall of communism. The CEE countries regained independence and introduced the process of transition from the centrally planned economy to the market economy in the beginning of the 1990s. The simultaneous operation of political democratization and economic liberalization is nowadays still one of the biggest challenges for this states. However, it should be stressed that there are a lot of differences in the level and mode of the transformation processes in the particular CEE countries.

---

[1] In this paper, the selection of Eastern and Central Europe countries is made in accordance with the 16+1 platform. It involves the post-communist countries: Estonia, Latvia, Lithuania, Poland, The Czech Republic, Slovakia, Hungary, Romania, Slovenia, Croatia, Serbia, Bosnia and Herzegovina, Montenegro, Bulgaria, Macedonia, Albania.

The paper aims to examine the geographical distribution of China's economic influence on the Central and Eastern Europe countries. The author used various data sources[2] to prepare an analysis of the China-CEE trade and investment relations. It takes into account the data from 2004 to 2014. The results of the study are visualized in different illustrations. The body of the article consists of three main parts. Firstly, there is a short introduction into the China-CEE relations. Secondly, the author examines the bilateral trade cooperation. Thirdly, the flow of Chinese monetary capital to the European post-communist countries is investigated.

China-CEE cooperation

There is a visible revival in the relations between China and the CEE countries in the last few years. Since 2011, there is a yearly meeting of the representatives of the sixteen Central and Eastern Europe countries and China. The first meeting took place in Budapest in 2011, the next summits were held in Warsaw, Bucharest, and Belgrade. The meeting in 2015 took place in Beijing. There are many reasons suggested for this by the scholars trying explain this rapprochement. "It is China who is the driving force behind the recent increase of contacts... The crisis of the European Union and the resulting financial vacuum revealed the potential opportunities in the CEE region. Even though these opportunities are modest in comparison to the usual Chinese appetite, Beijing has utilized every possible chance to find business projects for the overcapacity of its companies and for its abundant financial assets" (Turcsanyi, Matura & Fürst, 2014, p. 131) According to Song (2013), "While the EU faces a sovereign debt crisis, the CEE countries are confronted with additional financial difficulties. They find themselves in need of a new economic partner, and China may prove to be a good alternative. Moreover, it is in China's interest to develop a closer cooperation with CEE as this will help to upgrade and diversify both China's foreign trade and its overseas investment options" (p. 8). As we can see, both China and the CEE countries are eager to develop the cooperation. There are also some controversial concepts signalized by different scholars, e.g. describing the Central and Eastern Europe countries as a gateway to the European Union. Matura (2013) probably gives the best explanation of that matter

---

[2] United Nations Conference on Trade and Development, American Enterprise Institute and Heritage Foundation, Institute of Social Science, University of Tokyo (based on MOFCOM data).

"The trouble with this approach is that it is nonsensical and uninterpretable, or, at the very least, none of the parties concerned have given it any real substance. On the one hand, one of the biggest markets for Chinese goods has long been the European Union (...) On the other hand, Chinese direct investments have also found their way to Western Europe, whereas up till now only a small proportion of this has arrived in the Central and East European region". (p. 142)

Although it is incorrect to treat the CEE countries as a gateway to the European Union for Chinese companies, it seems to be feasible, that there is a connection between the rapprochement of the relations and the concept of the New Silk Road, promoted by China since 2013. The idea assumes establishing and modernization of the communication infrastructure between PRC and Europe, which is China's most important trading partner (Kaczmarski, 2015, p. 2). The project contains building several routes which should contribute to a significant increase of the value of Chinese export to Europe. It is also a possibility to develop the communication infrastructure in the regions where the New Silk Road is planned. One of this regions is the Central and Eastern Europe. There are two main logistic corridors crossing this area: the northern railway route and the southern route, which is going to be the extension of the maritime line that ends in the Greek Port of Piraeus (Pavlićević, 2015, p. 9).

China-CEE trade relations

The People's Republic of China is known as the country with the highest value of export in the world. It is also the second largest importer, behind the United States. Export from China is one of the most important factors of the growth of the Chinese economy. As it was mentioned earlier, European countries are China's most significant trade partners, therefore the concept of the New Silk Road, which should contribute to the increase in China-Europe trade relations, can considerably shape the global economic order. The Central and Eastern Europe countries can not only serve China's need for a logistic corridor, but they may also grasp an opportunity to develop the bilateral trade.

There are a few features that describe the China-CEE trade. Firstly, the value of export from China overwhelmingly surpasses the value of import, in 2014 for instance, it was six times greater. The difference is also visible in the geographic structure of China's global trade. The share of the CEE countries in global export from China is 2,7%, while their contribution in the PRC import is only 0,55%. This trade imbalance occurs in all of the sixteen post-communist countries. Nevertheless, it differs in particular states. It can be seen that in the Visegrad 4 countries[3], which are the main China's trade partners in the region, the value of export to China is more or less at the same level. The import from China contributes mostly to the imbalance rate. It is bigger in Poland and Czech Republic, whereas in Slovakia and Hungary, the value of import from China is only three times higher than the value of import. The lowest imbalance rate occurs in Bulgaria.

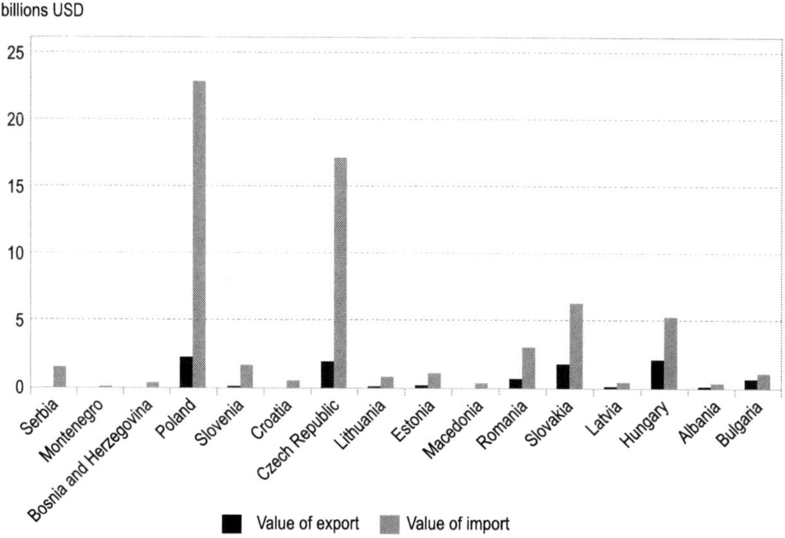

Graph 1: The value of China-CEE export and import in 2014
Source: own elaboration on the basis of UNCTAD data.

Secondly, we can observe a dynamic growth of the value of export from China in 2004–2014. Two countries, Czech Republic and Poland, contributed mostly to this relevant increase. Although in 2004 the value of export from China to none of the sixteen CEE countries exceeded 5 billion USD, it was greater than 15 billion USD in 2014 in Czech Republic and Poland. The latter is the biggest recipient of Chinese goods in the region. There was no such significant increase of export from China to any of the other countries. It was constantly growing in Slovakia. In Hungary, as well as in Romania, its value is rather stable from 2008. In all of this five countries we can see a relevant decrease of the value of export from China in 2009, due to the global financial crisis.

Thirdly, when we take into consideration the global structure of import to the post-communist European countries, the influence of trade with China is somewhat different. Import from China plays the biggest

---

[3] Czech Republic, Hungary, Poland, and Slovakia.

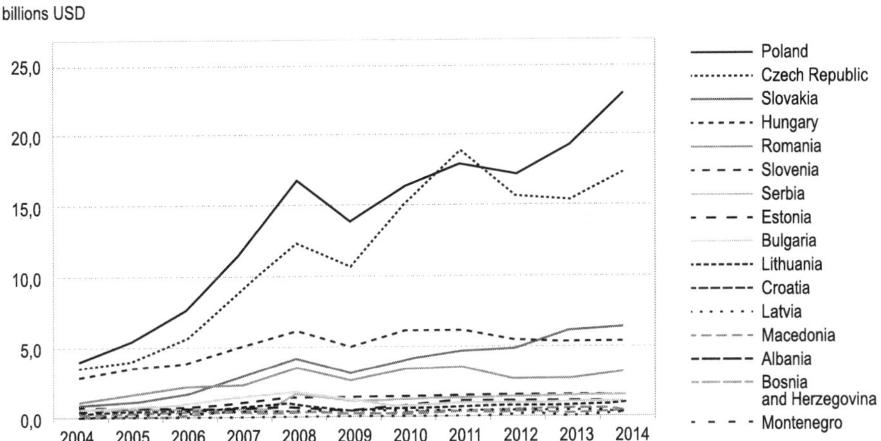

Graph 2: The value of export from China to the CEE countries from 2004 to 2014
Source: own elaboration on the basis of UNCTAD data.

role in Czech Republic, its share in the total value of import exceeds 11%. The Middle Kingdom is a significant exporter to Poland as well. Nevertheless, when we look at the other countries, the classification is different from the case of the absolute value. More than 7% of the value of imported goods is provided by China to Albania, Montenegro, Serbia and Slovakia. The lowest contribution in the geographical structure of import from the PRC occurs in Croatia, Latvia and Lithuania.

Fourthly, although there is a significant imbalance between the export and import in the China-CEE trade relations, the value of export from the post-communist European countries to the Middle Kingdom was growing during the last decade. As well as in import from China, Poland is likewise the greatest exporter to the PRC. There are four countries that rapidly developed the export to China and they are nowadays on a quite similar level of its value. These are the Visegrad countries. Among the remaining states, Bulgaria and Romania, the two eastern Balkans countries, stand out in this ranking. We can see that they started growing the export to China more rapidly from 2010. Unlike the export from China, export from the CEE countries does not show any decline in the time of the global financial crisis.

Fifthly and finally, the absolute value of export from Central and Eastern European countries to China does not correspond with the share of the PRC in the geographic structure of the global export from the post-communist states. Albaniais the only country that shows an outstanding share of export to the Middle Kingdom. The contribution of export to China in Albania is more or less three or four times greater than in the other countries. The strong trade cooperation between Albania and

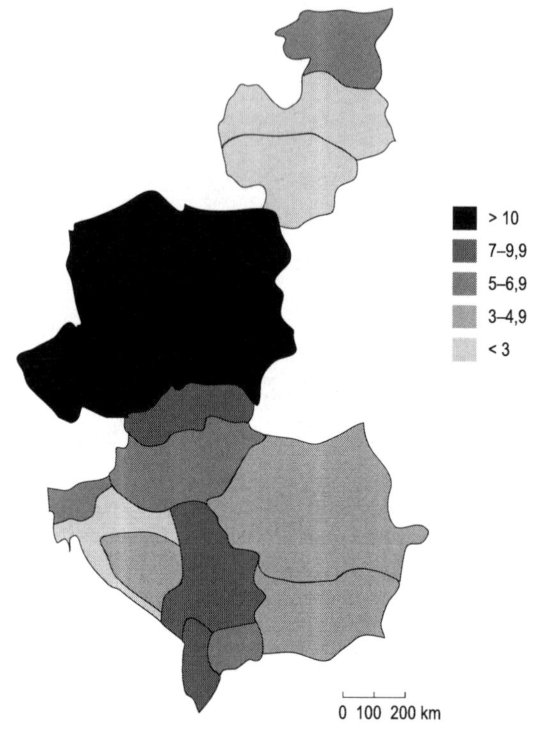

Graph 3: The share of import from China in the value of the global import in the CEE countries in 2014
Source: own elaboration on the basis of UNCTAD data.

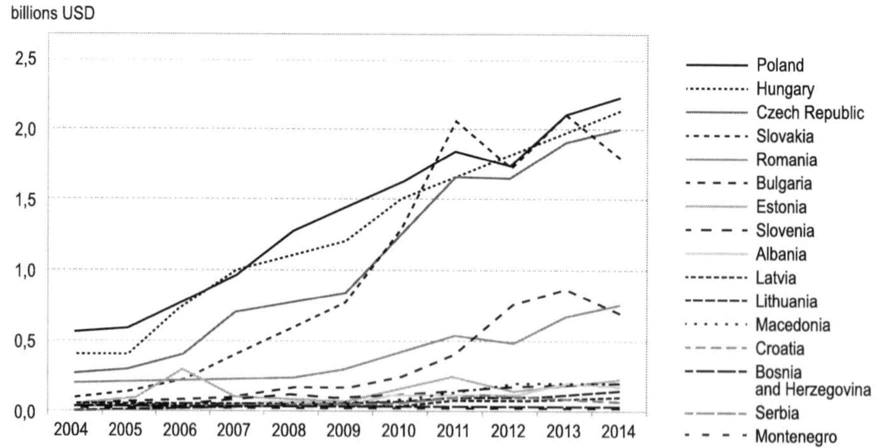

Graph 4: The value of import from the CEE countries to China from 2004 to 2014
Source: own elaboration on the basis of UNCTAD data.

the PRC can be explained by their traditional friendship. In the rest of the countries, the share of export to China in global export is less than 2,5%, with the highest rate in Bulgaria, Slovakia, Hungary and Macedonia. The lowest share of export to China occurs in Croatia.

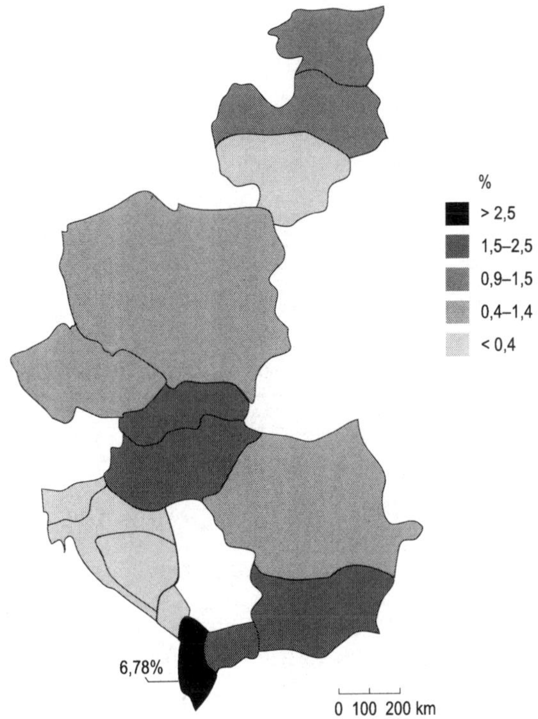

Graph 5: The share of export from the CEE countries in the value of the global export from CEE in 2014
Source: own elaboration on the basis of UNCTAD data.

Chinese investments in the CEE countries

The People's Republic of China is recently becoming one of the major global investors. For many years it was mainly perceived as an attractive place to locate the investments, mainly due to the cheap labour force. In 1999, the Chinese government introduced the *go out* policy to encourage national companies to undertake international activity. The process of overseas expansion proceeded very fast. According to KPMG report (2015), "it appears that China's outward direct investment (ODI) overtook inward foreign direct investment (FDI) in 2014, by a narrow margin, making the country a net capital exporter for the first time. China's Ministry of

173

Commerce estimates that the total ODI volume for 2014 stands at around US\$120 billion, a 10 percent rise from US\$ 108 billion in 2013" (p. 10).

The development of the Central and Eastern Europe countries in the last twenty-five years was, to a great extent, possible due to the inflow of foreign investments. The Western Countries were the main source of the financial capital. As it was mentioned earlier, the crisis of the European Union revealed opportunities for the Chinese companies to get an access to the region. This chance is often described as a window of opportunity (e.g. Liu, 2013, p. 1). It can be seen that both sides have significant reasons to develop the cooperation. On the one hand,

> "Chinese are in fact not only willing to lend financial support and credit; it is an economic necessity for them as well. The enormous domestic savings rate, the huge foreign trade surplus of the past decades and the PRC's status as net importer of capital, has accumulated a currency reserve of nearly 3,300 billion dollars, which is now inconvenient for the Chinese government. (...) That is, it is a much profitable (...) decision to invest a substantial portion of the reserves in the real economy rather than to keep it in state bonds barely earning interest". (Matura, 2013, pp. 143–144)

On the other hand,

> "What they (the CEE countries) truly want is an external source of financing to pull the region out of its cash-stripped problems after the traditional investors withdrew their money. Furthermore, as countries in transition and not yet on the same level as the Western Countries, they have some developmental objectives, including the establishment of new production and industrial facilities, the improvement of their infrastructure, etc. In all these sectors, China is perceived as a potential new partner capable of providing the necessary financing". (EIAS, 2014).

Although there are many opportunities to increase the Chinese investments in the CEE countries, there are also a few obstacles in developing this kind of economic cooperation. For example, "In the field of FDI issues there is a fundamental contradiction between Chinese an Central European intensions. While China is mostly looking for infrastructure investments opportunities (preferably through governmental public procurements), most of the CEE countries are keen to attract greenfield investments in order to create jobs and industrial production" (Turcsanyi, Matura & Fürst, 2014, p. 133).

As it was pointed out earlier on, there have already been a few summits of the representatives of China and the post-communist European countries. In order to enhance the investment in the region, in April 2012 the PRC announced a \$10 billion special credit line for Chinese companies engaged in CEE. Next, in September 2012 a Secretariat for China-Central and Eastern Europe Cooperation was created (Jacoby, 2014, p. 213). It is clear that the process of financial flow from the Middle Kingdom to this part of Europe is a rather new phenomenon. Although the inflow of Chinese investment to CEE developed just several years ago, after the financial crisis, it is worth to examine its scale and diversification.

The first part of the analysis is based on the number of the direct Chinese foreign investments, which were realized from 2004 to 2013. We can observe that there are six countries with a significant number of received Chinese FDI: Poland, Romania, Hungary, Czech Republic, Bulgaria, and Serbia. The tendency of a growing inflow of Chinese financial capital is constantly seen in the three Visegrad Countries and in Romania since 2007. In Bulgaria, the rapid growth of Chinese FDI started in 2010. Two years later, Serbia noted a significant increase of capital from the Middle Kingdom. It appears that the China-CEE political cooperation influenced mostly the Balkan states, Bulgaria and Serbia, although there is also a visible increase of the number of the PRC's companies in Poland and Romania since 2010. The illustration also shows that Hungary was the first to attract a significant amount of Chinese FDI.

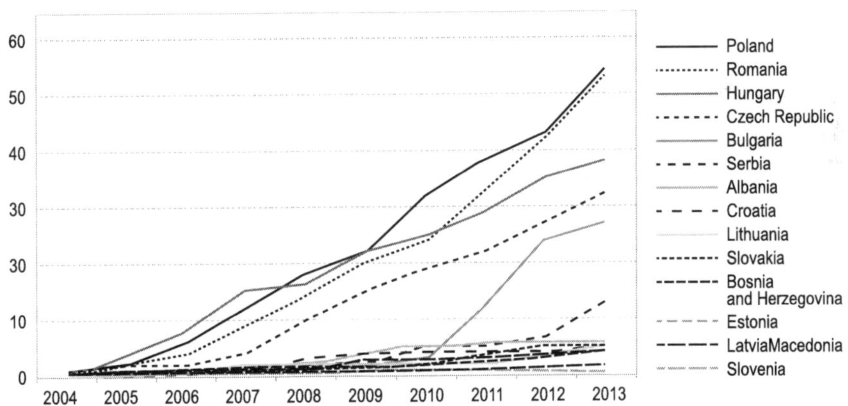

Graph 6: The number of Chinese FDI in the CEE countries from 2004 to 2013
Source: own elaboration on the basis of China's Outward Foreign Direct Investment Data (Marukawa et al., 2014).

It has to be noted that the number of transactions from China does not correspond with the value of Chinese FDI in the CEE countries. It is Hungary that has attracted the biggest amount of financial capital from the PRC, although the amount of enterprises which invested there was smaller than in Poland and Romania. Furthermore, the value of investment that flowed from China to Hungary was by far greater than in the other countries. The high number of investments in Romania and Poland did not correspond with the FDI stock. Although there was a large amount of transactions, the value of FDI was comparable to the Czech Republic and Bulgaria. It can be concluded, that there is a lot of small investments in Poland and Romania. The value of individual transactions was higher in Hungary, Slovakia, the Czech Republic, and Bulgaria.

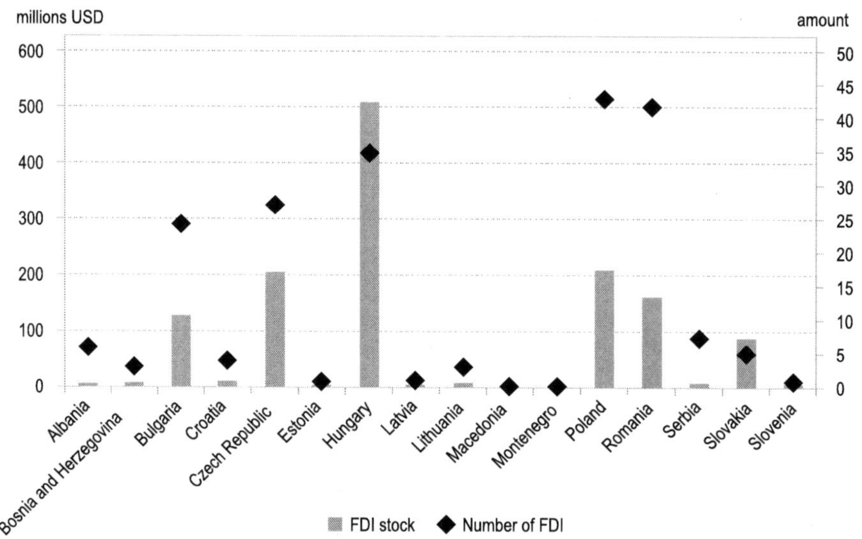

Graph 7: The number and accumulated value of Chinese FDI in the CEE countries in 2012
Source: own elaboration on the basis of China's Outward FDI Data (Marukawa et al., 2014) and UNCTAD data.

There are two main branches that predominate in the number of Chinese investments in CEE countries. These are Sales and Marketing and Administration and Service.[4] The manufacturing sector also plays an important role. The branches are various in particular countries. In Poland the three above mentioned industries appear in the largest number. They are also present in Romania, but that country received relatively great number of affiliates of Chinese companies which invest in other companies. A similar structure occurs in the Czech Republic and Hungary. The Administration and Service enterprises dominate in Bulgaria. The branches that FDI located in Serbia are more or less at the same level.

---

[4] Administration and Service includes facilities that provide services to customers, representative offices that support the operations of the parent company, and also restaurants and hotels.

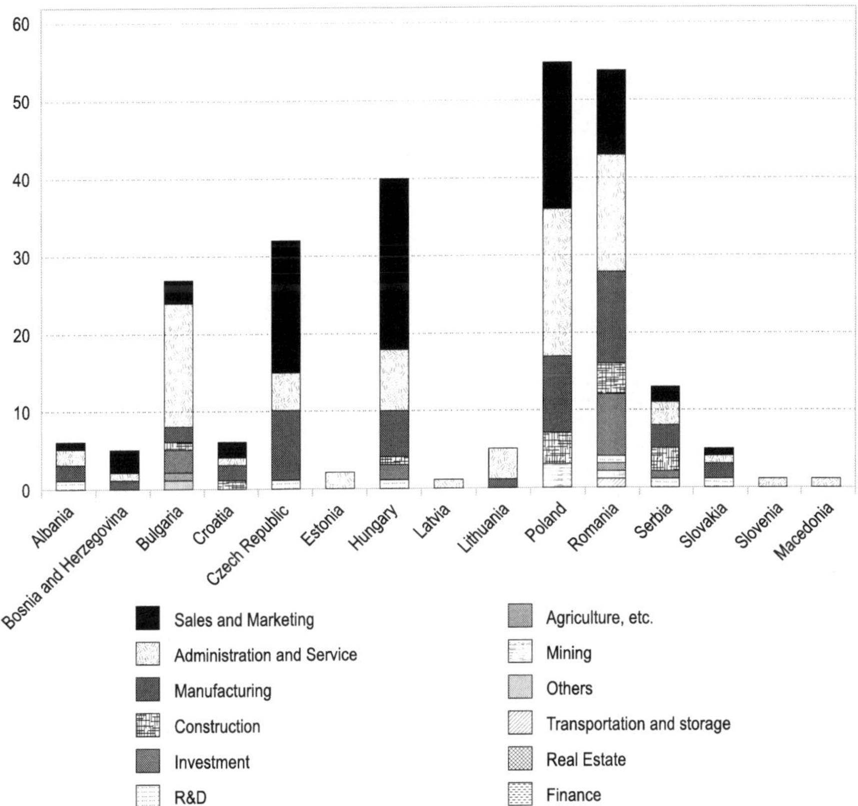

Graph 7: The number of Chinese FDI in CEE classified by branches in 2004–2013
Source: own elaboration on the basis of China's Outward Foreign Direct Investment Data (Marukawa et al., 2014).

China is a very large country, diversified in a lot of aspects. Its various provinces and cities develop in a different speed and mode. The companies that invest abroad also originate from different regions[5]. The Graph 8 shows the spatial distribution of the PRC's enterprises which conducted overseas expansion in the CEE region. It can be seen that the vast majority of these undertakings originated from the eastern coast of China. There is nothing strange about it, because this region is on the highest level of the economic development. The greatest number of investments come from the Zhejiang (40) and Jiangsu (33) provinces. The Zhejiang province

---

[5] As for the regional origin of investors, they are classified into 31 provincial-level regions, 5 large cities (Dalian, Ningbo, Xiamen, Qingdao, and Shenzhen), Central State Owned Enterprises and Ministry of Commerce SOEs. Investors originated from the five large cities are not included in the number of investors from the provincial-level regions, to which the cities belong.

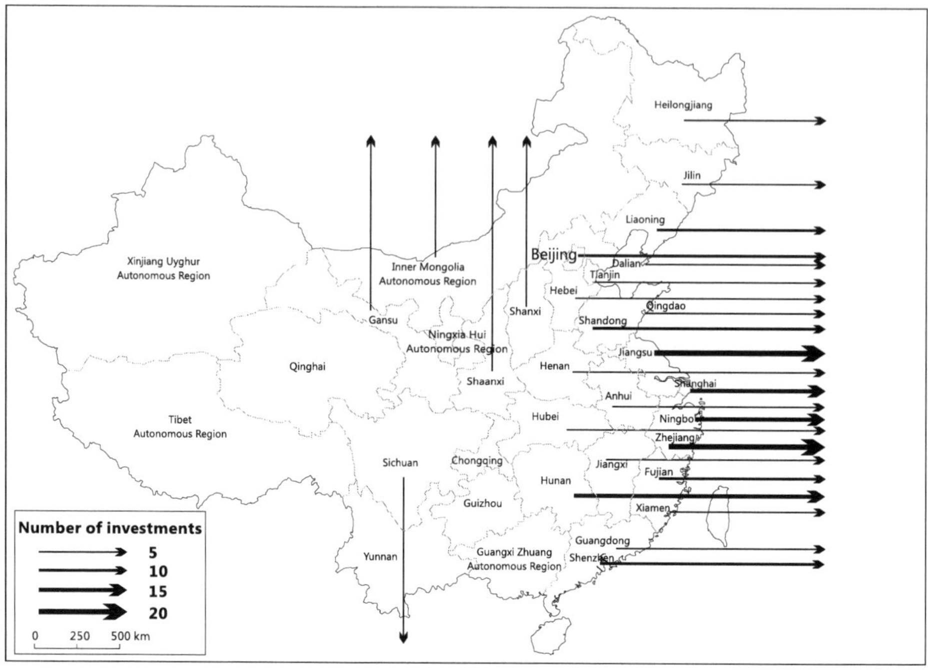

Map 1: The spatial distribution of the origin of Chinese FDI in CEE in 2004–2013
Source: own elaboration on the basis of China's Outward Foreign Direct Investment Data (Marukawa et al., 2014).

is also the origin of the largest number of FDI in Europe. There is also a significant number (20) of Central State Owned Enterprises which are not marked on the illustration. Taking into account the inland provinces, the highest number of investments originated from the Hunan province (18). It may be noticed that three large cities play an important role. These are Shanghai, Ningbo, and Shenzhen.

The second part of the analysis was conducted on the basis of the biggest, individual transactions.[6] It is important to note that it includes more recent deals; due to the dynamic changes in the China-CEE economic relations, they differ relevantly from the above findings. In the following section foreign direct investments and contracts are taken into account. As it appears, the latter is an important stream for the inflow of the Chinese monetary capital.

The following map and Table 1 show the distribution of the most significant Chinese transactions in the CEE region (The transactions conducted mostly since 2010). The number of contracts was much greater

---

[6] The minimum value of transaction was 100 million USD.

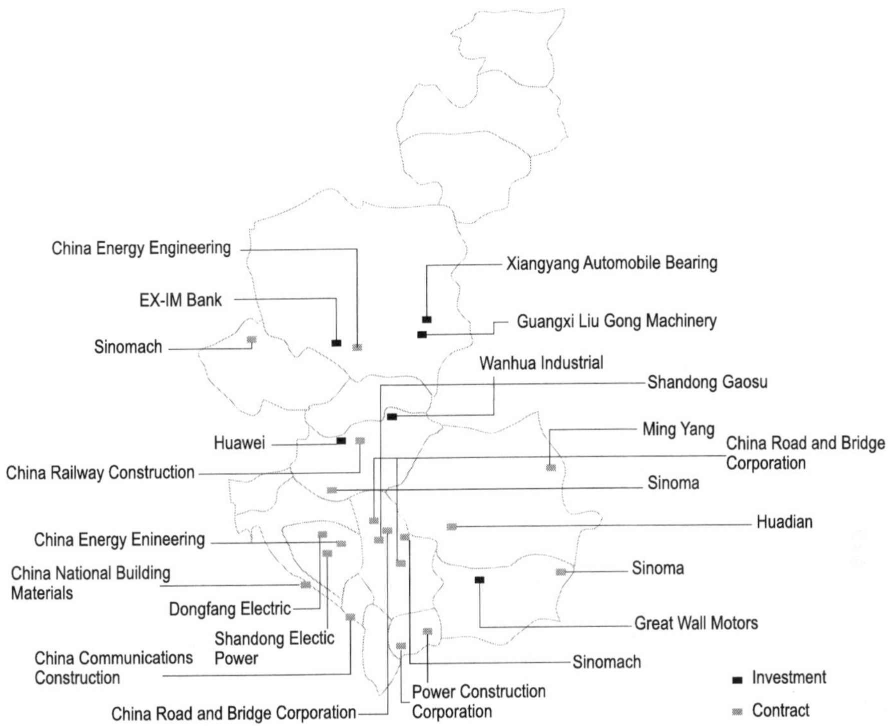

Map 2: The biggest Chinese investments and contracts in CEE from 2004 to 2014
Source: own elaboration on the basis of AEI, Heritage data, Vengali (2015).

than the number of FDI. The deals occurred in five sectors: Energy, Construction, Transport, Chemicals and Technology. We can observe that on the one hand, investments were concentrated in Hungary and Poland, on the other hand, the contracts were focused in the Western Balkans. The accumulated value of transactions was definitely at the highest level in Hungary. The two biggest investments, conducted by Wanhua and Huawei, were located in this country. In contrast, the value of financial inflow to Poland was more or less five times lower. As it was mentioned, the Western Balkans have attracted a great ammount of Chinese financial capital through contracts. They occurred in two fields: transportation infrastructure and energy production. The development of the transportation infrastructure in this area is connected with One Belt, One Road strategy. The Chinese aim to build a convenient and fast transportation route from the Mediterranean Sea ports (especially from the Greek port of Piraeus) to the markets of Western Europe – the major destination of goods exported from the PRC. The biggest contract in transportation infrastructure development was placed in Montenegro, however it must be noted, that there is a plan to construct a new railway link between Belgrade and Budapest, which will be the most significant Chinese deal in that field in Balkans. Serbia, Bosnia and Herzegovina, Macedonia are not the members of the European Union, therefore they are probably more "flexible" in their legal and political frameworks (Vangeli, 2015), what can contribute to the great amount of Chinese contracts in this region. The only FDI in the Balkan region was conducted by Great Wall Motors. The company, in cooperation with Litex Motors, founded a car manufacturing plant. There is a lack of big investments and contracts in five countries: Estonia, Latvia, Lithuania, Slovakia and Slovenia.

To conclude, the China-CEE economic relations recently show a growing tendency. As well as the significant diversification of the European post-communist states, the Chinese influence is also different in the individual Central and Eastern countries. The Visegrad countries are the most important PRC's trade partners. The trade imbalance is a major feature that apply to all the post-communist countries. It is import from China that mainly shapes the imbalance rate. Due to the biggest value of import from China to Poland and the Czech Republic, they have also the highest imbalance rate among the Visegrad group. Although the export from CEE to China is on a lower level, it grew constantly from 2004. There is a significant increase of the value of export to the PRC from Bulgaria and Romania since 2010. Perhaps it is one of the results of the China-CEE political rapprochement. Albania stands out in the share of export to China in the structure of its global export. Hungary is the country that attracted the greatest amount of monetary capital from China. The Western Balkan countries: Serbia, Bosnia, and Herzegovina, Macedonia and Montenegro are recipients of Chinese financial aid through contracts, which occur in the fields of transportation infrastructure and energy production. This Chinese financial engagement can be connected with One Belt, One Road strategy and the China-CEE16 political cooperation. As we can see, the monetary capital flow from the PRC to Western Balkans is complemented by a growing trade cooperation in the eastern part of the Balkans. One may assume that the China-CEE political rapprochement mostly applies to this European region. It is also visible that in four countries: Estonia, Latvia, Lithuania, and Slovenia, the Chinese economic influence is on a low level.

Table 1. The biggest Chinese investments and contracts in CEE from 2004 to 2014

Year	Country	Quantity $million	Chinese Partner/ Contractor	Sector	Project
2007	Hungary	170	Sinoma	Construction	Construction of a cement production line for Holcim
2009	Czech R.	100	Sinomach	Energy	Construction of a solar power station
2009	Bulgaria	120	Great Wall Motor	Transport	Founding a car manufacturing plant
2010	Serbia	260	CRBC	Transport	Construction of a bridge in Belgrade
2010	Serbia	340	Sinomach	Energy	Reconstruction of the Kostolac coal-fired power station
2010	Bosnia	710	Dongfang	Energy	Development of a thermal plant
2010–2011	Hungary	2 110	Wanhua Industrial	Chemicals	Acquisition of Borsodchem
2012	Bulgaria	210	Sinoma	Construction	Construction of a cement line
2012	Poland	100	Liu Gong	Transport	Acquisition of a part of Huta Stalowa Wola (construction machinery)
2012	Hungary	1 500	Huawei	Technology	Establishing a new logistic centre
2012	Hungary	990	CRC	Transport	Construction of a high-speed railway linking Liszt Ferenc Airport to the Eastern Railway Station in Budapest
2012	Romania	1 300	Huadian	Energy	Building a coal-fired plant
2013	Serbia	850	CRBC	Transport	Construction of two motorways: Pojate-Preljna and Novi Sad–Ruma
2013	Poland	560	CEE	Energy	Building of a coal-fired power unit
2013	Serbia	330	Shandong Gaosu	Transport	Construction of a section of a highway Belgrade–Obrenovac
2013	Bosnia	280	Shandong	Energy	Construction of a gas-fired power plant
2013	Macedonia	400	PCC	Transport	Building two stretches of highway: Kicevo-Ohrid, Miladinovci-Stip
2013	Romania	540	Ming Yang	Energy	Development of a wind farm
2013	Serbia	720	Sinomach	Energy	Further work in Kostolac
2013	Poland	n/a	Xiangyang Aut. Bearings	Transport	Acquisition of the Rolling Bearings Factory
2014	Montenegro	1 120	CCC	Transport	Construction of a 41 km section of the planned Bar-Boljare highway
2014	Bosnia	1 060	CEE	Energy	Building of a coal-fired power unit
2014	Croatia	130	CNBM	Transport	Equipping a new Bulk cargo terminal in the port of Ploce
2014	Poland	200	EX-IM Bank	Energy	Acquisition of a wind farm

Source: own elaboration on the basis of AEI, Heritage data, Vengali (2015).

References

European Institute for Asian Studies (2014). *China-CEE relations: Diving Line or Business as Usual?* Brussels.

Jacoby, W. (2014). Different cases, different faces: Chinese investment in Central and Eastern Europe. *Asia Europe Journal*, 12(1–2), 199–214.

Kaczmarski, M. (2015). The New Silk Road: a versatile instrument in China's policy. *OSW Commentary*, p. 2.

KPMG Global China Practice (2015). *China Outlook 2015*. Retrieved from: www.kpmg.com/cn (accessed: 10/10/2015).

Liu Zuokui (2013). The Pragmatic Cooperation between China and CEE: Characteristics, Problems, and Policy Suggestions. *Working Papers Series on European Studies*, Vol. 7, No. 6, pp. 1–9. Beijing: Institute of European Studies, Chinese Academy of Social Sciences.

Matura, T. (2013). China's Economic Expansion into Central Europe. *Asian Studies*, pp. 138–151. Budapest: Hungarian Institute of International Affairs.

Marukava, T., Ito, A., Zhang, Y. (2014). China's Outward Foreign Direct Investment Data. In: *ISS Contemporary Chinese Research Series*, No. 15. Tokyo: Institute of Social Science.

Pavlićević, D. (2015). China's New Silk Road takes shape in Central and Eastern Europe. *China Brief*, 15(1), 9.

Song Lilei (2013). From rediscovery to new cooperation: The relationship between China and Central and Eastern Europe. *EU-China Observer*, Issue 5, 8–14.

Turcsanyi, R.Q., Matura, T., Fürst, R. (2014). The Visegrad countries' Political Relations with China: Goals, Results and Prospects. In: Szunomár, Á. (ed.). *Chinese Investments and Financial Engagement in Visegrad Countries: Myth or Reality?* (pp. 127–141). Budapest: Institute of World Economics.

Vangeli, A. (2015). *The new kid in the block: a short intro to the China-WB relationship*. Balkans In Europe Policy Blog.

Michał Lubina

The New Silk Road and its Geopolitical Consequences for Poland

The New Silk Road has recently become the most famous worldwide Chinese political initiative. Although far from being complete, or even secured, The New Silk Road – providing its success – would present unique opportunities for Poland. It would not only benefit from the short-term economic benefits but could even reverse the effects of its inconvenient geopolitical position.

The New Silk Road: An Introduction

The New Silk Road, or, to be correct, Silk Road Economic Belt/Corridor (later: One Belt One Road) Initiative[1] was announced by the Chinese President Xi Jinping in Astana, in September 2013. During his speech at Nazarbayev university[2] on September 7th 2013, Xi presented five most important policy recommendations: to strengthen policy communication, to improve road connectivity, to promote trade facilitation, to enhance monetary circulation and to strengthen people-to-people exchanges (*President Xi Jinping Delivers...*, 2013). The most important part of his speech came when he urged to "improve traffic connectivity, so as to open the strategic regional thoroughfare from the Pacific Ocean to the Baltic Sea,

---

[1] There is also another name, The Silk Road Economic Belt and the 21st-century Maritime Silk Road; however, the One Belt, One Road, *Yidai yilu*, remains the most popular name, alongside The New Silk Road.

[2] The venue of this speech has a value itself. Kazakhstan remains China's most important regional partner ("strategic partner") and the announcement of New Silk Road in a speech at the University named in honor of Nazarbayev may be understood as Chinese way of "giving face" to Kazakhstan's leader.

and gradually move toward the set-up of a network of transportation that connects Eastern, Western and Southern Asia"; also, among other things, he urged the relevant countries to "enhance communication and green-light regional economic integration in terms of both policy and law" and to "promote local-currency settlement" (*Xi suggests China…*, 2013).

Xi's Astana initiative was soon followed by another step. On the 4th of October 2013, while visiting Indonesia and speaking in the parliament, he proposed a parallel initiative: "building a new maritime silk road", saying that China and ASEAN countries "share a destiny" and would both benefit from this new idea (*Xi in call…*, 2013). The content of Xi's Indonesia speech was similar to the viewpoint presented in Astana (though of course it differed on details): emphasis on a stronger economic cooperation, including financial aspects, very close cooperation on the joint infrastructure projects (e.g., building roads and railways), the enhancement of security cooperation, and the idea of a "21st century maritime Silk Road" through strengthened "maritime economy, environment technical and scientific cooperation (Szczudlik-Tatar, 2013). Since then, Central Asian and Southeast Asian components of New Silk Road became known in both Chinese media and within the expert circles under one slogan: "One Belt and One Road" (the belt being the maritime route whereas the road being the Central Asian one). There are slight differences in the official goals of these two routes (in Southeast Asia the emphasis is on trade security, in Central Asia on the trade itself (ibid.), but they should be considered combined. In this article, both routes would be understood as one concept: the New Silk Road.

First serious comments after Xi's Astana visit underlined the possible regional consequences for the newly created concept of the "New Silk Road". That isthe enhanced Chinese economic domination over the region: "it is a prelude to the closer integration of the region in the fields of infrastructure, trade & finance and energy" which, combined with "the rapid development of economic cooperation and China's de facto sponsorship of Central Asia's weaker states" is "inevitably leading to a situation where the Central Asian states are, to varying degrees, falling into political dependence on China, which in some cases is even taking on a neo-colonial character" (Jarosiewicz, 2013). This, of course, in the long term means some kind of a political confrontation with Russia, the previous political patron and geopolitical controller of Central Asia. New Silk Road in the regional context may be understood as China's response to the rival integration project promoted by Russia the Eurasian Economic Union (Wiśniewska, 2013). And, if successful, New Silk Road would give China a political advantage over Russia in the region, with the help of Beijing's economic instruments. So far, however, both sides were able to restrain and avoid any confrontation with each other. This was possible thanks to the very nature of the New Silk Road initiative: "the Chinese concept, which is based on different principles than the Russian idea, makes it possible for Beijing to protect its economic interests in Central Asia without the need to openly compete with Russia"; Beijing was able to win Moscow over: "by treating Russia as an essential element of the New Silk Road" the Chinese "were able to "reduce Russia's dislike of the project" and created an "impression that this is a positive-sum game, and thus Russia may be convinced that it is not worth opposing Chinese projects in Central Asia" (Kaczmarski, 2015). China avoided confrontation with Russia for a single reason. It is not Moscow that is Beijing's main global competitor (and a partner at the same time) but Washington (see below). Taking into account the geopolitical implications of the special US-China relations, Beijing cannot aggregate Moscow. It must maintain at least a neutral relationship, at all costs.

The disputes in the South China Sea (incidents, frozen dialogue, unfriendly statements) between China on one side, and Vietnam, Malaysia, Philippines and Taiwan on the other, overshadowed the comments after the announcement of the Maritime Silk Road. That is why, the New Silk Road policy seemed to be considered as a tool to defuse tensions. This new approach, based on a soft language, lucrative economic offer and security aspects was supposed to be "China's olive branch to the ASEAN states" (Szczudlik-Tatar, 2013). This olive branch, however, was soon replaced by China's firmer stand on the disputed islands, which means that the Maritime Silk Road project and the disputed islands should not necessary be combined. What China wants here, is to dominate the South China Sea and to impose her vision of regional (and global) development, without giving many concessions in return.

With time, the concept of the New Silk Road grew in importance. It became not only a plan for creating a network of infrastructural connections (mainly transport corridors, both on land and at sea, between China and its most important economic partner – Europe), but, "throughout 2014, the concept gradually came to be the pivotal issue in China's foreign policy and, to a lesser extent, in its domestic policy" (Kaczmarski, 2015). In November 2014, China announced establishing the Silk Road Fund worth $40 billion to "set up a Silk Road infrastructure fund to boost connectivity across Asia" (*China to establish...*). A month earlier, on the 24th of October 2014, China, together with 20 other Asian countries, founded the Asian Infrastructure Investment Bank, an additional source of money for the New Silk Road (*21 Asian countries...*, 2014). Moreover, in January 2015, China launched the Energy Development Fund worth $20 billion to "finance China's 'One Belt, One Road' initiatives", or in other words, the New Silk Road (*New fund...*, 2015).

All this is meant to provide sources for creation of a network of transport corridors, that will connect China with her trade partner nr 1: the European Union. It also means building or modernizing the transport infrastructure (railways, including high-speed railways, and road infrastructure, airports, inland and maritime ports) as well as creating the oil and gas pipelines and telecommunication infrastructure. All this makes the New Silk Road "a conglomerate of routes, and envisages more than ten variants of transport connections between China and Europe" (Kaczmarski, 2015). Laying down of such an elaborate and enormously expensive network of high-speed, high-volume railroads as well as oil and natural gas pipelines across the vast breadth of Eurasia is "a breathtaking project to put in place an infrastructure for the continent's economic integration" (McCoy, 2015).

Since 2014, the New Silk Road has also become, as Marcin Kaczmarski put it, "a versatile instrument of Chinese policy", in both the regional and global dimensions. According to him, this concept is becoming "a key element of China's public diplomacy and soft power" (it's being presented in information and propaganda setting, covering cultural events, expert meetings and tourist routes, and promoted as a "Chinese version of the Marshall Plan"). The concept is "a kind of 'packaging' for China's economic expansion, lending it an attractive form". China may present her expansion as beneficial for all ("win-win formula"), it is imagined as an "illustration of the Chinese philosophy of international relations where all the countries engaged are winners". Its aim is to promote (or enhance) the image of China as a 'benign' power. Moreover, it is a "flexible formula of dialogue": China can 'sell' this concept to the individual countries and regions, because the concept of the New Silk Road is an open political project, without clearly defined boundaries (Kaczmarski, 2015).

The openness of this project raises questions of how concrete it is. Its main objectives are not clearly defined, and its nature is imprecise. The Chinese analyst like to say that this project is planned for generations and for decades (*The 2nd Academic Conference...*, 2015), which raises questions, whether it is at all real. It may turn out to be a simple propaganda effort, without any real effects on China's foreign policy. Moreover, there are objective problems that may become crucial obstacles to the development of the existing railway connections between China and Europe (the core of the New Silk Road's land section concept), such as customs procedures, differences in railway systems, the lack of goods that could be exported to China and the fact that it's still cheaper to send containers by sea.

Nevertheless, while understanding all this reservations, this article considers the New Silk Road as a real possibility. It's China's geopolitical response to the US pivot towards Asia, a chance to break away from the USA's new containment policy. And what a response it may be!

The geopolitics of New Silk Road

The New Silk Road is a plain, though pretentious allusion to the famous Silk Road, that connected Europe with Asia. Here one may see a characteristic style of Chinese policy making. The Chinese like to hark back to history while pursuing their present policy. However, this is not only a pretentious way; it reveals yet another feature of the Chinese-style policy: in-depth understanding of history and its mechanisms.

"In these circumstances – wrote George Kennan in his famous Foreign Policy article – it is clear that the main element of any United States policy toward the Soviet Union must be that of long-term, patient but firm and vigilant containment of Russian expansive tendencies"("X", or George Kennan, 1947). Outdated? Not quite. Just remove the names "Soviet Union" and "Russian" and replace them with "China" and "Chinese".

The USSR collapsed in 1991, and the USA won the cold war. But – contrary to some optimistic claims (Fukuyama, 1992) – history did not end. On the opposite: it returned (Kagan, 2008), or rather, it has always been here. Since the 2000s, China became the new US global competitor. Beijing was beginning to develop its sea power and strategic interests beyond its border. China has also been astute in utilizing its financial and cultural power in order to win friends and gain influence around the world, particularly in Asia-Pacific. This was a possible threat to the US: if the US was to be pushed out of the Asia-Pacific region and to loose its control over maritime routes in Southeast Asia, then U.S. global hegemony would end (Bartosiak, 2015).

Faced by China's rise and its geopolitical consequences, Washington's answer was logical. Obama's terms saw reorientation of the US foreign policy away from the Middle East and back to Asia-Pacific. Negligence and political idealism were replaced by Kissinger-like realism. The containment policy was recycled from the dustbin of history. Thus, in 2011 with "US pivot/rebalance to Asia" or, in "plain language, the US's China containment policy" (Lintner, 2013) was born. Washington started TPP negotiations and strengthened cooperation with the Southeast Asian countries, particularly in the scope of security (Singapore, the Philippines, Indonesia, Malaysia, Thailand and Brunei). The most significant (and successful) American move was making a deal with Burmese generals. Before 2011, Myanmar was one of most important political vassals of China – Beijing's "icing on the cake" in Asia. Thanks to "US pivot to Asia" the Americans turned it almost completely upside down: the Sino-Burmese relations today are as bad as they had not been since 1980s, and the Burmese post-generals are conducting joint military drills with US army. From Washington's point of view, it was a huge success. For China, all this meant stopping the natural way of development in Southeast Asia. If the US was to succeed further (e.g. with TPP project) in the region, Washington would be able to block China's rise in Asia-Pacific for good.

Faced by this serious challenge, China had to find a way to break away from this policy of containment. Chinese leaders followed Sun Zi's advices: if you are faced by a stronger opponent, do not fight with him openly, but instead, try to get around and manoeuvre yourself to a better place (Chong Pin-lin, personal 2015). They simply looked at the map and saw the obvious. If the road to the East and Southeast Asia is blocked, then they must move to the West, to Europe. This was nothing new. They just dust off the century-old idea of the Silk Road. The scale as well as the possible global consequences was new. To understand them, one must go back to the very idea of geopolitics.

When Sir Halford Mackinder, the founder of this new modern science known as geopolitics, wrote at the beginning of 20th century his article "The Geographical Pivot of History", he simply redrew the map of the world. His new map showed Europe, Asia, and Africa as a one continent: "the world island". Beyond it, there was its broad, deep "heartland": a territory stretching some 4,000 miles from Volga to Yangtze. So enormous, that it could only be controlled from its "rimlands" in Eastern Europe (its maritime "marginal" in the surrounding seas) (Mackinder, 1903).

When Mackinder proclaimed his ideas, the world had been witnessing the peak of the British power, born out of the sea-dominance. This dominance, in turn, was then the result of more than 300 years of Western sea-powers global supremacy (Panikkar, 1953). In the sixteenth century, "the "discovery of the Cape road to the Indies (...) the revolution commenced by the great mariners of the Colombian generation", Mackinder wrote, "endowed Christendom with the widest possible mobility of power (...) wrapping her influence round the Euro-Asiatic land-power which had hitherto threatened her very existence". This greater mobility gave Europe's seamen "superiority for some four centuries over the landsmen of Africa and Asia" (Mackinder, 1903, p. 432). Since Henry the Navigator, the sea powers has been dominating the world for 400 years (first Portugal, then the Netherlands, then Britain and finally the USA) (Bartosiak, personal conversation 2015). They competed to control the globe via the surrounding sea lanes with their instruments: ships (first men-o'-war ships, then battleships, submarines, and finally, the aircraft carriers). Thanks to this, they'd been controlling of whole coasts and continents: "at the peak of its imperial power circa 1900, Great Britain ruled the waves with a fleet of 300 capital ships and 30 naval bastions, bases that ringed the world island from the North Atlantic at Scapa Flow through the Mediterranean at Malta and Suez to Bombay, Singapore, and Hong Kong. Just as the Roman Empire enclosed the Mediterranean, making it *Mare Nostrum* ('Our Sea'), British power would make the Indian Ocean its own 'closed sea,' securing its flanks with army forces on India's Northwest Frontier and barring both Persians and Ottomans from building naval bases on the Persian Gulf" (McCoy, 2015).

For Mackinder, however, sea dominance was not enough. He argued that the future of global power lays not in controlling the global sea lanes, but in controlling a vast land mass, the "Euro-Asia" (Mackinder, 1903, p. 429). He simply turned the globe away from America, and placed Central Asia in the global centre. For him, the Heartland was the key region worldwide. As he put it later: "who rules the Heartland, commands the World-Island, who rules the World-Island commands the world" (Mackinder, 1962, p. 150). He was not the only one. Zbigniew Brzeziński clearly followed this way of thinking when he wrote "a power that dominates 'Eurasia' would control two of the world's three most advanced and economically productive regions... rendering the Western Hemisphere and Oceania geopolitically peripheral to the world's central continent." (Brzezinski, 1997, p. 31). This rationale was that any power that controls the World-Island, would control well over 50% of the world's resources. And the Heartland's size and central position made it the key to controlling the World-Island. Therefore, the vital question was how to secure control for the Heartland. Or, just how to prevent any strong continental power to emerge, maintain the control over the Heartland and make full use of its vast resources.

According to his concept, maritime powers' geopolitical nightmare was that if any strong state were allowed to control the vast resources of Heartland, it would be able to control the world. He believed that the introduction of the railroad had removed the Heartland's invulnerability to land invasion and enabled faster transportation of goods. As Eurasia began to be covered by an extensive network of railroads, there was an excellent chance, that a powerful continental nation could extend its political control over Eurasian landmass. In his words, Russia or Germany might expand "over the marginal lands of Euro-Asia," allowing "the use of vast continental resources for fleet-building, and the empire of the world would be in sight" (Mackinder, 1903, p. 436).

Moscow was the first capital to become a continental rival for the sea-powers. In the 19th century Russia challenged British supremacy. Their Great Game in Central Asia was a strategic rivalry of sea power versus land power or – to use Mackinder language – "the World-Island and the Heartland." Although the Great Game ended with a "strategic draw" (Russia and Britain settled their zones of influence), this enabled lasting of a status quo favourable for the British. Then came the two World Wars fought over his "rimlands" (from Eastern Europe through the Middle East to East Asia). The First World War was "a straight duel between a land-power (Germany) and a sea-power (Great Britain)" (Mackinder, 1962, pp. 78–79). The Second War World was "a strategic overtime", where the sea-powers (Great Britain and the USA) fought to prevent Germany from taking the Soviet-controlled Heartland and to create Hitler's "Living Space". *Following Allied victory, the USA took the global lead from Britain, but continued to follow the British global policy* to contain China and Russia inside that Eurasian heartland. They built an arc of military bases "that followed Britain's maritime template and were visibly meant to encircle the world island"; they contained the Soviet land power by the U.S. Navy; they created layers of encircling military alliances, and finally, added a global network of 450 military bases. As Alfred McCoy summarized, "stripped of its ideological foliage, Washington's grand strategy of Cold War-era anti-Communist "containment" was little more than a process of imperial succession" (McCoy, 2015).

U.S. ultimate success after 1991 seemed to indicate the continuum of sea-power dominance. This is, however, not so obvious. Russia's and Germany's failure proved that Mackinder was wrong when he identified them as potential mortal challengers to the sea-powers' dominance. This, however, does not mean his theory was falsified.[3] Today we have a new global competitor, who may make full use of Heartland's vast resources. It is China, with her New Silk Road.

Beijing does not try to build a strong navy (like the British) or a global aerospace dominance (like the USA). Instead, China moves deep towards the World Island. By doing so, China is trying to – as McCoy coined it – "thoroughly reshape the geopolitical fundamentals of global power: build a transcontinental infrastructure for the economic integration of the world island from within and at the same time mobilize military forces to surgically slice through Washington's encircling containment" (McCoy, 2015). In other words, China wants to overturn the global dominance of the sea-powers in favour of continental (Heartland) power. Even the very down-to-earth analysts notice that the New Silk Road concept "in the long term is becoming an element of the construction of the Chinese international order, which is alternative to the one dominated by the United States" (Kaczmarski, 2015).

The New Silk Road is the tool to reverse the global geopolitics. Construction of enormously expensive network of high-speed, high-volume railroads as well as oil and natural gas pipelines across the vast

---

[3] The theory itself has never been falsified nor verified.

breadth of Eurasia means fulfilling Mackinder vision: "for the first time in history, the rapid transcontinental movement of critical cargo – oil, minerals, and manufactured goods – will be possible on a massive scale, thereby potentially unifying that vast landmass into a single economic zone stretching 6,500 miles from Shanghai to Madrid". In this way, "the leadership in Beijing hopes to shift the locus of geopolitical power away from the maritime periphery and deep into the continent's heartland" (McCoy, 2015).

China started from integrating her own territory. Here, infrastructure was the key: road, railways (including high-speed railways), and pipelines, entwined the whole country, with highways cutting the remote mountain ranges and new investments seen everywhere (McCoy, 2015). This all-out development was a prelude to another step: "zou chu qu", or the "going out policy" (Stargardt, 2002). In Central Asia that meant (besides planned transportation routes), constructing a comprehensive network of trans-continental gas and oil pipelines to import fuels from the whole Heartland: from Russia in the north, Turkmenistan and Kazakhstan in the centre, Pakistan in the south and in the southeast from Myanmar. And now, Beijing proclaims the New Silk Road: a project that combines and unites all the previous initiatives with the newly planned ones.

If succeessful, the New Silk Road would change the global geopolitics. It would turn the centre of global power away from the maritime powers and back to the land powers. It is easily forgotten that until the 15th century, the global centre of power was Asia, in the Heartland. This is where the most dynamic global empires existed and it was the contact with Asia,that gave Europe her power and dominance. It ended with the great geographic discoveries and the colonial period that followed them. It resulted in Asia's decline and subordination by the Western powers and, consequently, with the dominance of sea-power of Great Britain and the USA (Panikkar, 1953).

Nothing, however, is granted forever. The history may reverse again. And the hypothetical success of the New Silk Road may even make China the first sea and land superpower (Bartosiak, personal conversation, 2015). Of course, this vision is only a future possibility, and by no means a necessary scenario (given the fact that the U.S. would do anything to prevent it from happening). Furthermore, the result of this struggle will be visible in the next decades only. Nevertheless, it is intellectually interesting to speculate about possible consequences for Poland, should the New Silk Road succeed.

New Silk Road's Implications for Poland

The implications of the hypothetical New Silk Road's success for Poland may be divided into two categories. First: short and mid-term economic (and regional) chances, opportunities and consequences. And second, much vaguer, long-term, strategic, geopolitical ones.

The short-term opportunities are mainly economic and regional ones. Poland, as the key country in Central Eastern Europe plays an essential role as a transit area and a place of entry to the Western European markets. Although China's trade with Central Eastern Europe is only about 10% of Beijing's total trade with the UE, the region will not be the main beneficiary of the influx of Chinese goods. It may, however, become a key transit point, a "gateway" to the Western Europe via inland and maritime ports. Regional infrastructure is the main challenge here, particularly the lack of standards; incomplete double tracks railway lines and the lack electrification. Here, China may help with modernization and electrification of railways (Szczudlik-Tatar, 2013).

On the wider scale, being the transit point is nothing to be ashamed of. From Beijing's point of view, this is one of the region's main advantages, if not the only one. One can notice this perception in creating the (quite bizarre from European perspective), 16+1 group.[4] In this respect, Poland is quite privileged by geography: Chinese products going via Poland need to cross only two borders. Furthermore, China considers Central Eastern Europe as a "testing ground" for Chinese products, before they fully enter the Western European market. Beijing believes that the absence of history of conflicts will help to decrease social resistance to Chinese initiatives and win the ideological war over hearts and minds of Eastern Europeans. China has one trump card here: the hopes for Chinese funding: grants, loans and investments (Szczudlik-Tatar, 2013). For Poland this may be the way to escape from "middle income trap".

The New Silk Road's land route has a particular significance for Poland – its shortest variant leads to Germany via Poland. Furthermore, Poland may hope to become the main hub on the western end of the future supply line of Chinese goods going via the New Silk Road, providing that Beijing would not consider Hungary a better place for such an investment (*The 2nd Academic Conference...*, 2015).

The most important economic consequence of the New Silk Road project for Poland may be connecting Poland with Western China. Although most of the Polish investments are concentrated in the costal part of East-

---

[4] 1+16 means China plus Albania, Bosnia and Hercegovina, Bulgaria, Croatia, Montenegro, Czech Republic, Estonia, Lithuania, Latvia, Macedonia, Poland, Romania, Serbia, Slovakia, Slovenia, and Hungary.

ern and Southern China, the real chance for success lies in Western China. Regions and provinces of Qinghai, Gansu, Ningxia and Xinjiang (most notably, with Lanzhou New Area, the economic hub of Western China) present more economic opportunities than the cooperation with the entire country or only with the eastern provinces, where the "Chinese cake" has already been eaten by a (too) strong competition from Western companies. This regionalisation of efforts, an element previously non-existent in Poland's strategy, could become the hallmark of the Polish economic presence in China. Opportunities are open for Polish companies in industries and sectors such as mining, petrochemical, environmental protection, biomedical, pharmaceutical, green technologies, agriculture processing, chemicals. Moreover, there are prospects for boosting trade, most notably the Chengdu-Łódź direct cargo rail link. This link may become Poland's trump card due to the basic facts: the "rival" link Chongqing-Xinjiang-Duisburg takes 16 days, whereas Chengdu-Łódź 12 days. Furthermore, Chengdu-Łódź is much faster than the sea passage (40–50 days) and is much cheaper than air cargo.

Providing that Poland finds a way to fill the trains to China with goods (so far the trains return almost empty to Chengdu due to the lack of desirable goods for Chinese markets), and to establish a handling center for goods moving in both directions and/or link the container terminal in Małaszewicze near the Belarusian border with the project; then the New Silk Road may become one of Poland's main economic assets (Szczudlik-Tatar, 2013). It may even be a successful way of reinvigorating the entire region of Łódź, which fell behind the other Polish provinces in the country's development after 1989 (the same can be said about the Eastern provinces of Poland).

So, the economic opportunities for Poland are there. The questions is whether we would be able to make use of them, whether the Polish elites would be competent enough to bargain a good position vis-à-vis China, and whether the external factors, most notably the American influence, would not hamper, or even topple the whole New Silk Road project. The answers to these questions remain to be seen.

Much more fascinating or perhaps even fantastic, are the long-term, geopolitical consequences for Poland, should China be able to reverse the global geopolitics. Again, before presenting this point of view, we must present the historical context here.

The geographical discoveries and colonialism that followed them, created what Immanuel Wallerstein called the "world-system". He characterized the "world system" as a set of mechanisms of inter-regional and transnational division of labour which redistributes surplus value from the periphery (poor, underdeveloped part of the world, usually raw-materials exporters) and semi-periphery to the core (industrialized part of the world) by the means of the tool called market. Core countries have a high-skill, capital-intensive, technologically advanced production, whereas the peripheral and semi-peripheral countries focus on a low-skill, labour-intensive production and the extraction of raw materials (Wallerstein, 1974, pp. 347–57).

The system constantly reinforces the dominance of the core countries, but it also has dynamic characteristics (technological revolutions, new transport means etc.) – individual states can gain or lose their core/semi-periphery/periphery status over time. Some, like the Netherlands, Great Britain or the USA, become hegemons (ibid.). All of them were sea-powers in the past, but not continental ones, and indeed, the creation of the world-system shifted (to use Mackinder's terminology), the power status from the Heartland to the World Island.

Wallerstein's world-system emerged from the "long" sixteenth century 1450–1550 and then geographically expanded across the entire planet by around 1900. The West used its advantages to gain control over most of the world economy, which resulted in industrialization and creation of capitalist economy – this in turn led to unequal development. Thus a tripartite division of labour emerged, with core, semi-peripheral, and peripheral zones. The developed, core countries dominate the other, less developed "semi-periphery" states; which, at the same time dominate over the others in the "periphery". The core nations dominate by owning and controlling the major means of production in the world and perform the higher-level production tasks (productivity, financial and trade dominance). The periphery nations own very little of the world's means of production and provide less-skilled labour. The semi-peripheral countries fall somewhere in-between, in a midway (ibid.).

Using these categories, one may say that China is a country that transformed from being peripheral to semi-peripheral and is now on the way to overthrow the entire system and to become the core of the new system (providing it ever happens). Poland, similarly, though on a less scale: at the formation of the world-system it was a peripheral country, and it developed into being semi-peripheral country only in the 20th century. Now it is a classic case of a semi-peripheral country. It fits well with the basic semi-peripheral countries' characteristics: it must keep itself from falling to the category of peripheral nations and, at the same time, strive to join the category of the core nations; it is relatively developed and has diversified economy, but is not dominant in international trade and tends to export more to peripheral nations and import more from core nations in trade; and it acts as buffer between cores and peripheries (ibid.).

Finally, one more comment is needed here: from Janet Abu-Lughod that argued with Wallerstein by arguing that before the emergence of world-system there was a pre-modern world system extensive across Eurasia existed in the 13ᵗʰ Century. The Mongol Empire stitch together the Chinese, Indian, Muslim and European regions in the 13ᵗʰ century, before the rise of the modern world system (Abu-Lughod, 1991). In other words, Abu Lughod shows that global epicenter of powers in the Eurasian Heartland existed already before the emergence of sea-powers "world-system". Only later, after geographical discoveries and colonialism, the global epicenter shifted in favor of sea-powers.

By agreeing with Janet Abu-Lughod in this point, we may conclude one thing: the formation of Wallerstein's world-system, or the shifting the global epicentre of power from the continental Heartland to the maritime World Island, pushed Poland towards the margins of Europe and consequently, to the margins of the global world. The geographical discoveries, colonialism and reshaping of the world economy that followed afterwards, all this adversely affected the Kingdom of Poland. It fell to the peripheral category – an exporter of raw-material to the West, which in the long term resulted in a political subordination and the loss of independence (Bartosiak, personal conversation, 2015).

So now, if China is able to overthrow the world-system again, in favour of the continental Heartlandand back to dominance of Eurasia, then Poland would be positively affected. In other words, the geopolitical consequence of successful implementation of New Silk Road means a reversal of the negative consequences of geographical discoveries and colonialism (the dominance of the sea powers). Thus, this constitutes a great chance for Poland's development. For now it may look vague or even unbelievable, but we must remember that the opportunity is there: "we may notice it, even within the life our generation" (ibid.).

Conclusions

The New Silk Road is far from secured or even certain. This impressive political project may reverse the global geopolitics and shift the epicentre of world power back from the maritime powers to a continental one – China. Whether China would fulfil this dare dream is yet to be seen. However, if it should happen; Poland, assuming it pursues a wise policy, would not only benefit from the short-term economic benefits but also escape from the middle income trap or even reverse the effects of its inconvenient geopolitical location. It's a dream worth dreaming – even if it looks an incredible dream.

References

Books:

Abu-Lughod, J. (1991). *Before European Hegemony: The World System A.D. 1250–1350*. Oxford: Oxford University Press.

Aung Zaw (2013). *The Face of Resistance. Aung San Suu Kyi and Burma's Fight for Freedom*. Bangkok: Mekong Press.

Brzezinski, Z. (1997). *The Grand Chessboard. American Primacy and It's Geostrategic Imperatives*. New York: Basic Book.

Fukuyama, F. (1992). *The End of History and the Last Man*. New York: Free Press.

Kagan, R. (2009). *The Return of History and the End of Dreams*. New York: Random House.

Mackinder, H.J. (1962). *Democratic Ideals and Reality*. New York: W.W. Norton [orig. published in 1919].

Panikkar, K.M. (1953). *Asia and Western Dominance*. New York: the John Day.

Wallerstein, I. (1974). *The Modern World-System, Capitalist Agriculture and the Origins of the European World Economy in the Sixteenth Century*. New York: Academic Press.

Articles and chapters:

"X" (George Kennan) (1947). The sources of Soviet conduct. *Foreign Policy*, July. Retrieved from: https://www.foreignaffairs.com/articles/russian-federation/1947–07–01/sources-soviet-conduct (accessed: 30/10/2015).

21 Asian countries sign MOU on establishing Asian Infrastructure Investment Bank. Xinhuanet, 24.10.2014. Retrieved from: http://news.xinhuanet.com/english/business/2014–10/24/c_133740149.htm (accessed: 30/10/2015).

Bartosiak, J. (2015). *Air-Sea Battle and Its Implications for Grand Strategies in the Western Pacific and Eurasia*. Lecture in Potomac Foundation. Washington, D.C., 21.10.2015.

Belt with Central Asian Countries, Ministry of Foreign Affairs of the People's Republic of China, 7.09.2013. Retrieved from: http://www.fmprc.gov.cn/mfa_eng/topics_665678/xjpfwzysiesgjtfhshzzfh (accessed: 10/10/2015).

China to establish $40 billion Silk Road infrastructure fund. Reuters, 8.11.2014. Retrieved from: http://www.reuters.com/article/2014/11/08/us-china-diplomacy-idUSKBN0IS0BQ20141108#GatK4rPKwIIv8BGg.97 (accessed: 30/10/2015).

Jarosiewicz, A. (2013). *A Chinese tour de force in Central Asia*. OSW Analyses, 18.09.2013. Retrieved from: http://www.osw.waw.pl/en/publikacje/analyses/2013–09–18/a-chinese-tour-de-force-central-asia (accessed: 30/10/2015).

Kaczmarski, M. (2015). *The New Silk Road: a versatile instrument in China's policy*. OSW commentary, 10.02.2015. Retrieved from: http://www.osw.waw.pl/en/publikacje/osw-commentary/2015–02–10/new-silk-road-a-versatile-instrument-chinas-policy (accessed: 30/10/2015).

Lintner, B. (2013). *Myanmar North Korea Stay Brothers in Arms*. Asia Times Online, 5.09.2013. Retrieved from: http://www.atimes.com/atimes/Southeast_Asia/SEA-01-050913.html (accessed: 30/10/2015).

Mackinder, H.J. (1904). The geographical pivot of history. *The Geographical Journal*, 23(4). Retrieved from: http://www.thinkorbebeaten.com/Library/M/MacKinder%27s%20Heartland%20Theory.pdf (accessed: 30/10/2015).

McCoy, A. (2015). *Washington's Great Game and Why It's Failing*. Tom Dispatch. Com, 6.07.2015. Retrieved from: http://www.tomdispatch.com/post/176007/tomgram%3A_alfred_mccoy,_washington (accessed: 30/10/2015).

New fund initiated for Silk Roads. China Aggregates Net, 28.01.2015. Retrieved from: http://www.caggregate.com/?p=3361 (accessed: 30/10/2015).

President Xi Jinping Delivers Important Speech and Proposes to Build a Silk Road Economic Seminar Chinese New Silk Road: Polish Point of View. PISM, Warsaw, 5.11.2015.

Stargardt, J.M. (2002). *China Awakes*. Offshore Investment, Issue 226, May. Retrieved from: http://www.offshoreinvestment.com/pages/index.asp?title=China_-_Issue_226 (accessed: 30/10/2015).

Szczudlik-Tatar, J. (2013). *China's New Silk Road Diplomacy*. PISM Policy Paper, No. 34(82), December. Retrieved from: https://www.pism.pl/files/?id_plik=15818 (accessed: 30/10/2015).

Wallerstein, I. (1974). *The Rise and Future Demise of World Capitalist System: Concepts for Comparative Analysis*. In: Comparative Studies in Society and History, Volume 16, Issue 4 (Sept. 1974).

Wiśniewska, I. (2013). *Eurasian integration. Russia's attempt at the economic unification of the Post-Soviet area*. OSW report, 30.07.2013. Retrieved from: http://www.osw.waw.pl/en/publikacje/osw-studies/2013-07-30/eurasian-integration-russias-attempt-economic-unification-post (access: 30.10.2015).

Xi in call for building of new 'maritime silk road'. China Daily USA, 4.10.2013. Retrieved from: http://usa.chinadaily.com.cn/china/2013-10/04/content_17008940.htm (accessed: 30/10/2015).

Xi suggests China, C. Asia build Silk Road economic belt. Xinhuanet, 7.09.2013. Retrieved from: http://news.xinhuanet.com/english/china/2013-09/07/c_132700695.htm (accessed: 30/10/2015).

Personal conversations:

Bartosiak, J., personal conversation, Washington, D.C., 22.10.2015.

Chong Pin-lin, personal conversation, Krakow, 15.03.2015.

The 2nd Academic Conference on China-Central and Eastern Europe (CEE) Cross-Cultural Dialogue, Education and Business, Jagiellonian University, 22–24.09.2015.

Agnieszka McCaleb, Ágnes Szunomár

Comparing Chinese, Japanese, and South Korean FDI in Central and Eastern Europe

Introduction

Chinese outward FDI is one of the most spectacular cases of today's international economics in terms of rapid growth, geographical diversity and cases of takeovers of established western brands. Chinese firms mainly invest in Asia, Latin America and Africa, where they search for markets and natural resources. Developed economies however also became their important targets, offering markets for Chinese products and assets, that Chinese firms lack. Moreover, Chinese firms increasingly invest in Central and Eastern European countries (CEECs). These investments constitute a small share of China's total FDI in Europe (10%) and are quite a new phenomenon; but since 2006, rising inflows of Chinese investments could be observed, which are expected to increase (McCaleb & Szunomár, 2013).

Chinese companies however are not the first investors in CEECs from East Asia, as Japanese and South Korean FDI started to flow into the region in the early 1990s. Among the East Asian investors, South Korea has a dominant role in the Czech Republic and Slovakia, Japan is the main investor in Poland, while China recently acquired a dominant position in Hungary.

The aim of the paper is to analyse and compare motivations and location determinants of Chinese, Japanese and South Korean FDI in the largest recipient countries within the CEECs – namely Hungary, Poland, the Czech Republic and Slovakia – with special focus on the role and impact of host country macroeconomic and institutional factors.

After the introductory section, the paper presents the theory and literature on FDI location determinants with special focus on FDI determinants in CEECs. The paper's main section contains findings on similarities and differences in characteristics and motivations of Chinese, Japanese and South Korean FDI in CEECs. In addition, it provides a detailed description of the impact of both macroeconomic and institutional factors.

1. Theory and literature review

Majority of research on motivations for FDI apply the eclectic or OLI paradigm by Dunning (1992, 1998) that states that firms will venture abroad when they possess firm-specific advantages, i.e. ownership and internalization advantages, and when they can utilize location advantages to benefit from the attractions these locations are embedded with. Different types of investment incentives attract different types of FDI which Dunning (1992) divided into four categories: market-seeking, resource-seeking, efficiency-seeking, and asset-seeking. Localization advantages "comprise geographical and climate conditions, resource endowments, factor prices, transportation costs, as well as the degree of openness of a country and the presence of a business environment appropriate to ensure to a foreign firm a profitable activity" (Resmini, 2005, p. 3). Much of the extant research and theoretical discussion is based on FDI outflows from developed countries for which market-seeking and efficiency-seeking FDI is most prominent (Janicki & Wunnava, 2004; Buckley et al., 2007; Leitao & Faustino, 2010).

The rapid growth of OFDI from emerging and developing countries resulted in numerous studies trying to account for special features of emerging MNCs behaviour that is not captured within mainstream theories. For example, Mathews extended OLI paradigm with linking, leverage, learning framework (LLL) that explains rapid international expansion of companies from Asia Pacific (Mathews, 2006). Where linking means partnerships or joint ventures that latecomers form with foreign companies in order to minimize risks involved with internationalization as well as to acquire "resources that are otherwise not available" (Mathews, 2006, p. 19). When forming links with incumbents, the latecomers also analyse how the resources can be leveraged. They look for resources that can be easily imitated, transferred or substituted. Finally, repeated processes of linking and leveraging allow the latecomers to learn and conduct international operations more effectively (Mathews, 2006, p. 20).

Nevertheless, traditional economic factors seem to be insufficient in explaining FDI decisions of MNCs. In the last decade international economics and business researchers acknowledged the importance of institutional factors in influencing the behaviour of MNCs (e.g., Tihanyi et al., 2012). According to North, institutions are the "rules of the game" which are "the humanly devised constraints that shape human interactions" (North, 1990, p. 3). Institutions serve to reduce uncertainties related with transactions and minimize transaction costs (North, 1990). Meyer and Nguyen (2005, p. 67) argue that informal constraints are "much less transparent and, therefore, a source of uncertainty". As a result, Dunning and Lundan extended OLI model with the institution-based location advantages which explains that institutions developed at home and host economies shape the geographical scope and organizational effectiveness of MNCs (Dunning & Lundan, 2008).

2. Characteristics and motivations of Chinese, Japanese, and South Korean OFDI in CEECs

Although CEECs differ in many respects, they have some common features as possible locations for far-east investors. Their economies have been in the process of catching up over the last decades, defined mainly by European powers and FDI has a key role in their restructuring. There was investment from East Asian countries in the CEECs as early as the nineties (Japanese Suzuki factory in Hungary). In the past decade, most of these countries became increasingly interested in boosting trade relations with and attracting investments from East Asian economies. The global economic and financial crisis of 2008 intensified these ambitions.

The largest recipient countries of East Asian investments within the CEECs are Hungary, Poland, the Czech Republic, and Slovakia. Altogether in the four countries around 90 percent of foreign investments are from Europe, only an average of 7.4% of FDI comes from other countries, mainly from the USA, South Korea, Japan and China. Typically, equity capital and reinvested earnings dominate in East Asian invested capital, while other forms are not that significant. The only exception is Poland, where the "other investment" category (meaning mainly intercompany loans) outnumbers equity capital and reinvested earnings in the case of Chinese and Japanese investments.

As table 1. shows, according to selected CEECs' national banks data South Korea has a dominant role in all countries except Poland; Japan is the largest East Asian investor in Poland, and the second largest in the Czech Republic, Hungary and Slovakia; while China is less significant.

Table 1. FDI stock in selected CEECs from the main East Asian countries, 2012 (million EUR)

	China	Japan	South Korea
Czech Republic	−7.1	1058.1	1228
Hungary	65.4	772.6	1047.7
Slovakia	47.1	92.9	1899.1
Poland	218.5	1093.1	625.8

Data source: national bank data and OECD data for Slovakia.

In fact, the role of Chinese capital in CEE countries is still relatively very small, but recently this capital inflow has accelerated significantly and has also played an important role in the region's recovery from the crisis. According to Chinese statistics, Chinese FDI in the Czech Republic started to increase from 2006 and reached 202 million USD in 2012. The official statistics explain this huge increase with the recalculation of stock for 2012, however, the components of this supposed growth are unknown. There is an inverse discrepancy in the case of Hungary as, according to Chinese data, the amount of Chinese investments reached 507 million USD by 2012.

Nevertheless, this amount is far greater when taking into account cumulative Hungarian data, since a significant portion of Chinese investment is received via intermediary countries or companies, therefore it appears elsewhere in Chinese statistics. According to Hungarian reports, Chinese investment in Hungary by 2013 was around 3 billion USD.[1]

Chinese investors typically target secondary and tertiary sectors of the selected countries. Initially, Chinese investment has flowed mostly into manufacturing (assembly), but over time services attracted more and more investment as well, for example in Hungary and Poland there are branches of Bank of China and Industrial and Commercial Bank of China as well as offices of some of the largest law offices in China, Yingke Law Firm (in Hungary in 2010, in Poland in 2012) and Dacheng Law Offices (in Poland in 2011, in Hungary in 2012). Main Chinese investors targeting these countries are interested primarily in telecommunication, electronics, chemical industry and transportation. In addition to the largest investor, Wanhua, major investors are Huawei, ZTE Corporation, Lenovo, Sevenstar Electronics Co., BYD Electronics, and Comlink.

---

[1] More than 1.5 billion USD from that is the investment of the Chinese chemical company Wanhua, which acquired a 96 percent stake in the Hungarian chemical company BorsodChem through its Dutch subsidiary in 2010 and 2011 and later also invested in the development of BorsodChem. It is the largest Chinese investment in the CEE region so far.

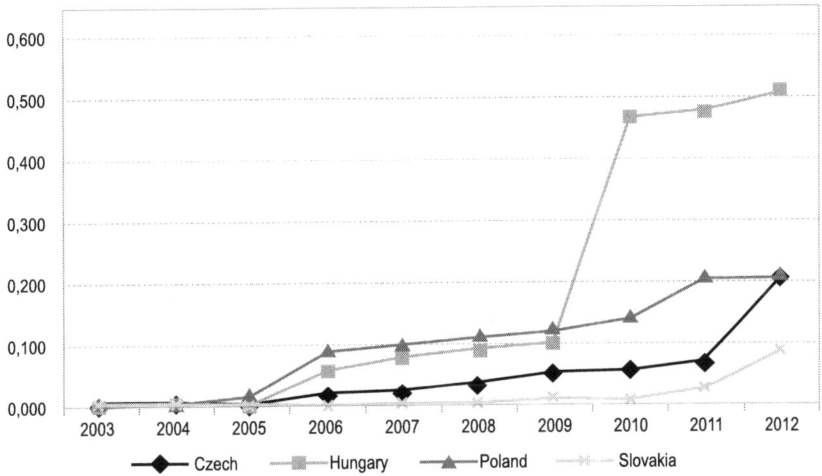

Figure 1. China's OFDI stock in Visegrad Countries, 2003–2012 (USD billion)
Source: MOFCOM, NBS 2013.

Major Japanese investors are Suzuki Motor Corp., Sumitomo Group, Toyota, Denso, Matsushita Electronic Components, Panasonic, Sanyo and Mitsui. Majority of Japanese FDI is concentrated in the electronics and automotive industries. Only recently Japanese investors expanded their interests towards other industries such as food (Lotte's acquisition of Wedel and Pijalnie Czekolady), financial services (Meiji Yasuda's interest in Europa Group and Warta Group), fleet management (Hitachi Capital's acquisition of Corpo Flota), and cosmetics (Rohto's interest in Dax Cosmetics).

Korean investments are also focused in the electronic and automotive industries as well as chemical industry. LG Electronics, Daewoo, Kia, Hyundai and Nexen are one of the major investors. According to researcher Vilém Semerák of the Prague-based CERGE-EI Institute, the South Korean firms are following the footsteps of German ones in CEE.

"…South Korea is trying to replicate the German influence in Central and Eastern Europe. When you look at what Kia and Hyundai have been doing in the past two years, they are clearly trying to imitate what Volkswagen and other car producers have been doing. They have moved their development centres to Germany and try to produce Europe-designed cars for European customers (…), they are also making use of cheap labour and relatively good production conditions in Central and Eastern Europe". (Richter, 2014)

When entering the CEE markets, Japanese and Korean MNCs most often choose greenfield entry mode. Korean MNCs initially engaged only in productive investment, but recently also carry out research and development activities (Szczudlik-Tatar & Mejssner, 2014). Regarding the Chinese entry mode, there are examples for greenfield or quasi-greenfield[2] investments (Huawei, ZTE, Lenovo), as well as M&As (Wanhua) and joint ventures (Orient Solar, BBCA).

2.1. Motivations of OFDI – macroeconomic aspects

When searching for possible factors which make the CEE region a favourable investment destination, Ikemoto (2007, p. 92) found the following advantages:

> "(1) the country's tradition of manufacturing; (2) many qualified and skilled workers; (3) qualified production managers; (5) advantageous geographical location for the EU market; (6) relatively well established infrastructure (roads, railways, electric power, etc.); (7) lower labour costs than the EU-15 countries; and (8) FDI incentive programs (several years' tax holidays, duty free import of equipment, job creation grants, site development support, etc.)."

In fact, the selected CEECs' workforce is skilled compared to other Central and Eastern European countries, while labour costs are lower in the CEE region than the EU average. However, there are differences within the region as well, unit labour costs are cheaper in Bulgaria and Romania than in Hungary, Slovakia, the Czech Republic and Poland but these differences don't necessarily influence investors as, for example, there is more Chinese investment in Hungary, Poland and the Czech Republic than in Romania and Bulgaria. An explanation for that can be the theory of agglomeration effect, as generally OFDI in these countries is the highest in the region.

Concerning market size, Poland is the biggest in terms of the size of population, while the others are medium-sized or small. The Czech Republic and Slovakia are relatively affluent markets as well based on GDP per capita in purchasing power standards. In addition to the size of the market, the CEECs' convenient location in the centre of Europe, generally positive overall business conditions also play an important role when searching for possible investment locations. For example, according to a survey by JETRO of Japanese manufacturing investors in Europe, cited in KPMG (2014, pp. 24–25), Poland is assessed better in terms of management problems than the Czech Republic and Hungary. When choosing

---

[2] Parent companies of Huawei, ZTE or Lenovo haven't built up new operational facilities (as they chose the form of contract manufacturing) but created new long-term jobs by hiring new employees.

a location in CEE for its new factory, Hyundai chose the Czech Republic arguing proximity of their other plants, strength of the Czech economy, the fact that the country is the largest exporter of cars, components and electronics in the region. Chiappini (2014) found that Japanese overseas investments are mainly driven by host market size, yen real exchange rate, macroeconomic stability, resource endowments and some policy variables, such as confidence societal rules, control of corruption, government effectiveness, political stability and private sector policies.

Concerning Japanese multinationals, a large majority of Japanese FDI in CEECs was directed at the manufacturing sector, especially transport equipment and electronics (like Yazaki, Toyota, Suzuki, Sumitomo, Panasonic, Sony). Toyota built a joint venture factory (TPCA) with Peugeot in the Czech Republic in 2001 (producing since 2005) and opened a transmission factory in Poland during the same year, and an engine factory in 2005, that supplies TPCA. TPCA produced 200,000 cars in 2014, but has cut back planned production and employees for 2015.[3] Several Japanese investors in the CEECs manufacturing sector preferred countries with lower corporate tax and a high rate of GDP growth. Thus, overall, Japanese FDI in CEECs is characterized by efficiency-seeking and market-seeking motives (Kawai, 2006).

Access to EU markets was an important market-seeking factor (Woon, 2003). The very first big Japanese investment in the transition countries was of Suzuki: in 1991 Hungarian Suzuki Corporation was established and serial production of cars started in 1992. By July 2014, over 2.5 million cars had rolled off the assembly line. The main motivation here was to get behind "the EU walls", as Hungary had signed an association agreement in 1991 and had prospects for membership. Suzuki continually invested in developing its factory and increased the share of local supplies (in order to reach the local content level required for tariff-free exports to the European Union) (Éltető & Szunomár, 2015).

South Korea has had similar motives. Among the first, being a risk-taker and market seeker, Daewoo established a basis in Poland in the automotive industry and in electronics. The large Korean producer exploited the opportunities of the Polish privatisation process when taking over FSO automobile factory in 1996. Its suppliers followed and also invested in Poland. Later, other South Korean car producers (Kia and Hyundai) made use of cheap labour and relatively good production conditions and moved their development centres to the V4 to produce cars for European customers. The Hyundai Mobis plant is the third major South Korean

---

[3] http://www.praguepost.com/technology/43340-tpca-to-lay-off-workers (accessed: 17/09/2015).

investment project in the Czech Republic[4], started its production in 2009 and is still following an increasing trend in output. A Nexen tyre factory is built in 2015 in Zatec, the agreement was signed in June 2014.[5] In 2004 KIA Motors started to operate in Slovakia employing 3500 workers and producing five car models and also engines (ICEG, 2012). These heavily export-oriented investments had the aim of acquiring markets utilising a qualified labour force (Éltető & Szunomár, 2015).

Although generally, Chinese OFDI are characterized by natural resource-seeking and market-seeking (Buckley et al., 2007), in developed economies – including CEECs – Chinese investment are more concerned with the wide range of objectives, including market-, efficiency- and strategic assets-seeking motives (Rosen & Hanemann, 2013). Describing Chinese investments in the CEE region, Jacoby (2014) observes that their characteristics differ somewhat from those in the EU. Among the three forms of FDI (greenfield investment, mergers & acquisitions and strategic alliances) we can find more greenfield projects and fewer strategic alliances from the Chinese side than in the EU.

Parallel with the increasing number of mergers and acquisitions in the region, strategic asset-seeking motives have become more and more important for Chinese MNCs in recent years. Chinese investments are also motivated by the seeking of brands, new technologies or market niches that they can fill in European markets.

2.2. Motivations of OFDI – institutional aspects

The change of institutional setting of CEECs due to their economic integration into the EU (in 2004 and 2007) has been the most important driver that spurred OFDI in the region, especially in the manufacturing sector. Majority of Chinese firms that invested in CEECs after their EU accession were motivated mainly by accessing the old EU-15 markets and the CEE markets were of secondary importance. CEECs' EU membership allowed investors to avoid trade barriers and the countries served as an assembly base due to the relatively low labor costs. The motive of overcoming trade barriers shows similarity with Japanese investments in CEECs in the second half of the 1990s. Japanese MNCs established as-

---

[4] In July 2014 the investment agreement was signed about the construction of the company for production of headlamps in Mošnov. The construction of the company is planned for September 2015 offering around 6–900 jobs. http://www.mobis-auto.cz/en/aktuality/140804.php (accessed: 17/09/2015).

[5] The firm will have a capacity estimated at 6 million units annually with more than 1,000 employees. http://www.rubbernews.com/article/20140627/NEWS/140629958/south-koreas-nexen-tire-signs-czech-plant-deal# (accessed: 17/09/2015).

sembly plants in CEECs, but sold their products mainly in the affluent Western European markets (Woon, 2003).

Another aspect of the EU membership that is inducing investments in CEECs is institutional stability (e.g., protection of property rights). According to Morck et al. (2008), one of the drivers of Chinese OFDI is unstable institutional, economic and political environment of their home country. It is in line with the findings of Clegg and Voss (2012, p. 101) who argue that Chinese OFDI in the EU shows "an institutional arbitrage strategy" as "Chinese firms invest in localities that offer clearer, more transparent and stable institutional environments. Such environments, like the EU, might lack the rapid economic growth recorded in China, but they offer greater planning and property rights security, as well as dedicated professional services that can support business development" (Witt & Lewin, 2007).

In their investment decisions in CEECs, East Asian firms might also be attracted by Free Trade Agreements between the EU and third countries such as Canada, the USA (being negotiated), and the EU neighbouring country policies etc. as they claim that their CEECs subsidiaries are to sell products in the host, EU, Northern American or even global markets. Moreover, East Asian firms' CEE subsidiaries allow them to participate in public procurement. Example is Nuctech company that established its subsidiary in Poland in 2004 and initially targeted mainly Western European market. Recently Chinese firms also interested in investing in CEECs became more inquisitive about food safety standards and certificates. They would be interested in exporting agricultural products with the EU safety certificates to China where food safety has been a problem.

Characterising Asian investments and their motivation in the Visegrad region we have to mention the role of state subsidies and incentives. Especially before the EU membership, but also afterwards, governments and local authorities applied sometimes tailor-made incentives to attract large investors.[6] In the case of Hungary the so-called "customs free zones" were highly attractive for greenfield foreign investors during the nineties. These export oriented automotive, electronics and other firms provided a huge share of foreign trade of the country. Poland and Slovakia too, provided corporate tax allowances and other incentives for foreign investors, for example, there are special economic zones in Poland with support services. The Czech government has also given subsidies, for example about €200 million in tax allowances, partial funding for employee training and other investment incentives to draw Hyundai to a high un-

---

[6] It must be highlighted that CEE countries usually compete for foreign investment by offering different types of incentives.

employment region (Walewska, 2014). Similarly, TPCA[7] was granted generous incentives from both the Czech state and from the town of Kolín, which paid for the complete development of the industrial zone, costs of traffic route extensions, sound barriers, new housing units and other adequate infrastructure. As a result, the town of Kolín is indebted until 2019 (Guidote, 2008). The recently concluded agreements with Hyundai and Nexen have also included state incentives.[8]

Chinese MNCs seems to pay more attention to the level of political relation than Japanese and Korean firms. The smaller amounts of Chinese investments in the Czech Republic or Slovakia can be explained by the colder political relations of the past years (see Fürst & Pleschová, 2010). By contrast, Hungary – which is the major recipient of Chinese OFDI in the CEE region according to Hungarian cumulative data – has had historically good political relations and earlier than other CEECs, since 2003, intensified bilateral relations in order to attract Chinese FDI. Hungary is the only country in the region that introduced special incentive for foreign investors from outside the EU, which is a possibility to receive a residence visa when fulfilling the requirement of a certain level of investment in Hungary.[9] Moreover, Hungary has the largest Chinese diaspora in the region which is an acknowledged attracting factor of Chinese FDI in the extant literature that is a relational asset constituting firm's ownership advantage (e.g. Buckley et al., 2007). Example is Hisense's explanation of the decision to invest in Hungary that besides traditional economic factors was motivated by "good diplomatic, economic, trade and educational relations with China; big Chinese population; Chinese trade and commercial networks, associations already formed" (CIEGA, 2007).

In case of Poland only recently Chinese firms became also attracted by privatization of state enterprises which provide access to technology (patents), brands, distribution networks, and manufacturing capacity for European markets. Examples are: in early 2012 Liugong Machinery's acquisition of Huta Stalowa Wola's construction equipment division and its distribution subsidiary, Dressta. Until 2005, Dressta was a joint venture

---

[7] The company is situated in the industrial zone Kolín-Ovčáry with around 3500 employees. Eighty percent of all parts for cars are sourced in the Czech Republic. More than 100 supplying firms (about 60 of them Japanese and a similar number of them from Western Europe) followed TPCA to the Czech Republic to work also for other car factories.

[8] Under terms of the Nexen contract, the Czech state will provide incentives at a maximum of $190 million, of this, $100 million tax relief on corporate income, $50 million financial support to strategic investment, $15 million for job creation, $15 million from the Ústí region as a discount on the land and $4.5 million in financial support for training.

[9] Third country nationals are allowed to acquire Hungary's permanent residency status through investing in Special Hungarian Government Bonds that have a minimum 5-year maturity. The minimum initial investment by each subscriber is 250,000 EUR.

between Komatsu America and Huta Stalowa Wola and has sales offices around the world. Secondly, in 2013 China's Tri Ring Group Corporation acquired Polish Fabryka Łożysk Tocznych (the biggest Chinese investment in Poland so far), producer of bearings for automotive sector.

Conclusion

The investigation of the motivations of East Asian OFDI in CEECs shows that Chinese, Japanese, and Korean MNCs mostly search for markets. CEECs' EU membership allows them to treat the region as a 'back door' to the affluent EU markets (tariff-jumping FDI). Investors are attracted by the relatively low labour costs, skilled workforce, and market potential. It is characteristic that their investment pattern in terms of country location resembles that of the world total FDI in the region. Our paper also showed that the CEE region (including the selected group of countries) is not homogeneous and that there are differences in the economic relations between the CEE countries and East Asia, too.

Having examined the CEECs-East Asian economic ties, we can conclude that while Japan and South Korea previously had larger roles, recently China is pushing forward. Analysing the difference in motivations before and after the global financial crisis it can be assessed that although it did not have an impact on East Asian investments in CEECs directly but it did have indirectly because as a reaction to the global financial crisis CEECs started to search for new opportunities for their recovery from the recession. For example, Hungary's "Opening to the East" policy was initiated after (and partly as a result of) the crisis, but the crisis also made Poland look eastward. China took these opportunities and has increased sectoral representation of Chinese firms in CEECs in recent years. Another reason for this higher Chinese representation could be a diversification strategy, because recently, the Chinese global investment strategy places great emphasis on diversification in all respects.

According to our research results, the characteristics, motivations and location determinants of Chinese investments in CEECs differ somewhat from Japanese and South Korean FDI: while in the case of the latter two countries macroeconomic factors (such as labour costs, market size, corporate taxes, etc.) had and still have a decisive role in selecting FDI locations, Chinese firms in addition to macroeconomic factors seem to attach more importance to institutional factors. Country-level institutional factors that impact Chinese MNCs' location choice within CEECs seem to be the size of Chinese ethnic population, investment incentives such as special economic zones in Poland, resident permits in exchange for given amount of investment (in Hungary), privatization opportunities, etc., but also good political relations between host country and China (example Hungary's good relations and very high level of Chinese FDI when compared with other CEECs; while it is said that Liu Gong's acquisition of HSW might have been delayed because of COVEC's problems with building part of Polish highway).

References

Buckley, P.J., Clegg, J.L., Cross, A.R., Liu Xin, Voss, H. & Zheng, P. (2007). The determinants of Chinese outward foreign direct investment. *Journal of International Business Studies, 38*, 499–518.

CIEGA (2007). *Investing in Europe. A hands-on guide*. Retrieved from: http://www.e-pages.dk/southdenmark/2/72 (accessed: 4/11/2013).

Clegg, J. & Voss, H. (2012). *Chinese Overseas Direct Investment in the European Union*. ECRAN. Retrieved from: http://eeas.europa.eu/china/docs/division_ecran/ecran_chinese_investment_in_the_european_union_jeremy_clegg_and_hinrich_voss_en.pdf (accessed: 4/11/2013).

Chiappini, R. (2014). Institutional determinants of Japanese outward FDI in the manufacturing industry. GREDEG Working Papers Series, No. 2014–11. Retrieved from: http://www.gredeg.cnrs.fr/working-papers/GREDEG-WP-2014-11.pdf (accessed: 21/05/2015).

Dunning, J. (1992). *Multinational Enterprises and the Global Economy*. Cambridge, UK: Addison-Wesley Publishers Ltd.

Dunning, J. (1998). Location and the multinational enterprise: A neglected factor? *Journal of International Business Studies, 29*(1), 45–66.

Dunning, J.H. & Lundan, S.M. (2008). Institutions and the OLI paradigm of the multinational enterprise. *Asia Pacific Journal of Management, 25*, 573–593.

Éltető, A. & Szunomár, Á. (2015). *Ties of Visegrád countries with East Asia – trade and investment*. Working Paper, No. 215, Institute of World Economics – MTA KRTK. Retrieved from: http://vki.hu/files/download_909.html (accessed: 17/09/2015).

Fürst, R. & Pleschová, G. (2010). Czech and Slovak relations with China: contenders for China's favour. *Europe-Asia Studies, 62*(8), 1363–1381.

Guidote, M.B. (2008). *A Case Study on the Car Industry of the Czech Republic. Tracing FDI Trends in Central and Eastern Europe after the 1990s*. Retrieved from: http://www.euroculture.upol.cz/ (accessed: 19/09/2014).

ICEG (2012). *V4 Trade and FDI Observer. Panorama of the Automotive Industry*. October.

Ikemoto, S. (2007). *Globalization and Japanese Investment in the Czech Republic*. Retrieved from: http://www.eco.nihon-u.ac.jp/center/economic/publication/journal/pdf/37/37ikemoto.pdf (accessed: 19/05/2015).

Jacoby, W. (2014). Different cases, different faces: Chinese investment in Central and Eastern Europe. *Asia Europe Journal, 12,* 199–214.

Janicki, H.P. & Wunnava, P.V. (2004). Determinants of foreign direct investment: empirical evidence from EU accession candidates. *Applied Economics, 36,* 505–509.

Kawai, N. (2006). The Nature of Japanese Foreign Direct Investment in Eastern Central Europe. *Japan aktuell, 5.* Retrieved from: http://www.giga-hamburg.de/openaccess/japanaktuell/2006_5/giga_jaa_2006_5_kawai.pdf (accessed: 15/08/2013).

KPMG (2014). *Poland's Position as a Business Partner for Japan.* Retrieved from: http://www.kpmg.com/PL/pl/IssuesAndInsights/ArticlesPublications/Documents/2014/Raport-KPMG-Polands-Position-as-a-Business-Partner-for-Japan-2014-online.pdf (accessed: 19/05/2015).

Leitao, N.C. & Faustino, H.C. (2010). Portuguese Foreign Direct Investments Inflows: An Empirical Investigation. *International Research Journal of Finance and Economics, 38,* 190–197.

Mathews, J. (2006). Dragon Multinationals: new players in 21st century globalization. *Asia Pacific Journal of Management, 23*(1), 5–27.

McCaleb, A. & Szunomár, Á. (2013). *Chinese FDI in Central and Eastern Europe: institutional perspective.* Paper presented at the 39th European International Business Academy, 12–14 December, Bremen, Germany.

Meyer, K.E. & Nguyen, H.V. (2005). Foreign investment strategies and sub-national institutions in emerging markets: Evidence from Vietnam. *Journal of Management Studies, 42*(1), 63–93.

Morck, R., Yeung, B., Zhao Minyuan (2008). Perspectives on China's outward foreign direct investment. *Journal of International Business Studies, 39,* 337–350.

North, D. (1990). *Institutions, Institutional Change and Economic Performance.* Cambridge: Cambridge University Press.

Resmini, L. (2005). FDI, Industry Location and Regional Development in New Member States and Candidate Countries: A Policy Perspective, Workpackage No 4, *The Impact of European Integration and Enlargement on Regional Structural Change and Cohesion,* EURECO, 5th Framework Programme, European Commission.

Richter, J. (2014). *South Koreans step up investments in Czech Republic.* Retrieved from: http://radio.cz/en/section/marketplace/south-koreans-step-up-investments-in-czech-republic (accessed: 19/05/2015).

Rosen, D.H. & Hanemann, T. (2013). China's direct investment in advanced economies: the cases of Europe and the United States. *China Economist, 8*(5), 65–79.

Szczudlik-Tatar, J. & Mejsnner, P. (2014). *Stosunki Polska–Korea Południowa: nowe ścieżki współpracy* (Poland-South Korea Relations: New patos of cooperation). Retrieved from: https://www.pism.pl/files/?id_plik=17123 (accessed: 18/05/2015).

Tihanyi, L., Devinney, T.M. & Pedersen, T. (2012). *Institutional Theory in International Business and Management.* Emerald Group Publishing, pp. 481.

Walewska, D. (2014). *Polska znów przegrała z Czechami*. Retrieved from: http://www.ekonomia.rp.pl/artykul/1128823.html (accessed: 23/05/2015).

Witt, M.A. & Lewin, A.Y. (2007). Outward foreign direct investment as escape response to home country institutional constraints. *Journal of International Business Studies, 38*, 579–594.

Woon Lim Jia (2003). Asian FDI in Central and Eastern Europe and its impact on the host countries. *Asia Europe Journal, 1*, 349–369.

Anna H. Jankowiak

Partnership through Investment – Chinese Foreign Direct Investment in CEE Countries

Introduction

China's accession to the World Trade Organization (WTO) in 2001 was the impetus for the creation of a new economic power and the search for new directions in foreign economic policy of this country. Simultaneously, the change of political and economic conditions in the global economy in the 21st century, and especially the outburst of the global economic crisis 2007/2008+, contributed to the increase in interest from the Chinese central authorities to energize diplomatic relations and the development of economic cooperation with the countries of Central and Eastern Europe (CEE). During his visit in Warsaw in April 2012, at the Economic Forum 'Poland – Eastern Europe – China', the then Chinese Premier Wen Jiabao, emphasized the growing importance of multi-faceted and long-term cooperative and financial relations with sixteen countries in CEE, as a source of potential economic benefits for all parties involved.

Foreign economic policy of China, due to the economic slowdown in the G3 countries, will concentrate on actively seeking partners in the markets of developing countries, including Central and Eastern Europe. What is worth mentioning, is that the multi-faceted efforts to establish contacts with developing countries from different regions of the world is evident in China's economic strategy since the beginning of the 21st century. This is reflected in rising of Chinese investment turnover with those countries. It should also be noted, that the Chinese people perceive Central Europe as a separate region, which is not a part of the German or Russian sphere of influence. This trend should be used in building relations with Beijing. It is a fact that China prefers the bilateral relations activities, rather than multilateral, and it should be taken into account (Clegg & Voss, 2012, p. 11).

The aim of the article is to present the involvement of China in the CEE region through their foreign direct investment. On the one hand, Prime Minister Wen Jiabao's visit and the strategy of cooperation with the Central European region presented by him, on the other hand, the increasing importance of the region, contributed to the exploration of this very issue in the article. In addition, the article attempts to identify future directions of cooperation between CEE and China, which directly affects foreign economic policy currently pursued by the Chinese authorities. The paper initially presents the inflow of Chinese capital in the form of FDI to the CEE countries. Analysis of the directions of investment relations in China been carried out and particular attention is paid to the relationship with the CEE countries. This article is based on a descriptive method and the analysis and comparison of secondary sources mainly related to the inflow of Chinese foreign investments to the countries of the CEE region. The analysis covered the available Polish and foreign literature dealing with topics related to the investments attractiveness of the market and the individual countries of the CEE region.

1. Foreign Direct Investment – theoretical background

Pursuant to the definition of the transnational corporation, in order to consider a company a TNC, it must have affiliates or branches in other countries. They are established by making foreign direct investments (FDI), i.e. by transferring the capital outside the territory of their native country. Transnational corporations and foreign direct investments are two inseparably intertwined concepts, but not perfect synonyms. Nowakowski defines FDI as "investments that establish long-lasting relationship, which manifests in permanent interest of the entity seated in specific geographical area (direct investor) in an entity seated in the economy other than the economy of the investor" (Nowakowski, 2000, p. 109). According to S.D. Cohen, FDI is a financial process associated with operating and controlling income-generating facility in at least one country outside the country of origin (Cohen, 2007, p. 36). According to the definition of OECD, foreign direct investment is a type of investment aimed at holding a long-term control by a resident entity in one economy (foreign direct investor) in an enterprise resident in an economy other than the economy of the foreign direct investor (FDI enterprise). The investor is to gain permanent benefits due to long-lasting influence on the management of the FDI enterprise. The minimum number of shares held in a given enterprise is 10%; however, the influence on management, with such level of shares, may be exerted only if the other shares are highly dispersed (OECD, 2008, p. 234).

The definition of FDI comprises both primary capital transaction between the direct investor and the FDI enterprise (either directly or through other related enterprises) and later the flows of FDI. FDI has three components:

- equity capital is the foreign direct investor's purchase of shares of an enterprise in a country other than its own country,
- reinvested earnings that are not transferred by the investor outside the country of investment location,
- intra-company loans or intra-company debt in the form of short- or long-term borrowing and lending of funds between direct investors (parent enterprises) and affiliate enterprises (World Investment Report, 2008, p. 249).

In order to make foreign direct investment by an enterprise, three basic conditions must exist, which gave the basis for Duning's formulation of the eclectic theory of foreign direct investment. He joined the theory of monopolistic advantage (that explains why the investments are made outside the territory of the country of origin but does not indicate why these investments are located on specific markets), location theory (that explains why FDI is made on specific markets without giving the reason why they are made) with the theory of internalization (that explains the mechanisms of using benefits by the enterprise from making the foreign investment) (Rymarczyk, 2014, pp. 47–48). OLI paradigm was made on this basis (OLI meaning ownership, localization, internalization). An enterprise will transfer capital – in the form of foreign direct investment – under the following conditions:

- a company must display specific advantages that result from the resources and abilities it has, which make the company competitive on the international market,
- a company should use the competitive advantage it has gained by establishing its own structures on foreign markets, not to transfer it by means of selling (e.g. licences),
- a company should join its own advantages with the advantages of the location market, meaning it should effectively use the advantages of given location in order to maximize its own profit (Nowakowski, 2000, p. 79).

According to the above-specified paradigm, making a foreign direct investment at a given moment should be conditioned by the configuration of the three forces specified above. Enterprises will enjoy various advantages that result from the specific character of their operations, the country of their origin and the country of the target investment (Dunning, 2001, p. 176). The first two factors closely depend upon the capabilities and resources of the company, the third factor decides about the direction of transferring the capital in the form of FDI.

2. Chinese FDI and ODI in the world

China was for many years a target market for foreign investors. The stream of foreign capital inflows in the form of FDI was always impressive, and China was ranked at the forefront. Investors sought cheaper labour to manufacture their goods, and the Chinese economy offered both lower labour costs and its vast resources. Chinese investors, however, were not active on the international scene. In 2005, inflow of investment from abroad was nearly five times greater than the outflow of Chinese capital to other countries. With the development of the country and due to changes in the international market, Chinese companies and corporations have been increasingly active in the global economy. Now we can observe the increased activity of Chinese investors in most national economies. Investment activity abroad has led to a situation, in which outward foreign direct investment (ODI) exceeded the foreign investment flowing into China. In 2013, Chinese ODI exceeded 108 billion of USD, and increased by 10% to 120 billion USD in 2014 (Graph 1). For the first time in the history of China, the Chinese invested more capital in the form of a foreign investment, making China a net capital exporter.

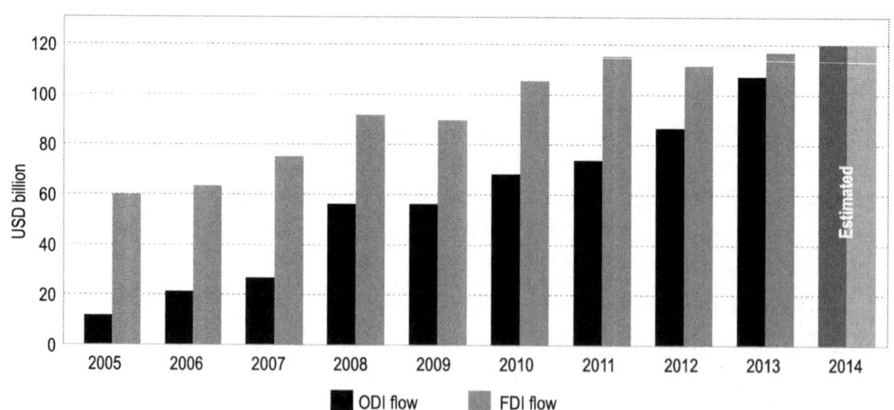

Graph 1: Value of China's ODI and FDI flow, 2005–2014 in billions of USD
Source: *China Outlook 2015*, KPMG's Global China Practice, KPMG International Cooperative, 2015, p. 10.

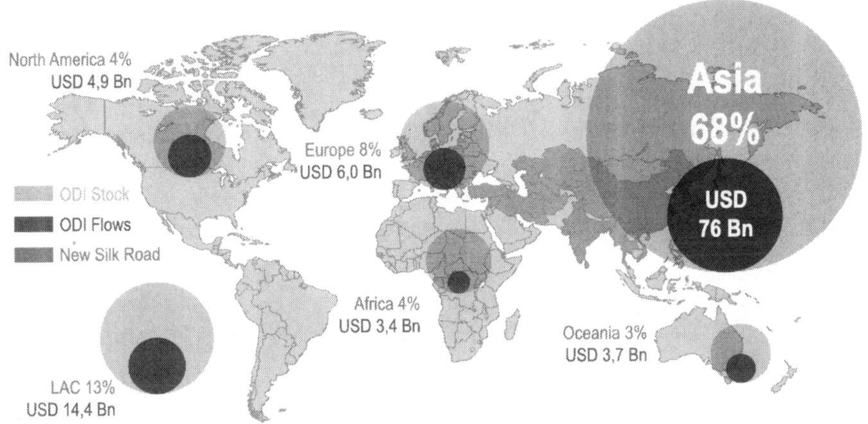

Graph 2: Continental distribution of Chinese ODI stock in 2013
Source: Ministry of Commerce of the People's Republic of China (MOFCOM), Bruegel, http://brue-gel.org/2015/06/chinas-outward-foreign-direct-investment/ (accessed: 20/09/2015).

As global players, the Chinese investors are active mostly in Asia, where 68% of all Chinese FDI are located (Graph 2). The most popular destination is Hong Kong. 13% out of the 32% that is being invested outside Asian countries are going to Latin America, 8% to Europe, 4% each to North America and Africa, and 3% to Oceania.

For many years, Chinese corporations were looking for the investment opportunities in the developing countries. The main goal was to seek natural resources. In the year 2010, the top countries attracting Chinese overseas M&A were Brazil, Canada, Argentina, US, Australia, Israel, the Nederlands, Sweden, Guinea and the UK. The situation has changed, and at present, Chinese investors are active in the well developed countries, where they can find access to new technologies, advanced IT products or distribution networks. In the year 2014, the most popular countries for Chinese M&A were the US, Peru, the UK, Australia, France, Italy, Singapore, Portugal, Canada, and the Nederlands (China Outlook, 2015, p. 12). The new global Chinese investor is searching for advantages that can improve the company's competitiveness on the international market.

The change can be seen not only in the level of growth of destination countries for Chinese investments, but also in the preferred sectors. In 2010, Chinese overseas M&A (see Graph 3) were made in the oil and gas sector, then the mining and automotive industry. In 2014, the most popular sector was computers and electronics, then mining, and the real estate as the third sector (ibid., p. 11). The evolution in Chinese ODI is very visible. First, the Chinese companies are active on a very big scale. They haven't been so open for the foreign direct investment before, but

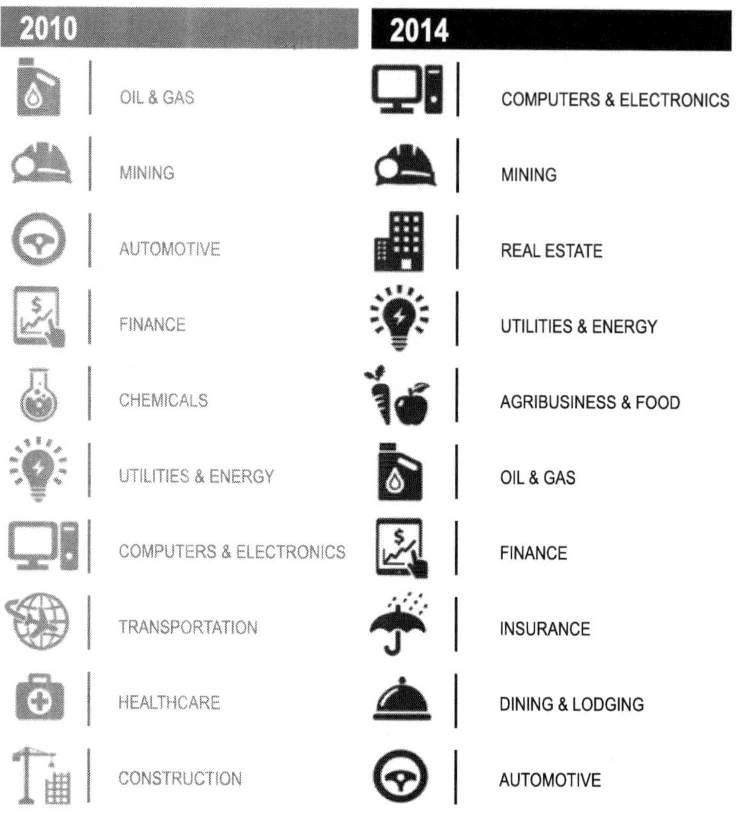

Graph 3: Top industry sectors attracting Chinese overseas M&A investment, by deal value
Source: *China Outlook 2015*, KPMG's Global China Practice, KPMG International Cooperative, 2015, p. 11.

the domestic situation in China and the downturn in the world economy allowed them to go global. Secondly, they invest in countries more developed than they used to before. Thirdly, the sectoral structure is diverse. The less technologically advanced areas had given way to more complicated goods.

3. Chinese FDI in Europe and the CEE countries included

As it was mentioned above, Europe is not the most common and important destination of the Chinese foreign direct investment. It must be noted, that the volume of China's FDI in Europe grows at a steady rate. In

2005, Chinese investment in Europe reached the value of 189.54 millions USD (*Statistical...*, 2010, p. 100) and in 2010, it was over 5 billion USD (see the Graph 4). In the years 2005–2010, total value of China's FDI in the region increased over 16 times, and more than doubled in the years 2009–2010. 2011 was a very good year for Chinese investors in Europe, as they invested 3 times more than in the previous year. It is estimated that in 2014, the Chinese investments in Europe will increase to the level of 25 billion USD. It can be a result of new investment regulations adopted by the Chinese authorities. According to the law, only the high value investments (over 1 billion USD) and the investments in the sensitive areas and sectors, require the approval. It can be the beginning of the process of going global on a big scale for Chinese investors.

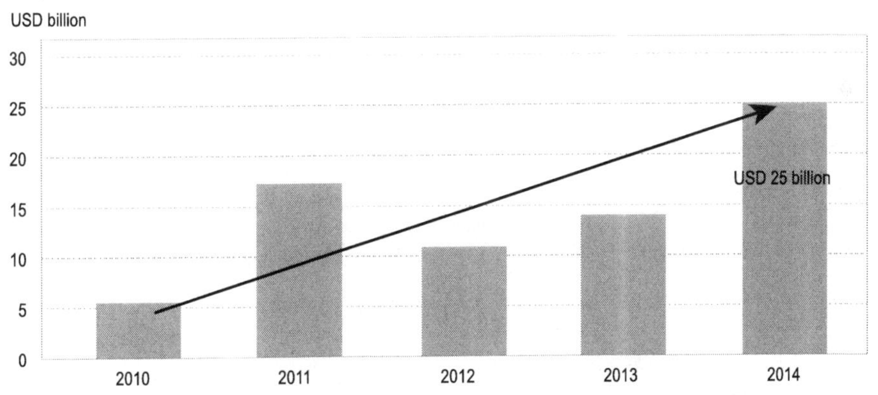

Graph 4: China's FDI to Europe 2010–2014
Source: *Riding the Silk Road: China sees outbound investment boom. Outlook for China's outward foreign direct investment*, EY Knowledge, March 2015, p. 15.

Out of the EU-10 countries, the largest FDI flow was observed in the United Kingdom, Germany and France, so the largest EU economies are at the same time the biggest recipients of Chinese capital in the form of FDI. In the period from 2000 to 2014, the majority of cumulative Chinese investments went to the three countries mentioned above (over 50%) (Hanemann & Huotari, 2015, p. 14) (see Graph 5). The bilateral relationship between China and Germany is very strong, not only in the scale of investments, but also in the terms of the trade exchange. The German economy is getting stronger after the crisis of 2008+, so the economic relations with China are more efficient. Chinese foreign direct investments are seen not only in Germany, but also in other Western European countries.

In 2005, Chinese companies made 12 M&A transactions in Europe (5 in Germany). In 2007, right before the economic crisis, the number

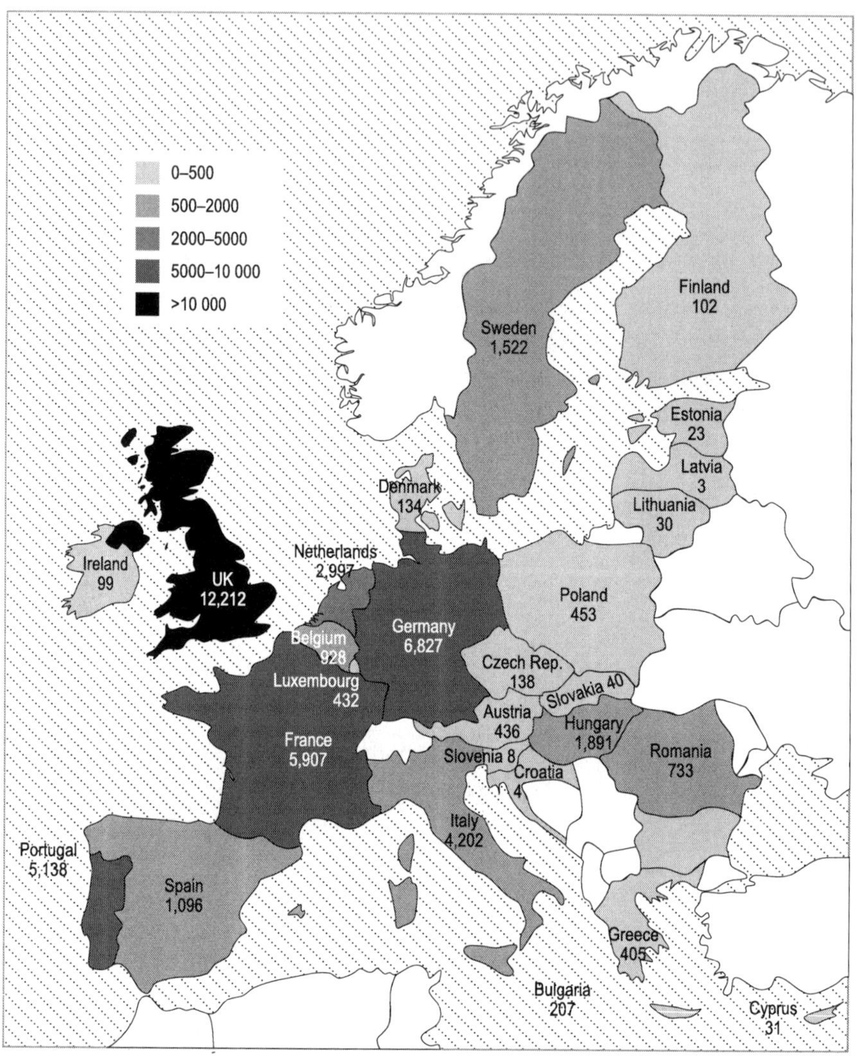

Graph 5: Chinese FDI in the EU-28 in 2000–2014 (Greenfield and M&A transactions by geographic location; value of cumulative investment in million EUR)
Source: T. Hanemann, M. Huotari, *Chinese FDI in Europe and Germany Preparing for a New Era of Chinese Capital*, Mercator Institute for China Studies and Rhodium Group, June 2015, p. 15.

of transactions reached 15 (only 2 were made in Germany). Chinese ODI in Europe increased over 300% over the years 2010–2014. In 2014 Chinese corporations were responsible for 116 M&A projects in Europe. 21 projects were made in Germany (see Graph 6), 14 were in France and 13 in the UK (*Riding...*, 2015, pp. 15–16). Analysis of aggregated value of China's foreign direct investment in Europe shows the dominant position of the EU-10, so Chinese investors fulfil the strategy to invest in the well developed countries. In 2005, according to data published by the Ministry of Commerce of the People's Republic of China, as much as 97% of the FDI flow was directed to the EU-10 countries. Similar trend was observed in 2007 (97%), and 2010 (93%) (*Statistical...*, 2010, p. 100).

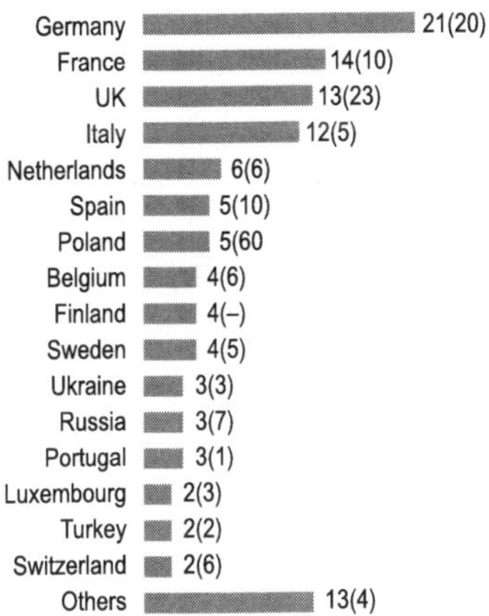

Graph 6: Volume of Chinese M&A transactions in Europe in 2014 (2013)
Source: *Riding the Silk Road: China sees outbound investment boom. Outlook for China's outward foreign direct investment*, EY Knowledge, March 2015, p. 16.

At present, the CEE region is not a target of major foreign direct investment for China. Only 8% of Chinese investments were located in the CEE countries between 2000–2014 (Hanemann & Huotari, 2015, p. 14). Chinese investors display marked preference for countries of Western Europe. While Chinese businesses are not a major investor group for the new member states, the volume of Chinese investment in the CEE region grows steadily. At the beginning of Chinese investment expansion to Europe, the target countries were from Western Europe. Now, the situation is changing, and more and more investments are being made in Central Europe and some in Eastern Europe.

This trend is particularly strong in Hungary, Poland, and the Czech Republic (Table 1). In 2010, those three countries received a joint 92,5% of total China's FDI directed to the new EU member states (Bilateral, 2014). In 2012 (the latest available data published by UNCTAD), the situation was different, because of the negative flow to Poland. The analysis of the Chinese FDI flow to Hungary and Poland is extremely interesting. Based on data presented in Table 1, it can be noticed that those two countries are competing with each other for Chinese investments. In one year (e.g. 2010), Hungary is more popular amongst Chinese investors and the

Table 1: Chinese FDI flows to the CEE countries in 2008–2012 (millions of USD)

	2008	2009	2010	2011	2012
Bulgaria	3	2	7	68	20
Czech Republic	−19.2	−26.6	12.3	−118.0	76.8
Estonia	4.1	6.4	−2.6	2.6	0.3
Hungary	−105.0	−22.2	136.4	−170.7	141.2
Latvia	-1	−	1	−	1
Lithuania	−	−	−	1	2
Poland	139.6	−191.7	0.4	101.2	−148.4
Romania	−4	−	-9	-3	-3
Slovak Republic	2.1	−20.8	15.9	34.8	−9.9
Slovenia	0.3	0.0	−0.3	−0.2	0.3

Source: author's own work based on *Bilateral FDI Statistics*, The Division on Investment and Enterprise of UNCTAD, Geneva 2014, http://unctad.org/en/Pages/DIAE/FDI%20Statistics/FDI-Statistics-Bilateral.aspx (accessed: 20/09/2015).

next year (e.g. 2011), Poland receives more capital from FDI. That shows that Poland and Hungary are the strongest partners for Chinese investors in Central and Eastern Europe.

In addition to the two aforementioned countries, also Bulgaria, Romania and the Slovak Republic are final destinations for Chinese invest-

Table 2: Chinese FDI stock to the CEE countries in 2008–2012 (millions of USD)

	2008	2009	2010	2011	2012
Bulgaria	9	14	19	82	103
Czech Republic	75.8	53.8	59.4	−17.2	−5.2
Estonia	0.3	12.3	7.0	9.2	12.1
Hungary	41.6	10.7	131.8	−32.3	86.2
Latvia	−	−	1	−	1
Lithuania	3	3	3	2	3
Poland	336.1	188.7	303.7	413.7	288.1
Romania	82	49	69	61	91
Slovak Republic	36.0	21.6	26.7	59.6	62.1
Slovenia	0.2	0.4	0.1	−0.1	0.2

Source: author's own work based on *Bilateral FDI Statistics*, The Division on Investment and Enterprise of UNCTAD, Geneva 2014, http://unctad.org/en/Pages/DIAE/FDI%20Statistics/FDI-Statistics-Bilateral.aspx (accessed: 20/09/2015).

ments. In 2012 (see Table 2), Bulgaria was the second country in CEE if we analyse the Chinese FDI stock (Poland was the first). Over 103 million USD were invested in this country, and every year, the FDI stock is increasing progressively. The third country was Romania (91 million USD) and the fourth was Hungary (86.2 million USD).

The CEE countries are a desirable location for the manufacturing of textiles, leather goods and luggage, television sets, communication equipment, computers and other electronic equipment (especially Poland and Romania), as well as electrical machinery and equipment (here, the target countries are the Czech Republic, Hungary, Poland). Chinese FDI in the CEE countries can be encouraging trade-substituting and import barrier-avoiding investments in the lower-cost EU countries. Some of the investments are focused on the natural resources, which results from the country specific, natural factors (e.g. forestry in Poland and the Czech Republic as well as mining in Poland). The number of attractive sectors identified in the CEE countries for Chinese investments is quite impressive. In Romania, 8 sectors are consider to be attractive, 7 in Poland, 6 in Hungary, 5 in Estonia, 4 in Bulgaria, 3 in Slovenia, 2 in Slovakia, 1 in Lithuania. None of the sectors in Latvia are attractive for Chinese investors (Clegg & Voss, 2012, pp. 65–66).

4. Chinese FDI in CEE – Partnership through investment

Directions of economic cooperation between China and the countries of Central and Eastern Europe (CEE) were presented by the prime minister Wen Jiabao, in his speech made on April 26 2012 in Warsaw at the Economic Forum "Poland – Central Europe – China". The main directions of this policy were outlined in 12 points, presented below[1]:

1. Setting up a China-Central and Eastern European Countries' Cooperation Secretariat, situated at the Chinese Ministry of Foreign Affairs. The Secretariat will be in charge of communication and coordination of all the matters of economic cooperation, preparation of governmental meetings and business forums, as well as implementation of the tasks agreed upon during those meetings. The 16 countries of the CEE, on voluntary principle, will set up an institution and a co-ordinator as their representatives in the Secretariat's proceedings.

2. Chinese government will set up a special credit line of 10 billion USD, partly in the form of subsidized loans to facilitate the bilateral co-

---

[1] Main topics of PM Wen Jiabao's speech presented at the International Economic Forum "Poland – Central Europe – China" in Warsaw, April 26, 2012.

operation in the IT industry, infrastructure construction and green economy. The 16 countries of the CEE region may submit their project applications to the National Development Bank of China, Export and Import Bank of China, Industrial and Commercial Bank of China, Construction Bank of China, Bank of China or China CITIC Bank.

3. A special fund for investment cooperation between China and the CEE countries will be set up, with 500 billion USD directed to the fund in the first phase of the project.

4. China will send assignments to promote trade and investment in the CEE region and will initiate active measures to form bilateral economic and trade cooperation. China intends to cooperate with CEE in order to boost the volume of bilateral trade to 100 billion USD by the year 2015.

5. In the light of practical needs of the CEE countries, China will actively promote cooperation with CEE among its local business, with the intent of setting up special economic zones in each of the CEE countries within the next five years, or participating in the existing SEZ and technological parks in the region.

6. China is open to active pursuance of financial cooperation with the CEE countries, in the form of: currency swaps, settling cross-border trade in local currencies, and setting up local branches of banks on principle of mutuality, to facilitate flexibility in bilateral cooperation.

7. An advisory board will be set up to discuss the potential of establishing a direct transportation route between China and CEE. Chinese Ministry of Trade (as a co-ordinator) and the 16 countries of the CEE region (voluntarily) will explore the possibility of support for local road networks or construction of a model railroad network in joint venture form, or using other forms of cooperation.

8. China postulates setting up a forum of cultural cooperation with the CEE countries in China in 2013, and to promote regular meetings of governmental and expert panels to propagate bilateral exchange on the cultural level, in the form of arts and culture festivals and other cultural activities.

9. Chinese government declares their intention to grant 5 thousand scholarships to young students from the CEE countries in the next 5 years, as well as their support for Confucius Institutes and a 'Confucius class' program in those countries. Within the next 5 years, Chinese government will invite 1 thousand students to study Chinese language at the Chinese universities. Actions will be taken to support university exchange programs and bilateral research programs. One thousand Chinese students and researchers will be sent to the CEE countries within the next 5 years. In 2013, Chinese Ministry of Educa-

tion plans to host an international panel to discuss the issues involved in the international dialogue in education with the CEE countries.

10. China postulates setting up an association to promote tourism in China and the CEE countries, to be coordinated by China Tourism Administration. The postulated body will include representatives of civil aviation authorities, travel agencies and aviation companies from all parties involved. The postulated alliance will serve the purpose of promoting business relations and tourism, as well as examining the potential of increasing direct air links between China and the 16 countries of the CEE region. China Tourism Administration has already been involved in promotion of tourist products of both China and the CEE countries at the Chinese International Travel Fair in Shanghai in autumn 2012.

11. Setting up a research fund to promote studies of bilateral relations between China and the CEE. China declares its intention to direct 2 million CNY[2] annually, to support academic exchange between research institutes and scientists of both parties.

12. China plans to organize the international summit of political leaders from China and CEE; representatives of young generation of political activists from both parties will be invited, with the intention to promote understanding and friendship (Skulska, Bobowski, Jankowiak & Skulski, 2014, pp. 149–174).

Based on the arguments mentioned above, it is very clear that the CEE countries are important for Chinese government and the investors as well. The CEE countries have the potential and resources, but on the other hand, costs of labour and capital are lower than in the countries of Western Europe. That can be the key argument for Chinese investors looking for an alternative place for FDI. Chinese companies are active on the European market by international trade. The export to Europe and import from Europe are significant parts of Chinese trade relationship with the world. The next steep after the bilateral trade could be in a form of foreign direct investment, which can be beneficial for both parties. In a globalized world, trade itself is not enough for a developing company, so the natural way of progress is a capital transfer in the form of FDI. Investments straighten bonds between companies and countries. By the increasing number of Chinese FDI in the CEE region, the links and presence of Chinese companies are expressly visible. That is needed, because Chinese companies are not well recognised not only in the CEE countries, but also in western part of Europe. A study carried out on a group of students of economics showed that none of the respondents could name

---

[2] Based on 2011 average yuan exchange rate, this corresponds to ca. 310 thousand USD.

a single Chinese company that is located in their country, or are ranked as one of the biggest companies in the global economy. During the same research, students didn't have any problem with American or Japanese companies.[3] This simple research shows that the recognisability of Chinese companies is lower in comparison to other countries. The Chinese investments can change the perception of Chinese companies in Europe. The image of China can be improved by effective FDIs.

FDI made by Chinese companies may affect the bilateral partnership between China and the CEE countries. The cooperation made by trade at the beginning, , is getting stronger when the investor is actively present in the host country. The activities and daily cooperation with domestic companies can built a strong network, not only between companies, but countries as well.

Chinese FDI in the CEE countries can bring a lot of benefits for the bilateral partnership. For European countries it can be:
1. Meeting funding needed in the host nation.
2. Creating employment in the host nation.
3. Increasing the value of host nations' assets.
4. Increasing productivity in the host nation.
5. Expanding market share for host country firms.
   China and its investors can achieve following profits:
1. Demonstrating China's economic power.
2. Obtaining advanced European technology.
3. Diversifying foreign exchange reserves and assets.
4. Reducing EU dissatisfaction over the trade imbalance (Jiang, 2014, pp. 7–9).

5. Conclusions

Chinese FDIs are expected to grow in the coming years. According to the data provided by MOFCOM (Statistical, 2010, p. 79), Chinese FDI are located in 178 countries globally. It is worth mentioning that Chinese investors are active in the regions not very popular amongst other investors, where the risk is higher than in any other countries, like Libya, Myanmar or Sudan.

The strong connection between Europe and China will become strategically important, especially in the context of the New Silk Road. The new

---

[3] Author's own research carried out on a group of 100 students of economics made in January 2015. Students were asked the question: Can you name any Chinese/American/Japanese companies located in Poland or ranked in any world's ranking (e.g. Fortune Global 500)?

initiative created by Chinese government in 2015 called "One Belt, One Road" will open the possibilities for Chinese investors to go global. The directions of Chinese investments in Europe will change. That is a very good scenario for the countries from Central and Eastern Europe. Foreign direct investment is one of the most important areas of potential development in bilateral relations. Investment relations between China and the CEE countries are expected to develop, based on the strategy aimed at this region, announced by the Chinese central authorities. Meanwhile, the mutual commitment of the CEE countries and China in the form of a capital cooperation does not reflect the current opportunities, despite the fact that the three rapidly developing countries in the CEE group i.e. Poland, alongside Hungary and Romania are treated by the Chinese government as the three most important locations for foreign direct investment in this part of the world.

There are a lot of obstacles in the way of the partnership between China and CEE. They are seen mostly in the cultural differences, various political view and social standards. The problem mentioned above can be a barrier for FDI or just one of the elements, that are needed to be taken under consideration in the decision making process. The understanding of Chinese perception of making business with the CEE countries is critical for the future size and shape of the investment cooperation. Chinese investors need to be seen as partners, rather than competitors or the enemy. Europe and the CEE countries got used to the large scale of trade with China (export and import flow) and now, we need to work on the method on how to deal with the investors from China. The wise cooperation can be beneficial for both sides. The partnership through investments is potentially attainable. The CEE countries were neglected by Chinese companies for many years and for many reasons (e.g. unfriendly environment (*World Class...*, 2010), lack of natural resources or less developed IT technologies). As it was showed in data presented above, the situation is changing, and the bilateral relationship is getting stronger, because of the FDIs.

References

Bilateral FDI Statistics (2014). Geneva: The Division on Investment and Enterprise of UNCTAD. Retrieved from: http://unctad.org/en/Pages/DIAE/FDI%20Statistics/FDI-Statistics-Bilateral.aspx (accessed: 20/09/2015).

China Outlook 2015 (2015). KPMG's Global China Practice. KPMG International Cooperative.

Clegg, J. & Voss, H. (2012). *Chinese Overseas Direct Investment in the European Union*. London: Europe China Research and Advice Network.

Cohen, S.D. (2007). *Multinational Corporations and Foreign Direct Investment. Avoiding Simplicity, Embracing Complexity*. Oxford: Oxford University Press.

Dunning, J.H. (2001). The Eclectic (OLI) Paradigm of international production: past, present and future. *International Journal of the Economics of Business*, *8*(2).

Hanemann, T. & Huotari, M. (2015). *Chinese FDI in Europe and Germany Preparing for a New Era of Chinese Capital*. Mercator Institute for China Studies and Rhodium Group.

Jiang, S. (2014) *Chinese Investment in the EU*. Beijing: Working Paper Series on European Studies Institute of European Studies Chinese Academy of Social Sciences Vol. 8, No. 1.

Ministry of Commerce of the People's Republic of China (MOFCOM), Bruegel. Retrieved from: http://bruegel.org/2015/06/chinas-outward-foreign-direct-investment/ (accessed: 20/09/2015).

Nowakowski, M.K. (2000). *Biznes międzynarodowy – obszary decyzji strategicznych* (*International Business – Areas of Strategic Decisions*). Warszawa: Wydawnictwo Key Text.

OECD Benchmark Definition of Foreign Direct Investment (2008). OECD.

Riding the Silk Road: China sees outbound investment boom. Outlook for China's outward foreign direct investment (2015). EY Knowledge.

Rymarczyk, J. (2004). *Internacjonalizacja i globalizacja przedsiębiorstwa* (*Internationalisation and Globalisation of an Enterprise*). Warszawa: Polskie Wydawnictwo Ekonomiczne.

Skulska, B., Bobowski, S., Jankowiak, A., Skulski, P. (2014). *China's Trade Policy Towards Central And Eastern Europe In The 21st Century, Example Of Poland*. Folia Oeconomica Stetinensia. Volume 14, Issue 1. Szczecin: Wydwnictwo Uniwersytetu Szczecińskiego.

Statistical Bulletin of China's Outward Foreign Direct Investment (2010). Ministry of Commerce People's Republic of China.

World Class Aspirations – The perception and reality of China outbound investments (2010). KPMG. Hong Kong.

World Investment Report 2008. Transnational Corporations and the Infrastructure Challenge (2008). New York and Geneva: UNCTAD.

Luciano Segreto, Magdalena Popowska

Chinese Foreign Direct Investments in Europe. The Polish Case

Foreign Direct Investment (FDI) has been one of the most discussed topics in the economic globalization. In effect, Multi-National Corporations (MNCs) consider FDI as an important means to reform their production activities across the borders, maintaining the corporate strategies while using the competitive advantages of the host country. The inflow of FDI in the host country has seen as a significant opportunity to integrate their economies into the global market, and to promote their economic development. Host country's government, in order to maximize FDI's benefits, employs a variety of policies and measures. Nowadays, China becomes one of the biggest players in this FDI global game.

This paper aims to present an updated vision of Chinese foreign investments in Europe, focusing particularly on Poland. The internationalization process of Chinese companies, which is perceived as the consequence of the greatest economic phenomenon that can be described as the progressive integration of China in the global economy, occurred in the last decades. It has been worth noticing how nowadays, enterprises compete among them through international strategies, not only on a trade relation basis, but also increasingly through overseas foreign direct investment (FDI). The framework in which the Chinese enterprising is evolving is taking enormous proportions, and it is expanding throughout the global market, seeking new opportunities and resources. Hence, seeking more favourable conditions than those found within their own national borders.

Short historical background

The inflow of FDI in China over the past 20 years, has significantly influenced its economic development. Since the opening-up to the global economy, China became one of the most important host countries for FDI flows (Wei & Liu, 2011). Therefore, the foreign companies established in the Mainland did not only provide financial capital, but also human capital such as management expertise and new technologies. In addition, FDI have helped to integrate the country into the regional and the global manufacturing and sales process, which has been determinant in intensifying its export-driven economic growth. Accordingly, it is now widely recognized that foreign investment has contributed significantly in the Chinese process of modernization (Jiang, 2012).

Nowadays, the trend has changed; from China's impressive economic development, and after its accession to WTO in 2001, the Chinese government decided to adopt a policy aiming at encouraging Chinese outbound investments. Therefore, China is becoming one of the most important exporters of investment capital. The Ministry of Commerce announced that China's outbound FDI would exceed its inward FDI in a few years to come. This is explained by the fact that Chinese FDI outflows kept rising since 2004, notwithstanding the global financial crisis.

The first flux of Chinese FDI overseas markedly followed the government investment strategy; in fact, they were mainly directed towards developing countries in Asia, Africa, and Latin America, due to the abundance of natural resources necessary for Chinese industrial production. While the resource-seeking strategy continues to be fundamental in China's foreign investment policy, the second flux of Chinese investors targeted the industrialized economies, such as the US and the European Union, looking for their advanced technologies, management skills, and human capital or for their local distribution networks. With the global financial crisis, this phenomenon has been more intense and has raised several concerns among the researchers, policy makers and the public opinion. In the aftermath of the economic crisis of 2007, that afflicted the Euro zone; the European Union became one of the major recipient of Chinese outbound investment. At that time, many important and famous European firms have been acquired by Chinese investors, if not for that fact, a lot of these companies would have been bankrupted, bringing heavy consequences on the labour market.

Respectively, China's rising power today produces a combination of enthusiasm and concern, because its outbound FDI increased dramatically from zero in 1978 to a record 105.7 billion USD in 2011–2012. The reduction of barriers on outward FDI and the increasing encouragement by the Chinese government in promoting the global expansion of its multinational companies is an attempt to gain a major role in the international financial sector. This impressive expansion of the Chinese outbound investments in the European Union in the mist of the Euro zone's debt crisis, have induced fear about the possible threat of "China buying up Europe." This expression is just a step away from posing the question, whether China is "buying the world" (Nolan, 2012).

Since China's entry to the WTO till 2011, China received the largest FDI inflows compared to other developing or transition economies. However, in 2009, the global crisis caused China's FDI inflows fell to 95 billion USD; then it strongly recovered, reaching 115 billion USD in 2010, and it rose further to 124 billion USD in 2011.

In 2012, the foreign direct investment confidence index showed that China was maintaining its ranking at the first position. In fact, it is still the first recipient of FDI inflows worth 124 billion USD, well ahead the other developing countries such as Brazil, India and Russia (Davies, 2012, p. 1).

China's rise as a global direct investor

Over thirty years of openness has made the People's Republic of China one of the world's largest recipient nation to foreign direct investment (FDI). Foreign-funded enterprises have played a catalytic role in the processes of market-based economy, about half of China's foreign trade contributed by providing an enormous amount of foreign exchange reserves. These elements show just one side of China's "open door" policy.

The high level of inward FDI has cast a shadow over the growing levels of Chinese outward investment. The recent rapid expansion of Chinese overseas investment has captured an extensive attention; because this trend appeared particularly after the financial crisis of 2008, when the global FDI decreased, China's presence in the world remains very small compared to that of the developed economies (Salidijanova, 2011). However, considering China as a source of FDI, it has to be interpreted as an important step in the country's economic development, and as an evident element to indicate, that China will continue to strengthen its opportunity to invest overseas in the years to come. China's investments have developed not only in size, but also geographically, by following the government's economic commitments.

Even though China's overseas investments are still very small, its manufactures have been gaining importance by the virtue of new international capital source. In the light of the principal FDI determinants, such as market size, economic growth, availability of skills and good infrastructure as well as the presence of enabling regulatory framework, China attracts a big size of FDI. Therefore, thanks to this environment created since the beginning of the economic opening up, Chinese companies had the opportunity to become more competitive, and to gain the capacity to invest overseas (Buckley et al., 2007, pp. 499–518).

The central authority has created a complex structure with several governmental bodies to administrate FDI. The system regulates the details of several issues, as for example the examination and the approval process, it encourages specific types of projects, regulates the system of foreign exchange control, and the SOE assets management. As the government's approach to FDI changed, shifting from a tight and restrictive capital outflow, to encouraging Chinese manufactures to invest overseas, also the policy keeps changing following the government's strategy. Literature have outlined four stages explaining the historical development of China's FDI. Before the process of economic liberalization began in 1978, the Chinese economic policy was based on self-reliance and economic independence, because there was practically no outward investment, for the reason that the government was strongly against every form of FDI. A different attitude towards FDI was embraced, after the economic liberalization, when its importance was recognized. Consequently, China did not only welcome the capital, but also technology and foreign management experience, furthermore, it started to encourage Chinese investments abroad.

During the first stage, from 1979 to 1985, foreign trade and investment were under state's control. Therefore, solely state-owned trading corporations and local enterprises had the opportunity to undertake foreign investment, exclusively after the approval of the State Economic and Trade Commission (SETC). During this period, the foreign investment policy was not established, because the government was concentrated more on setting down policies to attract FDI into China rather than on encouraging Chinese FDI overseas. Nevertheless, state-owned enterprises were the first investors trying to enter into the international business framework, by taking advantage of their already existing business links, bestowed upon them by the central and local authorities (Voss et al., 2009, pp. 146–148).

In 1979, the State Council released a document announcing that overseas investment was recognized as one of the thirteen official policies for opening up the economy. Notwithstanding the efforts, the policy framework regulating Chinese overseas investments was incoherent, and, in addition, the State Council was in charge of approving every project. For instance, it approved the establishment of four SOEs specialized in overseas investments, which were expected to play a fundamental role helping manufactures in entering into the international market (OECD, 2008, pp. 81–82). However, the new SOEs introduced and approved by the government used to operate outside of the standard administrative framework. Moreover, the official statistics of the activities of the Ministry of Foreign Economic Relations and Trade (MOFERT), did not register their investments. Chinese FDI projects were strictly linked to the government's political strategy, rather than to the enterprise's business motivation; giving the reasons that the approval was based on its contribution to the Chinese economic and political influence onto the international system (Voss et al., 2009, pp. 148–149).

Subsequently, Chinese government decided to change its strategy, by giving more importance to trade-related issues, besides the political objectives, in order to develop new markets, increasing exports and obtaining new resources. However, the shift was very slow, because Chinese foreign investments were still politically oriented. Therefore, Chinese investments motives changed from seeking resources to the combination of resource-market, and seeking technology (Wu & Chen, 2001, pp. 1238–1241).

Until 1985, the enterprises having the permission to establish subsidiaries abroad were mainly interested in the following sectors: engineering, finance, insurance and consultancy. Just a few of Chinese manufacturers overseas were involved in the activities abroad. This trend changed around the mid-1980s. The first step in 1984 was the introduction of "The Notice about Principles and the Scope of Authority for Examination and Approval of Establishing Non-trading Enterprises in Foreign Countries, Hong Kong and Macau". The further step in 1985, was the approval of the "Interim Regulation on the Administrative Regulations on the Administrative Measures and Procedures of Examination and Approval of Establishing Non-trading Enterprises Abroad". These regulations brought further liberalization of the existing policies and authorized any legal-entity enterprises, including non-state-owned companies, to apply for the permission to invest abroad, it required a sufficient capital, an adequate technical and operational expertise and a suitable overseas partner (OECD, 2008, pp. 81–82).

Afterwards, in accordance with this liberalization, overseas investments turned to be diversified into new industries, such as metallurgy, minerals, petrochemicals and chemicals, electronic and light industry, transportation, finance, medicine, and tourism.

This policy framework constitutes the core of China's FDI administration, which is still in vigour notwithstanding several revisions. The liberalization led to a sharp rise of the Chinese outflow investment, increasing on a yearly basis, from 134 million USD to 850 million USD in 1988

(Kaartemo, 2007, pp. 7–9). It is evident that the rise was justified by the government's retightening of central control and suspension of the approval procedure.

The third phase, from 1992 to 1998, implied a sort of delocalization of the decision process. Local authorities, instead of the central one, sustained the big increase of overseas investments by local and provincial enterprises. Some of them were engaged in the real estate sector and in the stock market speculation in Hong Kong. Consequently, many of the subsidiaries overseas suffered from heavy losses, due to the reasons of nepotism and the corrupt management. As a result of this massive loss of state assets and leakage of the foreign currency, the Ministry of Foreign Trade and Economic Cooperation (MOFTEC) decided to introduce a stricter and more rigorous control (Poncet, 2007, pp. 117–118). Nevertheless, all these elements appeared but a quite evident strategy of the Chinese government to discourage FDI (Yuan & Pangarkar, 2015, p. 275).

However, by the late 1990s, the government attitude towards FDI changed from merely allowing and/or encouraging Chinese investment overseas. The support program was focused at specific industries, such as the enterprises engaged in processing and assembling raw materials, or machinery export. Light industry, such as textiles and electrical equipment, were promoted by export tax reductions and by foreign exchange as well as by financial assistance for their projects overseas (OECD, 2008, p. 83).

The encouragement, was basically given to large SOEs investment overseas, operating in strategic sectors, which were expected to spearhead the country's industrialization and raise the level of competitiveness at the global market. The development of China's foreign investment is interpreted as a success of China's market-oriented reforms. These reforms brought to two opposite effects on the progress of Chinese FDI outflow. While the Chinese companies gained more autonomy in their foreign operations, the maturing Chinese market reduced the benefits of an international network as the advantage of the barriers between domestic, and international market became less privileged. The reduction of international barriers consequently decreased the profit margins of indirect investments, benefiting from the commodity chains overseas (Peng, 2012, pp. 97–107).

The first contribution in the "go global" strategy came from the former President Jiang Zemin 1990. He believed that in order to spread China's economic opening to the outside world it was necessary to expand Chinese business overseas. The first initiatives started around 1995, but it was the National Foreign Investment Work Conference in 1997 that paved the way for a more decisive step: Jiang Zemin promised strong support by the government to the Chinese firms willing to invest abroad. Nonetheless, clearer effects of this strategy were visible only years later. In 2001, the former Prime Minister Zhu Rongji, in his report to the National People's Congress on the work of the government officially announced the new policy (Shambaugh, 2013, pp. 174–183).

Subsequently, the Tenth Five-Year Plan (2001–2005) listed the Chinese outward investments as one of the four primary goals to integrate the Chinese economy into the international dynamics. Afterwards, at the Tenth National People's Congress in 2004 Prime Minister Wen Jiabao declared, that China should accelerate and implement the strategy of "go global", to guide Chinese investment abroad. All forms of enterprises were encouraged to invest overseas and to expand their market shares. The "go global" strategy was identified as the priority goal again in the last Eleventh Five-Year Plan (2006–2010) and in the Twelfth Five-Year Plan (2011–2015). Moreover, it has been set a new goal, in order to achieve a "balance" between outward and inward FDI, this means that while inward FDI will continue to grow, it will have to do so more slowly, as an effort to promote outward investment (Davies, 2012, p. 7).

The Government encouragement in promoting Chinese outbound investment has also always been manifested through the high level diplomatic missions to other countries (Zhou et al., 2013). The Government, both directly and indirectly, has always assisted Chinese enterprises. For instance, after President Hu Jintao's tour to several Latin American countries in November 2004, more than 400 agreements were signed by China. The FDI administration reform brought in a more efficient system, as the approval authority shifted from the central to the local level, implementing a simplified process with fewer items to submit to the authority, besides, it has introduced online application to enhance transparency (OECD, 2008, pp. 83–84).

The government has also adopted other systems to liberalize the restrictions over Chinese overseas investment. For example, it has abolished the compulsory relocation scheme of the overseas profits back to China, determined to allow Chinese manufactures to re-invest their gains. Moreover, in 2006, it abolished the long-imposed quota of 5 billion USD per annum on foreign exchange allocation for FDI.[1]

In addition to the administrative reform, other specific measures reflecting industrial policy on FDI were adopted. In 2004, the government announced that the National Development and Reform Commission (NRDC) and the Export-Import Bank in China (EIBC) were committed to promoting Chinese overseas investment through favourable loans in specific areas:

---

[1] This quota had been gradually raised from the original level of US dollar 1bn, to US dollar 3.3bn in 2004 and to US dollar 5bn in 2005, before being abolished.

- Resource exploration projects to mitigate the domestic shortage of natural resources;
- Projects to promote the export of Chinese products, technologies, equipment and labour;
- Overseas R&D (research and development) centres to utilize internationally advanced technologies, managerial skills, and professionals;
- M&A (mergers and acquisitions) that could improve the international competitiveness of Chinese enterprises and stimulate their entry into foreign market (UNCTAD, 2006, p. 210).

As mentioned above, the Government supports FDI through different policies, such as financialand fiscal incentives as well as indirect assistance to overseas investment through its Official Development Aid (ODA) programs and diplomatic missions.

Nevertheless, the most powerful tool provided by the Government, are the financial incentives, for the reason that it allows Chinese enterprises from the priority lists, to access to below mentioned rate loans. Two banks provide this service, the China Export and Import Bank (Exim Bank) and the China Development Bank (CDB); furthermore, other state-owned commercial banks are lined up with the Government's strategic shift in supporting FDI (OECD, 2008, p. 84).

The current China's FDI expansion, encouraged by the government's "go global" strategy, reflects two aspects of the Chinese economy: macroeconomic and microeconomic. On the one hand, at the macroeconomic level, the Mainland has to balance its international capital flows, in order to handle the raising pressure to revalue its currency. The unprecedented level of foreign exchange reserves, resulted from the persistent trade, caused the Chinese authority to adopt a more flexible regime. In fact, it allows an incremental appreciation of the exchange rate, but this form of adjustment is not enough to stave off the revaluation pressure effectively. China's successful expansion into exports caused protectionists reaction in many host countries. The large accumulation of foreign exchange reserves in China created the rise of pressure, since the early 2000s, and, to a larger extent, between 2006 and 2010, from the international community on revaluating the renminbi.[2] For the reasons mentioned above, the

---

[2] Yongnian Zheng, Jingtao Ji, Minja Chen, Revaluation of the Chinese Currency and its impact on China, The University of Nottingham, Discussion paper nr. 24, 2007. Until 2005, the RMB was pegged to the US dollar, but after that year, under significant pressures of the US administration, China shifted to a managed float system, based on a basket of major foreign currencies. Since then, and until the summer of 2015, RMB was revaluated against the US dollar by 25% (W. Cline and J. Williamson, *Updated estimates of Fundamental Equilibrium Exchange Rates*, Peterson Institute for International Economics, Policy Brief, 2012; F. Bergsten, *Currency War, the Economy of United States and the reform of the International Monetary System*, Testimony before the Committee of ways and means, US House of representatives, May 16, 2013).

government saw the outbound investment as a friendly measure to avoid trade frictions and, to some extent, to mitigate revaluation pressure.

On the other hand, at the microeconomic level, more Chinese manufacturers possess incentives and capacities to put into practice international strategies in order to improve their comparative advantage and profitability. Many Chinese firms within the FDI inflow gained the knowledge and the experience to settle business abroad thanks to their foreign partners. Moreover, China's production over capacity observed in some industries within the domestic market, such as textile industry, colour TV production, almost every sector of home appliance production, air conditioner, washing machine, fostered the Chinese central government motivation to encourage its enterprises to invest overseas (Gugler & Boei, 2008, p. 12).

At that time, the "go global" project was still fragmented among different government bodies; therefore, the only beneficiaries of the FDI project incentives are the large SOEs, operating in strategic sectors. In many cases, the successful conclusion if this decision process is linked to the intergovernmental general agreements. By 2007, Chinese state owned business groups were responsible for around 35% of national FDI, a proportion that increases considerably, if one takes into account figures concerning FDI to tax havens (Suthwerland & Ning, 2015, p. 107). To promote overseas investments by SMEs, the government should intervene in two ways. Firstly, the central authority should provide more information to Chinese investors, not only about the policy framework of the host countries, but also concerning its practical issues, such as labour, environment and social practices. Secondly, the exchange rate volatility may be considered as a significant risk in outward investment, because the gradual liberalization of the exchange rate management system in China may bring more uncertainty in the future (Gugler & Boei, 2008, p. 12). In recent years, the Chinese government has shown a more determined commitment to SMEs outgoing strategy, encouraging them to participate in foreign management and competition. Nevertheless, results are still not too optimistic (Wang, 2014, pp. 61–64).

Chinese investments are influenced in many ways by the imperfections of the capital market. In virtue of the bank system, strictly controlled by the Chinese government, it is easy for any Chinese company to borrow loans below the market rates. In addition, the sovereign wealth funds of the China International Trust and Investment Corporation (CITIC) and the China Investment Corporation (CIC), with allocated assets from enormous stock of foreign exchange reserves, have supported Chinese firms in their outbound investments (Gugler & Boei, 2008). Particularly, the large SOEs and some private manufacturers have benefitted from this mechanism, in order to secure the financial resources for their domestic-operations .. Additionally, the Chinese government has protected the national champions firms from competition on the Mainland and granted them special permits in order to set up financial companies, or to acquire a majority of local banks and to establish joint ventures with foreign insurance companies (Child & Rodrigues, 2005, pp. 381–383).

Drivers for Chinese outbound FDI

Throughout the years, the controls on Chinese FDI have been constantly relaxed, however, as explained previously, this is not sufficient, because China's FDI projects need to successfully pass two stages before being approved. Firstly, Chinese enterprise has to demonstrate the profitability and commercial viability of the project. Secondly, the government has to agree that the project respects the country's interest. Nevertheless, the majority of FDI are the large, state-owned enterprises, in which the decision process is frequently dominated by the government's intention. Given the important role played by the government in driving the economy, Chinese FDI are often seen more as part of the economic reform process, rather than a real business activity (Rosen & Hanemann, 2006, pp. 167–168).

In accordance to the FIAS/MIGA/IFC/CCER survey on China's FDI in 2005, 150 Chinese companies were interviewed, and the result was that the most common motive for Chinese ODI was market seeking (85% of the questioned companies considered it as an important motive for their investment), then strategic asset seeking (51%), resource seeking (40%) and efficiency seeking (39%) accordingly (UNCTAD, 2006, pp. 167–168). Similar information can be derived from Deng's survey made in 2009. It showed that market seeking was considered to be the most frequent motive for Chinese FDI, even though Deng found that the strategic assets and efficiency seeking were an equal motivation. Additionally, the OECD study made in 2008, considers another important motive for China's FDI, that being diversification-seeking project, which mainly interests large SOEs (OECD, 2008, p. 94). The excessive competition in the domestic market, due to the increasing multinational companies investing in China, caused the overcapacity production in certain industries, and obliged Chinese enterprises to leave the domestic market and to move to new markets overseas, in which it is possible to gain direct access to the host market. Furthermore, concerning the deregulation of the services sectors after China's accession to the WTO, competitive pressures pushed more Chinese firms from the service sectors to invest abroad.

Since the late 1990s, strategic asset seeking has been one of the major motives for Chinese FDI. This means that all the foreign enterprises holding technologies protected with intellectual propertyrights, or brand names recognized globally after establishing strong sales channels, are theoretically a scope of the Chinese interest. Acquiring strategic assets is an easy method to obtain technologies without incurring large expenses on research and development, on international marketing campaigns and or creating an efficient distribution channel. Furthermore, the acquisition of such assets will also prevent the possibility of other competitors purchasing these strategic companies. As Chinese enterprises are fully aware of the increasingly competitive market, they recognized the necessity to shift their investment strategy to the one based on low cost production and low prices, to the one based on competitive innovation, or a brand image that produces higher profit margins (OECD, 2008, p. 98). Chinese strategic asset-seeking companies are focused on the highly developed countries with attractive technologies and brands, as for example Europe and North America. There are many reasons to justify such strategic assets motivation. It provides an opportunity for a market and innovation seeking company from a developing country to overcome these deficiencies, by simply acquiring another asset, one that already possesses all the above mentioned elements (Gugler & Boei, 2008, p. 19).

According to what we said above, it seems evident that the key to success of the internationalization strategy of a Chinese firm is determined by its relationship with the Chinese government; but, it also depends on its ability to take advantage of this support while escaping from the institutional restrictions. Because the business needs independence in order to take the required strategic decisions on the market rather than to satisfy the institutional instructions. Furthermore, foreign partners may have a critical view of the strong interference on the internationalization strategy of Chinese firms on behalf of the government. However, the invasive domestic institutional interference can be interpreted as an important element in driving Chinese firms to escape from the Mainland framework. In particular, the precarious legal system, the domestic acquisition obstacles, the regional protectionism of the Chinese companies are seen as challenges to be faced. Therefore, FDI represent the solution to access to an unrestricted business development without the government interference.

Considering the Chinese Ministry of Commerce data, by the end of 2007, barely 7000 Chinese enterprises have established more than 10000 subsidiaries abroad, spreading in almost 200 countries all over the world. The geographic distribution of Chinese outbound operations sees Asia as the most attracting destination, it isfollowed by Latin America; however, its weight is decreasing over time, while Africa, North America and the European Union are becoming larger recipient of Chinese investments, even though they still account for a limited percentage of the total outbound FDI (Gattai, 2009, p. 250). Furthermore, in the recent years, the economic recession in the US has transferred the attention of Chinese firms towards the European Union. Therefore, the European Union became the fastest growing destination for Chinese investment.

Chinese Foreign Direct Investments in Europe

By focusing our attention on the European Union, it is necessary to point out to the evidence, that Chinese investments in the Old Continent are still relatively small, although the number of investment projects funded by China have been increasing steadily (500 percent since 2000). Even if we limit the observation period just to the most recent years, this trend is confirmed: between 2009 and 2011, Chinese FDI to the EU countries increased 30 fold (EUSME, 2014, p. 3). Furthermore, as the data source suggest, the amount of the total Chinese FDI outflows is unequally distributed across the European Member States. Literature argues that Chinese firms proove a strong investment concentration into a small number of countries, which are of a high income and developed economies as well. In fact, the United Kingdom is the first destination for the Chinese outbound investment in Europe, followed by Germany, the Netherlands, and France; while Sweden, Italy, Spain, Poland, Romania and Hungary receive a very limited percentage of the investment. Later on, we will also analyse in detail the relevance and the function of the new European member states (Nicolas, 2009, p. 5).

The European Union symbolizes a very particular case of China's overseas investment strategy, justified mainly by the European integration. Its peculiarity is based on the fact that by entering into one member state, a Chinese firm de facto gets an access to the entire European Single Market. Moreover, the European member states are highly distinguished among them. Moreover, there is a lot of differences in between the investments in the particular European Union member states. This difference is particularly evident between the markets of the "Old Europe" and the markets of the new, enlarged European Union, specifically, in the Central and Eastern part of the continent (Zhang et al., 2012, p. 103). In addition, the Eurozone economic crisis offered the Chinese firms a great opportunity to invest in the European integrated market. Because of the crisis, legendary and famous European assets became affordable; ergo, many opportunities became available for Chinese companies looking for overseas investment. Before focusing our attention on the various entry modes, it is also necessary to explain more clearly, what factors are behind Chinese outward direct investment in Europe.

As already said, the main driving forces of Chinese outbound investment are varied. They include the desire to access the foreign markets, technologies, natural resources; however, the first two factors are the principal motives justifying the investment in Europe. Behind these strategies, there are is also a variety of push and pull elements that foster and stimulate Chinese companies to invest overseas. All these aspects are essential in order to understand why the Chinese entrepreneurs from different sectors prefer to invest in Europe rather than to export their sales to foreign investors. It is evident that pull and push factors are interrelated amongst them.

Among the pull factors, protectionism of many of the major markets is perceived as the major threat. Therefore, as in the past it was also the case of the firms belonging to advanced economies, Chinese investors now are increasingly motivated to invest overseas instead of exporting (Dunning & Lundan, 2008). Moreover, the Chinese record on trade surplus with the United States and the European Union, brought an anxiety to Chinese exporters concerning the possibility of the establishment of high tariffs to tackle the problem of the goods coming from China. For instance, in 2003, the US government has introduced anti-dumping duties (that reached a level of 22.36 percent) against four China based TV producers, including the TCL television sets (Hong & Sun, 2004, p. 626).

From the Chinese point of view, entering into the European Single Market is more complicated than for instance, entering into any another country, because the European Union consists of 28 different states; but, at the same time, it has one integrated market with common rules and regulations. Therefore, Chinese companies have to consider not only the European regulations, but also the single member state own laws and regulations. As a result, the selection of the entry mode becomes fundamental. Since the beginning of the economic crisis, the main European firms targeted by Chinese companies are of a competitive niche producers, and former partners or suppliers, with a serious, critical economic and/or financial situation. In most cases, the acquisition is immediate, or it starts through a strategic investment, followed by a complete takeover. To strengthen the relationship with the European partner, Chinese acquirer prefers to engage firstly in a minority-stake acquisition. Surely, different ways of investments are related to their different purposes. Independently to the form of investment, the Chinese primary goal has always been to gain an access to the brand name and to its distribution network, and undoubtedly, to its technology expertise and its customer networks alike (Milelli et al., 2009, pp. 207–209).

Recent studies have discovered that some of the Chinese firms have demonstrated their preference to enter into the European market not only through the traditional FDI modes, but also by creating strategic alliances with the European enterprises. This last kind of investment – largely perceived as less risky – guarantees more adaptability, and implies fewer obligations when a foreign company decides to enter into a new market for the first time. In the past, the scholars studied the phenomenon of the strategic alliance from the perspective of the Western firms, as they usually were the main actors. More recently, research has shown that the strategic alliance was often established between the Western and Chinese companies in China (Zhang et al., 2012, p. 103).

Most of the time, there is an instant, major acquisition or a start of a strategic alliance, followed by a complete takeover by a Chinese firm. From time to time, the Chinese enterprise decides to establish a minor acquisition, in order to consolidate the relationship with its European partner. This kind of investment is used in sectors like services and manufacturing. The decision to acquire certain kind of companies is dictated by the already existing distribution network and the technology utilised by a certain company, as this is the quickest and easiest way to enter and to succeed in the European market (Nicolas, 2009; Sanderson, 2015).

It is widely recognized that acquisitions provide a direct access to technologies and skills, as well as the distribution networks and well-known brands. For this reason, in the recent years, Chinese enterprises have increased their acquisition of European companies. This trend has rapidly accelerated after 2002; it represents the turning point, after China's access into the WTO. The Chinese firms have acquired renowned European enterprises such as Schneider Electronics, Thomson, Volvo, Marionnaud, MG Rover and more; recently also Pirelli, the group delivering the tires to Formula one cars (Nicolas & Thomsen, 2008, p. 15).

Filippov and Saebi (2008) defined this new phenomenon as "Europeanisation". It is a broad concept characteristic to a lot of Chinese companies, that are increasingly seeking the access into the European market. This new expression refers to the strong efforts made by Chinese companies to enter into the competitive European market, in the attempt to strengthen their presence in Europe, pursuing their main objective that is the access to superior technologies, competencies and expertise. The new concept of "Europeanisation" does not consist of just a simple strategy of investment carried by single business entity. It appears to be a well-made strategy, planned by the Chinese government. This idea is justified by the investments strategies adopted by every single company, because they are trying to strengthen their presence on the European territory by increasing the production, for the purpose of capturing new markets. However, it gives the impression that the main goal is to acquire strategic positions, in order to use the European base as the launch for global operations. For this purpose, they take the advantage of the European skills, methodologies, technologies and are trying to conform to the European code of conduct, in order not to avoid problems with the competitive pressure. For the Chinese companies manufacturing in Europe, it is very expensive, and the barriers to the market entry are excessively high and strict. Therefore, the only solution available is to acquire a domestic company in Europe. Despite that, even after the acquisition, the acquirer has to sustain the competitive advantage, for example, by maintaining high quality standards, because European consumers pay particular attention to the quality of products. Additionally, the new acquirer will have to face yet another, new challenge, the strong European labour regulation (Filippov & Saebi, 2008, p. 17).

Notwithstanding the recent enlargement of the European Union, the powerful purchasing power is still being held by the Western European consumers. For this reason, for a Chinese investor, the chances to survive after having entered in this competitive and unfamiliar market are very low. As a consequence, Chinese firms found that due to the last enlargement of the European Union in 2004 and 2007, there are new opportunity to access the Single Market through the former communist states of the ex URSS. The new European member states are seen as a commercial entrance, enabling access to Europe's half a billion market of consumers. It is defined as the backdoor to Europe, because it grants the Chinese investors a leap over the European tariff barriers.[3]

Filippov and Saebi argue that Chinese investors target the Western European members for their competences in new technology and knowhow; in comparison the new Eastern EU members represent the destination for foreign direct investment looking for establishing company's subsidiary, aiming to export to the Western European consumers without customs duty. The only European regulation to respect in order to be allowed to export into the Single market without customs duty, re-

---

[3] Tariff jumping is considered the only strategic investment solution, considering all the trade wars between China and the European Union. The European Union after having accused China of price dumping, it has introduced several duties on different goods. For instance, in the 1990s, the European Union accused China of exporting TV sets at too low prices; consequently, it has introduced duties of 40% for all the TV sets produced in China. This duty has been lifted only in 2002, but the European Union has then fixed quotas on quantity imports and it has introduced minimum prices of products. If more than 50% of the product is made within the European borders (by a Chinese subsidiary), there are no applicable duties.

quires that more than half of the manufacturing of the product comes from within the European Union borders. Therefore, it permits the Chinese companies to choose between capitalizing on their low cost base in China (as the cost of production in Eastern Europe is higher in comparison to the Mainland) and the manufacturing inside the European borders and selling duty-free in the Single market. The second solution justifies the necessity to produce inside Europe, instead of importing these goods from China. This strategy enables Chinese multinational companies to decrease logistics costs and escape from the payment of tariffs and duty.

Greenfield investments of the Chinese firms in Western Europe are established for the basic functions, as for example, to support the trade or to establish a sales representation. While in Eastern Europe, they have different functions and furthermore, since they focus on low cost manufacturing. Acquisitions in Western Europe targeted engineering companies with strong competences and know-how, in order to transfer these new knowledge to the headquarters. Differently, the acquisitions in Eastern Europe are made to take advantage of the lower cost of manufacturing. The strategic alliances established in Western Europe are most of the time a technology alliance. On the contrary, the strategic alliances with the Eastern European companies are logistics and marketing based alliances, established to help Chinese companies to understand and adapt to the European standards and technological requirements (Filippov & Saebi, 2008, pp. 11–13).

Foreign direct investments structure and distribution across the European Union

Through the examination of the distribution of Chinese outward investment across the European Union, it is possible to highlight the capability of Chinese companies in the investment competition. Although, it is hard to understand and determine the specific distribution of Chinese firms through the European member states, because there are limits in the measure of the aggregate data. In accordance with the Chinese Government data, 87% of the total Chinese outward investment during the period 2004–2010 flowed to Asia, and precisely 72% destined to Hong Kong (National Bureau of Statistics of China, 2011). Therefore, it is obvious that a relevant part of this outward investment is routed from China through Hong Kong, due to monetary reasons; accordingly, the final destination is somewhere else (European Commission, 2013). Moreover, the private equity fund "A Capital" based in Beijing, Brussels and Shanghai, declared that Europe was among the top destination of Chinese outbound investments in 2012, which rose by 21% over 2011, and totalled 12.6 billion USD. The Chinese investment in Europe tripled between 2006–2009 and again, between 2009 and 2012 (Silk, 2014).

A more recent research has shown that data concerning Chinese FDI have several limitations and that in general, literature remains elusive. Usually, data concerning FDI have been overstated, and this evaluation is particularly relevant since the Chinese Ministry of Commerce announced that in 2014, the outflow of capital for the first time overtook the inflow. A complex work of readjustment of both flows and stocks has permitted to modify any previous evaluation. The new data are of the year 2013 (Ferrero et al., 2015).

Table 1: Chinese ODI Stocks and Flows by region before and after adjusting for round-tripping and offshoring (USD bn)

Stocks					
MOFOCM			**Adjusted**		
Region	**Total**	**% Total**	**Region**	**Total**	**% Total**
Asia	447.41	68%	Asia	245.32	49%
Latin America	86.09	13%	Latin America	23.15	5%
Europe	53.16	8%	Europe	95.19	19%
North America	28.61	4%	North America	63.19	13%
Africa	26.19	4%	Africa	38.88	8%
Oceania	19.02	3%	Oceania	32.70	7%
TOTAL	660.62	100%	TOTAL	498.46	100%
Flows					
MOFOCM			**Adjusted**		
Region	**Total**	**% Total**	**Region**	**Total**	**% Total**
Asia	75.6	70%	Asia	40.69	50%
Latin America	14.36	13%	Latin America	4.39	5%
Europe	5.95	6%	Europe	13.87	17%
North America	4.9	5%	North America	11.42	14%
Africa	3.37	3%	Africa	5.38	7%
Oceania	3.66	3%	Oceania	5.87	7%
TOTAL	107.82	100%	TOTAL	81.62	100%

Source: Alicia Garcia Ferrero, Le Xia, Carlos Casanova, *Chinese outbound foreign direct investments: how much goes where after round-tripping and offshoring?*, BBVA Research, Working Paper No. 15/17, Hong Kong, June 2015.

Data are showing a strong reduction of the data concerning Asia and an increase, particularly significant for Europe. Inside the Old Continent, this process reinforces the already high figures for Germany, Luxemburg, France and Great Britain. However, the investments carried by Chinese firms in economically developed countries prove the intention to acquire technologies, brands, as well as the intrinsic competitiveness of the company targeted. Although this new strategy of investment is becoming important; as after the enlargement of the European Union, many Chinese firms are focusing on low cost production investments, located in the new European Union members. For those new European Union member states, that in general receive low FDI; investments established by Chinese firms are seen as a great opportunity to implement and catalyse the industrialization process of their internal economy.

Besides the factors attracting Chinese investments described above, the bilateral economic relation between the single member state and China is an important element in the analysis of the distribution of Chinese investments across the European Union, because it encourages and promotes inwards investment in the particular, interested European Union member state. Therefore, it is necessary and fundamental to consider the European member state FDI in the context of China, in order to understand the strong interest that both countries share on mutual economic relations. The large investment undertaken by a member state in China encourages and galvanizes the trust between the two countries, and consequently, it stimulates the European member state to adopt governmental support to host Chinese investment (Clegg & Voss, 2012).

Therefore, in order to understand the distribution of Chinese investment across the European market, it is required to analyse the single European member state FDI into China against the individual member state importance within the European market overall size. The results elaborated by the researchers Clegg and Voss (2012), give evidence of the size of the Chinese FDI pouring into each European Union member state. This study shows a positive correlation between the GDP of the single EU state member, its FDI to China and Chinese FDI into the same country. In Germany for example many firms have initially enjoyed a long lasting relation with their Chinese investors, before the acquisition was made by the Chinese partner. Therefore, the acquisition is the outcome of a meaningful economic relationship. Accordingly, we can expect a connection between the investment carried out by a member state in China, and the Chinese investment following suit in that interested state.

Clegg and Voss' study does not consider some other very complex processes, which statistical data can only suggest, without being able to explain them. The mutual perception between single European countries and China, the presence of a Chinese community, the potential of the local market, the geographical position, all of these are just some of the elements we must consider. For instance, a large Chinese emigration that had started already in the 1980's and was reinforced during the following decade, explains the disproportion of the Chinese FDI to Hungary, where the largest amount of these investments amongst all the areas is located (Lathan & Wu, 2013).

Chinese FDI in Poland

Poland is experiencing a similar process, but at a lower rate. In fact, a recent research seems to confirm the correlation between the increase of Chinese immigrants into Poland and the rise of Chinese FDI, but the figures are still too low to permit confirming a long-term trend (Wiśniewski 2012; Kaczmarczyk et al., 2013). Among all of the CEE countries, Poland seems to have a better profile, considering all of these points of view: a growing economy, even during the recent economic crisis, a large market, a barycentric position in Europe, with an infrastructure that is undergoing a deep process of modernization (PAIiIZ, 2015).

Despite the asymmetry of data and information offered by the official statistical institutions in China and in Poland, Chinese investments in Poland are falling behind those of Hungary and Rumania, considering the importance in all the CEE countries. According to Chinese sources, which sometimes show a very big, and not always justified difference, the total amount in 2012 was 130 million USD, while the Polish sources were declaring around 180 million. The revised data seem to offer even more positive picture, since the level of Chinese investments should be around 390 million USD. Data provided by the Central statistical office of Poland for 2013 affirm that there are 799 firms in the country, whose capital is in its majority in Chinese hands. According to this figure, China takes the eighth place in the Polish national ranking of foreign investors. The same source also says that there are 829 firms with Chinese capital. Out of these firms, 706 are of a small size (up to nine employees) and only 120 have more than nine employees. There were 509 companies in 2010, and 433 out of them had less than nine employees, which means that the large majority of Polish firms controlled by Chinese investors is a part of the micro-firm universe. The largest increase occurs in this section, while the companies with more than nine employees increased proportionally less. Statistical data, once again, do not offer any detailed information about the bigger firms. The financial information simply does confirm this picture. The average of capital of the smaller firms is around 206,000 PLN, while the 120 bigger companies by average, have a capital of almost one million PLN. Unfortunately, the statistical exercise is soon to be completed, because no other figure (even aggregated) is available, since the total amount of capital invested by China remains quite far away from the one offered by the biggest European and American investors. Nevertheless, data concerning Chinese investments in Poland must be compared with the situation within a couple of years after Poland had entered the EU. In 2006, there were only 75 firms with Chinese firms. The trend is quite similar in the other CEE countries (Polish Information and Foreign Investment Agency, 2014).

The Polish case seems to offer a clear evidence of the feature that can be defined as "political" decision, leading to invest more in this country. On both sides, there has been a convergence process in preparing the conditions for a real jump in Chinese FDI in Poland. The visit to China of the Polish President Komorowski in December 2011 was the first step of a real common strategy.[4] A few months later, in April 2012, Prime Minister Wen Jiabao visited Poland. It was the first time in the last 25 years for a Chinese Prime Minister to visit this country. During the visit, he also took part in the China-Central Europe-Poland Economic Forum, held in Warsaw.[5] Both events created a strong institutional framework, that permitted establishing a new conduct line and, to some extent, providing Poland with a sort of a new status in front of the Chinese eyes but also, even in the eyes the other countries of the region. However, from the Chinese point of view, the pragmatic approach to a very complex and long-term issue prevailed over any more symbolic meaning of the new strategy (Liu, 2013).

During his visit, Prime Minister Wen Jiabao presented the "Twelve measures" that should permit to reinforce the cooperation not only with Poland, but also with all of the Central Eastern European countries. The proposals included firstly the setting up of a secretariat for cooperation between China and the Central and Eastern European countries in order to coordinate all the future activities foreseen by the Chinese proposals. From the economic point of view, the establishment of a special credit line of 10 billion USD for cooperation projects (a part of the strategy to reach 100 billion dollars in trade between China and Eastern and Central Europe by 2015), and sending to CEE countries Chinese trade missions set to revamp the bilateral economic cooperation, were the most relevant

---

[4] *President Komorowski urges China to invest in Poland*, 19.12.2011. Retrieved from: http://www.thenews.pl/1/12/Artykul/80728,President-Komorowski-urges-China-to-invest-in-Poland#sthash.loudlbTN.dpuf (accessed: 15/10/2015).

[5] *Prime Minister Wen addresses China-Central and Eastern Europe Business Forum in Warsaw, Poland*, 27.04.2012. Retrieved from: http://english.cntv.cn/20120427/112488.shtml (accessed: 15/10/2015).

aspects. In the medium term (2012–2017), Wen Jiabao suggested creating economic and technological zones in each country, affirming that his government would push Chinese firms to take part in the development of the existing economic and technological zones in the relevant countries. The documents also described a series of monetary and financial measures, including the opening of branches of the Chinese State owned banks; establishing a special advisory committee on the construction of transportation network between China and the Central and Eastern European countries. Some other points were mentioning cultural aspects, such as the opening of Confucius institutes. The development of the cultural, academic and tourism initiatives both in China and in the CEE countries in order to reinforce the mutual understanding and knowledge. The "Twelve measures" strategy officially was officialy launched in September 2012 along with the establishment of the China-CEE Secretariat (Simurina, 2014).

However, one should not overestimate the weight of Chinese investments in Poland. In 2011, according to an official source, there were only six Chinese companies among the biggest FDI in Poland. Germany was leading this ranking with 382 firms, followed by France with 122. Even India (not to mention the small European economies), was ahead China with eight firms. This number remained stable also in 2012 and 2013, while the last data available (for 2014) show an increase up to 13. Nevertheless, the distance between the Polish figures and the German ones (486 firms) or the French ones (261) increased dramatically between 2011 and 2014 (Polish Information and Foreign Investment Agency, 2012–2014).

Do this data diminish the importance of the Chinese strategy for Central and Eastern Europe and particularly for Poland, or do they contradict the wider Chinese strategy analysed in the first part of this paper? The difficulties in collecting not only the data, but also qualitative information suggests a very low profile in any statement concerning Chinese investments in Poland. An analysis of the impact of the most relevant Chinese investments shows that the general strategy outlined especially from the early 2000's, seems to be finding its road. The fact, that the most recent investments are following the main points included in the "Twelve measures" highlighted by the Chinese Prime Minister in 2012 is even more important. They are actually showing that Chinese firms are entering in the special economic and technological zones, accessing high tech production via direct control of important Polish companies, that might be in financial troubles, but that allows to keep a long tradition in quality production. According to a recent study on Chinese FDI at the European level, however, most of the investments in Poland seem to be directed at the high-tech manufacturing sector. However, too much aggregated data, in the end, cannot allow to detect the preciseness of this evaluation (EUSME, 2014). They are also establishing infrastructure and service companies, permitting the Chinese goods to enter by the front door into not only the Central Eastern European market, but also the whole European market.

The last point merits some more detailed analysis, because it has a strategic impact, since one of the most important aspects of the Chinese foreign economic policy is to create the best conditions to permit the trade to grow. For instance, in 2013, a new transportation service link was established, the Chengdu-Europe express rail cargo service, that has its terminal in Poland, in Łódź.[6] The train tracks runs along 9,826 kilometres of the legendary Silk Road, from Chengdu (Sichuan Province), through Kazakhstan, Russia, Belarus, before entering into Poland and reaching Łódź. Despite the fact that the transportation costs by train are 25% higher than by a cargo-ship, the time of transport is dramatically reduced, from about 35–45 days to 12–14 days (Ocicka, 2015, p. 125). The shareholders of the company running the service are Hatrans Logistics (a firm based in Hong Kong), Vailog (controlled by a British company), and YH Global (a Chinese enterprise based in Shenzhen). There is official enthusiasm about the project, a part of a larger strategy strongly sponsored by the Chinese president Xi. However, a more critical approach highlights the tough competition with the classical maritime alternative, and suggests that only important government (central and local) subsidies can permit, at least, in an early phase, to give a chance to the rail service.[7]

The terminal is just a huge hub for the whole Europe, since from Łódź, Chinese goods (or products manufactured in China for Western customers) can also reach Western European markets within three days. Recently, it has been announced that Chinese investors will set up a logistic centre to handle all the operations and functions connected with the management of the Łódź terminal. In fact, at the end of 2015 the goods were stored in the structures of the container terminal in Łódź Olechów, administrated by Spedcont company (Ocicka, 2015, p. 124).

The importance of this strategy and of the future investment in logistics has been increased since 2014, when Chinese president Xi Jinping announced the "New Silk Road strategy", the "One Road, one Belt" project, a sprawling set of trade and infrastructure agreements which aims to foster free trade and bolster Chinese soft power amongst China's neighbours

---

[6] *China to Poland railroad begins operations*, 14.01.2013. Retrieved from: http://chinadaily-mail.com/2013/01/14/china-to-poland-railroad-begins-operations (accessed: 15/10/2015).

[7] *Silk Road subsidies undermine rail link*, 8.12.2014. Retrieved from: http://www.scmp.com/business/economy/article/1657286/silk-road-subsidies-undermine-rail-link (accessed: 15/10/2015).

to the West and Southeast (Min Ye, 2014). In November 2014, the Chinese government announced the creation of the special, 40 billion USD Silk Infrastructure Fund, to finance the construction or improvement of a series of railways, bridges, ports, and roads; to permit all the countries included in this strategy to take part to this new strategy at the best conditions (Clover & Hornby, 2015).

The recent developments of Chinese FDI raise the question, whether negative experiences with Chinese investors did or did not provoke any long-term consequences. The most famous case is connected with the construction of a segment of the A2 highway from Warsaw to Berlin, a strategic infrastructure project, co-financed by European Union. A 30-mile stretch of the road, the section leading from Warsaw to Łódź «fell victim to poor planning, strict regulations, higher-than-expected costs and – in a small part, frogs» – wrote the *Wall Street Journal*. The Chinese company that acquired the contract – China Overseas Engineering Group Co Ltd (COVEC), a Beijing-based subsidiary of the China Railway Engineering Corporation – withdrew from a 447 million USD construction project in the first half of 2011, after incurring potential losses of 394 million USD, just two years after winning the important tender of the Polish government. Mismanagement, unprecise calculations of some of the costs (COVEC won the contract by reducing the price limit proposed by the government by 50%), incomplete knowledge of the EU's and Polish rules concerning publicly financed works, unfamiliarity with the European laws, regulation system and record-keeping, all these issues have been the factors, that obliged the Chinese company to withdraw. The impact of Covec's mistakes has been partly increased also by the negative attitude shown by many Polish firms that were supposed to deliver raw material and semi-finished products to the Chinese constructor, a subtle strategy aiming to discourage any further Chinese presence in one of the wealthiest Polish investment sectors.[8]

At the Polish-Chinese summit in April 2012, the issue remained out of the official agenda. In fact, as a Polish newspaper wrote, "during Wen Jiabao's visit, Chinese companies may sketch out rosy visions of future businesses. But these visions are ruined by the putrid smell, rising from the mess of the Chinese investment on the A2." Some other personality familiar with the issue affirmed that the Chinese "thought they came to Africa" (Cienski, 2012).

Beijing semi-official point of view recognized that "Chinese companies still have a lot to learn about managing infrastructure projects in Europe, despite their successful experiences in the developing countries"

---

[8] Chinese Builder Loses Showpiece Polish Highway Deal COVEC stops Polish highway construction. *China Daily*, 18.06.2011 (accessed: 15/10/2015).

(Areddy, 2011). A critical analysis by Chinese journalists confirmed that the "Chinese construction model", based on offering a very low price for the job, before asking for a readjustment due to negative weather conditions, unfavourable exchange rate or the cost of raw materials, successful elsewhere in the world, did not work in a country of the European Union (Le Van, 2012). However, China resisted the Polish government's request to pay the 200 million USD guarantee fund for the project. China's reputation is under examination, and consequences are still strong, more than three years after the end of Covec's story in Poland. Recent attempts by major Chinese companies, such as Shanghai Electric bids to build three power plants in Poland, have been rebuffed by Warsaw's government.[9]

Nonetheless, regardless of the unlucky conclusion of the highway investments, and despite all the efforts made on both sides, it remains quite difficult to substantially increase the amount of Chinese FDI in Poland, when one considers that Poland's ministry of Economy has just one official dedicated to brokering trade and investment relations with China. Major western European nations have more than 50 (Foy, 2015).

Conclusions

In a country like China, FDI are playing an increasing role in shaping the new profile of the Chinese economy. Literature underlines that their increasing importance is linked with the development strategy of the country. China needs outbound FDI today and in the future, as in the past decades it needed inbound investments and, to some extent, it still needs – for the modernization of its economy as well as to allow for a more balanced economic growth. Most of the Chinese FDI are aimed at the access to energy and raw materials. However, in the more recent times, the search for the advanced technologies, technical expertise and knowledge is becoming an increasingly important factor for Chinese FDI. As for the advanced economies, FDI have also the purpose to permit the companies to avoid any trade barriers or tariffs. Chinese manufacturing industry, the biggest in the world, requires a stable and easy access to markets, especially those of the advanced economies. Increasing Chinese trade has been for a long time the opposite side to the country's development strategy. Today, there is an important evidence showing the reconsideration of this growth's mechanism, although the new direction – more domestic market

---

[9] Shanghai Electric Group was interested in three contracts for the construction of three power plants in different regions of the country for the Polish state-owned company PGE (Agata Geppert, *Trade and investments in China*, "Polish Market", Special Edition 2013, p. 26).

oriented - does not appear solid enough because of the growing difficulties Chinese economy is facing in the recent times (Ghemawat & Hout, 2016).

Despite radical reforms, Chinese political and economic systems are still largely dominated by the State, and particularly by the Communist Party of China, which are defining the long-term strategies for economic growth and social and political stabilization. Outbound FDI are possible and are decided only in this framework. Despite the increasing autonomy of the firms, even the state-owned ones, and despite the still initial decentralization process in for the procedures concerning FDI, there is still a very strong political control over them. Their geographical direction as well as the sectorial distribution depend on political evaluation.

Chinese investments in Europe respond mainly to the need to access some of the most dynamic and rich markets but also to acquire technologies via the acquisition of companies with a tradition and a precise competitive advantage in the technical field. This kind of investments are mainly directed towards Western European countries. Only recently, after 2004 EU enlargement, Chinese government established a strategy of penetration into Central Eastern economies. The strategy has sufficiently elastic to permit to adequate it to the economic development of this area, and from 2012 – with the establishment of the "Twelve Measures" policy – it has become a pillar of the new foreign economic policy of Beijing. Nevertheless, the total amount of FDI going to these countries remain quite low compared to Western Europe.

Chinese investments into Poland are second by importance, only to those directed to Hungary, where a solid and stable Chinese emigration permitted to establish a set of political and social relations, that played an important role in Chinese decision making process. The structure of Polish economy is largely based on small and medium size firms, with a still relevant presence of the state-owned companies, especially within the coal and energy sector. This feature is not the most suitable for the big Chinese foreign investments, considering that the Western countries, including the US, developed a wide and deep penetration strategy already in the 1990s, and even greater after 2004. Firms controlled or set up by Chinese investors remain insignificant in numbers. Available data permit just a few considerations in this part of our analysis. Nevertheless, some qualitative aspects do allow to affirm that these investments are following State directives, regardless of being the initiative of a private, or a state-owned company.

In the more recent years, Chinese investments have been directed to the infrastructure system, still one of the most dynamic branches of the economy ,that did not stop to grow, despite the economic and financial crisis of the last years. Poland is becoming sort of a hub for Chinese exports to Europe, and Łódź is now the terminal of the new railroad link service, bringing trains full of Chinese manufactured goods to the Old Continent. Nevertheless, some problems remain in place. The troublesome end of an important contract in the public investment works in 2011, which could represent the beginning of a new form of Chinese penetration, is affecting new opportunities of investments for the big Chinese groups into the same sector. The investors' reputation – a value that is usually very important in the Chinese business culture – is still under scrutiny. Chinese investors are not unfamiliar with a very old attitude of any business community: to build a reputation needs years, to destroy it, just a few seconds are enough.

References

Areddy, J.T. (2011). COVEC stops Polish highway construction. *China Daily*, 18.06.2011; European Project Trips China Builder. *The Wall Street Journal*, 4.06.2012.

Bergsten, F. (2013). *Currency War, the Economy of United States and the reform of the International Monetary System*, Testimony before the Committee of ways and means, US House of representatives, May 16.

Buckley, P.J., Clegg, L.J., Cross, A.R., Liu, X., Voss, H. & Zheng, P. (2007). The determinants of Chinese outward foreign direct investment. *Journal of International Business Studies, 38*, 499–518.

Child, J. & Rodrigues, S.B. (2005). The internationalization of Chinese firms: A case for theoretical extension? *Management and Organization Review, 1*(3), 381–410.

China going global: The experiences of Chinese enterprises in the Netherlands. Ernst & Young, 2012.

China to Poland railroad begins operations, 14.01.2013. Retrieved from: http://chinadailymail.com/2013/01/14/china-to-poland-railroad-begins-operations (accessed: 15/10/2015).

Chinese Builder Loses Showpiece Polish Highway Deal COVEC stops Polish highway construction. *China Daily*, 18.06.2011 (accessed: 15/10/2015).

Cienski, J. (2012). Wen/Tusk: don't mention the builders. *Financial Times*, 25.04.2012.

Clegg, J. & Voss, H. (2012). *Chinese Overseas Direct Investments in the European Union.* London: ECRAN.

Cline, W. & Williamson, J. (2012). *Updated estimates of Fundamental Equilibrium Exchange Rates*, Peterson Institute for International Economics, Policy Brief.

Clover, Ch. & Hornby, L. (2015). Road to a new Empire. *Financial Times*, 13.10.2015.

Coase, R. & Wang, N. (2012). *How China Became Capitalist.* London: Palgrave.

Davies, K. (2012). Inward FDI in China and its policy context 2012. *Columbia FDI Profile.*

Dunning, J.H. & Lundan, J.S.M. (2008). *Multinational Enterprises and the Global Economy*. Cheltenham: Edward Elgar Publishing.

European Commission (2013). *Facts and Figures on EU-China trade*. Retrieved from: http://trade.ec.europa.eu/doclib/docs/2009/september/tradoc_144591.pdf (accessed: 15/10/2015).

EUSME Centre (2014). *Chinese Outward Foreign Direct Investment in the EU*, p. 3, July.

Ferrero, A.G., Le Xia & Casanova, C. (2015). *Chinese outbound foreign direct investments: how much goes where after round-tripping and offshoring?* BBVA Research, Working Paper No. 15/17, Hong Kong.

Filippov, S. & Saebi, T. (2008). *Europeanisation Strategy of Chinese Companies: Its Perils and Promises*, UNU-Merit Working Paper.

Foy, H. (2015). Chinese-backed fund steps up investments in Central and East Europe. *Financial Times, 9*(3).

Gattai, V. (2009). EU-China foreign direct investment: a double-sided perspective. *European Studies* (Amsterdam. Online), Vol. 27.

Geppert, A. (2013). *Trade and investments in China*, "Polish Market", Special Edition (pp. 24–26).

Ghemawat, P. & Hout, T. (2016). Can China's companies conquer the world? The overlooked importance of corporate power. *Foreign Affairs*, March-April, 86–98.

Gugler, P. & Boei, B. (2008). The Emergence of Chinese FDI: Determinants and Strategies of Chinese MNEs, paper presented at the Conference "*Emerging Multinationals. Outward Foreign Direct Investments from Emerging and Developing Economies*", Copenhagen Business School, Copenhagen.

Hong Ensuk, Sun Laixiang (2004). Go Overseas via Direct Investment – Internationalization Strategy of Chinese Corporations in a Comparative Prism, SOAS discussion paper, No 40, January, Centre for Financial and Management Studies, SOAS, University of London.

Jiang Xiaojuan (2012). FDI in China: Contributions to Growth, Restructuring, and Competitiveness in the 21st century, Nova Science Publishers, Inc., 2004.

Kaartemo, V. (2007). The Motives of Chinese Foreign Investments in the Baltic Sea Region, PEI Electronic Publication, 7.

Kaczmarczyk, P., Szulecka, M. & Tyrowicz, J. (2013). *Chinese investment strategies and migration – does diaspora matter? Poland – case study*. Florence: Robert Schuman Centre for Advanced Studies, European University Institute.

Lathan, K., Wu Bin (2013). *Chinese Immigration into the EU: New Trends, Dynamics, and Implications*. London: ECRAN.

Le Van, J. (2012). A road accident: the inside story of the Polish highway that wasn't built by Chinese firms, *Facing the risk of "Going out strategy"*, European Council on Foreign Relations.

Milelli, C., Hay, F. & Shi, Y. (2009). Chinese Firms Enter Europe: Some Empirical Evidence. In: Wu, Z. (ed.). *Financial Sector Reform and the International Integration of China* (p. 198–214). London: Routledge.

Min Ye (2014). China's Silk Road Strategy. Xi Jinping's real answer to the Trans-Pacific Partnership. *Foreign Policy*, November.

Modern Trains to Revive Ancient Silk Road, 8.06.2015. Retrieved from: http://www.gochengdu.cn/mobile/modern-trains-to-revive-ancient-silk-road-a118.html (accessed: 15/10/2015).

National Bureau of Statistics of China, 2011, Annual Report 2011 (This source considers Europe as the Great Europe zone, which includes Russia and other non-EU27.)

Nicolas, F. (2009). Chinese Direct Investment in Europe: Facts and Fallacies. Chatam House, Briefing Paper, *International Economics*.

Nicolas, F. & Thomsen, S. (2008). The Rise of Chinese Firms in Europe: Motives, Strategies and Implications, Draft Paper for presentation at the Asia Pacific Economic Association Conference, to be held in Beijing, December 13–14.

Nolan, P. (2012). *Is China Buying the World?* Malden: Polity Press.

Ocicka, B. (2015). Perpectives for development of logistic potential of Łódź region (Perspektywy rozwoju potencjału logistycznego regionu łódzkiego). Research Papers of Wrocław University of Economics nr 383, pp. 121–131.

OECD, China (2008). Encouraging Responsible Business Conduct.

Peng, M.W. (2012). The global strategy of emerging multinationals from China. *Global Strategy Journal*, 2(2), 97–107.

Polish Information and Foreign Investment Agency (2012). List of Major Foreign Investors in Poland – December 2011, Warsaw.

Polish Information and Foreign Investment Agency (2013). List of Major Foreign Investors in Poland – December 2012, Warsaw.

Polish Information and Foreign Investment Agency (2014). List of Major Foreign Investors in Poland – December 2013, Warsaw.

Poncet, S. (2007). Inward and Outward FDI in China, Panthéon-Sorbonne-Economie, Université Paris 1 CNRS and CEPII), this version: April 28.

President Komorowski urges China to invest in Poland, 19.12.2011. Retrieved from: http://www.thenews.pl/1/12/Artykul/80728,President-Komorowski-urges-China-to-invest-in-Poland#sthash.loudlbTN.dpuf (accessed: 15/10/2015).

Prime Minister Wen addresses China-Central and Eastern Europe Business Forum in Warsaw, Poland, 27.04.2012. Retrieved from: http://english.cntv.cn/20120427/112488.shtml (accessed: 15/10/2015).

Rosen, D.H. & Hanemann, T. (2009). China's changing outbound foreign direct investment profile: drivers and policy implications. Peterson Institute for International Economics, Policy Brief, ed. I. Kolstad and A. Wiig. What determines Chinese outward FDI? Bergen, Christian Michelsen Institute, CMI Working Paper, no 3.

Salidijanova, L. (2011). Going out: an overview of China's outward direct investments. *US-China Economic and Security Review Commission*.

Shambaugh, D. (2013). *China Goes Global. The Partial Power*. Oxford: Oxford UP.

Silk, R. (2014). Chinese investment in Europe jumps. *The World Street Journal*, 16.04.2014.

Silk Road subsidies undermine rail link, 8.12.2014. Retrieved from: http://www.scmp.com/business/economy/article/1657286/silk-road-subsidies-undermine-rail-link (accessed: 15/10/2015).

Simurina, J. (2014). *China's Approach to the CEE-16*, ECRAN.

Suthwerland, D. & Ning, L. (2015). The Emergence and Evolution of Chinese Business Groups: Are Pyramidal Groups Forming? In: Naughton, B. & Tsai, K.S. (eds). *State Capitalism, Institutional Adaptation, and the Chinese Miracle* (p. 102–153). Cambridge: Cambridge UP.

UNCTAD, World Investment Report 2006: FDI from developing and Transition Economies: Implications for Development. New York, United Nation Press.

UNCTAD's FDI/TNC database. Available at: http://stats.unctad.org/fdi/ (accessed: 28/08/2015).

Voss, H., Buckley, P.J. & Cross, A.R. (2009). An assessment of the effects of institutional change on Chinese outward direct investment activity. In: Alon, I., Chang, J., Fetscherin, M., Lattermann, C., McIntyre, J.R. (eds). *China Rules: Globalization and Political Transformation* (p. 135–165). London: Palgrave Macmillan.

Wang Qianfeng (2014). Analysis on the policies of FDI from SMEs about Chinese outgoing strategy. *International Journal of Business Administration, 6*(6), 61–64.

Wei A. Yingqi, Liu Xiaming (2011). *Foreign Direct Investment in China: Determinants and Impact*. Cheltenham: Edward Elgar Publishing Ltd.

Wiśniewski, P.A. (2012). The activity of Chinese companies in Poland (Aktywność w Polsce przedsiębiorstw pochodzących z Chin). *International Journal of Management and Economics, 34,* 108–127.

Wu Hsiu-Ling, Chen Chien-Hsun (2001). An assessment of outward foreign direct investment from China's transitional economy. *Europe-Asia Studies, 53*(8), 1238–1241.

Yuan Lin & Pangarkar, N. (2015). Performance implications of internationalization strategies for Chinese MNCs. *International Journal of Emerging Markets, 10*(2), 272–292.

Zhang Ying, Duysters, G. & Filippov, S. (2012). Chinese firms entering Europe: Internationalization through acquisitions and strategic alliances. *Journal of Science and Technology Policy in China, 3*(2).

Zhou Jianhong Jiang Jiangang, Zhou Chaohong (2014). Diplomacy and Investments: the case of China. *International Journal of Emerging Markets, 9*(2), 216–235.

Sebastian Bobowski

Fourteen EU States Already in, Japan and USA Still not Interested – What Lies Behind China-led AIIB?

Introduction

The Asian Infrastructure Investment Bank (AIIB) has gained a lot of attention recently, mainly due to the geopolitical context of China's proposal. A newly established development bank has been described by observers as an unprecedented project by a Northeast Asian emerging market with hegemonic ambitions.

The AIIB was proposed by the Chinese president, Xi Jinping, and the prime minister, Li Keqiang, during a series of visits in Southeast Asia in October 2013. Massive interest of both regional and non-regional states in obtaining a Prospective Founding Member (PFM) status, as well as quasi-ostentatious absence of the United States and Japan in the proposed framework, assign an extra meaning to discussions over new financial institution.

The aim of the paper is to study the evolution of Asian financial regionalism through the prism of the China-led Asian Infrastructure Investment Bank (AIIB) in order to understand hegemonic aspirations of Beijing, draw implications of establishment of new financial institution on mega-regional relations between China and Asian and non-Asian prospective founding members of AIIB. The author would like to study China's project addressing the scope of membership, investigating motivations laying behind the decisions of individual states such as the United States, Japan, Australia or the EU countries, including the United Kingdom and Poland. A theoretical context is drawn basing on the theories of financial regionalism and hegemonic stability.

1. Theoretical frameworks

1.1. Financial regionalism

The author would like to address the concept of financial regionalism as proposed by Hamanaka, while indicating lack of cohesive definition of this term.

Following Hamanaka, there are two types of financial regionalism, namely financial or macroeconomic forum or meeting, engaging regional states, and regional financial arrangement, involving two or more states.

The financial forums used to act as platforms for the purposes of regular information exchange between representatives of regional financial authorities. In this context, extra importance is assigned to regional, macroeconomic surveillance forums, gathering various market and financial data, enabling policy coordination and peer pressure. Such meeting may involve senior, deputy or deputy-deputy level of ministries, as well as directors of national central banks. Noteworthy, involvement of institutional apparatus gives an opportunity for constructive discussion and provision of reliable commitments.

The second type of financial regionalism is more formal, it embraces a spectrum of financial arrangements that may take form of monetary funds or development banks of a regional scale; while swap or repurchase agreements, as well as rescue/stabilization/reserve funds, shouldn't be perceived as manifestation of regionalism in itself. However, such bilateral or multilateral initiatives to pool some resources for the purposes of mutual support or shielded actions against adverse effects of financial turbulences, if necessary, may evolve consequently towards single, regional contracts that induce further institutionalization, as it was expected; for instance, when Chiang Mai Initiative was multilateralized in 2009, potentially providing the basis for the future Asian Monetary Fund (AMF). Importantly, regional financial frameworks tend to be accompanied by macroeconomic surveillance mechanism to monitor each country's performance for the purposes of securing individual contribution, as well as repayment of loans provided to the signatory parties.

Aforementioned manifestations of financial regionalism imply substantial contribution of the dominating state, institution-supplier, embracing both intellectual and financial dimension of institution's activities.

1.2. Hegemonic stability theory

Hegemonic stability theory (HST), rooted in the studies by Kindleberger, points out the importance of stabilizing state, namely, a hegemon, that is powerful enough to deliver international shared goods such as international organizations (The World Bank, GATT, etc.) or economic order (Kindleberger, 1973, p. 305). According to Russett, neither benefits, nor costs of the hegemonic state, resulting of establishment of a new international institution, should not be underestimated.

Noteworthy, criticism addressing HST theory centred around instrumental usage of the regional framework by hegemon, in order to secure and expand its own material potential, mainly through imposing the rules on the other states, as well as charging them with quasi-taxes. For instance, the International Monetary Fund (IMF) used to be criticized for subordination to the United States' political, economic, and financial interests, manifested, among others, through quota shares, and effective veto rights assigned to Washington.

The other side of the same coin, however, embraces various costs borne by hegemon as a result of establishing international financial institution. Hegemon, as the leading state within the framework, is expected to provide short-, mid-, and long-term capital in the form of loans, swap lines, and foreign investments. Therefore, financial regionalism is expected to impose concrete, tangible economic and financial liabilities on hegemonic state, that cannot be neglected by critics.

Following Hamanaka, an important intangible aspect of hegemonic position within the framework is prestige gained by dominating state (Hamanaka, 2010, p. 18). According to Morgenthau, establishing international institutions, organizing and hosting summits, and official meetings, strengthen hegemon's prestige, as well as economic contribution, however, prestige gains are not necessarily accompanied by material gains of a hegemon (Morgenthau, 1978, Chapter 6).

It should be noted, however, that regional hegemon, acting on the behalf of the other member states at the international level, gains additional prestige. When considering financial regionalism, costs of acting as stabilizer might be partially shared with the others through national contributions to regional support facilities, reserve funds, etc.

2. The Asian Infrastructure Investment Bank (AIIB) – genesis

As already mentioned, the Asian Infrastructure Investment Bank (AIIB) project has been announced by the Chinese president, Xi Jinping, and the prime minister Li Keqiang, in the mid-2013 during diplomatic offensive in Southeast Asia.

It appeared to be a counter reaction to slow pace of reforms and poor quality of governance in traditional western institutions i.e. the International Monetary Fund (IMF), the World Bank (WB), and the Asian Development Bank (ADB), dominated by the U.S., European and Japan's interests, while providing far inadequate representation of Beijing's potential and importance,[1] as well as demonstration of the a more assertive course of China's diplomacy. According to the official declarations, new multilateral development bank is expected to promote interconnectivity, and regional economic integration, while being complementary to already existing, aforementioned financial institutions, namely the ADB, the IMF, as well as the WB.

Asian financial regionalism gained an impetus again, being boosted by international financial, and economic turbulences, as well as a threat of regional contagion after 2008, similarly to 1997–1998. As a consequence, regional state manifesting hegemonic ambitions, namely China, tried to supply new regional framework addressing the needs and concerns of the neighbours. This has been found as a source of significant costs, related to financial contribution of the founding country to the institution, so as political prestige, when considering higher-profile regionalist financial project, namely a regional development bank.

An important breakthrough was the keynote speech, given by Chinese premier Li Keqiang at the opening of the Boao Forum for Asia (BFA) Annual Conference 2014 in Boao, South China's Hainan Province, on 10th April 2014, in which he called upon the Asian nations „to find fresh ideas to re-energize the region in the face of new developments and challenge" (GB Times Beijing, 2014), while indicating the critical role of economic integration to achieve common development, undisrupted by various bottlenecks such as backward infrastructure. As a result, consultations with relevant parties intensified, paving the way to establishment of mega-regional financial institution.

The AIIB was expected to be a modern knowledge-based institution, focused on development of infrastructure, and productive sectors of Asia,

---

[1] For instance, China accounts for 3,81 percent of votes in the IMF, 5,47 percent of votes in the ADB, while the U.S. – 16,74 percent and 12,75 percent, respectively, while Japan – 6,23 percent and 12,84 percent, respectively (International Monetary Fund, 2015; Asian Development Bank, 2015).

including transportation, energy, telecommunication, rural infrastructure, water supply, sanitation, environmental protection, urban development, logistics etc. As it was stated, the AIIB project has been inspired by experiences of development banks, and private sector, assuming "lean, clean, and green"[2] nature of the newly established institution (Asian Infrastructure Investment Bank, 2015).

Following the Asian Development Bank Institute Report 2010, Asian region requires approximately 8 trillion USD for infrastructure projects, to continue economic development; then, China-backed regionalist financial project with initial registered capital of 50 billion USD, doubled in May 2015 as a consequence of three-day consultations of the AIIB chief negotiators in Singapore (Yoshida & Okoshi, 2015), may be found as valuable contribution to regional strategic investments. According to *World Economic Situation and Prospects 2015* report by United Nations, the AIIB "present potential for scaling up financing for sustainable development", however, operational modalities and institutional frameworks need to be developed, addressing lending models in accordance with the governance structures, volume of additional resources allocated, fragmentation of the development finance system, as well as competition among institutions, and incentive structures to encourage sustainable development (United Nations, 2015, p. 73). Noteworthy, Jim Yong Kim, the World Bank Group's president, found the China-led bank to be an important new partner that shares a common goal: "ending extreme poverty (...) with strong environment, labour and procurement standards, the AIIB will join us and other development banks in addressing the huge infrastructure needs that are critical to ending poverty, reducing inequalities, and boosting shared prosperity" (The World Bank, 2015).

Finally, Takehiko Nakao, the ADB's Japan's president stated, that creation of the AIIB was "understandable" given regional realities (Panda, 2015).

As some experts state, the AIIB may potentially go beyond typical infrastructure projects to address demand in healthcare or education sectors, including interventions within African continent. Undoubtedly, new bank might enable massive Chinese capital to finance regional development projects, while boosting economic and political hegemony of Beijing within Asia-Pacific region.

Next few months passed under the sign of bilateral and multilateral consultations, and discussions over key principles and core issues concerning new, China-backed financial institution. Till October 2014, 22 Asian states signed a Memorandum of Understanding to establish

---

[2] Lean stipulates small efficient management team; clean equals lack of tolerance for corruption; green means respect for environment.

the AIIB, Beijing has been chosen as the location of headquarters. Three rounds of discussions among Prospective Founding Members (PFM) took place between November 2014 and late March 2015 in China, India, and Kazakhstan. According to the formal statement by Chinese authorities, AIIB project should be finalized and enter into force till the end of 2015.[3] It is worth mentioning, that till the 20th of September 2015 only one country, namely Myanmar, ratified the Articles of Agreement (AOA), becoming formally the first of the AIIB's founding members on the 1st of July 2015. In order to launch operations, the AOA, providing a legal basis and institutional frameworks of the proposed bank, has to be ratified by at least 10 countries, comprising 50% of the initial subscriptions of capital stock. On the 29th of June 2015, 50 out of 57 PFM signed the AOA (Malaysia delayed decision till 21st August 2015), while absent Denmark, Kuwait, Philippines, Poland, South Africa, and Thailand will probably follow the remaining possibility, namely, ratify the document without previous signing in accordance with internal jurisdictions, however, not later than the 31st of December 2016, following Article 58 of the AOA.

3. The AIIB – controversies on the issues of membership and agenda

Following Article 3 of the AOA, "membership in the Bank shall be open to members of the International Bank for Reconstruction and Development or the Asian Development Bank" (AIIB, 2015a), thus, the concept of membership appears to be inclusive.

When studying the AIIB project it terms of membership, both its mega-regional scope, embracing 57 states,[4] as well as great absentees, with special regard to Japan's and the U.S., should be stressed. Deeper analysis of the AIIB voting system[5] indicates massive China's dominance, that

---

[3] In order to meet this date, AIIB hired a team consisting of former WB and ADB bankers.

[4] Noteworthy, India was invited to join new bank as one of the first in June 2014 on the occasion of the visit of Chinese foreign minister Wang Yi soon after the Modi government assumed office. It should be stressed, that the AIIB membership may facilitate New Delhi's access to infrastructural funding. Moreover, while opening Indian market to Chinese capital seeking for development projects to finance, New Delhi could be awarded with full membership in China and Russia-led Shanghai Cooperation Organization (Aneja, 2014).

[5] There are three types of votes, namely: basic votes, share votes and Founding Member votes. The basic votes are equal for all members and constitute 18% of the total votes, while the share votes are equal to the number of shares. Each Founding Member furthermore gets 600 votes. The allocated shares are based on the size of each AIIB member's economy, calculated as follows: 60% of the nominal GDP and 40% of the GDP PPP. Importantly, the number of shares determines the fraction of authorized capital in the bank. Three PFM, namely, Malaysia, Portugal, and Singapore, decided not to subscribe to all allocated shares (Asian Infrastructure Investment Bank, 2015a).

may translate perspectively into absolute control over all the decisions to be made or blocked, then, veto power[6] (for further studies: see Table 1).

Till the 15th of April 2015, therefore, two weeks following the deadline for submissions, 37 regional countries were provided with PFM status and entered the project, including, among others, the ASEAN member countries, Australia, India, Iran, Qatar, Russia, Saudi Arabia, South Korea, and United Arab Emirates, as well as 20 non-regional, such as Brazil, Egypt, France, Germany, Poland, South Africa, and United Kingdom.[7]

An overview of AIIB voting system indicates findings as follows.

Firstly, China's pool of votes – 26,06 percent, makes the institution-supplier an unquestioned dominator,[8] able to concentrate control over any decision in its hands at an incomparable degree when compared to the U.S. position in the IMF or Japan's in the ADB – 16,74 and 12,84 percent, respectively.

Secondly, China combined with the other BRICS states, namely, Brazil, Russia, India, and South Africa, accounts for 43,29 percent of votes, thus, five leading emerging markets may constitute an unconquerable coalition against, for instance, the AIIB members representing western world, including Japan's and the U.S. allies.

Thirdly, the G7 grouping, embracing most advanced economies in the world, represented in the AIIB by France, Germany, Italy, and the United Kingdom,[9] has been provided, when combined, with 12,74 percent of votes, therefore, less than a half of China's.

Fourthly, the world leading region in terms of nominal GDP, namely, the European Union (EU), represented by a half of its members (14 states), namely, Austria, Denmark, Finland, France, Germany, Italy, Luxembourg, Malta, the Netherlands, Poland, Portugal, Spain, Sweden, and the United Kingdom, disposes of 20,2 percent of votes, thus, less than a half of BRICS' pool.

Fifthly, 20 non-regional members of the AIIB account for 26,71 percent of votes, therefore, slightly more than one third of the regional pool shared by 37 states, while nearly equal to China's.

Noteworthy, Japan, same as the United States declared accordingly, that under the current circumstances, the AIIB project does not address

---

[6] However, as Wall Street Journal reported in March 2015, China declared its readiness to resign of veto rights.

[7] Noteworthy, both North Korea and Taiwan were rejected by China as prospective founding members of the AIIB, while Belgium, Czech Republic, Hungary, and Ukraine officially considered the membership. Next to Japan and the United States, Canada and Colombia expressed no intention to enter the China-led bank.

[8] Worth mentioning that China's contribution will exceed 29,78 billion USD, thus, 30,34 percent of the AIIB shares (Huang & Chen, 2015).

[9] Absent G7 members are as follows: Canada, Japan, and the United States.

Table 1. The AIIB Prospective Founding Members (PFM) and voting system

Country	PFM status	Percent of votes	Country	PFM status	Percent of votes	Country	PFM status	Percent of votes
Australia	3rd April 2015	3,46	Italy	2nd April 2015	2,49	Philippines	24th October 2014	1,11
Austria	11th April 2015	0,7	Jordan	7th February 2015	0,37	Poland	15th April 2015	0,98
Azerbaijan	15th April 2015	0,48	Kazakhstan	24th October 2014	0,89	Portugal	15th April 2015	0,32
Bangladesh	24th October 2014	0,83	South Korea	11th April 2015	3,5	Qatar	24th October 2014	0,79
Brazil	12th April 2015	3,02	Kuwait	24th October 2014	0,73	Russia	14th April 2015	5,93
Brunei	24th October 2014	0,31	Kyrgyzstan	9th April 2015	0,29	Saudi Arabia	13th January 2015	2,47
Cambodia	24th October 2014	0,32	Laos	24th October 2014	0,3	Singapore	24th October 2014	0,48
China	24th October 2014	26,06	Luxembourg	27th March 2015	0,32	South Africa	15th April 2015	0,77
Denmark	12th April 2015	0,58	Malaysia	24th October 2014	0,36	Spain	11th April 2015	1,79
Egypt	14th April 2015	0,83	Maldives	31st December 2014	0,27	Sri Lanka	24th October 2014	0,5
Finland	12th April 2015	0,53	Malta	9th April 2015	0,27	Sweden	15th April 2015	0,81
France	2nd April 2015	3,19	Mongolia	24th October 2014	0,3	Switzerland	28th March 2015	0,87
Georgia	12th April 2015	0,31	Myanmar	24th October 2014	0,49	Tajikistan	13th January 2015	0,29
Germany	1st April 2015	4,15	Nepal	24th October 2014	0,33	Thailand	24th October 2014	1,5
Iceland	15th April 2015	0,28	Netherlands	12th April 2015	1,16	Turkey	10th April 2015	2,52
India	24th October 2014	7,51	New Zealand	5th January 2015	0,66	United Arab Emirates	5th April 2015	1,29
Indonesia	25th November 2014	3,17	Norway	14th April 2015	0,74	United Kingdom	28th March 2015	2,91
Iran	7th April 2015	1,63	Oman	24th October 2014	0,49	Uzbekistan	24th October 2014	0,45
Israel	15th April 2015	0,91	Pakistan	24th October 2014	1,16	Vietnam	24th October 2014	0,84

Source: own elaboration based on: Huang & Chen, 2015.

high standards of governance, lacking also environmental and social safeguards, therefore, both Tokyo and Washington explicitly expressed no interest in membership. According to Reuters, the AIIB is an attempt to change the unwritten rules of global development finance. Even though submitted projects will be assessed in terms of their legal transparency, as well as social and environmental interests of various stakeholders, the AIIB probably dictates no requirements regarding privatization and deregulation of businesses from its future borrowers; then, rejects free market economic policies recommended by the World Bank when providing loans. The AIIB representatives admitted, that, prospectively, loans would be combined with i.e. government subsidies to defray costs and avoid "hiking prices", while simplifying the internal review and risk assessment system of projects, in order to reduce costs and cut red tape. Worth mentioning, the decision making procedures are expected to be more efficient and less-time consuming, probably, at least to some extent, at the expense of "due diligence" rule (Qing Koh Gui, 2015). It is hard to assume that China may be willing to threaten future AIIB credit rating by adopting imprudent approach.

Both the US and Japan's optics seem to be ambiguous, especially when considering AIIB membership of close allies of Washington, namely the United Kingdom, Australia, New Zealand, India, Israel, and South Korea. The White House officially declared respect for those decisions, however, it also expressed hope, that the membership of countries such as the United Kingdom will help to push for adoption of high standards. Unofficially, the U.S. authorities felt disappointed and angry. As the U.S. government officially admitted, "we are wary about a trend toward constant accommodation of China, which is not the best way to engage a rising power" (Dyer & Parker, 2015), however, representative of the British prime minister seemed to ignore Washington's criticism stating that "(...) there will be times when we take a different approach ... We think that it's in the UK's national interest" (Branigan, 2015). Worth mentioning, the UK's decision to enter the AIIB on 28th March 2015, was followed by West European powers, namely Germany, France, and Italy on the 1st and 2nd April, respectively.

The official statement of German government regarding the AIIB membership might be reflected by finance minister Wolfgang Schäuble stating as follows: "we want to contribute our long-standing experience with international financial institutions to the creation of the new bank by setting high standards and helping the bank to get a high international reputation" (Thomas & Hutzler, 2015).

Consequently, 14 EU members already joined China-led bank, including Poland – a strategic ally of the U.S. in Central Europe.

Next to the British AIIB membership, Australia's and South Korean engagement in the China-led bank, despite intensive efforts of the U.S. diplomacy, should be studied.

The Australian's Treasurer Joe Hockey announced the decision to join the AIIB as a founding member in June 2015, declaring five-year contribution up to 930 million USD, therefore, the sixth largest amongst the 57 PFM. Following the official statement of the government, the AIIB is expected to provide Australia with "great opportunities to work with (...) neighbours and largest trading partner to drive economic growth and jobs", while attempting to dispel Japan's and the U.S. doubts and concerns, stating that "the governance of the AIIB will be based on best practice, ensuring that all members will be directly involved in the direction and decision making of the bank in an open and transparent manner" (BBC News, 2015; Tay, 2015). Importantly, a joint statement of the Australian prime minister, Tony Abbott, the foreign minister, Julie Bishop, and the treasurer, Joe Hockey stressed the importance of "the bank's board of directors having authority over key investment decisions, and that no one country control the bank" (Murphy, 2015).

Furthermore, Hockey's argumentation seemed to be followed by South Korean government, discouraged unsuccessfully from the AIIB membership by the strategic western security ally. Consequently, Seoul announced joining China-backed institution on the 28th of March 2015, as the last close ally of the U.S. among PFM, while being urged by Washington not to join a year before. This time, however, as the consequence of decisions of numerous allies of the U.S. to enter China's project, the American voice of disapproval seemed to fell silent (Kang, 2015). According to the official statement by South Korea's finance ministry, "the government will make efforts in close cooperation with the major countries to help the AIIB possess a high level of standards in the areas of responsibility, transparency, governing structure and debt sustainability", while demanding, following, among others, the UK's and Australian stance, improvements in the AIIB's governing structure and safeguards (Yoo Choonsik, 2015). Noteworthy, South Korea's finance minister, Taro Aso, reiterated Japan's concerns regarding fair governance at the AIIB, establishment of the board of directors, debt sustainability and respect for social and environmental issues (Kim & Choonsik Yoo, 2015), while pointing out opportunities provided by the AIIB membership, namely, an access to numerous construction, telecommunication and transportation projects for local businesses, as well as strengthening position of the country within the international banking sector (Mundy, 2015).

Finally, Poland's decision to join the AIIB, as the only country belonging to the EU from Central and Eastern Europe, and one of the closest allies to the U.S. in this part of the world, deserves extra attention. The Polish government announced officially its will to join the AIIB as the founding member on the 25th of August 2015, perceiving membership as an opportunity for the Polish companies to expand into Asia (Szary, 2015). As already mentioned, Poland refused to sign the AOA in June 2015, while being expected to do so after being officially accepted as the future AIIB's PFM on the 15th April. However, as government officials argued, it is a matter of time, that was too short to consult all the ministries and agencies before late June (Węglarczyk, 2015). The Poland's decision, probably encouraged by the other large EU members' decision to join the China-led project, including important U.S. allies, seemed to manifest both pragmatism and political realism of the Polish government, being aware of the rising importance of China for Central and Eastern Europe, as well as whole EU and the global economy. Therefore, Polish "yes" to the AIIB may be found as an intention to take root in the "main stream" of the EU. Warsaw probably did not feel the U.S. pressure at a degree comparable to Seoul, Sydney or London to stay outside China's project, due to lesser strategic importance as an American ally.

Interestingly, Hong Kong's representatives attended the third Chief Negotiators' Meeting held for Prospective Founding Members (PFM) in the late March 2015, by joining the Chinese delegation, however, official status will be determined after completing the negotiations. Similarly, Chinese Taipei hasn't been accepted so far, without indicating any reason; however, Beijing declared to keep the door open for the future membership of Taiwan (Kim & Choonsik Yoo, 2015).

From Japan's perspective, that appeared to be consistent with the U.S. stance, the AIIB was found as an instrument of expansion of China's soft power within the region, that could potentially challenge Washington's and Tokyo's influences. However, in an official statement, Tokyo seems to be inconsistent and ambiguous. In March 2015, after the statement of Japan's ambassador to China, Masato Kitera, that Tokyo's membership in the AIIB is likely, Chief Cabinet Secretary Yoshihide Suga, unequivocally denied this fact. According to Suga, Japan is truly concerned, whether the AIIB will be properly governed, and would not damage other creditors (Yahoo!News, 2015). As mentioned above, a key regional rival of the AIIB is the ADB, dominated by Tokyo's interests.

As a consequence of a lack of China's response to Japanese, as well as the American concerns, Suga declared that Tokyo is no longer considering AIIB membership. The latter statement has been confirmed by the Japan's prime minister Shinzo Abe, who argued, that Tokyo doesn't need to enter a new regional bank. Meanwhile, South Korea's decision to enter the AIIB was officially welcomed calmly in Tokyo, however, experts found this movement to be an attempt to gain an advantage over Japan, as well as a source of concerns for Japanese businesses being afraid of excluding them from the race for infrastructure projects in developing countries (The Japan Times, 2015; Gale & Taylor, 2015).

4. A brief look into the future

In May 2015, following the official acceptance of 57 PFM by the AIIB designated bodies, Japan seemed to try to seize the initiative in the region, while attempting to legitimate its own disapproval regarding membership in the China-led bank. Namely, Japan's prime minister Shinzo Abe announced the new five-year aid package of 110 billion USD, dedicated to „high-quality" infrastructure developments in Asia (Kameda, 2015). Following Abe's statement, Japan is willing to support the region regarding its demand for energy and innovation, however, an emphasis is put on the innovative dimension of the infrastructure projects to be financed. Also, the funds provided would probably manifest Japan's primacy over China's concept of regional development assistance, while confirming that "the game is still going on" (Kihara & Sieg, 2015). Noteworthy, aid package is to be distributed through the Asian Development Bank to counter newly established China's institution, as well as Japan's own national, specialized agencies and organizations (Channels NewsAsia, 2015). Additionally, Japan's government declared support in terms of building capacity, providing training for 8 thousand specialists from the medical sector in ASEAN, and 5 thousand from the energy sector across Asia in the five-year period.

But next to establishment of the AIIB, China's multifaceted activities embrace support for the India's project of the New Development Bank, (NDB) formerly referred to as the BRICS Development Bank, involving five large emerging markets, namely Brazil, Russia, India, China, and South Africa,[10] thus BRICS grouping, with a treaty signed in June 2014, and already in force. Another regional development bank headquartered in China, however, in Shanghai, is aimed at mobilizing "resources for infrastructure and sustainable development projects in BRICS and other emerging economies and developing countries", therefore, it may potentially complement the AIIB's acitivities to go beyond Asia-Pacific region to expand BRICS' members influences within different regions; while countering, alike partner financial institution located in Beijing, aforementioned Japan- and U.S.-led counterparts. It is worth mentioning, that

---

[10] Among which, China, India and Russia are simultaneously the three largest AIIB shareholders.

according to the Agreement on the New Development Bank signed at the 6th BRICS Summit held in Fortaleza, Brazil on the 15th of July 2014, each country holds equal number of shares, while possessing one voice and lacking any veto power (BBC News, 2014; Desai & Vreeland, 2014). The total capital amounted to USD 100 billion, then, equal to AIIB, 12,5 percent of which need to paid directly by the members in the seven-year period.[11] Moreover, additional 100 billion USD has been agreed under special reserve currency pool, potentially to counter the western-backed lending institutions (Government of Brazil, 2014). Last but not least, an agreement on cooperation between BRICS export credit agencies was signed, as well as an agreement on cooperation in innovation.

Finally, the Silk Road Fund, the China's state-owned 40 billion USD investment fund was established in 2014 to finance economic development projects under "One Belt, One Road" (Belt and Road Initiative, abbreviated OBOR) framework proposed by Beijing, announced in October 2013 by the president, Xi Jinping (Wu Jiao & Zhang Yunbi, 2013; Caixin, 2014). The main purpose is to enhance and support cooperation and connectivity of Eurasian states, while exporting China's production capabilities and increasing the role in the global affairs. OBOR is expected to proceed within two components, namely, the land-based Silk Road Economic Belt (SREB) and the oceangoing Maritime Silk Road (MSR). The Karot hydropower project in Pakistan, unveiled in April 2015, is the first investment financed by China's Silk Road Fund (Xinhuanet, 2015).

Conclusion

The Asian Infrastructure Investment Bank seems to be pretty attractive for both academics and policy makers, gaining attention and inducing debates on the regional and global governance issues. The new development bank, accompanied by parallel initiatives of the New Development Bank and the Silk Road Fund, significantly boost Beijing's influence within the international financial system, while raising various concerns and expectations.

On the one hand, China proved to be ready to establish multilateral financial framework, address development goals and infrastructure demand, attract many regional and non-regional governments to par-

---

[11] Initial capital of 50 billion USD had to be contributed on equal shares by all the members. Following AOA, individual shares may be increased, however, only under permission of the other members, as it was requested by India, when creating NDB's treaty. Additionally, even though membership is inclusive, thus, new entrants are welcome, BRICS' shares in capital cannot fall under 55 percent of total.

ticipate. On the other hand, Chinese leaders proved to be pragmatic when manifesting flexibility and persuasibility in regards to the AIIB's governance structures, including, among others, voting system and veto rights, while declaring multilateral character of the newly established institution, headquartered and dominated by China, though.

Following Jin Liqun, president-designate of the Asian Infrastructure Investment Bank, "AIIB will be a good global citizen", following the principles of transparency, openness, independence and accountability. Noteworthy, according to Liqun, at least twenty states are still considering the AIIB membership, thus, China-led bank may potentially overshadow the Japan-led ADB engaging 67 members (Watts, 2015; The Times of India, 2015).

Even though China is attempting to distance itself from any confrontational aspects of the newly established financial institutions, it is hard to question the essence of the message sent to the western world and institutions, when Chinese Finance Minister Lou Jiwei introduced the AIIB as "the new type of multilateral bank for the 21st century" (Salze-Lozac'h, 2015). Moreover, the NDB and the Silk Road Fund, accompanied by BRICS emergency reserve fund, seem to support China's geopolitical expansion toward "hollowing out" and breaking the monopoly position of the IMF, the WB and the ADB in the international development finance system. What is worth mentioning is thatChina's "One Belt, One Road" initiative will be connected with the Russia-led Eurasian Economic Union (EAEU), while BRICS cooperate more and more intensively with the China-led Shanghai Cooperation Organization (SCO) (The Economic Times, 2015).

Consequently, Japan's or the U.S. dilemma whether to join the AIIB or to stay outside, appears to be a wrong question in the wrong time. When addressing governance issues or environmental safeguards, it seems that optimizing new development bank in terms of agenda and structure, could be done better from the inside, thus, being a founding member of this multilateral institution, through building coalitions and imposing a pressure in favour of expected reforms. It seems probable that such a hypothetical U.S.-led coalition in the AIIB, engaging potentially, amongst others, the EU representatives, Japan, South Korea, Arab States, as well as India, may counter China's dominance and enhance significant improvements that could provide the AIIB with global legitimacy and recognition, to replace institutional competition with the IMF, the WB or the ADB with complementarity and strategic alliance in fighting against poverty and boosting global sustainable growth and prosperity. Many of the U.S. allies, with special regard to the United Kingdom, Australia, and South Korea, seemed to choose pragmatism and political realism at the expense of absolute and unconditional loyalty towards Washington and, as a last resort, erosion of bilateral ties.

China has entered the stage manifesting geopolitical hegemonic ambitions to influence and manage global governance processes, challenge multilateral institutional order, while drawing a vision of better, bright future for the Asia-Pacific region, prospectively also other emerging regions. However, hosting the AIIB's headquarters in Beijing, as well as the NDB's in Shanghai, combined with the "One Belt, One Road" initiative to connect Eurasia, while inducing a prestige and political radiation, expose the world largest emerging market to various risks resulted of eventual institution's poor governance, moral hazard, wrong targeting of aid, as well as ignorance of non-economic aspects of investments or surveillance mechanisms. One thing is certain for China – the whole world is watching.

References

Aneja, A. (2014). China invites India to join Asian Infrastructure Investment Bank. *The Hindu*, 30th June. Retrieved from: http://www.thehindu.com/todays-paper/tp-national/china-invites-india-to-join-asian-infrastructure-investment-bank/article6161311.ece (accessed: 14/07/2015).

Asian Development Bank (2015). Retrieved from: http://www.adb.org/sites/default/files/institutional-document/158032/oi-appendix1.pdf (accessed: 20/07/2015).

Asian Infrastructure Investment Bank (2015). Retrieved from: http://www.aiibank.org/ (accessed: 10/08/2015).

Asian Infrastructure Investment Bank (2015a). *Articles of Agreement*, 21st July. Retrieved from: http://www.aiibank.org/uploadfile/2015/0629/20150629094900288.pdf (accessed: 10/08/2015).

BBC News (2014). *Brics nations to create $100bn development bank*, 15th July 2014. Retrieved from: http://www.bbc.com/news/business-28317555 (accessed: 21/07/2015).

BBC News (2015). *Australia to join China-led AIIB as founding member*, 24th June. Retrieved from: http://www.bbc.com/news/business-33250847 (accessed: 14/07/2015).

Blustein, P. (2000). *The Chastening: Inside the Crisis that Rocked the Global Financial System and Humbled the IMF*. New York: Public Affairs.

Branigan, T. (2015). Support for China-led development bank grows despite US opposition. *The Guardian*, 14th March. Retrieved from: http://www.theguardian.com/world/2015/mar/13/support-china-led-developmentbank-grows-despite-us-opposition-australia-uk-new-zealand-asia (accessed: 22/05/2015).

Caixin (2014). *One Belt, One Road*, 12th October 2014. Retrieved from: http://english.caixin.com/2014–12–10/100761304.html (accessed: 30/06/2015).

Channels NewsAsia (2015). *Japan PM unveils US$110b plan for Asian infrastructure*, 21st May. Retrieved from: http://www.channelnewsasia.com/news/business/japan-pm-unveils-us-110b/1863328.html (accessed: 11/06/2015).

Desai, R.M. & Vreeland, J.R. (2014). What's the new bank of BRICS is all about. *The Washington Post*, 17th July. Retrieved from: http://www.washingtonpost. com/blogs/monkey-cage/wp/2014/07/17/what-the-new-bank-of-brics-is-all-about/ (accessed: 2/07/2015).

Dyer, G. & Parker, G. (2015). US Attacks UK's constant Accomodation with China. *Financial Times*, 12th March. Retrieved from: http://www.ft.com/intl /cms/s/0655b342-cc29–11e4-beca-00144feab7de,Authorised=false.html? siteedition=uk&_i_location=http%3A%2F%2Fwww.ft.com %2Fcms%2Fs%2F0 %2F0655b342-cc29–11e4-beca-00144feab7de.html%3Fsiteedition%3Duk&_i_re ferer=&classification=conditional_standard&iab=barrier-app#axzz3m5Zuw VYe (accessed: 24/06/2015).

Eichengreen, B. (2009). Can Asia Free Itself from the IMF? *Project Syndicate*, June, 22. Retrieved from: http://www.project-syndicate.org/commentary/ eichengreen6/English (accessed: 14/07/2015).

Gale, A. & Taylor, R. (2015). Decision to Join China-Led Bank Tests South Korea's Ties to U.S. *The Wall Street Journal*, 24th March. Retrieved from: http:// www.wsj.com/articles/decision-to-join-aiib-tests-south-koreas-ties-to-u-s-1427185565 (accessed: 31/05/2015).

GB Times Beijing (2014). *China eyes closer Asia's economic integration through Asian infrastructure bank*, 11th April. Retrieved from: http://gbtimes.com/ china/china-eyes-closer-asias-economic-integration-through-asian-infrastructure-bank (accessed: 10/07/2015).

Glaser, B.S. & Murphy, M. (2009). Soft Power with Chinese Characteristics: The Ongoing Debate. In: McGiffert, C. (ed.). *Chinese Soft Power and Its Implications for the United States*. Washington, D.C.: CSIS, March. Retrieved from: http://csis.org/files/media/csis/pubs/090403_mcgiffert_chinesesoftpower_ web.pdf (accessed: 14/07/2015).

Government of Brazil (2014). *Agreement on the New Development Bank – Fortaleza, July 15*, 15th July 2014. Retrieved from: http://brics.itamaraty.gov.br/ media2/press-releases/219-agreement-on-the-new-development-bank-fortaleza-july-15 (accessed: 11/07/2015).

Hamanaka, S. (2010). *Asian Regionalism and Japan*. London and New York: Routledge.

Huang, C. & Chen, A. (2015). China to have 30 per cent stake, veto power under AIIB deal. *South China Morning Post*, 30th June. Retrieved from: http://www. scmp.com/news/china/diplomacy-defence/article/1829342/aiib-deal-seals-chinas-big-stake-new-lender (accessed: 10/07/2015).

International Monetary Fund (2015). Retrieved from: https://www.imf.org/external/np/sec/memdir/members.aspx (accessed: 1/07/2015).

Jiao Wu & Yunbi Zhang (2013). Xi in call for building of new 'maritime silk road'. *China Daily*, 4th October. Retrieved from: http://usa.chinadaily.com.cn/china/2013–10/04/content_17008940.htm (accessed: 7/07/2015).

Kameda, M. (2015). Abe announces $110 billion in aid for 'high-quality' infrastructure in Asia. *The Japan Times*, 22th May. Retrieved from: http://www. japantimes.co.jp/news/2015/05/22/business/abe-announces-110-billion-in-aid-for-high-quality-infrastructure-in-asia/#.Vf-z-3200pT (accessed: 7/07/2015).

Kang Tae-jun (2015). South Korea Torn Between US and China. *The Diplomat*, 20th March. Retrieved from: http://thediplomat.com/2015/03/south-korea-torn-between-us-and-china/ (accessed: 14/07/2015).

Kihara, L. & Sieg, L. (2015). Japan just took a $110 billion shot a China's new infrastructure bank. *Business Insider*, 21st May. Retrieved from: http://www.businessinsider.com/r-japan-unveils-110-billion-plan-to-fund-asia-infrastructure-eye-on-aiib-2015–5 (accessed: 2/07/2015).

Kim, Ch. & Yoo Choonsik (2015). *South Korea sees gains for its infrastructure firms from joining AIIB*. Reuters, 27th March. Retrieved from: http://www.reuters.com/article/2015/03/28/us-asia-aiib-idUSKBN0MN08L20150328 (accessed: 23/07/2015).

Kindleberger, Ch. (1973). *The World in Depression, 1929–1939*. London: Allen Lane.

Morgenthau, H. (1978). *Politics among Nations: The Struggle for Power and Peace*, 3rd edition. New York: Alfred A. Knopf.

Mundy, S. (2015). South Korea to join China-led development bank. *Financial Times*, 27th March. Retrieved from: http://www.ft.com/cms/s/0/7587ad1c-d429–11e4-b041–00144feab7de.html#axzz3mDgFcCdU (accessed: 14.07.2015).

Murphy, K. (2015), Australia confirms it will join China's Asian Infrastructure Investment Bank. *The Guardian*, 28th March. Retrieved from: http://www.theguardian.com/business/2015/mar/29/australia-confirms-it-will-join-chinas-asian-infrastructure-investment-bank (accessed: 24/06/2015).

Panda, A. (2015). South Korea Joins the AIIB. *The Diplomat*, 28th March. Retrieved from: http://thediplomat.com/2015/03/south-korea-joins-the-aiib/ (accessed: 14/07/2015).

Qing Koh Gui (2015). *China's AIIB to offer loans with fewer strings attached*. Reuters, 1st September. Retrieved from: http://www.cnbc.com/2015/09/01/chinas-aiib-to-better-world-bank-adb-on-loan-terms.html (accessed: 11/09/2015).

Salze-Lozac'h V. (2015). To Be or Not To Be Part of AIIB. *The Asia Foundation*, 22th July 2015. Retrieved from: http://asiafoundation.org/in-asia/2015/07/22/to-be-or-not-to-be-part-of-aiib/ (accessed: 14/08/2015).

Szary, W. (2015). *Poland says to join Asian Infrastructure Investment Bank*. Reuters, 25th August. Retrieved from: http://www.reuters.com/article/2015/08/25/poland-investment-aiib-idUSL5N1103FK20150825 (accessed: 10/09/2015).

Tay, H.F. (2015). Asian Infrastructure Investment Bank: Australia sixth-biggest shareholder in China bank. *ABC*, 7th July. Retrieved from: http://www.abc.net.au/news/2015–06–29/australia-sixth-biggest-shareholder-in-new-china-investment-bank/6580682 (accessed: 14/07/2015).

The Economic Times (2015). *BRICS bank, AIIB to break IMF, World Bank monopoly: China think tank*, 14th July. Retrieved from: http://economictimes.indiatimes.com/news/international/business/brics-bank-aiib-to-break-imf-world-bank-monopoly-china-think-tank/articleshow/48053695.cms (accessed: 15/07/2015).

The Japan Times (2015). *Japan reacts calmly to South Korean decision to join China-led AIIB*, 27th March. Retrieved from: http://www.japantimes.co.jp/news/2015/03/27/world/japan-takes-south-koreas-decision-join-china-led-aiib-calmly/#.Vf3Jp32oopR (accessed: 5/06/2015).

The Times of India (2015). *Over 20 countries on 'waiting list' to join AIIB: China*, 19th September. Retrieved from: http://timesofindia.indiatimes.com/business/international-business/Over-20-countries-on-waiting-list-to-join-AIIB-China/articleshow/49025887.cms (accessed: 19/09/2015).

The World Bank (2015), *Statement by World Bank Group President Jim Yong Kim on the Establishment of AIIB*, 28th June. Retrieved from: http://www.worldbank.org/en/news/press-release/2015/06/28/statement-by-world-bank-group-president-jim-yong-kim-on-the-establishment-of-aiib (accessed: 10/07/2015).

Thomas, A. & Hutzler, Ch. (2015). Germany, France, Italy to Join China-Backed Development Bank. *The Wall Street Journal*, 17th March. Retrieved from: http://www.wsj.com/articles/germany-france-italy-to-join-china-backed-development-bank-1426597078 (accessed: 10/07/2015).

United Nations (2015). *World Economic Situation and Prospects 2015*, New York. Retrieved from: http://www.un.org/en/development/desa/policy/wesp/wesp_archive/2015wesp-ch3-en.pdf (accessed: 25/06/2015).

Wang Yunjong (2000). The Asian Financial Crisis and its Aftermath: Do We Need a Regional Financial Arrangement? *ASEAN Economic Bulletin, 17*(2).

Watts, J.M. (2015). Up to 20 Countries Waiting to Join China-Led AIIB, President-Designate Says. *The Wall Street Journal*, 19th September. Retrieved from: http://www.wsj.com/articles/up-to-20-countries-waiting-to-join-china-led-aiib-president-designate-says-1442666572 (accessed: 20/09/2015).

Węglarczyk, B. (2015). Polska nie przystąpiła do banku Azji. *Rzeczpospolita*, 30th June. Retrieved from: http://www.rp.pl/artykul/1212237.html (accessed: 1/07/2015).

Xinhuanet (2015), Commentary: Silk Road Fund's 1st investment makes China's words into practice, 21st April 2015. Retrieved from: http://news.xinhuanet.com/english/2015-04/21/c_134170737.htm (accessed: 14/05/2015).

Yahoo!News (2015). Retrieved from: http://news.yahoo.com/japan-denies-plan-join-china-led-development-bank-041742313--finance.html (accessed: 22/07/2015).

Yoo Choonsik (2015). *Another U.S. ally, South Korea, seeks to join China-backed AIIB*. Reuters, 26th March. Retrieved from: http://www.reuters.com/article/2015/03/26/us-asia-aiib-southkorea-idUSKBN0MM1ES20150326 (accessed: 24/04/2015).

Yoshida, W. & Okoshi, M. (2015). AIIB doubles funds to $100 billion. *Nikkei Asian Review*, 22nd May. Retrieved from: http://asia.nikkei.com/Politics-Economy/International-Relations/AIIB-doubles-funds-to-100-billion (accessed: 16/06/2015).

Alice Rezková

What Can CEE and China Learn from Each Other in Innovation?

Innovation, viewed in general terms as a tool to overcome economic growth slowdowns, has become a buzzword for many decision-makers and scientists. It is usually presented as a rescue path for economies that have already reached a certain, relatively comfortable income level, but are unable to move forward with their current economic growth model. Emerging economies have been attempting to alter their economic strategies to recover their growth rates in a sustainable manner. In addition, the governments with upper-middle income or high-income status think about creative reconstruction of their economic growth models.

The global financial crisis caused economic detriment in many sectors, and no economy was spared. Some managed to resume decent economic growth, while others never really recovered. Similarly, many East Asian economies, for example South Korea and Taiwan, overcame the financial crisis in the 1990s very well, while others like Japan, experienced a "lost decade" of economic stagnation. It seems as though as these economies were trapped in a pre-crisis stage missing out on essential economic reforms and remaining at the same level of development. This situation can be a natural growth slowdown that usually appears after strong growth periods, or it can represent a more sophisticated condition that can be called a "middle income trap."

The term "middle-income trap" (MIT) was first introduced by World Bank economists in relation to economic development in East Asia (Gil et al., 2007), and is therefore a relatively new term to describe the slowdown of previously very rapidly growing economies. Although the current literature does not offer a formal MIT definition, it can be described as a situation when "middle-income economies have a low probability of sustaining sufficiently high growth rates to join the high-income group" (Han et al., 2015). The World Bank uses gross national income (GNI) per capita to measure economies' capacity to provide well-being to its citizens. "Countries with average incomes of $12,476 (measured at 2011 prices) or more are classified as high income or developed economies" (World Bank, 2013). Therefore, countries need to exceed this threshold to become members of the high-income club, and for some, reaching this threshold was a difficult task. The most evident victim of this trap, often cited as retrospective proof of the MIT theory are Latin American economies that struggled to achieve high-income levels despite achieving middle-income status decades ago.

According to available literature there are two schools of thought. One sees the trap as "growth slowdown" that usually follows several years of strong growth (Eihengreen et al., 2013; Aiyar et al., 2013). The second sees the trap in a perspective of developing countries relative to the United States. Lee infers that "countries are most likely to fall into the middle income trap when their income levels rise to about 20–30% of the US level" (Lee, 2013). For example, China will very soon reach the World Bank middle-income status threshold, but its economy will also fit the definition of a middle income country with the income level of 20–30% of the US level.

If middle-income countries tend to be trapped at that level, what would this imply to the Central and Eastern European countries? Based on the World Bank criteria, Croatia, the Czech Republic, Hungary, the Slovak Republic, and Slovenia successfully moved into the high-income range. Bulman and his team define middle-income countries as those with per capita incomes between 10% and 50% of the US (Bulman et al., 2014). The threshold of 30% of the US income level further divides countries into lower and upper middle income groups. A Polish report argues that the threshold for being trapped is at the level between 45% and 65% of USA GDP per capita (Bukowski et al., 2012). According to these definitions, none of the countries from Central and Eastern Europe would fit into the high-income club, as shown in Figure 1. Therefore, any of them can be potentially threatened by the MIT.

Some researchers consider the MIT to be a myth, because so far not enough statistical evidence for unavoidable traps in middle-income status can be found. Therefore, they argue that the MIT concept cannot be broadly applied to every economy. Furthermore, the chances of middle-income economies catching up with very rich economies are less probable, as these income leaders represent moving targets. Notwithstanding the theoretical debate, an economic growth slowdown usually indicates a need to initiate structural changes, and inspire innovative solutions for new jobs creation and improvement of general well-being.

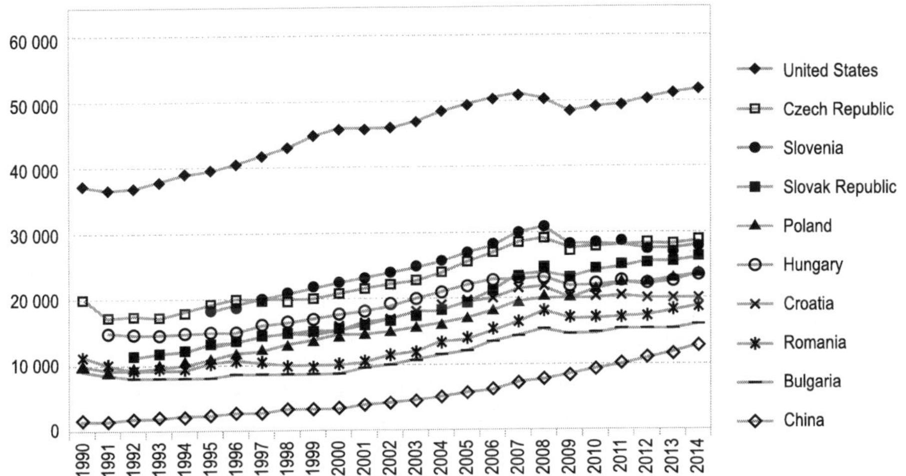

Figure 1: GDP per capita PPP (constant 2011, international $)
Source: World Bank Database.

1. Innovation drivers for sustainable economic growth

Even though China and the CEE[1] economies are defined by different geographical location, history, size or economy character, it seems that they are similar in terms of trying to initiate measures to stimulate economic growth. China together with India and the CEE belonged to the fastest growing regions in the world prior to the global financial crisis. Although the economic growth in the CEE region lagged behind China's incredible growth in the past decade, its results were impressive in comparison with other regions, as shown in Figure 2. Yet currently, many of the CEE countries experience a sluggish growth after the financial crisis began, as shown in Figure 1. However, not all individual countries are undergoing stagnation as some countries, for example Slovakia, experienced mild growth. China's economic slowdown during 2015, combined with the near-panic in its stock markets, reflect the planned transformation of its economy from agriculture and heavy industry into one focused on higher-value added products and services. But China's situation also raises questions about its underlying economic health, as there is obviously a strong need for reforms that would facilitate this transformation.

In addition to strong pre-crisis growth, both the CEE and China share one very similar comparative advantage within their regions. As shown

---

[1] Central and Eastern European countries definition following EU member states: Bulgaria, Croatia, the Czech Republic, Hungary, Poland, Romania, the Slovak Republic, and Slovenia.

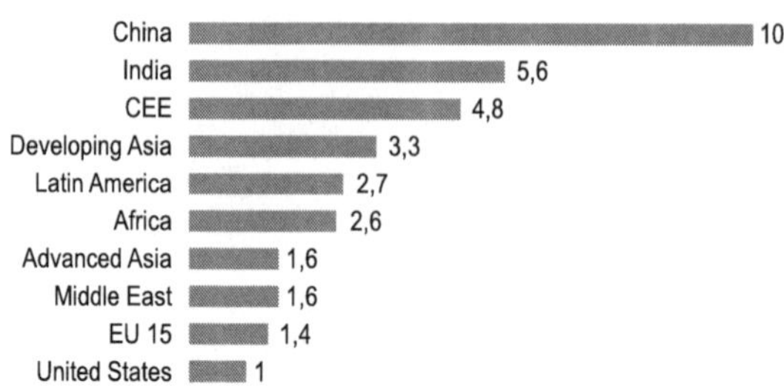

Figure 2: GDP per capita (real $), annual growth rate, 2000–2008
Source: IMF.

in Figure 2, both the CEE countries and China rely on comparatively low labour costs. The CEE utilizes its lower costs within the European Union as China does globally. As a result, both entities have successfully attracted foreign investors, who build low-cost production factories, lines assembling higher-value added products, as well as back-office centres. But their low cost comparative advantage will erode in the coming year, as competition increases from other countries with even cheaper labour. Thus, for both China and the CEE, productivity improvements through innovation and upgrading of production will be needed to drive growth.

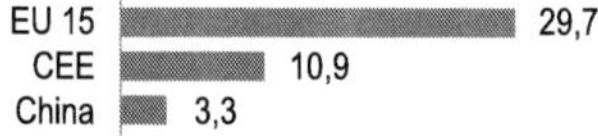

Figure 3: Average labour cost per hour, 2014
Source: Eurostat, National Bureau of Statistics of China.

Apparently, then, the MIT is not unavoidable, but is rather a situation linked with productivity gaps, as well as technological and structural changes. Based on his extensive research, Kanchoochat has identified three basic strategies for exiting the MIT: (1) improving education and governance, (2) changing export composition by following comparative advantage, (3) changing export composition by defying comparative advantage (Kanchoochat, 2014). The main difference between following and defying comparative advantage depends on the degree of governmental involvement in the acquisition of advanced technology. Lee confirms that "many developing countries will initially begin by selecting industries according to their initial comparative advantages, which is driven usually by their initial endowment conditions" (Lee, 2014). But he also stresses that countries should not remain at that middle stage, and should develop comparative advantages based on advanced technology and innovation.

Both the CEE countries and China now ask what strategies to implement in rebuilding their economies, creating new jobs and re-initiating economic growth. Such questions are obviously posed in different contexts, as China and the CEE countries face quite complex economic situations that cannot be comparable in all aspects. Also, innovation as a universal solution has to be perceived in its broader definition within various industries, not only the stereotypical linkage with high-tech industries. This research paper will evaluate some of the elements important for MIT exit strategies in both entities. The analytical criteria are based on available literature on innovation-oriented MIT solutions. The final set of criteria includes: (1) Governance, (2) Education, (3) Research and development, (4) Infrastructure, and (5) Urbanization.[2] Are there any areas where China and the CEE can share any lessons learned, or alternatively, define a weak approach?

2. Governance

Good governance is crucial for growth. It is indisputable that the quality of a country's legal institutions, corruption control and promotion of the rule of law can support the creation of better economic performance. They may enable a middle-income country to achieve high-income status. Research on this topic finds „evidence that corruption undermines the positive effect of institutions and trade openness on growth" (Campos et al., 2010).

While the CEE economies have eased regulations and created better environments for businesses, other reforms that could encourage entrepreneurship and attract more investment still lag behind, particularly in areas related to the rule of law and control of corruption. The situation in China is particularly alarming, as can be seen in Figure 4, which analyses 4 criteria based on Worldwide Governance Indicators: government effectiveness, regulatory quality, rule of law, and control of corruption. Each indicator can reach values between –2.5 and 2.5. Except for government effectiveness, China has negative values in all other criteria. Even though the CEE countries achieved higher values, they are very far below the EU-15 average, particularly in control of corruption.

Both the CEE countries and China demonstrate their weak points relative to the rule of law and control of corruption. These are areas where it can be very difficult to share experiences due to significant differences in legal systems. However, both parties can further support their efforts

---

[2] For example Aiyar completed a study in which he analysed determinants of growth slowdowns (institutions, demography, infrastructure, macroeconomic environment and policies, economic structure) on a set of 1125 observations with 123 slowdown episodes from 1960 to 2005 (Aiyar et al., 2013).

in increasing government effectiveness through enhancement of governmental e-services, their accessibility, and digital solutions for emergency crises. Similarly, many countries currently strive for convergence of their regulatory frameworks. The CEE countries follow the EU lead, and it could be beneficial for China to concentrate not only on tariff reductions in their bilateral trade, but also on convergence to international standards, which would also ease the situation for Chinese entrepreneurs.

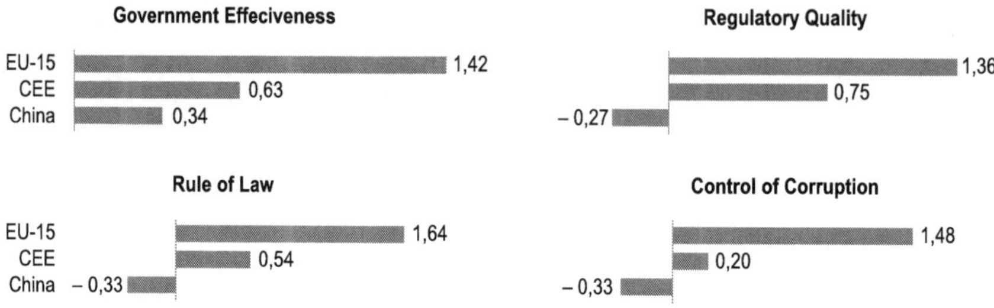

Figure 4: Comparison of government effectiveness, regulatory quality, rule of law, and control of corruption indicators in EU 15, CEE, and China (2014)
Source: The Worldwide Governance Indicators.

3. Education

Knowledge in the form of human capital can be considered as a public good that spills over into the economy and represents a source and driver of sustained growth (Jimenez et al., 2012). Grossmann found that the most effective measure to promote R&D is "to increase public expenditure targeted to the education of scientists and engineers" (Grossmann, 2007). Hanushek and Woessmann analysed PISA international test scores and found that education quality affects economic growth. They presented strong evidence that cognitive skills, rather than school attendance length, affected individual earnings, distribution of income and, finally, economic growth. They suggested that "one standard deviation higher cognitive skills of a country's workforce is associated with approximately two percentage points higher annual growth in per capita GDP" (Hanushek et al., 2012). While it is not very probable for a country to improve by one standard deviation, "it is plausible to think of getting schooling improvements that would lift a country's average by ¼ standard deviation (25 points on a PISA scale)", which was, for example, observed in the cases of Poland and Bulgaria during the past decade.

Table 1 below presents the results of the last available PISA testing in 2012. It shows that students from the CEE countries do not score as well in math, reading and science, as do students from the EU-15, Shanghai or OECD countries. In math, Chinese students hold number one position in PISA international rankings followed by Singapore, Hong Kong and Taiwan. Similarly in reading and science, China, Hong Kong and Singapore occupy the top three positions. Furthermore, all the other countries lag more than 40 points behind the China-Shanghai score. Even though the Chinese scores are not representative for the whole country, it indicates a positive trend in Chinese educational efforts. Interestingly, Poland is the only CEE country either in the top 15 in math, or in the top 10 in reading and science. Poland has also significantly improved its results over the past decade.[3] Most of the other CEE countries have rather worsened their positions.

Table 1: PISA International test scores comparison, mean score, 2012

	Math	**Reading**	**Science**
EU-15	496	499	504
CEE	479	478	488
China-Shanghai	613	570	580
OECD average	494	496	501

Source: OECD.

Although there is an intense discussion about PISA methodology and its relevance in the contemporary world (Zhao, 2014), PISA rankings can indicate certain direction and focus on providing quality education for future generations, as demonstrated by Poland. There should be more attempts to encourage people-to-people contacts in educational fields between China and the CEE countries. Even though particularly technically-oriented universities have begun to cooperate, mutual dialogue is also needed at other educational levels. It is apparent that both European and Chinese educational styles have certain benefits, and certain risks and increased sharing of experience could lead to the creation of "a golden middle way" that could encompass both systems.

4. Research and development

As previously argued, research and development stimulate economic development in any country. According to Lee, industrial upgrading and R&D lead to the production of high-value added products indispensable to any MIT exit strategy. In general, researchers agree on the linkage be-

---

[3] +27 points in maths, +39 points in reading, +28 points in science.

tween innovation and income growth. However, the resources invested into R&D do not always trigger innovation outcomes, as Ulku points out.

"There is a strong positive relationship between innovation (patent stock) and per capita GDP in both OECD and non-OECD countries, while only the OECD countries with larger markets, which include the G-7[4], Australia, the Netherlands, Spain, and Switzerland, are able to increase their innovation by investing in R&D. The results also suggest that the OECD countries that do not have effective R&D sectors seem to promote their innovation through technology spillovers from other OECD countries" (Ulku, 2004).

On the contrary, Grossmann's analysis suggests that productivity growth and welfare may not increase in response to higher R&D subsidies, although knowledge spillovers are the only externality coming from R&D spending of firms (Grossmann, 2007). Furthermore, Sterlacchini found that the weak relationship between actors of innovation systems – government, universities, research centres and business enterprises – hinders many European regions from reaping the fruits coming from R&D and skilled human capital (Sterlacchini, 2008).

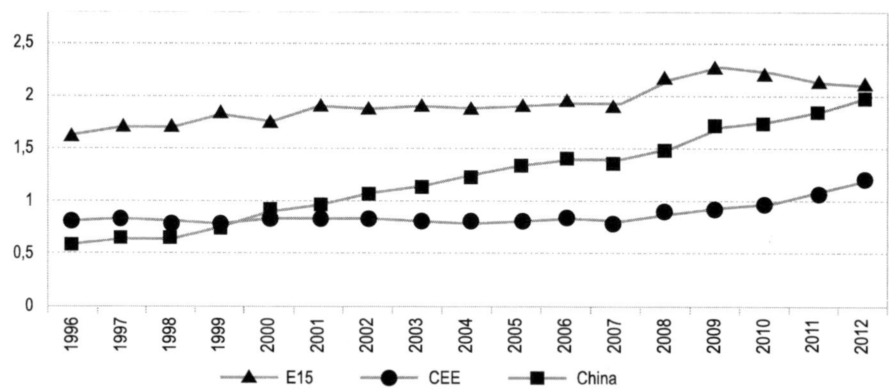

Figure 5: Research and development expenditure (% of GDP)
Source: World Bank Database.

The Chinese government is investing huge resources into the transformation of China from a world factory to a innovation nation. China now ranks second in terms of national research and development (R&D) expenditures, new universities and science parks are springing up around the country, and almost every day another successful innovation company is praised in the Chinese headlines. However, these successes and

---

[4] Canada, France, Germany, Great Britain, Italy, Japan, and the United States.

large investments do not truly describe anything about the state of the innovation environment in China. The development is still at a very early stage, and even though China is the world's largest high-tech exporter, a very high proportion of these products are processed with low domestic value added. Therefore, China stresses the importance of its R&D sector, and it is one of the top priorities for the Chinese government in its upcoming five year plan, particularly through its "Made in China 2025" programme, which seeks to expand the integration of innovation into industrial and service industries.

These Made in China 2025 goals are facilitated not only through high R&D investments, but also with related activities, such as business incubators. China is also inviting multinational companies to establish their R&D hubs in the country, even though China struggles with the protection of intellectual property rights. Since 2012, the number of business incubators has increased from 400 to more than 1,200 all around China, and the R&D centres followed a similar path with almost none in 2002 rising to 1,600 in 2011. More than 80% of these centres were supported or created by multinational companies. In contrast, the R&D efforts in the CEE countries are still very limited, as R&D investments in Figure 5 indicates that many CEE countries possess very strong industrial bases, and further investments would facilitate industrial upgrading.

The area of research and development may be the most natural field for further sharing of lessons learned. In order to foster its own innovation, Chinese companies are seeking cooperation mainly in western EU states. But even though the R&D potential of the CEE countries has recently advanced and many CEE countries can boast strong industrial bases with innovative potential, they are yet to be included in these R&D initiatives. Major limitations of joint R&D attempts are prejudices on the side of CEE entrepreneurs related to the protection of intellectual property, technology transfers and overall societal attitudes in China. CEE entrepreneurs need more encouragement, case studies, good practices exchange and inspiration sharing, in order to establish cooperation with Chinese partners.

5.1. Infrastructure

A broad definition of infrastructure includes sectors such as transport, water, power or telecommunications, and represents large public investments in most countries. A solid infrastructure network can help to reduce costs of production, thereby affecting companies' profitability, level of production output, income and employment. It helps to diversify the choices in rural areas by offering alternative options in employment and consumption. Furthermore, telecommunications networks in particular enable access to modern technology, which can help an economy in its transition to higher-income levels.

China is currently promoting its new "One Road, One Belt" strategy focusing on connectivity in the broader sense. Its main goal is to connect Europe and China via various infrastructural networks. At this stage of cooperation, it is not very probable that Chinese companies would be engaged in construction of the CEE network, be it transport or energy. Yet, both entities could cooperate quite well in third-party countries on the "One Road, One Belt" projects, and build up the mutual confidence needed to extend the cooperation in the future.

The Figure 6 below compares actual and required infrastructure investments from 1992 to 2011 in the the EU-15, the CEE and China. It is apparent that infrastructure development in CEE countries is underinvested compared with the EU-15. In contrast, China has spent 8.5% of its GDP in infrastructure from 1992 to 2011 and it clearly contributed to Chinese economic growth. According to a survey from the World Bank, "if the level of Latin America's infrastructure development rose to match Korea's (the median of East Asian countries), in countries such as Bolivia, Guatemala or Peru, growth would speed up by at least 5 percentage points per year" (Calderón et al., 2005). The CEE countries are not low income countries, but higher connectivity within the region could significantly ease the trade flows.

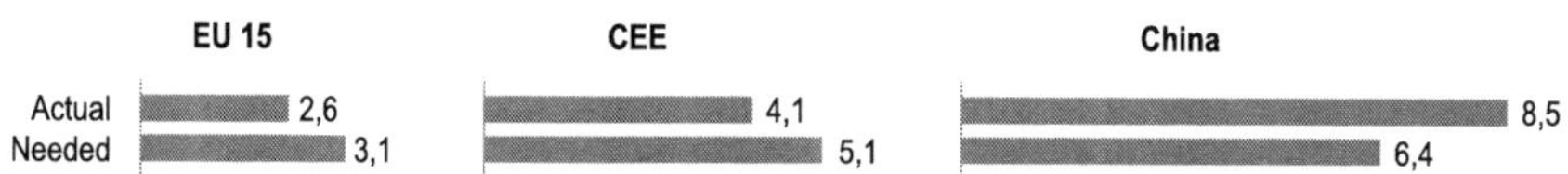

Figure 6: Infrastructure investment from 1992 to 2011 (% of GDP)
Source: McKinsey Global Institute (Labaye et al., 2013).

6. Urbanization

To many researchers and policy-makers, the correlation of urbanization and economic growth has been a puzzle. There is evidence for linkage between urbanization level and economic development, as the latter usually involves the transformation of a country from a rural agricultural based economy, to an industrial-service based economy. However, "in the long run, the increasing level of urbanization is a natural consequence of economic development. Even though accelerated urbanization without parallel economic growth often occurs in the world, a higher rate of urbanization does not, as a rule, lead to more economic growth" (Chen et al., 2014). Even though there is no agreement that urbanization per se may not lead to the expected economic development, other indirect factors of urbanization can help in raising living standards, as for example urban concentration or removal of barriers to rural-urban mobility. Henderson argues that "the form that urbanization takes, or the degree of urban concentration, strongly affects productivity growth" (Henderson, 2003).

The countries of Central and Eastern Europe are less urbanized then those in Western Europe (EU-15). In the CEE, 62% of their residents live in urban areas, compared with 79% of residents in the EU-15. Furthermore, there was almost zero urban growth in the past decades compared with the EU-15. Today, the urbanization rate in China has passed the turning point of 50% and the number of people in cities jumped to almost 700 million. It is expected that in 2030, China's urbanisation rate should reach around 70%, and nearly one billion people will live in cities (UNDP China, 2013). This speed of urbanization exerts enormous pressure that may be very difficult to manage in such a short time. Furthermore, the statistics show, that in 2014, up to 270 million people in Chinese cities are migrant workers from the countryside who do not have urban residence permits.

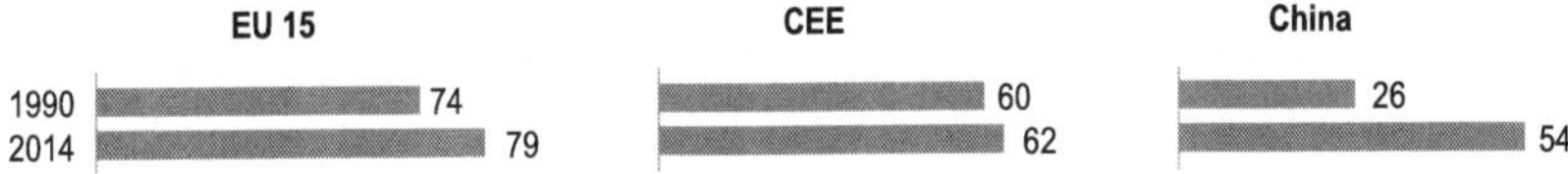

Figure 7: Urbanization rate in EU 15, CEE and China, 1990 vs. 2014
Source: World Bank Database.

Both entities could cooperate on increasing the quality of urbanization. There are already various initiatives of cooperation in the field of smart cities running between the EU and China[5], that can serve as flagships in other cities and there are many areas where companies from the CEE countries can contribute. Areas of potential cooperation include reduction of traffic congestion, use of public transportation or smart grids, and renewable energy systems, to name just a few.

---

[5] For example vertical farms in cities, eco-friendly taxis in Shenzhen or public bicycle sharing.

Conclusions

The CEE countries and China have shared their interests in the initiation of economic reforms, support of innovative industries, and launching of institutional reforms. For both regions, these steps can represent important moves on their way to restarting their economic growth. Even though economic situations for the CEE countries and China can be very complex, there are areas where they can share innovative approaches and solutions to possible MIT-related problems. Institutions, education, research and development, infrastructure and urbanization were among the areas analysed.

Both parties can further support their efforts in increasing government effectiveness, be it enhancement of governmental e-services, their accessibility and digital solutions for emergency crises. Similarly many countries currently strive for convergence of their regulatory frameworks. The CEE countries follow the EU lead, and it could be beneficial for China to concentrate not only on tariff reductions in their bilateral trade, but also on convergence to international standards, which would also ease the situation for Chinese entrepreneurs who depend on exports to European markets.

There should be more attempts to encourage people-to-people contacts in the educational field between China and the CEE countries. Even though technically-oriented universities in particular have started to cooperate, the mutual dialogue is also needed at other educational levels. It is apparent that both European and Chinese educational styles have certain benefits and certain risks, and increased experience sharing could lead to the creation of the golden middle way that could encompass both systems.

The area of research and development can represent the most natural field for further sharing of lessons learned. Chinese companies have set up join cooperation in research and development mainly with western EU states, however, even though the R&D potential of the CEE countries has recently advanced and many CEE countries can boast strong industrial bases with innovative potential, they are yet to be included in these R&D initiatives. Chinese companies are currently trying to boost their presence in the CEE region. Therefore a smooth transition from unilateral involvement in the secondary sector to a more balanced collaboration in applied science should be a priority.

China is currently promoting its "One Road, One Belt" strategy, focusing on connectivity in the broader sense. At this stage of cooperation, it is not very probable that Chinese companies could be engaged in construction of the CEE network, be it transport or energy. Yet both entities could cooperate quite well in third countries on the One Road, One Belt projects, and build up the mutual confidence needed to extend the cooperation in the future.

Both entities could cooperate on increasing the quality of urbanization. There are already various initiatives of cooperation in the field of smart cities running between the EU and China[6] that can serve as flagships in other cities, and there are many areas where companies from the CEE countries can contribute.

References

Aiyar, S. et al. (2013). *Growth Slowdowns and the Middle-Income Trap*. International Monetary Fund.

Bukowski, M., Szpor, A. & Śniegocki, A. (2012). *The Potential and Barriers of Polish Innovation*. Warsaw: The Structural Research Institute.

Bulman, D., Eden, M. & Nguyen, Ha (2014). *Transitioninig from Low-Income Growth to High-Income Growth*. Policy Research Working Paper 7104. World Bank Group.

Calderón, C. & Servén, L. (2005). *The Effects of Infrastructure Development on Growth and Income Distribution*. Dynamics, Economic Growth, and International Trade (DEGIT).

Campos, N.F., Dimova, R. & Saleh, A. (2010). *Whither Corruption? A Quantitative Survey of the Literature on Corruption and Growth*. Bonn: Institute for the Study of Labor.

Chen Mingxing, Zhang Hua, Liu Weidong & Zhang Wenzhong (2014). *The Global Pattern of Urbanization and Economic Growth: Evidence from the Last Three Decades*. PLoS One.

Collier, P., Kirchberger, M. & Söderbom, M. (2015). The cost of road infrastructure in low and middle income countries. *World Bank Economic Review*.

Eichengreen, B., Park Dongyun & Shin Kwanho (2013). *Growth Slowdowns Redux: New Evidence on The Middle-Income Trap*. National Bureau of Economic Research.

Faber, B. (2014). Trade integration, market size and industrialization: Evidence from China's national trunk highway system. *Review of Economic Studies, 81*(3).

Gil, I. & Kharas, H. (2007). *An East Asian Renaissance: Ideas for Economic Growth*. Washington, D.C.: The International Bank for Reconstruction and Development/The World Bank.

Grossmann, V. (2007). How to promote R&D-based growth? Public education expenditure on scientists and engineers versus R&D subsidies. *Journal of Macroeconomics, 29*.

---

[6] For example vertical farms in cities, eco-friendly taxis in Shenzhen or public bicycle sharing.

Han Xuehui & Wei Shang-Jin (2015). Re-examining the Middle-Income Trap Hypothesis: What to Reject and What to Revive? *ADB Economics Working Paper Series*, July, No. 436.

Hanushek, E.A. & Woessmann, L. (2012). Do better schools lead to more growth? Cognitive skills, economic outcomes, and causation. *Journal of Economic Growth*, 17(4).

Henderson, V. (2003). The urbanization process and economic growth: The so-what question. *Journal of Economic Growth, 8.*

Jimenez, E., Nguyen, Vy, Patrinos, H.A. (2012). *Stuck in the Middle? Human Capital Development and Economic Growth in Malaysia and Thailand.* Policy Research Working Paper 6283. The World Bank, Human Development Network, Education Unit.

Kanchoochat, V. (2014). *The Middle-income Trap Debate: Taking Stock, Looking Ahead.* Tokyo: National Graduate Institute for Policy Studies (GRIPS).

Labaye, E. et al. (2013). *A new dawn: Reigniting growth in Central and Eastern Europe.* McKinsey Global Institute.

Lee Keun (2013). *Schumpeterian Analysis of Economic Catch-up (Knowledge, Path-Creation, and the Middle-Income Trap).* Cambridge: Cambridge University Press.

Sterlacchini, A. (2008). R&D, Higher Education and Regional Growth: Uneven Linkages among European Regions. *Research Policy*, Vol. 37.

Ulku, H. (2004). *R&D, Innovation, and Economic Growth: An Empirical Analysis.* International Monterary Fund.

UNDP China (2013). *China National Human Development Report 2013, Sustainable and Liveable Cities: Toward Ecological Civilization.* China Translation and Publishing Corporation.

World Bank (2013). *Atlas of Global Development: A Visual Guide to the World's Greatest Challenges.* World Bank Publications.

Zhao Yong (2014). *Who's Afraid of the Big Bad Dragon: Why China Has the Best (and Worst) Education System in the World.* New York: John Wiley & Sons.

Ciril Kafol, Metka Tekavčič, Ljubo Drakulevski, Atanas Kochov

Comparison of Telecommunications Development Pattern in China and the Republic of Macedonia

Introduction

Telecommunication operators market has been growing fast in the last two decades. Convergent telecommunication operators operated in four major areas: mobile telephony, fixed telephony, broadband or Internet services and lately, delivery of television services over existing telecommunication platforms. The telecommunication industry boomed especially in the mobile and broadband segment. There is a difference in telecommunication in the developed and developing countries.

According to ITU (2015), 3.2 billion people globally are using the Internet by the end of 2015, out of which 2 billion are from developing countries. For every Internet user in the developed world, there are 2 in the developing world. However, 4 billion people from developing countries remain offline, representing 2/3 of the population residing in developing countries. Of the 940 million people living in the least developed countries (LDCs), only 89 million use the Internet, corresponding to a 9.5% penetration rate.

ITU (2015) study also claims that by the end of 2015, there are more than 7 billion mobile cellular subscriptions, corresponding to a penetration rate of 97%, up from 738 million in 2000. Between 2000 and 2015, global Internet penetration grew 7-fold, from 6.5% to 43%. Mobile broadband is the most dynamic market segment; globally, mobile-broadband penetration reaches 47% in 2015, a value that increased 12 times since 2007. The proportion of households with Internet access at home increased from 18% in 2005 to 46% in 2015. Fixed-broadband uptake is growing at a slower pace, with a 7% annual increase over the past three years, reaching 11% penetration by end 2015. The proportion of the population covered by a 2G mobile-cellular network grew from 58% in 2001 to 95% in 2015.

The Peoples Republic of China and the Republic of Macedonia went through fast development phase of telecommunication operators market over the last two decades. Study of the development patterns may give useful information and improve trending ability also uncovering available co-operation possibilities. For the purpose of this article, we compare historical data and trends of the current data on main telecommunication identifiers between the PRC and the Republic of Macedonia. We also add information on historical data and trends of the development of telecommunication systems in the Republic of Slovenia in order to compare results. The purpose is to determine whether we may see the same development patterns in one of the biggest telecommunication markets in the world and one of the smallest telecommunication markets in the CEE Region.

1. Analysis of historical data

In this section, we analyse historical data and the trends of China (Mainland) and the Republic of Macedonia.

1.1. The Republic of Macedonia

Macedonia, officially the Republic of Macedonia is a country located in the central Balkan peninsula in Southeast Europe. It is one of the successor states of the former Yugoslavia, from which it declared independence in 1991. It became a member of the United Nations in 1993, but, as a result of an ongoing dispute with Greece over use of the name Macedonia, it was admitted under the provisional description of the former Yugoslav Republic of Macedonia abbreviated as FYROM. It has approximately 2 million inhabitants and 564.000 households.

This research is based on official reports data from the Agency for Electronic Communications in Macedonia (2014).

Fixed telephony

The fixed telephony market is facing a downward trend, due to the migration towards VoIP technologies. Both the total number of fixed lines and the number of fixed lines per population 100 have been continually decreasing.

Table 1: Electronic communication market in Macedonia

Fixed telephony	2009	2010	2011	2012	2013	2014
Number of fixed lines, mn	0,44	0,42	0,42	0,41	0,40	0,38
Fixed lines per 100 inhabitants	21,35	20,22	20,56	19,82	19,22	18,59
Mobile telephony	2009	2010	2011	2012	2013	2014
Number of mobile subscribers, mn	1,94	2,15	2,21	2,24	2,24	2,22
Mobile penetration per 100 inhabitants	94,85	104,9	107,82	108,52	108,48	107,86
Broadband	2009	2010	2011	2012	2013	2014
Broadband subscribers, mn	0,22	0,26	0,28	0,31	0,34	0,35
Annual growth, %		19,23%	8,98%	10,59%	8,39%	4,61%
Digital TV	2009	2010	2011	2012	2013	2014
Total users, mn	0,20	0,24	0,25	0,28	0,34	0,36
Annual growth, %		19%	5%	11%	22%	6%

Source: Agency for Electronic Communication in Macedonia, 2014.

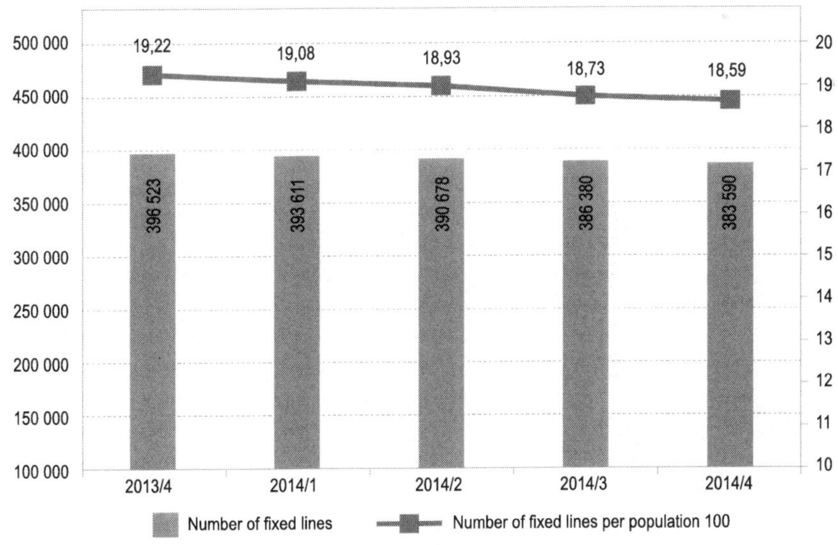

Graph 1: Number of fixed telephone lines in Macedonia
Source: AEC, 2014.

Mobile telephony

The mobile telephony market is saturated, with a decrease in Q4 2014. This is due to the decreased number of active, pre-paid residential subscribers. Postpaid subscribers have increased in both residential and business segments.

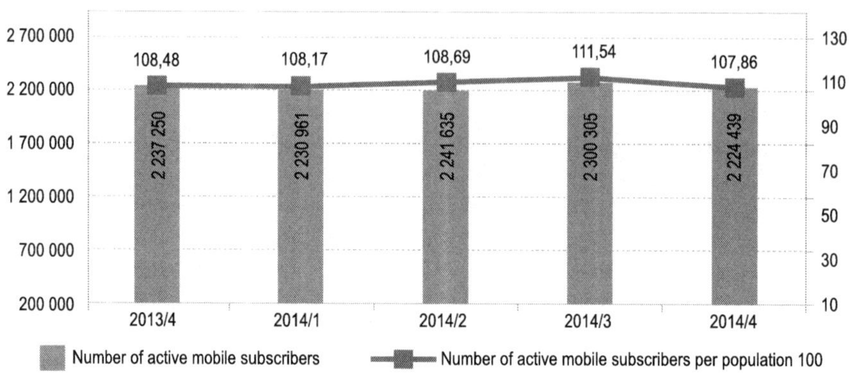

Graph 2: Number of active mobile subscribes in Macedonia
Source: AEC, 2014.

Broadband

The broadband market faces low growth, with a small increase in number of subscribers in all available technologies. The number of subscribers using baseband has a decreasing trend. Current state of broadband subscribers for Q4 2014 shows Cable and xDSL subscribers with 75% of the broadband market, with low growth of <5%.

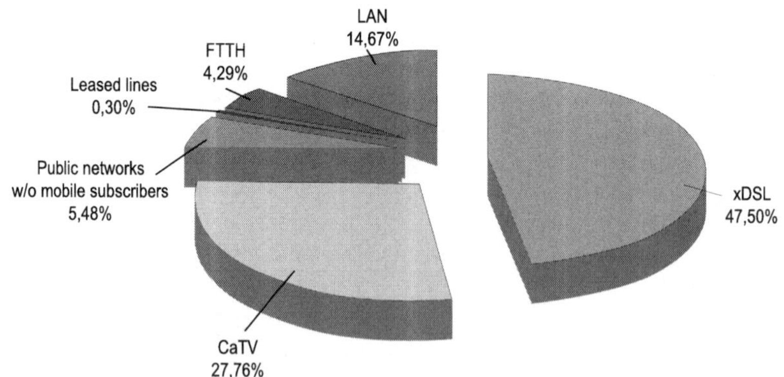

Graph 3: The broadband market in Macedonia
Source: AEC, 2014.

Table 2: Internet, access speed %

<1 Mbps	1 Mbps ≤ download <2Mbps	2 Mbps ≤ download <4Mbps	4 Mbps ≤ download < 8Mbps	8 Mbps ≤ download <20Mbps	20 Mbps ≤ download <30Mbps	30Mbps ≤ download <50Mbps	50 Mbps ≤ download <100Mbps	≥ 100Mbps
12	4.074	14.966	107.046	192.652	8.197	2.946	11.180	300

Source: AEC, 2014.

Television

The TV market is saturated, with a small increase in the number of subscribers in all available technologies. Current state of broadband subscribers for Q4 2014 shows Cable subscribers with 52% of the TV market.

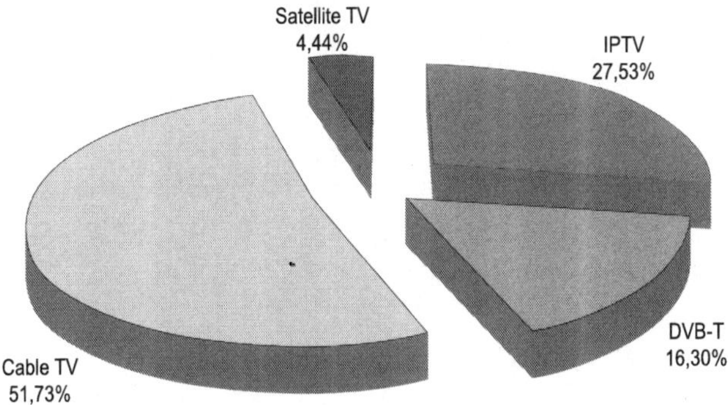

Graph 4: Television market in Macedonia
Source: AEC, 2014.

1.2. China (Mainland)

Mainland China, Chinese mainland or simply the Mainland, is a geographical and political term used to describe the geopolitical area under the direct jurisdiction of the People's Republic of China (PRC). It generally excludes the Special Administrative Regions of Hong Kong and Macau; however, it usually includes Hainan. The Peoples Republic of China is the most populated country in the world with approximately 1,35 billion inhabitants.

This research is based on a EMIS (2012) report data on China ICT sector.

Fixed telephony

The fixed telephony market is facing a downward trend, due to the migration towards VoIP technologies and abandonment of fixed services. Number of fixed lines has decreased further, both in 2013 (at 266.9 mn), and 2014 (at 251.7 mn).

Table 3: Electronic communication market in China

Fixed telephony	2003	2004	2005	2006	2007	2008	2009	2010	2011	2012
Number of fixed lines, mn	262,7	311,8	350,4	367,8	365,6	340,4	313,7	294,3	285,1	278,2
Fixed lines per 100 inhabitants	21,1	21,4	27	28,1	27,8	25,8	23,6	22,1	21,3	20,7
Mobile telephony	2003	2004	2005	2006	2007	2008	2009	2010	2011	2012
Number of mobile subscribers, mn	270	334,8	393,4	461,1	547,3	641,2	747,2	859	986,3	1112,2
Mobile penetration per 100 inhabitants	21	25,9	30,3	35,3	41,6	48,5	56,3	64,4	73,6	82,5
Broadband	2003	2004	2005	2006	2007	2008	2009	2010	2011	2012
Broadband subscribers, mn	n/a	25,8	37,5	38,2	66,4	83,4	103,6	126,3	150	175,2
Annual growth, %	n/a	91,00%	45,40%	38,20%	28,20%	25,60%	24,20%	21,90%	18,70%	16,80%
Digital TV	2003	2004	2005	2006	2007	2008	2009	2010	2011	2012
Total users, mn	n/a	n/a	n/a	n/a	n/a	49,2	76,9	110,5	141,2	186
Annual growth, %	n/a	n/a	n/a	n/a	n/a	81%	56%	44%	28%	32%

Source: EMIS, 2012.

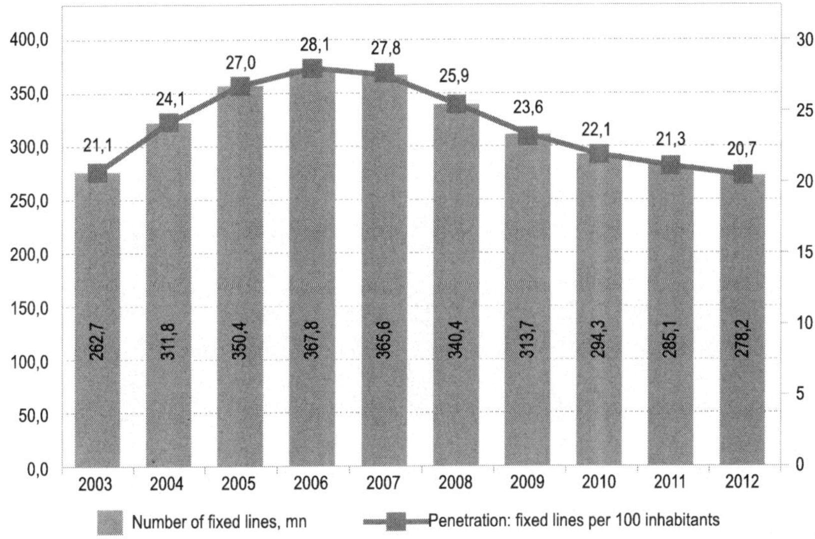

Graph 5: Fixed telephony market in China

Source: EMIS, 2012.

Mobile telephony

The mobile telephony market is on an upward trend, with a continuous increase since 2003. Mobile penetration per 100 inhabitants has further increased, both in 2013 (89.0), and 2014 (92.7).

Broadband

The broadband market is on an upward trend, with an increase in the number of subscribers in all available broadband technologies. Household broadband penetration has increased continuously since 2004, reaching 40% in 2012.

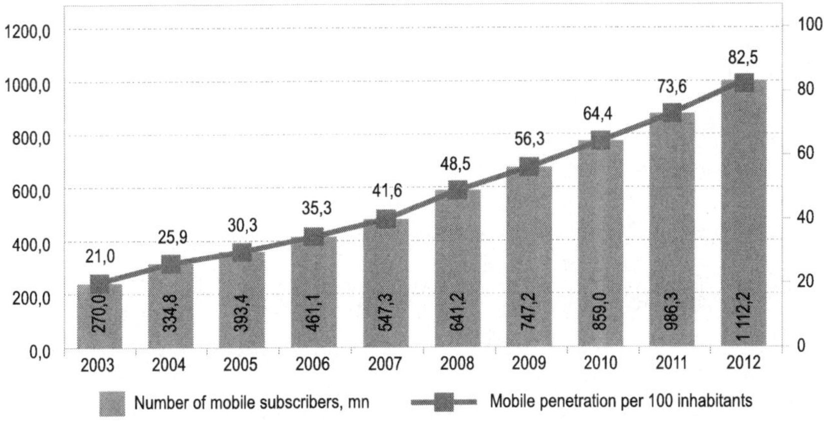

Graph 6: Number of mobile subscribes in China

Source: EMIS, 2012.

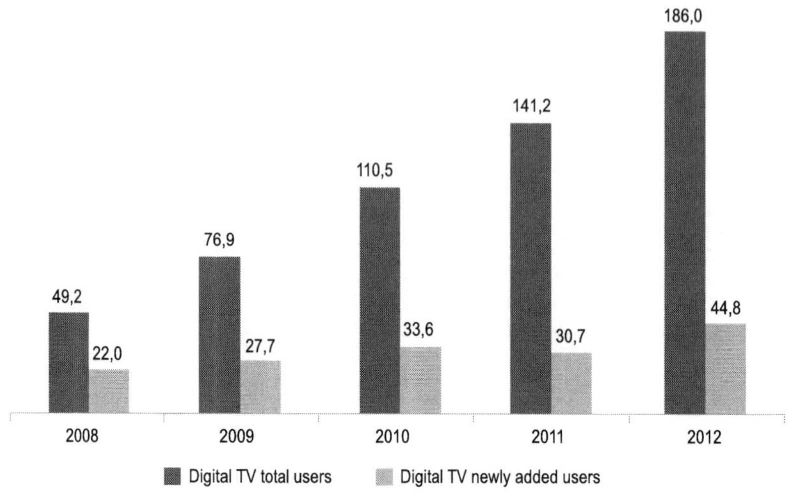

Graph 7: Number of digital TV users in China
Source: EMIS, 2012.

Television

The digital TV market is on an upward trend, with an increase in the number of subscribers. Number of subscribers has increased continuously since 2008, reaching 186 million in 2012.The market is still nowhere near saturation and continues its overall expansion.

2. Comparison of data

If we compare the development trend in China (Mainland) and the Republic of Macedonia, we can conclude that the development patterns are similar. Downward trend in fixed telephony is evident in the fixed lines per 100 inhabitant criteria, while the rising trend in mobile telephony is also evident with the sharp rise in years 2006 to 2008 in Macedonia, due to entry of a third mobile provider. The difference in size of the market is also clearly visible from the enclosed graphs. Annual growths in broadband are similarly decreasing, but the number of subscribers continuously raising. Digital TV annual growth is also slowing down, but the number of subscribers is continuously rising.

For the purpose of comparison, we also add the data for Slovenia. Based on a report from Agency for Communication Networks and Services of the Republic of Slovenia (2014), data show that the number of operators is larger in Macedonia and Slovenia, while the penetration of active subscribers per 100 inhabitants is smaller in China. It indicates that the smaller countries tried to bring down the prices, hence the increase in the penetration of mobile telephony, allowing for a larger competition in the market.

Mobile	MK 2014 Q3	SL 2014 Q4	CHN 2012 Q4
Number of operators	4	4	3
Number of active subscribers	2.300.305	2.283.375	1.110.200.000
Number of active subscribers per 100 population	111,5	112,8	80,6

Conclusion

The market for fixed telephony shows a downward trend in both countries, same as the global trend. The trend is existing due to the migration to other technologies and abandonment of fixed telephony usage.

The market for mobile telephony in Macedonia has been saturated since 2010/2011. The market penetration has been steady or has decreased since 2010.

The market of mobile telephony in China (Mainland) is far from saturated, still facing continuous growth. The penetration is still growing, as of 2014e.

Number of mobile operators is higher in Macedonia (4, as of 2014e) than in China (3, as of 2014e).

Annual growth in the broadband market in both countries is slowing down. In Macedonia, the latest data for 2014 shows 4.6% growth, while in China, the latest data for 2013 shows 7.8% growth.

Annual growth in the TV market in both countries is slowing down, but growth is still much higher in China. In Macedonia, data for 2012 shows 11% growth, 6% in 2014. In China, data for 2012 shows 32% growth.

From above, we may conclude that despite the differences in size and structure, development trends in telecommunication sectors are similar. China is still experiencing high growth rates due to lower penetration on all segments. We may conclude that it is possible to use comparisons in order to determine and forecast market and user behaviour. Future studies may add more complex research on the subject, adding complexity and accuracy to the findings.

References

AEC Agency for Electronic Communications of the Republic of Macedonia (2014). *Report on market developments (Q3 2014)*. Retrieved from: www.aek.mk (accessed: 28/09/2015).

ACNS Agency for Communication Networks and Services of the Republic of Slovenia, *Report on market developments (Q4 2014)*. Retrieved from: www.akos-rs.si (accessed: 28/09/2015).

EMIS (2012). *China ICT Sector Report (Q4 2012)*. Retrieved from: https://www.securities.com/emis/sites/default/files/EMIS%20Insight%20%20China%20ICT%20Sector%20Report.pdf (accessed: 28/09/2015).

ITU Facts and Figures (2015). Retrieved from: http://www.itu.int/en/ITU-D/Statistics/Pages/facts/default.aspx (accessed: 28/09/2015).

Appendix

Macedonia – Fixed telephony

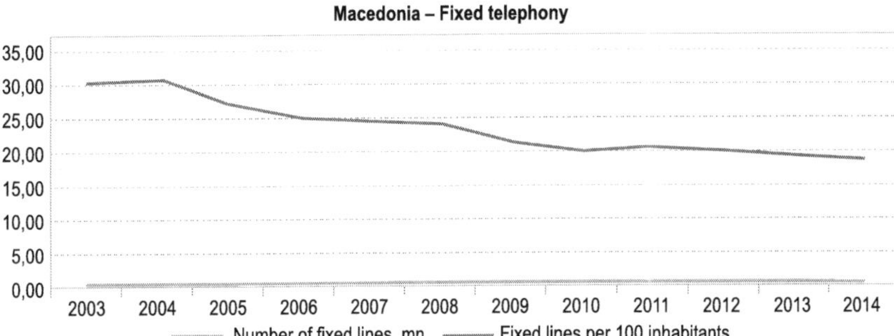

Macedonia – Mobile telephony

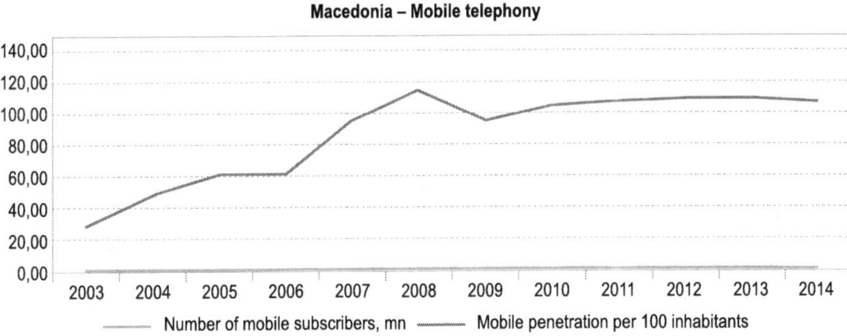

Macedonia – Broadband

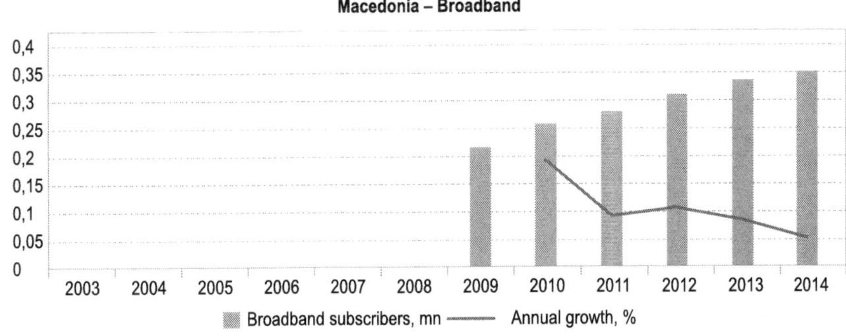

Macedonia – Digital TV

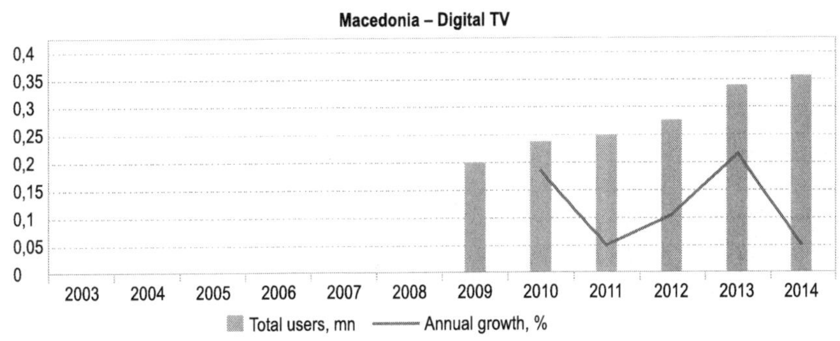

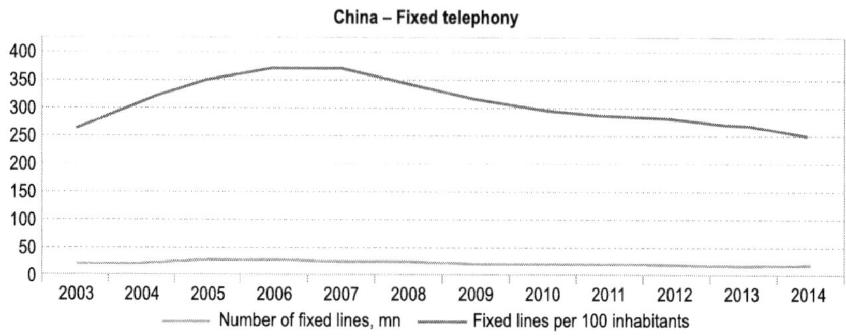

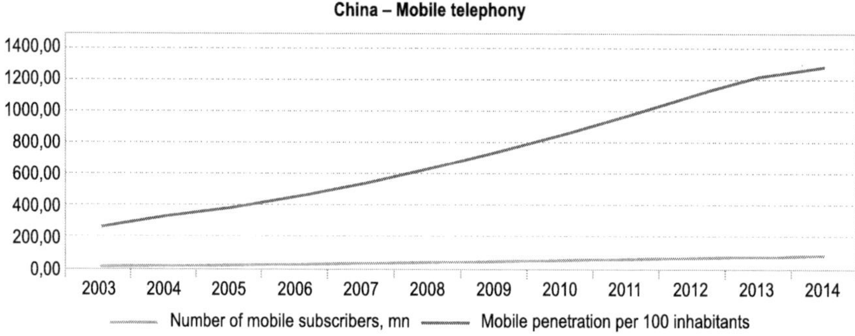

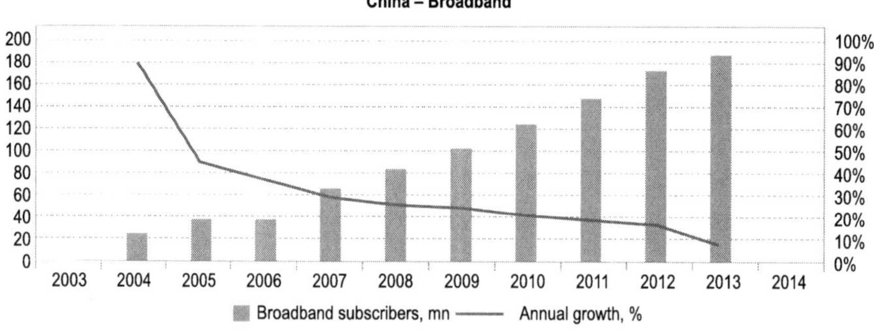

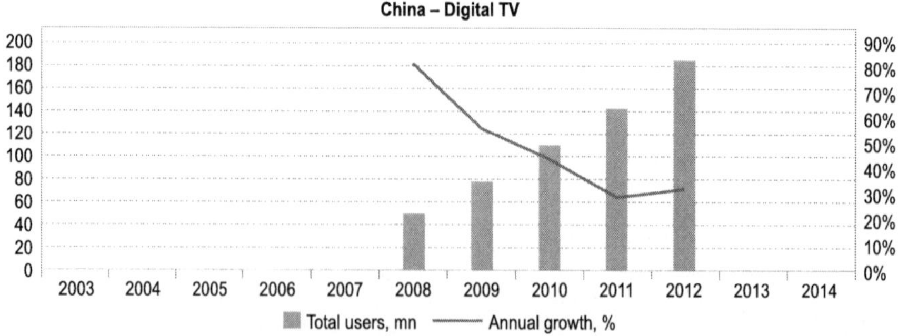

Source: AEC, 2014; ACNS, 2014; EMIS, 2012.

Tomasz Bieliński

Development of Chinese Mobile Phone Game Market as an Export Opportunity for CEE Mobile Game Producers

In 2014, China was the second leading importer of commercial services in the world. During the years 2000–2013 Chinese imports of computer and information services grew on the average pace of 27%, amounting to 5,94 billion USD in the end of that period (WTO, 2015, p. 4).

Two sectors of computer and information services in China that are developing especially dynamically are the mobile applications market and video game market. The market that seems to be the most promising for foreign imports is the one that emerges from the combination of these two sectors – mobile phone game market. Out of around 1600 companies active in the mobile games sector globally, around 150 are based in the CEE (The Multimedia Research Consultancy, 2008, p. 11). Unfortunately, most of the CEE markets are too small for locally focused content publishers, so most of the game producers try to enter other, bigger markets (Nostromo Wireless, 2012, p. 7). The aim of this article is to verify if the Chinese mobile game market can be treated as an attractive export opportunity for the CEE game developers, and if such expansion is possible.

Theoretical background

Fast development of smartphone and tablet market brought new possibilities for software developers all around the world. A completely new market of applications for mobile devices emerged. A mobile application (or mobile App) is software application that runs on a mobile device (smartphone, tablet, iPod, etc.), that has an operating system supporting standalone software. Mobile Apps can come preloaded on the mobile device, they can also be downloaded by the users from mobile App stores or the Internet (Wang, Liao & Yang, 2013, p. 11). Games are the most popular mobile applications, and mobile phones are potentially dominant game platforms in the future (Feijoo, Gómez-Barroso, Aguado & Scolari, 2012, p. 3). Technological innovations that improve device quality, greater mobile device ownership and broadband transmission offered by wireless communication networks, lead to further development of mobile gaming market (Soh & Tan, 2008, pp. 35–39).

Companies operating on the global mobile game market use many different ways of monetization. The term monetization refers to the method and the ability to generate a revenue (Fields, 2014, p. 21). Majority of mobile games in China are distributed free of charge, but the game producers can base their revenue model not only on the direct payments for the games, but also on advertising (Shintaro & Barwise, 2011, p. 60), product placement (Torrano, 2011, p. 124), or in game payments for virtual objects or premium content (Teitelbaum, Elders & Alavian, 2012, p. 377). A unique online gaming culture has developed in China (Kshetri, 2010, p. 159). Despite the fact that Chinese companies were initially a second mover in this industry with a limited technological competence; they managed to move up the value chain within a few years, from operators of foreign-developed games to game developers (Ström & Ernkvist, 2014, p. 6). In 2015, Chinese companies were leading on local market, but western competition was also present, proving that success on this demanding market is possible.

Global and Chinese mobile game market

Games are the most popular mobile applications downloaded by users all around the world. There were more than 1,4 billion mobile gamers in 2014 (Newzoo, 2014, p. 2) The global mobile gaming market revenues amounted to over 24,5 bn USD with the annual growth of 33% (Song & de Vit, 2015, p. 3). Four major video game markets in the world in terms of revenues are: China, the USA, Japan, and Korea. Chinese market is the most dynamic of them all. In 2015, China's mobile games market will reach 6,5 bn USD in revenues, more than one fifth of the 30,1 bn USD generated worldwide. This positions China as the world's biggest market for smartphone and tablet games, ahead of the US with an anticipated 6,0 bn USD in revenues in 2015 (Meng & McDonald, 2015). According to Newzoo (2015a) estimations, in 2017 Chinese mobile game market will reach 9,3 bn USD. Development of the mobile games market in China depends on the growth in the number of smartphone and other mobile devices users.

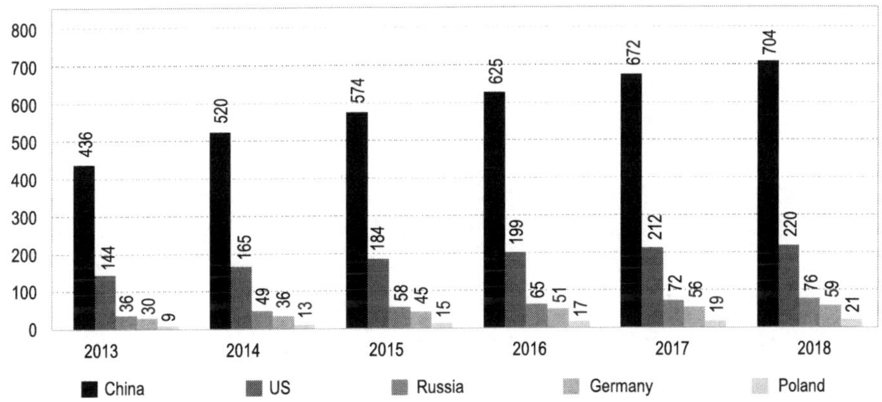

Figure 1: Number of smartphones (million, forecast from 2015)
Source: Emarketer (2014). 2 Billion Consumers Worldwide to Get Smart (phones) by 2016. Retrieved from: http://www.emarketer.com/.http://www.emarketer.com/Article/2-Billion-Consumers-World wide-Smartphones-by-2016/1011694 - sthash.eVhIrSLU.dpuf (accessed: 10/09/2015).

China is the biggest smartphone market in the world. Number of such devices in China in 2014 reached 520 million, and it was over 3 times bigger than in the United States. There is no market in CEE that would be even comparable in size. In Russia, the number of smartphones reached 49 million in 2014, in Germany it was 36 million and in Poland 13 million. What is more, the Chinese market is expected to grow dynamically during the next 4 years to reach over 704 million devices by 2018 (see Figure 1). Since 2012, more Chinese access the Internet using mobile phones than by desktop or laptop computers (China Internet Network Information Center, 2013, p. 5), so the Chinese people not only possess phones that have the ability to connect to the Internet, but they actually do it. This leads to the conclusion that China is the country, in which mobile gaming has globally the biggest growth possibilities. Size and growth of the Chinese market is an unquestionably strong argument for the CEE game developers to enter it.

To fully understand the Chinese mobile game market it is necessary to know the characteristics of Internet market in that country, which is much different than its Western counterparts. It is the biggest single Internet market in the world. By June 2015, there were 668 m Internet users in China, which accounted for 48,8% of population (China Internet Network Information Center, 2015, p. 7), giving enough space for further growth. Compared to the developed countries, where in 2015 on average 82,2% of population had an access to the Internet (Sanou, 2015, p. 3), Chinese market seems to be far from saturation, and it is growing fast. Between June 2014 and June 2015, there was 5,6% of annual increase that added 35,7 m new Internet users. According to Emarketer forecast (2014), the number of Internet users in China will reach 777 million by 2018.

Majority of the Internet users are relatively new. In 2005 only 111 m Chinese (8,5% of population) had access to the Internet. It means that they are not yet accustomed to the services of any particular company, and that gives an opportunity to the CEE software developers to enter the market. One of the studies on mobile gaming sector has revealed that an average Chinese user plays over 12 different games during every 30 days. Chinese respondents also expect to download another 7,5 gaming applications during next 30 days, which is a number more than 20% higher than in America and South Korea (Inmobi, 2014, p. 22). It means that the potential customers in China are not loyal to any game or producer, and if they will be offered a better product developed by the CEE engineers, they will download and play it.

There are many governmental restrictions that block a large part of international competition (like Google). This seems to be a big obstacle, but it can be also treated as an opportunity. Overcoming legal and cultural barriers can become an important competitive advantage for any CEE company over other Western competition. What is important in that matter is that good political relations between countries that used to be a part of the Eastern Block and China have longer history, and used to be much better than with the USA or any other countries that are major game producers. Political support from the local governments of the CEE countries might become necessary, but in many cases, this kind of help is possible though many public or private organizations like for example chambers of commerce. The Chinese government's consent for such operations may become an important competitive advantage.

China had 668 million Internet users in June 2015, and a vast majority (594 million) used mobile phones to access it. It was much more than just desktop or laptop computers. What is interesting, the number of people using desktop computers to access the Internet fell from 459 million in December 2014 to 457 million in June 2015 (see Figure 2). Most probably, these people started using mobile devices or laptop computers. There is also a growing market of people using their TV sets to access the Internet (probably as a secondary, additional device).

Another important fact is that in China, smartphone penetration is most prevalent among consumers ages 16–34 (Nielsen, 2013, p. 11), whereas in the United States, consumers ages 45–54 comprise a slightly higher percentage of smartphone usage than the other age demographics (comScore, 2013, p. 12). It is a very important information for the mobile game producers, as they need to adjust their products to different age groups.

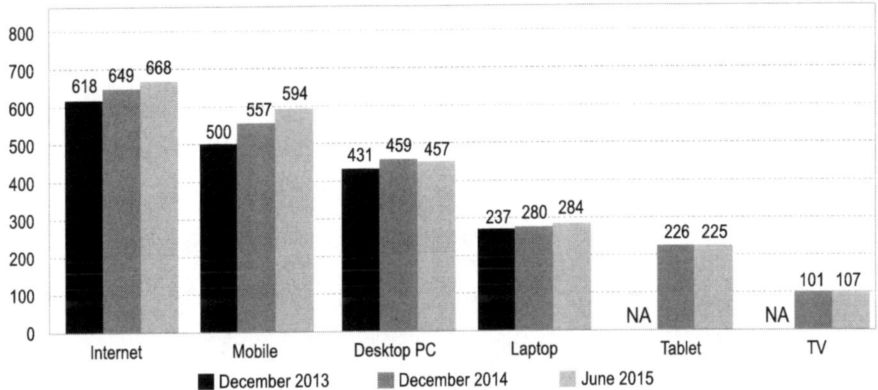

Figure 2: Total number of people and devices used to connect to the Internet in China in millions of users
Source: China Internet Network Information Center, *35th Statistical Report on Internet Development in China*, 2014, p. 13; China Internet Network Information Center, *36th Statistical Report on Internet Development in China*, 2015, p. 14.

One of the major barriers of the Chinese mobile games market is that major distribution platforms for Android phones are not global, as it is in case of a majority of countries, but local. On the global market 38% mobile game payments in 2015 was done though Google Playstore, which is not available for the majority of Chinese users. In May 2015, Android users in China downloaded their applications mainly though Myapp (26%), 360 Mobile Assistant (26%), Baidu Mobile Assistant (17%), and MIUI app store (14%). Myapp, the leader of the ranking, belongs to Tencent, which is the biggest mobile game producer in the world, which makes Android based distribution even more complicated. The China Mobile Games Monitor shows that in May 2015, Tencent published 29 of the top 100 grossing Android games and 59 of the top 100 grossing iOS games. Tencent will not allow foreign competition to successfully enter their local market though their own distribution platform.

Another problem that should be considered by the CEE game producers that would like to enter the Chinese market is a way of monetization. Even if the game distribution is a success and it would be downloaded by millions of players, the game producers need to find the way to get paid. The question is, if the citizens of China, who on average earn less money than the people in CEE, could afford to become a source of decent income from that region for the game producers. The easiest way would be to put a fee for downloading and subscription of the game. Unfortunately, the study of Inmobi Corporation (see Table 1) shows that this might not me the best way to enter the Chinese market.

Table 1. Paid App Download Behavior, by Country

	All free	**Mostly free**	**Mixed**	**All or mostly paid**
USA	56%	24%	18%	2%
China	54%	32%	13%	1%
South Korea	57%	24%	16%	3%

Source: Inmobi (2014). *Mobile Gaming Cross-Market Analysis*, p. 23.

Mobile game users in China are even less likely to pay for downloading a game than in some of the other countries. It is possible to base the main source of revenues on advertising, but then the average revenue per user is usually very low. The micro-payments for in-app purchases seem to be much more promising way of monetization.

Table 2. Frequency of inn-app payments made by game users

	Frequently	**Occasionally**	**At least once**	**Never**
USA	9%	16%	18%	57%
China	9%	21%	15%	55%
South Korea	13%	17%	26%	44%

Source: Inmobi (2014). *Mobile Gaming Cross-Market Analysis*, p. 25.

Study shows that the Chinese mobile game users do in-app payments more frequently than the wealthy Americans. They are not as good customers as the Koreans, of which 13% claim to frequently buy something in games, but 30% of Chinese do in-app micro-payments occasionally or frequently (see Table 2). Chinese players are willing to pay to beat the level, upgrade characters and resources, unlock level or even to buy virtual currency. This feature of the Chinese market is extremely important for any company that wishes to operate on it. The CEE companies entering China should consider adjusting their earning models and concentrate on inn-app payments, rather than other forms of monetization that could be ineffective.

It may appear that Chinese companies should have cost advantages over the CEE companies because of the low wages, and that it is more profitable to create games on the local market. In fact, in this specific sector wages in the CEE countries and in China are very similar. According to Glassdor (2015) survey results median software engineer salary in Poland in 2015 was 22,6 thousand USD per year, whereas in China 22,9 thousand USD. Programmers are highly qualified specialists, and their wages are relatively high all over the world.

Case studies of CEE companies on Chinese mobile game market

Case studies of the game producers from Poland prove that the success of CEE companies on the Chinese game market is possible, but hard to achieve. The first Polish studio to enter the Chinese online game market was Can't Stop Games, with a game called Pirates Saga in 2011, but they did not manage to succeed on any of the Asian markets (Mmwroclaw, 2011). Another company that attempted to enter China was Bloober, with a game Paper Wars: Cannon Fodder. Without any experience on the Chinese market company representatives went to the ChinaJoy digital entertainment expo to show their products to Chinese companies. They managed to attract attention of a Chinese venture fund and signed an agreement with a company The9 Limited (based in Shanghai) to distribute Paper Wars: Cannon Fodder in China (Newconnector, 2011). This first attempt was not successful, but the company gained an experience which resulted in a success of their next game called Brawl, on the Chinese market. Bloober has managed to publish Brawl for PlayStation 4 and a Chinese console – Tron. This two versions of the game were successfully distributed in China. Manager of Bloober claims that 40–50% of income in 2014 (which was more than PLN 6 million) come from Chinese market (Wolak, 2015).

The second CEE game company that achieved success on the Chinese market is Vivid Games, producer of mobile applications from Kraków. Their major product is a mobile game called Real Boxing. To enter the Chinese market Vivid Games used a Beijing based partner, Autothink Technology, which is responsible for publishing and distribution of the game in China, Hong Kong, Macau and Taiwan. Chinese company localized the game and adjusted it to the characteristics of this demanding East Asian market. Autothink Technology has a close partnership with China Mobile, China Unicom and China Telecom, the only three mobile carriers in mainland China. What is even more important. it has an access to more than 200 distribution platforms, which are mainly Chinese Android stores (Parkiet, 2015). Vivid Games does not reveal how many copies of the game have been downloaded, but on the 28th of June 2015, 55 days after the publication, it had over 600 thousand downloads on Muzhiwan (2015), 487 thousand on Zhushou (2015), 219 thousand on Ccplay (2015), 110 thousand on Appchina (2015), 93 thousand on Down Ali (2015), 51 thousand on Mumayi (2015), 37 thousand on Nduoa (2015), 25 thousand on Doyo (2015), and 17 thousand on Itunes (2015). Unfortunately, not all of the Chinese app stores revealed their download statistics, so it is not possible to count how many people in that country play the game. Real Boxing is also available on a new gaming device named Funbox, produced by Chinese company ZTE (Rzeczpospolita, 2014). The game took the 6th place on the Funbox toplist, platform with around 100 million users (Funbox, 2015). Real Boxing uses monetization model that is called Free2Play, which means that users do not have to pay anything for downloading the game or its subscription, but they are encouraged to do some in app payments, for example, to buy virtual currency and perks for the development of the boxer created by the player.

There is also another Polish company, Forever Entertainment S.A., that entered the Chinese mobile game market though joint-venture with a Chinese firm, China Smart Holding Company Limited, in May 2015. The aim of the joint-venture company is to translate, localize and publish European and American games on the Chinese and other Asian markets, and translated Chinese games on the European and American markets (Bankier, 2015a). New company has already managed do publish one game Teddy Floppy Ear – Kayaking on the China Mobile platform in the end of June 2015. It is not possible yet to give a verdict if that venture will be successful, but if Chinese consumers will like the game, it might become highly profitable (Bankier.pl, 2015b).

All of the Polish companies that successfully entered the Chinese market did that with local partners who provided distribution channels and good relations with the local authorities. Although there are no games produced by the CEE developers that would ever become the most popular game in China, examples of some European companies prove that it is possible. In May 2015, a game called Minecraft created by the Swedish video game developer Mojang was the second on the list of highest-grossing Android games in China. Another European company, Supercell from Finland, succeeded in the Chinese market with two products. Clash of Clans gained the 8th place on the list of top Android and 14th on the list of top iOS grossing games in China. Their second product, a game called Boom Beach was ranked 8th on the May's 2015 top iOS games by revenues (Newzoo, 2015b).

Key findings

Chinse mobile game market is the biggest in the World, and is still far from saturation. Analysis of the number of smartphones and Internet penetration proves that the Chinese market still has a high growth potential. Chinese game users are not loyal to any particular brand or product, so they can become customers of the CEE game developers, if only they would be offered good quality products. There are many barriers like the cultural differences and bureaucracy, that block foreign competition from entering the Chinese market. On the one hand, they can effectively stop the CEE game producers, but on the other, overcoming this barriers can become an important competitive advantage over other Western competition. Majority of the barriers can be bypassed by cooperation with Chinese companies, which is the easiest way of entering that market. Chinese partners can also support the distribution of games, especially on the Android operating system, a market which is divided into hundreds of local application stores. As far as monetization method is concerned, the Chinese users are more likely to do micro in app payments, than to pay for downloading a game. Case studies of the Polish companies that succeeded in China prove that the success of the CEE mobile game developers in the Middle Kingdom's market is possible.

Research contribution

There are not many CEE game producers that tried to enter the Chinese mobile game market. Game developers from the CEE countries that look for the opportunities of growth in the foreign markets should consider entering the Chinese market, which has recently become the biggest in the world. Chinese online game market is not yet as developed as the European or American ones, but also not as competitive, and far from saturation; so the perspectives of exporting products to China are very promising.

References

Bankier.pl (2015b). Kayaking na platformie China Mobile (Kayaking on a China Mobile Platform). *Bankier.pl*. Retrieved from: http://www.bankier.pl/wiadomosc/FOREVER-ENTERTAINMENT-Premiera-gry-Teddy-Floppy-Ear-Kayaking-na-platformie-China-Mobile-7271464.html (accessed: 10/09/2015).

Bankier.pl (2015a). Podpisanie istotnej umowy (Important Agreement Signed). *Bankier.pl*. Retrieved from: http://www.bankier.pl/wiadomosc/FOREVER-ENTERTAINMENT-Podpisanie-istotnej-umowy-7258633.html (accessed: 10/09/2015).

Bose, I., Yang Xinwei (2011). Enter the Dragon: Khillwar's Foray into the Mobile Gaming Market of China. *Communications of AIS*, 29, 551–564.

China Internet Network Information Center (2013). *34 Statistical Report on Internet Development in China January 2013*. Beijing: CINIC.

China Internet Network Information Center (2014). *35 Statistical Report on Internet Development in China January 2014*. Beijing: CINIC.

China Internet Network Information Center (2015). *36 Statistical Report on Internet Development in China January 2015*. Beijing: CINIC.

Emarketer (2014). *Internet to Hit 3 Billion Users in 2015*. Retrieved from: http://www.emarketer.com/Article/Internet-Hit-3-Billion-Users-2015/1011602 (accessed: 10/09/2015).

Feijoo, C., Gómez-Barroso, J.L., Aguado, J.M. & Scolari, C. (2010). *Mobile gaming prospects: the challenges to become a serious industry*. 21st European Regional ITS Conference.

Fields, T. (2014). Mobile & Social Game Design: Monetization Methods and Mechanics, 2nd edition. Boca Raton: CRC Press.

Hjorth, L. (2011) *Games and Gaming: An Introduction to New Media*. Oxford, UK: Berg Publishers.

Meng, G., McDonald, E. (2015). *Android vs. iOS Battle Heats Up in China, World's #1 Mobile Games Market*. Retrieved from: http://www.newzoo.com/insights/android-vs-ios-battle-heats-up-in-china-worlds-1-mobile-games-market/. http://www.newzoo.com/insights/android-vs-ios-battle-heats-up-in-china-worlds-1-mobile-games-market/ (accessed: 10/09/2015).

Mmwroclaw (2011). *Pirates Saga z Wrocławia dopłynęła do chińskich łączy (Pirates Saga from Wroclaw Sailed to Chinese Shores)*. Retrieved from: http://www.mmwroclaw.pl/artykul/pirates-saga-z-wroclawia-doplynela-do-chinskich-laczy,3184953,art,t,id,tm.html (accessed: 10/09/2015).

Newconnector (2011). Bloober Team – polska spółka podbija chiński rynek gier mobilnych. (Bloober Team – Polish Company conquers Chinese Mobile Game Market). Retrieved from: http://www.newconnector.pl/bloober-team-polska-spolka-podbija-chinski-rynek-gier-mobilnych (accessed: 10/09/2015).

Newzoo (2014). *Global Games Market Report Premium*. Retrieved from: http://www.newzoo.com/trend-reports/mobile-games-trend-report/.http://www.newzoo.com/trend-reports/mobile-games-trend-report/ (accessed: 10/09/2015).

Newzoo (2015a). *Global Games Market Premium, Q1 Update*. Retrieved from: http://www.newzoo.com/trend-reports/mobile-games-trend-report/ (accessed: 10/09/2015).

Newzoo (2015b). *Top 20 Android Grossing Games China*. Retrieved from: http://www.newzoo.com/free/rankings/top-20-android-games-china-grossing/#tMkYVc7vyFLAbYV6.99 (accessed: 10/09/2015).

Nielsen (2013). *Global Mobile Report*. Retrieved from: http://www.nielsen.com/content/dam/corporate/uk/en/documents/Mobile-Consumer-Report-2013.pdf.http://www.inmobi.com/ui/pdfs/Mobile_Gaming_Cross-Market_Analysis_(First_Edition).pdf (accessed: 10/09/2015)

Nostromo Wireless (2012). *Global Wireless Entertainment Market from a CEE Perspective*. Retrieved from: www.tmtevents.pl/files/nostromo.pdf.http://www.tmtevents.pl/files/nostromo.pdf (accessed: 10/09/2015).

Parkiet (2015). *Vivid Games rusza na podbój Chin* (*Vivid Games to Conquer China*). Retrieved from: http://www.parkiet.com/artykul/1416420.html.http://www.parkiet.com/artykul/1416420.html (accessed: 10/09/2015).

Sanou, B. (2015). *ICT Facts and Figures*, International Telecommunication Union. Retrieved from: http://www.itu.int/en/ITU-D/Statistics/Pages/facts/default.aspx (accessed: 10/09/2015).

Shintaro, O. & Barwise, P. (2011). Has the time finally come for the medium of the future? *Journal of Advertising Research, 51*, 59–71.

Soh, J.O.B. & Tan, C. (2008). Mobile gaming. *Communications of the ACM, 51*, 35–39.

Song, D. & de Wit, M. (2015). *The 2015 GMGC Global Mobile Games Industry Whitebook*. Retrieved from: http://2015.gmgc.info/ENG_GMGC_Newzoo_Global_Mobile_Games_Market_Whitepaper_Final.pdf (accessed: 10/09/2015).

Ström, P. & Ernkvist, M. (2014). Product and service interaction in the Chinese online game industry. *Technology Innovation Management Review*, 6–17.

Teitelbaum, D., Elders Ming-Hsuan & Alavian, R. (2012). Issues for payments in virtual economies. *Journal of Payments Strategy & Systems, 5*, 373–389.

The Multimedia Research Consultancy (2008). *Mobile Games Enterprises – The Essential Contacts Database*. Retrieved from: http://www.marketresearch.com/Multimedia-Research-Consultancy-v3465/Mobile-Games-Enterprises-Essential-Contacts-1686783/ (accessed: 10/09/2015).

Torrano, J. (2011). Gaming with my mobile. Product placement in video games. *Advances in Consumer Research – Asia-Pacific Conference Proceedings, 9*, 123–124.

Wang Hsiu-Yu, Liao Chechen & Yang Ling-Hui (2013). What affects mobile application use? The roles of consumption values. *International Journal of Marketing Studies, 5*, 11–22. Kshetri, N. (2010). The evolution of the Chinese online gaming industry. *Journal of Technology Management in China, 4*(2), 158–179.

Wolak, D. (2014). (100 mln Chinese will play Vivid Games's "Real Boxing"). *Rzeczpospolita*, November 20. Retrieved from: http://www.ekonomia.rp.pl/artykul/1158752.html (accessed: 10/09/2015).

Wolak, D. (2015). (Bloober Grows Thanks to China). Retrieved from: http://www.parkiet.com/artykul/1410428.html (accessed: 10/09/2015).

World Trade Organization (2015). *International Trade Statistics 2015*. Geneva, Switzerland: WTO.

Internet websites:

Appchina (2015). Retrieved from: http://www.appchina.com/app/com.vividgames.realboxing (accessed: 10/09/2015).

Ccplay.cc (2015). *Zhenshi Quanqi Pojie Ban / Real Boxing*. Retrieved from: http://ccplay.cc/package/94150/com.vividgames.realboxing/detail.html (accessed: 10/09/2015).

comScore (2013). *MobileLens Report 2013*. Retrieved from: http://www.inmobi.com/ui/pdfs/Mobile_Gaming_Cross-Market_Analysis_(First_Edition).pdf (accessed: 10/09/2015).

Down Ali (2015). Retrieved from: http://down.ali213.net/pcgame/RealBoxingI-SO.html (accessed: 10/09/2015).

Doyo (2015). Retrieved from: http://www.doyo.cn/game/18112?from=360onebox.

Funbox (2015). Retrieved from: http://www.funbox.com.cn/TVGame/TopRecommend.aspx (accessed: 10/09/2015).

Glassdoor 2015 survey results (2015). Retrieved from: www.glassdoor.com (accessed: 10/09/2015).

Inmobi (2014). *Mobile Gaming Cross-Market Analysis.* Retrieved from: http://www.inmobi.com/ui/pdfs/Mobile_Gaming_Cross-Market_Analysis_(First_Edition).pdf.http://www.inmobi.com/ui/pdfs/Mobile_Gaming_Cross-Market_Analysis_(First_Edition).pdf (accessed: 10/09/2015).

Itunes (2015). Retrieved from: https://itunes.apple.com/cn/app/zhen-shi-quan-ji/id534473264?mt=8 (accessed: 10/09/2015).

Mumayi (2015). Retrieved from: http://mpk.mumayi.com/386928.html (accessed: 10/09/2015).

Muzhiwan (2015). Retrieved from: http://www.muzhiwan.com/com.vividgames.realboxing.html (accessed: 10/09/2015).

Nduoa (2015). Retrieved from: http://www.nduoa.com/package/detail/207048.

Zhushou (2015). Retrieved from: http://zhushou.360.cn/search/index/?kw=%E7%9C%9F%E5%AE%9E%E6%8B%B3%E5%87%BB (accessed: 10/09/2015).

PART THREE

EDUCATION IN TRANSITION

Dong Xixiao

Opening the Two-Way Fast Lane for China-CEE Cultural Exchange by Equally Valuing the International Promotion of the Chinese Language and the CEE Languages Teaching

Languages are the bridges of communication and exchange across different cultures. Demands for Chinese talents in foreign languages, especially translators can date back to the pre-Qin period (before 221 B.C.). But judging by the will and the methods of communication, the communication between China and the outside world had been unidirectional in the long historic period, after Zhangqian went to the west of China on a diplomatic trip. The Chinese rarely show interest in exploring the outside world. There were only a limited number of professionals in foreign languages and they were not influential. The bridge of languages wasn't a two-way street. Like Professor Ge Jianxiong said, the famous Silk Road "is not built or promoted by Chinese. The Silk Road cannot take form without foreign demands for Chinese silk" (Ge, 2015). The overseas communication of Chinese culture was also led by foreigners in the beginning: in the 5th year of Dazhong in Tang Dynasty (851 A.D.), the "Travel notes in China and India" by the Arabian Suleyman are the first books introducing Chinese culture to Westerners. Then Marco Polo, Matteo Ricci, Michal Boym, George Macartney, Nicolae Milescu and others went to China in different ways. They all wrote books or travel notes. But not all of them were experts in Chinese language.

After the Opium War of 1840, the Chinese wanted to see the world. This wish became more stronger than ever before. Their demand for talents in foreign language kept on rising. A number of great translators turned up in the Republic of China period (1912–1949). They translated classic literature of different countries into Chinese. At that time, the culture of communication between China and the foreign countries was still mainly unidirectional, it was just the direction that had changed. It was only possible after entering into this new century, to promote Chinese language and culture, while cultivating talents in foreign languages to realize two-way fast passing of Chinese and foreign languages on the bridge of culture exchange.

1. The history of building a two-way passage between Chinese and the CEE cultures

After the People's Republic of China was founded, it was first recognized by former Soviet Union and the other CEE (Central and Eastern Europe) countries. Learning each other's language became a significant foundation of deepening communication and cooperation and the basis of building a two-way passage between Chinese and the CEE cultures. This process can be divided into the following three stages:

1.1. 1950s – the end of 1970s: the unsmooth development period

In 1949, China established diplomatic relations with the Soviet Union, Bulgaria, Romania, Czechoslovakia, Hungary, Poland, Albania, and other countries. Large numbers of officials who knew foreign language, especially the CEE languages were urgently needed. Therefore, China sent students to the best universities in these countries to study language, on the other hand, the CEE languages also started to be taught in China. In 1954, the two majors of Polish and Czech philology were founded at the Beijing University. In 1959, these majors were combined with the Romanian major at the Beijing Foreign Languages Institute as the Faculty of Polish, Czech and Romanian. In the beginning of the 1960s, as new majors like Hungarian, Bulgarian, Albanian, Serbian-Croatian were established, the pattern of the CEE languages teaching took basic form (Dai & Hu, 2009, p. 420).

According to the bilateral cultural cooperation agreement, Chinese language major and Chinese language course were established at the colleges of CEE countries. In the beginning, teaching Chinese as a foreign language was also targeted at overseas students from the CEE countries. It can date back to the "Chinese language courses for the exchange students of the Eastern European countries" (1950) and "Higher preparatory school for foreign students" (1962) (the predecessor of the Beijing Language and Culture University). Famous linguist, Mr. Zhu Dexi, used to teach Chinese language at the Sophia University of Bulgaria in the 1950s. He also compiled the first Chinese textbook for overseas students with professor Zhang Sunfen – *Chinese Textbook* (Ge & Dong, 2009, p. 415). "Teaching Chinese foreign languages" and "teaching foreigners the Chinese language" became the two footings of the cultural exchange between China and the foreign countries. The basic pattern of the two-way cultural exchange passage between China and the CEE countries gradually took shape.

In this period, the CEE language majors in China were mainly targeted at educating translators for the diplomatic purposes. The teaching notion of viewing the national interests above everything else, the strict and practical teaching tradition, the hard study trend and resources for the multiple language teaching had laid the foundation for future survival and development of less commonly taught languages of China (Ge & Dong, 2009, p. 415). During this period, relations between China and some of the CEE countries fluctuated. Chinese teaching in some countries had ceased, when the relations between China and Soviet Union worsened. Teaching of the CEE languages in China also went through a lot of great difficulties during The Cultural Revolution. But the above-mentioned teaching notion and tradition was passed on. In this period, teaching of the CEE languages had the features of a limited teaching platform, focusing on language skills, narrow demands for talents under the influence of the current political environment. The cultivation of Chinese language talents in target countries also shared similar characteristics.

1.2. 1980s – end of 1990s: the depression period

China and the CEE countries were in a transitional period. Most people's eyes were fixed on the Western political systems and cultural forms, they lacked attention to languages and the cultures of other countries. This kind of social trend directly influenced people's choices of foreign languages education. Chinese language or the CEE languages were not popular.

In the late 1970s, the reform and opening-up policy was implemented in China. Within the new trend of the market economy, languages such as English and Japanese were very popular. The CEE languages met the "cold shoulders." There were common problems, like the insufficient student quantity, of confidence in their majors, serious outflow of teacher talents, obsolete teaching content, outdated teaching equipment, shortage in schooling funding and library resource. Many majors were facing a survival crisis. The Ministry of Education agreed that the Beijing Foreign Studies Institute and relevant majors of Beijing University should enrol targeted-area students and separately enrol students in advance. This measure slightly relieved the problem of insufficient student numbers.

In the 1990s, the CEE countries went through long restructuring period in terms of politics and economy. There were many domestic problems. Chinese language teaching and the overseas promotion of their native languages were not sufficiently valued. Like the Chinese students learning the CEE languages, many Chinese language students also were founding it hard to find a job.

1.3. The 21st century: the booming development period

After entering the new century, China and the CEE countries found new development opportunities. China entered the WTO in 2001. Most of the CEE countries also have completed political and economic transformation. In the course of globalization, they share more common interests and concerns and have more interactions in trading and economy. The requirements on foreign language talents have also become more diversified.

Year 2004 has been an uncommon year for China and the CEE countries: in this year, the first Confucius Institute in world was opened, which marked the beginning of international promotion of the Chinese language; in the same year, the first batch of 8 CEE countries entered the EU and started to embrace the world with a brand new attitude. By now, 11 out of the 16 CEE countries have become the EU members. At the same time, number of Confucius Institute and Confucius Classroom has also risen to 48 in this region.

After the transformation, the CEE countries value the standardization even more, as it is the case when it comes to the protection and promotion of their own languages. Taking Romania as an example, we can say that the "Romanian Constitution" (in 1991) only planned to position an official language, then the "Law on Romanian language used in public places, relations and institutes" (2004) becomes the planning of the language itself, and finally, the "Law on establishing the Romanian Language Day" (2013) shows the real extent of the Romanian people's language belief in their own language. Many of the CEE countries became the mainstay power of keeping the cultural and language diversifications in Europe. An important way for China to show its understanding of the issue, and respect and support the European language diversification, is to value the cultivation of the CEE language talents, while making efforts in promoting the Chinese language.

2. Some suggestions on "accelerating" the two-way lane of China-CEE cultural exchange

China has become the second biggest economy in world. The voices of the CEE countries in international affairs has also been rising continuously. The joint development of China and the CEE countries has a great significance to the relevant countries, regions and even the whole world. From 2012, China has had three times of "1+16" leader meetings with the CEE countries and established the China-CEE National Cooperation Secretariat (2012). They've issued "The Bucharest Outline for China-CEE Cooperation" (2013) and "The Belgrade Outline for China-CEE Cooperation" (2014). The proposed "One belt one road" strategy has not only brought opportunities of bilateral cooperation in terms of trading and the economy, but also expanded cultural possibilities for exchange and cooperation. Both parties are willing to learn each other's languages and promote their native languages. This common will is the key of "accelerating" the two-way lane of China-CEE Cultural Exchange.

Talent cultivation has been converted from the "planned" mode of national control and arrangement, to the "market" mode of free competition. Insufficient teacher reserves, lack of teaching resources, difficulties in guaranteeing cultivated talent quality, and other problems start to become obvious. At the same time, after more than a decade of Chinese language promotion around the world, it has also met difficulties in some of the Western countries. We've heard some voices of objection from the USA, Canada, Sweden and other countries. It is a question worth thinking about, how can we combine the cultivation of the CEE language talents and the international promotion of the Chinese language to make them support, learn from and promote each other. Therefore, we've made the following suggestions:

So far, the majors established at the BFSU have basically "covered all" of the CEE languages. Many other universities have also established relevant majors, after realizing the future of the CEE language development. Their cultivated object students have been extended to high schools (such as the 7-year thorough talent cultivation mode made by the Beijing International Studies University).

2.1. Comprehensive arrangement and utilization of human resource

Talent reserves of the less commonly taught languages are an "old, big difficult" problem. On the one hand, as bilateral relation keeps deepening, the gap of the high-level foreign language talents keeps expanding; on the other hand, many majors don't enrol every year, which makes the cycles of demand and supply somewhat inconsistent. Some students cannot find appropriated work after graduation, and their professional skills keep degenerating. I think that the Confucius Institutes in the CEE countries are not only international promotion centres of the Chinese language, but also reserves and incubators for the language talents in the CEE countries.

If the Chinese headmasters, teachers and volunteers working in Confucius Institutes can master the languages of their target countries, it shall undoubtedly be a great driving force for the international promotion of the Chinese language. Although some personnel sent by the BFSU and the BLCU have this ability, English is still the main working language for most people. The BFSU undertakes the work of organizing many Confucius Institutes in CEE, but the quantity of professional teachers in their relevant languages still cannot meet the demands of the overseas assignments. In recent years, some graduates that had majored in the CEE languages and had chosen to achieve a Master's degree in Teaching Chinese as a foreign language, go to relevant countries to work as a teacher combining the two majors. This practice has had good effects. If the CEE language majors in Chinese universities can establish long-term relation with NOCFL (Hanban) and provide language training, the national strategy can be served better and more directly.

Insufficient teacher resources have always been the bottleneck for building the CEE language majors. As the personnel system at the universities is being reformed, the requirements on teachers' discipline background, degree and overseas studies have become stricter. The work experience at the Confucius Institutes can greatly help the teachers to develop personal abilities, improve degree level and expand career choices. Some high-degree scholars with outstanding language level can supplement the foreign teacher resources at the universities. There is a successful example of a teacher from the BFSU obtaining a doctors degree in the target country during her work period in the Confucius Institute as the Chinese Headmaster. If this mode can be further promoted, we can realize the "triple win" of Confucius Institutes, universities in China and the individuals.

2.2. Establishing of evaluation mechanism

Evaluation and testing is an important process to guarantee the quality of talent cultivation. In 1992, the HSK tests formally rose to the level of national exams. By 2014, the HSK test site number has reached 860 around world, including 25 sites in the CEE countries, mainly in the Confucius Institutes. HSK has become a highly authoritative and standardized evaluation mechanism, which is widely recognized by global Chinese language learners.

On the contrary, language level tests for the CEE language majors in China have always been organized by different teaching and research offices separately, without any unified standards. In the recent years, relevant majors were established at more and more universities. But their testing standards are not unified. Some of the CEE countries organize language level tests for their native languages according to *The common reference framework of European languages: study, teaching and evaluation* and the language competence evaluation mechanism established by ALTE. However, only a small number of Chinese students undertake the tests. The causes include: (1) The language teaching goals and textbook systems are different between China and the EU countries; (2) Due to the limited number of learners, the costs of establishing long-term test sites are too high; (3) Many CEE countries don't make much effort in promoting their native languages and cannot organize tests alone.

Considering the above conditions, I suggest that relevant universities in China can consider the CEE countries as a whole, and build a language level testing mechanism after referring to the European standards, practical demands on foreign language talents in China and the successful experience of the HSK tests. The experience accumulated and problems happen in this process should also be timely reported to NOCFL and other institutes as a reference.

2.3. Valuing the symbolic significance of languages teaching

The China-CEE cooperation at present is mainly developed around the economic and trade ties. But cultural exchange shouldn't be measured mainly by interests. Instead, it should represent greater inclusiveness and mutual trust. As the important basis of cultural exchange, foreign language teaching should be both practical and symbolic. When the Foreign Ministry of China was compiling *The Language Books for Leaders in Foreign Affairs*, Jiang Zemin, the Ex-President of China who is proficient in Romanian, suggested to add the Romanian version in addition to the English, French, Russian, German, Spanish, Italian, Arabian and Japanese versions. Some Romanian media exclaimed in surprise that "China has positioned Romanian as an international common language". This report is obviously somewhat exaggerated. However, we can see that the foreign language study does not only suit the practical needs, but also shows recognition and respect to object countries. It is based on such consideration that we've made the grand plan of establishing majors for all official languages of the countries in diplomatic relation with China.

China doesn't seek economic interests or promoting its ideology by opening the Confucius Institutes around the world. Instead, China aims at building a smooth exchange channel between various countries across the bridge of languages. This is not only the wish of China, but also a common wish of the people in the CEE countries. Mutual trust in culture cannot be built without sufficient expression of both parties' wills and two-way interaction in language popularization and cultural communication. Within the China-EU Language Cooperation Seminar (Beijing, 2009), more than 60 representatives from EU and China discussed the theme of "Languages build a diversified world". One of the main topics is transmission of Chinese language into Europe and the EU official languages in China. Zhang Xinsheng, Deputy Minister of Education in China stressed at that time, that diversification of human culture relies first and foremost on the diversification of languages. But diversification of world languages faces serious challenges against the background of globalization. The Chinese government highly values improvement of foreign language education for the Chinese people and has cooperated with language promotion institutes of many countries in the world. They are welcomed to establish branches in China (Xinhua, 2009). In this aspect, language and cultural promotion institutes of the CEE countries in China can learn from experience of Confucius Institutes and cooperate with the CEE language majors of Chinese universities to share resources and complement each other in advantages.

Conclusion

There is not only competition and confrontation, but also the communication and cooperation within international relations. Mutual cultural understanding and learning from each other need a wide basis. Languages play the role of a bridge and bond it in. There's no way to eliminate disagreement and establish a mutual trust without mastering each other's languages. Languages also pave the road for communication and cooperation in other aspects.

The experience of the success of Confucius Institutes can be a reference and an example for many countries. But the focus of cultural exchanges is in equality and interaction. The "two-way fast lane" of China-CEE cultural exchanges cannot be successfully built, unless we protect the diversity of the world languages and cultures by respecting other countries' language culture, while promoting our own native language, cooperating with cultural promotion institutes of other countries, and actively encouraging various foreign language talents.

References

Dai Weidong (戴炜栋), Hu Wenzhong (胡文仲) (2009). *The Research on Foreign Language Education in China (1949–2009)* (《中国外语教育发展研究 （1949–2009）》). Shanghai: Shanghai Foreign Language Education Press.

Fu Ke (付克) (1986). *The History of Foreign Language Education in China* (《中国外语教育史》). Shanghai: Shanghai Foreign Language Education Press.

Ge Jianxiong (2015). The history of one belt one road is misinterpreted, quoted from: http://club.china.com/baijiaping/gundong/11141903/20150310/19363154.html (accessed: 11/03/2015).

Ge Zhiqiang (葛志强), Dong Shuhui (董淑慧) (2009). Zhu Dexi and Zhang Sunfen – the founders of Chinese language teaching in Bulgaria (保加利亚汉语教学奠基人朱德熙和张荪芬). In: *Research on European Language and Culture* (《欧洲语言文化研究》). Beijing: Current Affairs Press.

Hu Wenzhong (胡文仲) (2011). Thoughts on the Chinese plan of foreign language education (关于我国外语教育规划的思考). *Foreign Language Teaching and Research* (《外语教学与研究》), *1*, 130–136.

Li Yuming (李宇明) (2011). Some thoughts on improving national language abilities (提升国家语言能力的若干思考). *The Linguistics Periodical of Nankai University* (《南开语言学刊》), *1*, 1–8.

Liu Yingsheng (刘迎胜) (1998). Research on foreign language education history in China from Song and Yuan dynasties to the beginning of Qing dynasty (宋元至清初我国外语教学史研究). *Jianghai Academic Journal* (《江海学刊》), *3*, 112–118.

The Higher Education Research Institute of Sichuan International Studies University (四川外语学院高等教育研究所) (1993). *Chronicle of Events in Foreign Language Education in China* (《中国外语教育要事录》). Beijing: Foreign Language Teaching and Research Press.

Xinhua (2009). China EU work together to protect linguistic diversity (中国欧盟携手保护语言多样性). Xinhua. 30.03.2009. Retrieved from http://news.xinhuanet.com/newscenter/2009–03/30/content_11101549.htm (accessed: 3/07/2015).

Wang Yan

A Contrastive Analysis of Traditional Chinese and Western Teaching Styles – A Case Study

In the process of second language teaching, both Chinese and Western teachers show their distinctive teaching styles as demonstrated by their different teaching approaches and roles. Generally speaking, the mainland ELT teachers prefer a more instructor-centered style of class management than Western teachers do, which is characterized by the form of "knowledge transmission from teacher to students" (cited in Xiao, 2006), while Western teachers tend to take a communicative approach and encourage students' participation in class. There is no doubt that different teaching styles can exert different impacts on students' learning processes and outcomes. Since teaching styles have become particularly important in the context of teaching English as a second language, identifying the teaching style can help language teachers, especially Mainland ELT teachers, gain a clearer insight into the embedded strengths and weaknesses so as to ensure positive learning outcomes and effective teaching.

1. Literature Review

"Teaching style is a teacher's individual instructional method and approach and the characteristic manner in which the teacher carries out instruction. Teachers differ in the way they see their role in the classroom, the type of teacher-student interaction they encourage, their preferred teaching strategies and these differences lead to differences in the teacher's teaching style" (Richards et al., 2005, p. 699). The difference between traditional Chinese and Western teaching styles, to a large extent, can be traced back to cultural influence. German linguist Hofstede (1980) points out the three cultural dimensions which affect Chinese L2 teaching and learning, including the "Power Distance Dimension" of Chinese teachers' authority image and students' submissiveness in the instructor-centered classroom, and "Collective-Individualistic Dimension", focusing on the Asian value of seeing individuals as an inseparable part of an in-group and the Westerners' stressing individual goals, needs and rights rather than the community (Hall, 1977; Hoftstede, 1980). In addition, teaching styles may vary from person to person, and there is no absolute criterion for judging a good style of teaching. The traditional Chinese teaching style may be an effective way to enable students to grasp fundamental facts, grammatical rules or sequences, while the Western teaching style emphasizes student engagement in classroom activities and fosters their critical thinking and independent learning. When a teaching style matches the learning style, students can gain more knowledge, obtain more information and perform far better (Lage & Treglia, 2000). However, since the major goal of any effective course is to develop students' ability to communicate in the target language (Davies & Pearse, 2002), a flexible and dynamic teaching style will enjoy popularity among students and the traditional teaching style, characterized by its monotonous teaching approach and teacher's authoritative roles, will inevitably fail to meet the needs of students in modern times.

2. Methodology

This research project is a case study which aims at investigating and analyzing the differences between traditional Chinese and Western teaching styles. In order to better understand the purpose, the main focus is on different teaching approaches and teacher's roles performed by both Chinese and Western teachers. In addition, two questions were posed in the case study:

1. In what aspects are Chinese and Western teaching styles different from each other?
2. What can mainland ELT teachers gain by analyzing teaching styles?

2.1. Instruments

The study was viewed as a qualitative research, since it could present a more accurate picture of reality and reveal more complexities (Cohen et al., 2000; Merriam, 2001; Freebody, 2003; Wen, 2004). Pre-interviews and participant observations were used as data-collecting instruments.

In the research project, we chose the former to obtain useful information about the subjects' syllabuses and objectives of their writing course, their teaching approaches and the students' academic performance. The interviews lasted about 5 minutes each, which allowed us to "fish" the subjects' personal styles, motives and feelings based on their tone of voice, facial expressions, etc.; thus, we could probe certain information (Moser & Kalton, 1971; Cohen, 2000; Bell, 2005). In addition, classroom observation was an important part of the study, since this naturalistic approach allowed us to observe what actually happened in class, and consequently obtain valuable data (Allright, 1988; Bell, 2005). The classroom observations averaged 50 minutes in length. Both pre-interviews and classroom observations were audio- and video-recorded for later verbatim transcription and analysis. In this case study, different teaching styles constituted independent variables, in which different teaching approaches and teachers' roles were variations. The dependent variable is mainland ELT teachers' self-improvement and more effective teaching. In other words, an in-depth study on different teaching styles can provide mainland ELT teachers with a clear insight into the nature of a teaching style and at the same time enable them to reflect on their teaching performance in order to enhance their professional development and pedagogical outcome.

2.2. Subjects

Table 1. Background Information on the Two Subjects

Subjects	Sex	Title	Academic qualification	Years of teaching	Teaching courses
CT	F	Professor, dean	Master	24	Writing
WT	F	Assistant Professor, program leader	PhD	20	Writing

Note. CT and WT are short forms of the Chinese teacher and the Western teacher.

Source: results of research.

The subjects involved in this case study were two English language teachers with their 31 English major students from two universities in mainland China and Hong Kong. The two subjects' academic qualifications and training were in English and their experience of teaching English was 24 and 20 years respectively. The Chinese teacher obtained a Master degree in English literature in China and was professor and dean of the English department; The Western teacher from the UK had a Med, PGCE and PhD in education. She was assistant professor and program leader in MAELT in the English department of a university in Hong Kong.

The choice of observing their classes was based on the fact that they were both expert teachers, one a program leader of MAELT, the other the dean of the English faculty, and they taught first-year college students writing during the observation.

In addition, the subjects selected in this case study constituted a convenient sample simply, because the Western professor was working at the same university in Hong Kong, where I was doing my master's degree in English language teaching – and the Chinese professor was my colleague, before I came to Hong Kong for further studies. However, owing to the fact that the sampling was not randomly selected, no claim is made herein that the two main subjects chosen constituted a representative sample of all college English teachers in L2 teaching.

2.3. Ethical Considerations

As a qualitative researcher, I adopted three safeguards to protect the subjects of the study. Firstly, the research objectives were honestly articulated to the subjects in person so that they could understand and express their concerns. Secondly, written consent was obtained to conduct the research and to film the classes of both teachers. Lastly, to ensure confidentiality, the names of the two subjects were changed simply to "Chinese teacher" and "Western teacher".

3. Data Analysis

The study reveals that generally both Chinese and Western teachers were deeply involved in their instructions. The objectives of the writing session were clearly introduced and the class time was used effectively. However, a closer look at their classroom teaching and a careful analysis of the data indicate that there was a striking difference between traditional Chinese and Western teaching styles as reflected by the subjects' teaching approaches and teacher's roles.

3.1. Teaching Approaches

In his review of the development in teaching writing, Platridge (2004) has listed different approaches based on a chronological order: controlled composition from the mid 1940s to the mid 1960s; product approach in 1960s, process approach in the 1970s and genre approach, which is regarded as the most effective approach to this day.

The Chinese teacher adopted the traditional product approach, in which students were encouraged to mimic a model text (Steele, 2007). The teacher organized her teaching plan in 5 stages:

- Stage 1. Introduction to classification and its purpose initiated by teacher's questions and students' answers.
- Stage 2. Model text – "The Two Types of Clouds" was read.
- Stage 3. Organization of ideas by offering strategies in doing classification.
- Stage 4. Teacher's deconstruction of the model text.
- Stage 5. Mimicking the model text in groups with the teacher's feedback.

One of the encouraging findings is that the Chinese teacher did not dogmatically follow the content of the product-driven approach as was demonstrated by her encouraging the students' collaborative work in class. The product approach, focuses on the layout, style, organization and grammar. In addition, the exposition's features are very much fixed. Therefore, the approach adopted by the Chinese teacher may help students in handling this type of writing tasks. However, the book-based, instructor-centered approach also has its defects. In the whole session, the teacher controlled the flow of the content which the students were expected to receive and absorb. The monologue-like instruction created a static and monotonous learning atmosphere, which prevented the students from active involvement in learning.

By contrast, based on the classroom observation, the Western teacher's way of teaching was different from that of the Chinese teacher and the effect produced was also not the same accordingly. In her teaching of writing, she employed a genre-based approach, centered on the language and discourse of the text, and the context in which the text was produced (Paltridge, 2004). In her writing session, the teacher explicitly explained to her students the "code of conduct" through a genre-based Curriculum Cycle (cited in Gibbons, 2002, p. 60). In the course of teaching, the teacher followed the stages identified by Derewianka (Gibbons, 2002):

- Stage 1. Building background knowledge of the code of conduct
  - Based on a video in a previous lesson about Jamie Oliver, a famous chef who wanted to enact a code of conduct for his new chefs, students were encouraged to share other information on the type of genres, the nature of the code of conduct, authentic materials from interviewing Jamie and the model text.
- Stage 2. Modeling "Boeing Code of Conduct"
  - Choose "Boeing Code of Conduct" as a model text which was similar to the target one.
  - Deconstruct the text together with students by identifying the three stages from the text, students' marking interesting word fea-

tures like negative words "inappropriate", "violation", "conflict of interest" and the negative polarity and pointing out some grammatical features by using "meta-language" (Gibbons, 2002).

- Stage 3. Writing in pairs.

  In the process of teaching writing, the Western teacher provided scaffolding for her students at each step until they gained the competence to do the writing task independently. What is more, active interaction between T-S and S-S created a very lively and dynamic classroom atmosphere. However, it would be much better if a teacher-guided joint construction was added to the teaching procedure, because it is viewed as a very important stage in the Curriculum Cycle, from which students can get a clear idea of both process and product in the writing course (Gibbons, 2002).

3.2. Teacher Talk Time

There is no denying the fact that in the process of classroom teaching, teacher talk plays a very important role in guiding students' learning. However, if the classroom discourse is dominated by teacher talk, students will have less chance to practice themselves in the target language. Harmer (2000) believes that it is a vital part of a teacher's job to offer opportunities for students to express themselves in class. In his opinion, Teacher Talking Time (TTT) should be minimized while Students Talking Time (STT) should be maximized. Zhao (cited in Hu, 2007) in her study of analyzing Teacher Talk argues that in a teacher-centered classroom setting, TTT usually occupies 70%-90% of the total classroom discourse. Thus, the students hardly have an opportunity to engage in classroom activities and express their viewpoints in class.

The data from classroom observation indicates that compared with Western TTT (47.6%), Chinese TTT covered 77% of the total class discourse. As for STT, Western STT (54.2%) was twice the amount of the Chinese's and occupied more than half of the total discourse. Therefore, students in Chinese teacher's class had less opportunity to participate in class activities and the development of their inter-language will be halted accordingly.

Table 2: Discourse Amount

Discourse Amount / Teacher	Overall Time	Total Discourse Amount		TTT		STT	
	t (min.)	t (min.)	%	t (min.)	%	t (min.)	%
Western teacher	50'	42'	84	20'	47.6	22'	52.4
Chinese teacher	50'	44'50"	89	34'50"	77	10'	23

Source: results of research.

3.3. Teacher-Students' Interactions

Language teaching is a continuum of teachers' instructions and students' learning, the essence of which is interaction. Based on this, modern pedagogy indicates that the process of language teaching is T-S communication, active interaction and mutual development. Appropriate and manifold interactions can make lessons more lively and dynamic than traditional teacher-centered, students-silent lessons (Davis & Pearse, 2002). During the classroom observation, we found that the interactions between T-S and S-S in the Western teacher's class were very impressive.

(*The Western teacher*) T-S: individual interaction (25 times)

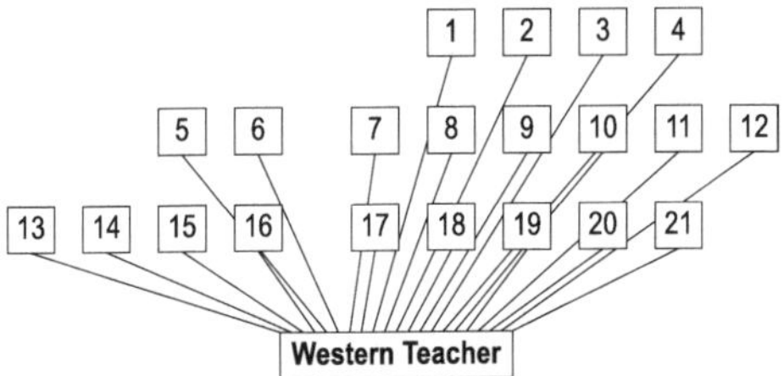

Diagram 1: Individual Interaction between T-S in Western Teacher's Class
Source: results of research.

(*The Western teacher*) T-S: interaction in pair work (12 times)

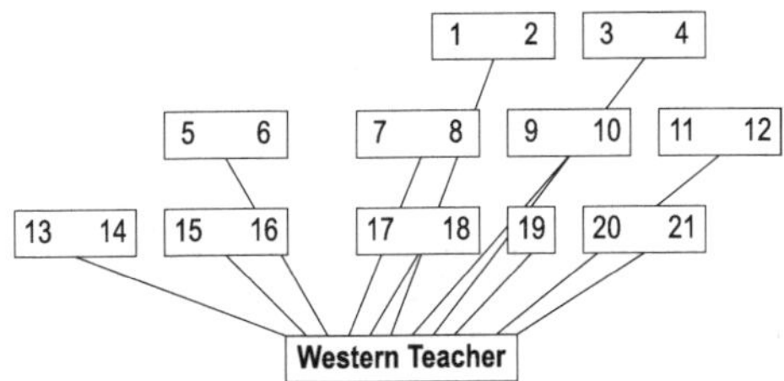

Diagram 2: Interaction between the Western Teacher and Pairs
Source: results of research.

(*The Chinese teacher*) T-S: individual interaction (13 times)

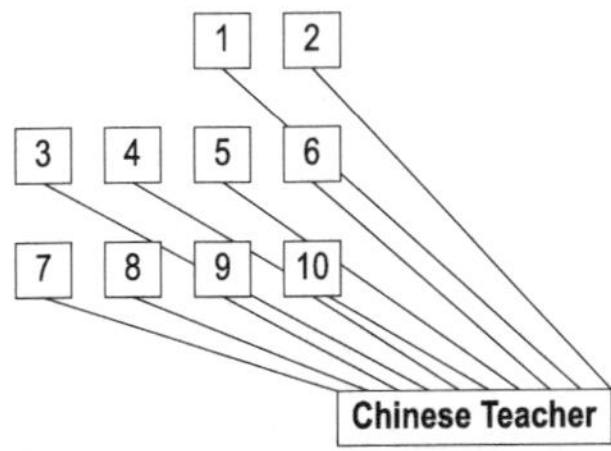

Diagram 3: Individual Interaction between T-S in Chinese Teacher's Class
Source: results of research.

From the above diagrams, we can conclude that the Western teacher involved herself in interacting both with individuals (25 times) and pairs (12 times). Besides, two students came to the board, marking language features from the text on the overhead projector with the help of others. In contrast, the Chinese teacher's interaction with her students only amounted to 13 times.

3.4. Teacher's Roles

Clearly, a teacher should assume great responsibility to create a context in which students' thirst for knowledge can work most effectively. The following table shows the different roles both Chinese and Western teachers performed in their writing sessions

Table 3: Teacher's Roles

The Chinese teacher	The Western teacher
An authority figure	A facilitator of learning
A teacher of the textbook	A developer of materials
A bystander of group work	A director and involver of group work
An island in the learning community	A psychologist, sister and educator

Source: results of research.

As for the Chinese teacher, she appeared to be an authority figure (Hedge, 2002), who stood still behind the platform throughout the whole session. The platform was like a gap separating her from her students and hindered meaningful interaction between the teacher and her students. Standing there, the teacher assumed the airs of a sage on the stage with the students sitting in rows, showing respect. By contrast, the Western teacher played a role of a facilitator who questioned, encouraged and stimulated her students in their thinking, problem-solving and independent learning.

In terms of choosing teaching materials, it seems that the Chinese teacher was an instructor of the textbook, who regarded it as the sole teaching material in the classroom instruction, while the Western teacher acted as an information provider whose teaching materials were beyond textbooks. They covered various authentic materials ranging from an interview with Jamie Oliver, a model of the code of conduct from "Boeing" to the handout of the tasks for the students. Tomlinson (2001) holds that no textbook can be an ideal choice for any particular class and firmly believes that an effective teacher should be able to produce and provide additional teaching materials over and above textbook material.

The findings concerning the two teachers' roles indicate that the students involved all took an active part in their collaborative work. However, the teachers concerned performed quite different roles in the student group work. In the whole process, the Chinese teacher looked like a bystander, holding fast to her "fortress" and leaving her students alone with their discussion. Conversely, the Western teacher played the role of a director and an involver who gave instructions for the pair work, initiated it, monitored it and organized feedback (Hedge, 2002). Rather than standing on a platform, she strolled across the room, from one group to another, monitoring, guiding, and even being involved in their collaborative work. She was also a keen observer. When noticing a pair student at the back row unwilling to start their work, she went up to them, helping them break the ice and guiding them onto the right path.

Charles Curran (cited in Richards et al., 2005) developed a method of second and foreign language teaching – Community Language Learning, by which teachers are expected to counsel students learning in small or large groups. These groups are "communities" (Richards et al., 2005). In this sense, if we compare the classroom to an intact learning community, the teacher's role is assumed to be the "counselor" who should help the students with their problems (Richards et al., 2005). From the observation, the Chinese teacher seemed like an educational island (Terry, 2005) that is separate from the outside world (here he refers to the whole learning community). There is a lack of counseling and communicative atmosphere. In the whole session, the Chinese teacher was indulged in her monologue-like instruction, looking ahead without any eye contact with her students. As a consequence, the atmosphere in the classroom appeared to be oppressive and dull.

An interesting finding from the research is that the Western teacher played the role of an educator when explaining the new word "integrity" from the text: "Boeing Code of Conduct." She stated that she had "integrity" as a teacher and believed in sharing knowledge and helping people to learn. She also asked the students what they had "integrity" in. Some students responded with "doing an assignment, and do it well" and so on. At last, she summarized that being a good student was the reflection of their "integrity." The interesting point is that the Western teacher's belief coincides with the mottoes of every Chinese teacher. They are: *jiao shu yu ren* (it is the teachers' duty to not only impart knowledge to their students but also teach them morals) and *yan chuan shen jiao* (teaching by personal examples as well as verbal instructions). Leng (cited in Xiao 2006) holds that personalized approach is believed to be more effective than mere verbal instructions.

Another finding which should be highlighted reveals that the Western teacher acted as a psychologist in her class when monitoring and guiding the students' group work. Being a psychologist, you should be capable of reading your clients' mind: what are they thinking about? And what do they need? When the students started group discussion, the teacher moved all the time, strolling among each group, listening to them attentively and joining in their discussion. When doing so, she usually did a deep-knee bend, looking amiably in the speaker's eyes with an eye contact and smiling with encouragement. The teacher's deep-knee bend proved to be very effective in communicating with her students. In Halliday's SFL theory, the social context of language can be analyzed in three factors: the field of discourse, the tenor of discourse and the mode of discourse (Richards, 2005). In the classroom context, the participants of tenor are teacher and students. Compared with students, a teacher is in a higher position. Interpersonally, there is a social distance between a teacher and students. The Western teacher sensed the importance of setting up a reasonable close relationship with her students (Christie, 2005), so she made an eye contact and deep-knee bend while communicating with her students. As a result, it bridged the gap between the teacher and students, and helped the students remove the teacher's authoritative image from their minds. Looking down at her, the students at this moment saw her as their sister or friend rather than a teacher. Hence, their feeling of tension and timidity in front of her were completely gone. Followed that was their fluent and meaningful argument.

3.5. Implications

Some of my Chinese colleagues who teach writing often complain that their students are fed up with the writing course since the lesson always follows the same sequences of teacher's deconstruction of the text → students' imitation → final product. They find it hard to interact with students in class. However, the case study enables us to gain knowledge from the Western teacher's practical teaching approach, her responsibility, the dynamic interaction and the rapport with her students in class. In spite of the fact that the Chinese teacher's teaching style is viewed as a specific subject in the case study, it still reflects some problems existing among the Mainland teachers. Even if the Chinese teacher admitted that her traditional teaching style could no longer cater to the students' learning styles in a modern classroom context, the conception of teacher-fronted, whole-class mode (Davies & Pearse, 2002) influenced by the Chinese culture of teaching has taken root among many Mainland Chinese teachers.

When mentioning the expectation of how teachers should appropriately behave, Hedge (2002) claims that it may require far more than a simple change in pedagogy: a change in self-perception is needed. That is to say, if a teacher desires to transform from the traditional image of an authority figure to a facilitator and helper of the students, he or she, above all, should change their self-conception. Therefore, some suggestions are provided as follows.

- Overseas immersion is a good way to broaden the teachers' minds and adjust their teaching styles.
- Panel activities and in-service training are very helpful for teachers to gain experience and receive professional input.
- Self-reflection enables the teacher to reflect on his or her experience in teaching and bring light to the possible problem areas in teaching and redesigning the class plan. Just as Ye (1998) said, "He who devotes his lifetime to designing teaching plans may not be an expert teacher. However, he can become an excellent instructor if he keeps on self-reflection for three years".
- Most importantly, it is high time ELT Mainland Chinese teachers realized the importance of education and bore in mind that teaching is a profession as well as a vocation. Teachers must shoulder great responsibility to cultivate their students' physical, mental and psychological competence. Moreover, they should love their students and give them individual attention (Hedge, 2000). In classroom teaching, they ought to do their utmost to make the classroom a supportive environment where students can be motivated to participate in various activities, and experience their academic progress. This in turn can facilitate students' self-confidence, self-esteem and positive motivation, enabling them to achieve greater success (Davies & Pearse, 2002). The teacher's dedication to teaching embodies this lofty vocation.

Conclusion

The research of the case study suggests that there are some striking differences in traditional Chinese and Western teaching styles as reflected by the different teaching approaches, teacher talk time as well as teacher's roles. The findings indicate that the Western teacher pays more attention to cultivating her students' communicative competence and independent learning ability more than her Chinese counterpart does. Moreover, her student-oriented teaching style has proven to be more suited to her students' learning style. The objective of the case study is to provide Mainland ESL Chinese teachers with insights into the Western teaching style from which they can adjust their own teaching styles so as to improve their professional competence and teach their students more effectively.

Since the data collected and the time spent on the research were limited, the findings might not represent all the Chinese and Western teachers' teaching styles. Therefore, the study cannot generalize its findings. Moreover, the case study still needs further research and some questions should be explored. For example, what are the underlying paradigms influencing the difference between the traditional Chinese and Western teaching styles? How should the Mainland Chinese teachers transfer what they have learned from the Western teaching style into their own classroom teaching?

References

Allright, R.L. (1988). *Observation in the Language Classroom*. London and New York: Longman.

Bell, J. (2005). *Doing Your Research Project*. Berkshire: Open University Press.

Campbell, C. (2003). *Teaching Second Language Writing: Interacting with Text*. Beijing: Foreign Language Teaching and Research Press.

Cohen, L. et al. (eds) (2000). *Research Methods in Education*, 5th ed. London and New York: Routledge Falmer.

Davies, P. & Pearse, E. (2002). *Success in Language Teaching*. Shanghai: Shanghai Foreign Language Education Press.

Firkins, A. & Forey, G. (2006). Changing the literacy habitus of a Hong Kong secondary school. In: Bokhorst-Heng, W., Osborne, M.D. & Lee, K. (eds). *Redesigning Pedagogy: Reflection on the Theory and Praxis* (pp. 33–46). Rotterdam: Sense Publishers.

Freebody, P. (2003). *Qualitative Research in Education Interaction and Practice*. London: Sage Publications Ltd.

Freeman, D. (2005). Second language teacher education. In: Carter, R. & Nunan, D. (eds). *The Cambridge Guide to Teaching English to Speakers of Other Languages* (pp. 72–80). Cambridge: Cambridge University Press.

Gibbons, P. (2002). *Scaffolding Language, Scaffolding Learning: Teaching Second Language Teachers in the Mainstream Classroom*. Portsmouth, NH: Heinemann.

Hall, S. (1997). *Cultural Representations and Signifying Practices*. London: Routledge.

Harmer, J. (2000). *How to Teach English*. Beijing: Foreign Language Teaching and Research Press.

Hedge, T. (2000). *Teaching and Learning in the Language Classroom*. Shanghai: Shanghai Foreign Language Education Press.

Hofstede, G. (1980). *Culture's Consequences*. London: Sage.

Hu Qingqiu (2007). A contrastive analysis of English classroom discourse of a foreign teacher and a Chinese teacher. *Foreign Language Teacher Abroad*, 4(1), 32–37.

Hyland, K. (2005). *Teaching and Researching Writing*. Beijing: Foreign Language Teaching and Research Press.

Lage, M.J., Platt, G.J. & Treglia, M. (2000). Inverting the classroom: A gateway to creating an inclusive learning environment. *Journal of Economic Education*, *31* (Winter), 30–43.

Lightbown, M.P. & Spada, N. (2002). *How Languages Are Learned*. Shanghai: Shanghai Foreign Language Education Press.

Lin Kai (ed.) (2006). *Pedagogical Research at Tertiary Level*. Tianjin: Tianjin Science and Technology Press.

McCarthy, M. (2005). Discourse. In: Carter, R. & Nunan, D. (eds), *The Cambridge Guide to Teaching English to Speakers of Other Languages* (pp. 48–56). Cambridge: Cambridge University Press.

Merriam, S.B. (2001). *Qualitative Research and Case Study Applications in Education*. San Francisco: Jossey-Bass Publishers.

Mitchell, R. & Myles, F. *Second Language Learning Theories*. London: Hodder Headline Group.

Moser, C.A. & Kalton, G. (1971). *Survey Methods in Social Investigation*. London: Heinemann.

Nunan, D. (2002). *Research Methods in Language Learning*. Beijing: Foreign Language Teaching and Research Press.

Paltridge, B. (2004). Approaches to teaching second language writing. Retrieved from: http://www.arts.usyd.edu.au/committees/ArtsTLCtee/Projects/CIW/paltridge.htm (accessed: 1/11/2007).

Reid, J. (2001). Writing. In: Carter, R. & Nunan, D. (eds.). *The Cambridge Guide to Teaching English to Speakers of Other Languages* (pp. 28–34). Cambridge: Cambridge University Press.

Richards, J.C. et al. (eds) (2005). *Longman Dictionary of Language Teaching and Applied Linguistics*. Beijing: Foreign Language Teaching and Research.

Terry, K. (1996). The changing role of teachers. Retrieved from: http://vathena.arc.nasa.gov/project/document/teacher.html (accessed: 16/10/2007).

Tsui Amy (2005). Classroom interaction. In: Carter, R. & Nunan, D. (eds.). *The Cambridge Guide to Teaching English to Speakers of Other Languages* (pp. 120–126). Cambridge: Cambridge University Press.

Wang Si (2007). New choice in English language teaching – genre approach. Retrieved from: http://cet.cavesbooks.com.tw/htm/mo50926.htm (accessed: 16/09/2007).

Wen Qiufang (2004). *Applied Linguistics: Research Methods and Thesis Writing*. Beijing: Foreign Language Teaching and Research Press.

Xiao Lixin (2006). Bridging the gap between teaching styles and learning. *TESL-EJ*, *10*(3), 23–35.

Ye Lan (1990). *Education Research and Approach*. Beijing: People's Educational Press.

Li Xiaomei, Ma Xiaoxue, Hu Tongtong

How Does Learning Style and Teaching Style Jointly Relate to Cultural Intelligence? A Study of Chinese Overseas Students

According to a recent global education report, Chinese overseas students are the largest group among international students in most countries. As the US 2013 Open Doors report mentioned, "The growth of international students' number is largely driven by students from China. The enrolments of Chinese student soar by 21 percent in total and reach almost 235,000 students, while those of other countries only take less than 5 percent of the total." With more and more Chinese students going abroad, some inconspicuous cross-cultural problems emerge. Not only do these problems disturb the students' families and the students themselves, but also pose some unnecessary trouble for host universities and culture in general. Recently, those problems have become much more serious due to the fact that most of overseas students who were born after 1980 under the Chinese "one-child policy" always assume self-central thinking style.

Nowadays, there are more and more training programs in China, offered by home universities, host universities, and even some special training institutions, aimed at improving students' understanding of the new culture and helping them adapt to the new environment more easily and quickly. More and more literary sources are focused on setting up effective cross-cultural training courses to assist outsiders in adapting to the oversea environment more smoothly. But the nature of these training programs is that they have to cater to the needs of overseas students and allow for the cultural background of host universities and countries (Hodgetts & Luthans 2000; Hutchings 2005). Because that kind of training programs is generally intensive and only provides surface knowledge, there is only little improvement observed in students after taking that kind of training. The most important point to be taken is how to gain knowledge about a new culture rather than superficial content. Having the habit of self-educating is very important for students who stay aboard and adapt to a new social environment. And the increasing emphasis on the students learning style could promote students' practical adaption, especially in the case of Chinese students, most of whom develop their basic knowledge through self-study in high school under high pressure from the National College Entrance Examination (NCEE), and they first gain their social knowledge in their college life, so, from the phenomenon noted above, we could infer that the importance of effective learning style has been neglected by cross-cultural practitioners.

In addition, a learning style is a kind of process: how we perceive and process information, how we acquire experience and how we react to new things (McCarthy, 1996). In the Chinese culture, there is an old saying "live and learn". A divergent learning style focuses on cognitive adaptation by observation rather than by taking action; a convergent learning style concentrates on the ability to learn from both the problem and the context/setting of the problem (Harvey & Novicevic, 2001). This style is much better for learners to adopt when they need to adapt to a new and complex global environment.

According to the contingency theory of the human resource learning process, the balance between teaching and learning is critical to achieve better performance in a cross-cultural context, and the results of achieving this balance include satisfaction, commitment and involvement of expatriates in work places (Kolb, Osland & Rubin, 1995). Different training behavior should suit different kinds of learning styles (Kolb et al., 1995; McMurray, 1998). To enhance cross-cultural adaptability, English teachers (English as a second language) play a very important and special role in the students' learning performance by familiarizing the students with the outside world. Thus, the balance between the English teachers' teaching methods and students' learning styles is a key factor in improving cross-cultural adaptability.

With regard to the research gaps mentioned above, we address three questions here: (1) How does learning style relate to cross-cultural adaptability? (2) If students' learning skill is certain, could teachers' typical behavior in class influence students' cross-cultural adaptability? (3) How do teachers' typical teaching behaviors and students' learning styles jointly influence students' cross-cultural adaptability? To explore the answers to these questions, we integrate two streams of research to form our research topic: firstly, we adopt Kolb's (1984) experiential learning theory (ELT) to explain the learning style of Chinese overseas students;

secondly, we consider cultural intelligence – CQ (Ang & Van Dyne, 2008; Earley & Ang, 2003), an individual's capability to function effectively in culturally diverse contexts, as a key factor to improve cross-cultural adaptability.

This paper is organized into five sections. After the introduction, theoretical background and hypotheses are explained. Sections three and four demonstrate the methods and results of hypotheses testing in this paper. The final part outlines discussions with theoretical implications, practical significance and research limitations.

1. Theory and hypotheses

Nowadays, more and more Chinese students go abroad to pursue their education. Those students with overseas experience may be the majority of multinational corporations' staff and immigrants in the future. What may influence people's ability to adapt to an exotic culture into which they must be integrated? The answer could be their experience, the knowledge of the new country/culture, their interpersonal relationships, and so on. Four-year college life is a very important period because most of people start to learn about the world in that time. For Chinese college students, this period is much more important. In China, almost all high school students learn English merely for college entrance examinations, so the information about foreign country/culture mainly comes from textbooks. Some schools may provide foreign teachers, but students can only communicate with foreigners once or twice a week. Therefore, the experience in college becomes quite imperative: more time learning English and more contacts with foreign teachers and exchange students mean less confinement to exams and more openness to the diverse world. Apart from all the interaction with foreign cultural background in college, English teaching in class seems indispensable, as it trains students systemically, introduces foreign culture, and most importantly, allows students and teachers to interact with each other in short-term communication instead of teachers delivering lectures and students just listening in high schools. How the coordination between teaching and learning processes give results in improving a person's cross-cultural adaptability in their college life becomes the key topic. We need to develop a comprehensive model to involve all interrelationships between the learning style, the teaching style and individual cultural intelligence, especially in the case of Chinese college students.

Cultural Intelligence

Since intercultural communication was established in 1950s, cultural intelligence (CQ) has been put forward in the successful development of cross-cultural adaptation research.

In 2003, the term CQ, first described by Earley and Ang (2003), could be defined as "a person's capability to collect and deal with information, make judgments and corresponding uses, and adapt to a new culture in a different cultural environment", and it has three aspects: behavioral, motivational, and metacognitive. Currently, CQ research has extended the conceptualization and theoretical basis of CQ (Ang & Van Dyne, 2008; Ng & Earley, 2006; Triandis, 2006) to examine relationships with cultural adaptation and performance (Ang, Van Dyne, Koh, Ng, Templer, Tay & Chandrasekar, 2007), expatriate effectiveness (Kim, Kirkman & Chen, 2008; Shaffer & Miller, 2008; Templer, Tay & Chandrasekar, 2006), personality (Ang, Van Dyne & Koh, 2006; Oolders, Chernyshenko & Stark, 2008), intercultural training (Earley & Peterson, 2004; Lievens, Harris, Van Keer & Bisqueret 2003), and multicultural teams (e.g., Earley & Mosakowski, 2004; Janssens & Brett, 2006; Rockstuhl & Ng, 2008). Going beyond the existing research on CQ that has theorized and demonstrated the importance of CQ for performance in cross-cultural contexts, we shall focus on CQ as a set of learning capabilities that are important for global leaders. Emerging from a four-factor structure in CQ (megacognition, cognition, motivation, and behavior) (Sternberg & Detterman, 1986), and combined with Intelligence and Emotional Intelligence research, a new four-factor structure has been put forward, consisting of Mega-cognitive, Cognitive, Motivational, and Behavioral Cultural Intelligence. On the basis of Earley and Ang's description about the four-factor structure of Cultural Intelligence, we could comprehend each factor in detail: Mega-cognitive Cultural Intelligence refers to the individual's feelings in cross-cultural communication; Cognitive Cultural Intelligence deals with how well a person knows a different culture (such as customs, religion, laws, etc.); Motivational Cultural Intelligence relates to the positive adaptation an individual undergoes to be better involved in a new cultural environment; Behavioral Cultural Intelligence is about the appropriate and acceptable behaviors outsiders adopt when they are in intercultural communication.

Learning Style

Herbert Thelen (1954) was the first to have raised the concept of learning styles. A learning style is the manner in which information is processed. Keefe (1979) regarded a learning style as a kind of a physical activity; it represents the way information is received, as a relatively stabilized interaction with study circumstances, which is more general. Kinsella (1995) had a more complete statement: a learning style is a customary, favoured, and to some extent lasting way adopted during the process of perceiving and processing information. Curry (1983, 1987) invented the Onion Model for a learning style; from outer to inner sphere, there are: guidance tendency, social interaction, information processing method, and cognitive style. Guidance tendency refers to one's preference for the learning environment, such as light and sound; social interaction means that being with others becomes a part of learning; information processing method is the way one encodes information; and cognitive style is related to one's personality. In the early 1990s, an Alabama University professor, Rebecca Oxford, and Lavine (1991), divided learning styles into five categories. 1) Sensory preferences: auditory, visual, haptic, and operational; 2) personality traits: extroversion and introversion; 3) information processing methods: intuitive and concrete sequential; 4) information perceiving methods: close and open; 5) thinking methods: analytic and global. For the purpose of our study, we are trying to define the learning style as a way in which information is perceived and processed by a learner.

Kolb (1981) identified learning as a process of creating knowledge through transforming experience. He used the Learning Cycle to demonstrate the learning process which includes four steps: Concrete Experience (CE), Reflective Observation (RO), Abstract Conceptualization (AC), and Active Experiment (AE). Kolb's Learning Cycle starts at Concrete Experience, the knowledge and feeling of the actual environment, emphasizing learning through experience; the next step is Reflective Observation that embodies one's introspection of what happened. In this step, learners are encouraged to observe carefully and try to understand the same thing in various perspectives; then we move to step 3 – Abstract Conceptualization – the learner uses his/her own knowledge to rethink, analyze matters, and construct meaning; the final stage is Active Experimentation, applied to test the constructed meaning and to solve the real problem. It hinges on learning from doing, and being brave enough to explore.

Knowledge creation cannot occur without the transformation of experience. Facing a complex cross-cultural environment and undergoing ability improvement triggers a cycle of a learning process, which includes experiencing, reflecting, thinking, and acting, as well as interactions between the person and the environment (Kolb, 1984). The holistic nature of Kolb's learning style fits the complexity of international assignments, given that leaders are exposed to, and required to manage, a multitude of demands and cues from their new environment (Ng, Van Dyne & Ang,

2009). Learning is a continuous process where new knowledge change existing ideas and perspectives, relearning, and integrating old and new ideas are important aspects (Kolb, 1984). This emphasis on a continuous and dynamic cycle of learning is particularly crucial for global leaders given the uncertainties and complexities of culturally diverse business settings.

Kolbs learning style has been widely applied in management development literature (Kolb, 2005; Yamazaki & Kayes, 2004). Much of this research (e.g., Cassidy, 2004; Furnham, Jackson & Miller, 1999; Mainemelis, Boyatzis & Kolb, 2002; Yamazaki & Kayes, 2007) describes preferred learning styles based on Kolb's (1999a, b) Learning Style Inventory. Kolb's learning style was adopted in our research due to its dynamic process-oriented approach in order to meet our research topic on exploring intervening mechanisms in studying. It is particularly crucial and essential to adapt to the uncertainties and complexities of culturally diverse business settings for our future global leaders. Thus, we propose the following hypotheses:

Hypothesis 1: Students' learning style will influence their cultural intelligence. Classroom Interaction.

The Input Hypothesis Theory (Krashen, 1981; Swain, 1985), also called Comprehensible Language Input, enriches the theoretical research on language learning, and also opens a new direction – Classroom Interaction. According to these theories, teaching can be seen as a circulation of "teachers inputting – students receiving – students outputting", and when the cycle is completed, teaching is regarded as having achieved its goal. However, with the development of research, scholars found that this circulation is not that simple in practice, especially in the "teachers inputting – students receiving" phase. Since the information teachers input may vary in completeness and acceptability, and the students' receiving abilities are different, teachers and students need to communicate repeatedly in order to complete the circulation. In this situation, the pattern may change to "teachers inputting – students receiving and giving feedback – teachers verifying and modifying the feedback, and inputting again – students understanding and then receiving – students outputting". If students do not receive successfully or give any feedback, they may suspend the teaching circulation, resulting in failure. Based on the above-presented case, Long (1983) proposed the Interaction Hypothesis, which considers the interaction between people as interaction modification – both sides would affirm and modify the information again and again in the communication. Classroom interaction applies Long's theory into classroom teaching. According to H.D. Brown and Qiufang Wen (1994), interaction means the process of two or more people exchanging their feelings and information and the influence exerted in that exchange. Therefore, we can define classroom interaction as follows: teachers construct a certain environment in the classroom and encourage students to participate in the environment, express their thoughts, and exchange opinions with teachers and other classmates. Classroom interaction focuses on the teaching environment construction and election of communication modes. We propose:

Hypothesis 2: When students' learning skill is certain, teachers' typical behavior in class may influence students' cultural intelligence.

Hypothesis 3: The interaction between students' learning skill and teachers' typical teaching behavior in class may influence student's cultural intelligence.

2. Data and Methodology

A survey was applied to test the proposed model. Since a survey is able to provide accurate individual data on social facets, belief, and attitude, by adopting designed survey, researchers could enjoy high generalizability of the research findings.

Survey Measurements

With all the appropriate measurements and valid procedures mentioned above, most of the measurements of items in this study (i.e. learning style, teaching style and Cultural Intelligence) were adopted from existing literature. Since all these items were originally written in English, then translated into Chinese by a Chinese researcher and the Chinese version was then translated back into English by a bi-lingual US researcher to ensure the precise content of the items in the literature, there was no difference between the accuracy of the two contents. Furthermore, the questionnaires in this study were represented both in Chinese and English versions on the survey website. According to several principles of questionnaire design, we developed and finalized a questionnaire (de Vaus, 1995) in which all items were scored on the 5-point Likert-type scale, ranging from 1-point ("strongly agree") to 5-point ("strongly disagree").

Independent variables. Learning style and teaching style. With regard to the measurements of the learning style, we learned from LSI measurement (Kolb, 1984) and devised 48 questions applied to four learning styles, including Concrete Experience (CE), Reflective Observation (RO),

Abstract Conceptualization (AC) and Active Experiment (AE), each with 12 questions. As for the teachers' typical behavior in class, She and Fisher (2000) put forward five-question measurement of the teaching style to test the teaching behavior in class, and this measurement is widely accepted by researchers nowadays. In this study, we merged these 5 questions into a sorting question to shorten the questionnaire.

Dependent variable. Cultural Intelligence. Based on the classical CQ measurement of Ang et al. (2007), we designed a diagnostic scale concerning four basic elements of Cultural Intelligence (meta-cognition, cognition, motivation, and behavior) five questions for each element and 20 questions in total.

Control variables. We controlled the participants' gender, major, education background, studying region, and the duration of time spent abroad. Notably, these control variables could potentially affect the students' cultural intelligence.

Survey Design

The survey questionnaire adopts the recall method, a useful tool to collect individuals' long-term perceptual data so as to facilitate the formation of current perceptions and behaviors (Olguín, Waber, Kim, Mohan, Ara & Pentland, 2009).

The questionnaire is divided into three parts and consists of 70 questions. To better recall the learning style and teaching style during college life, the first question asks: "please write down the name of one of your most memorable English teachers and the date you met him or her". This could serve as a retrieval cue to trigger a memory of that experience (Tulving, 1985). The second part is the main body of the questionnaire with 69 questions based on the above measurements. The third part includes the basic demographic characteristics, such as age, gender, Internet experience and frequency of Internet use.

Data Collection

The online survey is addressed to Chinese young generation (born from 1985 to 1990), who graduated from Chinese universities and now study aboard for their Master or PhD degree or has been working aboard for less than 5 years, since only these people could clearly and accurately recall events to help measure the possible effects of teaching styles and learning styles in college life on their cultural intelligence. At the beginning, in order to ensure the validity of the measurement before the final version, a pre-survey was delivered to 30 people, including young Chinese faculties who obtained their PhD degrees abroad in less than 2 years, and students who study overseas. In order to ensure the consistency of the questionnaire, we only modified the description of 2 items. During the formal investigation from February 22, 2014 to April 22, 2014, we completed the final version of the questionnaire by using "SOJUMP", an online questionnaire platform, and then posted the website link to the questionnaire on Social Network Sites, such as Renren, QQ, wechat, and the BBS online campus. We also successfully contacted overseas students through the teachers of the Confucius Institutes and professors from the US, Australia and European countries.

During the procedure, we released 680 questionnaires and received 330 questionnaires back, among which 112 questionnaires were incomplete or did not qualify and 218 were valid. The demographic variables are presented in Table 1. The data showed: 1) Gender: the number of males and females is basically the same; 2) Majors: in the sample, science students are the majority, there is slightly less business students and liberal arts students are the least numerous group; 3) Education Background: bachelor and below constitute the largest group (about 62.1%) of the sample; 4) Studying region: most of the respondents study in Europe and North America; 5) Time duration of staying abroad: most students stay abroad for less than three years, of which 39.0% stay for less than one year and 43.6% for over one year.

Table 1: Demographic data (N=218)

Item	Option	Number	Percentage
Gender	Male	105	48.2
	Female	113	51.8
Majors	Science	88	40.3
	Business	86	36.7
	Arts	44	23.0
Educational background	Doctor	13	6.0
	Master	72	31.9
	Bachelor and below	133	62.1
Studying on which continents	Europe	99	44.0
	North America	91	42.7
	Oceania	17	7.8
	Asian	11	5.5
Duration of staying abroad	Less than one year	84	39.0
	One to three years	95	43.6
	More than three years	39	17.4

Source: results of research.

Table 2: Descriptive Statistics, Reliabilities and Intercorrelations among Measures (N=218)

Measurement	Mean	Std	1	2	3	4	5	6	7	8	9	10	11	12	13	14	15
1. Metacognitive	3.78	0.62	(0.69)														
2. Cognitive	3.31	0.69	0.21**	(0.81)													
3. Motivational	3.89	0.70	0.23*	0.20**	(0.73)												
4. Behavioral	3.49	0.74	0.48***	0.34***	0.45***	(0.74)											
5. Concrete Experience	2.60	0.37	0.18**	-0.01	0.07	-0.07	(0.73)										
6. Reflective Observation	2.49	0.39	0.20**	0.48***	0.25**	0.33***	0.19**	(0.75)									
7. Abstract Conceptualization	2.50	0.40	0.04	0.11†	-0.10	0.16*	-0.08	0.47***	(0.71)								
8. Active Experimentation	2.60	0.44	0.10	-0.06	0.08	0.06	0.11	0.27***	0.34***	(0.69)							
9. Challenging	3.54	1.36	0.09	0.15*	-0.07	-0.02	0.10	0.15*	-0.02	0.07	1						
10. Non-verbal Support	2.63	1.15	-0.06	-0.08	-0.10	-0.06	-0.01	0.05	0.19**	-0.12†	-0.33***	1					
11. Friendly	3.28	1.03	-0.07	-0.04	-0.03	-0.03	-0.04	-0.01	0.12†	-0.06	-0.05	-0.19*	1				
12. Controlling	2.44	1.57	0.01	0.12†	-0.11	0.10	-0.16*	-0.13†	-0.17*	-0.11	-0.20**	-0.42***	-0.24**	1			
13. Specialty	1.83	0.84	0.14*	0.07	0.07	0.17*	0.11	-0.06	-0.20*	-0.06	-0.12†	-0.09	-0.19**	0.31***	1		
14. Gender	0.48	0.50	-0.15*	-0.08	-0.12†	-0.17*	0.11	0.04	0.09	0.06	0.11	0.04	0.03	-0.24**	-0.33	1	
15. Duration of stay outside	1.76	0.70	-0.18*	0.23**	-0.14*	0.01	-0.12†	-0.07	-0.06	-0.14*	-0.14*	0.24**	-0.07	0.02	0.03	0.20**	1

† Correlation is significant at the 0.1 level (2-tailed). * Correlation is significant at the 0.05 level (2-tailed).

Source: results of research.

In general, the demographic data on the valid samples is balanced and the sample is representative. Cronbach's alpha for each measurement is reported in Table 2. Presenting the descriptive statistics and correlations for all the variables in this study, Table 2 also shows that Cronbach's alpha is over 0.6 and the correlation of challenging and encouraging is high (β = -0.438). That is to say, if we keep these two variables challenging and encouraging, a multi-collinearity problem may occur in later analysis. In order to avoid this, we interviewed 10 students by phone and deleted one variable.

3. Results

To examine the relationship between students' learning skills, teachers' typical behavior in class and their interactions' influence on the students' cultural intelligence, we conducted OLS regression to test hypothesis 1.

The Interrelationship between learning style and CQ

In order to identify the relationship between a person's learning style and cultural intelligence, we applied OLS regression in Model 1.

$$CQ_i = a_i + \sum_{t=1}^{4} b_t * LS_t \qquad (1)$$

where CQ_i are 4 measurements of cultural intelligence (i=1, 2, 3, 4). CQ_1 is Meta-cognitive CQ, CQ_2 is Cognitive CQ, CQ_3 is Motivational CQ and CQ_4 is Behavioral CQ. LS_t is 4 measurements of Learning Style. (t=1, 2, 3, 4). LS_1 is concrete experience, LS_2 is reflective observation, LS_3 is abstract conceptualization and LS_4 is active experiment. The results are shown in Table 3.

The overall effects of teaching style on the relation between learning style and CQ

To test the second hypothesis of this study, we applied teaching style as a direct independent variable in Model 2.

$$CQ_i = a_i + \sum_{t=1}^{4} b_t * LS_t + \sum_{j=1}^{4} g_j * TS_j \qquad (2)$$

where TS_j represents the teaching behavior (j=1, 2, 3, 4). TS_1 is *Challenging*, TS_2 is *Non-verbal Support Challenging*, TS_3 is *Friendly* and TS_4 is *Controlling*.

The effect of interaction between teaching style and learning style on CQ

To explore how the interaction between learning style and teaching style affects the CQ, we applied the interaction between teaching style and learning style into analysis in Model 3.

$$CQ_i = a_i + \sum_{t=1}^{4} b_t * LS_t + \sum_{j=1}^{4} g_j * TS_j + \sum_{t=1}^{4}\sum_{j=1}^{4} d_{(t,\,j)} * (LS_t * TS_j) \quad (3)$$

We found that ΔR^2 (test for the whole model) in Model 3 is larger than that in Model 2 and Model 1. This means that the interaction model could give a better explanation on CQ.

Results on Metacognitive CQ. From Tables 3 and 4, we could infer that Reflective Observation has a strongly significant and relatively positive effect on the Meta-cognitive CQ, and Non-Verbal Support and Controlling in the teaching style interact with Reflective Observation, having a positive effect on Meta-cognitive CQ. Moreover, no teaching style shows a significantly direct influence on Meta-cognitive CQ. In all three models, students who major in science and engineering have a stronger Meta-cognitive CQ than those who are liberal arts and business students. The gender and duration of stay abroad show no significant effect.

Results on Cognitive CQ. From Tables 3 and 4, we could infer that Reflective Observation does a strongly significant and relatively positive effect on *Cognitive* CQ, and Challenging and Controlling in teaching style both have positive effects on Cognitive CQ, and interacted with Reflective Observation and Active Experimentation to do a negative effect on Cognitive CQ. In all three models, longer duration of being abroad shows a higher result in Cognitive CQ.

Results on Motivational CQ. From Tables 3 and 4, we could infer that Reflective Observation shows a strongly significant and relatively positive effect on Motivational CQ, while Abstract Conceptualization has a strongly significant and relatively negative effect on Motivational CQ. All four teaching styles show negative overall effects on Motivational CQ, and a weak negative influence of interaction between Abstract Conceptualization and Non-verbal Support was exerted on Motivational CQ in Model 3. Students who major in science and engineering have a stronger effect on Motivational CQ than those who are liberal arts and business students in Model 1. The gender and duration of stay abroad show no significant effect.

Results on Behavioral CQ. From Tables 3 and 4, we also infer that Reflective Observation shows a strongly significant and relatively positive effect on Behavioral CQ, while Concrete Experience is not as strong in that respect. Controlling teaching style interacting with Reflective Observation has a negative effect on Behavioral CQ. No teaching style shows a significant overall effect on Behavioral CQ. In all three models, students' majors show a significant and positive effect on Behavioral CQ, with the highest coefficient of science and engineering students and the lowest to liberal arts students. The gender and duration of stay abroad show no significant effect.

Table 3: Learning Style and Teaching Style effects on Metacognitive CQ (N=218)

	Metacognitive CQ		Cognitive CQ		Motivational CQ		Behavioral CQ	
	Model 1	Model 2	Model 1	Model 2	Model 1	Model 2	Model 1	Model 2
Interception	2.46*** (0.46)	3.33*** (0.46)	1.57*** (0.44)	0.79 (0.51)	3.58*** (0.51)	5.45*** (0.50)	2.09*** (0.52)	2.61*** (0.61)
Concrete Experience	0.18 (0.12)	–	-0.16 (0.11)	–	-0.12 (0.12)	–	-0.30* (0.13)	-0.30* (0.13)
Reflective Observation	0.24* (0.12)	0.29** (0.10)	1.04*** (0.11)	0.95*** (0.10)	0.65*** (0.13)	0.69*** (0.12)	0.65*** (0.14)	0.72*** (0.12)
Abstract Conceptualization	-0.04 (0.12)	–	-0.16 (0.12)	–	-0.54*** (0.14)	-0.44*** (0.13)	0.04 (0.14)	–
Active Experimentation	0.15 (0.10)	–	-0.19† (0.10)	-0.22* (0.09)	0.17 (0.11)	–	0.06 (0.12)	–
Challenging	–	0.02 (0.04)	–	0.07* (0.03)	–	-0.18*** (0.04)	–	-0.03 (0.04)
Non-verbal Support	–	-0.04 (0.05)	–	-0.07 (0.05)	–	-0.23*** (0.06)	–	-0.09 (0.06)
Friendly	–	-0.06 (0.05)	–	-0.01 (0.04)	–	-0.13** (0.05)	–	-0.03 (0.05)
Controlling	–	-0.01 (0.04)	–	0.06† (0.03)	–	-0.17*** (0.04)	–	0.01 (0.04)
Gender	-0.06 (0.09)	-0.04 (0.09)	-0.14 (0.09)	-0.14 (0.09)	-0.04 (0.10)	-0.14 (0.10)	-0.10 (0.11)	-0.09 (0.11)
Duration of stay outside	-0.07 (0.06)	-0.08 (0.06)	0.27*** (0.06)	0.34*** (0.06)	-0.09 (0.07)	-0.05 (0.07)	0.08 (0.07)	0.10 (0.07)
Specialty (Science)	0.36** (0.11)	0.38 *** (0.11)	0.36** (0.11)	0.17 (0.10)	0.36** (0.11)	0.13 (0.12)	0.43*** (0.13)	0.43*** (0.13)
Specialty (Business)	0.14 (0.10)	0.15 (0.11)	0.14 (0.10)	-0.01 (0.10)	0.14 (0.10)	0.02 (0.11)	0.30* (0.12)	0.24† (0.12)
R^2	0.15	0.14	0.15	0.41	0.16	0.26	0.21	0.22
Adjust R^2	0.11	0.10	0.11	0.38	0.13	0.23	0.18	0.18

† Correlation is significant at the 0.1 level (2-tailed). * Correlation is significant at the 0.05 level (2-tailed).
Source: results of research.

Taking into account the statements mentioned above, we could partly support the hypothesis.

Table 4: Interactions of Teaching Style, Learning Style Effect on CQ (N=218)

		Challenging		Non-verbal Support	Friendly	Controlling	
		CQ_2(0.07*)	CQ_3(−0.18***)	CQ_3(−0.23***)	CQ_3(−0.13**)	CQ_2(0.06†)	CQ_3(−0.17***)
Concrete Experience	CQ_4(−0.30*)						
Reflective Observation	CQ_1(0.24*)	CQ_1(0.23†)		CQ_1(0.28*)			CQ_1(0.23*)
	CQ_2(1.04***)	–					
	CQ_3(0.65***)						
	CQ_4(0.65***)						CQ_4(−0.41***)
Abstract Conceptualization	CQ_3(−0.54***)			CQ_3(−0.29†)			
Active Experimentation	CQ_2(−0.19†)	CQ_2(−0.25*)		CQ_2(−0.39**)			

Color [dark grey] means significant positive result; color [light grey] means significant negative result.

† Correlation is significant at level 0.1 (2-tailed). * Correlation is significant at level 0.05 (2-tailed).

Source: results of research.

4. Discussion and Conclusion

The goal of this research is to explore the mechanisms and relationships between students' learning styles, teachers' teaching styles and Cultural Intelligence more thoroughly. We try our best to discover the way to improve students' cultural intelligence through a proper learning style and teaching style, and the best type of interaction between these two styles. Through systematic testing, refinement and analysis, we believe we managed to prove the correctness of our hypothesis that a learning style could influence Cultural Intelligence, and that a teaching style may help improve Cultural Intelligence only when it is combined with a proper learning style. The findings of this research bring the theoretical implications and practical significance to cross-cultural management.

Theoretical Implications

Much empirical research suggests that a learning style is strongly connected to adaptation in a cross-cultural context. Learners with the divergent learning style show cognitive adaptation to a cross-cultural environment (Harvey & Novicevic, 2001). Our study shows a great support of the relation of the learning style and CQ. Three major conclusions could be drawn from the results of this study, based on cross-cultural theory, learning theory and communication theory.

The first conclusion drawn from the research is that different learning skills will exert different forms of influence on CQ. From the four learning styles described by Kolb (1984), Reflective Observation is the most important skill to improve CQ comprehensively; the co-efficiency between Reflective Observation and cognitive CQ is higher than that between Reflective Observation and meta-cognitive CQ. Reflective Observation embodies one's introspection of the past; thus, learners are encouraged to observe carefully and try to understand the same thing from various perspectives (Kolb, 1984). CQ refers to an individual's understanding and behavior in a different cultural context, and is encouraged by the style of Reflective Observation.

The second conclusion shows that a teaching style has a great direct effect only on Motivational CQ. Meta-cognitive CQ and behavioral CQ do not appear to be influenced by the teaching style whatsoever. Challenging and Controlling teaching styles show slightly positive relations to Cognitive CQ. Challenging is to encourage students to obtain a better and more thorough understanding of the knowledge. And in China, students are too passive to accept knowledge in most situations. Controlling was usually applied to require students to go over more knowledge in most classrooms in China. But recently, it has been changing significantly. More and more universities embrace the concept of a "Flipped Classroom", which gives a dominant position to students rather than teachers; that is to say, Controlling exerts a less direct influence on the learning performance. Any kind of teaching style showed a strong negative effect on Motivational CQ. Motivational CQ mainly focuses on interests and driving forces. More pushy behaviors from teachers and less subjective initiative from students will lead to less Motivational CQ. If we look at the young Chinese generation born during 1980–1985 under China's "One-child policy", we can find that their strong rebellious thoughts strengthen their self-controlling thinking style. And that is why the outside pressure is likely to make them unwilling to accept knowledge.

The last conclusion is that in combination with a certain learning style, a teaching style will have an effect on CQ. Challenging, Non-verbal Support and Controlling – these three teaching styles will exert a strong positive influence on Meta-cognitive CQ through Reflective Observation. Interaction with Non-verbal support will have a much higher result. Teachers' supporting behaviors could provide a good environment for students to deepen their Reflective Observation and consequently encourage them to acquire new knowledge when they are immersed in a distinct culture. Furthermore, communication between students and teachers will accelerate the knowledge process and improve Meta-cognitive CQ. As does real experience in original culture, Active Experimentation shows a negative effect on Cognitive CQ when it interacts with Challenging and Non-verbal Support. As for experimentation, it will have a strong and sustainable influence on "home culture feeling"; that is to say, more Challenging and Non-verbal Support behaviors would strengthen feelings towards home culture and inhibit outsiders from accepting the customs or thinking of the host culture, so a match between a given learning style and teaching style could exert a catalytic influence on cultural intelligence.

Practical Implications

The findings presented in this paper have some practical significance. Although many previous studies have suggested that both the learning style and teaching style are highly related to the adaptation ability, empirical validations on the two variables put together and interacting with each other have been limited. The results of this study confirm three points: firstly, a match between a learning style and teaching style could have a great effect on CQ; secondly, students ought to apply more reflective observations into their cross-cultural studies; thirdly, an English teacher should adopt behaviors corresponding to the students' different learning skills and processes,. Only a proper match between a learning style and teaching style could help students develop and show a high CQ which means a higher adaptability to a new culture.

5. Limitations and Future Study

Due to limited research conditions and resources, this research has some defects: 1. With relatively small samples, 218 questionnaires could not properly represent the whole community of Chinese outsiders, so the applicability of the findings in this paper is under restriction; 2. With regard to the research participants, various education backgrounds are not balanced; the proportion between MA and PhD is still small, so the conclusion of this research could not be fully tested among students with master's or doctoral degrees; 3. There are still other moderating variables between interaction patterns in the classroom and the cultural intelligence of students that need to be studied; 4. This research does not concentrate on the CQ of overseas students from a diachronic perspective.

In the future, researches should adopt more balanced and broader data, and pay much attention to the comparison from a diachronic perspective to further validate the relationship between interaction patterns in the classroom and the cultural intelligence of students.

References

Ahmadi, S., Safarzadeh, H., Hozoori, M. & Dehnavi, F. (2013). The role of cultural intelligence of managers in promoting employees' collaboration. *Management Science Letters*, 3(7), 1915–1926.

Ang Soon & Inkpen, A.C. (2008). Cultural intelligence and offshore outsourcing success: a framework of firm-level intercultural capability. *Decision Sciences*, 39(3), 337–358.

Ang Soon, Van Dyne, L. & Koh, C. (2006). Personality correlates of the four-fact or model of cultural intelligence. *Group & Organization Management*, 31(1), 100–123.

Ang Soon, Van Dyne, L., Koh, C., Ng, K.Y., Templer, K.J., Tay, C. & Chandrasekar, N.A. (2007). Cultural intelligence: Its measurement and effects on cultural judgment and decision making, cultural adaptation and task performance. *Management and Organization Review*, 3(3), 335–371.

Ang Soon & Van Dyne, L. (eds). (2008). *Handbook of Cultural Intelligence: Theory, Measurement, and Applications*. Armonk, NY: ME Sharpe, pp. 3–15, 71–90, 107–125, 145–173.

Ang Soon & Van Dyne, L. (2008). Conceptualization of cultural intelligence: Definition, distinctiveness, and nomological network. In: Ang Soon & Van Dyne, L. (eds.). *Handbook of Cultural Intelligence: Theory, Measurement, and Applications* (pp. 3–15). Armonk, NY: ME Sharpe.

Brown, H.D. & Wen Qiufang (1994). *Teaching by Principles: An Interactive Approach to Language Pedagogy*. Vol. 1. Englewood Cliffs, NJ: Prentice Hall Regents.

Cassidy, S. (2004). Learning styles: An overview of theories, models, and measures. *Educational Psychology*, 24(4), 419–444.

Curry, L. (1983). *An Organization of Learning Styles Theory and Constructs*. Prepared for presentation at American Educational Research Association Annual Meeting, April, Montreal, Canada.

Curry, L. (1987). *Integrating Concepts of Cognitive or Learning Style: A Review with Attention to Psychometric Standards*. Ottawa: Canadian College of Health Service Executives.

Darvish, H., Khalili, M. & Farahani, M. (2013). The relationship between cultural intelligence and bank performance: A case study of a private bank. *Management Science Letters*, 3(2), 415–418.

De Vaus, D.F. (1995). *A guide regarding the formulation and interpretation of a research problem*. Unpublished paper. Pretoria: University of South Africa.

Earley, P.C. & Ang Soon (2003). *Cultural Intelligence: Individual Interactions across Cultures*. Stanford: Stanford University Press.

Earley, P.C. & Mosakowski, E. (2004). Cultural intelligence. *Harvard Business Review*, 82(10), 139–146.

Earley, P.C. & Peterson, R.S. (2004). The elusive cultural chameleon: Cultural intelligence as a new approach to intercultural training for the global manager. *Academy of Management Learning & Education*, 3(1), 100–115.

Furnham, A., Jackson, C.J. & Miller, T. (1999). Personality, learning style and work performance. *Personality and Individual Differences*, 27(6), 1113–1122.

Ghonsooly, B. (2013). Cultural intelligence and writing ability: Delving into fluency, accuracy and complexity. *Novitas Royal – Research on Youth and Language*, 7(2), 147–159.

Harvey, M. & Novicevic, M.M. (2001). Selecting expatriates for increasingly complex global assignments. *Career Development International*, 6(2), 69–87.

Herrmann, E., Call, J., Hernández-Lloreda, M.V., Hare, B. & Tomasello, M. (2007). Humans have evolved specialized skills of social cognition: the cultural intelligence hypothesis. *Science*, 317(5843), 1360–1366.

Hodgetts, R.M. & Luthans, F. (2000). *International Management: Culture, Strategy, and Behavior*. New York: McGraw-Hill.

House, R.J., Hanges, P.J., Javidan, M., Dorfman, P.W. & Gupta, V. (eds.) (2004). *Culture, Leadership, and Organizations: The GLOBE Study of 62 Societies*. Thousand Oaks, CA: Sage Publications.

Hutchings, K. (2005). Koalas in the Land of the Pandas: Reviewing Australian Expatriates? China Preparation. *International Journal of Human Resource Management, 16*(4), 553–566.

Isfahani, A.N., Jooneghani, R.B.N. & Azar, M. (2013). Analyzing the effects of cultural intelligence on employee performance in Azaran Industrial Group (Isfahan Province). *International Journal of Academic Research in Business and Social Sciences, 3*(5), 363–376.

Janssens, M. & Brett, J.M. (2006). Cultural intelligence in global teams: A fusion model of collaboration. *Group & Organization Management, 31*(1), 124–153.

Joy, S. & Kolb, D.A. (2009). Are there cultural differences in learning style? *International Journal of Intercultural Relations, 33*(1), 69–85.

Keefe, J.W. (1979). Learning style: An overview. In: *Student Learning Styles: Diagnosing and Prescribing Programs* (pp. 1–17). Reston, VA: National Association of Secondary School Principals.

Kim Kwanghyun, Kirkman, B.L. & Chen Gilad (2008). Cultural intelligence and international assignment effectiveness. In: Ang Soon & Van Dyne, L. (eds.). *Handbook of Cultural Intelligence: Theory, Measurement, and Applications* (pp. 71–90). Armonk, NY: ME Sharpe.

Kinsella, K. (1995). Understanding and empowering diverse learners in ESL classrooms. In: Reid, J.M. (ed.). *Learning Styles in the ESL/EFL Classroom* (pp. 170–194). Boston, MA: Heinle & Heinle Publishers.

Kolb, A.Y. (2005). *The Kolb Learning Style Inventory – Version 3.1 2005 Technical Specifications*. Boston, MA: Hay Resource Direct.

Kolb, D.A. (1981). Learning styles and disciplinary differences. In: Chickering, A. (ed.). *The Modern American College* (pp. 232–255). San Francisco: Jossey-Bass.

Kolb, D.A. (1984). *Experiential Learning: Experience as the Source of Learning and Development*. Vol. 1. Englewood Cliffs, NJ: Prentice-Hall.

Kolb, D.A., Osland, J. & Rubin, I. (1995), *Organizational Behavior: An Experimental Approach*. Englewood Cliffs, NJ: Prentice-Hall.

Kolb, D.A. (1999a). *Learning Style Inventory, Version 3*. Boston, MA: TRG Hay/McBer, Training Resources Group.

Kolb, D.A. (1999b). *Learning Style Inventory – Version 3: Technical Specifications*. Boston, MA: TRG Hay/McBer, Training Resources Group.

Krashen, S.D. (1981). *Second Language Acquisition and Second Language Learning*. Oxford: Oxford University Press.

Kumar, N. & Rose, R.C. (2008). The effects of personality and cultural intelligence on international assignment effectiveness: a review. *Journal of Social Sciences, 4*(4), 320.

Lievens, F., Harris, M.M., Van Keer, E. & Bisqueret, C. (2003). Predicting cross-cultural training performance: the validity of personality, cognitive ability, and dimensions measured by an assessment center and a behavior description interview. *Journal of Applied Psychology, 88*(3), 476.

Li, M., Mobley, W. & Kelly, A. (2012). When do global leaders learn best to develop cultural intelligence? An investigation of the moderating role of experiential learning style. *Academy of Management Learning & Education*, 24th January.

Long, M.H. (1983). Native speaker/non-native speaker conversation and the negotiation of comprehensible input1. *Applied linguistics, 4*(2), 126–141.

McCarthy, B. (1996), *About Learning*. Barrington, IL: Excel, Inc.

Mainemelis, C., Boyatzis, R.E. & Kolb, D.A. (2002). Learning styles and adaptive flexibility testing experiential learning theory. *Management Learning, 33*(1), 5–33.

Nafei, W.A. (2012). The impact of cultural intelligence on employee job performance: An empirical study on King Abdel-Aziz Hospital in Al-Taif Governorate, Kingdom of Saudi Arabia. *International Journal of Business and Management, 8*(1), 26.

Ng, K.Y. & Earley, P.C. (2006). Culture + intelligence: old constructs, new frontiers. *Group & Organization Management, 31*(1), 4–19.

Ng, K.Y., Van Dyne, L. & Ang Soon (2009). From experience to experiential learning: Cultural intelligence as a learning capability for global leader development. *Academy of Management Learning & Education, 8*(4), 511–526.

Olguín, D.O., Waber, B.N., Kim, T., Mohan, A., Ara, K. & Pentland, A. (2009). Sensible organizations: Technology and methodology for automatically measuring organizational behavior. *Systems, Man, and Cybernetics, Part B: Cybernetics, IEEE Transactions on, 39*(1), 43–55.

Oolders, T., Chernyshenko, O. S. & Stark, S. (2008). Cultural intelligence as a mediator of relationships between openness to experience and adaptive performance. In: Ang Soon & Van Dyne, L. (eds.). *Handbook on Cultural Intelligence: Theory, Measurement and Applications* (pp. 145–173). Armonk, NY: ME Sharpe.

Osland, J.S., Kolb, D., Rubin, I. & Turner, M. (2007). *Organizational Behavior: An Experiential Approach*. Upper Saddle River, NJ: Prentice-Hall.

Oxford, R.L. & Lavine, R.Z. (1991). Conflicts in the language classroom. In: Magnan, S.S. (ed.). *Challenges in the 1990s for College Foreign Language Programs*. Boston, MA: Heinle & Heinle Publishers.

Peterson, B. (2004). *Cultural Intelligence: A Guide to Working with People from Other Cultures*. Yarmouth, ME: Intercultural Press.

Petrovic, D.S. (2011). How do teachers perceive their cultural intelligence? *Procedia – Social and Behavioral Sciences, 11*, 276–280.

Rockstuhl, T. & Ng, K.Y. (2008). The effects of cultural intelligence on interpersonal trust in multicultural teams. In: Ang Soon & Van Dyne, L. (eds.). *Handbook of Cultural Intelligence: Theory, Measurement, and Applications* (pp. 206–220). Armonk, NY: ME Sharpe.

Rose, R.C. & Subramaniam, N.K. (2008). A review on individual differences and cultural intelligence. *The Journal of International Social Research, 1*(4), 504–522.

Shaffer, M. & Miller, G. (2008). Cultural Intelligence: A key success factor for expatriates. In: Ang Soon & Van Dyne, L. (eds). *Handbook of Cultural Intelligence: Theory, Measurement, and Applications* (p. 107–125). Armonk, NY: ME Sharpe.

She, H.C. & Fisher, D. (2000). The development of a questionnaire to describe science teacher communication behavior in Taiwan and Australia. *Science Education, 84*(6), 706–726.

Soldatova, G. & Geer, M. (2013). "Glocal" identity, cultural intelligence and language fluency. *Procedia – Social and Behavioral Sciences, 86*, 469–474.

Sternberg, R.J. & Detterman, D.K. (eds.) (1986). *What Is Intelligence?: Contemporary Viewpoints on Its Nature and Definition.* Norwood, NJ: Ablex.

Swain, M. (1985). Communicative competence: Some roles of comprehensible input and comprehensible output in its development. *Input in Second Language Acquisition, 15*, 165–179.

Templer, K.J., Tay, C. & Chandrasekar, N.A. (2006). Motivational cultural intelligence, realistic job preview, realistic living conditions preview, and cross-cultural adjustment. *Group & Organization Management, 31*(1), 154–173.

Thelen, H.A. (1954). *Methods for Studying Work and Emotionality in Group Operation.* Chicago: University of Chicago, Human Dynamics Laboratory.

Triandis, H.C. (2006). Cultural intelligence in organizations. *Group & Organization Management, 31*(1), 20–26.

Tulving, E. (1985). Memory and consciousness. *Canadian Psychology / Psychologie Canadienne, 26*(1), 1.

Yamazaki, Y. & Kayes, D.C. (2004). An experiential approach to cross-cultural learning: A review and integration of competencies for successful expatriate adaptation. *Academy of Management Learning & Education, 3*(4), 362–379.

Yamazaki, Y. & Kayes, D.C. (2007). Expatriate learning: Exploring how Japanese managers adapt in the United States. *The International Journal of Human Resource Management, 18*(8), 1373–1395.

Jaroslava Kubátová

Preparation of University Students from Western Cultures for Cooperation with China: Reasons and Methods

This paper highlights the reasons why it is necessary to prepare university graduates for cooperation with China. Based on the current experience of the Department of Applied Economics, Faculty of Arts, Palacký University in Olomouc, Czech Republic, the possible ways and scope are suggested.

According to the statistics of the International Monetary Fund (2014), China was the world's largest economy when it comes to the size of real GDP in 2014. It is estimated (Businessinfo, 2014) that by 2020 China will have had a 17% share of the world trade. Czech trade with China has increased sharply in the last twenty years. China is an important business partner for the Czech Republic, with Czech import from China being sharply higher than export to China (Czech Statistical Office, 2015). The most important traded commodities are machinery, vehicles, hard goods, and soft goods. There has also been an increase in Chinese investments in the Czech Republic and Czech investments in China. For example, an important Chinese private company, CEFC, is currently planning to invest CZK 20 billion in the Czech Republic. Czech investments in China are primarily aimed at the automotive industry and services (Businessinfo, 2014b). Another area with a big growth potential is tourism. In 2014, 200 000 Chinese tourists came to the Czech Republic (Czech Tourism, 2014).

The short summary of Czech trade with China presented above clearly implies that the labor market will experience an increase in the demand for workers who can speak Chinese and who are well-oriented in economics, the Chinese culture, business etiquette and so on. Even today, the demand for such workers is high. This fact is confirmed by surveys of Czech employment websites (e.g. jobs.cz, careerjet.cz) and by confirmed easiness with which graduates of Applied Economics combined with Chinese Philology at the Faculty of Arts of the Palacký University find jobs. Many of these students are already employed in the course of their studies.

Important factors to be considered when preparing students for cooperation with China

It is necessary to strengthen, extend and update the preparation of graduates who would possess the currently demanded qualifications and competencies in response to the development of Czech-Chinese relations and the social and technical development in general. Many factors must be taken into consideration when preparing students for cooperation with Chinese partners.

The Czech Republic belongs to the Western culture, while China is a representative of the Eastern culture (Hofstede, 2007). Geert Hofstede (1984) defines culture as "...the collective programming of the mind that distinguishes the members of one group (a nation, in our case – author's note) or category of people from others". Czechs, who graduate from Czech schools, experience difficulties in imagining differences between Czech and the Chinese cultures. The Czech education system is based on the western concept of science: on categorization, analysis, synthesis, and comparison. Critical thinking, based on logic, rationalization and scientific argumentation is required from students. The literature used in management and economy courses is of western origin. The Czech Republic is a part of low-context cultures whereas China is a part of high-context cultures. This fact can lead to misunderstandings if Czechs are not familiar with the Chinese way of communicating. The culture of the Czech Republic is monochromic, i.e. the time is perceived as linear, processes are strictly planned and deadlines are determined and expected to be kept. The Chinese culture is polychromic, i.e. the perception of time in this culture is vastly different. The knowledge of these and many other characteristics of the Chinese culture, like the sociological concept of face, the importance of hierarchy and so on, is either rare among the Czech, or highly inaccurate, like their knowledge of Guanxi. Rudolf Fürst (2005) pointed out in his study that the Czech view of China still shows signs of stereotypes and downright deficiency of awareness. According to Fürst, the image of China among the Czech ranges from fascination through romanticism to criticism. The experience with freshmen suggests that this image has not changed much over the last ten years. On the other hand, despite the current freshmen generation being demographically weak, there is an increase of students' interest in study programs related to the Chinese langue, which is a very positive trend.

Given the above, there are many reasons to prepare university graduates who possess knowledge of the Chinese language and cultural background combined with knowledge of economics and management. The development of economic relations and the significance of China is only one of these reasons. The question which remains is: what is the best way to accomplish this task in the terms of quality?

Suggestions for further development of Chinese Studies

The most important areas on which students need to concentrate are: language and cultural competencies. Cultural competencies can be improved by raising the cultural intelligence of students. Cultural intelligence is defined as an ability to be effective across various cultural contexts: national, ethnic, organizational, and generational (Livemore, 2011). This ability can be also effectively developed by staying in touch with members of different cultures and by short- or long-term stays in relevant given country. The Confucius Institute can significantly help with the whole preparation of students and without its support the preparation of students in the current system applied in state universities in the Czech Republic would be much harder.

It is in the interest of both national economics and universities to create study programs focused on China and the Chinese language. High-quality study sources and personnel will provide objective information about China which would then be spread to the wider society by the graduates. These study programs must be prepared comprehensively and in a balanced manner to correspond with the required graduate profile. Courses focused on entrepreneurship should be ideally taught by an experienced teacher from the relevant country. This fact creates a significant opportunity for academic personnel exchange between the Czech Republic (or other countries in Central or Eastern Europe) and China. It is also desirable to enable Czech students to travel to China to study or work for at least one semester.

Courses on the Chinese language are very important. The Confucius Institute helps by providing lecturers and it would be also desirable to secure Business Chinese lecturers with higher academic degrees. The experience with teaching at the Department of Applied Economics of the

Faculty of Arts of the Palacký University shows how difficult it is to obtain literature concerning the Chinese approach to management, human resources, marketing and other areas strongly influenced by national culture and values, in languages different than Chinese.

Potential of cooperation with Chinese experts illustrated on the basis of a management course

We would like to use a specific example to show how cooperation with Chinese experts can help students from Western cultures to gain insight into the Chinese managerial thinking. The word *insight* might be too optimistic, since good management and leadership are part of tacit knowledge which is very hard to pass on. However, it is important for students who aspire to be employed in an intercultural environment to have at least some awareness of the Chinese approach to management. Such knowledge is very difficult to obtain, as the literature focused on Chinese management is written almost exclusively in the Chinese language. A teacher from a Western culture can obtain a translation of Chinese literature and teach accordingly; however, with regard to their natural mindset, they cannot pass the knowledge as effectively as a Chinese expert can. The most effective way to obtain knowledge about the Chinese managerial methods would be student work placement in Chinese companies. The translation of the Chinese managerial literature that is currently being done at the Department of Applied Economics at the Faculty of Arts of the Palacký University is the first step (Bedáňová, 2015). These translations allow us to see the areas where Western cultures most struggle to understand the Chinese way of thinking.

The Chinese approach to management has two aspects. The first one places emphasis on ethics and morality, and the other one stresses benefit. All of the major philosophical schools in China (Confucianism, Taoism, and Buddhism) can be useful in management due to their principles. A manager seeking to enhance his or her own managerial skills should focus on Taoism; if they seek to improve their behavior and comprehension, their focus should be on Buddhism. A company as a whole should focus on Confucianism if it wishes to improve its management (Zhu, 2008).

The teachings of Confucius have been a source of inspiration for more than 2000 years and they also influence management. The Chinese approach to management has been influenced mainly by the Confucian emphasis on the cultivation of one's own morals. The purpose of education should be to enable a human being to become a "noble person"

(Cheng, 2006, p. 54), and as such serve the society, be an asset to it and follow moral principles. An executive must first focus on themself to be able to manage and lead other people.

Self-improvement, self-education and self-formation are often emphasized in the Chinese culture; aside from Confucianism, they are also a part of Taoism and Buddhism. Self-cultivation has been traditionally recommended to politicians, for it could help them change their personality and become perfect/ideal rulers of their country. Human high-mindedness can be constantly developed through self-cultivation (learning). Zeng (2010) formulated three specific steps of self-cultivation that are based on the ideas of Confucius and on the traditional values of the Chinese culture, in particular the sociological concept of face. These steps are self-awareness, self-discipline and keeping the initiative in one's own hands.

- Self-awareness enables the manager to listen to other people and be compassionate. Compassionate attitude helps the manager to save other people's face.
- Self-discipline is necessary when criticizing others. According to Chinese values, it is important to save the face of everyone involved. To manage such a task successfully, one needs self-discipline and prudence, especially when dealing with a situation where more than one side claims to be right. The approach to problem-solving in China is different from the one in western cultures, so more truths can actually coexist (see below). For these reasons, a manager must be able to empathize with employees and to be compassionate.
- Maintaining initiative is a task of every manager but not everyone is courageous enough to do it. Managers must realize that keeping initiative is crucial, as without it, projects and tasks cannot develop the way they were desired.

The problem with maintaining initiative can be related to the Chinese management's approach to objectives. In western cultures, objectives are defined and systematic steps are taken in order to achieve them. A manager from a western culture, on the one hand, is responsible for achieving the goal and their remuneration depends on it. On the other hand, Chinese managers may or may not reach their goals. The Chinese are very much aware of the fact that if the goal is reached, the next one will be much harder to reach and this will only lead to the manager being "worn out." Therefore, the Chinese do not always feel the need to chase after goals. Moreover, in China, reaching a goal does not automatically equal reward and failing to reach it does not have to lead to punishment. Important as they are, according to the Chinese management, objectives and results cannot be considered to be the most important aspects. This is because circumstances can differ. If we find ourselves in times when business is smooth, good results are easy to achieve and therefore they are not special or worthy of a reward. On the other hand, when business is slow, the manager would not achieve great results even if they wore themself out and there is no reason for punishment (Zeng, 2010).

According to the western management, a problem must be solved once it emerges. There are only two options: either solve the problem or do not. To solve a problem is to fulfill one's duty; to not solve it is to fail in fulfilling that duty. The Chinese management is able to create a third option. On the one hand, a Chinese manager knows that not solving a problem is not an option, because then the problem remains and worsens. On the other hand, to solve a problem is not good either because solving a problem will certainly cause more problems, maybe even greater and more complicated. According to the Chinese, there is a way to achieve balance between solving and non-solving: namely, mitigate the problem, dismantle it and if needed, tune it up. The Chinese like to change big problems into small ones, and small ones into "no ones." with the originator of this thought is not known and therefore it is not attributed to any philosopher (Zeng, 2010).

This type of approaching problems, called neutralization, is not stressful and has no negative effects or impacts. The method of transformation originated in taiji. Three types of moves are used in taiji: *tui, tuo*, and *la*, hence the name of the method of dealing with problems: "*tui, tuo, la*." The advantage of the "*tui, tuo, la*" method is that it does not make the atmosphere at work unpleasant and it takes human feelings into account. The words *tui, tuo, la* can have more meanings, when used with other expressions. This is yet another that it is hard to imagine for someone with education based on western culture.

Tui can be translated as "push" and it can mean:
- To use strength to widen/open/solve problems
- To put problem aside to be thought through
- To find a reason to deny (get rid of) a problem.

In practice, *tui* means that a problem should by "pushed" towards the person responsible for the problem or to a specialist who deals with this kind of problems. *Tui* in the sense of "put aside to be thought through" is good for employees. If a supervisor comes up with a task and asks his or her subordinates whether they are willing to assume responsibility for it, no one should apply right away. The one who is willing to assume responsibility for a task right away gives an impression of being irresponsible, because he or she did not think the task through. Such an employee can also cause an unpleasant working environment since their co-workers might be envious and try to push them out of the team. In an ideal situation, the employee says that they will think about the task. The manager appreciates the effort to think the task through and assigns it to the employee. Another possibility is that when no one else wants to assume responsibility for the task, then the employee can actively do so.

Tuo can be translated as "gently drag behind" and can also have other meanings:
- To drag gently, not leave behind
- To avoid delays
- To avoid executing tasks or solving problems in a hurry.

La means "pull"; the difference between *tuo* and *la* lies in intensity. *La* means to pull vigorously and can have other meanings as well:
- To pull inside
- To simplify a situation so it can be finished more easily
- To neglect or ignore.

All of these methods, *tui*, *tuo*, and *la*, should be used in harmony, with regard to the people and circumstances related to the problem. Only then will the method be an asset. Naturally, all of these methods have their pros and cons and it is up to the manager to choose what method he or she uses and how. When deciding which method will bring the desired effect, the manager must take into consideration the people who will apply it and the motivation they have. Moreover, the way of executing the method must be harmonic. There is a Chinese proverb that says "rules are dead, people are alive." Rules and methods must always be adjusted to the people and circumstances they apply to. This attitude is one of the hardest to understand for western cultures. The western culture tends to generalize much more, meaning that the norms and rules that are established apply to everyone under any circumstances.

Another thing typical for western cultures is duality: manager – subordinate; decision-making according to circumstances – decision-making according to laws and rules; right – wrong; done – not done, etc. The Chinese, however, always look for a "grey zone," according to the philosophy of taiji. They try to find a midpoint between opposites, e.g. a midpoint between decision-making according to circumstances and decision-making according to laws and rules, a midpoint between a manager and a subordinate, a midpoint between the right and wrong, a midpoint between done and not done. With the help of harmony, they find a third principle in the middle. For a western mindset, the idea of achieving and not achieving a goal or solving and not solving a problem at the same time is hardly comprehensible.

Academic workers from western cultures often examine the thoughts of Confucius and other Chinese philosophers. Nevertheless, according to Zeng, they often reach wrong conclusions and misunderstand the message. The main problem lies in the fact that western attitudes and approaches are used in this research to judge the Confucian thought. While it is completely understandable, it is not possible to understand the original Chinese thought this way. Therefore, the following conclusions often appear. We present them with Zeng's explanatory notes (2010, pp. X–XIV):

- Chinese politics is too centralized and has dictatorial tendencies
- The history of China shows that dictators were the minority and were quickly removed from power. Not one dictator was loved by their people
- The Chinese have no principles; almost all situations are solved on an individual basis and therefore it is very hard to make any predictions.

While it is true that completely identical problems can have a different solution based on time, people and place, it does not mean that Chinese people lack principles. On the contrary, the Chinese have principles that they hold in very high regard and they stick to them. Still, they would make rational adjustments according to time, place, the people involved and other circumstances. Chinese principles are not immutable and will not "fight to the last breath," but at the same time, they will not change every time someone wants them to. The truth is that even nowadays many Chinese fail to provide complete explanation of this issue. They would only mention a number of contradictory "pearls of wisdom," sometimes providing people from western cultures with incorrect information, and consequently decreasing their understanding of the Chinese even further.

- The Chinese blindly reminisce about the past and former glory, therefore they are unable to concentrate on current goals or to have a positive attitude towards new things and changes.

The Chinese divide time into three parts: the past, the present and the future, the main focus being on the present. "A hero is silent about his former glory," meaning that the former achievements are in the past and it is truly unnecessary to remember them. Only when discussing the achievements of their ancestors will the Chinese exaggerate. The intention, however, is not to exaggerate past but to motivate grandchildren to strive for perfection. Also, the Chinese cannot allow their ancestors to lose their face.

From early childhood, a child is taught by their parents to be flexible, to be able to adapt and to like changes. The Chinese would never openly say it, but they constantly demand innovation and change. However, the western culture and modernization is different from the Chinese one and it is necessary to be careful not to judge Chinese modernization based on the criteria assumed by western cultures.

- The Chinese lack the concept of control and balance of power.

The Chinese do not like to be controlled publicly, because such an act is an expression of mistrust towards the executive. This causes the executive to lose their face and also, the authority to control can be used for blackmail. The Chinese prefer a non-public control of power. When making plans concerning human resources and redistribution of others, the executive must be careful to keep everything in balance; otherwise, they might influence stability and harmony as a whole. The communication between an executive and others is effective only when the executive is aware of these subtle relations and respects them.

- It is necessary to submit to Chinese authorities unconditionally.

This is a big misunderstanding. The Chinese lay emphasis on mutuality. Almost all relations are based on mutual help and by no means can they be compared to unconditional obedience. The first impression may be that the Chinese obey in every way and that a subordinate will agree to anything that their executive implies. In reality, however, the subordinate may not agree with their supervisor, but they are not used to express their feelings immediately. When working on a task, they may not necessarily do it according to their supervisor's instructions but according to their own judgment. This is not considered as deceiving or cheating the supervisor; on the contrary, it is an expression of respect. On the outside, it looks like the Chinese obey completely but in reality they have their own opinions.

- The Chinese place great importance on the form and etiquette.

The Chinese do not like formalities that are not necessary. However, in China, the form expresses an important intent. For example, the main goal of a wedding is to give the newlyweds a sense of responsibility and, there should be only one wedding in one lifetime.

Many analytics from western cultures believe that in western cultures, a father raises his children with love, whereas in China, he has a strict attitude and the children do not feel his love. In reality, the strict attitude proves the real love of Chinese parents, who care for their children's destiny.

- The Chinese constantly demand a sense of belonging to a group.

According to Zeng, the Chinese feel strong mutual attachment but not a sense of belonging in general. A good job and a good attitude of a manager are needed for the sense of attachment to become a sense of belonging to a working environment. As everything changes, even mutual trust and the sense of belonging may change back to the sense of attachment.

- The Chinese do not tolerate different opinions and do not allow them to be expressed in a company.

In reality, the Chinese want to hear different opinions but everybody knows that an honest piece of advice is not always a flattering one. Different opinions are helpful in the search of new ideas and better plans;

nevertheless, the Chinese do not like a public debate or a situation where a different opinion appears in a public debate. They prefer to express different opinions in private and keep the communication clear so the opinion is acceptable. It is easy to communicate before or after a meeting, but it is hard to lead an effective discussion during.

- The Chinese managerial style is suitable only for quiet times and stabilized society, not for an environment of quick transformations.

The Chinese have gradually came to the conclusion that 80% of changes are bad and only 20% of changes are good. Therefore, when undergoing change, they are trying to avoid worsening the situation. They have established a principle of "dealing with changes by not allowing ourselves to change and resort to unchangeable principles." Unfortunately, according to Zeng, many Chinese do not understand this themselves and cause further misunderstandings among people from western cultures. There is no doubt that the Chinese management is suitable and applicable also to times of rapid changes and extraordinary situations.

- Chinese like to put the blame for their mistakes on other people and do not like to claim responsibility themselves.

The truth is that it definitely looks like this is the case. Nevertheless, the Chinese only pass the responsibility on someone else in order to save their own face. In the end, the real responsibility impacts the one truly responsible as it cannot be discarded easily.

In western cultures, people often admire managers – heroes who can gain influence but claim allegiance to democracy. On the other hand, the Chinese do not admire heroes at all. A manager who resembles a hero and, like most heroes, uses their power and influence, would end up being removed from the office very quickly. Chinese people prefer a manager who resembles a sage, because the Chinese worship wisdom. According to Confucius, a manager/leader should have a good heart and be humane. This way, he will be naturally considered a leader (Zeng, 2010).

These wrong conclusions are unfortunately quite widespread, even in academic circles. Therefore, the decisions about the extent of cooperation with Chinese institutions can be short-sighted. We believe that another Chinese virtue, Chilku Nailao, which means "patience and resilience", can be helpful in such negotiations.

The Confucius Institute might significantly contribute to removing these misconceptions by securing translation of Chinese publications into English or other relevant languages. Securing Chinese lecturers and supporting working placements of foreign students in Chinese companies would be an even greater contribution.

Future education in China-related fields at the Faculty of Arts of the Palacký University

Chinese Philology has been taught at the Palacký University for a very long time. A new master's degree program, Chinese as a foreign language, is currently being prepared in cooperation with the Confucius Institute. A dual study program, Applied Economics combined with Chinese Philology, is an ideal option with regard to usefulness. As a next step, the Faculty of Arts of the Palacký University and the Confucius Institute in Olomouc may prepare a new Bachelor's degree program, called "economic studies focusing on China" in order to improve the readiness of graduates to cooperate with Chinese entities. The Confucius Institute can mainly help with securing lecturers to teach technical Chinese language and the specifics of the Chinese business behavior. Cooperation between the Department of Applied Economics and Beijing Foreign Studies University – International Business School was already established last year, thanks to the efforts of the Confucius Institute. First exchanges of scholars and students are already taking place under the terms of the agreement which is currently being prepared. We also plan scientific and research cooperation in the future.

The western society is currently interested in traditional Chinese values. This fact favors activities leading to the exploration of these values. *Emotional Intelligence*, a book written by David Goleman, became a bestseller for managers in the second half of 1990s. The recommendations which are found in this publication can also be found in the teachings of Confucius or Xunzi. The ideas based on Buddhist and Confucian values, like mindfulness and happiness at work, currently spread from the USA, which is a traditional representative of the western approach to business and management. The Confucius Institute can significantly contribute to China being presented not only as a country with a unique combination of political and economic system, but also as a society based on many highly regarded values. One possible method is to support study programs focusing on China, the Chinese language and the Chinese economy.

References

Bedáňová, H. (2015). *Management in Contemporary China*. Unpublished master's thesis.

Businessinfo (2014a). *Čína: zahraniční obchod země*. Retrieved from http://www.businessinfo.cz/cs/clanky/cina-zahranicni-obchod-zeme-19056.html (accessed: 14/09/2015).

Businessinfo (2014b). *Čína: investiční klima*. Retrieved from: http://www.businessinfo.cz/cs/clanky/cina-investicni-klima-19059.html (accessed: 14/09/2015).

Cheng, A. (2006). *Dějiny čínského myšlení*. Praha: DharmaGaia.

Czech Statistical Office. (2015). *Zahraniční obchod s Čínou*. Retrieved from: https://www.czso.cz/csu/czso/zahranicni-obchod-s-cinou-2005-az-2012-63zz81k8k1 (accessed: 14/09/2015).

Czech Tourism (2014). *Čína jako strategický zdrojový trh pro cestovní ruch*. Retrieved from: http://www.czechtourism.cz/getattachment/Institut-turismu/Aktuality/Cina-jako-strategicky-zdrojovy-trh-pro-cestovni-ru/29_01_15_analyza_cina.pdf.aspx (accessed: 14/09/2015).

Fürst, R. (2005). Czech Perceptions of China: Between Matter-of-Factness and Imagination, Between Orientalism and Occidentalism. *Mezinárodní vztahy*, 3, 25–45.

Hofstede, G. (1984). *Culture's Consequences: International Differences in Work-Related Values*. Thousand Oaks: Sage, p. 21.

Hofstede, G. (2007). Asian management in the 21st century. *Asia Pacific Journal of Management*, 24(4), 411–420.

International Monetary Fund (2014). *World Economic Outlook Database*. Retrieved from: http://www.imf.org/external/data.htm (accessed: 14/09/2015).

Livemore, D. (2011). *The Cultural Intelligence Difference*. AMACOM. Kindle Edition.

Zeng, S. (2010). *Zhongguo Shi Guanli Jingdian* [*Classics of Management in Chinese History*]. Beijing: Beijing Daxue Chubanshe.

Zhu Fu (2008). *Ma Yunru Shi Shuo – Zhongguo Dingji CEO de Shangdao Zhenjing* [*Ma Yunru says – Practical Knowledge on Trade for China's Senior Executive Directors*]. Beijing: Zhongguo Jingji Chubanshe. Retrieved from: http://data.book.hexun.com/book-1826.shtml (accessed: 14/09/2015).

Tina Ilgo

Facing the Challenges of Teaching Chinese through Confucius Classrooms in Slovenian Schools: Current Situation and Prospects

With the growing demand for the Chinese language and culture in Slovenian schools and the establishment of Confucius Classrooms (CCs), Slovenian schools are facing many challenges. The present paper examines important issues in teaching Chinese through CCs in Slovenian kindergartens, primary schools, and secondary schools.

The first Confucius Classroom in Slovenia was established in Maribor at the 2nd High School in Maribor in 2013. It was followed by Confucius Classroom Ljubljana at Trnovo Primary School in 2013, Confucius Classroom Kranj at the Krnaj High School in 2014 and Confucius Classroom Koper at the University of Primorska in 2014. The Slovenian Ministry of Education, Science and Sport has confirmed the curriculum for the Chinese language in Slovenian primary schools (2011) and high schools (2013). The "Chinese culture and language" pilot project was first introduced in two Slovenian primary schools: France Prešeren Primary School and Gorje Primary School. In the school year 2012/2013, the project started in the form of an enrichment of activities as extracurricular activities involving the Chinese culture and language in H.C. Andersen Kindergarten, Trnovo Primary School, Koseze Primary School, and Tone Čufar Primary School in Ljubljana. In the school year 2013/2014, in cooperation with and under the sponsorship of the National Education Institute of the Republic of Slovenia, Trnovo Primary School, introduced the "Chinese culture and language" project to the Slovenian education system. Since 2012, presentations of Chinese culture and language are held on a regular basis every year in the form of creative workshops at Trnovo and Koseze primary schools.

During the three years of teaching and learning Chinese in Slovenian primary schools and secondary schools, a survey on teaching the Chinese language through CCs was conducted among Slovenian sinologists and Chinese teachers. The results of the survey yield some important data and insights on how to improve teaching Chinese in Slovenia. The key research questions addressed in this paper are:

1. What do we need for a successful introduction of the Chinese language and culture classes to the Slovenian education system?
2. How to create a sequenced, articulated curriculum?
3. How to promote Chinese language learning in Slovenia?
4. How to face the shortage of qualified teachers?

The final goal is to form recommendations for future Chinese language teaching in Slovenian schools based on the experience and the theoretical framework of teaching the Chinese language as a foreign language.

Chinese language teaching and learning in the Slovenian education system

According to Wang (2010), "historically two major private initiatives were instrumental for introducing Chinese to the U.S. schools: the Carnegie Foundation's initiative in the early 1960s throughout the 1980s and the Geraldine Dodge Foundation's initiative from the 1980s through the early 2000s" (p. 15). When reading this, we can undoubtedly claim that the Chinese language in the Slovenian education system is a newcomer. The first initiative in the scope of Chinese language teaching and learning was undertaken by three individuals: one of the first Slovenian researchers in the field of japanology and sinology, Andrej Bekeš, Jana S. Rošker, and Mitja Saje, who established the Department of Asian and African Studies at the Faculty of Arts of the University of Ljubljana in 1995. The initiative of implementing Chinese as an elective subject in Slovenian primary and secondary schools also came from the Department of Asian and African studies. The Slovenian Ministry of Education, Science, and Sport has confirmed the curriculum for Chinese language classes in Slovenian primary schools (2011) and high schools (2013).

The second initiative came in 2010, when the Confucius Institute Ljubljana (CI Ljubljana) was established at the Faculty of Economics of the University of Ljubljana.[1] It is a business-oriented CI, but has been closely

---

[1] CI Ljubljana is a non-profit organisation established for the purpose of promoting and teaching Chinese language and culture, operating under the supervision of Hanban (Office of Chinese Language Council International).

engaged in introducing the Chinese language and culture to the Slovenian education system for the past three years. From 2013 to 2015, it has established four Confucius Classrooms (CC), which are covering four Slovenian regions: central Slovenian region (Ljubljana and its surroundings), Pomurska region (Maribor and its surroundings), Gorenjska region (Kranj and its surroundings) and Primorsko-notranjska region (Koper and its surroundings). The long-term goal of CCs is to establish a vertical link in the field of Chinese culture and language teaching and learning between kindergartens, primary schools, high schools and universities. CCs are trying hard to form a good basis for teaching and learning Chinese in the Slovenian school system. The current situation concerning kindergartens, primary schools and secondary schools offering the extracurricular activity of studying the Chinese culture and language or/and the Chinese language as an elective subject in Slovenia in the school year 2014/2015 is the following:

CC Maribor	CC Ljubljana
– Tezno Kindergarten, 40 – France Prešeren Primary School, 15 – II. High School Maribor, 15 – Ptuj High School, 8	– H.C. Andersen Kindergarten, 66 – Trnovo Primary School, 84 – Koseze Primary School, 28 – Savsko naselje Primary School, 18 – Bežigrad High School, 6 – Jože Plečnik High School Ljubljana, 4
CC Kranj	**CC Koper**
– Matija Čop Primary School Kindergarten, 19 – Živ Žav Kindergarten, 16 – Janina Kindergarten, 17 – Mojca Kindergarten, 18 – Orehek Primary school, 29 – Mavčiče Primary school, 11 – A.T. Linhart Primary School Radovljica, 3 – Kranj High School, 13	– Mornarček Kindergaten, 10 – Barčica Kindergarten, 12 – Lucija Primary School, 18 – Ciril Kosmač Primary School, 22 – Diego del Castro Primary School, 18

The above situation is a result of three years of cooperation between CI Ljubljana at the Economic Faculty of the University of Ljubljana, the Department of Asian and African Studies at the Faculty of Arts of the University of Ljubljana, and Slovenian sinologists and volunteer Chinese teachers sent to Slovenia by Hanban. The interest in the Chinese language and culture in Slovenia is growing, mainly due to the growing interest in economic cooperation with China and cross-cultural studies. Most countries in the world, such us the USA, the United Kingdom or Sweden, just to name a few, are aware of the importance of the Chinese language, which is the most widely spoken language in the world, especially in international business, and one of the six official languages of the United Nations. Introducing Chinese language to Slovenia, where commonly taught European languages such as English, German, French, Spanish or Italian are still dominating the field, poses a major challenge.

What do we need for a successful introduction of Chinese culture and language classes in Slovenian schools?

During the three years of teaching and learning Chinese in Slovenian primary and secondary schools, a survey determining the strengths, weaknesses, opportunities, and threats involved in teaching the Chinese language in Slovenian schools through CCs was conducted among Slovenian sinologists and Chinese teachers. In the school year 2012/2013, the survey was conducted on six teachers (4 sinologists and 2 Chinese teachers); in the school year 2013/2014 on twelve teachers (7 sinologists and 5 Chinese teachers); in the school year 2014/2015 on thirteen teachers (6 sinologists and 7 Chinese teachers). The factors listed in the SWOT matrix

STRENGHTS

Creative workshops
Social engagement
Effective lesson planning
Team-teaching
Student interest
Language & culture combo
Chinese bridge contest

WEAKNESSES

Yearly Chinese teacher replacement
Heterogeneous student groups
No articulated curriculum
Not compulsory class/no grades
Students overloaded with activities

OPPORTUNITIES

Enhance Chinese culture promotion
Translation of teaching materials
Enhance cooperation between schools

THREATS

Student drop-out rate
Shortage of trained teachers
Lack of funding

are presented in the form of *word clouds*, whereby the font size of the visual representation of individual factors correlates with the frequency of listing this particular factor by the respondents. For example, 84% of all respondents listed *team teaching* as a strength; 57% percent asserted that the *lack of an articulated curriculum* constitutes a weakness. Since the sample size of the respondents varies from year to year, the resulting frequencies have been calculated as a weighted average over the entire observed period from 2012 to 2015.

The results of the SWOT analysis provide some important data on how to improve teaching and learning Chinese in Slovenia. The most interesting findings are explained in the following subsections.

Team teaching

In his contribution, Everson (2011) describes the challenges Chinese teachers face when teaching Chinese in the United States: "Teachers of Chinese always seem to remark that when they enter a new teaching assignment, they are not only *a* Chinese teacher, but usually the *only* Chinese teacher. What this means is that they have no help or mentoring from a senior Chinese teacher and are often responsible not only for teaching Chinese, but also for designing the entire Chinese curriculum in their school" (p. 3). In Slovenian schools, Chinese teachers are not the only teachers as they are teaching together with Slovenian sinologists, who help them adapt to the Slovenian school system and methodology, and who prepare teaching plans for each lesson. According to Slethaug (2007), team teaching is an activity in which several instructors work together to fulfil teaching tasks (pp. 88–89). In Slovenia, team teaching and cross-cultural work are intertwined. As Zhu (2010) remarks, cross-cultural work adds another complication as teachers from different countries (using their native languages as the medium of instruction) teach in the same classroom and try to learn from one another (p. 161). Team teaching is a successful model of teaching Chinese culture and language in the form of extracurricular activities in Slovenian primary and secondary schools. According to the SWOT matrix, 84% of all respondents listed *team teaching* as a strength. Since Slovenia is not an English speaking country, Chinese teachers cannot conduct classes without the assistance of Slovenian teachers. Firstly, the language of instruction in Slovenian primary schools is Slovenian. Secondly, kindergarten children, and students from the first to the sixth grade of primary school do not have sufficient or any knowledge of the English language needed to understand

Chinese teachers. Thirdly, since Chinese teachers are not familiar with the teaching methodology in Slovenian schools, it is difficult for them to maintain discipline in the classroom without a Slovenian teacher present their side, let alone conduct classes according to standards. In the last three years of teaching and learning Chinese in Slovenian primary and secondary schools, team teaching proved to be a very successful method of teaching and learning Chinese.

The cooperation between Slovenian sinologists and Chinese teachers is an important experience that allows both partners to gain a deeper insight into team teaching. It is important to combine expertise and to complement one another. At the beginning, such cooperation requires some degree of mutual adaptation, tolerance and openness to different methodological approaches. When teachers reach a consensus about the methodology, topics and forms of teaching, classroom discipline, etc., team teaching constitutes an important contribution to the personal and professional growth of both teachers. One Chinese volunteer teacher described team teaching as follows: "We have to do much work to complement the ideas, but actually these ideas are the key reasons that attract me to work with full energy".

Combining Western and Eastern teaching approaches delivers innovations that can lead to a balanced coexistence of different methodological approaches, and thus to a new model of teaching that has to be adjusted to the cognitive abilities of pupils and the Slovenian education system. The participation of a Slovenian sinologist and a Chinese teacher enriches the learning process. For students, the presence of a native speaker is a significant benefit. In addition, a weekly meeting with a Chinese teacher becomes a routine for the students and allows them to internalize the acceptance of the "Other" as something natural. The working languages are Chinese and Slovenian. Teachers plan the lesson together. The Chinese teacher focuses on the linguistic part, whereas the Slovenian sinologist plans the cultural part of the lessons and is responsible for the compliance of the methods and forms of teaching to the Slovenian educational system, and for the smooth running of the activities, translation and explanation. The linguistic and cultural parts complement each other.

National teacher training courses and teacher development programs for Chinese teachers as well as Slovenian sinologists would significantly raise the quality of team teaching, and, in turn, increase the quality of curriculum articulation as well as teaching and learning Chinese in general.

Social engagement

According to the SWOT matrix, 60% of all respondents listed *social engagement* as a strength. By social engagement, we mean various performances, events, exhibitions or other out-of-class activities related to Chinese culture and language. CC Ljubljana, in cooperation with CI Ljubljana and primary schools, organizes several out-of-class activities for students in the form of projects, where students are able to present what they have learned in Chinese language classes to the wider Slovenian public. The fact that most of the schools did not organize out-of-class activities, and that only some of them cooperated in doing so, makes the resulting percentage even more significant. In the school year 2014/2015, all primary schools which belong to CC, cooperated in all major out-of-class activities organized by CC Ljubljana[2] and/or CI Ljubljana. The future goal of CC Ljubljana is to encourage social engagement in kindergartens and secondary schools and to engage students in out-of-class activities. In the last three school years, the following out-of-class activities were organized:

- The Chinese New Year gathering (2013, 2014, 2015)
- Chinese lanterns exhibition
- Celebration of Chinese Spring Festival in Nova Gorica
- Filming of a movie at the Confucius Institute in Ljubljana
- Chang E Flying to the Moon exhibition
- Terracotta warriors exhibition in Nama shopping centre in Ljubljana and at Ljubljana Old Town
- Tree metamorphosis exhibition in Cankarjev dom (cultural and art centre) in Ljubljana and in Ljubljana City Hall
- Closing event on the Chinese culture and language, China through children's eyes in Ljubljana Old Town (2013, 2014, 2015)
- Chinese summer school, Chinese summer experience at Trnovo (2014, 2015)
- Chinese culture and custom day (2014, 2015)
- Traditional Slovenian breakfast with representatives of the Chinese and Slovenian governments
- Visit from Chinese teachers and students from Beijing Foreign Languages School, BFSU in cooperation with 2nd High School in Maribor
- Performance of CC Ljubljana students at the opening of an exhibition entitled *Ferdinand Augustin Hallerstein: A Slovenian in the Forbidden City* in Slovenia's National Assembly
- Several occasional exhibitions

---

[2] The headquarters of the CC Ljubljana are at Trnovo Primary School.

These out-of-class activities not only help students strengthen their speaking, listening, reading and writing skills, but also stimulate their interest in the Chinese language and culture, broaden their general knowledge, their rhetorical and public speaking skills, and encourage creativity, team-work and project work. The response from students and parents to out-of-class activities is extremely positive.

Creative workshops

Similarly to team teaching, creative workshops are also a great advantage of Chinese culture and language teaching and learning in the Slovenian school system. According to the SWOT matrix, 57% of all respondents listed *creative workshops* as a strength. By creative workshops, we do not mean workshops like papercutting, Chinese fan or lantern painting, etc., but artistic creations by children of different age groups related to Chinese culture. Creative workshops encourage students' creativity, critical thinking, broaden their knowledge of Chinese art, literature, history, philosophy, geography, customs, traditions, etc. Children get involved in project work and enhance their teamwork skills. Creative workshops are based on a five-step didactic model.

- Step 1: opening the senses
- Step 2: getting familiar with a certain topic
- Step 3: establishing a dialogue
- Step 4: creative process
- Step 5: social engagement

The five-step didactic model is a modified version of experiential learning developed as part of an international project entitled "European identity of multiple choices" (Štirn Janota et. al., 2012, p. 24). According to the five-step didactic model, each topic the teacher chooses begins with activities aimed at the individual's sensitivity towards a certain subject and at evoking personal experiences in order to open the senses of every individual participating in the world of differences. The second step focuses on acquiring knowledge about specific content and making sense of it. The third step revolves around dialogue. Students apply the acquired knowledge and exchange experiences, ideas, and obtain feedback on their research; they establish a dialogue with the subject, themselves and others. The fourth step focuses on creativity. Students report on the content through artistic creation. The fifth step is social engagement, the essence of which is to enter into relationships with others and present the findings and creations to a wider public (ibid., p. 25).

Following the examples in the chapter "Social engagement", we can engage the children in different creative activities by intertwining Chinese culture and language, and taking into account the five-step didactic model.

- Chinese five elements and their symbolic meanings
- The legend of Chinese zodiac signs
- Discovering Chinese culture through myths, legends and stories (e.g. Creation of Heaven and Earth by Pangu, Chang E Flying to the Moon, Fuxi and Nuwa, The Legend of Nian Monster, The Legend of the White Snake, etc.)
- Beijing opera masks and their symbolic meanings
- Chinese festivals: customs and celebration (e.g. Chinese New Year, Lantern Festival, Qingming Festival, Dragon Boat Festival, Double Seventh Festival, Mid-Autumn Festival, etc.)
- Chinese paper cutting and creativity
- Chinese and European art: differences and encounters
- Chinese attractions through history and art (e.g. the Great Wall of China, the Forbidden City, the Terracotta Warriors, etc.)
- Discovering the silk road
- Chinese songs, dances and martial arts
- Chinese cuisine and eating habits
- "Let's touch China" (meeting children with different artefacts from China)

To Chinese volunteer teachers, creative workshops represented a completely new approach to creative teaching and learning Chinese. Their response was extremely positive.

"I was impressed by our first creative workshop. I played the role of an assistant for the students, instructing them and helping them finish their works. Although I could not communicate with them in Chinese, neither in English fluently, I found a way to help them to specify and realize their ideas. The dragon they were drawing was four meters long. They thought a lot before putting their pencils to the paper. I tried to encourage them to draw and paint as they liked, helping them to start. Surprisingly, they understood me quite well. Good interaction between students and myself made me realize that people of different nationality, different age groups, speaking different languages, share common interest in culture which connects them."

Promotion of Chinese language learning

To fulfil one of the essential long-term goals of teaching and learning Chinese in Slovenia, and to establish a vertical link from kindergartens to universities, the promotion of Chinese culture and language should focus on all levels of education, from kindergartens, through primary and secondary schools, all the way to universities. Firstly, the "Chinese culture and language in the Slovenian education system" project should be presented at the Slovenian Ministry of Education, Science and Sport and the National Education Institute of the Republic of Slovenia. Clear goals of the introduction of Chinese culture and language teaching and learning into the Slovenian education system should be established, with an emphasis on the strategy and funding possibilities. Secondly, the "Chinese culture and language in the Slovenian education system" project should be presented to the management sector (principals of schools and kindergartens and deans of faculties), parents and teachers. Thirdly, yearly presentations involving the Chinese culture and language should be carried out among children and students in all education institutions that belong to different CCs. The themes should include interesting cultural chapters from Chinese history, society, art, literature, etc., Chinese calligraphy, Chinese writing system development, Chinese stories, children's songs, games etc. The themes should be carefully selected and suitable for different age groups.

The promotion directed at the management sector should include reasons why children should learn Chinese, along with strategies, the methodology, the program and an articulated curriculum for learning Chinese in Slovenian kindergartens and schools, long distance goals, the outcomes of the program and its benefits to the children.

The promotion addressed to the parents should highlight the importance of Chinese language as a global language, the current state of Chinese teaching and learning in the global society, the added value of learning a foreign language, the possibility of associative learning, the possibility of creating a vertical link (kindergarten, primary school, high school, university), general knowledge competence, the development of tolerance and understanding of cultural diversity, presentation of the curriculum etc.

The promotion aimed at children should be carried out in the form of presentations as well as creative and cultural workshops.

How to create an articulated curriculum?

According to Xing (2006),

"to implement successful use of materials of foreign language acquisition, pedagogical specialists have to design and develop curricula adequate for various types of learners. Learners may be divided roughly into two groups: adult learners and young learners. These groups may be further subdivided thusly: college students, professionals, grade school students, and weekend school students. Each of these groups has different patterns of learning and moves at a different pace; hence each requires a different curriculum to meet its goals of learning and to optimize its learning potentials." (p. 30)

As mentioned before, The Slovenian Ministry of Education, Science, and Sport has confirmed the curriculum for Chinese language classes in Slovenian primary schools (2011) and high schools (2013). The curriculum for primary schools refers to students from 7th to 9th grade, whereas a curriculum for younger students has not yet been formalized. Since the opening of CC Ljubljana, the number of students from 1st to 6th grade applying for extracurricular activity Chinese culture and language is constantly growing. Slovenian sinologists and volunteer Chinese teachers conduct their classes according to the teaching plans they jointly prepare, but they have no formal standards or articulated curricula to follow. Groups of students are often heterogeneous, which means that teachers have to adapt the lectures to students of different ages. Furthermore, they need to prepare teaching plans for advanced levels. To enable these young students to learn Chinese efficiently and effectively, experts would need to design a curriculum tailored to young learners' psychological learning patterns. As Xing notes, "Chinese curricula for young learners still appear to be in the early stage of development" (ibid., p. 37).

Firstly, according to Xing, there are three essential elements in a Chinese language curriculum: "(1) to choose a Romanization system, (2) to decide upon a version of characters and (3) to select a procedure in the acquisition of sounds and characters" (ibid., p. 32).

Secondly, "teaching materials are an indispensable component in the development of an adequate curriculum." (ibid., p. 40) For the time being, there are no teaching materials in the form of textbooks, workbooks or AV teaching materials in Chinese-Slovenian for primary or secondary schools. Some teaching materials are being translated and designed. The SWOT analysis results show that 57% of all respondents listed *translations of teaching materials* as an opportunity.

Thirdly, the curriculum needs to define the stratification of the pedagogical grammar of Chinese. This step includes elementary materials (e.g. tones and tone change, initials and finals, stroke order of the characters, character structure, numerical expressions, time expressions, etc.), intermediate materials (e.g. word order, topic-comment construction, complex sentences, modal auxiliaries, etc.) and advanced materials (e.g. discourse connectors, discourse devices, formal vs. informal speech, speech acts, etc.).[3]

Fourthly, curriculum development involves choosing those content areas which enable students to learn how to use grammatical elements in real communicative situations (e.g. greetings, numbers, family members, body parts, animals, colours, hobbies, school life, etc.).

The fifth element of an articulated curriculum is cultural topics. According to Hammerly (1985, pp. 145–146), culture is divided into achievement and informational culture (art, architecture, literature, religion, history, philosophy, etc.) and behavioural culture (common daily practices and beliefs that define an individual and dictate behaviour in a specific society) (Christensen, 2011, p. 20). The SWOT matrix shows that 60% of the respondents listed *combination of language and culture* as a strength.

How to face the shortage of qualified teachers?

The SWOT analysis shows that one of the threats to Chinese language teaching and learning in Slovenia is the *shortage of trained teachers*. Volunteer Chinese teachers have no knowledge on the Slovenian education system and teaching methodology in Slovenian schools. They are young graduates, with very little or no practical teaching experience. They come to an environment which is completely new and unknown to them, and they need to adapt to it almost "at the speed of light". In the first two years of teaching and learning Chinese in Slovenia, they had to enter the class in less than a week after coming to Slovenia (most of them had never been to Europe before), without any preparation. Last year, CI Ljubljana organized the first *teacher training* for Chinese teachers in cooperation with sinologists. Thus, Chinese teachers had a longer adaptation period, but still less than two weeks. For successful adaptation, Chinese teachers should first attend teacher training; further, the school management should enable them to *observe* lectures in different classes conducted by different teachers in the form of *pedagogical practice* at the school where they work. This would enable them to understand the methods

---

[3] For more information on this topic, see Xing, 2010, pp. 52–59.

of teaching in Slovenian schools. Furthermore, sinologists should introduce the school and the employees to the Chinese teacher and plan Chinese culture and language lessons with them. That way, volunteer Chinese teachers from diverse backgrounds could adapt more efficiently to the Slovenian teaching environment and expectations. One of the weaknesses that have been identified in the SWOT matrix is the yearly Chinese teacher replacement, as Chinese teachers need at least two to three months to adapt to the new environment, the way of life and their work duties. It would be a great benefit to the system of Chinese language teaching in Slovenia, as well as to the children and students, if Chinese teachers stayed in Slovenia for at least three years.

A great step forward would be the accreditation of a pedagogic program for Chinese language teaching at the Faculty of Arts of the University of Ljubljana. In Slovenia, sinology is a non-pedagogic program, which means that sinologists do not have proper teacher training in the field of teaching Chinese in primary and secondary schools. If they had not studied another pedagogical program, they would have to enrol on a special Pedagogic and andragogic education program at the Faculty of Arts of the University of Ljubljana, which would enable them to teach in primary and secondary schools; however, there is no specialisation for Chinese language teaching. Professional teacher training for Slovenian sinologists and volunteer Chinese teachers would bring great benefit to the Chinese language and learning program.

Conclusions

The high interest and motivation expressed by students is an important benefit in implementing Chinese culture and language classes in the Slovenian education system, but it does not guarantee success. An articulated curriculum that would include the strengths shown in the SWOT matrix, such as team teaching, effective lesson planning, creative workshops, social engagement and language and culture combination, is a foundation of a successful introduction of Chinese language teaching and learning in the Slovenian education system. A well-designed curriculum can achieve its objectives only through excellent and professional teaching performance. Excellent teaching performance requires highly competent, professional, and personally engaged teachers, which further requires funding and professional teacher training.

Here are some recommendations on how to raise the quality of teaching and learning Chinese in the Slovenian education system:

- Provide funding for the Chinese language teaching and learning program in the Slovenian school system at the national level and through Hanban.
- Increase the number and effectiveness of Chinese language teachers and Slovenian sinologists.
- Provide full-time teaching positions for one Slovenian sinologist in each CC.
- Organize coordination of Chinese language planning at different levels, particularly at the state level.
- Develop language learning programs and an articulated curriculum for all levels (kindergarten, primary, school and high school).
- Provide teaching materials (textbook materials, software, dictionaries and online programs), materials for creative, cultural, and other workshops.
- Create a network of institutions cooperating with CCs to enable out-of-class activities.
- Enhance cooperation between CCs.
- Enhance cooperation with Chinese schools and universities.

As Wang (2010) writes,

"there exist complicated and interwoven channels of needs, supplies and demands for various elements: students, teachers, policy, funding, programs, curriculum, materials, assessments of student learning outcomes, program evaluation, and community/parental support, to name just a few examples. Taken together, these elements and mechanism of needs, supplies, and demands for language learning and teaching play important roles in the evolutionary process of language spread, maintenance, or loss. The stronger and the more developed these elements and mechanisms for a particular language are, the more successful the learning and teaching of the language will be, with satisfactory results and greater sustainability over time." (p. 6)

For the time being, we would need to focus on quality rather than quantity concerning Chinese language teaching and learning in Slovenia, and build a solid foundation for future teaching and learning that would bring great benefit to the school system, teachers involved, and to the children's future in the globalised world.

References

Christensen, B.M. (2011). Bringing culture into the Chinese language classroom through contextualized performance. In: Everson, M.E. & Xiao Yun (eds.). *Teaching Chinese as a Foreign Language: Theories and Applications* (pp. 19–34). Boston: Cheng & Tsui Company.

Everson, M. (2011). The importance of standards. In: Everson, M.E. & Xiao Yun (eds.). *Teaching Chinese as a Foreign Language: Theories and Applications* (pp. 3–18). Boston: Cheng & Tsui Company.

Hammerly, H. (1985). *An Integrated Theory of Language Teaching and Its Practical Consequences*. Blaine, WA: Second Language Publications.

Sleathaug, G. (2007). *Teaching Abroad: International Education and the Cross-cultural Classroom*. Hong Kong: Hong Kong University Press.

Štirn Janota, P. et al. (2012). *Lahko v šoli tudi drugače? Reševanje konfliktov in oblikovanje vzgojnih projektov (Can the school do it other way? Conflict resolution and the creation of educational projects)*. Retrieved from: http://www.cpi.si/files/cpi/userfiles/Datoteke/evalvacija/LahkoVSoliDrugace/Knjiga.pdf (accessed: 1/10/2015).

Wang Shuhan (2010). Chinese language education in the United States: A historical overview and future directions. In: Chen Jianguo, Wang Chuang, Cai Jinfa (eds.). *Teaching and Learning Chinese: Issues and Perspectives* (pp. 3–32). United States of America: Information Age Publishing, Inc.

Xing Janet Zhiqun (2006). *Teaching and Learning Chinese as a Foreign Language: A Pedagogical Grammar*. Hong Kong: Hong Kong University Press.

Zhu Weibin (2010). Learning for all: Cross-cultural, interdisciplinary team teaching between China and USA. In: Ryan, J. & Slethaug, G. (eds.). *International Education and the Chinese Learner* (pp. 161–171). Hong Kong: Hong Kong University Press.

Zakon o osnovni šoli (Official Gazette of the Republic of Slovenia) (2013). Retrieved from: http://pisrs.si/Pis.web/pregledPredpisa?id=ZAKO448 (accessed: 1/10/2015).

Velimir Stojkovski, Deng Shizhong, Elena Damjanoska

The Role of the Confucius Institute at Ss. Cyril and Methodius University in Skopje in Promoting the Chinese Language, Culture, and Business in the Republic of Macedonia

The Republic of Macedonia and the People's Republic of China have strengthened their relations and cooperation since establishing diplomatic relations more than two decades ago. This cooperation has increased in the past ten years, which only emphasizes the importance and the role which the Confucius Institute has had in this process.

The purpose of this paper is to determine the extent of the need for the development of culture-specific Chinese business classes, due to the demand for business Chinese in companies and for personal use. We will focus on those Chinese classes that have been offered and conducted thus far. We plan on providing a concise overview of our teaching program as well as past experiences and results. In our research, we will use the data gathered from the surveys we have conducted among the current Confucius Institute students.

1. Historical Background of the Sino-Macedonian cooperation

The Republic of Macedonia and the People's Republic of China established diplomatic relations in 1993. In the past, Macedonia and China continued to develop and maintain close bilateral economic relations. This has later been emphasized through the increase of trade between the two countries, as well as the great number of investments and projects funded by the Chinese government in areas such as hydro power plants, IT sector, etc. In 2012, PR China established a USD 10 billion fund for infrastructure projects in Central and Eastern Europe. Macedonia is the first country to have signed an agreement to use part of the funds in the amount of EUR 580 million for the largest-ever Sino-Macedonian joint infrastructure project. The project involves the construction of two new sections of a highway: Miladinovci – Shtip and Kichevo-Ohrid, which is being constructed in Macedonia by SINOHYDRO. One of the biggest investments in the public transport sector was the purchase of 313 buses from Zhengzhou Yutong Bus Company for the purposes of the Skopje Public Transport company – JSP in 2012. In 2014, a contract was signed with CSR Zhuzhou for the procurement of four diesel and two electric trains by the Macedonian national railway operator MZ Transport.

Chinese companies have also left a footprint in the telecommunications sector in Macedonia. In 2006, ZTE signed a contract with the second largest data communication operator Neocom to construct the first optical transmission network in Macedonia. Furthermore, the two biggest telecommunications companies, Telekom and VIP Macedonia, have installed and used equipment by Huawei and ZTE. In order to provide support and enhance the relations and cooperation between business sectors in Macedonia and China, the Macedonia China Chamber of Commerce was established in 2015, dedicated to promoting and increasing business and cultural links between Macedonia and China. Furthermore, we have observed an upswing in the bilateral trade volume, experiencing a year-on-year growth of 8.5 percent, which reached USD 525 million in 2014 and USD 267 million in the first half of 2015. This has made China Macedonia's seventh-largest trading partner third year in a row.

PR China and the Republic of Macedonia have also built strong relations in the area of education and medicine. The country's first Confucius Institute was founded in Skopje in 2013, and just one year later, with the support and funding of the Chinese government, the elementary school "Rajko Zhinzifov" was built in Skopje, where Chinese is taught to elementary students.

As Mr. Wen Zhenshun, Ambassador to the Republic of Macedonia, said in a recent interview:

> "Future cooperation also has great potential. China and Macedonia have strong desires to cooperate in the areas of agriculture, energy and tourism. Macedonia is open to China regarding new energy exploration and investment. And more and more Chinese tourists visit Macedonia, attaining a growth of 76 percent in the first half of 2015... The Belt and Road Initiatives proposed by China also offers new opportunities for mutually beneficial cooperation." (Ambassador Wen Zhenshub on 4th Summit Meeting of 16+1, November 24, 2015)

This only further validates our belief that the strong political, economic and cultural ties between the two countries will continue in the future, thus also reaffirming the need for learning Chinese in the business community. This development has emphasized the importance and the role which the Confucius Institute has had in this process.

2. Confucius Institute's work: the role and activities

The Confucius Institute at Ss. Cyril and Methodius in Skopje was established in September 2013, in cooperation with Hanban and the partner university Southwestern University of Finance and Economics from Chengdu. The main goal of the Confucius Institute (CI) is to promote studying the Chinese language and culture, as well as to facilitate the cooperation of the two universities and countries in different areas like education, culture and business.

The Confucius Institute started giving Chinese language classes in November 2013. At first it offered only beginner's level Chinese language courses, but as the interest in the Chinese language grew, intermediate level Chinese and Business Chinese were offered. The teachers who conduct the lessons are from China, and they are recruited through the Hanban teacher network on a year or two-year basis. The Chinese classes are conducted by Chinese teachers with the use of English as the language of instruction. Thus, Macedonian students learn Chinese via another foreign language. We use different kinds of textbooks, teaching materials and multimedia aids which are provided by Hanban. These teaching materials are also in English.

Currently, the Confucius Institute provides Chinese language classes and tends to the needs of around 300 students of all ages. The classes are organized and held at several different teaching locations in Skopje. Primarily, the classes take place at the CI, as well as at the Ss. Cyril and Methodius University in Skopje, namely the Faculty of Philology and Faculty of Philosophy. Furthermore, we cooperate with the Ss. Cyril and Methodius elementary school and NOVA International high school, where Chinese is an extra curriculum class and an elective class, respectively.

The intensification of the cooperation between the business sectors of the two countries has helped open up opportunities to expand the work of the Confucius Institute in new fields. In 2015, the CI in cooperation with the Secretariat for European Affairs of the Government of the Republic of Macedonia started providing Chinese language courses for civil servants from various line ministries and state agencies: the Ministry of

Foreign Affairs, the Ministry of Education and Science, the Ministry of Environment and Physical Planning, the General Secretariat of the Government, Prime Minister's Office, the Secretariat for European Affairs, the Financial Police, the Customs Administration, and the Agency for Foreign Investments.

The business community during this period has often turned to the CI for information and consultative services. Big companies from various industries as well as small entrepreneurs reach out to the CI for different kinds of assistance, from procuring quality translation to cultural advice and contacts, as well as Chinese language instruction. While a number of business professionals are enrolled in the regular Chinese courses offered by the CI, the largest wine producer Tikveš requested a specially designed Chinese language course for its mid and upper level management. This course includes instruction and introduction to the Chinese language, Chinese business customs, as well as wine-related terminology and phrases.

3. Research

Based on the above, we set out to determine the extent of the need for the development of culture-specific Chinese business classes. This is due to the demand for Business Chinese in companies and for personal use, a demand we expect will only grow in the future.

For this purpose, we have decided to conduct research to assess the quality and effectiveness of Chinese teaching in Macedonia and solicit suggestions for improving the Chinese courses. In order to have a more comprehensive outlook, we decided to base our research on a multidisciplinary approach which includes both qualitative and quantitative analysis and methodology. We conducted a qualitative analysis of the teaching materials and methodology applied in the CI's Chinese language courses, which includes an overview of the past experience of the teachers and students. We conducted a survey among CI adult students, university students, Macedonian companies, members of the China Macedonia Chamber of Commerce and Chinese companies working in Macedonia as well as government civil servants. We applied the cross-sectional approach, which is best suited for quantitative analysis. According to Larsen-Freeman and Long, it entails "controlled measurement, it is outcome-oriented and generalizable (involves a large group of subjects)" (Larsen-Freeman & Long, 2012, p. 12).

3.1. Qualitative analysis of the teaching materials and methodology

This analysis is based on the written feedback received from the CI students regarding the teaching materials and methodology used by the CI teachers in the Chinese courses, as well as documented experience and insights of the CI teachers in the CI internal reports.

3.2. Teaching materials

The CI's four teachers use *The New Practical Chinese Reader* series of teaching materials in classes for adult students and civil servants. This series is part of Hanban's teaching material program, and has received "the Excellent International Chinese Teaching Materials Award". For the purposes of the business course, the teachers use *Winning in China – Business Chinese* teaching material series.

According to the teachers' assessment, the textbooks are well-written and the accompanying teaching materials are useful. The materials provide a wealth of applicable linguistic and cultural knowledge. The students can learn a lot of basic concepts and grammar structures, while the teaching materials are suitable for different levels. It is important to note that the English explanations are thorough, detailed and easy to understand. The lessons content is interesting, and the vocabulary and grammar sections contain diverse and practical exercises.

Even though the textbooks are very practical, due to the different levels of the student's command of grammatical and linguistic terms, additional explanations and clarifications need to be provided by the teacher. Since English is not the mother tongue of neither the students nor the teachers, the use of dictionaries and other reference materials is required. This takes up quite a lot of valuable class time, which the teacher could use for practicing or learning something new.

The students are not satisfied with the fact that each unit requires learning a great amount of new vocabulary, but not enough time is spent on exercises and practicing sentence patterns and the usage of new words. At times, students are not able to understand cultural references, and the material seems to them as if it is compiled for learners who are learning in China. In this respect, they find it does not meet their needs.

3.3. Teaching methodology

In the classroom, the CI teachers use methodology that attempts to facilitate the learning process for the students by following the principle of moving from simple to complex tasks and from easy to difficult levels.

One of the teachers goes even further, by e-mailing a weekly overview of what was studied in class along with a reminder about homework and tests, thus creating customized additional learning and review material for the students. Other teachers have introduced additional exercises and use visual aids, which they either create or adopt from the Hanban teaching aids. They use these methods in order to enable students to learn creatively and strengthen their motivation.

However, their best efforts are at time thwarted by imposed teaching targets, which cause accelerated speed of teaching, making students fall behind. In general, the students praise the positive attitude, readiness to help and the teaching style of their teachers. However, the most common comment is the need for a slower pace of learning, so the students can master the necessary grammatical knowledge, sentence patterns, vocabulary, speech and pronunciation.

On the other hand, the teachers feel limited within the confines of the traditional classroom, especially in locations that are not part of education institutions. Due to objective reasons, they are not able to use multimedia, which would enable them to convey certain cultural and linguistic knowledge more vividly, quickly, succinctly and effectively.

3.4. Survey of current and potential Chinese learners in Macedonia

As it was mentioned in the introduction, in 2015 we carried out a survey of the students of Chinese, also to assess their needs, views and proposals for the improvement of Chinese instruction in Macedonia. The survey was conducted in various educational institutions, business companies and government agencies, specifically:

1. Education:
   - Confucius Institute at Ss. Cyril and Methodius University in Skopje
   - Faculty of Economics – Ss. Cyril and Methodius University in Skopje
   - University of Southeastern Europe in Tetovo
2. Business:
   - Macedonia China Chamber of Commerce
   - Tikveš wine company
   - SINOHYDRO
   - ZTE
3. Government institutions:
   - General Secretariat of the Government
   - Secretariat for European Affairs
   - Customs Administration
   - Ministry of Environment and Physical Planning

The survey included a total number of 392 subjects, which we consider to be a sufficient and representative sample size for the purposes of our research. As stated previously, these are subdivided into the following categories: students in higher education, business community, civil servants and CI adult students. The following is a breakdown of each category of the subjects by the number of participants and their age:

The first category, students in higher education, consisted of 144 subjects, mainly 93.1% between the ages of 18–20, while only 6.9% were between the ages of 21–30. The business community included 135 respondents, of whom 55% were aged 20–30, while 45% were aged 31–40. Finally, the total of 113 civil servants and adult CI students completed the questionnaire, whose ages ranged 18–60; of those, 19.5% were aged 18–20, 32.7% – 21–30, 27.4% – 31–40, 14.2% – 41–50, and 6.2% – over 50.

The research was conducted via questionnaires which were distributed electronically and on paper. In total, there were 4 types of questionnaires, distributed in 3 languages: Macedonian, English and Chinese:

1. Type 1 questionnaire designed for university students
2. Type 2 questionnaire designed for company employees
3. Type 3 questionnaire designed for company management
4. Type 4 questionnaire designed for existing CI students, including adult students and civil servants.

Each type of questionnaire contained 10 to 12 multiple-choice questions; however, in the interest of brevity and limited space in this paper, we will focus only on the key areas of interest for this research.

4. Survey results

4.1. Business community

Macedonian companies that do business with China and Chinese companies that do business in Macedonia have a need for employees with a working knowledge of Chinese, so they encourage their current staff to enroll in Chinese language classes. A number of these employees are attending the Chinese language courses provided by the CI. However, the Tikveš wine company has approached the CI with a request for a customized Business Chinese course for their mid and senior management. Since China is a big market in which they have important partners, and which they visit frequently, in addition to Chinese language instruction they expressed a need to learn more about the Chinese Business culture. Since the nature of their business entails long working hours and frequent business trips, they needed a more intense and focused course.

Thus, a Chinese volunteer teacher used the *Winning in China – Business Chinese* teaching materials and textbook as a base for the course, supplementing it with materials relating to wine, wine culture and business, and used English as the language of instruction. This is only one example of the level of interest in Business Chinese courses expressed by the business community.

However, in order to assess the need for Chinese language learning at the local Macedonian companies and Chinese companies in Macedonia more fully, the Confucius Institute at the Ss. Cyril and Methodius University in Skopje conducted a survey with a questionnaire. The CI asked for the assistance of the Macedonian Chamber of Commerce to reach out to Macedonian companies working with China to fill in the questionnaire. Furthermore, the questionnaire was sent by e-mail to Chinese companies in Macedonia, which include Huawei, ZTE and SINOHYDRO. In total, 168 questionnaires were sent out, of which 135 were filled in completely, from which data presented below was extracted and a subsequent analysis was made.

The questions that were most conducive to the purposes of our research can be divided into three groups: 1. Reasons for learning Chinese; 2. Expectations from the course; and 3. Structure of the course. From the information contained in the survey's questionnaire, there is a realistic need for Chinese language courses expressed by both the Macedonian local companies and Chinese companies in Macedonia, which indicates a necessity and possibility for these kinds of courses. The information in the questionnaires also shows that managers of these companies would like to learn Chinese as well. As can be seen in Figure 1, the motivation behind learning Chinese is almost equally divided between the interest in the language and the necessity of knowing Chinese for the purposes of work. This shows both the rising popularity of the Chinese language

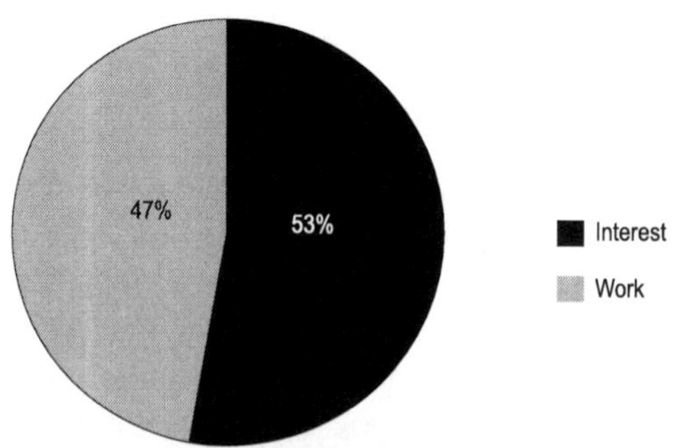

Figure 1: Reasons for studying Chinese

and culture in Macedonia and the region, and the ever-increasing presence of Chinese business in Europe, which requires better knowledge of Chinese in order to have better communication with Chinese companies, thus improving business relations.

The obtained data about the content of the course shows that the survey participants are equally interested in the Chinese culture and the Chinese language, which means that language and culture will have to be integrated equally in the course materials, and taught in class. At the same time, the classes need to be supplemented with events and activities rich in subjects pertaining to the Chinese culture, organized by the CI, which will enable students to experience and understand the different aspects of the Chinese culture and nurture their commitment to studying the Chinese language. However, the survey shows that the area the respondents are most interested in during the course is business Chinese, with 40% of the respondents providing this answer (Figure 2). This was expected and understandable, since their main motivation for studying Chinese is the ability to apply it at work.

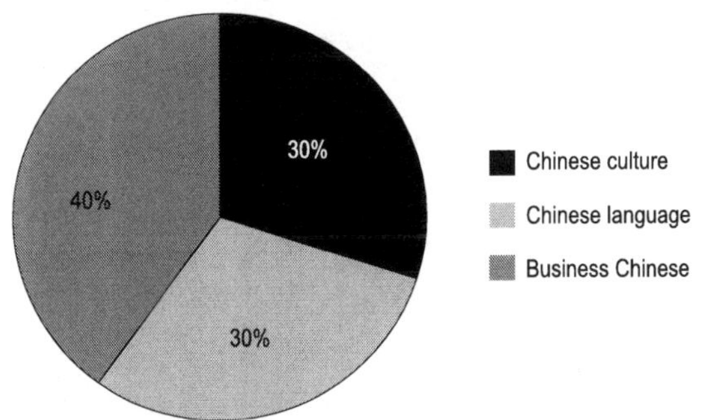

Figure 2: Preferred course content

The preferred frequency of the classes (45 min/class) is 2 classes per week (Figure 3), with 80% saying that this is the structure of the course best suited for them. This is due to the fact that more than 2 classes per week do not leave them with enough time to study, review, acquire and absorb the material, combined with their work obligations during the week. On the other hand, less than 2 classes per week would cover very little material and would not provide enough time for practical work during classes. All of this leads us to conclude that the overall language acquisition process would be too slow and insufficient to ensure adequate improvement of language skills and knowledge.

Over 90% of the participants (Figure 4) expressed a preference for a local Chinese language teacher that would use Macedonian as the in-

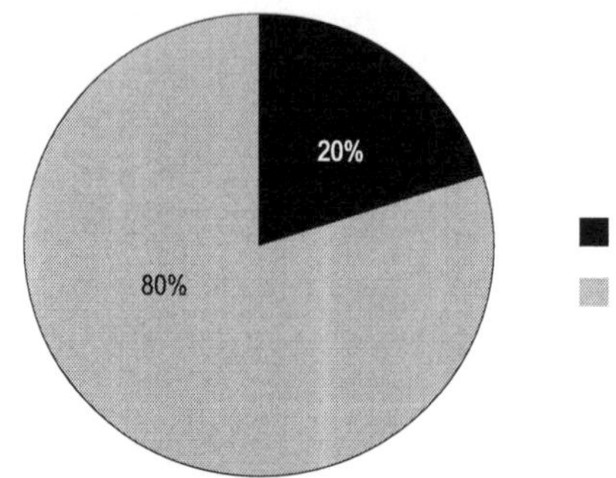

Figure 3: Preferred number of classes per week

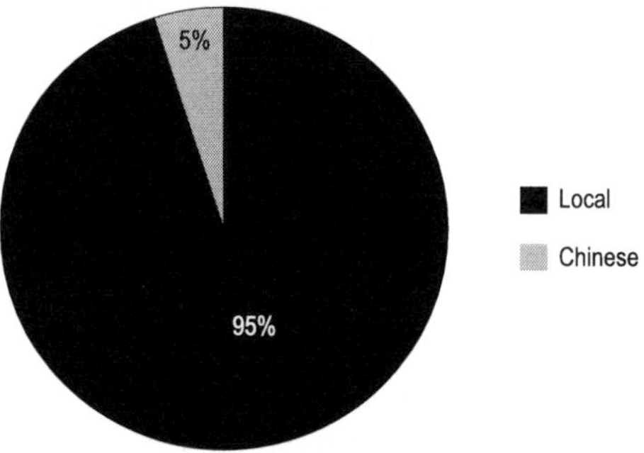

Figure 4: Chinese language teacher preference

struction language to teach them Chinese. This is quite an overwhelming response, which cannot be overlooked when designing and organizing courses for the business community. This creates immediacy for the Confucius Institute to increase its efforts to train competent local teachers in the foreseeable future, as well as to expand and upgrade the teaching capacity of the Confucius Institute.

4.2. Government (civil servants) and CI adult groups

We also conducted a survey among a wider range of students which are not specifically focused on Business Chinese. This category includes one homogenous group of civil servants, and a heterogeneous group of adults with different backgrounds that attend the CI classes. The age structure is quite wide-ranging and comprehensive, including students from the ages of 18 up to the age of 60, which shows that all generations and people from all walks of life are interested in studying the Chinese language and culture. This is why we consider their answers to be quite beneficial, as well as representative and indicative of what is expected and needed by the Macedonian public with regard to the services and courses provided by the Confucius Institute.

The survey consisted of 127 questionnaires, out of which 113 were fully answered and could be used for our research. The set of questions was similar to the ones submitted to the business community, thus making it suitable for comparison and a wider analysis. The data was collected and aggregated as a whole, but the professional structure of the subjects was as follows: civil servants – 39.8%, students – 31.9%, teachers – 5.3%, businessmen – 3.5%, technical staff – 1.8%, and other – 0.9%.

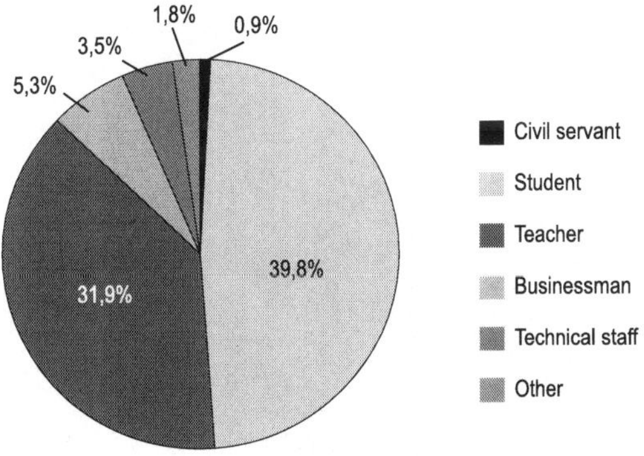

Figure 5: Professional profiles of the respondents

In our analysis we shall concentrate on the same topics of interest as with the business community in order to make a viable and well-based comparison. Subsequently, with regard to the reason for learning Chinese, the biggest reason chosen is interest (73.4%), the second most popular reason is further development (33.6%), followed by work (8.8%).

With regard to the preferred course content, a large majority of the respondents chose topics centered on learning the Chinese language (88.5%). However, it is worth noting that Chinese culture (61.8%) and Business (20.4%) also received considerable percentage which indicates an expressed interest in these topics.

Regarding the length of the classes, the majority of the students (58%) consider the current arrangement of lessons suitable (civil servant groups: 3 classes per week, NOVA International Secondary School: 3 classes per week, adult groups: 4–6 classes per week). At the same time, there are students (42%) who would like to increase the number of classes per week, so we need to meet the needs of students regarding the number of classes they would like to attend on a weekly basis. Finally, when asked what type of teachers they would prefer, 91.2% answered in favor of native Chinese teachers from China, while 8.8% preferred a local language teacher (Figure 7).

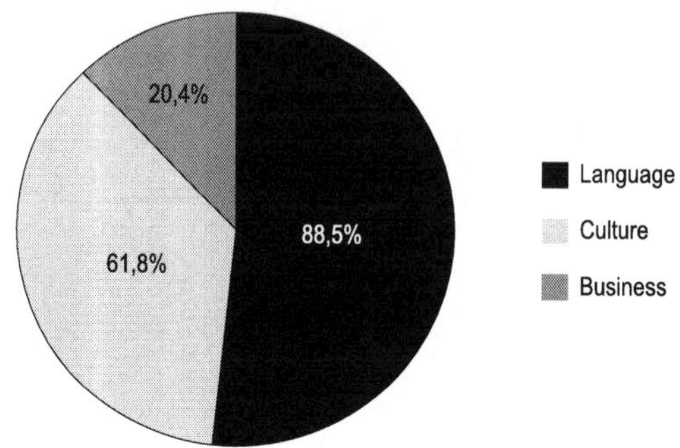

Figure 6: Preferred course content

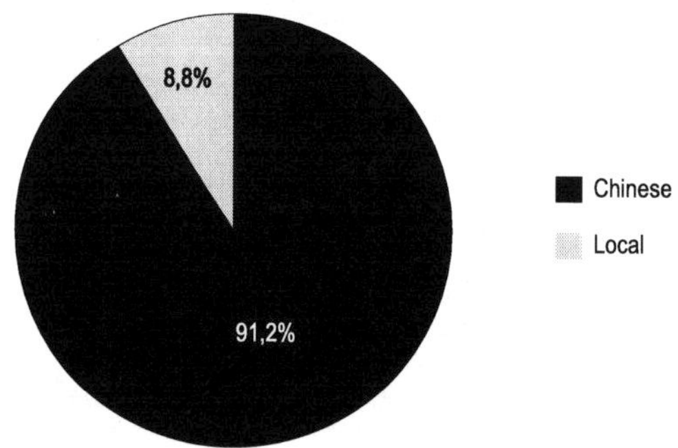

Figure 7: Chinese language teacher preference

4.3. University students

University graduates are the future of the business community and the source of young, creative, ambitious and qualified staff. That is why we decided to include in the survey students with Business and Economics majors from the Faculty of Economics at Ss. Cyril and Methodius University in Skopje (100 survey respondents) and the South East European University in Tetovo (44 survey respondents). The total of 144 students who had not studied Chinese were surveyed in order to assess their interest in learning Chinese and ultimately determine if there was a need for Business Chinese courses, and if so, how large.

Based on the replies to the survey, 72% are interested in China and 34% would like to go to China. However, only 48.6% of the respondents would like to learn Chinese. Out of the 51.4% that are not interested in

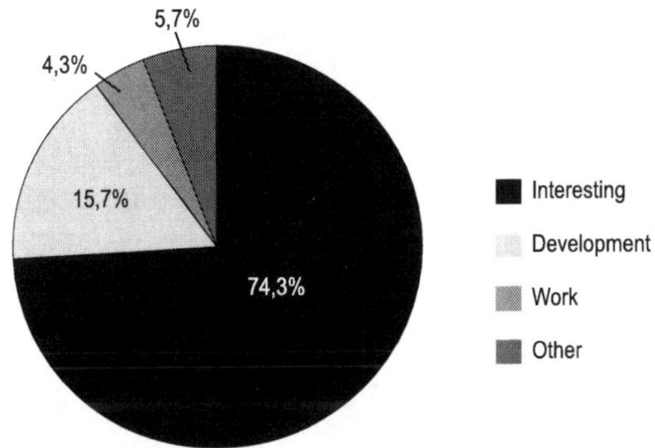

Figure 8: Reasons for learning Chinese

Chinese, 50% cite "not interesting" as a reason for not wanting to learn Chinese, while 32.4% claim there is "no benefit" in learning the language and 12.2% say they do not have the time. This means that in our future promotion of Chinese language courses targeted at this group, the CI will have to highlight and demonstrate the interesting and practical aspects of learning Chinese.

The respondents that are interested in studying Chinese have listed the following reasons: 74.3% consider it to be an interesting endeavor, 15.7% want to learn because of their future development, 4.3% would learn for work, and the rest (5.7%) have cited "other" as a reason (Figure 8).

The topics and content that the interested students would like to focus on in their Chinese courses are as follows: Chinese language – 45.7%, Chinese culture – 42.9%, and only 7.1% would like Business content.

Regarding the preferred number of classes per week, 71.4% consider 2 classes per week as most suitable, 10% would like one class per week and 8.6% would prefer 1.5 classes per week.

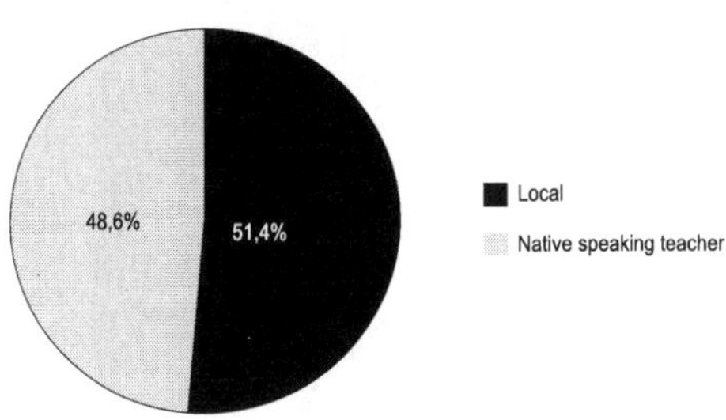

Figure 9: Chinese language teacher preference

Unlike the two previous groups that predominantly preferred either a local Macedonian teacher or a native speaking Chinese teacher, this group is fairly divided in this regard, with 51.4% who would prefer a local Macedonian teacher, and 48.6% who would prefer a native speaking teacher (Figure 9). Based on this feedback, the CI could consider establishing a course where both a local teacher and a native speaker would teach one class, so that students could benefit from the native speaker introducing the basics of the Chinese language and focusing on speaking and culture.

5. Summary

In the previous part of the paper, we provided an overview of the situation with Chinese classes, the feedback and recognized needs for improvement and developing new teaching services that will ultimately contribute to the cooperation of education and the development and expansion of business opportunities for individuals, entities and companies from both countries. Now, we would like to propose strategies, measures and activities that could be implemented in the coming period for the purpose of expanding the role of the Confucius Institute in Macedonia.

5.1. Proposed strategies: moving forward

When selecting volunteers and teachers from China, preference should be given to candidates with a strong command of a foreign language, especially to candidates with working knowledge of other European languages, especially Slavic languages. The Beijing Foreign Studies University is in the process of setting up a course for teaching the Macedonian language, so in the future volunteers should primarily be selected from this pool of students. During the training conducted before the selected teachers and volunteers leave for their posts, the future teachers should undergo country-specific local language training.

We should also consider investing resources in developing local qualified Chinese language teachers. We have the opportunity to select ambitious and willing candidates from the Macedonian students studying Chinese in Macedonia and/or China. This would require developing in-house training and also arranging for them to visit China to receive language teacher training.

Along with developing local teaching talents, continuous efforts should be made to develop local teaching and reference materials. Chinese language teaching materials should be compiled, which suit the particular needs of the students of the Macedonian Confucius Institute. This would make it easier for them to learn the target language by making references to familiar topics related to Macedonian culture, habits and customs in Chinese.

Based on the data from the survey, we can conclude that the teaching methods should entirely be learner-centered and guided by the students' needs. If the aim is successful target language acquisition, more emphasis should be placed on the communicative function while obtaining firm grasp of the language structure. Due to the differences in age, professional commitments, interests, motivation, availability and ability, etc. within the groups attending the regular CI language courses, there is a need for more diverse content to be included. We feel that this would help students to better understand the Chinese culture and society so they can use Chinese more effectively. Most importantly, though, the subject needs to be delivered in a dynamic way and with the use of multiple teaching and media platforms, like smartphone apps, e.g. Hanban's free online courses are ideal for individual study.

As the need for Business Chinese courses has been explored and showcased by the survey, the CI needs to devote resources to developing not just business courses, but industry-specific courses that will cater to the specific needs of business professionals. Furthermore, beside business and culture content, these courses need to be structured in a cyclical way that will enable constant review of the language structure and function together with cultural and industry-related information. Based on the CI's experience, business professionals, due to their professional commitments, tend to be plagued by time constraints, business travel and changing schedules, which leads to missed lessons and time lapses between tutorials. Consequently, a course that has a linear structure would be detrimental to successful target language acquisition.

In order to offer better services, the CI needs to establish and maintain strategic partnerships and cooperation with institutions that have similar goals and cater to the same communities. The cooperation with the Macedonia China Chamber of Commerce provides their members (over 1000 companies) with direct access to the CI services, and gives CI the opportunity to expand its reach and influence to the business community. On the other hand, the cooperation with the Faculty of Economics at Ss. Cyril and Methodius University provides scholarships for the students and gives them the opportunity to experience firsthand, both in theory and practice, the Chinese economy, which in turn helps CI perform its role as a promoter of education, culture and business cooperation, and understanding.

6. Conclusion

We hope that the research results presented in this paper will contribute to the improvement of the quality of Chinese language teaching, impact subsequent design of Business Chinese reference materials and ultimately lead to the creation of new business opportunities. Finally, future research may use our work as basis for more comprehensive studies of this subject to contribute to the development of Chinese studies in the Republic of Macedonia.

References

Larsen-Freeman, D., Long, M.H. (1991). *An Introduction to Second Language Acquisition Research*. London: Longman.

Liu Xun (刘珣) (2012). *Xin shiyong Hanyu keben* (新实用汉语课本: *The New Practical Chinese Reader*). Beijing: Beijing Yuyan Daxue chubanshe.

Ji Jin (季瑾) (2011).*Ying zai Zhongguo – Shangwu Hanyu xilie jiaocheng* (赢在中国 – 商务汉语系列教程: *Winning in China – Business Chinese*). Beijing: Beijing Yuyan Daxue chubanshe.

Bilateral Relations, Embassy of the PR China in the Republic of Macedonia. Retrieved from: http://mk.chineseembassy.org/eng/zmgx/t374485.htm.

Diplomatic Relations with the PR China, Ministry of Foreign Affairs of the Republic of Macedonia. Retrieved from: http://www.mfa.gov.mk/index.php/mk/nadvoresna-politika/bilateralni-odnosi/vonevropski.

Ambassador Wen Zhenshun on 4th Summit Meeting of 16+1. Retrieved from: http://mk2.mofcom.gov.cn/article/chinanews/201512/20151201199928.shtml.

Stanislav Južnič

Education in Transition of China-Based Jesuits from the Austrian Province

The publications and readings of China-based Jesuits' provide a deep insight into their know-how in light of statistical and historical analysis (Južnič, 2015, p. 126). The Social Network and Academic Genealogy of China-based Jesuit mathematicians and physicists uncovers the way they were educated in Europe. The Academic Genealogy of China-based Jesuits is a comparatively new approach offered in this article. For the time being, the research is limited to the data concerning China-based Jesuits from the Old Society of Jesus in the Austrian and Bohemian Jesuit provinces and to Tyrolean part of the Upper German Jesuit province, which is geographically situated on the territory of modern Austria and Italy. The aim is to get an insight into China-based Jesuits who came from the political unit of Habsburg-hereditary Mid-European lands (*Österreichische Erblande*), acquired by the Habsburgs in 1278, and from the Lands of the Bohemian Crown, annexed in 1526.

The political borders in those times do not quite match the borders of Jesuit provinces. In a broader sense, the *Österreichische Erblande* consisted of the Archduchy of Austria (Upper Austria and Lower Austria), Inner Austria, and the County of Tyrol. The Lands of the Bohemian Crown were a separate unit. The modern areas of *Österreichische Erblande* are the states of Austria, Slovenia, Northwestern Croatia with Istria, and Northeastern Italy. The modern area of the greatest part of the Lands of the Bohemian Crown is the state of Bohemia, but its northern part now belongs to the Southeast Germany and Southwest Poland. The previously independent Crown-lands of Bohemia and the Hungarian Monarchy were both incorporated into the Habsburg Empire in 1526, but Bohemian contributions to the Chinese Jesuit missions were much greater because Jesuits from the Hungarian Kingdom did missionary work in their neighboring Turkish lands. In contrast, there were at least thirty-seven Hungarian and five Romanian Jesuits who successfully worked in China in 20th century. Another contrast is that many Croatian Jesuits from the Old Society worked in the Americas, including Ivan Ratkaj, Ferdinand Konšćak, Ignacije Szentmartony, and Franjo Ksaver Haller. Ivan Ureman (Vreman, Wo Jowang Tchan-Yu, * April 6, 1583 Split; SJ February 1, 1600 Rome; † April 22, 1621 Nanking) was the only Croatian sent to China, but he was born in Split under the Venetian rule and therefore not directly connected with the Continental Kingdom of Croatia in the Austrian Jesuit province. He studied in Rome under Clavius and Grienberger, put down his roots in China in 1615, and lived mostly in Macao. Kircher in Rome published Ureman's travel notes on the magnetic declination. The Jesuits from the Old Society in the Bohemian Crownlands preferred destinations opposite to the ones favored by Croatians because at least eight of them went to China, and only the Moravian Valentin Stansel (* 1621 Olomouc; † 1705) and few others served in the Americas. In the southeast, the Austrian province of Jesuits included the Hungarian Kingdom's part of the Habsburg Monarchy with lands which belong to the modern states of Hungary, Slovakia, Croatia, Northern Serbia (Vojvodina), Romania, and Western Ukraine (Trans-Carpathia, or Zakarpattia) with the Jesuit College in Uzhhorod (Ужгород). To be sure, the Kingdom of Croatia was in a formal personal union with the Kingdom of Hungary, although in reality Croatia was in a subordinate position. Strange as it may be, the Hungarian part of the Habsburg Empire provided no China-based Jesuits from the Old Society.

Politically speaking, the areas in question included the Habsburg possessions of the Archduchy of Austria, Inner Austria, the County of Tyrol, and the Lands of the Bohemian Crown. The border of the Austrian province of Jesuits from the Old Society was not identical to the border of the Austrian part of the Habsburg Empire. In the European history, the church-related borders responded to the political changes with considerable delay. The modern Bavarian town of Passau and its surroundings belonged to the Austrian Jesuit province, as did its most-north-western part. Trieste and Gorizia with Friuli which today are part of modern Italy used to belong to the Austrian province of the Jesuits from the Old Society as its Southwest part.

The Austrian province of the Jesuits from Old Society changed its borders during the two centuries of its operation from 1551 to 1773. The College of Vienna was established in 1551, but it belonged to the province of Germania until 1556. In 1663 the German province was divided into the Lower German province and the Upper German (Germania superior) province with Vienna, Prague and Ingolstadt colleges. In 1563, the Upper German province was divided into the Austrian province, which included Vienna, Prague, and Trnava colleges, and the Upper German province with Trident (Trento), Hall, Ingolstadt, Munich, and Innsbruck colleges (http://www.encyclopedia.com/doc/1G2–3404900484.html, accessed: 5/09/2015; Dehergne, 1973, p. 277; Dolmanits, 1991, p. 2). Today, the ancient province of Tyrol is divided among the modern states of Italy and Austria. The Bohemian Jesuit province with colleges in Bohemia, Moravia and (Moravian and Polish) Silesia was created from the Austrian Jesuit province during the early stages of the Thirty Years War in 1622/23. The China-based members of the Austrian and Bohemian Jesuit provinces are examined in detail in the present work, as well as the China-based Jesuits from Tyrol, which belonged to the Upper German province. The Jesuits of the Bohemian Crown lands within the borders of modern Republic of Bohemia with Silesian areas originally belonged to the German Province and after 1563 to the Austrian province. The old Bohemian province was one of the strongest among all Jesuit provinces, and many of its members were active overseas missionaries. The Bohemian Jesuit province was geographically much smaller compared to the Austrian Jesuit province, from which it separated. The Austrian province kept fourteen colleges (Vienna, Passau, Linz, Krems, Graz, Leoben, Judenburg, Klagenfurt, Ljubljana, Trieste, Gorizia, Trnava, Humenné, and Zagreb), while the Bohemian province had twice as less colleges, namely seven: Jičín (Giczin), Prague, Chomutov, Český Krumlov, and Jindřichiv Hradec in Bohemia and Brno as well as Olomouc in Moravia. The Bohemian province incorporated colleges of Klodzko, established in 1598, and Nysa from Polish Silesia, and later on the college of Wroclaw as well. Today, those three towns belong to Poland (Lukács, 1978, 1: 2*-3*, 42*; Lukács, 1982, 2: 3*), but their colleges were excluded from the Bohemian Jesuit province after the Prussian occupation of Silesia in 1742. The Bohemian province had some regular scholars in Leipzig and Dresden, but none in Prussian Wroclaw, Klodzko, and Nysa in 1773. The Mid-European geopolitical situation was always very complicated with different nations using different names for the same urban centers. In spite of efforts led by Jesuits, Bohemia became the most secular state in Europe.

Most of the Jesuits from the Austrian and Bohemian provinces joined the Society in Vienna, Leoben in Styria, Trenčin, or Brno, but frequently also Graz, Linz, Klagenfurt, Ljubljana, or other colleges. The biggest colleges for novices in the Austrian and Bohemian provinces worked in Slovakian Trenčin, Vienna, and Moravian Brno, but none of them in Bohemia. The professors of the third approbation provided the third (final) approbation in Vienna, Judenburg, Slovakian Banská Bystrica, Bohemian

Jičín (Giczin), or Moravian Telč (Telczi, Telczen) in 1772–1773. The houses of the professors with third approbations were only in Vienna and Prague in 1773. They offered rooms to distinguished guests, for example to Bošković during his stay in Vienna. In 1718–1773, the most important university colleges for which the Jesuit catalogues listed affiliated students were in Vienna, Graz, Košice, Trnava, Prague, and Olomouc, although courses were also offered in smaller colleges of Austrian Province. In 1772, the repetitions-specialization in mathematics with a chair for their professor, separate chairs for the prefects of mathematical museums and for the prefects of observatories with their assistants were offered in Graz, Trnava, Vienna, Olomouc, and in the Clementinum in Prague. The humanities specialization was offered in Hungarian Györ, Slovakian Skalica, Czech Klatovy (Glattovia), Moravian Uherské Hradiště, Brzeźnica (Brzezniz) southwest of Krakow, and in Vienna, where Jesuits offered specialization in linguistics. It is oblivious that the Jesuits paid special attention to the traditional geographical borders and also to the linguistic particularities. Therefore, the main educational institutions were distributed in fair shares in the traditional units of Austria, Hungary, Bohemia, and Moravia with the single exception of Moravian Brno novitiate, which also worked for the Czech and Silesian parts of the Bohemian Province. Vienna was certainly somewhat privileged, as beside the Viennese chairs and institutions, similar ones usually existed in Graz, Leoben, or Judenburg in Styria of the Inner Austria (*Catalogus... Austriae*, 1718, 1772; *Catalogus... Bohemiae*, 1710, 1773).

Previous scholarship on China based Jesuits education

Tracing European educational patterns and connecting them to the network of China-based Jesuits is not a new idea. Ugo Baldini has already identified the native places and the *alma mater* of the Jesuits who taught in Macao. In his dissertation, Vermote used the geographical term "Central European States" (Germany, Austria, Poland, Tyrol, and South Tyrol), which cover a broader area beside the Habsburg Monarchy, i.e. the central and northern parts of Germany and Poland. Vermote's Austria also covers the Lands of Bohemian Crown and the Hungarian Monarchy. According to Vermote, the number of Jesuits sent to China from "Central European States" in 18th century was 65. On average, 63% of the Jesuits sent to China were redirected or died on-board according to Vermote's calculations based on Dutei, Standaert, Wicki, and Dehergne's numbers. In the Mid-European case, 23% of the Jesuits sent to China were redirected, 23% died on-board, and 53% made it to the destination. Therefore, Mid-Europeans sent to China reached their destination much more often compared to the others.

Research method seen through the mid-european system of Jesuit education for future China-based missionaries

The bibliometrical analysis can provide some statistical insights into the supposed change of Beijing Jesuits from the full-time preachers to part-time scientists in 18th century (Baldini, 2008, pp. 55, 74, 78–79; Golvers, 2013; Vermote, 2013, pp. 29–30, 91, 93, 152–153, 275; Duteil, 1994; Standaert, 2001; Wicki, 1967). Another useful illustration of the change of approach of the Chinese Jesuits towards their own scientific achievements is the insight into their European training in mathematical sciences. The Social network analysis based on the academic genealogy of mathematically-trained China-based Jesuits gave additional insight into the supposed dynamics of the scientific research conducted by China-based Jesuits. The (European) Jesuits' educational system was a rigid one, but it did change with time. An 18th century China-based Jesuit was certainly not educated in the same scientific spirit as his predecessors.

The standard in those cases is that the academic predecessor of an individual is (are) his thesis advisor(s). In the special case of (China-based) Jesuits' mathematical sciences, two main points are taken into account when it comes to their education. The first of them were the philosophical studies of the individuals. In the first year of the triennium of the philosophical studies, called "logic", the student learned most of his mathematics from a professor of mathematics. The (applied) mathematics of those times covered all calculable aspects of the Natural Sciences, including geometrical optics, large parts of mechanics, including hydromechanics, and acoustics. The astrology of the earlier times dealt with all the numerical aspects of astronomy before some wild astrological predictions on the Pope's behalf caused the removal of astrology from University curricula after the papal bull of Sixtus V. During the second year of their triennium of philosophical studies, which was called "physics", the student learned physics with some chemistry, biology, meteorology, and astronomy included. The professors of physics usually had a great surplus of educational materials and the student was often unable to deal with all of it during one academic year. Therefore, he had to finish his physics lectures in the last (third) year of philosophical studies, called "metaphysics".

An individual Jesuit is presented as an academic descendant of his professors of mathematics in his first year of philosophical studies, and of his professors of physics in his second year of philosophical studies, although in some periods mathematics could be taught also in the second year of philosophical studies. It must be taken into account that in those times mathematics covered considerable aspects which today belong to physics, namely applied mathematics of mechanics and optics. More importantly, Jesuit professors of mathematics behaved like modern professionals and taught their subject for several years, while Jesuit professors of physics before 1750s taught triennium (logic-physics-metaphysics) and often switched to theological chairs or to high administrative posts after providing a triennium or two of philosophy. Advanced posts were available for mathematics professors, including chairs of the professors of repeaters of mathematics, curators of mathematical and astronomical museums (laboratories or observatories), sometimes with assistants called *socius*, but only in the main universities of Vienna, Graz, Trnava, Olomouc, and Prague. On the other hand, no Jesuit higher philosophical studies worked without the professor of philosophy who taught physics in the second year, but some colleges saved money with an empty chair for mathematics. For example, the college of Ljubljana did not hire professors of mathematics from 1718/19 to 1742/43 and from 1744/45 to 1746/47.

Jesuits had to finish their studies of triennium of philosophy before they began their studies of theology. The philosophical triennium was also necessary for the studies of medicine or law in Catholic Universities before 19th century, but Jesuits usually completed theological faculties. Even future Jesuits working as Far East Royal Physicians, like J. Koffler, did not study medicine in Europe. They went through ordinary Jesuit training of philosophy and theology and only later did they specialize in medicine. Hallerstein's travel companion, Carolus Slamenski, who had served Transylvanian dragoons as surgeon-major and entered the Jesuit Order in a comparatively advanced age, did not complete the faculty of medicine. In his times, Habsburg surgeons did not need to receive higher education from medical faculties before the reforms of Gerard van Swieten (* 1700; † 1772).

The other academic predecessor of an individual could be his professor of the repeaters of mathematics if the individual served as a repeater of mathematics during his pedagogical praxis after he finished his philosophical studies and before he began his theological studies. The specialization of the repeaters of mathematic was provided for masters of arts who had previously obtained a bachelor's degree of philosophy and the *venia docendi* (privatdozent) title. Professors of the repeaters of mathematics usually kept their posts for several years and guided the specialization of four up to dozen repeaters of mathematics per one academic year. They served only in the best universities of the Austrian and Bohemian Jesuit provinces in Vienna, Graz, Trnava, Olomouc, and Prague. The topic which their masters-repeaters specialized in was applied mathematics and they endorsed many questions which today belong to physics and other related sciences. In the academic genealogy, the professor of the repeaters of mathematics is treated as a more important predecessor of his student-master of philosophy, who practiced under the guidance of a professor of the repeaters of mathematics at least two years after he finished his studies of physics. Usually, an individual repeated mathematics for one academic year, but during the reform in 1750s, many repeaters of mathematics in Habsburg Universities served for two years. Of course not all China-based Jesuits had previously repeated mathematics, but many of them had, including Hallerstein and Laimbeckhoven, who had additionally been trained in mathematical-astronomical sciences in Portugal before they embarked for China.

European training of the future China-based Jesuits in mathematical sciences

It is evident that the older generation of China-based Jesuits from the Austrian Jesuit province, including Johannes Grueber and Fridelli, belonged to the same educational milieu as Swiss Paul Guldin and his Carniola collaborator Kobav at the Jesuit University of Graz. Their contemporaries, the future China-based Jesuits Koffler and J. Grueber's travel companion Diestel, also studied in Graz. But their professor of mathematics, Durandus, originally came from the Low Countries (the Netherlands) as did Durandus' professors, Saint-Vincent and d'Aguillon. Koffler's younger classmate, Philippus Miller (Müller), taught China missionaries Herdtrich and Johannes Grueber, and also Michael Heiniz. Heinz taught Fridelli's teacher, Paul Hansiz. Hansiz taught professor Amartina from Friuli and also Ernest Vols, who was a teacher of Hallerstein and Laimbeckhoven's professor, Franz Schmelzer. The Belgium and Luxemburg Habsburg province developed a broader influence on the Mid-European Habsburg education only a century after the Peace of Utrecht (1713), when Boerhaave's student at the University of Leyden, Gerhard van Swieten, reformed the technical-scientific part of the educational system in the Habsburg Monarchy. The academic genealogies of China-based Jesuits clearly show that the Belgian educators were instrumental in the Mid-European part of the Habsburg Monarchy already during the Thirty Years War.

The new (last) generation of the China-based Old Society of Jesus from the Austrian Jesuit province, including Hallerstein and Laimbeckhoven, was educated at the Viennese University. They repeated mathematical lectures in Vienna under the guidance of professor of the repeaters of mathematics Schmelzer, who was a student at Vols, Hansiz, Heiniz and Kobav, as Johannes Grueber and Fridelli were. Schmelzer and his Graz professor of physics, Müetinger, also repeated mathematical lectures with the students in Graz. But Müetinger's professor of the repeaters of mathematics, Luz, studied physics in the slightly different educational tradition of the Hungarian-Slovakian University of Trnava, where Gabriel Grueber was also later educated as a repeater of mathematical lectures. Trnava certainly also belonged to the Austrian Jesuit province, but its approach to mathematical sciences, especially to astronomy, was more sophisticated in Trnava compared to Graz, where the Jesuit observatory never produced any groundbreaking discoveries. G. Grueber's Trnava professor of the repeaters of mathematics was a famous astronomer, Franz Xavier Weiss, Bošković's follower and collaborator of Hallerstein's Viennese editor, Maximilian Hell (Udías, 2000, p. 160; Inglot, 2012, p. 230; Standaert, 2001, p. 731).

The mid-18th century was a turning point in Jesuit science and education, but it happened too late to save their order from suppression. The academic genealogy of China-Based Jesuits was used to illustrate the changes in the world view which they brought with them to China. The case study was limited to the Jesuits born or educated in the Austrian and Bohemian provinces and Tyrol. The group did not include many China-Based Jesuits, but some of those were extremely influential and their development probably has some relevance worldwide. There was evidently some transformation from the early education of the Jesuits from the Austrian province at the University of Graz, influenced by the experts from the Low Countries, to the later Viennese education, which had been based on the domestic forces before the Peace of Utrecht enabled the arrival of a new wave of experts from the Low Countries, including the physicians van Swieten, Jacquin and Jan Ingenhousz, trained in the universities of Leiden and Leuven. Speaking from the standpoint of science, the later China-Based Jesuits from the Habsburg Monarchy accepted some aspect of local research framework, which in second part of 18th century developed under influence of Bošković, who taught in the Habsburg universities of Pavia and Brera-Milano. The exact difference of this framework compared to other European centers was not easy to define before Bošković influenced physics in the Habsburg Monarchy. The China-Based Jesuit mission was eventually suppressed very soon after Bošković's ideas were widely accepted in almost all universities in the Habsburg Monarchy. Additionally, Bošković was never in Portugal and he was almost exclusively extremely popular only in the countries he personally visited during his many travels. Bošković' unpopularity in Portugal certainly influenced the spread of his ideas into the China-based Portuguese Jesuit mission. The Portuguese suppressed the Society of Jesus in their mainland and in their colonies in 1759, only few months after Bošković main book *Theoria Philosophiae...* was printed in Vienna in 1758, and before its second, more relevant edition was published in Venice in 1763. The Jesuits were suppressed in France in 1762 but even earlier d'Alembert and his group had heavily criticized Bošković, which directly influenced China-based Jesuits of the French mission because they were closely connected to the French academy.

Koffler

Andreas Xavier Wolfgang Koffler studied mathematics with Durandus. His teacher of physics was Zacharias Trinkelius from Bratislava in the Austrian Jesuit province. The total of twenty-three of his academic predecessors were identified, only seven of them born in the Austrian Jesuit province. Obliviously, he matured in an extremely international educational framework.

Picture 1: Andreas Xavier Wolfgang Koffler
Source: archive of the Author.

Johannes Grueber and his Travel Companion Diestel

Johannes Grueber was eventually one of the oldest and most influential China-based Jesuits from the Austrian province. He was born around Linz not far from Amstetten, where the grandfather of his relative Jesuit general, Gabriel Grueber (* 1740), was born.

Johannes Grueber's academic predecessors included many professors from outside the Austrian Jesuit province, besides Pedro Nonius, Clavius of Bamberg, The Belgians were Brussels-Bruges born Durandus, Saint-Vincent, and d'Aguilon. Among them was the professor of physics from Vienna (1604), Georg Elfinstonis from Scotland, Sigismundus Mogilnicki from Mogielnica in Poland, Volfgang Quelmetz (Quelmitz) from Meissen in Saxony, Johannes (Heumondt) Heumont from Lorraine, and Thomas Williams from Oxford. Among his sixteen predecessors, ten were born outside the Austrian Jesuits province.

Johannes Grueber's travel companion Diestel had similar academic predecessors to those of Johannes Grueber, except that his professor of physics was Paulus Rosmer (* 1605 Maastricht in Limburg). As of today, none of Diestel's known six academic predecessors from four generations was born in the Austrian province.

Herdtrich

Other examples of Mid-European academic (mathematical) predecessors of the Jesuits who later embarked for China were provided. One of them was a Viennese student of philosophy, Christian Wolfgang Herdtrich (* 1625; † 1684), who had thirty-one academic ancestors available. Among them was Georg Sigismundus from Litomyšl in Bohemia, which was separated from the Austrian Jesuit province shortly before Sigismundus' death. Sigismundus' teacher of physics was Adam Prionius from Kalisz in Poland. Other Herdtrich's academic predecessors outside the Austrian Jesuit province include Phrearius from German Henningen, Wright from English York, Sittarus from Jüllich west of Köln, Millius from Worms in German Pfalz (Palatinate), Georgius Vanderboom from Delft in Holland, Laelius from Priverno southwest of Rome, Guielmus Jonstonis from Newburgh in Scotland, Cossubus from Pischkowitz in Polish Silesia, and Michael Hagen from Viterne in Lorrain. Among his academic predecessors were also ten "foreign" professors who taught J. Gruebers' predecessors: Pedro Nonius, Clavius of Bamberg, and Brussels-Bruges born Belgians Durandus, Saint-Vincent, and d'Aguilon. Herdtrich's academic predecessors were also: the professor of physics in 1604 in Vienna, Georg Elfinstonis from Scotland,

Sigismundus Mogilnicki from Mogielnica in Poland, Volfgang Quelmetz (Quelmitz) from Meissen in Saxony, Joannes (Heumondt) Heumont from Lorraine, and Thomas Williams from Oxford. Therefore, Herdtrich's twenty academic predecessors outside the Austrian Jesuit province are available if we leave out Bohemian Sigismundus, which was at least 65%. If we take just five generations of Herdtrich's academic predecessors into account, we have twenty-seven professors. Of that number, seventeen were born outside the Austrian Jesuit province.

Fridelli and Mesar (Messari)

Fridelli's teacher of mathematics was Scaletari from Gorizia. Scaletari's academic predecessors were mostly from the Austrian Jesuit province. Fifteen of them in total, Scaletrari included, qualify as academic predecessors of Fridelli over five generations. Only four other were not born in the Austrian province, if we do not take into account the Bohemian Sigismundis, who was among them.

Fridelli repeated mathematics in 1607 under the guidance of Professor Paul Hansiz. Thirteen of his academic predecessors were identified, among them six born outside the Austrian province.

During Mesar's (Messari) studies in humanities in Gorizia, the teacher of philosophy and physics in Gorizia in the period between 1593 and 1695 was Valentino Amartina, born in Tricesimo north of Udine in the domain of Venice. Johan Baptist Mesar continued his studies in Graz, where his older brother Johan Paul studied rhetoric in 1681. Johan Baptist Mesar's classmate was Johan Baptist Praeschern, who later taught physics in Trieste, Gorizia, Zagreb, and Graz. Praeshern translated the anti-astrological work of an Italian Jesuit, Giovanni Pietro Pinamonti (* 1632; † 1703), into Latin in support of the papal bull of Sixtus V against judicial astrology in 1586. Pinamonti relied on the work of his fellow Bolognese Jesuit Riccioli, but he also briefly mentioned Copernicus, Peter Appian and King Alfonso. For one year, Mesar and Praeshern's younger classmate was Sigismund (Georg) Jenschiz (Jentschiz, Jenčič) from Kočevje, who taught physics in Ljubljana in 1714/15 and published his exam theses.

Among the five generations of Johan Baptist Mesar (Messari) and Praeshern's academic predecessors, we find eleven Jesuits born in the areas of the Austrian province, including Cluj in Transylvania, three ancestors from the Bohemian province, including Silesia, and eight "foreign-born" professors-ancestors. All his academic ancestors in the 5th generation taught in Graz, although they were born in Brussels, Loraine, Saxony, Central Poland, Silesia, Bohemia, and Graz. Mesar's professor of mathematics in Graz, Alexander Donati, was born in Venetian Tisana and two other ancestors in the 3rd generation were born in Verona and the Udine area, although all of them joined the Austrian Jesuit province (Pinamonti, 1701, pp. 12, 49, 110–112, 134; Dehergne, 1973; Hamy, 1893, pp. 78–79; Šmitek, 1994, p. 7; Andritsch 3: 135–136 [no. 50, 51, 91]; Mairold, 2013, pp. 18 [no. 20 and 21]; Stoeger, 1855, p. 226).

Picture 2: Messari
Source: archive of the Author.

Laimbeckhoven and Hallerstein

Hallerstein did not have a professor of mathematics during his studies of philosophy in Ljubljana. Laimbeckhoven and Hallerstein's professor of the repeaters of mathematics was Franz Schmelzer (Fischer, 1978, p. 179; Standaert, 2001, p. 310). If we examine the branches of the academic predecessors of Laimbeckhoven, there was no professor outside of the Austrian Jesuit province in the first four generations, and there was only one in the fifth generation, namely Otto Schimonsky from Twardogóra, northeast of Wrocław in Polish Silesia. Thirteen professors are known in the first five generations of Laimbeckhoven's educators, and only one of them was a "foreigner", which gives us only 8%. However, in the 6th generation of Laimbeckhoven's academic predecessors almost all educators were born outside of the Austrian Jesuit province apart from one professor of physics, Bernardus Geyer (* 1607 Stockerau in Austria). We are faced with the same situation when we take his professor of mathematics, Rospicher, and his professor of physics, Kapmiller, as predecessors, because we would have only one professor out of the eighteen born outside the Austrian Jesuit province in the 4th generation, namely the professor of mathematics, Alexander Donati from Latisana on Adriatic between Venice and Monfalcone, which was not far from the Habsburg border near Trieste. Rospicher was also Hallerstein's teacher of mathematics and his professor of physics was Sebastian Insprugger. Insprugger never repeated mathematic, but he was Rospicher's classmate during their studies of physics, when their first academic predecessor from outside the Austrian Jesuit province was Claudius Voragius from Venzone, 30 km north of Udine in the 4th generation (5th generation if we count Hallerstein and Laimbeckhoven's academic ancestors). Even in their 5th generation of academic predecessors, only Otto Schimonsky was a "foreigner", but even he was not born far from the northern border of the Bohemian Jesuit province.

Several China-based Jesuits from the Austrian and Bohemian provinces distinguished themselves by successful research in astronomy. Hallerstein and Laimbeckhoven's travel companion, box-manufacturer Joseph Chrysostom Neugebauer (* 15/5/1706 Ząbkowice Śląskie [Franckenstein] south of Wrocław in Silesia; SJ 27/10/1729 Vienna; † 1759 China), became the rare case of an astronomer and architect without completing any of the European university studies. Neugebauer was born in Ząbkowice Śląskie between the Jesuit colleges of Kłodzko and Nysa in today's Silesia, Poland. If we look at his family name, he could have been of a German origin, which was pretty common in Bohemian Sudetenland, which is nearby. In the time of Neugebauer's birth, the city of Ząbkowice Śląskie belonged to the Habsburg Empire, but King Frederick annexed it to Prussia in 1742 during Neugebauer's Chinese campaign. According to the geography of his native place, Neugebauer should have entered the Bohemian Jesuit province. Instead of that, he entered the Austrian Jesuit province in Vienna in 1729, probably due to the migration of his family from Silesia to Austria in his teenage years.

In Europe, Neugebauer was trained as a temporary helper to Jesuits. He became a skilled carpenter with great experience in construction. From 1730 to 1736 he was a Viennese novice, later in charge of practical work in the Viennese college as the keeper of grain supplies and carpentry (Južnič, 2012, p. 400; *Catalogus... Austriae*, 1730: column 24, 1732: column 30; *Catalogus... Austriae*, 1730: column 22, 1732: column 30; Vermote, 2013, p. 153). In 1737, he joined Hallerstein's group and sailed for China as one of rare temporal helpers (coadjutors) sent to China from Central Europe.

Brothers-coadjutors constituted only 5% of all Jesuits sent to China, certainly because coadjutors were recruited from the local Chinese converts. Usually, one quarter of coadjutors were needed in a Jesuit college, such as Ljubljana, for three quarters of Jesuit Fathers. After a brief stay in Macao in 1739, Neugebauer left for Cochinchina, where he became priest on May 28, 1741 and served as astronomer from 1743 to 1750. In 1750 the Jesuits were expelled from Cochinchina, and as a result he returned to Macao. In the field of astronomy, Neugebauer probably unofficially studied under Hallerstein.

Discussion

One of the most important China-based Jesuit missionaries, Martino Martini (Wei K'ouang-Kouo, Tsi-T'ai, * 1614 Trento [Trident]; SJ 8. 10. 1632 Roma; † 6. 6. 1661 Hangchow) was from Tyrol. He settled in China in 1637, but in 1650 he returned to Europe to discuss the Chinese Rites controversy with the authorities. Although born as Habsburg-subject in Trento, Martini never belonged to the Austrian Jesuit province because his native town's Jesuit College was a part of the Upper German Jesuit province all his life. It is interesting to note that Martino, J. Grueber and Diestel were among the rare China-based Jesuits who returned to Europe, although Diestel died en route. They were also among the exceptions who used the mainland path.

Another Tyrolean missionary, Eusebio Francisco Kino (* 1645; † 1711), worked in Mexico and Arizona. One of the most important Jesuit mathematicians of all times, Christoph Grienberger (Griennberger, * 1564 Hall in Tyrol; SJ 1590 Prague; † 11/3/1636 Roma), was also Tyrolean although he joined the Society of Jesus in the Bohemian Province. Grienberger never settled in China, but he trained a lot of Jesuits who did, such as: Schall von Bell, Terrentius (Schreck) and Kirwitzer. Another student of Grienberger's was Jesuit Gregorius a St. Vincentio; Grienberger's younger friend was Ch. Clavius' student, mathematician and physicist Marin Getaldić (* 1568 Dubrovnik; † 1626 Dubrovnik).

Eight Jesuits from the Bohemian province of the Old Society of Jesus have reached China. Several others worked in Cochinchina and also spent some time in neighboring China. Eight Bohemian, Moravian, and Silesian Jesuit Chinese missionaries were, in chronological order: Václav Pantaleon Kirwitzer (Wenzel Pantaleon Kirwitzer, Wenceslaus Kirwitzer, Wenceslas Pantaleon Kirwitzer, 祁維材 Qí Wéicái, 1588 or 1590 Kadaň in Bohemia; SJ 28/2/1606 Brno; † 22/5/1626 Macao), who worked in China in 1620–1626, musician Leopold Ferdinand Liebstein (Liebstain, 石克勝 Shí Kèshèng, * 1667 Nysa; SJ 14/10/1685; † 1711 Beijing), who was in China in 1707–1711, and horologer Franz Ludwig Stadlin (Franciscus Leonitus, 林濟各 Lín Jìgè, * 18/6/1658 Zug in German Switzerland; SJ 28/9/1687 Bohemia; † 1740 Beijing), who stayed in China in the years 1707–1740. In spite of the fact that all Jesuits from the Austrian province travelled to China on ships flying the Portuguese flag and worked in China in a Portuguese college and church, they never ceased to belong to their native Austrian Jesuit province, which published the data about them in its yearly Viennese Catalogues. Stadlin was probably the ablest inventor of them all, but he was a Catholic German Swiss and probably joined the Jesuits in Bohemia only to pave his way to China. Stadlin was probably the most appealing and one of the oldest China-based Jesuits of his time. He widely travelled through Europe to upgrade the horologic know-how of his native Switzerland, which was always considered superior. After his novice years he worked as the director of clocks (director horlogii) in Wroclaw from 1689 to 1700. Later on, he went to Brno, Legnica in modern Poland, Litoměřice (Leitmeritz) northwest of Prague, and Nysa (Neisse) in Poland. Hallerstein wrote a notice on the merits of deceased Stadlin's son after he dropped his anchor in China.

The most important mathematician among the China-based Jesuits from the Bohemian province was Franz Tillisch (Franciscus Thilisch, 楊秉義 Yáng Bǐngyì, * 16/01/1670 Wroclaw; SJ 1/10/1684 Brno;[1] † 1716 Beijing [Koláček, 1999, p. 17]). He was the student of a Jesuit professor of mathematics, Kresa, in Charles-Ferdinand University in Prague. From 1704 to 1707 Tillisch taught mathematics at the Universities of Olomouc and Prague, and worked as the imperial mathematician in China from 1710 to 1716.

Karel Slavíček (Carolus Slaviček, Slavizek, Slaviczek, Slawicek, Celavirchec, Slavisechett, Slavitchek, Slawiczek, Slawiezeck, 嚴嘉樂 Yán Jiālè,[2] * 24/12/1678, Jimramov in Moravia; SJ 9/10/1694 Brno; † 24/08/1735 Beijing) was the only China-based Jesuit from the Bohemian province of the Slavic nationality, while the remaining seven were of Germanic origin. The Slavic Nationals had the majority in Bohemia and Moravia, but they were socially and politically disadvantaged to such an extent that they had only 20% of all students at the University of Prague at the time of its establishment in 1348. The political circumstances of the Czech nobility worsened even further after their Protestant majority was defeated at Bila Hora (White Mountain) on November 8, 1620, and peasant Czechs

---

[1] According to Ricci Roundtable, or 14/10/1685, according to https://web.math.muni.cz/biografie/franz_tillisch.html (accessed: 10/09/2015).

[2] 嘉樂 is a transcription of Carolus or Charles.

only began to push into the towns in the times after the industrial revolution, which goes beyond the scope of this article. Slavíček was born to a teacher and town counselor and writer in Jimramov, east of Prague. His native settlement had less than one thousand inhabitants and for this reason it was unattractive to Germans. Most of his fellow China-based Jesuits from the Bohemian province were born in bigger cities. The Moravian epitaph *Carol[us] Slavicek Morav[us]* was written on his tombstone in Beijing. He knew the local language and preached in Czech as a professor of Hebrew in Olomouc in 1710. Slavíček was famous for his research into lunar liberation in China (Duteil, 1994, p. 289; Fischer, 1985). He made and repaired clocks and organs as a musician, horologer, and astronomer.

Other China-based Jesuits from the Bohemian Province included Florian Josef Bahr (Florianus Bahr, 魏繼晉 Wèi Jìjìn, * 1706 Niemodlin in Polish Silesia [Falkenberg] 25 km Northeast of Nysa; SJ 1726 Brno; †1771 Beijing; in China: 1738–1771). Bahr studied philosophy in Brno before he entered the Jesuit Order. In China, he worked as a musician and measured the lunar eclipse in Beijing on 12/11/1761. Bahr's colleagues were: music artist Johann Walter (Joannes Walter, 魯仲賢 Lǔ Zhòngxián, *6/01/1708 Žilina [Bilmae, Biline] in the northwest Bohemia; SJ 10/101729 Bohemia; † 24/06/1759 Beijing), who worked in China from 1741 to 1759, and painter of biological items and vacuum pump operator Ignác Sichelbart (Sichelbarth, Sickelbart, Sickelpart, 艾啓蒙 Ài Qǐměng, *26/09/1708 Neudeuk [Neudeck, Nedejk] in North Bohemia; SJ 20/10/736 Bohemia; † 6/10/1780 Beijing), who stayed in China form 1745 to 1780. Strictly speaking, out of all Bohemian Jesuits only Kirwitzer belonged to the Austrian Jesuit province before it was divided.

On average, Habsburg missionaries remained in China for twenty years, usually until their death, except for J. Grueber, Diestel, and Johann Koffler. Martini sailed to China twice as the only one among the Habsburg subjects. Most of the Habsburg Jesuit missionaries from Tyrol, Austrian and Bohemian provinces entered the society as teenagers, usually before or after their philosophical studies. The exceptions were Jesuits of humble origins from remote regions, like Mesar, whose father was from the Karst region, although he had already worked in Gorizia for several years, probably as a butcher, according to the meaning of his family name in Slovenian. Other examples of late entrance into the Order involved skilled craftsmen, like carpenter Neugebauer, horologer Stadlin, or painter Sichelbart. On average, the China-based Jesuits from the Bohemian province entered the Society of Jesus later; consequently, they settled in China at a later time compared to the Jesuits from the Austrian province.

The Jesuits from the Habsburg Monarchy who worked in Hué (modern Vietnam) were not taken into consideration if there is no strict proof of their work in China, as it is available for Johann Koffler (Coffe, * 19/6/1711 Prague; SJ 9/10/1726 Brno; † 8/1/1785 Sibiu). J. Koffler was a relative of an older China-based Jesuit from the Habsburg Monarchy, Andreas Xavier Wolfgang Koffler. In Olomouc, J. Koffler studied philosophy from 1729 to 1731 with a professor of mathematics, Karl Langer, who had studied mathematics in Prague. In 1730, his professor of physics was Jakob Hein and his professor of logic was Martin Raschdorff, who taught physics in 1731. Having obtained his masters in philosophy, J. Koffler taught the first rudimentary class of grammar school in Cĕský Krumlov in 1733, and the second class in 1734. He studied theology in Olomouc in 1735 and in the Prague college of St. Clement from 1736 to 1738. He arrived in Macao on 26/7/1740 and travelled to Cochinchina in 1742. From June 14, 1747 to 1755 he worked in Hué as the Royal Physician. In 1755, he was expelled three years after other Jesuits because his work was indispensable for a while. From 1755 to 1762, he stayed in Macao, and he was arrested there on 5/7/1762 in line with Marquise de Pombal's suppression of Jesuits in the Portuguese dominions in 1759. From 19/1/1764 to 10/7/1767, J. Koffler was a prisoner in Tour St. Julien in Lisbon, but Empress Maria Therese arranged for his transfer to Genoa and back home (O'Neill & Domínguez, 2001, 3: 2209; *Catalogus... Boëmiae*, 1714: column 19, 1715: column 19, 1716: column 19, 1730: columns 15–17, 1731: 15–17).

Other Hué-based Jesuits from the Habsburg Monarchy included Hallerstein's travel companion, Carolus Slamenski (* 1708 Bohemia; SJ 1736 Goa; † 7/06/1747, Cochinchine), who replaced a royal mathematician in Tonking in 1739, and later in Cochinchine Johann Sibert (Jan Siebert, * 28/05/1708 Iglau in Moravia; SJ 9/10/1723; † 12/09/1745 Hué). Slamenski first served with the dragoons in Transylvania as surgeon-major. Later he went to Danzig (Gdansk), and finally sailed to Amsterdam and Lisbon. Johann Hoppe (* 12/07/1708; SJ 20/10/1724 Świdnica [Schweidnizt] in today's Polish Silesia; † 1781 Tonkin) embarked for the Jesuit province of Japan, which included Hué, in 1737. In 1740, he was in China and went to Hué on June 9, 1743. Hoppe was in China for several years, but his Chinese offices were not cleared as far (http://ricci.rt.usfca.edu/biography/view. aspx?biographyID=664, accessed: 9/10/2015).

Johan Grueber from the Bohemian Jesuit province served in "Provicia Japonia" from 1736 onwards together with Siebert, but he is not included in the Ricci Roundtable. Their travel companion from the same Bohemian province was Wenceslas Paleczek (* 10/06/1705 Prague; SJ 28/10/1721 Brno; † 1758). They arrived in China in 1738, and Paleczek went to Tonkin,

Table 1: Academic Predecessors of China-based Jesuits from the Habsburg Monarchy Hereditary Lands, Tyrol, and Bohemian Crown. They belonged to the Tyrolean part of the Upper German province and to the Austrian province, which later split with the Bohemian Province. The predecessors summed on the right of the "/" sign were the Jesuit's professors of mathematics and physics, and those on the left side of the "/" sign were counted predecessors of the Jesuit's professor of the repeaters of mathematics, if the particular Jesuit repeated mathematics as a part of his specialization

Name	Years of work in China	Aged while joining the Jesuits/ and arriving in China	Academic Predecessors of first five generations born outside his domestic province	Academic Predecessors born in his domestic province in first five generations
Austrian province				
Kirwitzer	1620–1642	17/31	7 (64%) of 11	4 in Habsburg Monarchy
Andreas Xavier Wolfgang Koffler	1645–1652	15/34	16 (70%)	7
Johannes Grueber	1658–1661	18/35	10 (62%)	6
Diestel	1658–1660	16/35	6 (100%)	0
Herdtrich	1660–1684	16/35	17 (63%)	10
Fridelli	1705–1743	15/32	6 (46%) / 4 (32%)	7 / 15
Mesar (Messari)	1707–1715	28/34	11 (50%)	11
Neugebauer	1739–1743, 1750–1759	23/33	n/a	n/a
Laimbeckhoven	1739–1787	15/32	1 (6%) / 1 (8%)	17 / 12
Hallerstein	1739–1774	18/36	1 (6%)	17
Upper German province				
Martini	1642–1650, 1658–1661	18/28	1 (20%)	4
Bohemian province				
Liebstein	1707–1711	18/40	n/a	n/a
Stadlin	1707–1740	29/49	n/a	n/a
Tillisch	1710–1716	14/40	0	1 in Habsburg Monarchy, 1 in Polish Silesia part of Bohemian Jesuit province

Name	Years of work in China	Aged while joining the Jesuits/ and arriving in China	Academic Predecessors of first five generations born outside his domestic province	Academic Predecessors born in his domestic province in first five generations
Slaviček	1716–1735	16/38	0	1 in Habsburg Monarchy, 1 in Polish Silesia part of Bohemian Jesuit province
Bahr	1738–1771	20/32	n/a	n/a
Johann Koffler	1740–1741, 1755–1762	15/29	0	5 (100%)
Walter	1741–1759	21/33	n/a	n/a
Sichelbart	1745–1780	28/37	n/a	n/a
Total average	20	19/35	43%	57%
Average of Austrian province	21	18/34	52%	48%
Average Tyrolean part of the Upper German province	11	18/28	20%	80%
Average of Bohemian province	19.5	20/37	0	100%

Source: results of research.

probably to Hanoi. He arrived on 2/2/1739 or at least in 1742, and became the superior of the Jesuit mission in Hué in 1748 (Ricci Roundtable (http://ricci.rt.usfca.edu/biography/view.aspx?biographyID=1109, accessed: 10/09/2015); *Catalogus personarum, et officiorum Provinciae Boëmiae Societatis Jesu*, 1740: column 21).

It is evident that the education of future China-based Jesuits from the Austrian and Bohemian Jesuit provinces was gravely changed during the century that passed between Andreas Xavier Wolfgang Koffler's and Hallerstein's work in China. Not only were their *alma maters* in Graz widely replaced with Vienna or Trnava, but the geographical destination of their teachers was completely modified. All 17th century China-based Jesuits from the Austrian province had more than 60% academic predecessors born outside the Austrian province. For Herdtrich and later for Fridelli and Mesar (Messari), more domestic teachers were employed.

In Laimbeckhoven and Hallerstein's times, the Austrian Jesuit province had already at least five generations of domestic teachers. The Jesuits from the Bohemian province eventually had all domestic professors of mathematics and physics from the late 17th century onwards. It was certainly already a kind of academic tradition and it is fair to suppose that the Habsburg universities from Laimbeckhoven and Hallerstein's university time already delivered lectures on mathematical and technical subjects in their own way, which was influenced by Bošković's ideas a few years later. Bošković chose Vienna for the printing of his masterpiece *Theoria philosophiae naturalis* in 1758 because he noticed a strong support for his novelties in the Austrian Jesuit province and to the lesser degree in the Bohemian Jesuit province of Joseph Stepling (* 1716 Regensburg; SJ 1733 Prague; † 1778 Prague).

Nationality and nobility

Most of China-based Jesuits from the Austrian province, Bohemian Province, and Tyrol were of German nationality. Martino was the only one of Italian descent. Only Diestel, Mesar, and Slavíček were of Slavic origin (Pachtler, Montézon & Estève, 1861, pp. 339, 344, 350). Mesar was born in Gorizia and Diestel was born in much smaller Vipava. Hallerstein's mother was Baroness Erberg from mixed Gottscheer Area, predominantly speaking the German dialect, and his father was also a Baron, of Frankish origin. Baron Hallerstein certainly learned the Slovene dialect at least to be able to speak to his servants. His travel companion, Gottfried von Laimbeckhoven, was nominally lower in the ranks of nobility, but his mother was a child friend of the Emperors' daughter. His sister, Maria Elisabetha von Sumerau, married to Antonius Thadeus von Sumerau (* 23/03/1697 Lenz; † 17/02/1771 Freiburg im Breisgau), the first governor of Further Austria. Laimbeckhoven described to the couple his observations of the comets of 1755 and May–June 1759 in a letter signed bon May 28, 1760 (Laimbeckhoven, 2000, pp. 97, 110).

As for the others, J. Grueber's family probably originated from the peasant surroundings of Amstetten as did the ancestors of the Jesuit general Gabriel Grueber (* 1740). Fridelli was a son of a lawyer in nearby Linz. It is not easy to determine the actual noble origin of Jesuits because they did not use titles in their catalogues or published works, although in their diaries they expressed great familiarity with the noble titles of their visitors and benefactors.

Ljubljana College for future Chinese missionaries

When determining the origins, education, positions, and publications of China-based Jesuits from the Austrian province, it will be interesting to examine the accomplishments of the Ljubljana Jesuit College. Diestel, Andreas Xavier Wolfgang Koffler, and A. Hallerstein taught lower levels in Ljubljana, although Diestel formally specialized in humanities in Leoban, whereas in fact he taught newcomers at the Ljubljana lower

Table 2: Geography of the births of Ljubljana Jesuits

Number of births of Ljubljana Jesuits from the Old Society	Area
250	Vienna
144	Archduchy of Austria outside Vienna, Linz, and Krems
34	Linz
65	Graz
88	Styria outside Graz
110	Ljubljana
189	Carniola outside Ljubljana
46	Tyrol
53	Croatia
33	Klagenfurt
90	Carinthia outside Klagenfurt
188	German Lands north of Passau
22	Passau
11	Moravia
28	Bohemia
21	Slovakia
7	Italy west of Tyrol and Gorizia
38	Gorizia
9	Trieste
24	Poland
14	Switzerland
9	France
1412	Total Ljubljana Jesuits with known Birthplaces

Source: results of research.

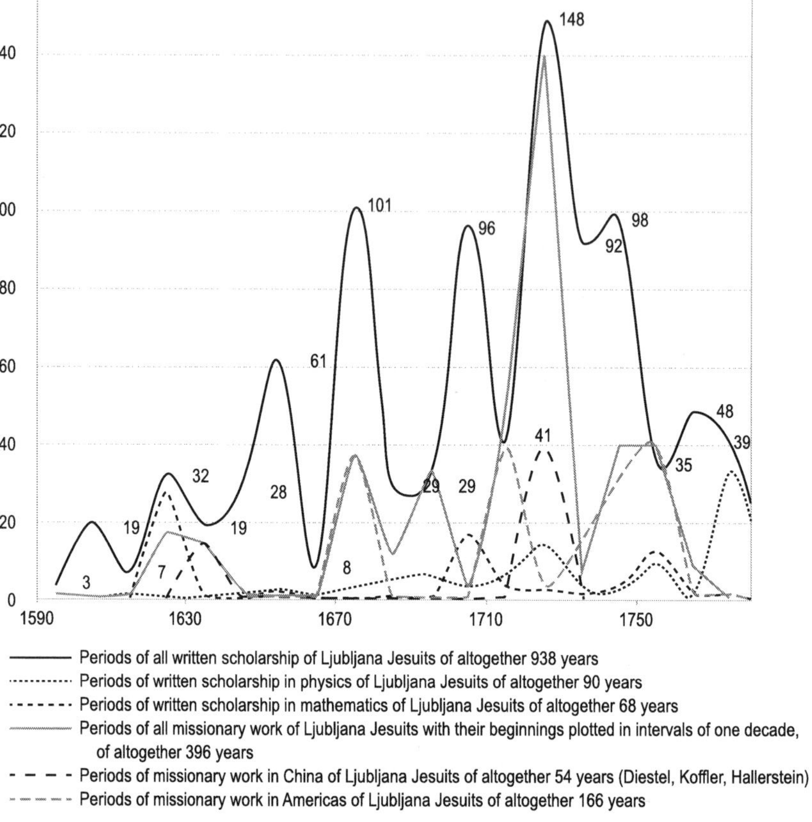

Figure 1: Missionary and scholarly work of Ljubljana Jesuits plotted

Source: archive of the Author.

school.[3] Diestel, A. Hallerstein, and Mesar were born nearby in Carniola, although Mesar was never given a position in Ljubljana. A good part of China-based Jesuits from the Habsburg Monarchy was therefore connected with Carniola-Ljubljana. Another important area was Sudetenland, on present border between Bohemia and Poland, where most of China-based Jesuits from the Bohemian province originated.

Nearly 400 (28%) of Ljubljana Jesuits were born in the Archduchy of Austria, most of them in Vienna. Nearly 300 were born in Carniola, including Ljubljana. The Inner Austria covered 425 (30%) births. The Inner, Lower, and Upper Austria, therefore, provided much more than a half (58,5%) of domiciles of Ljubljana Jesuits. 210 (15%) were from an area covered by today's Germany, which is not surprising because Outer Austria was considered somehow domestic, as well as Passau in Bavaria,

---

[3] Lukács, 1982, p. 573; Baraga, 2003, pp. 132–133.

which belonged to the Austrian province. Besides present-day Germany, modern Poland also had a considerable number of births (24.2%), mostly in Polish Silesia, which belonged to the Bohemian Jesuit province before the Prussian annexation. Among foreigners, the Swiss included 14 births (1%) and the French – 9. Foreigners were therefore not excluded, but they were also not common with the Scotsman professor of rhetoric Jacob Setonus (* 1590) as the only one from Great Britain. To be fit for the challenging journey to China, the Ljubljana Jesuits had to learn a lot about diversity and races.

Conclusion

The academic genealogy of China-based Jesuits from the Austrian Hereditary Lands and the Bohemian Crown mirrors the changes in the European educational system of the Jesuit Order. The universities providing the necessary mathematical training for future China-based Jesuits changed over the years from such schools as the comparatively new Jesuit university of Graz to the curriculum of the ancient Viennese University or in some cases to the developing university of Trnava with its excellent astronomical observatory. Simultaneously, with that slight geographical change also the kind of mathematics taught to Jesuits were modernized to involve a strictly Newtonian approach, which was slightly modified by Bošković's influence in the second part of 18th century. The new generation of China-based Jesuits from the Austrian province including Laimbeckhoven and Hallerstein had less than 10% professors of mathematical sciences in their academic genealogy in the first five generations born outside the Austrian Jesuit province compared to more than 60% in the cases of their older fellow China-based Jesuits Johannes Grueber and Herdtrich. The Jesuits from the Bohemian province were strict, and their teachers of mathematics and physics were all homegrown experts from the same province. Jesuit colleges matured, accepted the modern scientific trends, and foreign experts were not imported any more.

This soon became evident in the work and especially in the publications of China-based Jesuits. They ceased to publish monumental books and began to write more modern, shorter articles for the journals published by the European scientific societies. In a way, the work of China-based Jesuits became similar to the research of secular professionals in the last years before the suppression of the Society of Jesus.

After the Peace of Utrecht, a new wave of educated experts from Low Countries joined Habsburg universities, especially the University of Vienna, to reform the curriculum according to West European standards. Those changes, provided by van Swieten, who was the leader of the group, were introduced too late to exert a broader influence on China-based Jesuits from the Austrian province. Also, the influence of eleven years' younger van Swieten's contemporary, Bošković, came too late for China-based Jesuits from the Old Society.

References

Andritsch, J. (ed.) (1977). *Die Matrikeln der Universität Graz. 3: 1663–1710*. Graz: Akademische Druck- und Verlagsanstalt (Matriculations of Graz University).

Baldini, U. (2008). The Jesuit College in Macao as a Meeting Point of European, Chinese and Japanese Mathematical Traditions. Some Remarks on the Present State of Research, mainly Concerning Sources (16th-17th Centuries). In: Saraiva, L. & Jami, C. (eds). *The Jesuits, the Padroado and East Asian Science (1552–1773)* (pp. 33–79). London, Singapore et al.: World Scientific.

Baraga, F. (ed.) (2003). *Letopis Ljubljanskega kolegija Družbe Jezusove (1596–1691) (Historia annua Colegii Societatis Jesu Labacensis)*. Ljubljana: Družina (Yearly of Ljubljana Jesuit College).

Catalogus personarum & officiorum Provinciae Austriae Societatis Jesu, anno.... Wien (Catalogs of Austrian Jesuits).

Catalogus personarum, et officiorum Provinciae Boëmiae Societatis Jesu. Prag (Catalogs of Bohemian Jesuits).

Dehergne, J. (1973). *Répertoire des Jésuites de Chine de 1552 a 1800*. Rome: Institutum Historicum S.I. (Jesuits in China).

Dollmantis, F. (1991). *Ignatius von Loyola und die Jesuiten*. Wien: Österreichische Nationalbibliothek, 1.

Duteil, J.-P. (1994). *Le mandat du ciel*. Paris: AP éditions-Arguments (Mandate of Heavens).

Encyclopedic entry for Habsburg Monarchy. Retrieved from: http://www.encyclopedia.com/doc/1G2-3404900484.html (accessed: 10/09/2015).

Fischer, K.A.F. (1978). Jesuiten-Mathematiker in der deutschen Assistenz bis 1773. *Archivum Historicum Societatis Jesu*, 47(93), 159–224 (Jesuit Mathematicians).

Fischer, K.A.F. (1985). *Catalogus (generalis) provinciae Bohemiae (1623–1773) et Silesiae (1755–1773) Societatis Jesu*. Versio provisorica. ausgearbeitet auf Grund der Archivalien der Archivum Romanum SJ Roma. München: Rott im Elsass (General Catalogue).

Galerie illustreé de la Compagnie de Jésus (1893). Paris: Hamy.

Golvers, N. (2013). *Libraries of Western Learning for China. Circulation of Western Books between Europe and China in the Jesuit Mission (ca. 1650–ca. 1750). 2. Formation of Jesuit libraries*. Leuven: Chinese Studies XXVI.

Inglot, M. (2012). Páter Gabriel Grueber (1740–1805): študent Trnavskej univerzity, ktorý sa stal generálom Spoločnosti Ježišovej. = Pater Gabriel Grueber (1740–1805): Student der Tyrnauer Universität, der Generaloberer der Gesellschaft Jesu wurde. *Trnavská univerzita vo svetle dejín. = Die Tyrnauer Universität im Licht der Geschichte* (pp. 225–243 [Slovakian text], 256–277 [German text]). Kraków and Trnava: Ústav dejín Trnavskej univerzity – Towarzystwo Słowaków w Polsce.

Južnič, S. (2012). Building a bridge between observatories of Petersburg and Beijing. A study on the Slovenian Jesuit Avguštin Hallerstein. *Monumenta Serica, 60*, 309–404.

Južnič, S. (2015). Bibliometrics of Jesuit Mathematicians in China. *Historia Scientiarum (Tokyo), 24*(3), 126–151.

Koláček, J. (1999). *Čínské epištoly.* Velehrad: Refugium Velehrad-Roma (Chinese Letters).

Laimbeckhoven, G. (2000). *Der Bishof von Nanking und seine Briefe aus China mit Faximile seinem Reisenbeschreibung.* Sankt Augustin: Institut Monumenta Serica (The Bishop of Nanking).

Lukács, L. (1987–1988). *Catalogus generalis seu Nomenclator biographicus personarum Provinciae Austriae Societatis Jesu (1555–1773).* I-III. Romae: Institutum historicim S.J. (General Catalogue).

Mairold, M. (ed.) (2013). *Promotionen an der Universität Graz. 1682–1773.* Graz: Akademische Druck-v. Verlagsanst.

Martelanc, I. (1924). *Ivan Mesar misijonar v 18. stoletju.* Ljubljana: Martelanc.

O'Neill, C.E. & Domínguez, J.M. (2001). *Diccionario histórico de la Compañía de Jesús: Infante de Santiago-Piatkiewicz.* Univ Pontifica Comillas, 3 (Historical Dictionary).

Pachtler, G.M., Montézon, F. de & Estève, E. (1861). *Das Christenthum in Tonkin und Cochinchina, dem heutigen Annamreiche: von seiner Einführung bis auf die Gegenwart.* Paderborn: Schöningh (Christianity in Tonkin).

Ricci Roundtable. Retrieved from: http://ricci.rt.usfca.edu/biography/.

Standaert, N. (2001). *Handbook of Christianity in China,* Part 1. Leiden: Brill.

Stoeger, J.N. (1855). *Scriptores Provinciae Austriacae Societatis Jesu ab ejus origine ad nostra usque tempora.* Viennae: Typis congregationis mechitharisticae.

Šmitek, Z. (1994). Janez Krstnik Mesar – portret tonkinškega misijonarja iz 18. Stoletja. *Dve domovini, 5*, 7–17.

Udías, A. (2000). Observatories of the Society of Jesus 1814–1998. *AHSI, 69*, 151–178.

Vermote, F. (2012). *The role of urban real estate in Jesuit finances and networks between Europe and China, 1612–1778.* Dissertation, University of British Columbia.

Wicki, J. (1967). Liste der Jesuiten-Indienfahrer 1541–1758. *Portugiesische Forschungen der Görresgesellschaft. Erste Reihe: Aufsätze zur portugiesischen Kulturgeschichte, 7*, 252-450.

Huang Zhuoyue

Link in the History:
The Development of the Research on Avguštin Hallerstein and its Contemporary Meaning

Since the end of the 16th century, Jesuits carried out a huge plan of taking a sea-voyage eastward. Missionaries from Eastern Europe started arriving in China accordingly. For example, from the early 17th century to the mid-18th century, statistics show that four Polish missionaries came into mainland China, amongst whom Jean M. Smogolenski and Michal Boym (Wardęga, 2010[1]) were the most famous ones and both had the experience of studying theology in Krakow. Amongst other missionaries to China were also Karel Slavíček from Czech (Bohemia), Avguštin Hallerstein from Slovenia. They were the first Eastern Europeans getting to know China. In recent years, with the increasingly close communication between China and Europe, the research on Eastern European missionaries which concerns plenty of untapped materials and topics, begins to attract attention from academia. I attended a round table conference on Avguštin Hallerstein, held by Slovenian scholars at Ljubljana in 2006. From then on, I got myself involved with the historical character. Participating in a lot of activities in Europe or Beijing, I, to some extent, became a direct witness to the research plan on Avguštin Hallerstein. Therefore, I hope to take this opportunity to provide an academic overview to this important historical character. Since in contemporary academic context, as we can see, the Jesuits' coming to China is not an issue free of controversy, this paper intends to give reflective consideration to the activities of early Jesuit missionaries including Avguštin Hallerstein in China, with reference to some new theoretical discourses.

---

[1] The paper was also submitted to the international conference "On the Early European Missionaries coming to China" hosted by professor Huang Zhuoyue and sponsored by Sinology Institute of Beijing Language and Culture University in 2009.

1. A kind of Process: Retrospection on the research of Avguštin Hallerstein

As an international project, the research on Avguštin Hallerstein was undertaken mainly by the scholars from Slovenia and China. Yan Zonglin, a scholar living in Republican China, was the first one paying attention to Avguštin Hallerstein. At the end of the 1930s (or in the beginning of 1940) he published a paper named *The Document of Portuguese Envoy coming to China in the 18th Year of the Reign of Emperor Qianlong*, which illustrated in detail, how Avguštin Hallerstein, a man from "热尔马尼亚人", as a Portuguese envoy, had passed through customs in China (Yan, 2003, pp. 213–215). Then, in the 1980s, almost 40 years later, at the request of former Yugoslavian Archive, Chinese scholar Ju Deyuan made detailed textual research and published his paper *Liu Songling, Head of the Imperial Board of Astronomy in the Qing Dynasty* (Ju, 1985, p. 1). The greatest contribution of the paper lied in identifying for the first time *Liu Songling* (刘松龄) as Avguštin Hallerstein's Chinese name in historical records, which was an essential clue to linking the research in China and Slovenia. After that, along with the progress of Chinese academia, records about Hallerstein could be found in numerous books and papers that introduced early Sino-foreign relations as well as the missionaries to China. Papers written by Gao Wangling carefully investigated the case of Hallerstein in the discourse of Chinese imperial court (Gao, 2006, p. 2; 2008, p. 3; 2012, p. 1). Inspired by the studies of Chinese and overseas scholars, Han Yongfu, working in The First Historical Archive, published the paper *The Historical Archives of Missionary Avguštin Hallerstein* in 2011, which put together (in a form of a portfolio) some 27 special files of Hallerstein, selected and obtained from the cabinet, the court, the Ground Council and the imperial palace respectively (Han, 2011, p. 1). Meanwhile, the thesis *Research on Jesuit Augustin Ferdinand von Hallerstein of Emperor Qianlong* (Feng, 2014) written by Feng Jun, a relatively all-round study, covered broader aspects than the ones previously covered by the Chinese scholars, some parts of it were published in different magazines (Feng, 2003, p. 6; Feng, 2013, p. 14). The basic information on Hallerstein so far, was revealed clearly in Chinese academia.

Of course, the most important efforts were paid for by the scholars coming from Europe, mainly Slovenia. In general, their studies evolved along two ways: the first was to exploit and collect historical records, which was also the basis for the research of Hallerstein. It needed painstaking efforts, because most of historical materials (based on letters) were kept across Europe and written in different languages. The second was to study Hallerstein's life stories and scientific achievements, in which exports from Slovenia and other European countries were deeply involved.

In light of the existing research, August Dimitz (1827–1886) and Karel Dežman (1821–1889), with Carniola ancestry, were the most important representatives who paid attention to Hallerstein, carrying out investigations in the 19th century. August Dimitz presented life stories of Hallerstein exclusively in one of his essays written in 1861 (Dimitz, 1861), which was regarded as a starting point for the topic. Karel Dežman presented some of Avguštin Hallerstein's letters and in his paper published in 1881 (Dezman, 1881, pp. 50–51), he systematically studied the tasks and scientific cooperation undertaken by Jesuits (including Hallerstein) in China. Then, in 1928, a Dutch scholar, Johan W.J.A. Stein (1871–1951), gave a detailed account of Hallerstein's scientific work in Beijing (Stein, 1928). It seemed that for further consideration, all these research had something to do with the idea of national identification in Slovenia at different times (Juznic, 2003).

With growing sense of national independence in Slovenia, a large number of profound studies on Hallerstein sprang up since the 1990s. Hallerstein was taken as an essential part of national epics, and he was also a great figure, who initiated the friendship between China and Slovenia. At the same time, scholars like Zmago Šmitek, Pietro Corradini, and Josef Kolacek presented some vital publications. Yet, professor Stanislav Južnič and professor Mitja Saje, made the most significant contribution to promoting the research, as they conducted a more systematic analysis of Hallerstein. In 2003, professor Stanislav Južnič published the book titled *Hallerstein: The Last Great Jesuit Astronomer at Beijing* in Slovenian language. The book elaborated exhaustively on the astronomical and mathematical tradition that missionaries in Beijing had adopted. It also depicted Hallerstein's special achievements and position, such as his attainments on electronics and mapping in the history of missionaries in China. It is the most significant research result on Hallerstein. Published by Shanghai Joint Publishing Company, its Chinese version was translated by a Chinese scholar Zhou Pingping in 2014.

Professor Mitja Saje did a fantastic job with the research. First, he collected, sorted out and published many historical records of Hallerstein. In order to get the original documents, he spared no efforts in visiting numerous archives in China and across Europe (Saje, 2004, pp. 603–607). Meanwhile, his valuable papers promoted greatly the study on Hallerstein (Saje, 2008, Vol. VII). He actively organized international scholars to get involved in investigations on Hallerstein. In 2006, I attended the round table forum held by professor Mitja Saje in Lubiana, where I got to know Slovenian scholars and witnessed a great deal of work led and organized by him in the recent 10 years. In 2007 in particular, professor Mitja Saje as the initiator, successively applied an EU joint project (KIBLA) together with universities and institutions in China, Portugal, Austria, and other countires. As a person in charge of the Chinese side of the project, I participated in discussions and promotional events in different countries. In the meantime, an international conference "The Early European Missionaries to China and Sinology Studies" centered on Hallerstein, was held at my university (Beijing Language and Culture University). Many scholars of different countries and regions attended the conference and discussed in depth the scientific achievements of Hallerstein and his indispensable role of bridging early relations between China and Europe (Ren, 2010, p. 2). Hallerstein, thus, became a topic of an international research and as the result of the project, a well-designed collection of essays was published in English in 2009 (Saje, 2009).

In the whole process of research on Hallerstein, another important person, Wang Huiqin, professor Mitja Saje's wife, should not be neglected. In recent 10 years, she was involved in all the academic activities on studying Hallerstein and supervised the art and media products in KIBLA project. She presented her personal exhibition many times in Slovenia, Austria and China, as well as other countries which greatly extended the influence of the project in the world. What is also worth mentioning is that her picture book named *The Slovenian in Forbidden City*[2] was published in three languages. The picture book, winning awards from Slovenian government, was also highly appreciated by Hanban and Chinese experts and scholars after being shown at Beijing Language and Culture University in October 2014.

Although there is other countless research and promotion of Hallerstein, it was impossible to list them all in this paper. However, what can be seen is that Hallerstein the previously unknown historical figure, is foregrounded in the history and obviously symbolizes the friendship between China and Slovenia.

2. Beyond post-colonial theory: another way of distinction and interpretation

In general, there are two ways to evaluate Hallerstein's achievements in China: the first is an internal evaluation, made according to Hallerstein's life stories and their implied meaning in special heritage (such as in re-

---

[2] Beijing Yuyan Daxue Chubanshe (北京语言大学出版社) published the English-Chinese bilingual version in 2014.

ligious, diplomatic or scientific systems). Both Slovenian and Chinese scholars tend to settle Hallerstein's position in light of the history of science. His contribution, therefore, is fully displayed in the process of empirical studies and textual research. The second, is an external evaluation, which means to judge beyond empirical and heritagestudy, that is to say, to analyze and discuss with reference to historical development of the contact and collision between China and the West. Admittedly, it has something to do with theoretical orientations of different authors and does not confine in a personal assessment to Hallerstein. From an external and macro perspective, European missionary activities in China, from the late 16th century to the mid-20th century, followed and associated with the European overseas expansion which had lasted for many centuries. As we all know, since the Palestinian-American scholar Edward Said put forward the concept of "orientalism" in 1978, the reflection on orientalism which was known as post-colonialism, swept around the world. Thus, the entire European missionary activities initiated by Matteo Ricci were naturally brought into this reflection, which became particularly evident in the American sinology and Chinese academic world. It also exerted an impact to the first way of evaluation – internal evaluation. No matter what kind of attitude we hold, it seemed that we could not avoid the radical challenges raised by post-colonialism. Therefore, only by facing these challenges and distinguishing them from the academic perspective, the historical figures can be evaluated credibly and reliably.

This paper intends to extend and generalize the issue deriving from three aspects in order to explain the possible meanings embodied in missionaries represented by Hallerstein.

First of all, we have to take a look at the history of European missionary work in China that was a trend formed by people like Hallerstein. From a historical point of view, it covered ups and downs during a period of about 400 years. Therefore I think that an appropriate method should be used to further differentiate the process, rather than discussing it in an indistinct framework. In such a case, European mission in China could be divided into two stages: the first stage, known as the early missionary stage, spreading over the period from the late 16th century to the late 18th century, when Jesuits led the missionary work when most of them came from European continent; the second mission stage, referred as the later missionary stage, was led by Anglo-American protestant missionaries during the period from the beginning of the 19th century to the mid-20th century.

There is no doubt that these two stages witnessed differences in doctrines, canons and missionary policies, which will not necessarily be discussed in this paper. The wide differences, however, also lied in relations between China and Europe during the two stages. We have seen that the aim of early Jesuits to China was cultural enlightenment, which was relatively simple, and they did not show any interests to gain extra advantage over Chinese political power or economic benefits. Their activities in China were mainly limited within the dissemination of religion, science and knowledge. Moreover, they conducted friendly exchanges with Chinese court elites and the brightest from all walks of life by adopting the policy inherited from Matteo Ricci. Although there were some inevitable conflicts, mutual acceptance and pervasive tolerance were still the mainstream of the contact between China and Europe. This also admittedly was due to the fact that China and Europe were relatively comparable in national strength before the 18th century. During the reign of Emperor Kangxi, Yongzhen, and Qianlong Chinese imperial court was strong enough to control foreign forces (including missionary activities). Therefore, when the missionary work did not get the desirable effect in China, the remarkable Jesuits like Hallerstein, Tomé Pereira, Jean François Gerbillon, and Joachim Bouvet et al. began to spend their energy and talent on the exchange and dissemination of science, skills and knowledge. As the situation of missionaries coming to China was very complex after the early 19th century, it was hard to treat them as a whole. From a general perspective however, their mission was peculiarly related with the entire colonialism in either an intentional or a practical sense, because they came to China at a specified time, when European countries strongly penetrated into China with their political, commercial and military force. Hence, the equal situation used to be held in the relations between China and Europe was broken and labeled itself as "a strong west and a weak China".[3] At the same time, missionaries hold an arrogant and discriminatory attitude to China, which could be proved in their statements and behaviors (I have investigated some important facts about in one of my papers[4]). Missionary work, therefore, need to be further distinguished and arranged in the process of historical investigation during these two stages since they represented substantial difference in Sino-Europe relations.

In my opinion, the cultural ambition in a macro context needs to be separated from effects of specific activities. Cultural ambition refers to that all the missionary work inevitably brought with it a kind of an universal aim (It is cultural colonial orientation according to theories of postcolonialism). It could not be chosen or changed by any single missionary, instead, it was specified and endowed by a conceptual structure operated by history. Similarly, concept did not equal to practice, it transformed

---

[3] The difference in patterns of cultural exchanges during these two stages can be also seen in D.E. Mungello, 2005. Jiang Wenjun translated the book into English, and Xinxing chubanshe (新星出版社) published it in 2007, pp. 13–14.

[4] See Huang, to be published, Part one, "General Overview".

itself or yielded unexpected effects in the process of development, because of the complexity of practice environment and its own appealing, frightening and dissolving power. This must be noticed when studying how one culture spread out into the domain of the other.

The following is also a good example illustrating the above point. During debates within the European church some priests argued that early Jesuits in China had been involved in helping Chinese court handle domestic issues or introducing Chinese knowledge to Europe, more than in accomplishing their missionary work.[5] This was the exact reason why the Vatican had determined to ban Jesuit mission. The argument might be too strong to believe, since the ban from the Vatican could also be attributed to its complex relations with missionaries and their struggles for patronage (保教运动) (Zhang, 2003, pp. 438–502), as well as the negative reactions by Chinese court to the rites controversy. However, some peculiar implied meaning could still be identified in Jesuits' activities in China. Activities of Jesuits like Hallerstein in Beijing proved that Jesuit, in fact, conducted a great number of beneficial work for Chinese imperial courts and gained measurable achievements in delivering Western knowledge of sciences and arts to China. Moreover, they effectively promoted the interaction and exchanges between China and the Western world from the historical point of view.[6] It was well researched by many scholars and need not to be elaborated further. I think, therefore, if we study missionaries to China within the historical context and its complexity, their mission needs not only to be categorized according to different periods of time, but also to be distinguished from the special practice effect. It should not be simply presupposed as a fixed concept of "cultural colonialism" based on some abstract post-colonial theories regardless of time, area, level and individual distinctions. In addition, we should realize that missionaries living in China for a long time were capable of influencing Chinese people with their sense of cultural duty and the strong impulse. In return, they were, to some extent, also remolded by Chinese culture and were implicitly led to an unpredictable direction.[7]

---

[5] Jonathan D. Spence mentioned that the missionary work of European missions coming to China in the 17th century had been shifted to reporting China according to the information they sent back to Europe. See Spence, 1999, translated into Chinese by Ruan, and published by Guangxi Shifan Daxue Chubanshe, 2013, p. 62.

[6] Explanation of the interaction see Mungello, 2005. This kind of interaction is quite obvious in the dissemination of Chinese culture and thought in France and Germany, which has been fully studied by Chinese academia.

[7] Paul A. Cohen (1984) has ever mentioned that Western missionaries living in China for a long time became less like Westerners. They studied Chinese language and adopted Chinese tradition, which was a process of hybridization. They were more Westerner-in-china than real Westerners.

The fact that historical resources can either be in opposite or in harmony with contemporary policy, also needs to be mentioned. A good proof is that the historical image of Confucius underwent many changes in China since the 20th century. Although history indeed cannot be changed, it is by no means silent or meaningless. It was, if needed, often adopted by various positions to achieve their aims and involved directly in contemporary life, which formed a living connection between history and contemporary life. Therefore, it is unnecessary to forsake the chance to borrow and divert historical resources after distinguishing their reliability. As it can be seen in the decades of long research on Hallerstein in both China and Slovenia, as well as the resulting exchanges between these two countries, Hallerstein performed a role of glue, closely bonding China and Slovenia, and even Europe together. The huge geographical distance between Slovenia, a part of Eastern Europe, and China being a part of the East, is shortened immediately at the mention of Hallerstein. This is the contemporary effect caused by historical events, which cannot be reached by post-colonial discourse. It indicates that the adaptability of post-colonial theory is limited, and it is only one of the possible ways to interpret history. In this sense, all the related research should be encouraged to make history a kind of valuable source to promote peace and friendship between Europe and China.

References

Cohen, P.A. (1984). *Discovering History in China: American Historical Writing on the Recent Chinese Past*. New York: Columbia University Press.

Dezman, K. (1881). Ein Krainer als Hoffastromomer in Beijing 1739–1774. *Laibacher Wöchenblatt, Organ der Verfassungs-Partei in Karin, Gedr, bei Leykam in Graz*. Laibach: Kleinmayr & Bamber.

Dimitz, A. (1861). *Ein Beitrag Zur Biographie der Hallersteine, Mitteilungen des historischen Vereines Für Krain*.

Feng Jun (冯军) (2003). Yesuhuishi Liu Songling yu qinggong yiqi zhizao (Jesuit Hallerstein and Instrument Manufacture in Qing Imperial Court, 耶稣会士刘松龄与清宫仪器制造). *Heilongjiang Shizhi* (《黑龙江史志》), 6.

Feng Jun (冯军) (2013). Qianlongchao yesuhuishi Liu Songling shulun (乾隆朝耶稣会士刘松龄述论, Discussion about Jesuit Augustin Ferdinand von Hallerstein of Emperor Qianlong). *Sichou zhi lu* (《丝绸之路》), 14.

Feng Jun (冯军) (2014). Qianlongchao yesuhuishi Liu Songling yanjiu (乾隆朝耶稣会士刘松龄研究, Research on Jesuit Augustin Ferdinand von Hallerstein of Emperor Qianlong). Master's thesis from Xibei Minzu Daxue (西北民族大学).

Gao Wanglin (高王凌) (2006). Liu Songling: zuihou de yesuhuishi (刘松龄: 最后的耶稣会士, Hallerstein: the Last Jesuit). *Zhongguo Wenhua Yanjiu* (《中国文化研究》), 2.

Gao Wanglin (高王凌) (2008). Liu Songling bixia de qianlong shisannin (刘松龄笔下的乾隆13年, The Image of the 13th Year in the Reign of the Emperor Qianlong in Hallerstein's Writings). *Qingshi Yanjiu* (《清史研究, Studies in Qing History》), 3.

Han Yongfu (韩永福) (2011). Yesuhui chuanjiaoshi Liu Songling dangan shiliao (耶稣会传教士刘松龄档案史料, The Historical Archives of Jesuit Hallerstein). *Lishi Dangan* (《历史档案》), 1.

Huang Zhuoyue (黄卓越) (to be published). *Haiwai Hanxue yu Zhongguo Wenlun: Yingmei juan* (海外汉学与中国文论: 英美卷, *Overseas Sinology and Chinese Literary Theory: Anglo-American Volume*). Beijing: Beijingdaxue chubanshe. Part one, "General Overview".

Ju Deyuan (鞠德源) (1985). Liu Songling: Head of the Imperial Board of Astronomy in the Qing Dynasty. *Palace Museum Journal*, 1.

Juznic, S. (2003). *Hallerstein: The Last Great Jesuit Astronomer at Beijing* (刘松龄: 旧耶稣会在京最后一位伟大的天文学家, transl. by Zhou Pingping [周萍萍]). Ljubljana: Tanja Rejc.

Mungello, D.E. (2005). *The Great Encounter of China and West, 1500–1800* (1500–1800 中西方的伟大相遇, transl. by Jiang Wenjun [江文君]). Lanham, MD: Rowman & Littlefield Publishers.

Ren Zengqiang (任增强) (2010). Duowei shiye zhong de chuanjiaoshi hanxue yanjiu (多维视野中的传教士汉学研究, Missionary Sinology Study from multi-layered perspectives). *Zhongguo Wenhua Yanjiu* (《中国文化研究》), 2.

Saje, M. (2008). Difficult position of Augustin Hallerstein in Chinese Court. *Studia Orientalia Slovaca*, Vol. VII, Bratislava.

Saje, M. (2008). Rossija v pismah slovenskego iezuita Avgustina Hallerštejna (Russia in the letters of Slovenian Jesuit Augustin Hallerstein). In: *Kitaj v dialoge civilizacij: k 70-letiju akademika M.L. Titarenko* (pp. 603–607). Pamjatniki istoričeskoj mýsli. Moskva: Rossijskaja Akademija Nauk, Institut Daljnego Vostoka.

Saje, M. (2009). *A Hallerstein – Liu Songling 刘松龄: Multicultural Legacy of Jesuit Wisdom and Piety at the Qing Dynasty Court*. Maribr: Association for Culture and Education KIBLA. Daxiang Chubanshe (大象出版社) published the Chinese version in 2015, and the Chinese name of the book is Siluowenniya zai zhongguo de wenhua shizhe – Liu Songling (《斯洛文尼亚在中国的文化使者 – 刘松龄》).

Spence, J.D. (1999). The Chan's Great Continent: China in Western Minds (大汉之国:西方眼中的中国, transl. by Ruan Shumei 阮叔梅). New York: W.W. Norton & Company.

Stein, J.W.J.A. (1928). *Misionaris en astronoom: Augustinus von Hallerstein, Overdruck uit Studien: Tijdschrift wor Godsdienst, Wetenschap en Letteren wan de Nederlandse jezuienprovincie*. Malmberg: 's-Hertogenbosch, W. van Gulick.

Wardęga, A.K. (2010). *The Early Polish Missionaries coming to China*. Retrieved from: http://oldsite.sinologystudy.com/2010/0425/11.html (accessed: 13/10/2015).

Yan Zonglin (阎崇临) (2003). *Chuanjiaoshi yu Faguo Zaoqi Hanxue* (传教士与法国早期汉学, Missionaries and French Early Sinology). Zhengzhou: Daxiang chubanshe.

Zhang Guogang (张国刚) (2003). Cong zhongxi chushi dao liyizhizheng (从中西初识到礼仪之争, *From the First Sino-Western Contact to Rites Controversy*). Beijing: Beijing Renmin chubanshe.

Contributors

Tomasz BIELIŃSKI, Ph.D., Assistant at the University of Gdańsk, Institute of International Business, Department of International Economic Relations. His articles were published in *Międzynarodowe stosunki gospodarcze. Teoria i praktyka*, red. E. Oziewicz, T. Michałowski (Warszawa: PWE, 2013); *Globalizacja i regionalizacja w gospodarce światowej*, red. R. Orłowska, K. Żołądkiewicz (Warszawa: PWE, 2012); *Development of Internet Social Networks in China as a Chance for European Software Developers*, [in:] *Clusters, Networks and Markets in the Asia-Pacific Region* (Wrocław: Research Papers of Wrocław University of Economics no. 295, 2013); *China's increasing competitive advantage in research and development, and human resources*, [in:] *Competitiveness of Economies in the Asia-Pacific Region, Selected problems* (Wrocław: Research Papers of Wrocław University of Economics, 2011). His major scientific interests are: human capital, educational policy and innovation in China.

Sebastian BOBOWSKI, Ph.D., Assistant Professor, Lecturer, Faculty of Economic Sciences, International Economic Relations Department, Wrocław University of Economics, Poland; co-founder and a member of the Asia-Pacific Research Centre at the Wrocław University of Economics; author and co-author of 4 books and 54 articles in Polish and English concerning the issues of the Asian regionalism, international business, cluster structures, cohesion policy of the European Union (EU), innovations; director of Bachelor and Master Program in International Business (2014–), departmental coordinator of "Erasmus Plus" program covering UE-28, EFTA member states and Turkey (2010–); Visiting Research Fellow at the Center for Asian and Pacific Studies (CAPS), Seikei University, Tokyo, Japan (2014); Visiting Professor at the University of Applied Sciences in Schmalkalden, Germany (2011) and IPAG Business School in Nice, France (2013); presenter at the international conferences held in Singapore, Japan, Macau, Portugal, Austria, Czech Republic, Italy and India; deputy of the Central Europe in the European Association for Southeast Asian Studies Board 2013–2017 (EuroSEAS); author of the training modules/manuals and coach in the regional/national training and educational projects co-funded by the EU; co-author and contractor of international research project "Clusters as an innovation carrier of enterprises and regions. Verification and implementation of Asian models in terms of the Polish economy", funded by National Science Centre, Poland (2011–2014).

Elena DAMJANOSKA, M.A. (Confucius Institute at Ss. Cyril and Methodius University in Skopje). She holds degrees in Chinese Language and Literature and English Language and Literature. She has translated Mo Yan's novella Red Sorghum from Chinese into Macedonian and has compiled the first Basic Chinese – Macedonian Dictionary. Her academic fields of interest include Chinese Studies and Applied Linguistics.

DENG Shizhong, Ph.D., Professor, Chinese director of the Confucius Institute at Ss. Cyril and Methodius University in Skopje since 2013. Previously, he was a Vice-dean and a Professor of Mandarin Chinese Language and Literature at the College of International Education, Southwestern University of Finance & Economics. He holds a Ph.D. in Comparative Literature and is the author of several books, amongst which are *Rethinking the Teaching Chinese as a Foreign Language and Chinese Culture* (Chengdu: Sichuan University Press, 2007), *Comparative Literature Theoretical Research in Mainland China, Taiwan and Hong Kong* (Chengdu: Bashu Press, 2000). Deng Shizhong has also conducted research and published numerous articles in academic journals on topics such as Chinese as a foreign language, Chinese culture and literature, comparative literature, etc. He has been a member of various associations, such as Teaching Chinese as a Foreign Language Association and Chinese Comparative Literature Association. He also translated several books from English to Chinese.

DONG Xixiao (董希骁), Ph.D., Associate Professor, Vice-dean at the Beijing Foreign Studies University, School of European Languages and Cultures. Titles of the most significant books published and subject matter of published articles: *System of addressing terms in modern Romanian* (《现代罗马尼亚语称谓系统》, Beijing: Foreign Language Teaching and Research Press, 2008); *Analysis on re-acquisition of Romanian citizenship by citizens of the Republic of Moldova and on research reports issued by Soros Foundation* (摩尔多瓦共和国公民重获罗马尼亚国籍现象解析 – 兼评索罗斯基金会调研报告), *International Forum* (《国际论坛》), 6, 71–76. His academic interests and ongoing research: Romanian language and culture; language planning and language policy.

Ljubomir DRAKULEVSKI, Ph.D., is a Full Professor at the Faculty of Economics Skopje, Ss. Cyril and Methodius University in Skopje. He accomplished his Ph.D. in 1998, his Ph.D. thesis entitled: *Leadership: A Basis for Effective Strategic Management*. At present, he is engaged as a Full Professor of Strategic Management, International Management and Organizational Behaviour, at the first cycle (undergraduate) and second cycle (postgraduate) of studies at the Faculty of Economics in Skopje. He published 5 books: *Management Lexicon* (1993, 1996), *Strategic Management* (1996, 2001), *Leadership: A Basis for Effective Strategic Management* (1999), *Organization* (2012) and *Leadership* (2015). He participated in 20 research projects at the Faculty of Economics and MANU. Also, he published over 70 papers in the country or abroad. He realized a one semester study stay at the Arizona State University, Tempe, USA (1995), as a participant on the Program of Development of Business – Management in Macedonia. He also realized: a study stay at the Wolverhampton Business School, Wolverhampton, United Kingdom (November 1998); at Pantheon University, Athens, Greece (February 2000); at the Business School, Staffordshire University, Stoke-on-Trent, United Kingdom (August 2001), at Institute of Business Administration, LIUC, Università Cattaneo Castellanza, Milan, Italy (November 2001) at Rennes 2, Rennes, France (February 2003); at College of Business, Athens, Ohio, USA (May 2003); at the University of Iceland, Iceland (June 2005). Beginning from 2011 he has been engaged as a Dean of the Faculty of Economics, Ss. Cyril and Methodius University in Skopje.

Attila FARKAS, Ph.D., senior lecturer of philosophy in the Faculty of Economics and Social Sciences, Szent István University Hungary, where he teaches a variety of philosophy and ethics courses, and he is a research fellow at the Hungarian Academy of Arts. He earned his Ph.D. from the Doctoral School of Philosophical Sciences, Eötvös Loránd University, Budapest. His research specialities are moral philosophy, political philosophy and theory of art, he wrote two books, ten book-chapters and ten journal articles.

János FEHÉR, Ph.D. and a habilitation in Business Administration and Organizational Sciences and a "dr. univ." degree in Industrial Sociology. He is Associate Professor and Academic Director of Human Resources BSc Program at Károli Gáspár University of the Reformed Church in Hungary, Department of Economic Sciences and a Visiting Associate Professor at Szent István University, Gödöllő, Hungary. He has been a Lecturer and Trainer-Consultant to represent the market economy "Human Resource" paradigm since the 80-ies, and was the first Academic to teach HRM in Hungarian Graduate Programs in the era of the democratic transitions at International Management Center, Budapest, the first Business School and Management Development Institute in Central-Eastern Europe. He had been Visiting Associate Professor at Temple University Philadelphia, the Budapest Campus of Case Western Reserve University, Cleveland, the Budapest Corvinus University, and the Budapest Program Part of the University of Pittsburgh MBA Program. Dr. Fehér is author of 38 refereed publications (145 publications in all). He has authored/edited 3 books and a HRM Company Briefing Material Series for some of the largest Hungarian companies transforming their HRM systems. He has been a Consultant at and a Program Developer, Director and Instructor of Upper Level Management Programs of leading Hungarian and international companies.

Péter FODOR, M.A., Assistant Lecturer at the University of Pécs, Faculty of Business and Economics. Member of the board at Mevid Zrt. (MEVID plc) Pécs. From 2010: chairman of the board. In 2006-2009 PhD Student, doctoral candidate at the University of Pécs, Faculty of Business and Economics, Management Consulting Department. In 2014 exchange lecturer for one semester – Nanjing Audit University China.

Łukasz GACEK, Ph.D., Professor at the Institute of Middle and Far East, Jagiellonian University in Krakow. His research concentrate on political systems, security issues, and international relations in East Asia. He is also the author of numerous articles and books about China's foreign policy, China's energy security, ecological security, Asian political systems, and others.

HUANG Zhuoyue, Ph.D., Professor of Literary and Cultural Studies, Director of Institute for International Sinology Studies in Beijing Language and Culture University, Head of Center for Chinese Culture Translation and Communication Worldwide, Chairman of the Academic Committee of CCCTSS National Project. His research focuses on Chinese traditional ideology history and literary criticism of Ming and Qing dynasty, international Sinology Studies, comparative literature, Cultural Studies and contemporary Chinese culture. He published many books on the above research fields, and presided over a series of important projects in China and abroad. Significant publications: *Sixiangshi yu Pipingxue Yanjiu Wenji* (黄卓越思想史与批评学论文集, *Huang Zhuoyue' Collected Papers on the History of Ideas and Literary Criticism*), Beijing: Beijing yuyan daxue chubanshe, 2012; *Ming Yongle zhi Jiajingchu de Shiwenguan Yanjiu* (明永乐至嘉靖初诗文观研究, *Literary Trends form 14–16 Century in China*), Beijing: Beijing shifan daxue chubansh, 2000; "Hanzi Yunlv Shuo" (汉字韵律说, Chinese Written Characters and Versification), *Beijing daxue xuebao*, 2014; "Cong Wenxueshi dao Wenlunsi: Yingmei Guojia Zhguo Wenlun Yanjiu Xingchenglujing Kaocha" (从文学史到文论史: 英美国家中国文论研究形成路径, From Research of Literary History to Literary Criticism: The Path of Shaping of Chinese Theory in the United Kingdom and the United States), *Zhongguo wenhua yanjiu*, 2013.

Tina ILGO, Ph.D., Department of Asian and African Studies and Department of Sociology of Culture, Faculty of Arts, University of Ljubljana. Tina Ilgo works at Trnovo Primary School in Ljubljana as a Chinese language teacher and head of the project Chinese culture and language in Slovenian education system. She cooperates with Confucius Institute Ljubljana, Faculty of Economics, University of Ljubljana, she organizes and leads teacher trainings, Chinese summer school at Trnovo, various events and exhibitions related to Chinese culture and language, she coordinates Chinese teachers and sinologists at Confucius classrooms, and performs tasks related to the management of Confucius classroom Ljubljana. Her scientific monograph entitled *Pretrgan molk: Kritika tradicionalne kitajske družbe skozi simboliko v Lu Xunovih novelah* [Broken silence: Criticism of traditional Chinese Society through Symbolism in Lu Xun's Short Stories] was published in 2013. She has written several articles concerning modern Chinese literature. In her academic interests and ongoing research, Tina Ilgo is currently focused on teaching and learning Chinese as a foreign language.

Anna H. JANKOWIAK, Ph.D., Assistant Professor in the Department of International Economic Relations and Head of Science and Cooperation Section in the International Co-operation Office at the Wrocław University of Economics; co-founder of the Asia-Pacific Research Centre and the main coordinator of Asian Conference at Wrocław University of Economics; author and co-author of 35 articles and 7 books in Polish and English concerning the issues of the Asian regionalism, Asian economies, transnational corporation, international business, global production networks and clusters in global economy; Member of European International Business Academy; co-creator of the research project "Clusters as an innovation carrier of enterprises and regions. Verification and implementation of Asian models in terms of the Polish economy", funded by National Science Centre, Poland; co-author of the expertise *Niche markets for Polish products in China*, prepared at the request of Polish Information and Foreign Investment Agency.

Jarosław JURA, Ph.D., is a president of the Institute of Socio-Economic Enquiry. He obtained his Ph.D. in sociology from the University of Warsaw. Among his research interests there are sociology of communication, social anthropology, quantitative analysis of qualitative data, as well as the social issues of contemporary China and Chinese expansion in Africa. He is an author and co-author of numerous publications, including: Jura, J., Kałużyńska, K., de Carvalho, P., *Events over Endeavours. Image of the Chinese in Zambia and Angola*, Kraków: Jagiellonian University Press, 2015; Jura, J., Kałużyńska, K., Not Confucius, nor Kung Fu: Economy and Business as Chinese Soft Power in Africa, *African East Asia Affairs. Asian Monitor*, 2013; Jura, J., Eating and drinking interactions patterns and social women role transformation in contemporary urban China, *Polish Sociological Review* 2009.

Stanislav JUŽNIČ, Ph.D., Professor, head of Jesuit archive. Although he was born in San Francisco, he finished most of his studies on Ljubljana, including the graduate work with physicist academician Robert Blinc Ph.D. with historian academician Vasilij Melik (deceased). He finished his trilogy about the history of exact sciences in Slovenia, which included Astronomy (Radovljica: Didakta, 2008), Physics (2008), and Mathematics (2009) for the International Year of Astronomy 2009. He published almost 1000 scientific works in Slovenian, Croatian, Serbian, Ukrainian, Russian, English, Catalonian, Italian, and German languages in all continents including Australia and the Japanese land of the rising Sun. Dr. Južnič conducted profound studies of the history of science basically connected with Slovenians; after he had found in his philosophically related models of the development of physics that most of the attempts in that field did not consider enough facts relying mostly on unconfirmed information about the purposed scientific revolutions of Copernicus, Galileo, Newton, Faraday & Maxwell, Planck, and Einstein. In the year (2009) his project, supported by numerous collaborators on both sides of the Atlantic, was finished in its main points with the publication of the last part of trilogy on the Slovenian related history of science. Among his recent monographs are: *Hallerstein, a Chinese Astronomer from Mengeš* (2003, translated to Chinese and published in Shanghai in 2014), *History of the Vacuum Research and Vacuum Techniques* (2004), *History of Ko-*

stel 1500–1900: between two civilizations (Camp Hill, PA: SGSI, 2005, translated in 2008), *Gabriel Gruber: from Ljubljanian Canal to Jesuit General* (May 2006), *Professor Plemelj and Comet* (2006), *Fran Dominko and Slovenian Astronomy* (2007), *Blaž Kocen and the Beginning of Geography Teaching at Carniola* (2007), and *Valvasor at Slovene Astronomy* (2007). For the International Year of Astronomy 2009 he finished his trilogy about the history of exact sciences in Slovenia which includes *Astronomy* (Radovljica: Didakta, 2008), *Physics* (2008), and *Mathematics* (2009). He prepared the history of Franciscan physics and related sciences for the 800th anniversary of Franciscan order in 2009 and two volumes History of Vacuum and Vacuum Techniques in 2004 and 2010, published by the Slovenian Vacuum Society. In 2013 he published the annotated bibliography of Balthasar Hacquet for Slovenian Academy of Sciences and the biography of Nikola Tesla.

Ciril KAFOL, Ph.D., is CEO of Telekom Slovenije subsidiary in Republic of Macedonia. He has over 20 years of experience in the field of telecommunication and electrical engineering industry. He finished his Ph.D. in engineering management and published more than 20 articles referenced in COBISS.

Kaja KAŁUŻYŃSKA, M.A., is a Ph.D. candidate at National Chengchi University in Taiwan. She obtained her MA degrees in Chinese Philosophy at the Xiamen University and Far Eastern Cultures at the Jagiellonian University (Kraków). Co-author of Jura, J., Kałużyńska, K., de Carvalho, P., *Events over Endeavours. Image of the Chinese in Zambia and Angola* (2015) and several papers concerning the image of China in Africa. Her research interests include social change in contemporary rural China, media images, and development and application of data mining techniques.

Atanas KOCHOV, Ph.D., Professor at the Faculty of Mechanical Engineering in Skopje, University Ss. Cyril and Methodius – Skopje. He obtained his B.Sc. (1990) and M.Sc. (1994) in Mechanical Engineering, Doctoral study program University of Washington 1995–1996 – High temperature composites – US Navy Research project; Ph.D. (2002) from the Ss. Cyril and Methodius University in Skopje; Ph.D. thesis title: *Theoretical and Experimental investigation of composite materials and their implementation in metal forming tool design.* Dr. Kochov is a former US Fulbright Scholar – postdoctoral study program at the University of Washington, Composite materials based on recycled plastics – new technologies for designing composites (2004, Seattle, USA). Dr. Kochov is the current Dean of the Faculty of Mechanical Engineering (2008-) in Skopje, where he has been working since 1991. In addition to his teaching duties, between January 1996 and October 2000 Dr. Kochov was the Head of the Laboratory for Metal Forming Processes. Since 2007 Professor Kochov was the member of the Council of Science and research and national coordinator for research in technical sciences. He was re-elected in 2009 as a member of the Ministerial Council for science and technology up to 2012. Dr. Kochov was a General Manager of CIRKO

(Centre for Research, Development and Continuing Research) from 2005 to 2008. Dr. Kochov has been national coordinator and international expert for the UNIDO – Resource Efficiency and Cleaner production, and Low carbon technologies and economy, which was established in 2006. In additional to his teaching experience at Ss. Cyril and Methodius University, Dr. Kochov has taught at the University of Washington (Seattle, USA) and the University of Applied Sciences in Wildau, Germany. He participated in a several programs for professional and managerial trainees in USA, Germany, Sweden, Norway, Swiss, Japan, Slovenia. He previously held a variety of consultancy positions for organizations such as ALOKA Holding Europe for medical equipment, Engerosistem, and the United States Trade and Development Agency for definitional mission for Balkan gasification, TDI FDI – Ireland. He is a member of numerous professional bodies, including his country's Society of Mechanical Engineering (since 1995) and the American Society of Mechanical Engineering (since 1997).

Péter KOLLAR, M.A., is an assistant lecturer in the Faculty of Economics and Social Sciences, Szent István University, Hungary. He has been earning Ph.D. degree on topic of transformational leadership. He is lecturing human resource management, personnel administration and leadership subjects. During his career he has been doing research in topic of leadership, business ethics, competency measurements and "big data" analytics.

Rafał KOSZEK, M.A. in geography, graduated from the Pedagogical University of Kraków, interested mainly in three topics: Chinese foreign economic activity, the Way of Saint James and the ancient history of geography. Author of: *Chinese Investments in Europe during the Global Economic Crisis* and *Jakub Sobieski's Spanish Pilgrimage to Santiago de Compostela*.

Jaroslava KUBÁTOVÁ, Ph.D., is an Associate Professor at Palacky University Olomouc, Czech Republic,the Head of the Department of Applied Economics. Academic interests: Human Capital Management and Knowledge Management in intercultural environment with special emphasis on the Asia Pacific region. Ongoing research: Prediction of working behaviour of Generation Z. She is an author of books: Kubátová, J., Seitlová, K., *Řízení virtuálních týmů* [Virtual Teams Management], Olomouc: Univerzita Palackého, 2015; Kubátová, J., *Řízení lidského kapitálu v interkulturním prostředí* [Human Capital Management in Intercultural Environment], Olomouc: Univerzita Palackého, 2014; and articles: Kubátová, J. *Effective Knowledge Sharing Through Social Technologies*, [in:] *Leading Issues in Social Media*, London: ACPI, 2015, pp. 105–121; Kubátová, J., Kukelková, A., *Cultural Differences in the Motivation of Generation Y Knowledge Workers. Human Affairs* [online], October 2014, pp. 511–523; Kubátová, J., *Specifika využívání internetových sociálních médií v Asijsko-Pacifické oblasti* [The Specifics of the Use of Internet-based Social Media in the Asia-Pacific Region], *Dálný východ* 2013, 3(1–2), pp. 18–33.

LI Xiaomei, Ph.D., Associate Professor in College of Management and Economics, Tianjin University. She had been the visiting scholar at Purdue University, USA during 2012–2014. Her main research focuses on the cross-cultural management, including the talents circulation and management in current international higher education and innovation research in cross-country enterprises. She published over 20 articles in famous journal, including Higher Education Quarterly and Journal of General Management.

Michał LUBINA, Ph.D. in political science from the Jagiellonian University in Kraków. He works as an Assistant Professor at the Institute of Middle and Far East of the Jagiellonian University. The author of two books on Burma and one on China-Russia relations.

Tamás MATURA, Ph.D., is an Adjunct Professor at L'École Supérieure des Sciences Commerciales d'Angers (ESSCA) in Budapest and Shanghai. He started his career as a Research Fellow of the Hungarian Institute of International Affairs, while he also used to serve as a counsellor on China to the Minister of National Economy, he was a member of the editorial committee of the China Strategy of Hungary, and was one of the authors of the BRICS Strategy of Hungary under the supervision of the Ministry of Justice and Public Administration. At the same time, he is the founder of the Central and Eastern European Centre for Asian Studies.

Agnieszka McCALEB, Ph.D., is a lecturer and researcher at the East Asian Research Unit of World Economy Research Institute, Warsaw School of Economics. Her research focuses on Chinese Multinational Companies and the National Innovation Systems in East Asia. She holds a Ph.D. in Economics from the Warsaw School of Economics. Agnieszka McCaleb graduated from Warsaw School of Economics, major in International Economic and Political Relations, where she wrote her Master thesis on the economic changes in the second half of 20th century China. She simultaneously achieved her M.A. in Sinology, obtained at Warsaw University. From 2006 to 2009, she was in charge of marketing for Chinese markets at Selena Group, one of the largest Polish investors in China. Her research interests focus on Chinese multinational companies. She speaks Polish, English, Chinese, and French.

Natalia OŻEGALSKA-ŁUKASIK, M.A., works at Confucius Institute in Kraków and is a Ph.D. Student at Institute of Sociology as well as at Interdisciplinary Ph.D. Programme "Society-Environment-Technology", Jagiellonian University. In 2011 graduated Jagiellonian University with MA in Sociology and Cultural Studies (Far Eastern Studies). In the past 8 years she visited China numerous times also in the framework of governmental scholarships at Beijing Foreign Studies University (2007–2008), Central China Normal University (2011–2012) and as a participant of Summer School for Ph.D. Students at Nanjing University in 2013. She also enriched her education by studying Sociology and Anthropology at University of Copenhagen. Her scientific interest focus on transformation of Chinese social landscape, in particular with respect to changes in family model, elderly lifestyle and intergenerational relations.

József POÓR, Ph.D., is a Professor of Management in the Faculty of Economics and Social Sciences, Szent István University Hungary, where he teaches a variety of management courses. He earned his Ph.D. from the Hungarian Academy of Sciences Budapest. He is Professor of Management at J. Selye University Komarno (Slovakia). He served as guest professor at five different US universities (PAMI-Honolulu, Bellermine-Louisville, EKU-Richmond, Saginaw-Michigan, CSU-Cleveland) and taught thirteen summer semesters between. He lectured at Catholic University-Lyon, France three times. He was as a Erasmus guest lecturer at many other European universities (Cranfield, UK; University of Applied Sciences in Frankfurt am Main, Germany; University Arnhem, Holland, Bergen, School of Economics, Norway) and visiting professor at University Bucharest and University Cluj, Romania as well. He was senior manager (Managing Director, Country Manager and senior consultant) at different internationally recognized professional service firms (Mercer, HayGroup, Diebold) and at a private business school (International Management Center, Budapest). His scholarly publications have appeared in more than ten internationally referred journals. He wrote twenty seven books and book-chapters in Hungarian, one book (Wolters-Kluwer-Complex) and five book-chapters (Addison-Wesley, Chapman & Hall, Kogan Page, Prentice Hall, and Routledge) in English and one book in Romanian alone or as co-author.

Magdalena POPOWSKA, Ph.D., since 2008 Associate Professor, Associate-Dean for International and Public Affairs, Departmental Erasmus Coordinator, Faculty of Management and Economics, Gdansk University of Technology; 2006-present: Entrepreneur/Business owner, TRANSLINGUA Magdalena Popowska, Gdańsk; 2005–2008: Assistant Professor, Associate Dean for International Co-operation, Department of Management and Economics, Gdansk University of Technology; 2004: Research fellowship, École Supérieure de Commerce de Rouen, France; 1997–2005: Head of the Mission for École Supérieure de Commerce de Rouen, Administrative Director of Master in Banking and Finance, Gdańsk University of Technology; 1997–1998: Administrative Coordinator of the Tempus Project, Gdansk University of Technology; September–December 1996: Junior Consultant, Instytut Promocji Kadr, Gdańsk; July–August 1996: Trainee, Crédit d'Equipement des PME, Rouen, France; January–June 1996: Trainee, French Consulate, Sopot, Poland. Some short visiting professorships in France and Italy (Rouen Business School, La Rochelle, Florence); President and cofounder of the Association Alliance Française in Gdańsk and of the Foundation at the Department of Management and Economics, GUT.

Alice REZKOVÁ, M.A., graduated in International European Studies and Diplomacy at the University of Economics in Prague majoring in European Economic Integration. She accomplished a stipend study program at the Hong Kong University of Science and Technology focusing on international trade and political economic strategies of Southeast Asian countries. In 2007–2010 she worked as the director of the Association of International Affairs. Then she was assigned as a project manager on strategy and M&A projects in various industries. She also conducted research primarily on economic and political relations between Asian countries and the EU.

Roxana RÎBU, Ph.D., Transylvania University in Brasov, Romania, lecturer; 2012 – Ph.D. thesis title: *The Religious Dimension of Confucianism in the Discourse of Modern and Contemporary New Confucianists* – in print; translator of literature works of writers such as Jiang Rong ("Wolf totem"), Ma Jian ("Chinese noodles"), Yan Lianke ("Lenin's kisses", "Dreams of Ding village"); fields of research: Mind/ Political Confucianism, religion, ethics, works of Mao Zedong. Articles on Confucian ethics, Tu Weiming, Kang Youwei, New Confucianism published in *Studii de sinologie* [Sinology studies] and *Traditii in dialog* [Traditions in dialogue] vols I-III, Bucharest University Publishing House.

Balázs SÁRVÁRI, M.A., is a Teacher Assistant at Corvinus University of Budapest. Among his highlighted papers there is the book *On the Political Economics of Globalization* (co-authors are Pál Gervai and László Trautmann; 2015, Typotex Publishing House) and the article *Strategic Vision of Brzeziński* (Köz-Gazdaság Scientific Journal, CUB, 2012/3, pp. 234–242). His major fields of research are: political economics of globalization and cultural heritage and China's position in global issues.

Luciano SEGRETO, Ph.D., is a Professor of International Economic History at School of Political Sciences of the University of Florence, and Professor of Corporate Governance Models at the Gdansk University of Technology. His main interests are in the history of family capitalism, international business, foreign direct investments, and banking history.

Mateusz STĘPIEŃ, Ph.D., Associate Professor in the Department of Sociology of Law at the Faculty of Law and Administration, Jagiellonian University, Cracow, Poland. He conducts research on axiology of law, comparative law and comparative philosophy. He is also the author of publications on law and magic, placebo effect of law, human rights in China, Confucianism and Legalism. He recently published two papers directly related to Chinese philosophy: *The Three Stages of Judges' Self-Development* (Hart Pub., 2013), and *The Relationship between Human Nature and Human Rights. The Confucian Example* (Springer, 2014).

Velimir STOJKOVSKI, Ph.D., is the Rector of Ss. Cyril and Methodius University, Skopje since 2008. He is also a full professor at the Faculty of Veterinary Medicine in Skopje. He holds a Ph.D. in Biochemistry and is the author of 2 books – *Biochemistry Methods* (1994) and *Veterinary Clinical Biochemistry* (2001), of more than 180 printed papers in international academic and scientific journals and 3 monographs. His has headed and participated in numerous scientific and research projects and his fields of academic and scientific research include biochemistry, cell biology, and veterinary medicine. Prof. Stojkovski is the Chairman of the Advisory Board of the Confucius Institute at Ss. Cyril and Methodius University in Skopje. He has also been the President of the Consortium of the European Information and Innovation Centre in Macedonia, President of the Association of Biologists of the Republic of Macedonia and President of the Interuniversity Conference of the Republic of Macedonia. He is a Professor honoris causa of the Southwestern University of Finance and Economics, Chengdu, PR China, the University of Veliko Turnovo, Bulgaria, as well as the State University "M.V. Lomonosov", Moscow, Russian Federation. He is also a recipient of various important state awards, such as the State award "Sts. Clement of Ohrid" from the Parliament of Republic of Macedonia and the State medal "Pushkin" by decree of the President of the Russian Federation.

Ágnes SZUNOMÁR, Ph.D., is a research fellow at the Institute of World Economics, Centre for Economic and Regional Studies of the Hungarian Academy of Sciences, where she is the head of the Research Group on Development Economics. Her research focuses on China's foreign economic relations including the relation between China and Central and Eastern Europe. She also made research on foreign trade and foreign direct investment issues and related policies in the Central-East European countries, with special attention to developments in Hungary. She holds a Ph.D. in Economics from the Corvinus University of Budapest.

Metka TEKAVČIČ, Ph.D. is a full professor and a member of the Academic Unit of Management and Organization at the FELU. She was elected as dean of the FELU in 2013. From 2001 to 2007 professor Tekavčič was vice-dean at the FELU. From 1999 to 2001 she was also the Head of the Academic Unit of Management and Organization. Her research interest lies in the fields of cost and performance management, as well as non-profit and especially education management. She has attended many international conferences, where she has presented papers from her research areas. She has published several research articles in Slovene, other European, and US peer-reviewed journals. She is a member of editorial boards in several prominent journals from her research field. Professor Tekavčič is president of the FELU's senate and the Head of the Institute for Management and Organization. In 2014 she was awarded the Artemida award for Women's Excellence in Management. From 1992 till 2013 she was a member of the City Council of Ljubljana, Slovenia. She has long been and remains a member of the supervisory boards of many important Slovenian companies and other institutions. Professor Tekavčič is currently a member of the advisory board at the University of Primorska and was elected a Vice-dean of Challenge: Future.

WANG Yan, M.A., has been teaching Chinese language as second language in Confucius Institute in Krakow since 2014. She is an Associate Professor in School of English Studies of Tianjin Foreign Studies University before she came to work in Krakow. Her research interest focuses on the teaching and learning styles in ELT.

Joanna WARDĘGA, Ph.D., is a Director of the Confucius Institute in Krakow (since 2010), and the Deputy Head for General Affairs of the Institute of Middle and Far East (2012–2016). M.A. in sociology, Ph.D. in political science (Jagiellonian University). She studied Chinese at Shanghai University and Xiamen University. Research interests: the transformation of contemporary Chinese society, Chinese nationalism, and tourism in East Asia. Author of articles on the sociology and political anthropology of China, and two books: *Chiński nacjonalizm. Rekonstruowanie narodu w Chińskiej Republice Ludowej* [*Chinese Nationalism. The Reconstruction of Chinese Nation*] (2014); *Współczesne społeczeństwo chińskie. Konsekwencje przemian modernizacyjnych* [*Modern Chinese Society. The Consequences of China's Modernization*] (2015). Editor of a book Współczesne Chiny w kontekście stosunków międzynarodowych [Contemporary China in the Context of International Relations] (2013), and originator of a "Chińskie Drogi" [Chinese Ways] book series at the Jagiellonian University Press.

Patrick Ray WOOCK, Ph.D., received his doctorate in Entrepreneurship from the University of Science and Technology (USTC) at Hefei, China. He is a recipient of the People Republic of China National Scholarship, and was recently a subject of a documentary (Woock the Ironman). Patrick Woock is presently an international instructor at USTC, Social Chair for Foreign Investors Federation of Anhui (FIFA), and Co-founder of the International Entrepreneurship Institute. In America, Patrick Woock worked as Broker/Trader for SFI Investments, leaving to acquire Woock Insurance and then establishing an independent brokerage business.

TECHNICAL EDITOR
Mirosław Ruszkiewicz

PROOFREADERS
Aleksandra Christ
Mikołaj Skrzypiec
Agnieszka Toczko-Rak

TYPESETTER
Marian Hanik

Wydawnictwo Uniwersytetu Jagiellońskiego
Redakcja: ul. Michałowskiego 9/2, 31-126 Kraków
tel. 12-663-23-81, fax 12-663-23-83